A CONCISE HISTORY

OF

BUSINESS IN CANADA

A CONCISE HISTORY
—— OF ——
BUSINESS IN CANADA

Graham D. Taylor
Peter A. Baskerville

TORONTO · OXFORD · NEW YORK

OXFORD UNIVERSITY PRESS

1994

Oxford University Press
70 Wynford Drive, Don Mills, Ontario M3C 1J9

Toronto   Oxford   New York
Delhi   Bombay   Calcutta   Madras   Karachi
Kuala Lumpur   Singapore   Hong Kong   Tokyo
Nairobi   Dar es Salaam   Cape Town
Melbourne   Auckland   Madrid

and associated companies in
Berlin   Ibadan

Oxford is a trademark of Oxford University Press

Canadian Cataloguing in Publication Data

Taylor, Graham D., 1944–
A concise history of business in Canada

Includes index.
ISBN 0-19-540978-7 (pbk.)

1. Canada — Commerce — History.   2. Canada —
Economic conditions.   I. Baskerville, Peter A.
(Peter Allan), 1943–   .   II. Title.

HF3224.T38 1994   380.1'0971   C94-930049-7

Design: Michael van Elsen Design Inc.
Cover photograph: Courtesy of the Collection of the Gilcrease Museum, Tulsa.

1 2 3 4 — 97 96 95 94

This book is printed on permanent (acid-free) paper ∞

Printed in Canada

CONTENTS

LIST OF TABLES

PREFACE

Perhaps more than most, this book was written on the backs of others. Without the careful and often provocative research of scholars too numerous to list, this synthesis could not have been undertaken. Hopefully our endnotes go some way towards indicating our debt. Hopefully, too, those on whom we have relied for details, debate and inspiration will find something of value in our attempt to integrate their work with that of others. While we both share responsibility for the whole, Peter Baskerville wrote the sections up to 1885 and Graham Taylor wrote the introduction and the sections following 1885.

Greg Marchildon, Chris Inwood, Eric Sager, and David Roth read portions of our manuscript. We thank them for their helpful suggestions. Olive Koyama and Phyllis Wilson worked wonders in smoothing over discordant styles. Thanks, too, to Richard Teleky for his initial encouragement and Brian Henderson for his patience in seeing the work through to completion. June Bull did her usual amazing job of transforming Baskerville's penmanship into typescript. As always, Fran provided P.B. with the necessary encouragement and support.

INTRODUCTION

Twenty-five years ago, writing a study of Canadian business history would have been both harder and easier: harder, because of the absence of primary and secondary sources on the subject. Few companies maintained archives, and those who did limited public access to them. Reliable statistical information on industrial activities in Canada was equally difficult to procure, especially for the period before Confederation. Although some companies, the chartered banks in particular, had commissioned histories of their institutions, few were written by professional historians and they provided at best limited glimpses of the enterprises' internal workings.[1]

Easier, in that the pattern of Canadian business evolution seemed much more clear-cut, owing largely to the pioneering research and analysis undertaken in the 1920s and 30s by a small number of economists, notably Harold Innis and his followers. The views of the 'Innis school' had a pervasive influence on the writing of economic and business history in Canada for many years. Even today the basic concepts formulated by Innis from his studies of the fur trade, the fisheries, and the Canadian Pacific Railway undergird the work of many scholars, who style themselves 'political economists' and contrast their approach to the theoretical model-building of 'neoclassical' economists.

Although Innis's ideas were complex and his writing tended to be opaque, the main thrust of his 'staple thesis' was straightforward. Since the earliest European settlements in the 1500s, the economy of Canada was based on the development and export of a series of raw materials or 'staples': fish and furs in the period before 1800; timber in the early nineteenth century; wheat and mineral products in the period from the 1890s to World War II; oil and pulpwood emerging toward the end of that era. The country's economic infrastructure and virtually its entire business community was harnessed to the development of these staples, and fortunes rose and fell with shifts in foreign demand for them. The transportation networks, the banking system, merchant communities and isolated 'company towns' were all byproducts of the staples trade. Political arrangements, social structures, relations between Native peoples and European settlers were in turn shaped by the needs and constraints of the staple system.

The fundamental role of staples in the Canadian economy also determined the country's international position and the internal structures of its business institutions. Canada was essentially a resource hinterland, supplying its raw materials to developed commercial and industrial nations abroad and dependent upon them for capital, technology, and labour as well as markets. In economic terms, even after it achieved a measure of political independence Canada was vitally tied to foreign metropolitan centres: France and England in the early years of European settlement, Britain in the nineteenth century and the United States in the twentieth century. Although in the early 1900s Canada acquired a modest domestic manufacturing base it remained largely dependent on foreign imports of finished products and continued to rely on exports of raw and semi-processed goods for its economic growth. Canadian banks and commercial houses functioned principally as middlemen in the staple export trade and maintained close ties with larger counterparts in the financial centres of London and New York. Much of Canada's manufacturing sector (as well as its mining and forestry industries) was colonized by businesses headquartered in those foreign metropoles. Despite the relatively high standard of living achieved by Canadians in the twentieth century, the country did not develop a diversified, self-sustaining economy and its businesses remained, directly or indirectly, under the control of foreign interests.[2]

Persuasive as this interpretation was (and still is, in some quarters), it rested on a precariously small base of documentation: the histories of a handful of large enterprises, most notably the Hudson's Bay Company and the Canadian Pacific Railway. Since the 1960s studies of Canadian businesses have proliferated, revealing a more complex picture of the country's commercial and industrial system. Dozens of books, hundreds of articles and papers chronicled the careers of entrepreneurs, case histories of companies, the evolution of government policies affecting business, the social and political roles of business figures, and trends in trade, investment, labour relations, and technological developments.

What has not clearly emerged, however, is an agreed-upon line of interpretation that challenges, modifies or complements the staple thesis. In 1973 an American business historian observed 'drift and disunity' among his Canadian counterparts: the Innis school no longer commanded a consensus but there was no generally accepted alternative. More than fifteen years later another reviewer commented that 'there is not yet a kind of cohesion that is the hallmark of a developed subfield' in the area of Canadian business history.[3]

In fairness, this problem bedevils historians generally: as researchers focused increasingly on specialized and arcane subjects, grand and all-encompassing interpretations of history disintegrated. Scholars squabbled over details or, more recently, engaged in 'deconstruction' of one another's arguments, undermining any over-all view of the patterns of the past. In the field of business history, however, at least outside Canada, a fairly coherent (if not uncontested) conceptual framework has emerged over the past three decades that traces the evolution of business institutions and their impact on the industrialized world.

The basic concept of business as a system of social as well as economic relationships that changes over time was substantially formulated in the nineteenth century by its arch-critic, Karl Marx, and his followers. Marx did not invent the term 'capitalism' but he provided both a detailed description of its workings and a theory of its historical evolution which—whatever its flaws in predicting the future—recognized that business organizations had their own dynamic of change and an impact on the political and social environment in which they functioned. At the same time, Marxists were largely preoccupied with the rise and anticipated fall of capitalists as a social class rather than with the internal arrangements of business enterprises or divisions within the business community. In Canada some Marxist scholars embraced, or at least sought to accommodate, the staple thesis within their theoretical framework. Others, particularly historians, devoted their attention to the travails of the working class with capitalists generally playing a somewhat shadowy role in the background.

Before World War II the study of business organizations and practices was carried out by a few researchers, mostly resident in business schools, principally in the United States. Among the most noteworthy of these was a Canadian, Norman S.B. Gras, who taught at Harvard Business School where the 'case study' method of instruction was particularly congenial to historical approaches. During the 1920s and 30s Gras developed a general framework for the evolution of capitalism in Europe and North America, derived in part from the work of German economic historians such as Werner Sombart and Gustav Schmoller. But the utilitarian environment of business education, oriented toward training professional managers, imposed limits on the range of issues Gras and his colleagues addressed, focusing their attention on administrative and financial aspects of business organizations rather than the broader social, political, and cultural settings in which businesses developed.

During the 1940s and 50s the interests of historians of business began to broaden. Some set out deliberately to challenge the popular stereotype of the business tycoon as a modern-day 'robber baron', a view that flourished in the Great Depression and reflected widespread public distrust of the large corporations that emerged around the turn of the century, particularly in the US and Canada. Self-consciously presenting themselves as defenders of capitalism in the Cold War era, these writers lauded corporate empire-builders such as John D. Rockefeller and Andrew Carnegie as 'industrial statesmen' whose achievements laid the groundwork for economic prosperity in the mid-twentieth century.

Another group undertook to more clearly link the study of business institutions with the social sciences. At Harvard Arthur Cole and others, inspired in part by the ideas of an Austrian economist, Joseph Schumpeter, focused on the concept of 'entrepreneurship', seeking to determine how social institutions and cultural values as well as economic factors stimulated or retarded individual enterprise in different countries. Others traced the historical developments of large corporations and investigated their impact on the operations of the market system. By the 1970s the work of Alfred D. Chandler, Jr and others on the rise of 'managerial capitalism' in the US stimulated research on this subject in Europe and Japan, and ancillary analyses of the consequences of the rise of big business on government policies, labour relations, the development and diffusion of new technology and political ideas.[4]

In general the postwar business historians elaborated upon and fleshed out the framework of evolution enunciated by Gras, indicating a clear set of stages of institutional changes that took place in the 'capitalist' world, with some distinctive regional and national variations. Between the thirteenth and seventeenth centuries, basic techniques of commercial organization and market transactions were developed by merchant communities in western Europe, spreading through trade and colonization to North America and outposts in other parts of the world. During the late 1700s and the 1800s some merchants diversified into specialized fields such as banking and insurance; others applied their capital and organizing techniques to industrial production. Around the turn of the twentieth century finance capitalists and some ambitious industrialists orchestrated consolidations of many smaller and diverse enterprises into large corporate systems and developed methods of communication and control to run these large operations, ushering in the era of 'managerial capitalism'. In the twentieth century, some corporations that had functioned primarily within national boundaries began to expand their production and marketing activities into global systems. At the same time national governments which had hitherto functioned principally as guarantors of property rights and private market transactions began to intervene more directly in the market system through tax and regulatory measures and public ownership.[5]

This very generalized scheme should not be seen as consisting of completely self-contained stages nor as necessarily implying progress from lower to higher levels of institutional size or sophistication. The big trading enterprises of the 1600s and 1700s, such as the Hudson's Bay Company, for example, exhibited many features similar to present-day multinational corporations. The trading world of merchant houses in that earlier epoch was in its own way as complex as large industrial operations in the twentieth century. While from the late 1800s to the post-World War II era the trend has been from small to large-scale enterprises, this process was neither all-pervasive nor irreversible: witness, for example, the growth of medium-sized specialized firms and 'de-conglomerations' of the past decade in the United States.

This book examines the history of business in Canada in the context of these general themes and the framework of capitalist evolution developed by business historians here and abroad since the 1960s. It does not draw exclusively on this literature, but seeks as well to introduce concepts and conclusions from other disciplines whose research has enriched our understanding of the processes and character of business institutions. The practitioners of the 'new' economic history have applied increasingly sophisticated quantitative methods to analyse trends and test assumptions about business behaviour. Social historians have focused on the structure of customs and values within which enterprises and entrepreneurs operated. Historians of technology have not only linked technical and commercial development but have also examined the relationship between technological and cultural change.

We do not undertake to reject or replace the staple thesis with a new framework for Canadian business history; rather, we seek to indicate how Canada's position as a staple-producing country interacted with its emergence as part of the capitalist world from the fifteenth century. While in many respects Canada was indeed a resource hinterland, it also developed a diversified commercial system and an indigenous industrial sector; by the mid-twentieth century it also served as a base for multinational banks and manufacturing enterprises. The configuration of business development in Canada may not be unique (there are suggestive parallels, for example, in the history of Australia and some Latin American countries) but it is distinctive and deserving of a detailed account.

In this account we will highlight these dimensions of Canadian business evolution:

(1) *Changing patterns of business organization.* In Canada, as elsewhere, basic objectives of enterprises— profitability, growth, and survival— have remained fairly consistent; but the means of achieving those ends have varied over time, in response to changing markets, the advent of new technologies, alterations in political and social arrangements and other factors. Changes in business structures —the movement from general to specialized activities in merchant communities, for example, or the emergence of joint-stock corporations—have in turn had an impact on government-business relationships and the growth (or decline) of communities and regions.

(2) *The particular character of Canadian business arrangements.* In many respects these patterns of change and stability in business organization resemble developments elsewhere in the capitalist world. At the same time, Canada has some distinctive features that have produced a special configuration of business arrangements. These include of course the staple system, but also the persistent tensions among regions in a sprawling, underpopulated country divided along cultural as well as economic and geographic lines; a legal system that has placed constraints on the operations of private enterprises even though the degree of constraint has varied over time; and, at least over the past century, a political system that has uneasily tried to balance 'national' interests against regional and continental economic pressures.

(3) *The international setting of Canadian business.* Since the earliest period of European settlement, Canada has been part of a transatlantic (and more recently global) business environment, not only in terms of trade, capital flows and the migration of people but also in the diffusion of technology, ideas and business practices. Canadian staples producers have faced competition in other remote hinterlands as well as shifting markets in the industrial heartlands of Europe and the United States. Events in financial centres—London, New York, Tokyo—have repercussions on Canadian capital markets. Technological developments have created opportunities for some industries while spelling the ruin of others. New methods of production, concepts of labour relations, ideas about government regulation and other matters have been imported, along with foreign industrial products.

These processes have not been entirely one-sided. Canadian businesses have developed specialized techniques in shipbuilding, the mining industry, even in automated machine production. Merchant fleets from Atlantic Canadian ports competed vigorously in the carrying trade in the Pacific Ocean in the nineteenth century and Canadian-based firms operated utilities, mines and manufacturing plants in the US, Europe and Latin America from the early twentieth century.

The chapters that follow rely very much on the wide-ranging research of Canadian historians of business, labour, public policy, and the economy as well as the conceptual themes developed by business historians and social scientists in other countries, and their contributions are noted in references at the end of each chapter. Particular mention should be made of three important works of synthesis. In 1987 the historian Michael Bliss published *Northern Enterprise: Five Centuries of Canadian Business*, a book that was intended both to survey the field and to bridge a gap between the popularizing works on the subject by writers such as Pierre Berton and Peter C. Newman and the specialized studies of academic scholars. As might be expected, *Northern Enterprise* encountered a mixed reception from both quarters. One reviewer (a journalist) welcomed its 'demythologizing' approach but lamented that 'the details become a blur of . . . names, dates and commercial links whose obscurity is probably deserved.' Another reviewer (an academic historian) saw it as a 'carefully crafted cavalcade of rising and falling enterprises' which 'does not offer much insight into the . . . economic, organizational and technological influences shaping the evolution of businesses . . . in Canada,' and reflected a personal, rather idiosyncratic view of the subject.[6]

Whatever its strengths or weaknesses, Bliss's *Northern Enterprise* represented a major effort to bring together the disparate literature in the field. It offered a coherent, if controversial, set of themes: Canada is a difficult place in which to do business, owing to geographic factors, scarcity of capital and population, etc.; yet both business and political leaders have persistently exaggerated their ability to overcome these obstacles and to control the remorseless workings of the competitive market, usually with unhappy results. Various aspects of Bliss's interpretation will be addressed later in this book. It should be noted that *Northern Enterprise* emphasizes two dimensions that are not as exhaustively investigated in our work: public attitudes toward business and the business community's self-image, subjects which Bliss has also addressed elsewhere.[7]

In addition, two reference works deserve special notice. *The Historical Atlas of Canada* is a joint venture involving a large number of historians, economists and other social scientists as well as geographers; it is a major contribution to the discipline, and not just in the field of business history. Finally the multi-volumed (and still unfolding) *Dictionary of Canadian Biography* provides information on numerous Canadian business figures from the colonial era through the end of the nineteenth century.[8]

Notes

[1]On this subject, see Duncan MacDowall, 'Business History as Public History: One of Canada's Infant Industries', *Journal of Canadian Studies* 20 (Autumn 1985), 5–21.

[2]On Innis and the influence of the staple thesis, see Carl Berger, *The Writing of Canadian History* 2nd ed. (Toronto 1986), 85–111. The 'standard' survey of Canadian economic history for many years, reflecting the staple approach, was Hugh Aitken and W.T. Easter-

brook, *Canadian Economic History* (Toronto 1956). A more recent effort by a Canadian political economist is R. Tom Naylor, *Canada in the European Age, 1453–1919* (Vancouver 1987).

[3]Glenn Porter, 'Recent Trends in Canadian Business and Economic History' in Glenn Porter and Robert Cuff, eds, *Enterprise and National Development: Essays in Canadian Business and Economic History* (Toronto 1973), 6. Rosemary Ommer, 'Capitalism in a Cold Climate', *Acadiensis* XIX (Spring 1990), 197–8.

[4]On the early development of business history as a discipline, see Ralph Hidy, 'Business History: Present Status and Future Needs', *Business History Review* 44 (1970), 483–97; Alfred D. Chandler, Jr, 'Business History: What is it About?', *Journal of Contemporary Business* (1982), 47–63. Norman Gras's major work is *Business and Capitalism: An Introduction to Business History* (New York 1939). The classic example of the 'robber baron' approach is Matthew Josephson, *The Robber Barons* (New York 1934); see also the writings of Gustavus Myers: *The History of Great American Fortunes* (Chicago 1910); *A History of Canadian Wealth* (New York 1914; reprinted Toronto 1972). A prominent example of the 'industrial statesman' view is Allan Nevins, *John D. Rockefeller: The Heroic Age of American Enterprise* (New York 1940). The work of the 'entrepreneurial school' may be sampled in Hugh Aitken, ed. *Explorations in Enterprise* (Cambridge, Mass. 1967). In addition to the writings of Chandler *et al.* noted in later chapters, see Chandler and Herman Daems, eds, *Managerial Hierarchies: Comparative Perspectives on the Rise of Modern Industrial Enterprise* (Cambridge, Mass. 1980).

[5]For a more detailed discussion of these themes, see Graham D. Taylor, 'Writing About Business', in John Schultz, ed., *Writing About Canada: A Handbook for Modern Canadian History* (Scarborough, Ont. 1990), 121–43.

[6]Bruce Little, review of *Northern Enterprise* in Toronto *Globe and Mail*, 18 July 1987; H.V. Nelles, 'Commerce in a Cold Climate: Bliss on Canadian Business History', *Business History Review* 62 (1988), 310–16. For other appraisals, see Ommer 'Capitalism in a Cold Climate', 205-6; Jacques Ferland, 'Business History and the Buried Treasures of the Theory of Value', *Labour/Le Travail* 23 (Spring 1989), 242–5.

[7]See in particular Michael Bliss, *A Living Profit: Studies in the Social History of Canadian Business 1883-1911* (Toronto 1974).

[8]*The Historical Atlas of Canada. Volume* I: From the Beginning to 1800 (Toronto 1987); *Volume* III: Addressing the Twentieth Century (Toronto 1990) *Volume* II: The Land Transformed, 1800–1891 (Toronto 1993); *The Dictionary of Canadian Biography* 12 vols (Toronto 1966-90). There are also some useful collections of essays on Canadian business history: David S. MacMillan, ed., *Canadian Business History: Selected Studies, 1492–1971* (Toronto 1971); Porter and Cuff, eds., *Enterprise and National Development*; Tom Traves, ed., *Essays in Canadian Business History* (Toronto 1984); Douglas McCalla, ed., *The Development of Canadian Capitalism* (Toronto 1990); Peter Baskerville, ed., *Canadian Papers on Business History*, vols I (1989) and II (1993) (Victoria, B.C.). Two recent surveys of Canadian economic history are: Kenneth Norrie and Douglas Owram, *A History of the Canadian Economy* (Toronto 1991), and K.J. Rea, *A Guide to Canadian Economic History* (Toronto 1991). Articles on Canadian business history may be found in various periodicals, notably *The Business History Review* and *Business and Economic History*, both American publications; *Business History* (British); *The Canadian Historical Review*, *The Journal of Canadian Studies*, *Acadiensis* and *Labour/Le Travail*.

1

THE MERGING OF
EARLY COMMERCIAL
TRADITIONS
TO 1663

1 BUSINESS PRACTICE IN NORTH AMERICA AND EUROPE AT THE TIME OF CONTACT

It is commonplace to stress the significant cultural and material differences that existed between Natives and Europeans at the time of contact. From the perspective of business history, however, it is especially interesting that the zone of smoothest contact occurred in the sphere of trade and exchange. Examination of the business behaviour of Natives and Europeans on the eve of contact suggests both that Europeans were not as sophisticated in business endeavours as some modern historians assume, and that North American Natives were more sophisticated in such practices than many who stress contrasts have noted. Contact brought together business systems conditioned by complex social, political, and cultural beliefs and behaviours. Just as there was no one European way of doing business, so there was no single Native business system. Similar enough forms and structures did, however, provide a basis for interaction. A business history perspective allows one to focus closely on those bases.

BEFORE EUROPE: BUSINESS IN NORTH AMERICA TO CIRCA 1500

North America had a business past before the arrival of Europeans, and that past conditioned much of early business relations with Europeans. While most Canadian historians now acknowledge the central importance of Natives in early European-Native trade, there is nonetheless a strong tendency to accentuate difference, to view the Native as an 'other'. Two important and perhaps dominant interpretations of pre-contact Native business behaviour illustrate this tendency. The first perspective holds that Native business cannot be understood in market-oriented terms. 'Economic life', as Abraham Rotstein, an economic historian, has remarked, 'had not yet been differentiated as a separate and relatively independent sphere of social existence as in modern society.' Rather, trade was an adjunct to diplomacy. Trade occurred to affirm and reaffirm peaceful and stable interaction between bands and cultures.

Related to the depiction of trade as designed to realize larger cultural ends, is the contention that pre-contact Native cultures were fundamentally anti-materialistic. George Hamell, an archaeologist, has suggested that, from an early period in the pre-contact era, goods buried with Natives signify 'spiritual' rather than materialistic 'sanctions of status'. Such items as pan-pipes and smoking pipes, both closely linked with the spirit world in post-contact native societies, and reworked animal parts—cut paws, drilled teeth, and shaped skulls—associated with post-contact medicine bundles, are dominant in pre-contact graves. Hamell believes that these items were prized because they promised 'well being' in a spiritual and health sense. They were linked to and symbolic of a larger cosmology based on the spiritual essence of known and unknown beings.

The non-material notion of wealth, often and justifiably pointed to as a major difference between Native and European societies, is further supported by the Native practice of gift giving during trade, burial, and other ceremonies. While the origin of this behaviour is obscure, public redistribution of spiritual and functional goods was probably established before contact. Such behaviour reinforced an egalitarian ideal held to be central to Native culture by—as Bruce Trigger, an anthropologist, suggests— 'identifying human generosity with the bounty of the natural world, upon which all human beings depended for their survival'. It is not surprising, then, that the author of a recent survey of Indian-white relations could state that European expansion into North America 'brought together two dramatically different peoples' who nonetheless co-operated with 'remarkable' ease.

Given the dominant interpretative paradigm concerning Native business behaviour one can sympathize with the puzzlement suggested by the word 'remarkable'. Yet, perhaps, the facility with which early business relations were conducted is not so much of a miracle after all. No attempt will be made here to de-emphasize the importance of culture as a factor in conditioning behaviour. The authors of this book accept, as a central premise, the statement put forward by Thomas Cochrane, an American business historian, that since 'the business system also reflects [a people's] culture, it does not operate the same way in any two nations.' A brief survey of pre-contact business behaviour suggests, however, that Hamell's and Rotstein's interpretations present a somewhat idealized and abstract picture of Native business behaviour. In fact, such a review suggests that some Native practices were indeed congruent with market behaviour although they had emerged from within a non-capitalist oriented culture.[1]

* * *

There are, of course, no written records testifying to the ebb and flow of business activity in pre-contact North America. The extent and nature of such activity must instead be inferred from the existence of scattered material remains: skeletons, tools, pottery, faunal and fecal debris. From such evidence, however, much has been learned concerning the extent and nature of pre-contact business practice.

The first point to note is that from the earliest times hunter-gatherer bands traded throughout what is now called Canada. Along the west coast, from 8000 BC until the time of European contact obsidian, a volcanic glass substance used as a cutting tool, was quarried, crafted, and traded from points in Oregon, Wyoming and British Columbia along the coastal areas and into the interior. Such trade took place in a down-the-line step-by-step process. In this scheme 'middlemen' abounded. And it seems probable that those at the far end of the line received tools which had been well used after leaving the craftsperson's hands.

Three relatively well researched examples of production for trade in Ontario illustrate the complexity of business activity in the pre-contact era. Before 3000 BC, hunter-gatherers near Lake Superior quarried local copper and chipped and polished the raw material into tools which were traded east to Labrador, west to Saskatchewan and south to Ohio and New York. As along the west coast, these trading items travelled via broad-based networks of often genetically-linked bands.

A second example, that of the production and distribution of flint blades from the north shore of Lake Erie, suggests that trade rivalry existed in the early pre-contact era. Between 1000 BC and 300 BC the production of flint blades along Lake Erie's north shore greatly exceeded local needs. Local craftspeople built on a tradition of such activity, modifying past styles and distributing their product directly throughout the Ontario-Ohio-New York region. By *circa* 300 BC, however, flint blades from Ohio began to supplant local production. The distribution of the Ohio blades and of the powerful Adena culture which produced them soon extended into Quebec and New Brunswick. In the face of this competition the local Lake Erie industry declined quickly, making it, perhaps, the first known casualty of free trade.

In the Rice Lake area of southeastern Ontario a series of large burial mounds —one measuring 174 feet long by 25 feet wide—dating from AD 500 mark the landscape. Burial patterns and grave good distribution within these mounds suggest that social status distinctions existed in some early hunter-gatherer societies. Natives at the most privileged rank were buried in discrete sub-floor pits accompanied by a range of grave goods. Status would seem to have been bequeathed to heirs since those in sub-floor pits were genetically related. The bodies of the less important became part of the fill with which the mounds were constructed. Segregated burials and differential placement of grave goods point to the emergence of a production and trading élite. In two grave sites, for example, silver items were buried with only one individual, suggesting specialized control over the trade and reworking of this item. The unprocessed silver which came from Cobalt, 350 kilometres north of Rice Lake, was reworked into thin sheets or other artifacts and distributed through an élite-controlled trade system as far as southern Ohio, the centre of what has been called the Hopewellian exchange system. It would seem that Rice Lake had emerged as a northern node in this exchange system and that a local élite controlled transactions of luxury (silver) items and bequeathed such control to their heirs. The formal and hierarchical system at Rice Lake and Ohio contrasts with the broad-based down-the-line exchange process which characterized the distribution of Lake Superior copper products and West Coast obsidian artifacts in the earlier pre-contact period. Elite control may, however, have left the Hopewellian system especially vulnerable to political or economic disruption. A broadly based trading system characterized by a series of independent interactions could withstand interruptions more effectively than a narrowly funnelled process controlled by a relative few. That both the Rice Lake and Ohio centres declined at the same time suggests the intensity of the interaction and makes it clear that hunter-gatherer groups were far from isolated islands unto themselves.

The nature of the trading system at Rice Lake also suggests that élite individuals and groups within some migratory bands transformed raw materials into trade goods, hoarded rather than publicly distributed the results of such trade, protected their privileged trade routes, and bequeathed such control to their kin. There is evidence to suggest that some of this behaviour even characterized the Huron and northern Great Lakes Algonkian peoples on the eve of contact, peoples often pointed to as examples of simple, egalitarian societies. Thus, for example, Huron kin groups controlled trade routes which their kin had founded, and, via inheritance practices, maintained such control within their own kin. An even more pronounced ranking system based on the hereditary control of desired trade goods and central exchange routes existed in pre-contact times among the Tsimshian on the Pacific coast.

The Huron and Tsimshian are particularly interesting examples of business behaviour because both these cultures prized gift giving and the public redistribution of trade goods. Just as hoarding or stockpiling goods enhanced one's status in some Native societies, so, too, did redistributing and sharing such goods in other societies. Some Native societies displayed social rank through conspicuous giving rather than through conspicuous consumption. While such behaviour is at one level clearly antithetical to the capitalist imperative of acquisition and personal reinvestment, it is nonetheless similar in the sense that wealth display was firmly embedded in native notions of social status. Once, for example, one's goods were distributed, it was imperative to acquire more goods for future public disbursement in order to maintain social standing. This imperative facilitated exchange in pre-contact Native societies and provided a point of affinity for initial relations with Europeans following contact.

The Rice Lake example, however, provides little evidence of public redistribution of exotic goods. Rather, differential access to items like silver seems more the norm. These items may have been prized for spiritual rather than materialistic reasons, but it nonetheless seems clear that not all Native societies in the pre-contact era dealt with wealth, however defined, in the same manner. As Ian Hodder, an archaeologist, has noted, different 'exchange strategies represent different ways to legitimate power.' In some contexts the distribution of goods throughout the social structure followed by the acquisition of 'new valued goods' by the initial distributors underlay the nature and preservation of social stratification. In other instances, like the Rice Lake example, status depended on restricted access to material wealth by an élite group.

A practice of the Huron of southern Ontario further illustrates the diverse nature of business activity in pre-contact North America. From about AD 500 Natives in that region began to farm corn, beans, and squash. While, given the commodities' perishable nature, evidence of trade in farm products with northern Algonkian bands is impossible to document, it is certain that such trade existed in the immediate post-contact period. In all likelihood such exchange predated the arrival of Europeans.

Much, then, of what went on in the business world of North America before Europe prepared North Americans for Europeans. Craft production, trade, exchange, and even, in some cases, farming were commonplace. In some instances business activity abetted and fostered status differentiation. In most

Native societies trade was imbedded in cultural constraints and imperatives: a widely-practised ethic of sharing and public distribution of goods was the most obvious of such imperatives, yet underlining that egalitarian activity were both status considerations and the desire to foster obligations within one's band.

The notion of obligation, however reciprocal, may in fact have underlain much of the business of trade between bands. If, as Rotstein suggests, trade was an adjunct to diplomacy, it may be that both were motivated by the desire to create obligations. Allies could then be expected to provide succour and aid in times of material deprivation. That exchange networks were, according to one study, strongest in regions where resources were unstable lends credence to the hypothesis. By interacting and creating obligations with as wide a number of people as possible, an individual hunter-gatherer and his/her kin and band structured a form of 'subsistence insurance' to be called upon in times of need. Trade facilitated such ties and fostered such obligations. It is perhaps here that Natives were most vulnerable: the notion of obligation occupied only the tiniest of space in the business baggage brought by Europeans who crossed the ocean to North America.[2]

EUROPE AT THE EDGE: COMMERCE, COD, AND PROTO-CONTACT

Emmanuel Wallerstein, a vigorous proponent of a world systems approach to the study of history, has argued that the sixteenth century marked a great divide in the history of the world. For the first time a world system based on trade, war, migration of peoples, and diffusion of ideas began to link — albeit in unequal ways — all parts of the globe. For Wallerstein the most crucial distinction that emerged after *circa* 1500 was the accumulation of capital on an order never before attained. Large capital bases facilitated expansion and control on a scale unparalleled in past history. Profits from long distance trade, the fruits of hegemonic commercial ties to newly-discovered colonies, fuelled Europe's economy in the years following 1500. While most historians believe that Wallerstein has overstated his case — in the sixteenth century, for example, world trade represented only a small fraction of European commerce and the largest part of Europe's economic output was the production of locally-consumed agricultural products — it is nonetheless true that changes in the commercial sphere in the early sixteenth century did, gradually, revolutionize the patterns of European trade. Those changes underlay and were influenced by the expansion of Europe to North America and provided both the means and the motives for doing business in the new world.

EUROPE'S COMMERCIAL REVOLUTION

By 1500 developments in vessel technology and navigational techniques made it possible for traders and explorers to contemplate long-distance voyages. Three-masted vessels replaced the traditional single-mast craft. Sails were improved and

HENRI MEMBERTOU

The Micmacs of the Maritime region were among the first of North America's natives to have direct contact and business dealings with Europeans. There is every reason to believe that such contact led to the rapid spread of European disease and the decimation of Micmac peoples. The best estimate of their numbers in 1600 is 3,000, but local Natives often complained that since the coming of the French, their numbers had declined rapidly. In 1600 Membertou was the chief and shaman of one small Micmac band that hunted, fished, and traded in the Port Royal area of Nova Scotia. He is often remembered for having been 'the first Indian to receive solemn baptism in New France'. His business acumen, however, is perhaps equally significant as it suggests that despite disease Micmac resistance and adaptiveness remained impressive throughout the early contact era.

Stimulated by the prospects of trading for fur and worried that other European powers might, as indeed they were, establish permanent colonies in North America to achieve that end, in 1603 the French government chartered a company, under the control of Pierre de Monts, to colonize the Acadia area. Due to insufficient capitalization, and challenges to its fur monopoly from French rivals, this attempt at colonization seemed virtually dead by 1607. An infusion of capital and religious purpose from French Jesuits gave it a new lease on life. Such in skeletal form is the story of the beginnings of long-term French settlement in Acadia.

What this outline ignores is, as the historian John Reid has so well noted, the determining role played by the Native peoples of that region. Even Membertou's band of 40 to 100 persons outnumbered the French colonists. The French were there at the sufferance of the Micmac. Why, then, did the Micmac permit their presence? Simply put, they did so because it was in their interests to do so. After the initial colony had been vacated in 1607, Membertou had guarded the vacant buildings; when the French returned in 1610 all was intact. Moreover, Membertou willingly became baptized by the colony's Jesuit priest. By the early seventeenth century, Membertou and other Micmacs had long traded with fishermen for European goods. Those goods were prized for their utilitarian value. But supply was a problem. A permanent rather than seasonal floating European presence ensured stability in trade. By protecting the site of Port Royal Membertou also guaranteed his band first access to all trade at that site. He and his band could then engage in profitable trade as intermediaries with inland tribes. This was an early example of what was to be a consistent tactic of Native peoples across the North American continent. In the eighteenth and nineteenth century on the prairies such Natives were known as home guards: they encamped around European trading posts and thus preserved trade for themselves. Membertou, therefore, might also be remembered for having been perhaps the first exponent of that entrepreneurial tactic.

Sources

Campeau, L., 'Henri Membertou', *DCB* 1 (Toronto, 1979) 500-1.

Reid, John, *Acadia, Maine and New Scotland: Marginal Colonies in the 17th Century* (Toronto, 1976).

redesigned to better facilitate tacking and improve speed. Hulls were smoother in construction, thus more impervious to leaks and more durable in heavy seas. The ability to determine latitude—where one is, on a north-south axis—allowed ship crews to venture out of sight of land for prolonged periods with a reasonable assurance of knowing where they were at any point in time.

Incentives to explore and embark on long-distance trading voyages also existed. Until late in the century Italian city states controlled direct trade with the wealthy Orient via the Mediterranean Sea. Frustrated, Portugal and Spain had begun to seek out alternative routes (Portugal via Africa and both via the Americas) even before 1500. While America proved to be a land block, it was also a rich source of gold and other plunder. Throughout the sixteenth century Spain and Portugal profited immensely from the importation of gold bullion from the Americas. The more northerly nations, England, France, and Holland, were relatively late start-ers. Blocked from the Mediterranean and from the southern Americas, France, England, and later Holland looked for a northern route to the east. They found no such route. Nor did they find gold. But, as we shall see, they did find cod and fur and they founded colonies.

Despite their slow start in the arena of long-distance trade and colonial plunder, by the close of the sixteenth century the northern European nations became eco-nomically pre-eminent in Europe. Gold bullion from South America did not remain in Portugal and Spain. Both countries sent much bullion south to Asia and, increasingly throughout the century, north to France and especially to Hol-land and England in return for a wide range of agricultural and manufactured goods. Not only did Holland and England profit from trade (and wars) with Spain and Portugal but by the century's close both northern nations had also begun to dominate the Mediterranean trade.

Technological change and the desire to trade directly with the east are by them-selves insufficient explanations of what amounted to a major shift in European economic and commercial power in the sixteenth century. It is at this point that the term 'commercial revolution' takes on added significance. For most historians, the term implies more than simply a shift in trade routes or even the commence-ment of long-distance as opposed to traditional local short haul trade. Aided by and abetting these developments was the emergence of an entrepreneurial mood, the desire to accumulate, the willingness to risk capital in new business ventures, the drive to compete and triumph over others. A communitarian ethic was fast being replaced by a credo which exalted individual success. This spirit of enter-prise helped Holland and England, the most entrepreneurially-minded cultures in sixteenth-century Europe, achieve their commercial triumph within Europe.

The wholesale merchant, most historians agree, stood at the centre of this entrepreneurial culture. In fact Wallerstein and others have dubbed this the era of merchant or commercial capital. 'The king of the emerging system', the authors of a textbook on Canadian economic history assert, 'was the merchant-entrepre-neur who profited not by manufacturing but by buying, transporting and selling goods.'[3] Such a view has much to commend it. There can be little doubt but that the urban-based wholesale merchant played a major role in the commercial affairs of sixteenth-century Europe. Typically such men maintained their capital in short-term business ventures, invested in the movement of goods, the purchase of shares, the granting of short-term loans, and the renting rather than purchasing of warehouses. Merchants, in other words, possessed little fixed capital and could therefore adjust in a flexible way to changing economic trends. Yet such an interpretation is open to two qualifications. Firstly, and following Wallerstein, the assumption is too often made that merchant kings made their fortunes in foreign commerce and that colonial exploitation fuelled European growth. A close analysis of the capital sources of the fifty richest merchants in England at the end of the seventeenth century suggests that merchant wealth was not linked to foreign trade and that the top merchant princes made their fortunes from the 'manipulation of money rather than the exchange of goods'.

More importantly, by focusing almost exclusively on the urban wholesale merchant, proponents of the entrepreneurial thesis ignore or downplay the economic activity of ninety-eight per cent of the people who lived in Europe in the sixteenth century. In particular, the entrepreneurial thesis has little to say about the ninety per cent of the population who lived in rural areas. Recently, however, a strong corrective to this excessively urban- and merchant-oriented focus has emerged. A brief exploration of this literature is important—both for the light it sheds on the origins of the European commercial revolution and for the insights it provides into the study of business development in Canada. The major premise of this alternative interpretation is simply that a comprehensive approach is required in order to understand the nature of business development within nations. Business was never a purely urban phenomenon. Not surprisingly, then, Europe's commercial revolution resulted from the confluence of many streams, the flow of urban-centred merchant capital being only one of them.

Merchant capital was symbiotic with profound structural change in rural areas, change which commenced if not before, then certainly during, the sixteenth century. Rising population and declining real wages led, especially in England, to the emergence of large numbers of rural poor. At the same time some landowners, in an effort to deal with declining income, increased land holdings and agricultural production. Land enclosures increased the number of landless and diminished the amount of land held by those who were able to resist the full impact of enclosures. What, then, were the prospects for the rural poor, both the landless and the many who attempted to survive on small subsistence-oriented plots? One conceivable option was to migrate to urban areas and seek employment there. Some did. But urban craft and industrial development at the commencement of the sixteenth century was, throughout Europe, controlled by guilds. Urban guilds tightly regulated rate, quality, and price of production, and restricted employment (especially keeping women and children out of the workplace) all the while maintaining an acceptable standard of living for the master artisans. Sixteenth-century cities were not beacons of opportunity for the growing numbers of rural poor.

Within cities some entrepreneurially-minded merchants, however, frustrated by the lack of flexibility in the conservatively oriented guild system, were growing restive. They began to move out of the towns to take advantage of the rural poor in an environment free from guild restrictions. The opportunity to spin, weave, and produce clocks, small metal wares, and other items at home allowed the rural poor to maintain a rural existence. Under what has been called the putting-out system all family members could contribute to the household income. Some historians believe that it was at this point that merchant exploitation was most rigorous. Salaries for home production were rarely sufficient to satisfy all the needs of individual households. Many households had also to continue to depend on their garden plots. Over time, however, as other historians have pointed out, rural households stepped up their reproduction (number of children) in order to increase their production; because of this greater numbers of households began to be able to purchase food from the larger, commercially oriented farms. By 1600 some thirty per cent of the rural population may have been engaged in non-agricultural endeavours. In this way rural manufacturing and agricultural production stimulated reciprocal demand. Spurred by growing regional, interregional, and (to a degree) international demand, rural industry expanded rapidly. With its expansion, so too did the incomes of merchant entrepreneurs. Merchant capital pools derived not simply from the buying, transporting, and selling of goods, but also from the proliferation of merchant-dominated rural household industry.

In order to account for different rates of rural industrial expansion in various European countries, historians have broadened their analysis to include an appreciation of the influence of government on business development. In many European countries guilds and governments were closely linked. Traditionally governments looked to guilds as social and economic bulwarks against potentially disruptive change. In late sixteenth-century France, for example, the crown decreed that all craftsmen had to be guild members. The troubled and weak governmental system in England, especially in the seventeenth century, left guilds there bereft of similar support. In the Dutch Republic weak central government coupled with a dynamic and diversified agricultural zone left guilds with little purchase in that country as well.

While the putting-out system did, indeed, expand most dramatically in Britain and Holland, it is important to note that significant rural industrial growth also occurred in France, Flanders, Catalonia, northern Italy, Switzerland, and areas east of the Rhine. It was a European phenomenon, a transition led by several countries but not unique to those countries. Different governmental contexts may have facilitated or hindered the growth of rural industry, but the putting-out system spanned Europe and was one of the major factors underlying the commercial revolution of the sixteenth century and beyond.

Long-distance trade, then, emerged from and depended on developments in rural Europe. Such trade did not have the primary stimulative effect on Europe's economy in the sixteenth century that Wallerstein and others attributed to it. Nor, as we shall explore in more detail later in this book, were the mechanics of long-distance trade understood immediately and well by those who first engaged in it. Rather, strategies and tactics were refined over time and input into that process was far from limited to European traders. Those with whom the Europeans traded in North America were also active participants in setting the rules of long-distance enterprise. The fisheries were the first of such enterprises to involve North America and some North Americans.[4]

COMMERCE ON THE BANKS: COD, WHALES, AND
THE EUROPEAN FISHERY, 1500–1620

Much ink has been spilled determining whether John Cabot in 1497 or unknown Bristol fishermen before that date first (re)discovered Newfoundland. In most accounts the nod goes to Cabot. From the perspective of history writing on North America, this is not a surprising verdict. After all, Jacques Cartier was fêted on the 450th anniversary of his voyage to North America and Christopher Columbus was the focus of intense attention by historians and others on the 500th anniversary of his voyage of discovery. Perhaps a party will be held in honour of Cabot in 1997! It is certain that no anniversary celebration will be held for upwards of 300,000 fishermen who between 1540 and 1590 embarked on 10,000 or more voyages from well over a hundred European ports to fish, primarily for cod, off Newfoundland's shores. When one realizes that it may have cost 400 British pounds (the equivalent in today's buying power of $60,000) just to victual each voyage and that that cost excluded the expense of charter or purchase of boat and insurance, then something of the magnitude of the business enterprise that flourished off the coast of Newfoundland can be appreciated.

A fascination with explorers only partly accounts for the under-emphasis of the fishery's significance in the sixteenth century. Lured by potential returns of eighty per cent on capital invested, many Europeans who never went to the Grand Banks invested in the fishery. Small and large merchants owned much of that capital investment. Yet the financing process was extremely decentralized. Merchants and general investors did not reside in any single port. Nor did they normally invest heavily in a single voyage. In part because insurance only slowly became available, investors spread their risks by buying shares in various vessels and only in certain cases putting a great amount of capital in a single venture. In France and England investors borrowed their money at a normal rate of 25 per cent interest (although there are many instances of higher rates), the security being their share of the voyage's income. Should the boat sink or be raided by pirates, then the lender received nothing. Sailors were also generally paid on a share basis. Participation, then, was extremely dispersed both geographically and, within various locales, by the number and variety of people involved. In this sense the fishery resembled a giant fan, its handle resting on Newfoundland, and the various points of its circumference touching the myriad fishing ports throughout Europe. While the fishery had a significant impact on the economic life of many of Europe's Atlantic ports—in terms of boat building, provisioning, and marketing of the catch—it lacked a central locus of control. Historians therefore, partly because of the onerous problems of data collection and because of too great a fascination with the 'Great Men of History', have tended to underestimate or ignore its overall significance.

The characteristics of the cod fishery have been most often explained within the compass of the staple thesis. In fact the cod fishery has generally been considered a classic instance of the 'staple trap': the exploitation of a natural resource to satisfy a demand originating outside the region of that resource; limited transformation of, or value added to, the staple thus discouraging the emergence of linked entrepreneurial activity in the region; profits taken by non-residents; over-exploitation of the resource, with the exploiters leaving little other than debris in their wake. While the staple thesis is a valuable approach, it is nonetheless important to be clear about what that perspective highlights. With its focus on the size and locus of demand, the nature of transformation, the degree of linkage to other enterprises, and the characteristics of the resource itself, the staple approach fits well with neo-classical models of market behaviour. From this perspective the cod fishery might reasonably be seen as a relatively separate and independent sphere of activity characteristic of a society more economically advanced than that of the indigenous peoples of North America. Yet examining the cod business from the perspective of Native business behaviour reveals aspects obscured by the staple view and suggests comparison as well as contrasts with Native behaviour.

This dual perspective is useful for understanding the reasons for the rapid growth and (in some countries) equally rapid decline of the cod industry. The staple thesis points to the extent of exogenous demand. Clearly the rising European population throughout much of the sixteenth century created a growing need for good, reasonably priced food, a demand nicely met by the nutritious properties inherent in cod. Yet in several ways this demand was, as in Native societies, filtered through processes which existed alongside and outside the economic sphere. The demand, itself, was very much culturally embedded. Thus in the Catholic nations of France and Mediterranean Europe, people were required by their church to eat fish up to 166 days of the year. In England no such culturally fostered demand existed and accordingly the local market for cod was much weaker. Yet even in England forces outside the purely economic domain played a major role in the industry's growth. Although Cabot and Bristol fishermen were at the Banks at the beginning of the sixteenth century, British presence for much of the rest of the century was sporadic at best. Fishing fleets from Spain, Portugal, and France dominated the Newfoundland fishery until the 1580s. Reasons of state compelled the British government to intervene. In this era maritime powers like France, Spain, and England commonly viewed the fishery as the nursery of seamen, as a training ground for naval recruits to man their ships of war. Worried that the British fishing industry was being overshadowed by that of France and other European powers, the British government legislated extra fish-eating days in order to create more demand. To foster the building of more ships, the government also attempted to protect the exclusive carrying rights of British merchants should they wish to export fish to other countries. Clearly the demand for fish within each European nation was entangled with cultural and political, as well as economic, imperatives.

Reasons of state, rather than economic forces, were also important determinants of the shift of power within the fishery in the late sixteenth century. At times Britain, unlike France and Spain, provided armed escorts to protect her fishing fleet against pirates and raids from European enemies. When Britain decimated the Spanish Armada in 1588, the Spaniards were never again major actors in the fishery. Similarly, wars between Spain and Portugal weakened their capacities to engage in the fishery. While the west country ports of Britain were clearly the closest of any European ports to Newfoundland, naval power rather than proximity was the crucial factor which made England and, in the seventeenth century, France the pre-eminent players in the Newfoundland fishery.

The development of the Newfoundland fishery was not simply a function of demand, however determined. That development was also fuelled, as the staple thesis would suggest, by the nature of the technology and the skills required to process the staple. Two characteristics concerning the processing of cod are most commonly stressed in the literature. The first is simply that the skills and technology were in place. The Newfoundland fishery did not signify a new industry; it represented the transfer of well established business practices to a new and rich venue. Methods of transport, finance, fishing, preserving, and marketing were honed by Europeans who had fished off Iceland, Ireland, and even Spain. When the Grand Banks became known, the European fishing industry was poised to move swiftly and exploit efficiently.

The second point is the simple processing involved. In this view, cod was exported relatively untouched, a further contribution to the ease of the industry's expansion. In this case, however, the notion of simplicity inherent in the staple thesis is somewhat misleading. Two types of cod fishing took place. Both resemble the operations of what has been described as 'virtually unmechanized seasonal factories overseas'. The description is apt. It nicely suggests the artisanal component of the production process—unmechanized—while indicating the hierarchical organization and discipline employed to control the factory-like workplace. Yet it should be noted at the outset that the factory-like system arose in response to the characteristics of the staple itself. Cod was a perishable product that could be caught only within a limited period of time. Assembly-like routines were a response to a particular problem—the need for swift processing and preservation —to a set of characteristics inherent in the staple being mined and processed. It was never conceived by those involved as a system worthy of general application. In that sense these 'seasonal factories overseas' remained a part of the pre-modern economic system however much they foreshadowed twentieth-century fascination with Taylorism, time studies, and assembly-line production.

Fishing on the Grand Banks and only rarely touching the shores of Newfoundland, sixteenth-century French fleets operated what has been called the wet or green fishery. French crews brought sufficient salt to cure and preserve the fish on board. The green fishery required less labour than the shore-based, dry fishing technique but the catch was also more perishable. Even in the wet fishery, however, specialized skills corresponding to a series of interrelated functions gave to the process an assembly-line atmosphere. Fishermen caught cod via hook and lines and kept the tongue of each fish to prove their individual daily output. A boy then carried the cod to the header, who beheaded and gutted it; the liver was taken to a keg for the production of oil. A splitter then removed the backbone and dropped the cod into the hold where salters packed the fish in salt. On arrival back in Europe the fish were unpacked, washed, and dried on shore.

The inshore fishery was more complex and required a greater number of individual skills than did the offshore fishery. In the first place it required co-ordinating activities with the crews of other vessels in the immediate vicinity. Competition for the best drying areas within each bay was severe; over time a tradition arose that the captain of the first vessel to reach shore controlled the allocation of space in that bay. Under the supervision of a skilled carpenter, wooden platforms, called stages, for salting were constructed. Living quarters were also built, as were oil vats, wooden flakes for the drying of fish, and often a brewery for the wetting of workers. Small boats manned by three men caught the cod and unloaded it at the appropriate stage where headers, splitters, and salters did their jobs. An efficient splitter could process 480 fish in thirty minutes! Salters required high skill levels since too little salt would cause discoloration when the fish dried and thus lower its market value; too much salt would burn the fish and cause it to break apart, and impure salt could alter the taste, delay preservation, and even facilitate deterioration. After salting, the fish were left for several days and then spread on flakes to dry. Even in this process, skill was necessary since too slow drying caused decay and too hot or swift drying could cause the fish protein to coagulate 'like the boiled white of an egg'. The fishery was arduous and at times dangerous work, carried out under severe time constraints. Since the season was short and the product perishable, sleep was at a premium. Nevertheless, labour was plentiful and the potential pay-off in shares and bonuses probably better than many workers could hope to realize in their home ports.

Clearly much organization and skill was required to prosecute the cod fishery efficiently. These features were even more marked in the chase for whales. The vessels used were at least twice as large as those employed on the cod fishery (450 tons compared to usually under 200 tons). An average crew was three times larger than that for the fishing of cod (90 to 30). In the sixteenth century Spanish and French Basque whalers rendered whale flesh at at least nine sites off the Strait of Belle Isle on the Labrador coast. As recent archaeological excavations at Red Bay, Labrador testify, the whale works were large factory-like processing facilities. The material brought from Spain to construct these facilities included red roofing tiles, clay for the rendering ovens, barrel staves, hoops, iron spikes, nails, and axes. One part of the Red Bay complex encompassed 150 square metres within which four or five specially constructed fire boxes lined with clay from Spain heated a like number of metal cauldrons each a metre in diameter.

Capital investment was correspondingly great. Those vessels which left up to fourteen Spanish Basque ports in the sixteenth century were generally financed by the most prominent and powerful of the region's merchants. Each vessel carried back to Europe at least a thousand barrels of oil, each barrel weighing some

Painting of the whale-rendering plants at Red Bay, Labrador, illustrates the 'industrial' character of that 400-year-old enterprise. *(Richard Schlect/© National Geographic Society)*

four hundred pounds. Between 1560 and 1580, fifteen to twenty vessels whaled each year, killing at least three hundred whales and shipping at least fifteen thousand gallons of oil annually. One historian has speculated that by the 1580s the whale herds may have been declining since port records suggest that in that decade whaling ships were returning half empty. As in the case of the cod fishery, so too with the whaling industry: the staple thesis tends to underplay the sophistication and factorylike processes that characterized these undertakings.

In many ways the financing, technology, processing, workplace environment, and marketing features of the Newfoundland cod and whaling ventures reflected the intersecting spheres of mercantile and industrial endeavour which characterized Europe in 1600. The capital requirements, especially when dealt with on a share basis, were relatively small. The payment of wages via shares further spread the risks of investment and kept capital mobile. The technological requirements for undertaking the fishery were substantial. Boat construction required a variety of sophisticated skills and material inputs. Iron and clay products were essential components of the whale-processing works. Not surprisingly, many of the Spanish investors were also owners of large iron foundries in the Basque region. The workplace, itself, was characterized by an assemblylike repetition of tasks, severe time pressures, and a hierarchical gradation of skill levels which were reflected in the pay ultimately received by individual workers. The number of workers involved probably compared favourably to all but such large European industries as building construction, ship building, textile production, and iron foundries.

The several attempts at colonization on Newfoundland in the seventeenth century—the London and Bristol Company, 1610–24 and David Kirke's enterprises following 1638 were the most prominent of these ventures—were really analogous to the setting-up of a long-distance putting-out system. The resident families would, the colonizers hoped, be able to control the best inshore sites and thus dominate the fishery. By the last half of the seventeenth century some efforts had been successful enough to challenge the traditional migratory fishery operating out of the west country ports in England. And if some west country merchants adapted and began to supply provisions to those Newfoundland settlements, others lobbied the government to disallow any settlement, arguing that such development would weaken the naval nursery. Accordingly the government passed several regulations requiring the depopulation of Newfoundland. Once again matters of state and economy intersected.

The marketing of cod and, to a degree, whale oil reflected the growing integration and specialization of the European trading system. By the third quarter of the sixteenth century British ships, often financed by London merchants, sailed to the Banks to purchase cod on prearranged contracts from fishermen. These large cargo ships would then sail to Mediterranean ports where the captain or a merchant's agent would exchange the cod for spice and other Oriental goods to take back to England. From the perspective of native trade in North America, the central role played by barter in this triangular European trading system is significant. Clearly Europeans were hardly pandering to native simplicity when, as we shall see, they bartered for fur and other goods. Barter was still a basic aspect of the European economy as well. Indeed this trading system proved to be a very effective way for Britain to obtain luxury items while maintaining control of its specie.

The Newfoundland fishery reflected many of the essential features of Europe's developing economy. As such it was an integral part of, not a peripheral input into, that economy. At the same time, aspects of the fishery — culturally and politically generated demand, trade rivalry, war and economy, and barter exchange — were reminiscent of North American native exchange behaviours. While the European economy and technology (especially in relation to iron goods) was clearly more sophisticated and far ranging, points of similarity and contact did exist and, as we shall see, were well utilized.[5]

PROTO- AND EARLY CONTACT: TRANSFORMING EUROPEAN GOODS, 1520–1603

Proto-contact is an elusive concept; the term attempts to describe that period when North American Natives had contact with European goods (and diseases) but not with Europeans themselves. Clearly this concept describes a moving frontier: not all Natives had contact with Europeans at the same time. Nevertheless this predirect and early contact era is of crucial significance for the study of business and other relations between Natives and Europeans. Focusing on the period of indirect and early direct contact offers a corrective to the dominant 'catastrophic' interpretation of Native-white contact and in the process underlines the resilient and adaptive characteristics of Native cultures. With this understanding one is in a better position to appreciate the ongoing creative roles played by Natives in business dealings with Europeans.

Very likely initial direct exchange between fishermen and Natives was, from the European perspective, less commercially based than grounded in the desire to acquire goods like foodstuffs to meet immediate needs. There are indications, however, that as early as 1542 Basque whalers may have been trading with Inuit in Labrador for fur. Certainly in the last quarter of the sixteenth century, with the rising European demand for beaver hats, such trade became a regular feature of the Newfoundland fishery. In the 1580s chartered vessels leaving Bordeaux for the cod fishery had written into their contracts the right to 'traficq avec les Sauvages'. Indications are that these vessels fished the Grand Banks and then went into the St Lawrence to trade with Natives at Tadoussac, a rendezvous which swiftly became a major trading point. Goods traded at the water's edge were retraded by Natives further inland. As early as 1520 some European goods had reached Ontario. By the middle of the century a fairly steady trickle of cut-up copper kettles, blue glass beads, and some silver tubular beads were acquired by Natives in the southern Great Lakes region.

Why Natives desired baubles, beads, and cut-up kettles, items of little value to Europeans, puzzled Europeans at the time and scholars since. Some have argued that the desire for these goods reflected the primitive nature of Native societies at this time. Others, who recognize in aboriginal societies a greater degree of complexity, have had difficulty in explaining Native demand for what one anthropologist termed 'a few scraps of metal'. Yet as George Hamell has explained, one must attempt to understand what was ' "rational" within the cultural milieu of American Indian societies'. According to Hamell, in the formative proto- and initial contact era (*circa* 1550–1620) Natives made sense of Europeans and their trade goods in terms of their own traditional beliefs. Europeans were held to be other-worldly peoples arriving from either under the water or beyond the horizon, regions inhabited by such beings. The beads and copper kettles brought by the Europeans or, as the Natives construed them, culture heroes who had returned from far regions, were analogous to red copper and crystal shell artifacts, traditional spiritually charged substances. By 'seeing' their trade goods as the Natives saw them, one can begin to understand why Natives coveted copper kettles in order to cut them up and desired beads and baubles only of certain colours—thus over time forcing European manufacturers and dyers to adjust to native preferences. Moreover, the fact that Europeans prized greasy beaver, beaver skins worn by Natives for a year and therefore, as we shall see in the next chapter, more suitable for the manufacture of hats, puzzled Natives. Why, after all, would Europeans desire cast-off garments? Each had what the other wanted, although neither valued what the other desired.

The initial conceptualization of European goods by Native peoples was not static. By providing the basis for the increased interactions prompted by European demand for furs after 1580, that conceptualization sowed the seeds of its own transformation. In a way that defies precise dating, Natives acquired and accepted European interpretations of the technological worth of more utilitarian items such

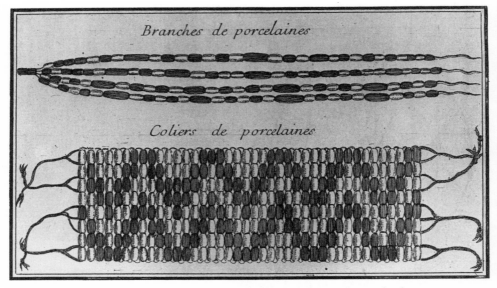

Branches de porcelaines

Coliers de porcelaines

Wampum—necklaces of shells—served as money, jewellery, and records of transactions. Native peoples gradually mixed glass, tin, and lead beads with the traditional seashells. *(National Archives of Canada/C10891)*

as axes, knives, and whole kettles. Only gradually, it must be stressed, did these utilitarian items begin to rival in importance the more spiritually prized materials. Even then the transition was never complete within any single Native society, nor did it proceed at the same pace within each Native society. Nevertheless the proto-contact period, especially in inland areas where it was of a longer duration than on the coast, did provide Natives with an opportunity to assess and integrate European goods free from the pressure of Europeans themselves.

In the Great Lakes region, the introduction of European goods accelerated processes of change already visible in the pre-contact era: increased trade competition, war, and growing centralization of settlement. In the late pre-contact period, south of Lake Ontario in what is now northern New York State the Five Nations Iroquois, from east to west the Mohawks, Oneidas, Onondaga, Cayuga and Seneca, had formed a Confederacy designed to minimize internal conflict. During the proto-contact era the Five Nations were safe from raids from the east and west and able to confront their northerly and southerly neighbours. During the proto-contact era most European goods arrived in the Five Nations area either from the northeast via the St Lawrence River or from the south via the Susquehanna river system.

Slightly north of Lake Ontario, hitherto dispersed groups of Huron began to coalesce at strategically based trading sites in the Humber and Trent Valley regions. Warfare with St Lawrence Iroquoian groups, which had begun before the known introduction of any European materials, escalated. At the same time, these St Lawrence Iroquoians were being attacked by Five Nations Iroquois. The Huron and the Five Nations natives wished to acquire control of a direct access to European trade. Warfare intensified after 1580, consequent on the growing demand by Europeans for fur. Sometime near the end of the sixteenth century the Mohawks successfully severed the St Lawrence as an artery for trade with the Europeans and southern Ontario groups, a trade route which remained closed for the next fifty years. In response, southern Ontario Hurons and an unknown number of St Lawrence Iroquoian captives moved northwest of Lake Simcoe to join Huron tribes who had lived in that area for several centuries. They did so, not simply to escape the depredations waged by the Mohawk — in fact they were probably at least as powerful as the Five Nations tribes. Rather they moved in order to take advantage of a more northerly access route to the European trading point at Tadoussac, through Algonkian natives based on Lake Nipissing and the Ottawa River and Montagnais who retained direct access to the Tadoussac trading station by waterways in central Quebec. A similar intensification of warfare and settlement consolidation took place within the Neutral group of Iroquoian people west of Lake Ontario and south of the Niagara escarpment. The Neutral, at times in alliance with the Petun, fought the Algonkians located in Michigan and engaged in trade with Huron, Susquehanna, and Senecas.

By the end of the sixteenth century, then, three (and if one includes the Petun about whom little is known, four) separate, often competing and warring nodes of native settlement—Neutrals in the west between modern Hamilton and Brantford, Hurons south of Georgian Bay, Petun between the Huron and Neutral, and the Five Nations south of Lake Ontario — had emerged, a settlement pattern at least in part encouraged by Indian understanding of and desire for European trade goods. Sometime in the same century, a fifth group of Iroquoian peoples, the St Lawrence Iroquoians, had been dispersed from their St Lawrence homeland, some to live with the Huron and others to live with various of the Five Nations tribes. Just as the fishery fitted nicely with traditional economic and political rivalries in Europe, so too did the trade goods brought by fishermen mesh with long-standing trade and diplomatic rivalries amongst North American Natives. Well before the arrival of Champlain and the commencement of European settlement in the St Lawrence-Great Lakes region, local Natives were ready for trade.[6]

Notes

[1]A. Rotstein, 'Trade and Politics: An Institutional Approach', *Western Canadian Journal of Anthropology* 3 (1972–73), 1; G. Hamell, 'Strawberries, Floating Islands and Rabbit Captains: Mythical Realities and European Contact in the Northeast during the Sixteenth and Seventeenth Centuries', *Journal of Canadian Studies* 21 (1986–87), 72–94; B. Trigger, 'Evolutionism, Relativism and Putting Native People into Historical Context', *Culture* 6 (1986), 69; J.R. Miller, *Skyscrapers Hide the Heavens: A History of Indian-White Relations in Canada* (Toronto, 1989), 4; T. Cochrane, *Frontiers of Change: Early Industrialism in America* (Oxford, 1981).

[2]R.C. Cole, ed., *Historical Atlas of Canada* 1 (Toronto, 1987), Plate 14; W.A. Fox and R.F. Williamson, 'Free Trade in Prehistory: A Lesson from the Past', *Ontario Archaeological Society Newsletter* 89, 4 (1989), 9–11; M.W. Spence *et al.*, 'Hunter-Gatherer Social

Group Identification: A Case Study from Middle-Woodland Southern Ontario', in S.P. De Atley and F.J. Fundlow, eds, *Frontiers and Boundaries in Prehistory* (London, 1984), 117–42; Ian Hodder, 'Toward a Contextual Approach to Prehistoric Exchange', in J.E. Ericson and T.K. Earle, eds, *Contexts for Prehistoric Exchange* (New York, 1982), 199–211; R.M. Stewart, 'Trade and Exchange in Middle Atlantic Region Prehistory', *Archaeology of Eastern North America* 17 (1989), 47–78.

[3]K. Norrie and D. Owram, *A History of the Canadian Economy* (Toronto, 1991), 31.

[4]E. Wallerstein, *The Modern World System*, 1 and 2 (New York, 1974 and 1980); A.K. Smith, *Creating a World Economy: Merchant Capital, Colonialism and World Trade, 1400-1825* (Oxford, 1991); H.G. Koenigsberger *et al.; Europe in the Sixteenth Century* (London, 1989); K. Norrie and D. Owram, *op. cit.*; Richard Grassby, 'English Merchant Capitalism in the Late 17th Century: The Composition of Business Fortunes', *Past and Present* 46 (1970) 87–107; J. Goodman and K. Honeyman, *Gainful Pursuits: The Making of Industrial Europe, 1600–1914* (London, 1988); H. Medick, 'Industrialisation before Industrialisation? Rural Industries in Europe and the Genesis of Capitalism', *The Indian Economic and Social History Review* 25 (1988), 372–84; P. Kriedte, *Peasants, Landlords and Merchant Capitalists: Europe and the World Economy, 1500–1800* (Cambridge, 1983); W.W. Hagen, 'Capitalism and the Countryside in Early Modern Europe: Interpretation Models, Debates', *Agricultural History* 62 (1988), 13–47.

[5]Papers by D.B. Quinn, J.A. Tuck and S. Barkham in G.M. Story, ed., *Early European Settlement and Exploitation in Atlantic Canada* (St John's, 1982); G.T. Cell, *English Enterprise in Newfoundland, 1577–1660* (Toronto, 1969); R.C. Harris, ed., *Historical Atlas of Canada*, 1, Plates 21, 22 and 23; L. Turgeon, 'Pour Redécouvrir notre 16ᵉ siecle: Les Pêches á Terre-Neuve d'après les Archives Notariales de Bordeaux', *Revue d'histoire de l'amérique français* (1985), 523–49; S.H. Backham, 'The Basque Whaling Establishments in Labrador, 1536–1632: A Summary', *Arctic* 37 (1984), 515–19; H.A. Innis, *The Cod Fishery* (Toronto, 1940); Jean-François Brière, *La Pêche Française en Amérique du Nord au XVIIIᵉ siècle* (Montreal, 1990); Jean-Pierre Proulx, *Basque Whaling in Labrador in the 16ᵗʰ Century* (Ottawa, 1993).

[6]B. Trigger, *Natives and Newcomers: Canada's 'Heroic Age' Reconsidered* (Montreal, 1985); L. Turgeon, 'Pêcheurs Basques et la traite de la Fourrure dans le Saint Laurent au XVIᵉ siècle', in B. Trigger *et al.*, eds, *'Le Castor fait tout': Selected Papers of the 5th American Fur Trade Conference* (1985), 14–24; J.A. Dickinson, 'Old Routes and New Wares: The Advent of European Goods in the St Lawrence Valley', in Trigger *et al.*, *'Le Castor tout fait'* . . ., Hamell, *op. cit.*; James Axtell, 'At the Water's Edge: Trading in the Sixteenth Century', in J. Axtell, *After Columbus: Essays in the Ethnohistory of Colonial North America* (N.Y., 1988), 144–81.

2 COMPANIES AND COMMERCE IN NORTH AMERICA: THE CASE OF FUR, 1603–1663

Just as Native peoples were adjusting to the changing nature of commercial relations even before direct contact with Europeans, so, too, significant structural changes were occurring within the world of European commerce. It is important to emphasize this point. Too often Natives are depicted as being mired in a stone-age culture and, by comparison, Europeans are viewed as harbingers of self-confident modern entrepreneurs. Perhaps long-distance overseas trade was an important catalyst leading to a world commercial system but in reality such a system only slowly evolved. The forms and structures which emerged to facilitate effective management of long-distance trade were honed only after centuries of experimentation. For both North American Natives and Europeans, the seventeenth and eighteenth centuries represented a period of uncertain adjustment to dramatic business and commercial change.

Most business in seventeenth and eighteenth century Europe did not take place within the structure of a joint stock, incorporated company. Economic collectivities, of course, pre-existed joint stock incorporated companies. Guilds were collective organizations but functioned more as trade associations composed of individual and, within the association, competing members. By the sixteenth century, the guilds' primary purpose was to restrict entry and protect the economic *status quo*. In England, regulated companies managed by a board of directors, who granted licenses to trade, controlled most sixteenth-century overseas trade. Such companies, however, were not joint stock ventures. They permitted individual and partnership activity and depended on government sanction of monopolistic privilege for success. Partnerships were the normal means of distributing risk, capital, and expertise within commercial endeavours. And the purchase of shares in fishing voyages was commonplace by the seventeenth century. Yet both of these collectivities tended to be contractually limited and of short-term duration. The joint stock, incorporated company offered the potential of combining the permanence of the guild organization with the focus of a partnership and the capital-raising potential of the fishery share system. Such a form of enterprise has, correctly, been called 'the most spectacular and the most novel type of business structure in the early modern period'.[1]

While the corporate form was utilized by entrepreneurs in the area of mining, metal works, and finance, its attributes seemed specially suited to the demands of long-distance colonial-commercial enterprise. Such enterprise accentuated certain difficulties already present in commercial life: poor communication, uncertain transport, problematic managerial control over long distances, and imperfect knowledge of limited and fluctuating markets. Colonial commerce also added a significant and onerous new burden: fixed capital investment in forts, factories, ships, warehouses, depots and, especially in North America, colonial infrastructure, far exceeding the fixed capital demands of any commercial venture engaged in by merchants up to that time. Compared to transitory partnerships, the corporate form promised the necessary long-term stability for investment in and management of such assets.

As they entered into an era of competitive commercial expansion and colonial acquisition, many European nations used early chartered companies as arms of the state. The mixing of state and entrepreneurial interests had already, as we have seen, taken place in the fishery. But in the context of the fisheries, the state had remained supportive, by way of regulations, military support, and exhortation. In the context of chartered companies the state gradually became an active partner, financier, manager and, at times, profit taker and loser. The corporate form provided a plausible home for the often conflicting time horizons of merchants and bureaucrats. Merchants who continued to desire short-term investments could do so through investment in and sale of corporate shares; governments, interested in more long-term strategic considerations, found the permanency of the corporate form suited to its ends.

If, at a general level, the above account of the emergence of chartered companies is useful, it nonetheless remains true that not all companies emerged in the same way or in response to an equally weighted set of pressures. French and British colonial and commercial behaviour in North America point to the importance of national commercial cultures as conditioning contexts for corporate endeavour. During the first half of the seventeenth century, chartered companies engaged in colonial commerce were really classic examples of old wine in new bottles: premodern business and cultural traditions dominated entrepreneurial activity. In the case of both countries such practice was insufficient for the commercial tasks at hand.[2]

THE FRENCH FUR TRADE IN NORTH AMERICA, 1603–1663

Near the end of the sixteenth century a number of market pressures converged to spark interest in the trade for furs in North America. The traditional supplier of beaver pelts for the European fur industry, Russia, was experiencing severe resource depletion. At about that time, in part because of the growing acceptance of Swedish style (Sweden was an aggressive and emerging military power), demand for broad-brimmed hats spread. The short barbed undercoat of the beaver's fur best provided the necessary properties for holding the shape of the broad brims. Beaver robes worn by Natives for a year (greasy beaver) were especially prized because the long guard hairs were worn off, exposing the barbed undercoat and thus minimizing the amount of processing required in Europe. In Paris, hatters had throughout the sixteenth century acquired substantial skill in felting wool hats and much of that skill and its attendant technology was transferable to felting beaver hats.

Market pressures alone, however, did not in France generate sufficient interest and the necessary capital to invest in North American trade. Many of those with money in France were reluctant to invest in any trade. For the nobility, trade was a grubby business and, in fact, in the late sixteenth century edicts were passed which stripped noble traders of their noble rank! Instead nobles preferred to invest their money in war, in landed estates, and in the purchase and sale of government offices—by the reign of Louis XIV there was some 60,000 such offices available. Yet, pressured by the growing commercial strength of the Dutch and the British, the French state was eager to facilitate North American colonial development. In the early seventeenth century the state took support where it could be found: from merchants in the Atlantic ports of Honfleur, Rouen, St Malo and La Rochelle. Between 1599 and 1604 the state granted ten-year monopolies of the fur trade to two chartered companies on the condition that the companies would colonize as well as engage in commercial activities. The first, headed by Pierre Chauvin, an experienced cod fisher and fur trader, failed in an attempt to establish a colony at Tadoussac. The second, backed by merchants at Rouen, La Rochelle and St Malo and headed by Pierre du Gua de Monts, was granted political and economic control of all land between the fortieth and forty-sixth degree of latitude. The company was to colonize, trade, and convert the native people to Christianity. It, too, failed to accomplish its ends.

In several ways these early attempts by the French crown to colonize by way of the agency of merchant-dominated chartered companies underlines the degree to which business practice was in a slow and halting state of transition from pre-modern to modern capitalist behaviour. Neither company operated on an open joint-stock basis. Rather, private invitations to participate in the venture were extended to select individuals. By this means these quasi joint-stock companies raised sufficient capital to prosecute the fur trade, but not enough to found a permanent colony. In each case the monopolies were challenged by competing fur-trade interests and the state, virtually bereft of a navy suitable for sailing the Atlantic, could do little about it. Since neither the state nor few of its most important supporters, the nobles, invested any capital in the ventures, incentives for interfering were somewhat limited. Moreover, the sense of permanency and monopoly implied in the company charter seem to have escaped even some of de Monts' backers who themselves engaged in private trade in competition with the company. Significantly, religion emerged as a motive for expansion equal to that of commerce and state. In de Monts' charter, the company was charged to convert the native people to Christianity. As a purely business form, the early chartered company left much to be desired: it encompassed aims often in conflict with those of commerce, while, at the same time, it did little to preclude private opposition even from some individual company investors. Small wonder that as the fur trade continued to expand, early chartered companies went quickly bankrupt.

Thanks to the persistence of Samuel de Champlain, a member of de Monts' company, colonization and trade in North America was kept before the eyes of royal authorities. After about 1614 Champlain and interested merchants in the Atlantic ports went their own way, forming a series of competing companies until, under Richelieu in the late 1620s, the Crown once again took an active role in

North American affairs. The formation in 1627 of the Compagnie de la Nouvelle France or Compagnie du Cent-Associés represented in terms of capital invested (300,000 livres divided into 100 shares of 3,000 livres each) the largest North American colonial enterprise at that time. The charter, drawn up by Cardinal Richelieu, the King's first minister, outlined the land-holding system, trading privileges, missionary ends, and governmental structures of the enterprise. By waiving the threat of loss of noble status and emphasizing the importance to France of North American colonization and missionary work, Richelieu attracted more investment participation from nobles than from any other single social group. Moreover, on condition of their participation he promised noble status to a number of merchants.

Despite the size and breadth of investment, the Cent-Associés much resembled its predecessor companies. Like them, it was a quasi joint-stock company: participation was limited to one hundred (a magic number in medieval times) and was initially by invitation only. As were the earlier companies, the Cent-Associés was formed to carry out several not always compatible ends, commerce being only one of them. And as with its precursors, the Cent-Associés quickly ran into aggressive competition—most disastrously from the Kirke brothers, British privateers who captured the company's vessels and controlled Quebec in the early 1630s, causing the company to lose some 240,000 livres in its first three years of operation. Nor were its own partners slow to pilfer company rights and profit from private trading. The Cent-Associés, strapped for money, subcontracted trading and other commercial rights — often to initial investors who paid a fixed annual sum and shifted to the parent company the most burdensome of overhead costs. Even Richelieu, one of the original one hundred investors, was quick to invest 17,000 livres in an affiliated company. In 1645 the Cent-Associés delegated all its trading rights to a group of New France residents, the Communauté des habitants, retaining control only of its seigneurial prerogatives. By that point, however, affiliated companies in the Acadian region were in open warfare on their 'parent'. Nor did the Communauté function for long as a collective enterprise: it, too, soon fractured into short-term competing associations. Even with respect to colonization — the Cent-Associés was required to bring 4,000 French to New France by 1643 — the company was upstaged by private entrepreneurs. A speculative trade in indentured contracts developed in Atlantic ports like La Rochelle. Merchants hired workers and sold their contracts in New France. This trade in indentured servants brought, before 1663, over half of all French migrants to New France, double the number brought over by the Cent-Associés. The Cent-Associés had become an impotent holding company to which accrued much of the expense of colonization, missionary work, and the promotion of enterprise and none of the profits generated by such activity.

What, then, can be said about the early French chartered companies? 'Royal charters', according to the historian Michael Bliss, 'were almost meaningless.' Many other writers have echoed that charge and have seen such companies as ventures which failed because of France's pre-modern commercial culture and infrastructure. Clearly the state had to appeal to other than simply commercial motives to attract participation from wealthy nobles. Clearly, too, missionary work was an essential feature of the companies' responsibilities. The Jesuits, who depended on Cent-Associés' support for their missionary work in the New World, never failed to extol the company's presence. 'Jesuit eulogy', as one historian has commented, 'seems slim recompense. Yet it reflects the prevailing notion that a commercial company could not live by profit alone.' Indeed, the Cent-Associés persisted for three and one-half decades without ever making a profit!

Nonetheless these early companies were more than corporate fronts for Catholic proselytizing. In ways unintended by their initial promoters and subscribers, the companies sparked commercial exchange and permanent colonial development in North America. Trade with Natives could certainly have occurred without permanent European habitation. As we have noted in Chapter One, by the early seventeenth century networks of Native middlemen were well in place for the transporting of inland fur to the coast. Strategic, religious, and commercial concerns on the part of Europeans, however, could not be satisfied by such a system. Yet small, short-term, competing enterprises could not alter the coast-based trading structure. In the early seventeenth century, centralized institutions on the order of well-financed and state-sanctioned chartered companies filled the breach by raising the capital and absorbing the losses so that short-term competing enterprises, often composed of individuals who had invested in the chartered companies themselves, could expand and profit at minimal cost. And such capital, as Pierre Boulle, an historian, has perceptively suggested, had 'to be lost outright: [a] permanent mortgage on profits would have discouraged further private backers' from participating in the future.

A broader perspective reinforces that conclusion. It is significant that early French chartered companies seem to have fulfilled functions similar to such enterprises in England, Scotland, and Holland. In those nations, too, the bankruptcies of chartered enterprises facilitated colonial commerce and European habitation in North America. Like New France and Acadia, Albany, Massachusetts, and Virginia owed their existence to chartered companies that failed to make profits. If, in the first half of the seventeenth century, none of the principal European countries had evolved centralized structures capable of mastering the challenges of long-distance multi-national enterprise, the foundations for the more mature development of such enterprise had nevertheless been laid.[3]

TRADE IN THE INTERIOR
European-Native Commercial Relations in the Great Lakes Region 1609–1670: A Case Study

Scattered evidence strongly suggests that in the early seventeenth century Atlantic coast Natives controlled the process of commercial exchange with Europeans. We have already noted the example of Membertou. Similarly at Tadoussac, a central site for early trade, Natives quickly found that if they waited for competitors to arrive before trading they could trade less for more. Not surprisingly, the cost of beaver pelts escalated quickly. In this context, limited Native carrying capacity rather than a limited desire for goods governed the extent of trade. Note has also been made of interior networks of Native middlemen that facilitated the movement of fur to the coast and of European goods to the interior, all of which would seem to have taken place along traditional trading paths. Europeans soon became impatient to short-circuit such enterprise. While middlemen groups resisted incursions, European traders like Champlain by a combination of guns, diplomacy, and trade goods ventured slowly west. By 1615 Champlain and Etienne Brulé had wintered with the Huron and, in Brulé's case, with the Algonkians, and on behalf of the Huron had fought their traditional enemy, the Five Nations Iroquois.

The full range of interrelations between Great Lakes Native societies and Europeans cannot be explored in any detail here. Yet an examination of their trading relationships is essential in order to appreciate the complexities of business and commerce in early seventeenth-century North America. Such an understanding cannot be attained by a simple focus on chartered companies and European entrepreneurs.

European trade accentuated but did not transform Native trading practice visible in the pre-contact period. The traditional role exercised by the Hurons in the northern trading relationship — supplier of agricultural goods in return for fish products and copper material — did, however, undergo elaboration as the result of increasing European trade. Well before the mid-1630s Hurons traded directly with the French at Quebec, paying tolls to various of the Algonkian tribes, especially the Kichespirini situated on the Ottawa River. Algonkian tribes such as the Nipissing and Cree of the northwest did not trade directly with Europeans but rather, in exchange for fur and fish, received some European goods from the Hurons in addition to traditional items like corn. After 1630 trading patterns in the northwest intensified since within Huronia beaver had been all but trapped out. Similar overtrapping may also have taken place within traditional Nipissing and Ottawa hunting territories, facilitated in part by Algonkian cultural beliefs that, treated properly, dead animals would return to earth and thus reincarnation would prevent extinction—a nice example of cultural beliefs mediating European inputs and pressures. The Nipissing and Ottawa became, like the Huron, intermediaries, drawing into the developing trade network the more northerly Cree as the initial suppliers of fur.

While continuing to attempt to control trade from the French, the easternmost tribe of the Five Nations, the Mohawks, began to deal directly with Dutch traders following the establishment of Dutch trading posts in the upper Hudson River valley in 1614. The Mohawk would not allow any other group, even other members of the Five Nations Confederacy, to trade directly with the Dutch. Like Membertou on the coast, the Mohawks were establishing a monopoly on European trade in northern New York.

The Hurons, in direct contact with the French, and the Five Nations, in direct contact with the Dutch, remained more or less loose alliances of several tribes linked by overlapping clan organizations. The nature of their trading links to separate European powers accentuated the traditional enmities between these two confederacies, and a third confederacy, the Neutrals, in southwestern Ontario, emerged to play a central trading role. Their traditional military strength and the very absence of direct European links allowed them to become, in addition to traders in their own right, an important port of trade—a neutral zone where the Hurons and Five Nations could trade in peace. In this way the two major trading circuits were linked. Dutch goods passing through the Five Nations could be traded for, among other items, French goods passing through the Huron and Petun confederacies. The Hurons and Five Nations did their best to keep Europeans out of direct contact with Neutralia. In fact, European trading posts and European traders were often hemmed in and could trade only with the permission of certain Native peoples. Yet these European establishments became, as one archaeologist has noted 'a set of fixed points to which the native trading system could be anchored'. The relatively loosely-focused exchange of the pre-contact era, had, by the mid-1630s, been supplanted by a more systematic flow of goods along fewer and more well-defined trade corridors.

Trade and politics were certainly intermeshed in this era. Elaborate ceremonies preceded trade between the Hurons and Champlain and much of the discussion focused, not on price, but on alliance and friendship. Yet even in this early era trade made for strange bedfellows. It would be wrong to think that the trading circuits—Dutch-Five Nations-Neutrals and French-Huron-Nipissing-Petun-Neutrals—were hermetically sealed against outside interference or, indeed, internal leakage. The Onondaga attempted to trade directly with the French. The Mohawk were constantly alert to any opportunity to partake of French trade whether by the agency of raiding parties or by the surreptitious activity of French smugglers. The Neutrals traded directly with enemies of the Five Nations to the south and may have traded with Algonkian nations to the north and west of Huronia. Algonkians in the southeastern Ontario region attempted, in the 1630s, to trade with both French and Dutch. When the occasion seemed appropriate, trade and politics could become separate spheres.

European trade fostered increased status differentiation within Native societies. In the early contact those already enjoying privileged hereditary positions consolidated their power. By the 1640s one European observer wrote of nobles and commoners within Huronia. Within Neutralia such a process of consolidation led to the emergence of a pre-eminent band leader, Tsouharissen, who controlled all aspects of Neutral affairs. Living in a central capital, Tsouharissen personally controlled a significant amount of trade material—including extensive pens for the management of his deer—and, typical of chiefdoms, he cemented trading alliances with southern tribes by a number of carefully chosen marriages.

Clearly Huron's 'nobles' and the Neutral chief Tsouharissen benefited from trade. But did they or other natives 'profit' from such activity? Certainly they sought a hard bargain. A close student of this period has concluded that Hurons and other middlemen traders demanded higher prices from interior tribes than they had paid Europeans. And these higher prices were often received despite the fact that the goods had been well used before being resold. Moreover status maintenance required the continued cultivation of a support or client group and

THE FISH TRADE

For many Natives in the Great Lakes region the fur trade was, before and after the arrival of Europeans, an economic activity of the second rank. This fact has often been lost sight of by historians who focus on the pursuit of fur by white Europeans and assume that Natives, too, saw fur as the trade item of first importance. The region's most numerous group of linguistically related peoples, the Algonquians, or in English 'spear fishermen', had for centuries before contact depended on fish as their staple diet and as their primary item for trade with other natives. Ojibwa, Ottawa, Potawatomi and Nipissing had by the fourteenth and fifteenth centuries AD evolved a society and culture which revolved around the rhythms of the fishery. The processing functions which accompanied spring and fall fisheries—net making and mending, spearing fish and setting fish traps, in the north freezing, in the south, drying and smoking for preservation—all became part of the religion or cosmology adopted by these peoples. Archaeological evidence has documented that fish was a 'hot' trade item as early as the 1350s. Hurons exchanged corn for

The Jesuit Louis Nicolas provided this sketch of Native fishing techniques, c. 1700. *(Louis Nicolas/ Codex Canadienses/#4726.7 page 15/From the Collection of the Gilcrease Museum, Tulsa)*

this was accomplished through extensive, public gift-giving. Evidence of status differentiation, gift-giving, and nodes of trade activity pre-exist European presence. These traditional behaviours intensified and mediated trade after those Europeans had arrived. Natives profited in traditional ways from European trade.

By the 1630s, if not before, Natives in the Great Lakes region had come to value European trade goods and Europeans themselves for utilitarian rather than more traditionally rooted spiritual ends. As early as the 1620s the Montagnais near Tadoussac had ceased to make birch bark baskets and stone cutting tools. Instead they used kettles, copper pots and metal cutting tools supplied by Europeans. The Five Nations and the Hurons became increasingly conscious of the utilitarian value of European goods and, by the 1630s, looked for metal cutting fish provided by their southern Algonkian neighbours. Fish-corn rather than fur-corn trade dominated pre-contact exchange relations in this region. Indeed, as late as 1648, a Jesuit priest who lived with the Hurons reported that fish 'is the ordinary money with which [the Algonkians] buy their main stock of corn'.

The centrality of the fishery to Algonkian peoples extended far beyond the mid-seventeenth century. Throughout the eighteenth and nineteenth centuries in the Rainy River region of northern Ontario, sturgeon was one of the main items traded in the Lake Huron district by Ojibwa with the Hudson's Bay Company. Between 1847 and 1857 Natives in the Lake Huron district traded 2,657 pounds of isinglass (a substance derived from sturgeon bladders and used in brewing and as an adhesive) to the Hudson's Bay Company. This represented a catch of approximately 26,134 sturgeon. For these people, reserves were useless without fishery rights. Yet despite the granting of such rights, non-Native commercial fishing had by 1900 eclipsed the Native fishery and, in the process, denuded the fish stock. Historical myopia combined with white rapaciousness and bureaucratic indifference rendered Native

access to Great Lakes fisheries impossible. That sorry story cannot be retold in detail here. It is enough to emphasize the vital role that the fishery business played in the lives of these people for centuries before and centuries after contact. Fish, not fur, sat at the centre of their economic trade and traditional culture. The loss of their fisheries undermined the core of their spiritual being.

Sources

Cleland, Charles E., 'The Inland Shore Fishery of the Northern Great Lakes: Its Development and Importance in Prehistory', *American Antiquity* 47, 4 (1982), 761-82.

Holyman, T.E., V.P. Lytwyn and L.G. Waisberg, 'Rainy River Sturgeon: An Ojibway Resource in the Fur Trade Economy', *Canadian Geographer* 32, 3 (1988), 194-205.

Lytwyn, Victor P., 'Ojibwa and Ottawa Fisheries Around Manitoulin Island: Historical and Geographical Perspectives on Aboriginal and Treaty Fishery Rights', *Native Studies Review* 6, 1 (1990), 1-29.

Schmaltz, Peter, 'The European Challenge to the First Nations' Great Lakes Fisheries', unpublished paper presented at the CHA, Charlottetown, 1992.

tools, pots, kettles and, in the case of the Five Nations, even woollen clothing. They also sought guns. These groups were not able to forge their own iron goods in this era, although they did rework and modify some metal tools. To the degree, therefore, that they gave up their old stone and flint working skills, to that extent they became more dependent on Europeans for increasingly essential tools and implements.

This subtle and slowly emerging dependence on European products coupled with a declining beaver stock intensified trade and political rivalries in the Great Lakes area. As well, the pressure of population loss due to disease and warfare further exacerbated tensions as Five Nations and Huron raided each other for captives to replace their human losses. French traders took what advantage they could from these escalating rivalries. While short-lived, the French-Mohawk treaty of 1645-46 provides an indication of the ease with which the French could abandon Native allies. The Mohawk were granted the right to hunt in new regions north of the St Lawrence and the French secretly assured the Mohawk that they would do nothing to protect pagan Algonkians living or hunting in those areas. Within Huronia, many sensed the ambivalent nature of French support and some willingly defected to, while many more were captured by, Five Nations warriors. In the summer of 1649 French traders, not French reinforcements, swooped into Huronia and returned to the St Lawrence with some 5,000 pounds of beaver fur. That winter many Huron died for lack of clothing, despite disinterring the dead and stripping them of the robes within which they had been buried. Soon after, the Huron were routed by the Five Nations and in the spring of 1650 French missionaries reached Montreal with three hundred survivors of the 30,000 people who had inhabited Huronia in 1600. By 1653, having defeated and dispersed the Petun and the Neutral, the victorious Five Nations seemed to have firm control of the Great Lakes territory and, with it, both major European trading circuits into that region. In fact, those victories helped to usher in a new stage in North America's business history, a stage which can only be properly viewed in the context of European developments.[4]

Notes

[1]B. Supple, 'The Nature of Enterprise' in E.E. Rich, ed., *Cambridge Economic History of Europe*, 5 (Cambridge, 1977), 436.

[2]D.H. Pennington, *Europe in the 17th Century* (London, 1989); T. Munck, *Seventeenth Century Europe, 1598–1700* (London, 1990); L. Blussé and F. Gaastra, *Companies and Trade* (Leeden UP, 1981); B. Supple, *op. cit.*, 393–461.

[3]R. Le Blant, 'Le Commerce compliqué des fourrures canadiennes au début du XVIIe siècle', *RHAF* 26 (1972), 53–66; J.F. Crean, 'Hats and the Fur Trade', *Canadian Journal of Economics and Political Science* 28 (1962) 373–86; Hugh Grant, 'Revenge of the Paris Hat', *Beaver* (1988–89), 37–44; John Reid, *Acadia, Maine and New Scotland . . .* ; biographies of Chauvin, de Monts and Champlain in *DCB* 1; Pierre Boule, 'French Mercantilism, Commercial Companies and Colonial Profitability', in L. Blussé and F. Gaastra, *op. cit.*; P.N. Moogk, 'Reluctant Exiles: Emigrants from France in Canada before 1760', *William and Mary Quarterly* XLVI (1989), 463–505; Michael Bliss, *Northern Enterprise: Five Centuries of Canadian Business* (Toronto, 1987); P. Goddard, 'Christianization and Civilization in 17th Century French Colonial Thought' (PhD thesis, Oxford, 1990).

[4]See Chapter 1, fn. 6; J.W. Bradley, *Evolution of the Onondaga Iroquois: Accommodating Change, 1500–1655* (Syracuse, 1987); W.C. Noble, 'Tsouharissen's Chiefdom: An Early Historic 17th Century Neutral Iroquoian Ranked Society', *Canadian Journal of Archaeology* 9 (1985); S.M. Jamieson, 'Economics and Ontario Iroquoian Social Organization', *CJA* 5 (1981); A. Rotstein, 'The Mystery of the Neutral Indians', in R. Hall *et al.*, eds, *Patterns of the Past: Interpreting Ontario's History* (Toronto, 1988), 11–36.

2

THE COLONIAL
BUSINESS
OF NEW FRANCE
1663–1763

3 CROWN, COLONY, AND BUSINESS ENDEAVOUR, 1663–1763: AN INTRODUCTION AND A FRAMEWORK

In a period of less than two decades in the mid-seventeenth century, three events helped set the contours of business behaviour on Canada's fur frontier for well beyond the next century: the dispersal of the Great Lakes people in the early 1650s, the coming of age of Louis XIV in France in the 1660s, and the chartering of the Hudson's Bay Company in England in 1670. These seemingly tangentially related occurrences were in fact linked by a common goal, the quest for control: the development of strategies and tools with which to structure and manage affairs, the pursuit of certainty in an uncertain environment.

In 1663 Louis XIV declared New France a Royal Province and henceforward part of France's normal governing structure. The Crown took direct financial responsibility, stripping intermediary companies of jurisdictional powers. By making the colony a department, similar to other administrative units within France, Louis XIV encouraged upwardly mobile élites to view positions in the colony as stepping stones to higher posts within European France. In economic terms, too, New France's 'place' in France became more clearly defined after 1663. It would exist to serve the imperial needs of the Mother Country. Some have called this mercantilism, a doctrine which allocated to colonies the role of supplying raw materials to the European heartland, receiving in exchange manufactured items from the mother country. The desire for self-sufficiency underlay the mercantilist doctrine. Self-sufficiency could be achieved via high tariffs, subsidies for domestic manufacturing and, most especially, an economically active and powerful central state.

In theory the head of the absolutist state which ruled France in the seventeenth and eighteenth centuries drew power from and was answerable to only God. In reality, however, the head of that state owed power to a combination of provincial, class, and familial groupings. The French monarch had constantly to appease, conciliate, and censure contending factions, social rivals, and provincial dynasties. In such a context there was only so much that a monarch could accomplish. The Crown could and did acquire the backing of the landed nobility through the sale of financial and judicial offices, offices which then became, for the life of the purchaser, tools to extort personal profits from the wider and mainly peasant-based population. In the time of Louis XIV royal offices and state pensions accounted for between one-half and two-thirds of the income of France's noble landed class. To conciliate support the French monarch had therefore to oversee the extreme decentralization of the state's financial system. Tax collection and other financial offices continued to be sold to private hands; the collection, spending and managing of state funds remained decentralized and without systematic checks from the centre. The resulting lack of financial control belied the reality of an absolutist state, even as the notion of such an entity gained more and more popular acceptance.

In his quest for supremacy Louis XIV also attempted to rule without a first minister, to become himself the first minister of the realm. For advisors he carefully chose men from clans or groups of the second, non-noble rank, men who did not carry with them an established power base in France. Yet, these men assiduously built up their own cadre of supporters using all the patriarchic and *rentier* tactics at their command. So extensive were such personal programs that one scholar has suggested that Colbert, the most famous of such appointees, directed more a family than a national enterprise. In this system men were attracted to government service less to serve national ends than to pad personal and patrimonial pockets. Like land, offices provided potential routes to ennoblement. Colbert realized this: he purchased a castle, traced his family tree to (Scottish) royal ancestry and married his daughter to French nobles.

The absolutist state mirrored the social classes and social pretensions of the social élite over which it ruled. In that context, mercantilism, rather than a centrally articulated and administered economic policy, was a reflection of the aspirations of various contending factions. Mercantilist ideas were, as D.C. Coleman has written in another context, 'utterances or moves in a bargaining process', and in France, the Crown was only one of many, albeit a powerful one, involved in the give and take of bargaining.[1]

* * *

Most historians argue that England far outdistanced France in moving into a capitalist-dominated, market-oriented economy in the seventeenth and eighteenth centuries. England's agricultural and political revolution in the seventeenth century led more swiftly than was the case in France to the creation of a wage-labour, consumer class, a mass market for which manufacturers and traders could provide goods other than simply luxury items purchased by a limited aristocratic clientele. By the end of the seventeenth century, some historians are of the opinion that a 'dictatorship of the bourgeoisie' reigned in England. No such argument is advanced for France. Most believe that it took the French revolution of the 1790s to create a similar political and economic structure. Until then peasants controlled small plots of land and only rarely produced more than they consumed or paid in various dues to others. In this context no mass consumer market could emerge. Merchants avoided investing in the production of such commodities and looked instead to commerce in luxury items to provide them with a way out of business, a means to acquire enough wealth to purchase land, government offices, and noble status. Nor did France create a centralized financial structure similar to that which emerged in England by the early years of the eighteenth century. England's more centralized structure permitted greater financial stability and the better possibility for coordinated state financial policy planning. France remained feudal, while England became capitalist.

These are compelling arguments. Yet overstatements must be guarded against. It took more than a century for England to emerge into a society dominated by mass consumer demand and diversified production. It is telling that in this and later periods British merchants continued to seek the trappings of the country gentleman: indeed some historians characterize British business behaviour even in the early nineteenth century as 'gentlemanly capitalism'.

Moreover, too often the term feudal is equated with stasis, no growth, lack of development or change. Yet in France, commercial agriculture emerged in certain areas; the putting-out system provided peasants with alternatives to subsistence farming; manufacturing did develop in the eighteenth century; some merchant traders operated firms on similar bases to those conducted by their English counterparts; officers and nobles and bureaucrats dabbled deeply in many commercial matters. By 1789 a large number of rural dwellers in France were neither commercial nor subsistence farmers. These underemployed rural dwellers enmeshed in a 'makeshift economy of the poor' were victims of unbalanced economic growth. In this sense the term feudal has merit. Social and political structures facilitated profiteering by privileged groups and discouraged the emergence of alternative money-making (however exploitative) élites. Marketing, financial, and cultural support for integrated and diverse economic development was therefore only slowly and even reluctantly put in place. In England, the Civil War of the mid-seventeenth century helped sweep away a social structure resistant to change. In France the Crown remained dependent on a noble class protective of traditional seigneurial privilege, resistant to direct taxation, and willing, for the most part, to live off the avails of small peasant *rentiers*. The persistence of this traditional social structure did not prevent all economic change, growth and diversification: it rather prevented the forging of effective links between various economic sectors. Even in England imbalance in economic growth occurred such that rural unemployment became a major problem at certain times and in certain places. The perpetuation of a feudal social system ensured that such imbalances and uneven growth, rather than static and no growth, were endemic in France in the seventeenth and eighteenth centuries.[2]

* * *

How does this Old World context facilitate an understanding of economic and business behaviour in New France? The contradictions inherent in the absolutist state rendered centralized, systematic economic policy-making and implementation problematic at best. The Imperial State did closely scrutinize economic development in the colony. Yet a rigid mercantilist doctrine was never enforced. As one historian of New France, while continuing to use the term, has admitted, 'This mercantilism became increasingly practical, supple, and even generous.'[3] After 1663 ministers concerned with the colony's economic affairs often stressed the need for economic diversity, including shipbuilding and iron works (to lessen France's dependence on Baltic nations), and multilateral trade with other French colonies as opposed to simple bilateral exchange with France. One Minister of the Marine, Jérôme de Pontchartrain (1699–1715), while officially opposing colonial manufacturers, did allow that 'their establishment in Canada ought not to be absolutely prevented, especially among the poor.'

An understanding of the Old World context also sensitizes the historian to the importance of social structures as mediators of economic and business behaviour. In the Old World merchants had little place. It has been said that 'Louis XIV hardly knew how to receive a merchant properly.'[4] Administered by office *rentiers*, mercantilist ends too often became subverted by empire-building and personal profit-taking.

This process occurred in New as well as Old France. In 1758 the Minister of Marine and Colonies admitted that 'In the colonies everyone trades more or less.' Those who did not, like one hapless 'civil servant', were often subject to sharp criticism, in this case from his mother-in-law:

> If you don't have enough wits to make some money where you are, you should be beaten since everyone knows what civil servants do and those who do not have a profitable trade are treated as idiots. You don't pay enough attention to these matters. It is all very well to do one's duty, but you should try to look after your own affairs as well.[5]

Most, however, would seem to have minded their own affairs quite well. Thus the Intendant, Jean Talon, Colbert's righthand man in the colony, is justly remembered for his energetic and often creative attempts to diversify the colony's economy in the 1670s. Yet even as he provided state subsidies for beer, iron, and other productive enterprises, he profited from personal economic endeavours. Louis Frontenac, perhaps New France's most famous Governor, went to the colony to make enough money to pay off angry debtors. He speculated in merchant shipping as well as the fur trade. In the 1730s Gilles Hocquart, another energetic intendant, sincerely attempted to raise the colony's economy by, as it were, its bootstraps. Yet he did so through the agency of a small number of personally appointed 'bureaucratic entrepreneurs' who saw no distinction between personal profit-making and state policy ends.

This system reached its nadir in the colony with the appointment of François Bigot as intendant in 1744. Bigot benefited from privately-held fur monopolies, and from partnership in mercantile ventures which received contracts from him to supply the state at inflated prices. He lived a sumptuous life. His penchant for aping the royal court at Versailles at a time when New France was under a virtual state of siege and when dismal poverty was the lot of most citizens typified the attitudes of his class. It is hard to know just how much money he grossed through private deals made possible by his public position. He may have overseen a cadre of fifty or so like-minded appointees. Much potential entrepreneurial energy was spent milking the profits to be had from speculation in offices in order to retire, as Bigot had dreamed, 'a country gentleman on a country property in an agreeable French province surrounded by family, friends and servants'.[6]

In fact Bigot and many of his cronies were arrested, tried and convicted of embezzling state money. Bigot was banished from France. This was not, however, an example of the State attempting to clean house. Rather, as John Bosher, an historian, has ably argued, it was more the case of the state seeking whatever scapegoats it could find in order to shift at least some of the blame for the British defeat of New France in 1759 to other shoulders. The conviction of major colonial officeholders also helped make it possible for the State to repudiate colonial debts — after all, how could the state know for sure which of these debts were legitimate? No law specified the correct mix of public and private endeavour; ultimately the Crown could, when it wished, when it was in its interest, render such a judgement. Speculators in office knowingly undertook that risk on their road to ennoblement.

Factional feuding, the inability to distinguish between state and personal ends, and the primacy of a noble life in France over a commercial career anywhere informed and curtailed business activity perhaps even more in New than in Old France. The perpetuation of the seigneurial system, the pervasiveness of a *rentier* officeholding mentality and a sparsely populated colony made the expectation of local economic diversification in New France somewhat unrealistic.

Does this mean, then, that from a business point of view the colony was a stagnant pond or—as Michael Bliss has colourfully argued—'a fur trading backwater, a couple of towns and a few thousand small farmers up a very large creek'. There are other interpretations. Some argue that after 1720 and before the Conquest the colony was modernizing in a manner every way comparable to that of the British colonies to the south. Only the conquest of New France by the English in 1763 ended such normal bourgeois-sparked growth. From this perspective the colony experienced similar business cycles to those which beset Old France. For France, 1650 to 1680 marked the worst years of a century characterized by falling prices and tight capital markets. Only slowly after 1713 did a turn-around in France's economy begin: between 1720 and 1745 her trade rivalled that of England and a major part of that trade involved her various colonial possessions. This controversy is of long duration and is permeated with ideological and national biases. We offer here an introduction to business life in New France, a portrait which highlights unbalanced growth and links that pattern to the strengths and weaknesses of the colony's Old World social structure.

Morris Altman, an economic historian, has provided the most recent and comprehensive statistical analysis of the colony's economy for much of the period under review.[7] His general finding is 'that Canada was economically dynamic and prosperous, even when compared to British North America' in the period 1695-1739. For much of the time before 1713 and after 1744 New France was beset by almost continual war. Its economy in those years was skewed and suffered accordingly. Only in the thirty years following 1713 did the colony experience peace and with it the opportunity for stable development. On the basis of census data for these years, Altman suggests that real per capita output for New France was 'similar' to that of British North America. Both economies experienced growth rates of about .05 to .06 per cent per year. Altman also argues that the colony's economy was 'fairly diversified': the agricultural sector dominated, contributing about 75 per cent of real growth domestic product, followed by the non-agricultural sector—shipbuilding, lumber, general trades—which generated

14 per cent and the fur trade which accounted for between 11 and 14 per cent in this time period.

If a colony of feudal France was indeed developing as rapidly as colonies of capitalist England, then one must rethink the relationship between the social structure and economic development. Before accepting such a conclusion (and, it should be noted, Altman does not make such a claim) one should be aware that the distribution of profits from the colony's economic activity is not measured here. In fact, as we shall see, profits generated by the significant colonial per capita output were distributed in a very unequal manner and in a way that retarded rather than encouraged continuous development.

A second point — and this is one concerning which Altman is too vague — concerns the meaning of 'fairly diversified'. It may be possible that per capita output was equivalent to that of British North America even while the structure of New France's economy remained different. Certainly, for example, New York exported a broader range of goods, fur, agricultural and manufactured items to a wider range of countries than did New France in this period, although the per capita value of their exports was roughly similar. In New France the fur trade dominated trade, probably representing in excess of seventy per cent of the value of exports for most years of the colony's existence. This strongly suggests that New York's economy was more diversified than that of New France and thus supports the proposition that relatively more balanced growth occurred within England and her colonies than within France and her Empire. It leaves open the social structural argument as accounting for much of the difference.

Altman's study clearly shows that economic growth occurred in New France. Yet that growth was of a relatively unbalanced sort and in that sense both the timing and the nature of colonial development reflected similar trends in Old Regime France. As in the mother country, the persistence of traditional social structures did not preclude economic output; rather, those structures impeded the development of linkages between various sectors, curtailed economic diversity, and ensured the continuance in power of a traditional élite. These factors, coupled with France's failure to encourage significant permanent settlement in New France, constituted severe obstacles to substantive economic growth. With these points in mind a closer look at business enterprise in New France, the operation of the fur trade, of general mercantile affairs, of craftsworkers and of farmers, is instructive.[8]

Notes

[1]D. Miquelon, *New France 1701–1744: 'A Supplement to Europe'* (Toronto, 1987); D. Miquelon, 'Canada's Place in the French Imperial Economy: An 18th Century Overview', *French Historical Studies* 15 (1988), 432–43; D. Parker, *The Making of French Absolutism* (London, 1983); D.C. Coleman, 'Mercantilism Revisited', *The Historical Journal* 23 (1980), 773–91.

[2]R. Hamilton, *Feudal Society and Colonization: The Historiography of New France* (Gananoque, 1988); M. Rosen, 'The Dictatorship of the Bourgeoisie, England 1688–1721',

Science and Society 45 (1981), 24–51; D. Parker, 'French Absolutism, The English State and the Utility of the Base Superstructure Model', *Social History* 15 (1990), 287–301; J.L. Goldsmith, 'The Agrarian History of Pre-Industrial France: Where Do We Go From Here?', *Journal of European Economic History* 13 (1984), 175–99.

[3]D. Miquelon, 'Canada's Place in the French Imperial Economy: An 18th Century Overview', *French Historical Studies* 15 (1988), 437.

[4]D. Parker, *The Making of French Absolutism*, 143.

[5]B. Young and J.A. Dickinson, *A Short History of Quebec: A Socio-Economic Perspective* (Toronto, 1988), 42.

[6]J.F. Bosher and J.C. Dubé, 'François Bigot', *DCB* 4 (Toronto, 1979), 69.

[7]Morris Altman, 'Economic Growth in Canada, 1695–1739: Estimates and Analysis', *William and Mary Quarterly* XLV (1988), 684–711.

[8]D. Miquelon, *New France 1701–1744* and 'Canada's Place in the French Imperial Economy . . . , 432–43; D. Parker, *The Making of French Absolutism*; John Bosher, 'The French government's motives in the *Affaire des Canada*, 1761–63', *English Historical Review* 96 (1981), 59–78; Hocquart and Bigot biographies, *DCB* 4; Michael Bliss, *Northern Enterprise* . . . ; Morris Altman, *op. cit.*; Denys Delage, 'Les Structures économiques de la nouvelle-France et de la nouvelle-York', *Actualité économique* 46 (1970), 67–118; Cameron Nish, *Les Bourgeois-Gentilshommes de la nouvelle-France, 1729–1748* (Montreal, 1968).

4 IN PURSUIT OF CERTAINTY: CANADA'S FUR FRONTIER, 1653–1763

Imperial powers were never very excited about the extent of economic return available from the trade in fur. For the Dutch the fur trade was, according to one historian, 'a mere flea-bite'. 'The most inconsiderable of all trades', a British politician declared: it accounted for under half a per cent of the total value of all English imports during the first seventy-five years of the eighteenth century. The company which controlled the trade in beaver in New France after 1718 received only about three per cent of its earnings from that endeavour. Yet the trade itself was a hotly contested affair. In part, that intensity was due to Imperial motives. But the very presence of Imperial states offered, for shrewd businessmen, the opportunity to reap high profits relative to the capital expended. If European powers were willing to underwrite infrastructural costs, then, private profit-taking seemed attractive. That trade also provided a stable income for a surprisingly large number of people especially in the Montreal region of New France. Moreover, the business strategies and commercial structures which evolved to carry out the trade in fur sheds light on the degree to which colonial business people could act independently of Imperial control and the pace at which commercial endeavour moved from a pre-modern to a more modern *modus operandi*.[1]

INSTABILITY IN THE INTERIOR, 1653–1715

At mid century the Iroquois had conquered several Native peoples living in southern Ontario. Despite the Iroquois' best attempts, however, those victories fell short of providing the power to control either trade flows or the activities of Natives living further to the north. Ottawa, Ojibwa, and Nipissing—not the Iroquois—took over the middlemen role vacated by the Hurons. Moreover, even as the Ottawa peoples travelled to and traded at Montreal, French traders moved inland to Ottawa territory north of Lake Huron and south of Lake Superior. In 1657 the French Governor, Lauson, who personally acquired 300,000 livres worth of fur, granted all settlers in New France the right to trade 'throughout the whole country'. An energetic Louis XIV, advised by his first minister, Jean-Baptiste Colbert, sent troops to quell the Iroquois and thus facilitated further French expansion into the interior. By the 1680s up to 800 itinerant salesmen, called *coureurs de bois,* travelled and traded throughout the Great Lakes hinterland. In addition, and often in competition with the Montreal based traders, state officials like the impecunious Governor Louis Frontenac set up a series of interior trading forts as part of what was virtually a private trading monopoly.

Colbert did not view the rampant commercial expansion on the part of the colonials with any enthusiasm. Rather he believed that too much expansion into

FORT FRONTENAC

AN INDEX TO COMMERCIAL POWER IN THE *PAYS D'EN HAUT,* 1671

As early as 1670, a Sulpician missionary situated in the Cayuga settlement at the Bay of Quinte near the Trent River warned his superiors about the extent of Iroquois hunting and trading as a middle group between Albany and northern Natives. He recommended the establishment of two French posts and a boat to patrol the Lake to stop this encroachment on what the French believed to be their private trading territory. Such was the context for the establishment in 1673 of Fort Frontenac, the first French trading post on the shores of Lake Ontario.

The selection of the site tells much about commercial relations on the north shore of Lake Ontario. The newly-appointed Governor, Louis Buade, Comte de Frontenac, trooped west in 1673 with a retinue of 400 men, 120 canoes, and two large bateaux. His destination was the Cayuga village at Quinte but, met en route by a delegation from the Five Nations, Frontenac acceded to their request to meet at the mouth of the Cataraqui River, the site of modern day Kingston. Since there was no Native settlement there, the Five Nations emissaries explained that Frontenac would not be seen to be favouring any particular tribe within the Confederacy. They neglected to say why there was no Native settlement at the mouth of an important link to the Ottawa River and the fur-rich interior: the surrounding land was of such low quality that it could not sustain any sizeable population. Nor was the site at all capable of being easily defended nor, even more importantly, appropriate as a location from which to exert control over Lake Ontario. Interested only in its trading potential, Frontenac mistook marsh reeds for meadows— 'of grass so good and so fine there is none better in France'—and declared in an imperious manner to the presumably suitably impressed Iroquois that this was where the French would erect their post.

The establishment of Fort Frontenac at a site deemed unfit by the Iroquois for Native habitation did little to disturb the Iroquois in their hunting and trading activities. The Cayuga chief put the matter most succinctly to Frontenac when he asked what the price for trade goods would be. To prevent 'roguish children', the Sachem hoped Frontenac could meet the competition at Albany. Frontenac did not reply and most current analyses suggest that the French were not able to compete in price with English goods. Over time some Natives did settle around and trade at the Fort but most tended to ignore the post, concentrating instead on fur trade routes near the Lake's western end and thereby maintaining their trading links with France's major European competitor, the English at Albany. Even those who continued to ply the Cataraqui River easily evaded the erstwhile French control by staying out of range of the Fort's guns. Despite military victories over the Iroquois in the mid-1660s, the French were far from being in a position to dominate events on the north shore of Lake Ontario.

Sources

Adams, N., 'Iroquois Settlement at Fort Frontenac in the 17th and Early 18th Centuries', *Ontario Archaeology* 46 (1986), 5–20

Konrad, V.A., 'An Iroquois Frontier: the North Shore of Lake Ontario during the Late 17th Century', *Journal of Historical Geography* 7 (1981), 129–44

Pritchard, J.S., 'For the Glory of God: The Quinte Mission, 1668–1680', *Ontario History* 65 (1973), 113–48

Webb, S.S., *1676: The End of American Independence* (New York, 1984).

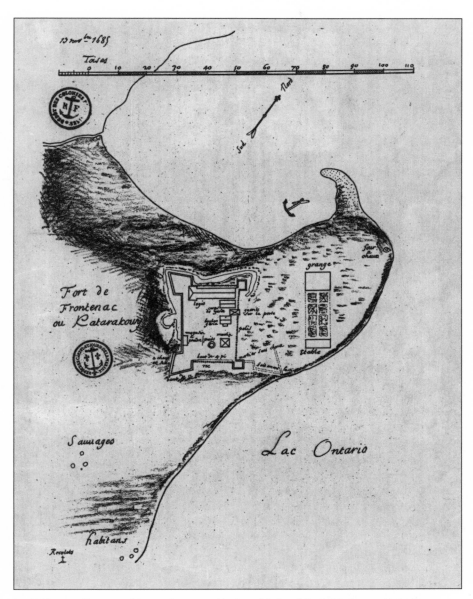

By 1685 a small group of Iroquois camped in the vicinity of Fort Frontenac. Note the missionary presence. *(Cartographic and Architectural Archives Division, National Archives of Canada/NMC4755)*

the interior would weaken the central colony and cause insurmountable problems of defence and supply. He desired a nucleated settlement focused on agriculture, lumbering, perhaps some shipbuilding, as well as the fur trade. Yet chartering the Compagnie des Indes Occidentales in 1664, 54 per cent financed by the state, and granting it monopoly trading rights in France for all beaver fur and moose pelts received at a fixed price from New France, facilitated the very expansion he opposed. In effect the guaranteed price assured the *coureurs de bois* a reasonable livelihood and teased state bureaucrats with prospects of windfall returns. Although the Compagnie was disbanded by the state in 1674, the policy of a state-regulated monopoly of beaver sales in France continued. Successor companies came and went. With guaranteed incentives still in place, *coureurs de bois* persisted paddling into the interior despite a licensing system established in 1681 restricting interior trade to 25 canoes per year.

The French state attempted to regulate the trade in fur under the aegis of chartered companies, and failed. It failed to put in place adequate mechanisms to control the expansive activity of local trader-colonists and speculating bureaucrats. Moreover, its guarantee of a fixed price in New France, an attempt to establish a stable economic base for colonial development, proved misguided. The market for fur in France and much of the rest of Europe could not absorb the escalating fur returns from the colony. This artificial disjuncture between supply and ultimate market cost the state, and at least some of those who invested in the various companies which managed the trade, dearly. By 1696 so great was the unsold glut of fur on the French market that the state virtually shut the trade down, although trading posts continued to exist at Fort Frontenac and, in the interior, at Michilimackinac and St Joseph, and some *coureurs de bois* continued to ply the interior waterways.

Ironically, even as the state attempted to end the fur trade, it was forced to delve even more deeply into public finances to provide subsidies for its continuance. Louis XIV depended on alliances with interior Natives to forestall expansion by Spanish and British into lands claimed by the French Crown in America. The curtailment of the fur trade upset those Natives who threatened to (and often did) turn to British competitors to trade. From the Imperial perspective, the fur trade had to become a loss leader in order to uphold French colonial ambitions in the New World.

That world also included the presence of the British who in 1664 ousted the Dutch from Albany; who in 1670 established, under the aegis of the Hudson's Bay Company, trading depots on the Bay; and who, throughout the later years of the seventeenth century, encouraged Iroquois aggression against the French even as they themselves fought pitched battles with armed French traders at the Bay. By the 1680s the French were engaged in commercial and military warfare in the north at James Bay and in growing military conflict with the aggressive Five Nations Iroquois in the south. Accordingly, they looked for aid from what most historical literature refers to as France's 'western allies', the unnamed Natives of a vaguely defined western interior. Far more than simply France's allies, these Natives were in fact independent actors who for a surprising length of time virtually controlled the central regions within which trading contact occurred. How, then, did what the historian, W.J. Eccles, has termed 'sovereignty-association' in the interior affect the conduct of fur trade affairs?

By the mid-1680s the Ottawa and Ojibwa peoples were successfully adapting to the changing dynamics of the French trade. Certainly the Ottawa and Ojibwa did lose some power, prestige, and status as the French moved further inland. Yet these same natives also adapted to the French presence. The Ottawa, for example, quickly settled around the central French trading post in the interior, Michili-mackinac, where they attempted to block other nations from direct French contact, supplied the French with native manufactured items such as canoes, provided food such as corn and fish, and continued to trade in furs. In fact the Ottawa exercised all the functions that Membertou had earlier on the coast, and that the homeguard Cree would do later in the northwest. Nor were the Ottawa simply dependent on the French in this period. They fought against tribes like the Miami and Sioux with whom the French wished closer relations. They entered into diplomatic negotiations with the Iroquois at various times. Whenever possible they traded with the British. Most importantly, and despite French *coureur de bois* intrusions, the Ottawa seemed to have maintained Native alliances first entered into during their period of dominance in the fur trade. Tithes, intermarriages, gift exchanges, and mutual war alliances held these tribes together even as the French began to undercut the Ottawa and Ojibwa as middlemen. Native relations and behaviours were far from simple reflections of and reactions to the French presence.

Thus in the 1680s when Governor Denonville asked the Ojibwa for assistance in his ongoing battles against the Iroquois, they swiftly moved south from Lake Huron and the southern shores of Lake Superior to further their own commercial and strategic ends. Their goal, like that of the French, was to subdue the Iroquois. Motivated in part by the desire for revenge and conquest, they had a further reason for action. The British-controlled fur trade operating out of Albany and through the Five Nations confederacy offered greater possibilities of return than did the French trade out of Montreal. To tap that trade required the conquest of the Iroquois. In effect the Ojibwa and Ottawa accepted French musketry in order to undermine French trade. By the late 1690s the Ojibwa had pushed the Iroquois out of Ontario and were attacking them in their villages south of the Lake. Vanquished, the Iroquois sought peace.

Following the Treaty of Ryswick in 1697, which ended hostilities in Europe between France and England, a series of colonial peace discussions commenced. These arrangements culminated in Montreal where the Peace of 1701 was concluded between the French, 200 representatives of the Five Nations and over 700 representatives of the Ojibwa, Ottawa, and other western tribes. They came to carve up Ontario and lands further west. The results have most often been interpreted from the perspective of the French, the Iroquois, and the latter's silent backers, the English at Albany, yet the participants who left the table with the fullest stomach were the Ojibwa. Before the gathering at Montreal, the Ojibwa and Iroquois had agreed to cease fighting in return for which the Ojibwa received an open path to trade at Albany and acquired control of the hunting territory north of Lake Ontario. The French were probably unaware of the Ojibwa-Iroquois agreement concerning the open path. In fact the French wanted the Iroquois to remain as a bulwark between the British and the western tribes. They wanted the Iroquois weak and subservient, not weak and impotent. They may have been, thanks to the Ojibwa, in a position to dictate to the Five Nations, but the French did not want a draconian peace. They wanted Iroquois-Ojibwa enmity to continue. By elevating themselves to the role of guarantor of peace, a sort of arbiter of last resort, they hoped to be in a position to kindle the fire while preventing a conflagration. If in 1701 the embers were warm enough to cause the Ojibwa to tread carefully en route to Albany, such would not always be the case.[2]

* * *

Compared to the aggressive commercial behaviour of the French, the English, especially those in the north associated with the Hudson's Bay Company, seemed at best passive and unaggressive, at worst, lazy and inconsequential. Because such a somnolent posture belies a long lived, successful corporate existence, historians have been somewhat at a loss as how best to explain the Hudson's Bay Company's early years. The fact that the Company survived its first fifty years is most often attributed to external factors: unlike the French commercial companies, the Hudson's Bay Company had no colony with which to contend; nor did it have private traders with whom to compete on the scale that French companies had; the inhospitable local terrain encouraged the underwriting of one activity— the fur trade, and prevented the expenditure of funds on a myriad of different ventures; the distance from the Bay to the English market was shorter than that from the western hinterland and New France to the French market and thus overall costs of doing business were lower. These are among the external factors by which historians have often explained how the company clung to the Bay in its early years.

More recently, other historians have adopted what might be called an internalist perspective in an effort to understand the company's success. These historians argue that the Hudson's Bay Company is best viewed as a prototype of a modern multinational enterprise. Much of their argument in support of this interpretation hinges on the nature of the company's internal organization. The strategies adopted by early chartered trading companies to deal with the uncertainties of long-distance trade in an era of poor communications and unreliable transport, to in effect manage the pre-modern market place, are very similar, such historians assert, to the managerial behaviour of modern multinational enterprise. In this context, the first half century of the Hudson's Bay Company's existence can be seen as an era of managerial experimentation. This was an era when the costs of shipping rose and the price of colonial products, in this case fur, dropped in Europe. In that context poor management led to disaster. Economic and efficient management became one of the fundamental prerequisites for success. In those years the Hudson's Bay Company evolved a set of managerial practices that set it apart from the strategies and structures adopted by its French competitors and provided it with a foundation for future development.

The central problem faced by early trading companies was how to lower the cost of transacting business in the sphere of long-distance trade. The Hudson's Bay Company, and several other early trading ventures, moved away from a 'free' market decentralized and dispersed trading system to one controlled as much as possible by salaried administrators. Operating within a hierarchical and bureaucratic structure, these managers were given responsibility for production, distribution, and pricing. Their central purpose was to devise systems for reducing cost, risk, and uncertainty in each of those areas. Instituting such a hierarchical structure was necessitated by the very large number of economic transactions such companies routinely undertook.

Although the Hudson's Bay Company was small compared to some of the companies operating in the Asian trade, it was nonetheless the third largest foreign trading company operating in England and by the early eighteenth century it engaged in thousands of economic transactions each year. Such transfers of goods and services took place between Natives and local traders, traders and ship captains, captains and Company principals in London, Company principals and British-European buyers, and Company principals and British suppliers. In an attempt to stabilize or at least 'predict' prices of supplies, 'futures' contracts were entered into with London manufacturers well in advance of delivery. Similarly, a constant price for fur, called the Standard of Trade, was instituted to help mesh markets separated by long distance in an era of pre-modern transport and communication. The number of economic exchanges—similar in volume to many late nineteenth-century enterprises— made it feasible and perhaps even essential for firms like the Hudson's Bay Company to attempt to generate, and to operate on the basis of, systematically gathered information concerning supplies, prices, and market preferences. It was during this period that the Hudson's Bay Company set up systems for handling efficiently these large numbers of linked affairs within one corporate structure. In so doing it became a precursor of a modern vertically integrated multinational enterprise.

The centralized management of such a large number and variety of transactions created its own costs and problems. We have already noted that many early trading companies failed abysmally in controlling their colonial representatives. Early economists like Adam Smith argued that the separation of investors from managers was a recipe for 'negligence and profusion'. This structural problem was exacerbated by the further difficulties inherent in long-distance control in an era when it took up to two years to issue commands and receive acknowledgement thereof. Some agency on the part of colonial managers was absolutely essential in such a context. Yet too much independence could and did lead to bankruptcy. Recognizing that such problems existed, many of the early trading companies, the Hudson's Bay Company among them, instituted mechanisms for controlling managers far from Head Office that are very reminiscent of modern practice.

To blunt the incentive for private trading the Hudson's Bay Company offered liberal wages and substantial bonuses. They also exacted oaths which included swearing commitment to the Company's goals and promising not to engage in private trade. Often they required the posting of bonds which would be forfeited if private trading took place. In an effort to emulate a family atmosphere or a corporate culture amenable to the Company's goals, the Directors praised, exhorted, and reprimanded whenever appropriate. Employee complaints were listened to and often, if directed against the alleged misconduct of others, quickly acted upon. As early as 1689 attempts were instituted to obtain young apprentices (fourteen-year-olds) and send them to the Bay to learn to read, write and trade in the hopes that they would become the nucleus of an effective and cohesive managerial cadre. Similarly by 1700 the Company began to hire its servants or workers from one area of Scotland, the cold and barren Orkney Islands, in an effort to find a homogeneous work force suitably disposed to the isolation and cold of the Hudson Bay region.

Even more importantly the Company instituted a series of measures that facilitated detailed monitoring and evaluation of managerial activity. Searching ships for contraband and reading employees' private letters were only the most crude of these measures. Detailed correspondence, increasingly systematic bookkeeping practice, and inventory control constituted an effective internal control system whereby the behaviour of individual managers (or factors) at the posts along Hudson Bay could be compared and evaluated.

For two centuries the Hudson's Bay Company's trading system revolved around the so-called Standard of Trade, a pricing mechanism that employed as its central unit of exchange the Made Beaver (MB), one prime beaver pelt, in terms of which all other trade goods and fur were assigned a value. Thus, for example, one pound of Brazilian tobacco cost two MB; one three-foot gun, seven MB, and six thimbles, one MB. The institution of fixed price and the conduct of bartered trade have often been seen as necessary qualifications of modern 'market-oriented' business practice in order to accommodate non-market Native trading behaviour. As corroboration of this interpretation, scholars like Abraham Rotstein and E.E. Rich point to the persistence of gift-giving, peace-pipe smoking and speech-making, practices embedded in Native tradition, that in the pre- and early contact era connoted more than reciprocal trade and extended to military alliances. Yet almost from the first presence of the British at the Bay, it was a case of new wine in old bottles. The British never allied with northern Natives, nor did those Natives expect them to. Speeches focused on trade matters, not on military or political affairs. More significantly, gift-giving quickly became less a testimony of friendship and more a means to achieve a profit. Natives offered low quality fur and local produce, not traditional symbolic items, and were, in turn, given gifts which would entice them to return with more followers the following year.

Rotstein and Rich, nevertheless, make a valid point. Some elements of Native culture did, indeed, set limits to the bargaining process. Natives had fixed needs and rarely varied from them. Their society abhorred hoarding. They also had limited carrying capacity in the canoes in which they travelled to the Bay each year. The combination of these factors undermined behaviour expected in a purely market-based exchange context. For example, the lowering of prices on Company goods would not necessarily attract more Natives bringing more fur. Rather the Natives would bring fewer fur since their needs and their carrying capacity could be more easily met. Gifts that could be consumed on the spot—rather than price reductions—were the most effective means of attracting Native traders.

Calculated bargaining occurred but was conditioned by the contrasting ethics of the two cultures: one predisposed towards no growth and the public distribution of goods; the other, towards growth and accumulation. Yet even here one should be wary of making too simple or stark a contrast between Native and European traders. In seventeenth-century Europe, the no-growth ethic conditioned the market behaviour of most agrarian dwellers. If the historian Fernand Braudel can claim, like Rich and Rotstein, that those peasants 'were not really integrated into the business of the market', it takes nothing from their ability to bargain shrewdly, nor from the fact that such a mentality was shared by the vast majority of rural Europeans in that era.

Similarly the system of bartered trade and a fixed price reflected Old World practice as much as New World needs. We have already noted that barter played a major role in the European trading system of this era, a sensible practice in a time of relative scarcity of metallic coinage. A well-used bookkeeping manual even had a separate chapter for barter transactions. The notion of a fixed price responded to several of what one writer has termed 'the structural weaknesses in the European economy' of the seventeenth and eighteenth centuries. At a time of uncertain market information occasioned by poor transport and communication over long distances, the fixed price provided an upper bound to trade at the Bay. The implementation of a constant trading standard or stable price structure did provide increased certainty and clarity in the pre-modern exchange system.

Equally importantly the Standard of Trade provided a means to check the agency of colonial traders. If the return in fur from a trading post did not match or exceed the Made Beaver value of the trading goods expended, the local factor was required to explain in written detail and, if such explanations failed to convince, he was then called back to London to account in person. While traders could when possible (that is, when it would 'not give any disgust to the natives') trade below the Official Standard, they could not exceed it. That Standard represented an upper bound to the price the Company was willing to pay the Natives for the fur they traded.

This price system should not be confused with the guaranteed fixed price offered by the various chartered companies operating within the context of the French fur trade. In the first place that price went to the independent French traders who themselves struck different bargains with interior Native traders. In this sense French traders competed against themselves as well as the British in their efforts to make as large a profit as possible from their guaranteed price. Nor did the French traders purchase all their trading goods from one company. And finally, they sold all other fur besides that of beaver and moose to a series of independent buyers situated in Atlantic ports in France.

When one also realizes that the Hudson's Bay Company did not send traders into the hinterland as the French did, the comparison suggests that in many ways the French system was the more flexible and aggressive. French traders in the interior should have been able to offer better prices and to adjust to market conditions—assuming an adequate guaranteed price for fur—than could their British competitors. But in fact, as the work of the historian Elizabeth Mancke has demonstrated, the Standard of Trade had built into it a competitive pricing system and a degree of flexibility not immediately apparent. The goods sent to the Bay for trade came with variable mark-ups. Those most sought after by the Natives —cloth, metal items, and guns—had the lowest mark-up, in part because they turned over more quickly, but mainly because the Company had to keep these items priced relatively low in order to compete effectively against the French and thus entice the Natives to the Bay. While these items were probably not loss leaders (we do not know what profits were on these items because packaging, transport, and labour costs are not deducted), they did serve to attract Natives to trade for items with higher mark-ups and presumably greater profits. As Mancke put it, 'Fixed prices did not preclude competitive pricing; they only established which goods would be competitively priced.' And, in fact, the pricing structure was carefully crafted. Accessories required for the proper use of guns, items like gun powder, powder horns, shot and flints, had mark-ups varying from 529 to 1900 per cent whereas the gun itself was marked up under 90 per cent. Over the first four decades of its history, as the Hudson's Bay Company directors began to be drawn from London's business and mercantile community, those directors responded to Native demand as conveyed by the traders along the Bay and shrewdly selected an inventory of saleable goods priced in a manner which permitted competition and promised adequate returns. It was a conservative strategy which sought stability and long-term return. And, as we shall see, such a strategy turned out to be quite appropriate for its time.[3]

As with so many other aspects of trade between Natives and Europeans, credit giving and taking emerged from past practices and represented the current interests of both parties. From the Hudson's Bay Company's point of view, granting Native hunters and traders credit helped to ensure their return to the company's northern posts the following year. It was a means of combating French competition. It was also a means of ameliorating the shocks occasioned by years of poor fur harvests, comparable to similar credit systems at that time in rural England designed to protect against poor wheat harvests. In years of distress, credit allowed Natives to continue to hunt fur and to trade the following year. As in seventeenth-century England, where credit 'was a common feature of life', so too by 1732 in James Bay credit had 'become a custom'.[4]

From the perspective of the Cree, who lived in the James Bay area, credit may have been viewed less as an economic transaction than as a moral imperative. Cree Natives, as Toby Morantz has pointed out, 'adhered to an ideology of reciprocity which permeated their natural and supernatural worlds'. If people looked after you, you looked after them. The Cree accepted credit and generally repaid advances because this was the moral thing to do. Just as they had fed Europeans by providing game and fish, Europeans could be expected to return that obligation by providing supplies in anticipation of future hunting returns. The Cree equated credit with the notion of reciprocity which lay close to the heart of their culture. Credit, rather than symbolizing the immediate dominance of one culture over another, represented, like barter, fixed prices, and gift-giving, a blending of traditional practices of Native and European.

'A DIVISION OF SPOILS': 1715–1763

Before 1715 few of the companies engaged in the North American fur trade made profits. Most of the large chartered companies in the French trade ended up bankrupt; the Hudson's Bay Company itself failed to declare a dividend between 1690 and 1718. After about 1715, however, demand for fur on the European market began to increase. Existing stockpiles were low in London and rotten in France and thus there was little usable inventory on hand to meet the demand. Following the Treaty of Utrecht in 1713 Europe experienced some thirty years of peace. Prospects for a profitable fur trade had rarely looked better.

The years leading up to the mid-eighteenth century are generally described as a 'crucial period' of intense competition in the fur trade. Because the era ended with the military conquest of New France by the British, there is a natural tendency to see that trade in terms of Imperial diplomacy, a context which relegates consideration of economic impact, profits, and commercial strategy to secondary importance. This tendency has been accentuated by the use made of the fur trade by the French state in the early eighteenth century. Even if such a perspective makes some sense in the French context, it makes none in the British. That state had little to do with governing the activities of the fur trade at Albany or at Hudson Bay. Moreover, and this is a point too often overlooked by those historians who view the trade simply from the perspective of Imperial diplomacy, for many in New France and some in France that fur trade continued to be first and foremost a business. Since colonial merchants were the linchpins of the Imperial system in North America, it makes sense to ask what was in it for them. Indeed even from the state's perspective a reasonably healthy colonial merchant group could only benefit Imperial ends. On the shifting foundation of Imperial subsidies and within the context of Native-French diplomacy and British competition, local colonial entrepreneurs evolved strategies appropriate to the context within which they operated. So, too, did their British competition and sometime Native allies.

The Ojibwa, busily establishing permanent settlements on the north shore of Lake Ontario, were quick to take advantage of the tense but relatively peaceful relations between the British and French after the Treaty of Utrecht in 1713. They encouraged English traders, selling them two hundred 33-foot canoes — each capable of carrying three tons of trade goods—in 1725 so that the British could travel to the north shore of Lake Ontario and trade with Ojibwa, virtually within sight of French posts. Nor did Ojibwa await British traders: canoe travel by Ojibwa across Lake Ontario increased eleven times between 1720 and 1724 over what it had been for the four previous years. The value of trade at the French posts on the southern Great Lakes fell by 47 per cent between 1724 and 1725.

Faced with severe competition from Oswego, the French closed their Toronto post even as more Ojibwa moved south.

The French were also pressed by the English from the north. In 1713 the Treaty of Utrecht had ceded the Bay to the English. A scant five years later the Hudson's Bay Company declared its first dividend in twenty-eight years. The French responded by attempting to cut into the Hudson's Bay Company's hinterland. Between 1717 and 1726, the French state reopened old northern posts at Temiskaming, Abitibi, and Nipigon and constructed new ones at Michipicoten followed, in the northwest, by Fort St Charles and a series of tributary posts in the 1730s. In the same decade some Ojibwa from Lake Superior moved north, pushing the inland Cree further west and north. The Ojibwa moved in order to maintain what control they could of the French fur trade. They did not want the French to initiate trading links with other western and northern tribes. There is also evidence that the Ojibwa, despite the French, traded directly with the British at James Bay, even as they did their best to prevent other Natives from doing so.

In its attempt to assist the fur trade the French state did more than supply infrastructure. It also reinstituted the brandy trade and abolished open bidding for monopolies at the interior posts, a system which had encouraged high prices and sharp trading practices. With leases now available at a lower cost and in a more regulated or stable environment, merchants could estimate with more certainty overall expenditures. The effect was immediate. Montreal merchants, who acquired licences to trade from the government, hired some 500 *engagés* to travel into the interior in most years of the 1730s. This represented about double the number hired in the 1720s. One-third of these *engagés* stayed the winter. Most travelled to one or other of the two major interior trading and trans-shipment posts, Detroit or Michilimackinac. Those who did not (*circa* 43 per cent in 1735 and 34 per cent in 1755) went mainly to a number of smaller posts established in the 1730s north and west of Lake Superior and further south in what is now northern Michigan and Illinois.

If these policies pleased colonial traders, the granting by the Crown of a monopoly over all beaver sales in France and the sale of all guns, shot, and strouds (a woollen product manufactured in England and essential to the fur trade) in the colony to one company, the Compagnie des Indes, did not. After a shaky start in 1718 as an essential part of the financier John Law's soon bankrupt commercial and financial empire, the Compagnie became in the early 1720s almost 'a department of the Controller General's Office'. The Compagnie consistently refused to accede to petitions from New France for freer trade and for the right to manufacture hats in the colony. Without doubt the Compagnie, on behalf of the state, viewed the colony as little other than a profitable source of raw material. And profitable it was: after expenses, the Compagnie between 1727 and 1743 netted about 200,000 livres profit per year. This represented a 26 per cent return on capital invested in the trade, over double what most mercantile businesses received in transatlantic ventures.

Historians have long suspected that the Compagnie reaped such substantial returns at the expense of colonial merchants. One study has suggested that in

1715 less than a dozen Montreal merchants had capital assets worth 50,000 livres. A second study has confirmed that Montreal's merchants on the eve of the Conquest enjoyed, at best, a moderate prosperity. Since the price charged by the Compagnie to French and European fur buyers was not above standard international rates, it follows that the price Montreal merchants received for beaver was low. It is tempting to conclude that the French fur trade business represents a classic example of the under-development of a colony by its mother country. As Wallerstein and others have argued, the emerging world system favoured the centre (Europe) at the expense of the periphery (in this case, New France).

Yet one of the problems with such a conclusion is that it portrays colonials as cardboard figures willingly cut to whatever shape French entrepreneurs and politicians desired. The denial of agency and ingenuity to colonial dwellers is of a piece with similar traditional depictions of Natives. A more supple perspective, one which allows for agency and creativity in the colony, is required. Clearly business in New France was conditioned and constrained by structures imposed from Europe. Yet within these structures merchants and others persisted in the fur trade. There is little evidence, before the wars following 1744 and the punitive commercial policies of the intendant François Bigot on the eve of the Conquest, of merchants quitting the colony. There is evidence, however, of increased mercantile control of that trade.

In the 1720s commandants had turned the various interior posts and forts into military commercial complexes resulting in great profit for themselves. But it would seem that in the 1730s and 1740s merchants, rather than commandants at interior forts and government placemen in Montreal, had taken firm control of the local trading companies that received the right to trade in the interior. Between 1720 and 1730, officers held 43 per cent of fur trade permits; between 1739 and 1752 they held only 16 per cent. Differentiation of function took place within the mercantile community. *Marchands voyageurs* hired *engagés* or canoemen and travelled with them into the interior to conduct trade. Others, known as *marchands équipeurs*, became outfitters, selling goods to those who travelled inland and remaining separate from the companies formed for the interior trade. There were perhaps as many as twenty who specialized in this trade at Montreal after 1720, and by the 1740s some outfitters began themselves to acquire trading leases from the government which they then subcontracted to a second company in return for the right to provision its trade and market its fur (save for beaver skin). This last arrangement anticipated the wintering partnerships that would typify the fur trade out of Montreal after the Conquest. There are also indications of technological upgrading by way of investment in larger boats. And finally, a trend towards concentration of ownership of fur permits is evident after 1739.

How, then, can one account for this evidence of colonial merchant prosperity in a context of plundering by metropolitans and predatory competition by the British? Some local merchants took advantage of the opportunities offered by the British market. Quite often British traders at Albany were able to offer higher prices for beaver than the Compagnie des Indes. When this occurred London's imports from Albany rose, suggesting an increase in smuggling. But ultimately smuggling was an unsatisfactory solution. Costs and risks were high. Moreover even at its peak, London's imports from Albany represented about one-fifth of Quebec's shipments to France. Smuggling did not compensate Montreal merchants for the low prices offered by the Compagnie des Indes.

A more telling strategy was to use the structure imposed by metropolitans against those who imposed it. From the Imperial perspective the trade remained an arm of the state, an enterprise primarily useful for maintaining the allegiance of interior Natives. Profits, while obviously appreciated, were a secondary concern. In this context Montreal merchants combated the low prices offered by the Compagnie des Indes by petitioning the Ministry of the Marine, warning that such prices would be scoffed at by the Natives who would then desert to British traders at Oswego, Albany and Hudson Bay. The French Empire, they warned, would be put at risk. Merchants also argued that state money for gift-giving in order to manage native 'mouvements dans les Pays d'en Haut' and maintain their allegiance to French trade and war aims was absolutely necessary. The strategy was effective. In response to such petitions, Compagnie prices were, if grudgingly, raised several times and colonial merchants benefited. And the state continued to issue payments to natives, the total of which represented in the 1730s about one-half the revenue received by the Crown from the fur trade and in the 1740s exceeded that revenue. Since merchants often acted as intermediaries, both in making known native demands and in distributing state largesse, the opportunity for fraud was palpable.

But for Montreal merchants to benefit from this strategy they would have had to pocket the increase in price rather than pass it on to the Natives. Since this, it would seem, is exactly what they did do, the question then becomes, how was British competition neutralized? Gift-giving helped. But the British also gave gifts. There is, moreover, a clear consensus in the historical literature that the British in Albany and at the Bay offered better value for fur than did the French. There is also strong evidence that suggests that Natives in the proximity of British and French competitors were shrewd traders and went where the best price could be had. Yet there would seem to have been a limit to the distance that Natives would travel in search of a bargain. As early as 1727 a disgruntled factor at Fort Albany on Hudson Bay complained

> I don't suppose the French trade so largely as we, but notwithstanding the natives being a people naturally inclined to laziness, they choose, rather to trade the goods up in the country than have the fatigue of coming down here.[5]

Natives in the northwest would seem, in fact, to have been discerning buyers who were very conscious of the costs of distance travel. They appreciated home delivery and thus paid higher prices for certain items offered by French traders in the interior. They continued, however, to go to the Hudson's Bay Company for essentials not available from the French. They simply went, as two close students of Native trading strategy have noted, 'at less frequent intervals'.

Should one conclude, then, that the French bested the British in the fur trade in this era? Certainly the French held their own in the hinterland area served by

Hudson's Bay Company posts at York, Albany, and Moose Factory. In 1755 the French shipped 615 packs of fur from posts in that area, while the British shipped 750. Moreover, following 1740, the three British posts had been experiencing rising prices and declining profits and throughout the early 1750s had been suffering losses. Yet the fact remains that, for the French, the northern shipment represented only twelve per cent of the total fur packs shipped from Canada to Montreal that year. In reality fierce competition only occurred in limited zones. In the era before the Conquest few posts were very close. The Hudson's Bay Company did not leave the Bay until the 1770s and few New York merchants went into the interior. Moreover the French state allowed only a fixed number of licensed French traders into the interior in any one year. As a result, the possibility of playing off one French merchant against another was restricted. Nor is this to imply that the British sacrificed profits in order to avoid competition. Unlike the French traders, the Hudson's Bay Company did not experience the same state pressure to expand into the interior and raise the flag on behalf of Empire. By remaining at the Bay in this period, the Company avoided the high overhead expenses incurred by Montreal traders and, as well, benefited from the tightly run managerial system described earlier. The Company paid close attention to market demands in Europe. It rarely shipped more fur from North America than it could sell in one year and keep as a small inventory to guard against ships failing at sea or other uncontrollable occurrences attendant on long-distance commerce. In this period it began to concentrate on other fur besides beaver and, in fact, the Company made its highest profits on the sale of marten, not beaver, skins. Without doubt the French were shipping a greater volume of fur to Europe. Yet one estimate of the Hudson's Bay Company's profits between 1739 and 1748 reports a thirty per cent return on capital invested and a second more conservative estimate nonetheless concludes that the Company turned a reasonable profit in all but seven years between 1737 and 1762. Not only did the Company not miss a dividend in these years, but it also invested considerable sums in other trading and banking enterprises in London. This last fact is of more than passing interest. Instead of reinvesting in and thus expanding the fur trade, the Company chose to avoid increased competition and invest substantial profits in other pursuits. All of this tends to confirm the suggestions of the historian, Thomas Wein, that the North American fur trade in the first half of the eighteenth century was characterized 'less [by] commercial trench warfare than a division of spoils'.

Nor, in the colony, were merchants the only ones who benefited from those 'spoils'. This point is often overlooked both by those who believe, *à la* Wallerstein, that little profit remained in colonies and by those who have approached the fur trade from the perspective of the staple approach, which generally assumes that little economic spin-off took place in staple trades. But profits did accrue to colonial merchants and, as one study of the fur trade's impact on the Montreal region has concluded, fur-trade money found its way into the pockets of other than merchants. Between 1714 and 1745 over 9,000 *engagés* were hired by Montreal merchants to transport goods into and fur out of the interior. These men were all from the Montreal region and they earned an average of 216 livres per trip. This was not a great deal of money in a period where a non-agricultural worker could normally earn between 300 and 400 livres per year. The fact that over sixty per cent of those for whom we have an occupation called themselves *habitants* or *habitant-voyageurs* suggests, however, that most regarded the fur trade as a profitable adjunct to other pursuits.

In some cases those pursuits may well themselves have been linked to the fur trade. Up to fifty per cent of the merchandise shipped to the interior each year was grown, milled, or manufactured in the colony. Money spent for goods in the colony varied from 60,000 livres in 1727 to over 100,000 livres in the early 1740s. The combined sum spent on fur-trade salaries and goods in the latter years in the Montreal region reached one-half of all money spent on the colony by the French government and one-tenth of the value of the colony's exports for those years. In the years before the Conquest, the fur trade, and enterprise occasioned by it, provided many in the Montreal region with at least a dependable income in an uncertain age.[6]

BUSINESS AND SOCIETY IN *LE PAYS D'EN HAUT*

No analysis of the fur trade in this period can ignore the fact that business relations fostered dramatic cultural change throughout *le pays d'en haut*. That trade encompassed and depended upon more than decisions made by male merchants in British boardrooms, state directives issued by French statesmen, daring exploits by male *coureurs de bois*, and shrewd dealing between Hudson's Bay factors and Native hunter/traders. The fur business was a gendered, multi-racial, and socially stratified affair. A brief look at activity around the Hudson's Bay posts in the north, and at the French posts in the central and southern Great Lakes regions in the pre-Conquest era, will indicate some of its social and cultural complexity.

Mention has already been made of those Cree and Ojibwa in the north and northwest regions of the upper country who traded with both the British and French. The British referred to these people as the uplanders, Natives who brought fur to trade at their posts, but who did not stay in the vicinity on any longer term basis. A second group of northern Natives, known as the homeguard, adopted a different role. Cree became homeguards for several reasons. Between 1670 and 1730, game began to become noticeably depleted in the area west of James Bay. As caribou, moose, and beaver became scarce, more Natives turned up at British posts in a destitute and 'almost starved' condition. In order to obtain food and trade goods, some of these Natives stayed and hunted geese for the traders. Knowledge that post food was available probably encouraged other Cree to hunt fur bearers rather than meat bearers such as caribou, and their dependence on the British for sustenance increased. Finally the demand for fur and the Cree's need to supply that demand created escalating pressures on the local fur-bearing populations; as these populations declined, Cree dependence on the British again increased.

Dependence did not lead to complete trust on the part of the British, nor did it lead to complete subservience on the part of the homeguard Natives. Sakie, a homeguard captain at Moose Factory, and his wife, Queen, had constantly to be cajoled, given presents, and watched carefully. The local trader often thought the homeguard feigned starvation in order to obtain food easily. Yet the Hudson's Bay factor generally acceded because when he did not Sakie threatened to, and on occasion did, go north to Fort Albany, leaving Moose Factory without their accustomed hunters and food providers.

Relations were further complicated by the fact that interaction between the homeguard and traders was as much social as economic. While the Hudson's Bay Company officially discouraged sexual and illicit trade between their employees and Natives, such regulations were widely ignored. Ship captains were only too happy to smuggle furs back to England. After the 1680s Hudson's Bay men were not allowed to bring European women to the Bay. As a result, the chief trader often took a Native woman into the post to live as his 'bedfellow'. Lesser traders could entertain Native women in their quarters during the day, but not overnight. Officially company servants, the lowest on the social and company hierarchy, were denied any contact. In reality the incidence of venereal disease suggests that such a ban was ineffectual.

The mixed-blood offspring of these many sexual liaisons soon became quite noticeable amongst the people who lived near the forts. These mixed-blood people symbolized an intermingling and merging of cultures that took place across many areas of activity. Fur traders began to use snowshoes and moccasins. In turn the homeguard Natives, like Sakie, wore a captain's coat, 'laced hat . . . stockings [and] a white shirt'. As early as 1721, Miscamote, a homeguard leader at Fort Albany, expressed his wish to 'be buried nigh the British' and in 1745 when Sakie died at Moose Factory he was buried, as was his wife two years later, 'after the English fashion'. This voluntary forsaking of sacred traditional burial practices is evocative testimony to the depth of cultural interaction at the Bay. And the term is interaction, not assimilation. If some Cree adopted British burial practices, Hudson's Bay traders conformed to Cree marriage formalities including obtaining the sanction of the bride's relatives and the payment of presents to the bride's family. Some traders upon retirement even took their Native wife with them to England. And many traders left, through their wills, bequests to their country wives. Interaction was conditioned by personal as well as economic needs.

Not all Cree accepted British customs to the extent evidenced by Miscamote and Sakie. Sakie, indeed, had a brother who traded with the French. Esquawenoe, an uplander leader, who frequented Moose Factory for a period of some twenty years, is another case in point. Termed 'the grand politician of all', and a 'sly cunning fox', Esquawenoe was known to trade with the French and had a son who was a prominent trader at French posts. During the tense years of conflict in the late 1750s, British fear and distrust of Esquawenoe's French connections increased to such an extent that they determined 'to take him into custody', although he was by that time a very old man probably not capable of much duplicitous activity. After four days' incarceration the uplander leader hanged himself in his cell. For some Cree, European rules remained anathema. In so many ways did events along this thin northern frontier of contact between European and Natives foreshadow the present.

A similar intermingling of Europeans and Natives took place at French posts in the central Great Lakes region. The most important of these posts, both as a fur trading and transhipment site, was Michilimackinac situated where Lakes Huron, Michigan, and Superior met. Life at Michilimackinac and at smaller French posts was simple in the extreme. Residents did little farming, depending on Ojibwa and Ottawa for crops and fish. Most who wintered were engaged in the fur trade, as a petty merchant, voyageur, clerk or boatman. Only a small garrison manned the Michilimackinac post (perhaps 35 men) and most of these men were engaged at some level in the fur trade. The largest building in these interior posts was, invariably, the local chapel or mission residence. Merchants and common voyageurs ate similar food, wore similar clothes, and occupied similar hewn log cabins which rarely exceeded 340 square feet in space and could be entered through two three-foot, five-inch high doors.

As did the British at the Bay, so too at Michilimackinac, French fur trade employees commonly married or lived with Ojibwa and Ottawa women. In the eyes of some, this relationship had about it the aura of sexual exploitation. In 1701, the Jesuit missionary at Michilimackinac averred that Native women 'found out that their bodies might serve in lieu of merchandise and would be still better received than beaver skins'. But Native women were more than sexual objects to French fur traders, just as the fur traders were other than simple sexual partners to Native women. Ojibwa and Ottawa women and their Métis offspring, like the Cree in the north, provided merchants with potentially lucrative links to Indian fur traders; ties of kinship helped French traders cultivate markets and influence in native society impossible by most other means. Native women helped European traders acculturate to the interior life, teaching them the use of the snowshoe, cooking appropriate meals, and acting as guides and general labourers. From the Native perspective, these liaisons facilitated access to powerful European traders, prized European goods, and the increased status that such relations conferred within Native society.

Small wonder, then, that between 1698 and 1765 almost one-half of the recorded marriages at Michilimackinac were between Canadian employees and Native or Métis women. During the same years about forty per cent of all recorded births were Métis offspring of those marriages. Indeed, the increased numbers of Métis required the Michilimackinac garrison to expand its walls at least three times before 1763.

Métis were truly offspring of the fur trade. A people between two cultures, the Métis mediated between Native and European in matters of war, trade, politics, and social affairs. In the course of so doing, the Great Lakes Métis, some historians have suggested, developed a sense of group consciousness, a vision of themselves as a distinct people. Other historians have disagreed, pointing out that Métis rarely intermarried. Rather they tended to marry outside their cultural group in order to better themselves within and strengthen their ties to the general fur trading community. This behaviour certainly made the emergence of a group consciousness more problematic. Nor did missionaries, merchants, and officers who worked in the interior in the eighteenth century commonly use terms which distinguished those of mixed blood ancestry from the interior residents. Such ascriptions did not become current until the 1820s. Specific gender roles may also have made difficult the emergence of a distinct identity. Male Métis tended to work more closely with white fur traders; female Métis more often remained in the geographical region of birth and maintained relatively closer and continued contact with their Native mother and her kin.

It may be that the resulting absence of cultural classification of the half breed by others and apparent resistance to cultivate a conscious distinctiveness themselves served the Great Lakes Métis well in their role as go-betweens linking Indians and whites in the fur trade society of *le pays d'en haut*. Lacking a specific cultural identity, they could be what others wished—white or Native as the occasion required. In this sense the children of the fur trade lived a chameleon-like existence, a life, as we shall see, increasingly difficult to maintain in the face of structural changes in the fur trade in the early years of the nineteenth century.

The social structure which emerged in and around Detroit, the major fur-trading transhipment centre in the southern interior, differed in several significant ways from that at Michilimackinac and the smaller western and northern posts. Starting in the 1730s, the French Governor, Beauharnois, encouraged settlers to take up land near the fort and by 1750 some 500 French Canadians farmed some 340 hectares of cleared land laid out in the seigneurial strip systems fronting on the banks of the St Clair River. Their produce helped provision the fur trade in that region. The emphasis on farming also lessened contact between Natives — of whom some 2,600 camped near the garrison in 1750—and settlers. Thus, relative to its larger population (200 at the garrison in winter and some 400 in the summer), Detroit probably did not contain proportionately as many Métis as did Michilimackinac. Detroit, in fact, reflected a mid point between the totally fur-trade structured societies of the central-northern regions and the increasingly agriculturally focused settlements further south and west in Illinois territory.[7]

* * *

This examination of the fur trade in early Canada sheds light on the degree to which business practice in the arena of long-distance trade was becoming ever more sophisticated. Possibly following the lead of much larger chartered trading companies operating in the Asian region, the Hudson's Bay Company gradually constructed a managerial system which facilitated some degree of control and some possibility of prediction in the volatile context of the colonial fur trade.

Operating in a different context, Native traders also adapted to change and evolved strategies to preserve and enhance their positions in the fur-trading system. In addition to playing French and British traders off against one another, Native traders also threatened British factors with the possibility of trading at a different British post in order to strike a better bargain. Yet in a context where competition occurred in only limited zones, Natives became discerning buyers, willing to pay higher prices to French *marchand-voyageurs* and thus avoid annual long-distance travel to the British at the Bay. Certain superior quality items would be acquired from the British by biannual visits. And, although direct documentation is not available, it is quite probable that the increased price paid French traders was passed on by the Natives to other interior tribes.

French traders operated in a context different from that of the British and Natives, and like the latter, they adapted effectively to that context. The French state structured the economic affairs of the fur trade to a far greater extent than did the British state. The Compagnie des Indes undoubtedly garnered the greatest profit from the beaver trade following the mid-1720s. Moreover, colonial fur-trade merchants competed against themselves as well as the British. Yet those merchants were able to trade non-beaver skins to a variety of French companies — in the 1730s such shipments exceeded the value of beaver exports — and we know almost nothing about the nature of profits in that sector of the business. As well, colonial merchants nicely turned Imperial rationales for the fur trade against the Compagnie and in the process extracted higher prices for their product. And, contrary to what the staple theory might predict, colonials other than merchants also benefited from the fur business. Some spin-offs did exist. The fur trade was a significant colonial business endeavour.

Such would seem, at least, to have been the case in the Montreal region of New France. From the perspective of colonial development as a whole, that trade is less impressive. Altman estimates that the trade only accounted for about 14 per cent of gross domestic output between 1695 and 1739. It is to the other areas of colonial business that we must, therefore, now turn.

Notes

[1] J. Israel, *Dutch Primacy in World Trade* (Oxford, 1989), 160; P. Tousignant, *RHAF*; T. Wien, 'Selling Beaver Skins in North America and Europe, 1720–1760: The Uses of Fur Trade Imperialism', *Journal of the Canadian Historical Association* 1 (1990) 293–317.

[2] Lauson, *DCB* 1; W.J. Eccles, 'Sovereignty Association, 1500–1783', *CHR* LXV (1984), 475–510; P.S. Schmaltz, *The Ojibwa of Southern Ontario* (Toronto, 1991); L.V. Eid, 'The Ojibwa-Iroquois War: The War the Five Nations Did Not Win', *Ethnohistory* 26 (1979) 297–324; Leo G. Waisberg, 'The Ottawa: Traders of the Upper Great Lakes, 1615–1700' (MA thesis, Carleton, 1978).

[3] Elizabeth Mancke, *A Company of Businessmen: The HBC and Long Distance Trade, 1670–1730* (Manitoba, 1988); K.A. Davies, 'Joint Stock Investment in the Later 17th Century', *The Economic History Review* 4 (1953), 283–301; Ann Carlos and Stephen Nicholas, '"Giants of an Earlier Capitalism": The Chartered Trading Companies as Modern Multinationals', *Business History Review* 62 (1988) 398–419; Carlos and Nicholas, 'Agency Problems in Early Chartered Companies: The Case of the Hudson's Bay Company', *The Journal of Economic History* L (1990), 853–75; E. E. Rich, 'Trade Habits and Economic Motivation Among the Indians of North America', *Canadian Journal of Economics and Political Science* 26 (1960) 35–53; A.J. Ray and D.B. Freeman, *'Give Us Good Measure': An Economic Analysis of Relations Between the Indians and the HBC Before 1763* (Toronto, 1978); F. Braudel, *Civilization and Capitalism* 2 (London, 1984),

55; Toby Morantz, "'So Evil a Practice'": A Look at the Debt System in the James Bay Fur Trade' in R. Ommer, ed., *Merchant Credit and Labour Strategies in Historical Perspective* (Acadiensis Press, 1990), 203–22.

[4]Craig Muldrew, 'Credit and the Courts: Debt Litigation in a 17th-Century Urban Community', *Economic History Review* XLVI (1993), 30; Toby Morantz, *op. cit.*, 205.

[5]A.J. Ray and D.B. Freeman, *op. cit.*, 179.

[6]A.J. Ray, 'Buying and Selling Hudson's Bay Company Furs in the 18th Century' in D. Cameron, ed., *Explorations in Canadian Economic History: Essays in Honour of Irene Spry* (Ottawa, 1985), 95–116; Thomas Wein, *op. cit.*; E. Mancke, *op. cit.*; J. Igartua, 'A Change in Climate: The Conquest and the Marchands of Montreal', *Historical Papers* (1974), 115–34; E.E. Rich, *The Hudson's Bay Company* 1 (New York, 1961); Jean Lunn, 'The Illegal Fur Trade Out of New France, 1713–1760', *CHAAR* (1939), 61–76; Gratien Allaire, 'Le commerce des fourrures à Montreal: Documentation et method d' analyse', in Trigger *et al.*, eds, *Le Castor tout fait*, 93–121; G. Allaire, 'Officiers et Marchands: Les Sociétés de commerce des fourrures, 1715–1760', *RHAF* 40 (1987), 409–28; G. Allaire, 'Fournitures et engagements, 1715–60: L'Impact économique du commerce des fourrures sur la region de Montreal', unpublished paper presented at CHA (Windsor, 1988); Catherine Desbarats, 'Amerindians and Colonial Government Finances in New France, 1700–1750', unpublished paper presented at CHA (Kingston, 1991); Michel Filion, 'La Traite de Fourrures au XVIIIᵉ siècle: essai d'analyse statistique et d'interprétation d'un processus', *Histoire sociale/Social History* 20, n. 40 (1987), 279–98.

[7]C.M. Judd, 'Sakie, Esquawenoe and the Foundation of a Dual-Native Tradition at Moose Factory', in S. Krech II, ed., *The Subaractic Fur Trade: Native Social and Economic Adaptation* (Vancouver, 1984), 81–98; E.S. Rogers, 'The Queen: A Cree Burial at Moose Factory, May 27, 1747', *Arctic Anthropology* 24, 1987; J.E. Foster, 'The Home Guard Cree and the Hudson's Bay Company: The First Hundred Years', in D.A. Muise, ed., *Approaches to Native History in Canada* (Ottawa, 1977), 49–64; Jacqueline Peterson, 'Many Roads to Red River: Métis Genesis in the Great Lakes Region, 1680–1815', in J. Peterson et al, eds, *The New Peoples: Being and Becoming Métis is North America* (Manitoba, 1985), 37–71; *Atlas*, I, Plate 41; H.R. Gorham, 'Ethnic Identity Among the Mixed Bloods of the Great Lakes Region, 1760–1830', MA thesis, Carleton, 1985.

5 OLD REGIME BUSINESS IN THE NEW WORLD: MERCHANTS, CRAFT PRODUCERS, AND PEASANT FARMERS

New France was never self-sufficient. The colony imported a wide variety of goods — brandy, spices, hardware, and at times grain among them. Merchants stood at the centre of this trade. They financed and outfitted and sometimes built the ships that sent people, mail, and goods between France and New France. They were, in many ways, the umbilical cord that linked colony and mother country. Merchants stood at the centre of the colony's trade with France and their business activity provided the essential connection between the two.

FRANCE, QUEBEC, AND THE CANADA TRADE

Merchants at La Rochelle, Bordeaux and several smaller ports in southwestern France controlled the Canada trade. At each port there lived a small cadre of Canada merchants who, over time, were linked by ties of credit and debt. General merchants specializing in the Canada trade were at the second rank of wealth within their home port and, in part for that reason, merchants from one port would often join those in another to finance voyages to Quebec. Yet kin relationships rather than port of residence are the key to understanding the structure of the Canada trade. That trade was virtually a family affair. In the first place, partners or agents in the colonial port of Quebec were generally relatives of the major partners in France. So, too, those who loaned and borrowed were often kin. Trading companies were structured along kin lines in order to meet the same objectives that the corporate organization of the Hudson's Bay Company sought: certainty and trust in the business of long-distance trade in an era of uncertain communication.

There was a second way in which the Canada trade was a family affair. Not only were sons partners with their father, but wives, too, played essential roles in business matters. Marriages were business propositions: in one businessman's journal he mentioned his marriage of that day and then entered into a long enumeration of the capital, business assets, and contacts which the union had made possible. Women brought more than capital to the business: Canada merchants who embarked on a long trading journey generally left their wives in charge, with a notarized power of attorney. Between 1720 and 1752, at least 27 women applied for and received the right to trade for furs in the *pays d'en haut*: while over half of them were acting on behalf of their officer-husbands stationed at an interior post, the remainder may well have been acting on their own. Many merchants willed their business to their widow for her to manage or as in the case of Mme

Pascaud, widow of one of the largest Canada traders at La Rochelle, to co-manage with her sons. And, from 1717 to 1751, manage she did. She extended the business by negotiating shrewd marriage contracts on behalf of her six children not only with merchant families at other ports but with nobility as well. By 1741, of the roughly 450,000 livres owed French merchants by Canadians, some 300,000 was due to the Compagnie des Indes and to the widow Pascaud.

Religion reinforced trading bonds forged by families. As J.F. Bosher, an historian, put it, 'the French merchant had a partnership with an Almighty God'. Those who allied with the same God allied with each other. Catholics, Jews, and Protestants would trade with each other but only rarely would they enter partnership. The extent to which religion mattered can be indicated by the French state's revocation of the Edict of Nantes in 1685, which led to the exile of 180,000 Protestants or Huguenots over the next decade. To succeed in Catholic France, one had to be a Catholic. Not surprisingly those Huguenot merchants who stayed in France after 1685 became New Converts and, gradually after 1720 and especially after 1740, New Converts came to dominate the Canada trade.

That New Converts became prominent in the Canada trade is significant on at least two counts. In the first place it suggests the low importance accorded that trade by those Catholic merchants who were better connected in France. Compared to other colonial ventures the Canada trade was a poor sister. Secondly, because New Converts could not hope for opportunities open to other Catholics for upward mobility in France, they gradually cultivated alternative client and support groups. Over time they became part of what has been called a 'Protestant International', an expanding nexus of financiers, merchants, and capitalists headquartered in the Netherlands and England and extending 'even to Quebec'. Such contacts would, for some, prove to be of great significance in the years following the Conquest.

Up to the mid 1720s the volume of shipping into and out of Quebec reflected the fortunes of the fur trade and the military plans of the Imperial state. Tonnage increased during the colonial wars of the 1690s and dropped thereafter, due to the declining fur trade and European wars, until almost the mid 1720s. Buoyed by a rising French economy and a revived fur trade, tonnage out of La Rochelle and Bordeaux nearly doubled in the twenty years after 1725. Trade with the French fort at Louisbourg and with the French colony at Martinique became increasingly significant in the 1730s, when, according to one source, the volume of shipping between Quebec and Louisbourg exceeded that between Quebec and France. Flour and biscuits from Quebec were traded at Louisbourg for dried cod which, with some lumber and wheat, then went to the West Indies in return for rum and spices and, perhaps most importantly, for bills of exchange which Quebec merchants used to help retire their constant deficit with French merchants.

For the Canada trade operated annually, with few exceptions, on a deficit basis: imports exceeded exports and much of the resulting shortfall had to be made up in bills of exchange arising from the French government's colonial expenditures on military and civil matters. In the aggregate, colonial merchants owed huge sums to their French counterparts: 250,000 livres in 1732 and perhaps 400,000 livres nine years later. In 1734 the widow Pascaud headed a deputation of Rochelais merchants who complained that merchants resident in the colony increased their trade on the backs of Rochelais credit. The view from Quebec and Montreal was, of course, different: far from feeling appreciative the colonial merchants, charged a high eight per cent for all advances, were quite put out. In this context, only a relatively few on either side of the Atlantic made a great deal of money out of the Canadian trade. Few prospered like the widow Pascaud who rose from humble Canadian origins (an innkeeper's daughter) to a position of financial and social prominence in France on the back of the Canada trade. Agents of French companies rather than colonial traders headed what was the equivalent of the Quebec chamber of commerce. Less than fourteen per cent of the Canada merchants active in La Rochelle and Bordeaux between 1713 and 1763 had Canadian origins. Even those metropolitan traders who extracted a fortune out of Canadian commerce 'frankly' warned their relatives to stay clear: 'this country is very poor'.

The difficulty in extracting profits from New France necessitated resident agents at Quebec. They, and other Quebec merchants, engaged in import-export, intercolonial, and regional trade. As in the French metropolitan posts, most Quebec City merchants lived in Lower Town close to the harbour: according to one study, just under half lived on three streets. In the course of handling the affairs of the metropolitan merchants the agents determined when and to whom to extend credit; set prices; assessed local market needs; evaluated and priced fur for export; prepared cargoes for shipment to French colonies in the Caribbean and after 1715 to Louisbourg; through Montreal merchants became connected to a hinterland beyond their direct reach; even, on occasion, built ships to be used in the Atlantic trade.

The return of war in 1744 altered the structure of the Canada trade in several ways. Wealthier merchants from Bordeaux began to eclipse the less well financed Rochelais traders as the state granted to favourites contracts for military supplies. These contracts involved large outlays, sums which might not be repaid for several years. Few of the Rochelais or local colonial-based merchants could afford to compete in these altered circumstances. As early as 1755 almost all of the old Canadian and La Rochelle merchants had left the trade, replaced by larger ventures generally from Bordeaux. Perhaps nothing better indicates the extent to which the Canada trade before 1744 was a matter of small consequence to wealthy French entrepreneurs.[1]

COD AND BUSINESS AT LOUISBOURG

Even in North America, New France did not rank as France's most important commercial colony. Not, at any rate, after the second decade of the eighteenth century. Isle Royale (Cape Breton Island), ceded to the French in 1713 by the Treaty of Utrecht, like New France specialized in the export of one commodity, in this case cod. Over one-half of all Isle-Royale adults worked in the fishery. By 1720 Isle Royale exported three times the value of New France's beaver; by 1737, the maritime colony exported eight times the per capita value of all products

This depiction of Quebec City, *c. 1680*, reveals a tiny but bustling port. *(National Archives of Canada/C107626)*

exported by New France. The merchant class that emerged to handle the colony's trade with France, New France, Acadia, New England, and the Caribbean differed in several ways from the inport-export traders at Quebec and their counterparts in the French ports.

In the first place that merchant community had either been born in North America or elected to make that area their principal residence. Few French commercial firms maintained agents at Louisbourg as they did at Quebec. The second major difference related to the mercantile community's control over the major export commodity. At Quebec import-export merchants did not generally participate as partners in the interior fur trade. They operated as middlemen, selling Montreal merchants goods and supplies and purchasing fur for export from Montreal companies. In the early years, ownership and control of the inland fishery was dispersed between some eighty to one hundred locally-owned *habitant-pêcheur* run firms. In 1734, women headed seven of these firms. These small, often family-run ventures operated close to the line and it may be that they made their greatest profits from their monopoly on the sale of liquor, clothes, and general necessities to their employees and from their right of first refusal on the purchase of all fish given their employees as wages, rather than from the cod fishery itself. Indeed these monopolistic rights may have been a significant attraction for merchants to become involved in the production of dried cod. By the 1750s, at any rate, eighteen merchant fishermen controlled almost fifty per cent of the cod catch. While these merchants only represented fifteen per cent of all fishery proprietors, their influence was obviously substantial.

Third, Louisbourg merchants participated in a far more diversified import-export trade than did Quebec merchants. Between 1713 and 1744 an annual average of 8,000 tons of shipping docked at Louisbourg; this was probably three to four times the yearly average docking at Quebec. While trade with France dominated, the West Indies trade increased over time, substantial exchange took place between New France and Isle Royale in the 1730s and, in some years, trade with New England overshadowed that with Canada and the West Indies and accounted for perhaps twenty per cent of the total trade at Louisbourg. Not surprisingly Louisbourg merchants were on average probably much wealthier than fur merchants at Montreal. They also enjoyed greater social prestige than their Quebec counterparts. They held a significant number of posts on the Superior Council as well as other administrative positions. And they used these positions well: for example, by the early 1740s they had successfully passed a series of decrees controlling and limiting the wages of fishers.

One historian has argued that the absence of institutional restraints—metropolitan commercial control and competing élites like the seigneurs and military in New France—created an atmosphere conducive to mercantile endeavour and thriving 'entrepreneurial enterprise'. To a degree this was, indeed, the case. Certainly Louisbourg's merchants were able to react more quickly during the war years of the 1740s and 50s in redirecting trade flows and revamping the local fishing industry than were the merchants in New France who were more closely tied to metropolitan centres in the Old Country. The Louisbourg example does contrast with New France. When freed from the fetters of economic bondage to French mercantile companies and the Old Regime state, colonials could profit from local commercial activity.

Yet one should not press this interpretation too far. Some Old Regime fetters remained in place. Military officers were active participants in the business of trade, often having a monopoly on the sale of goods to soldiers. They also engaged in the fishery. So, too, did government administrators, including members of the judiciary. In this sense, Louisbourg like all French colonies was ripe for the picking. To a certain extent the absence of metropolitan agents was offset by the fact that for much of the period French merchants owned the ships which transported goods to and from France. In fact, local merchants owned only about twenty-five per cent of the commercial ships at Louisbourg, and the ones they owned tended to be smaller than the overseas vessels.

Moreover, and perhaps most significantly, one must question the extent to which 'entrepreneurial enterprise' did indeed 'thrive' at Isle Royale. At best it was enterprise of a truncated sort. With the exception of ignoring the rules of mercantilism and trading with New England, Louisbourg merchants were a fairly conservative group. They did not diversify far from a dependence on cod, and their fortunes ebbed and flowed with the fishery's.

But is this simply yet again the tyranny of the staple at work? After all, how much economic diversification did the fishery facilitate? Perhaps only a little, but this question, similar to the staple thesis itself, is unduly restrictive. By themselves staples determine nothing: economic decisions are made by individuals; staple availability can shape but not dictate such decision. To be more concrete: why did Louisbourg merchants generally fail to diversify into boat building, coal mining, logging, or agriculture? Local resources existed to facilitate such enterprise. When the British controlled Louisbourg in the late 1740s they initiated coal mining, an enterprise which the French on their brief return in the 1750s continued. As for boat building, the frustrated local financial commissary lamented in 1743 that:

> I make every effort to enlist the inhabitants in building, but I am unable to suc-
> ceed because of the benefits they see in purchasing English ships, these
> purchases procuring for them the disposal of their rum and molasses, so if that
> harms construction, it on the other hand is good for the sale of the cargoes com-
> ing from the islands [the West Indies].[2]

As merchants, Louisbourg entrepreneurs focused on the disposal of goods, not their manufacture or production. While it is true that some merchants did become heavily involved in the production of dried cod, those who did only represented one-quarter of all merchants at Louisbourg and part of their motivation may have been to acquire a captive market for the sale of goods. Mercantile endeavour at Louisbourg led to little if any social and economic restructuring. Instead merchants attempted to buy cheap and sell dear and in doing so they looked to the sea, not the land. French and New England manufacturers profited from that orientation. The colony did not. As one scholar has concluded, 'With the fall of

ENTERPRISING WOMEN IN NEW FRANCE

Historians have yet to study systematically the role played by women in business in New France. With the exception of several short biographical studies, most of our knowledge of such activity is turned up, as it were, in the pursuit of other questions. Yet the results of such inadvertent attention are surprisingly rich and provocative. Combing a wide range of secondary sources, historian Jan Noel has determined that women were active on their own account and as partners with their spouses in general mercantile affairs, in fur trading, and in such industrial activities as pottery, iron forging, lumbering, tile making, tanneries, brick making, and textile production. Noel attributes such a seemingly high incidence of entrepreneurial activity on the part of women to several factors. This was an era, in the colony and in France, when separate spheres had yet to be carved out for women. Within families, the key social unit in this period, tasks were shared rather than apportioned by sex; space was public rather than private, tasks were diversified rather than specialized. The initial scarcity of women in New France added to their importance. So, too, did the fact that war often called husbands away, as did the pursuit of fur. Demographic, military, and economic realities reinforced the notion of shared roles and gave to many women opportunities to participate in economic matters denied their granddaughters.

These findings, as Noel herself points out, must be seen in relative, not absolute terms. Women, through a combination of circumstances, enjoyed some advantages that would not always be in existence. Even in New France, women certainly played a secondary role to men in economic affairs. Nor were all women equally advantaged. The *Coutume de Paris*, the colony's legal system, severely restricted independent access by married women to the marketplace. Upon marriage, the husband had absolute control of the management and fruits of all commercial property. He even enjoyed the return on his wife's property, although he could not sell that property without her consent. Nor could a wife sue in court (or be sued) or enter into business without her husband's approval.

Louisbourg, France disappeared from the scene and left so scanty a legacy from nearly half a century of occupation as to make clear that Cape Breton Island was largely undeveloped in the 1713-58 period.'[3]

ACADIAN COMMERCIAL RELATIONS

Acadia in the seventeenth and eighteenth centuries had two histories: one as a pawn used by international powers; the other, an internal life, separate from and in some ways resistant to international pressures. Those historians interested in the second perspective have, unfortunately, often stressed the alleged inward-looking, peasantlike mentality of the Acadians, subsistence farmers who never strayed far from their family plot of land. The economic reality of their 'inner

Spinsters and widows were not so disadvantaged. Widows, especially, would seem to have dominated the ranks of enterprising women. A careful study by Kathryn Young of merchants in the Port of Quebec has documented that only 7 per cent (five) of the top merchants were female, and the only one of them not a widow was the daughter of a widow in business. The reason for the prevalence of widows in business is not hard to understand. Mme Marie-Ann Fornel (née Barbel) assisted her husband Louis in business for some twenty years before his death in 1745. She used her experience to manage successfully those operations for another twenty years before retiring to live on carefully selected land investments. As with men, so too with women in business: family, kin, and religious contacts mattered. Louise de Ramezay's father was the Governor of Montreal. Through his contacts Louise operated a large lumbering industry and ultimately opened a flour mill and tannery. It may be, too, that business-women looked to trade with other women. Madame Perthius (née Roberge) took over her husband's business on his death and a large part of her subsequent trade was with the Ursuline Sisters and the Hospitalières at Trois-Rivières. The business correspondence of the wife of Quebec merchant Jean-Jacques Catignan, Marie-Ann Basquet, suggests, however, that in economic matters business took precedence over ties of gender. After inviting her Montreal agent, Mme D'Argenteuil, to come and visit her, she concluded her letter: 'I was mortified Mme by [the] manner in which you sent some of your merchandise.' We do not know whether Mme D'Argenteuil took up the invitation.

Sources

Dictionary of Canadian Biography, vols 1-4.

Noel, Jan, 'New France: Les Femmes Favorites', and Plamondon, Lilianne, 'A Businesswoman in New France: Marie-Ann Barbel, The Widow Fornel', in V. Strong-Boag and A.C. Fellman, eds, *Rethinking Canada: The Promise of Women's History* (Toronto, 1986).

Young, Kathryn, 'Kin, Commerce and Community: Merchants in the Port of Quebec, 1717-1745' (PhD diss., University of Manitoba, 1991).

history', however, belies such an interpretation and suggests, as did the Louis-bourg example, that local colonials could engage in commercial activity independent from the control of France and, at times, in direct contradiction to official Imperial ends.

The Acadians were very successful farmers. By 1750 some 10,000 people farmed about 20,000 acres of marshland. A skilfully constructed series of dykes allowed excess fresh water to flow out to the Bay of Fundy while preventing the inflow of salt water. Many of these farms produced surplus products, which facilitated an extensive set of trade relations with the local Micmac, with 'Nos Amis Les Ennemies', the English at Massachusetts, and, after 1717, with Louisbourg.

Acadians regularly ignored French restriction on trade with the English in part because France could not be depended upon to provide the Acadians with items like iron ware, salt, and some luxury goods. Surplus farm products including livestock, along with fur obtained from the Micmac (in return for guns, knives and pots), were shipped to Massachusetts in exchange for manufactured goods. So strong was this trade that in the late seventeenth century at least two English merchants had set up houses at Port Royal and others regularly travelled to Acadia to sell their goods. Some Acadian merchants continued to trade during periods of war. One even sought recourse for grievances in a Massachusetts law court. While aggregate statistics for this trade do not exist, documents left by individual trading companies suggest that in general the Acadians became increasingly indebted to their Massachusetts counterparts. Strong albeit unequal trade ties between Acadians and New Englanders were forged early in their respective histories.

When the English took possession of Acadia following the Treaty of Utrecht in 1713, Acadians continued to trade, this time with a new enemy, the French at Louisbourg. In 1740, for example, sixteen ships laden with livestock and agricultural products produced by Acadians went to Louisbourg. Acadians actively participated in intercolonial trade in circumstances which were often disruptive and even dangerous. These commercial ties were very much a part of Acadia's internal history.[4]

CRAFT PRODUCERS

The attention given by historians to merchants in New France has all but overshadowed the role played by craft producers in the colony's business affairs. Such a focus is understandable. Trade linked colonies and mother countries, and merchants managed trade. The economic utility of a colony was and is often measured by the type and value of its exports and by its role as a consumer of imports. This focus is intensified when viewed through the lens of the staple thesis. Colonial development centred on the export of raw materials from which the metropolitan state fashioned manufactured goods for resale in the colonies. This perspective is given credibility by the fact that New France's export statistics are comprised overwhelming of staple goods whereas its imports from France consisted of numerous luxury and manufactured items. Indeed exports from New France conform more readily to the staple model than do those of the British colony at New York, which exported a more diversified output. Moreover, much of what is known about craft producers in New France is derived from official governmental correspondence concerned with various state-sponsored and controversial attempts to foster manufacturing in the area of ship construction and iron works. Since neither initiative was an unqualified success, such correspondence is replete with carping and fixing of blame, all of which cast colonial craft producers in a poor light.

Some historians, however, have begun to put to one side the staple-export-led thesis of economic growth and to look instead at the colony's or region's internal economy for clues to the structure and practice of business endeavour. Focus on business activity which arises less from state initiative and export linkage and more from domestic demand suggests that local craft production comprised an important part of business activity in New France. Such production may have accounted for some fourteen per cent of total per capita output between 1695 and 1739. In the 1730s this sector's share of per capita production probably equalled or even exceeded that of the fur trade. Blacksmiths, bakers, butchers, leather workers, masons, carpenters, joiners, shoemakers, toolmakers, tailors, coopers, and other artisans comprised just over two-fifths of all workers in Quebec city in the eighteenth century.

Evidence drawn from notarial records concerning the apprenticeship system in New France suggests that the number of craftsworkers was sufficient to serve domestic demand. In the first place no guilds controlled allocation of trades as in France. Relative to France, as one historian has noted, 'the door [was] wide open to personal initiative and to the spirit of enterprise.' An apprentice was free to choose the area in which he or she wished to train and then to bargain with masters concerning the details of the apprenticeship contract. Such contracts were, compared to France, quite favourable to the apprentice. Many masters even paid their apprentices, rather than the reverse. Having completed their training, only a few apprentices elected to become journeymen, or paid employees of master craftsworkers. Instead they became masters themselves, at times setting up their own businesses in direct competition with those under whom they had apprenticed. These trends might suggest a shortage of skilled labour, yet the age of apprentices increased over time and the wages paid apprentices decreased after 1720, suggesting that the labour pool was in close harmony with domestic demand.

Craftsworkers like masons often entered into short-term partnerships, subcontracted work, and trained up to three apprentices at a time. In Montreal, at the turn of the eighteenth century, some twenty masons plied their trade in that manner, although few at that time had apprentices suggesting that the limits of the market had been reached. By the 1730s, however, the market would seem to have opened up as Paul Tessier, a 'master mason and stone-cutter', employed three journeymen stonemasons and one apprentice. Tessier, who slept in a bed worth 600 livres, would seem to have earned a reasonable income from his trade. Not all did. Evidence drawn from estate inventories suggests that in the period 1740–1755 about forty per cent of artisans in Montreal and Quebec died owing more than they owned.

In some instances mercantilist doctrine rather than local demand constrained craft production. The French state, for example, refused to permit a colonial hat industry to develop, probably because of the Compagnie des Indes' control of the beaver trade. Colonial potters were also disadvantaged as France exported to her colonies great amounts of earthenware goods manufactured in the homeland. Yet for the most part the French state allowed duplication of industrial enterprise and, in at least two celebrated cases, even encouraged it.

In 1732 the King authorized a 2½ per cent bonus on the price of constructing ships in New France. This further aided an already growing industry: between 1704 and 1745 private business constructed at least 132 ships in New France. Over half of those of which we know the tonnage were under 80 tons and were used in the Louisbourg trade. In 1739 shipbuilding accounted for about one-fifth of the non-agricultural sector's domestic output. With the advent of war private building came to a halt and the dozen ships built thereafter were constructed at the King's shipyard set up in 1739 at Quebec. In the early years that shipyard had difficulty acquiring sufficient skilled craftsmen; many historians have concluded that the colony suffered from a shortage of such labour and that craft production was accordingly underdeveloped. A more reasonable interpretation, however, is that sufficient craftsmen existed to service the civil or private sector; when the state suddenly added its own demands, then labour supply did become a problem.

More dramatic state intervention occurred in the development of an iron works industry at Saint-Maurice near Trois-Rivières. As Dale Miquelon has noted, the 'blast furnaces and forges themselves were in their time massive and costly structures.' The colony lacked the financial strength, transportation infrastructure, and technical skills to operate such an industry. In this sense the apprenticeship system can be seen to be a conservative factor in influencing growth. Such a system could generate skilled craftspeople for existing trades. It was less able to respond to new technological needs. Nonetheless, operated by French managers and workers the forges did produce between 1737 and 1741 a million pounds of primarily iron bars for shipment to France, the West Indies, and Louisbourg, and for local use. In the years following the forges generated an annual output of 400,000 tons. They failed, however, to generate a profit.

Michael Bliss has suggested that the Saint-Maurice venture was simply one of 'endless and mostly futile attempts' to develop industry in the colony and concluded that capital and labour deficiencies reflected the weakness of the colonies' geographical situation: 'there was a shortage of opportunities, a lack of products that could be made in Canada and sold profitably in or outside the colony.' This, 'the poverty of the North' thesis, has a nice sense of inevitability about it and speaks to many in a modern era of deindustrialization and free trade. While accentuating geographical constraints such an interpretation ignores the social-structure constraints that conditioned and limited business behaviour in New France. The colony, for example, received few permanent immigrants from France, primarily, as Peter Moogk has persuasively argued, because of factors relating to culture, not opportunity. Communal ties ran deep in France and French migrants more often received heartfelt letters from relatives pleading for their return than penned letters for others to join them. Other French colonies, including its most valuable American possession, Saint-Dominique, experienced similar problems in attracting migrants from France. Itinerant workers did go beyond France's boundaries but they tended to return home. As Moogk concludes they were for the most part 'migrant workers rather than intending colonists'. While this interpretation coupled with the conservative nature of the apprenticeship system might help to account for the lack of skilled labour complained of by the state, it does not account for the lack of local capital necessary to underwrite large industrial enterprises. Perhaps it is, as Bliss implies, simply a case of smart capital going elsewhere. Before concluding this, however, a closer look at the largest sector of New France's economy, the nature of agricultural production, is necessary.[5]

THE SEIGNEURIAL SYSTEM AND BUSINESS ENTERPRISE, 1663–1763

The agricultural sector accounted for about three-quarters of domestic output in New France between 1695 and 1739. Just under eighty per cent of New France's population lived in rural areas and the vast majority of those who did farmed. Not surprisingly, then, the size of the annual harvests went far towards setting the pace and extent of general business activity. Local craftsworkers depended to a great extent on business from the rural sector. Mercantile profits depended on good harvests: poor harvests cut import consumption and profits declined. Abundant harvests permitted a profitable export trade with Louisbourg and the West Indies. A series of uncertain harvests in the 1740s and 50s, coupled with a war, fatally weakened the import-export merchants. Like Old France, New France was an agricultural community and, to be successful, merchants and others had to adjust to that reality.

Historians have traditionally argued that agricultural production in New France could not be depended upon. A series of good years would be regularly offset by an equal number of poor crops. One historian has even suggested that, given the alleged primitive farming skills possessed by habitants, the short growing seasons, and often poor soils, a good harvest was a matter of luck. Subsistence-oriented agriculture and rough social equality characterized peasant life in rural seigneuries. Parts of this view are currently under revision. Historians now believe that the habitants farmed appropriately for an area of abundant land: thus intensive cultivation was superseded by the opening of new fertile lands for production. The rising agricultural output during the first third of the eighteenth century reflected increased land under tillage rather than increased yield per arpent. Such a strategy is commonplace and reasonable in a frontier environment.

Moreover, the notion of equality and subsistence has come increasingly under question. Recent studies suggest that at least twenty per cent of peasant farm households operated over 40 cleared arpents of land, 40 arpents taken as a rough measure of subsistence output. Some farm families with fewer than 40 cleared arpents may have worked off as well as on the farm, thus further complicating the notion of simple agrarian subsistence. Clusters of rural villages, especially near Montreal, are evident by 1760. These clusters suggest that exchange took place in rural areas. Many habitants received money, as well as bartered goods, for their farm produce: about one-third of habitant households in the Rivière du Sud region east of Quebec City had paper money to present for redemption after the conquest. François-Augustin Bailly de Messein, a general merchant situated in the rural area of Varennes, over a forty-year career, amassed a fortune exceeding 200,000 livres at his death in 1771. The wealth of this rural merchant probably ranked him as one of the richest men in New France! A study of landholding on one seigneurie between 1730 and 1765 had documented an increase, not a

PEASANT ACCUMULATION AND THE LAND MARKET
THE CASE OF RIVIÈRE DU SUD

Inheritance practices decreeing that all siblings should receive equal portions of the parent's estate have often been cited as reasons for equality amidst poverty in the countryside. After all, such a system would surely, if not preclude, then certainly retard the emergence of large estates capable of significant surplus production. At first glance, this would seem to be a system informed by an egalitarian ethic, an ethic incompatible with that of capitalist accumulation. Thomas Wien, however, in a remarkably sensitive and nuanced study, has in several ways qualified this standard portrait. In the first place, he has shown that peasants were active participants in local land markets. Such transactions went far beyond the limits of family affairs, or the subdividing of land amongst potential heirs. Between 1749 and 1754 in the Rivière du Sud region, some forty miles east of Quebec City, around one-third of such transactions worth about one-half of the total value, involved exchanges between non-relatives. Peasants accumulated this land often at the expense of other peasants. Even when aggregate average land holdings seem constant over time, that, by itself, should not be taken to mean that accumulation, and its reverse, dispossession, had not been occurring.

The activity of a select group known at the time by the felicitous phrase, *chefs habitans*, nicely illustrates this point. Michel Blais and his brother, Joseph-Marie, assembled a substantial block of productive land through at least forty separate transactions over a period of many years. Michel purchased land within a hundred-kilometre range of his home farm. He then used this outlying land to exchange with others for property, often yet to be received in inheritance, in his own region. He also loaned money and foreclosed on land in his neighbourhood. Other *chefs habitans* acted in a similar fashion, taking advantage of less advantaged peasant households and thus benefiting from and contributing to a process of differentiation and marginalization within rural society. The process of land accumulation meant that some households had more and better land to bequeath than others. Inheritance practices, then, did not provide for a homogeneous rural society.

Peasants accumulated land in order to provide for the future of their progeny. Yet constraints besides those exerted from customary inheritance practices underlay the process of land subdivision. Wien argues that subdivisions of land reflected material realities, more than cultural traditions. Peasants

decrease, in the disparity between farm sizes. Seigneurial agriculture under the Old Regime was not all of a piece. Some peasant farmers could and did accumulate. Others worked at non-agricultural jobs. Inequality was common.

In a sense, Morris Altman's controversial claim that not only did production increase in the eighteenth century, but that only rarely were harvests insufficient invested in land because there was very little else to invest in. They subdivided their accumulations, at times even before their old age and death, because large farms could not be managed productively in a context of expensive labour, poor and uncertain markets, and limited technology. What one author has termed the 'hegemony of small-scale production' set limits to the size of productive farms. Sixty cultivated arpents was about the maximum that could be effectively managed by one household. Subdivisions resulted in more manageable farms. Given the constraints of the rural economy, then, it made some sense to bequeath as well as sow the soil.

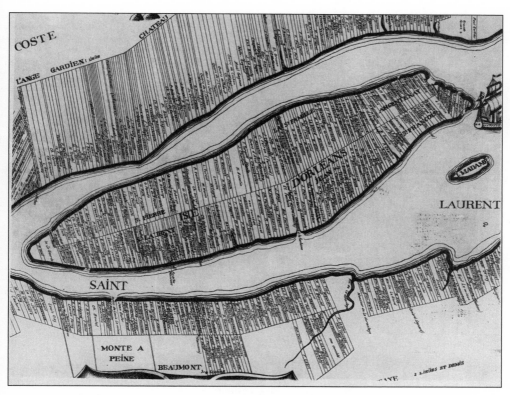

By 1709, land around Quebec City had been closely settled in the seigneurial system of narrow farms extending back from the river-front. (*Archives Nationales du Québec. Extrait de la 'carte du Gouvernement du Québec 1709'. ANQ-Q coll. into., D901-Nouvelle France, 1709*)

to meet local needs and unable to generate some surplus for potential export, sits well with evidence of inequality in the countryside. Some prosperity and inequality was clearly possible within a system that could generate exports. Indeed, Altman suggested that New France's inability to provide sufficient agricultural exports for Louisbourg and the West Indies—a role France had hoped the colony

73

could perform—rested with the small size of the farming community rather than with a stagnant and unprogressive agricultural sector. On the basis of an analysis of census data he concluded that wheat output was sufficient to feed 2,600 more people per year than lived in New France between 1795 and 1707 and that this surplus increased such that between 1728 and 1739, 27,600 extra people per year could be fed. Altman's generalizations were based on census data of questionable reliability for twenty-three of the forty-four years between 1695 and 1739, and he made no attempt to estimate output for the years without census data. Clearly then his findings are far from definitive. Although he bases his conclusions on far from ideal data, that data is nonetheless about the best available for measuring agricultural output. His conclusions, therefore, deserve to form at least the point of departure for all subsequent discussion of such output in this era.

If, then, the farming community as a whole produced increasing surpluses in the years before war racked the colony, to what extent did anyone in New France profit from such activity? The seigneurial system governed the landholding structure of New France. Seigneurs received grants of land from the Crown or acquired a seigneurie by purchase from a previous owner. They then allotted lots to individual tenants. These lots were subject to a series of charges payable by the habitant but, if these payments were met, the tenant was fairly free to farm, sell, or bequeath the lot. Some historians have suggested that seigneurs coveted land for social and cultural rather than economic motives. And, in fact, most seigneurs would seem to have made a greater part of their income in other pursuits. A close study of the ownership of 185 seigneuries in the 1720 to 1745 period, however, suggests that while Old Regime cultural values were obviously important spurs to owning land, economic calculations also played a part. Seigneurs from the noble and merchant classes chose their land with an eye to proximity to urban centres, good soil, water access, and the existence of fish and timber resources. In the period after 1700 merchants became especially active in purchasing seigneuries. The ones they bought were all well placed for farming and marketing produce, suggesting a strong economic motive as well as, perhaps, the desire to enter the landed class and thus enjoy the attendant social distinctions arising from such a position.

The state required that the habitant pay certain rents to the seigneur and the clergy. For some of these payments the habitant received services in exchange—for example, the use of the seigneur's mill for grinding wheat, and access to the clergy by payment of the tithe. For others he received nothing—*cens* and *rentes*, equivalent to a general rental charge; *lods et ventes*, surcharges on the sale of land by the habitant payable to the seigneur; and the *corvée*, a stipulated unit of time when the habitant had to work on the seigneur's or state's land. While similar exactions were made of peasants in France, any direct comparison is rendered difficult by the fact that the burdens varied greatly throughout the mother country. While the claim is often made that rents due seigneurs were lower in New France than in France, this was not invariably the case. It simply depends on the regions being compared. The point is that such exactions, all of which had feudal origins, were still in place. Land rental payments in the British colonies to the south, for example, were about seventy per cent less than in New France.

Any comparison of the economic and business structures of these two colonial systems must recognize that fundamental disparity. Rental payments for which the payee received nothing in return diminished surplus earnings and thus spending power and general economic growth. A number of detailed studies of the impact of seigneurial dues on habitant incomes have concluded that the abolition of such payments would have increased habitant spending power (that is, net profits after all expenses) by eleven to forty-five per cent depending on the time, period, and region studied. If individual seigneurs on average made only some 300 livres annually on such exactions, it is nonetheless clear that the habitant class as a whole lost much by their existence.

It is at this juncture that the continued existence of a feudal class structure and its economic relationships may have curtailed colonial business activity. Habitants spent most of their limited excess funds on land assemblage and to a lesser degree on clothing, appliances, leather goods, and assorted luxuries. Many of these items were manufactured by local craftsworkers. The nobility tended to spend their surplus funds on the purchase of luxury imports from France. To the extent that the habitant would have spent the surplus denied him by feudal exactions on local goods, colonial business development was thereby truncated. A significant portion of the surplus income generated by the agricultural sector was, thanks to state coercion, funnelled into the hands of a class that looked to France for the good things in life; local production and local demand for such production suffered. The perpetuation of a feudal landholding system did not preclude agricultural growth. It did retard economic diversification and thus limit opportunities for business people in New France. Nor should this surprise us. As we have already suggested, the persistence of a similar social structure led to similar problems in the mother country.[6]

THE CONQUEST AND BUSINESS ENTERPRISE

The Conquest looms large in the historiography of eighteenth-century Canada. Much of that debate focuses on the nature of the Conquest's impact on the colony's bourgeois class. Did the British victory lead to the decapitation of such a class and to its replacement by a politically connected British entrepreneurial group? Some have answered this question in the negative, arguing that a bourgeois class did not exist in New France. New France was a colony dominated by farmers. Those who were upwardly mobile looked for careers in the army, state, or church, not in entrepreneurial activity. There is much to support such an interpretation. The attraction of aristocratic values has already been alluded to. Clearly, agricultural business dominated the colony's gross national product. Yet in some years a significant amount of that produce was exported. While fur dominated trade, it did not account for all foreign commercial relations. Moreover, merchants in Montreal, while rarely ever rich, did persist and prosper within the structure of a state-run fur monopoly. Merchants at Quebec, according to Kathryn Young, were not all puppets manipulated by companies located in French ports. Indeed Quebec merchants regularly engaged in inter- and intra-colonial trade as well as shipping to and importing from the motherland. They invested in industrial pursuits, and in a city where most rented, they tended to own their homes and to buy property. Moreover, many Quebec merchants married into resident families and a large majority died in the colony. These merchants were not, as has often been argued, simple birds of passage. Most who came from France, stayed in Quebec. Many of their sons followed them into trade. Many of their wives provided them with entrées into colonial business life as well as money and, in many cases, personal entrepreneurial skills. A commercial community did predate the Conquest.

Most studies agree, however, that that community was not a very rich class. Montreal merchants earned a moderate income. Young has suggested that some Quebec merchants may have opted for a mercantile rather than military life simply because they could afford to do little else. Yet a study of the wills and property inventories of 73 merchants and 84 officers who died in Quebec city between 1670 and 1749 found that the average wealth of the merchants at the time of their death was about twice that of the officers. Sons of merchants may well have pursued a mercantile career, because, outside of government, it may have been the most lucrative way of making money in the colony. Colonial merchant fortunes were modest compared to the fortunes of many merchants in France. When measured against the fortunes of other urban colonials, however, merchants, on average, fared better.

A bourgeois class existed in Montreal and Quebec city, and rural merchants situated in villages close by, especially Montreal, were increasingly common on the eve of the Conquest. Yet one might wonder about the extent to which bourgeois values dominated even in urban centres. The average size of the dowry which officers received was twice that received by merchants in Quebec city. This suggests that Old Regime attitudes concerning social rank still dominated within the colony's premier post. On the eve of Conquest, a bourgeois class existed within a social milieu still strongly influenced by Old Regime values.[7]

This ordering of affairs changed only slowly after the Conquest. James Murray, the first British Governor, had little patience with the English and Scottish merchants who arrived after 1763, referring to them as 'licentious fanatics'. This attitude was far from uncommon in England in the eighteenth century. In England, as in France and New France, traditional societal attitudes changed at a slower pace than did economic growth. British merchants, like those in New France, had to ape the dominant values if they hoped to succeed: gentlemanly capitalism was the order of the day before and after the Conquest. British merchants in Quebec were quick to realize this. It made little sense to antagonize the British ruling class. While the odd merchant, like George Allsopp, did not know when to be quiet and suffered politically for his temerity, others like George Davison and his brother, Alexander, curried the favour of Governors and in return received a sixteen-year lease of the King's posts which gave them a monopoly of the fur and fish trade on the north shore of the lower St Lawrence, in one historian's opinion 'one of the choicest morsels of government patronage available'. George and Alexander also leased, successfully, the Saint-Maurice iron works from the government and in the 1790s acquired the very lucrative role of contractor for the British armed forces in North America. While the Davisons were exceptional in their ability to extract profit from government contacts, they were far from alone. For the most part, British merchants at Quebec realized that they were in a minority position, dependent both politically and economically on support from the mother country. Thus their desire for an elected parliament and the institution of British civil law took a back seat to the maintenance and extension of economic suzerainty.

If the importance of political patronage to commercial success remained unchanged after the Conquest, there can be no doubt that English rather than French merchants were better placed to win at that game. In the fur trade, British political appointees granted British rather than French merchants easier access to lucrative interior trading areas. Yet despite the sudden existence of a new market, new competition, and political bias, French fur traders/merchants persisted at the level they had enjoyed before the Conquest for the better part of the following two decades. A second influx of British merchants, this time from the south, following the passage of the Quebec Act and the American Revolution, tipped the scale firmly in favour of British control in this sector. The Quebec Act gave to the Quebec Governor control over the Ohio Valley and the northern interior. Albany fur traders, in competition with Montreal, took note and began to move their operations north to Montreal to deal more effectively with the new administrative order. The consolidation of the Montreal fur trade in the hands of the Scots-run North West Company by the end of the 1780s spelled the end of significant French managerial/mercantile involvement. It would be wrong to view this as the triumph of *laissez-faire* capitalism over Old World pre-capitalist values. The gradual nature of the change up to the eve of the American Revolution does not support such an argument. The fact is those merchants who moved north after 1775 tended to be better capitalized than those *in situ* and British as well as French merchants fell victim to the new arrivals.

The Conquest and its aftermath did exact a terrible toll on many of the French Huguenot merchants who had remained in the Canada trade. The Seven Years' War proved costly for many. The refusal by the French state to honour its debts ruined many others. Yet, as we have seen, not all Quebec city merchants relied solely on the French trade for their livelihood. Many were well integrated into colonial commerce and colonial society. Many of those remained and prospered serving local urban and rural trade after the Conquest.

Because of their established contacts in England, British merchants gradually took control of the import-export trade. Yet even in this sector, some French merchants persisted with success. Jacques Perrault lost much property during the Conquest but was able to re-establish his mercantile operations, using a London agent, and on his death in 1775 left an estate worth 150,000 livres. Pierre Guy had dealt with Huguenot merchants in France prior to 1763. After that date he salvaged what he could and went to London to, as he wrote, 'make acquaintances

OLD CORRUPTION REVISITED
BUSINESS AND GOVERNMENT IN POST-CONQUEST QUEBEC

It would be very wrong to give the impression that all merchants profited as easily as the Davisons from relations with or transactions involving government appointees. The Canada Affair of 1783 or, somewhat less grandiosely, the Thomas Cochrane scandal, is a case in point. A brief look at the affair helps to bring into focus the mercantile world at Quebec in an era of personal turmoil but structural stasis. Thomas Cochrane was the Quebec agent for the London banking firm of Harley & Drummond. Through a number of highly placed government contacts, the banking firm received the contract for supplying funds for the salaries and subsistence of the British army in the North American colonies from 1767 to 1783. Such contractors were popularly believed to pocket huge sums of public money and were widely excoriated as being throwbacks to an earlier era of peculation through government preferment. And, at least in the case of Cochrane's predecessor as Quebec agent, Jacob Jordan, such allegations were right on target.[1] Jordan had used some £15,000 of government money to speculate on his own account in the local wheat market. When found out he was dismissed as the banker's agent but kept his profits and other official government appointments. A scant three years later he became an agent for the government in purchasing huge amounts of wheat![2]

For some historians, the Cochrane affair is simply an extension of the Jordan scandal. Acting under express orders to the contrary, Cochrane advanced some £800,000 of credit to Quebec merchants between 1781 and 1783. When he became aware of the huge amount of such credit, Governor Haldimand, acting with support from government financial authorities in London, in effect foreclosed on the outstanding loans of some £155,000. Harley and Drummond dismissed Cochrane. Despite a series of bitter court cases, Cochrane would seem to have survived financially and, indeed, was a few years later in Quebec purchasing a seigneurie and leasing government saw mills.

Some historians see this incident as confirmation of the continued existence of systemic political corruption endemic in the old-regime, pre-modern political state. Such corruption crossed the ocean with the British and represented one more example of continuity with the political-financial world inhabited by Bigot and his compatriots in old regime France.[3] Without doubt, there is a grain of truth in all this. Yet from the perspective of business history, the Canada Affair takes on a different meaning: a meaning, which, while pointing to continuity with old regime France and pre-modern England, does so in terms of the persistence of outmoded financial structures rather than the prevalence of so-called corrupt behaviour.

Between 1779 and 1783 Cochrane remitted some £2,000,000 to Quebec. Less than 10 per cent of this money was actual hard currency or specie shipped to Quebec by the British Government. The rest had to be raised in local currency by selling to colonial merchants bills of exchange payable in London, England. The trading season at Quebec was only five months in duration—May to October—because the

St Lawrence River was not passable at any other time. This short season made it virtually impossible for colonial merchants to raise enough money from their local customers to pay cash for the government's bills of exchange before the end of the shipping season, when such bills had to be sent to England to pay their suppliers. Unless the government contractor advanced them credit, they could not purchase the bills and the trading system, under severe pressure to feed and equip the British military, would grind to a halt. During the war years, the contractor's agent at Quebec became the single most important source of mercantile credit for that colony. All major import-export merchants at Quebec and Montreal purchased the contractor's bills on credit, thus expanding their buying power and allowing them to order sufficient supplies to outfit and feed the military.

And this worked not simply to the merchant's advantage. Colonial and British currency were not the same. Transactions involving both currencies had to be calculated according to the prevailing exchange rate. That rate was in part a function of supply and demand, and demand was directly linked to the trading cycle. From the government's as well as the merchants' viewpoints, a stable exchange rate was most desirable: such a rate rendered future financial planning and ordering much less hazardous. By selling bills of exchange on credit Cochrane was able to maintain a stable exchange rate and thus save both government and merchants worry and money. Put simply, Cochrane was acting as a bank acts now: he was the old-regime equivalent of an institutionalized credit system.

Governor Haldimand and the British Government understood little of this. When Haldimand pulled the rug from

under Cochrane, he 'precipitated the most celebrated series of bankruptcies in the history of colonial America'. Twenty-two Canadian merchants were indebted to Cochrane as late as 1788, and nine of them became insolvent. Had Haldimand waited, it is probable that most of the monies due would have been paid up. As the historian Julian Gwyn has noted, 'the workings of the colonial money market in the absence of banks makes it clear that both British colonial policy and administrative practice lagged behind colonial economic realities.'[4] Yet at least some colonial merchants took heart from this episode. The United States responded by setting up a private banking system following 1782. It would be just under forty years before an institutionalized credit system would emerge in the Canadas. In the intervening period, merchants like James Dunlop, who owed Cochrane £3000 in 1787, competed with government contractors like the Davisons in the purchase and sale of bills of exchange. Indeed, Dunlop had learned well: by 1812, his biographers report, he had become 'the recognized channel through which the mercantile fraternity of Montreal and Quebec disposed of army bills. . . . [and should] be considered Canada's first large-scale bill broker'.[5]

Notes

[1]A.J.H. Richardson, 'Jacob Jordan', *DCB* 4, 402-3.

[2]For accounts of the scandal, see David Geddes, 'How "Habeas Corpus" Came to Canada: the Bills on Credit Scandal—Quebec, 1783', *Three Banks Review* 112 (Dec. 1976), 50-65; A.R.M. Lower, 'Credit and the Constitutional Act', *CHR* 6 (1925), 123-41; H. Neatby, *The Administration of*

⟶

Justice under the Quebec Act (Minneapolis, 1934); Julian Gwyn, 'The Impact of British Military Spending on the Colonial American Money Markets, 1760-1783', *Historical Papers* (1980), 77-95; D. Milobar, 'Conservative Ideology, Metropolitan government and the Reform of Quebec, 1782-1791', *The International History Review* 12 (1990), 45-64.

[3]The accounts by Geddes, Lower, Neatby and Milobar are of this general persuasion. For broader perspectives on corruption and the old regime, see W.D. Rubinstein, 'The End of "Old Corruption" in Britain, 1780-1860', *Past and Present* 101 (1983), 55-86; and J. Brewer, *The Sinews of Power: War, Money and the English State, 1688-1783* (London, 1989).

[4]Gwyn, 'The Impact of British Military Spending on the Colonial American Money Markets, 1760-1783', 91 and 94.

[5]D.S. Macmillan and A.J.H. Richardson, 'James Dunlop', *DCB* 5, 284-7.

here, which is very easy to do'. Significantly, Guy's first contact in London was with a Huguenot import-export merchant, Daniel Vialars. Huguenot connections facilitated Guy's entrée into the British mercantile world. In a sense that transition had begun even before Conquest when French Protestant merchants, denied succour within France, had been forced to seek contacts and business alliances in the international sphere. Even as the Conquest cut the cord which bound New and Old France, lines to a wider Protestant-dominated Atlantic community were being established. Such links did not put Quebec merchants in a position of equality with their English competitors, but they did provide a potential haven in a changing and often hostile world.

French merchants in the developing rural areas weathered the Conquest. English merchants began to move into the rural community of l'Assumption, forty kilometres north-east of Montreal, in the 1780s. But francophone merchants competed effectively and the most successful merchant in the area had first set up shop in the late 1750s. The anglophone merchants focused on outfitting the fur trade; francophone merchants operated a more general trade in retail, wheat, and lumber. And, as at the Port of Quebec, the merchant community prospered to a greater extent than did any other group. In the years 1785-1789 about 45 per cent of all the debt owed by farmers in the rural areas of l'Assumption was held by regional merchants. Their influence, in fact, extended beyond the economic realm: both anglophone and francophone merchants in l'Assumption held most local political and judicial appointments. They were the economic, social, and political élite of that rural area. And many merchants, like François Augustin Baillie of Varennes, invested heavily in land. By 1791 about one-third of all seigneuries in Lower Canada were owned by the English bourgeois, and one-third by the French bourgeois. In the rural area, it is clear, the French bourgeois class held its own against its British counterpart.

Although, as with all generalizations, significant exceptions exist, one can conclude that the Conquest did tend to funnel French business activity into the countryside: francophone merchants increasingly acted as the gatekeepers between rural and urban Quebec; anglophone merchants performed a similar function between urban Quebec and the wider world. Does this process warrant the term 'decapitation'? It does only if one views economic development through the narrowly focused lens of the staple thesis. If export activities are held to be the main determinants of economic growth, then the francophone bourgeoisie was indeed decapitated. Yet such a perspective is unduly restrictive. It trivializes the significance of economic activity in non-export oriented business endeavour. Rural francophone merchants would provide a basis for the emergence in Lower Canada of a group of business-minded politicians who in the second quarter of the nineteenth century would help lead Quebec into the era of steam, of industrial capitalism, of Confederation.[8]

Notes

[1] J.F. Bosher, *The Canada Merchants* (Oxford, 1987); J.F. Bosher, 'Success and Failure in Trade to New France, 1660–1760', *French Historical Studies* 15 (1988), 444–61; J.F. Bosher, 'French Colonial Society in Canada', *Transactions of the Royal Society of Canada*, Series 4, 19 (1981); A. Pascaud, biography, *DCB* 2; D. Miquelon, *New France 1701–1744*; J.S. Pritchard, 'The Pattern of French Colonial Shipping to Canada before 1760', *Revue français d'histoire d'outre-mer*, LXIII (1976), 189–209; Kathryn Young, 'Kin, Commerce and Community: Merchants in the Port of Quebec 1717–1745' (PhD diss., University of Manitoba, 1991); Michel Filion, 'La traite des fourrures au XVIIIe siècle: essai d'analyse statisque et d'interprétation d'un processus', *Histoire sociale/Social History* 20 (1987), 279–98.

[2] J.F. Bosher and J.C. Dubé, 'François Bigot', DCB 4.

[3] B.A. Balcom, *The Cod Fishery of Isle Royale, 1713–58* (Ottawa, 1984); A.J.B. Johnston, 'The Fishermen of Eighteenth-Century Cape Breton: Numbers and Origins', *Nova Scotia Historical Review* 9 (1989), 62–72; J.R. McNeill, *Atlantic Empires of France and Spain: Louisbourg and Havana, 1700–1763* (Chapel Hill, 1985); Terry Crowley, *Louisbourg: Atlantic Fortress and Seaport*, CHA Historical Booklet 48 (Ottawa 1990); Christopher Moore, 'The Other Louisbourg: Trade and Merchant Enterprise in Ile Royale, 1713–58', *Histoire sociale/Social History*, 12 (1979), 79–95; A.H. Clark, 'New England's Role in the Underdevelopment of Cape Breton Island During the French Régime, 1713–58', *Canadian Geographer* 9 (1965), 1–12; 'Bigot', *DCB*; 4. O.F. Chard, 'The Price and Profits of Accommodation: Massachusetts-Louisbourg Trade, 1713–44' in F.A. Allis, Jr, ed., *Seafaring in Colonial Massachusetts* (Boston, 1980), 131–51.

[4] J. Daigle, 'Nos Amis les ennemis: Relations commerciales des Acadians avec le Massachusetts, 1670–1711', *Le Petit Courrier* 6 (1987), 15–28; G. Wynn, 'Late 18th Century Agriculture on the Bay of Fundy Marshlands', in P. Buckner and D. Frank, eds, *Atlantic Canada before Confederation* (Fredericton, 1985), 44–53.

[5] Peter Moogk, 'Apprenticeship Indentures: A Key to Artisan Life in New France', *Historical Papers* (1971), 65–83; P. Moogk, 'Manual Education and Economic Life in New France', *Studies on Voltaire and the 18th Century*, v. 67; J.P. Hardy, 'Quelques aspects des niveau de richesse et de la vie matérielle des artisans de Québec et Montréal, 1740–1755', *RHAF* 40 (1987), 339–72; biographies of V. Brossard, *DCB* 2, J. Huppé, F. Jacquet, and P. Tessier *DCB* 4; Dale Miquelon, *op. cit.*; Michael Bliss, *Northern Enterprise . . .* ; J. Lunn, 'Economic Development in New France, 1713–1760' (PhD diss., McGill, 1942);

D.-T. Ruddel, 'Domestic Textile Production in Colonial Quebec, 1608–1640', *Material History Bulletin* 31 (1990), 39–49; R.C. Cole, ed., *Historical Atlas* 1, Plate 50.

[6]J. Lunn, *op. cit.*; M. Altman, 'Economic Growth in Canada', *William and Mary Quarterly* XLV (1988); M. Altman, 'Seigneurial Tenure in New France, 1688–1739: An Essay on Income Distribution and Retarded Economic Development', *Historical Reflections* 10 (1983), 335–75; Altman, 'Note on the Economic Burden of the Seigneurial System in New France, 1688–1739', *Historical Reflections* 14, 135–42; J. Mathieu *et al.*, 'La Propriété seigneurial au Canada au 18e siècle: Un Enjeu', unpublished paper presented to the CHA (Kingston, 1991); A. Greer, *Peasant, Lord and Merchant: Rural Society in Three Quebec Parishes, 1740–1840* (Toronto, 1985); R. Hamilton, *Feudal Society and Colonization* (Gananoque, 1988); J.L. Goldsmith, 'The Agrarian History . . . ', *Journal of European Economic History* 13 (1984); R.C. Cole, *Historical Atlas* 1, Plates 51, 52, and 53; L. Dechene, *Habitants et marchands de Montreal au 17e* siècle (Montreal, 1974); Louis Michel, 'Un marchand rural en Nouvelle France: François-Augustin Bailly de Messein, 1709–1771', *Revue d'histoire de l'amérique française* 33 (1979), 215–62; Thomas Wein, 'Peasant Accumulation in a Context of Colonization: Rivière du Sud, Canada' (PhD diss., McGill University, 1988).

[7]J. Igartua, 'The Conquest and the Merchants of Montreal', *Historical Papers*, (1974), 115–34; W.J. Eccles, 'The Social, Economic and Political Significance of the Military Establishment in New France', *Canadian Historical Review* 52 (1971), 1–22; Kathryn Young, *op. cit.*; Yvon Desloges and Marc Lafrance, 'Dynamique de croissance et société urbaine: Québec au XVIIIe siècle, 1690–1759', *Histoire sociale/Social History* 21 (1988), 252–68; Peter Moogk, 'Rank in New France: Reconstructing a Society from Notarial Documents', *Histoire sociale/Social History* 8 (1975), 34–53.

[8]David Milobar, 'Conservative Ideology, Metropolitan Government and the Reform of Quebec, 1782–1791', *The International History Review* 12 (1990), 45–64; P.J. Cain and A.G. Hopkins, 'Gentlemanly Capitalism and British Expansion Overseas: The Old Colonial System, 1688–1850', *Economic History Review* 39 (1986), 501–25; Michel Filion, 'La traite des fourrures au XVIIIe siècle: essai d'analyse statisque et d'interprétation d'un processus', *Histoire sociale/Social History* 20 (1987), 279–98; J. Mathieu, 'Jacques Perrault', *DCB* 4, 623–24; G. Joannette and C. Joron, 'Pierre Guy', *DCB* 5, 395–9; Allan Greer, 'George Davison', *DCB* 4, 197–9; Lise St-Georges, 'Commerce, crédit et transactions foncières: pratiques de la communauté marchande du bourg de l'Assumption, 1748–1791', *Revue d'histoire de l'amérique française* 39 (1986), 323–44; C. Harris, ed., *Historical Atlas of Canada*, Plate 51.

COLONIAL CAPITALISM
IN TRANSITION
1791–1871

6 SETTING THE CONTOURS FOR COLONIAL CAPITALISM: AN INTRODUCTION

Much current writing on the British industrial revolution argues against viewing the late eighteenth and early nineteenth centuries as a watershed era. Many historians now believe that industrial growth took place slowly and unevenly across various economic sectors: the term industrial revolution, while not lacking defenders, is increasingly qualified and contained. Words like 'take-off' and 'sustained economic growth' are being replaced by 'long and languorous' development.[1] In part, this revision of traditional views has emerged from the concerns of social historians to explain both the persistence of preindustrial artisanal/craft behaviour and the continued dominance of a business élite not intimately involved with manufacturing. Throughout the greater part of the nineteenth century the dominant British business person, it is argued, represented a blend of aristocratic landed values and gentlemanly commercial exploits. Persons of commerce and persons of land interacted: persons of industry remained subordinate. Some British historians have seen this as the era when Britain's entrepreneurial culture congealed. Because industrialization occurred so gradually, established élites were able to maintain economic and financial dominance and a new invigorating entrepreneurial spirit never took central hold. For these historians, many of the problems besetting modern Britain's economy had their origin in the late eighteenth and early nineteenth centuries.[2]

This debate is of some relevance for our understanding of business behaviour in British North America following 1791. That relevance is threefold: first, the gradual rate of structural change throughout the economy; second, the notion of cultural persistence, the continued power of old-world economic attitudes and behaviours in the face of gradual structural change; third, the role of the entrepreneur in economic change.

For the first fifty years of the nineteenth century mercantilist ideas set the contours of much colonial economic activity. The British Navigation Acts restricted British and colonial trade to ships of British registry, amd a series of sliding tariffs on lumber and wheat in the nineteenth century controlled colonial exports to the mother country. These measures were consistent with long-standing European (not simply British) imperial practice. Colonies existed to serve the mother country: those interests could be best met by importing colonial raw resources, when from the mother country's perspective it was economically or strategically advantageous to do so. Processed and manufactured goods could be shipped back for sale in the colonial captive market.

Yet, mercantilist notions gradually came under attack in Great Britain. As England industrialized, many entrepreneurs and politicians began to argue that their apparent economic dominance no longer required state support through tariffs and shipping protection. Free trade and a *laissez-faire* state could, it was believed, better foster the nation's trade and industrial growth. The idea was to break down the mercantilist barriers erected by other nations: to do so, their own had to come down first. Following the American Revolution, mercantilism ebbed as industrialism flowed. These currents, while slow-moving, were inexorable. Colonial business people had to tack their courses accordingly: some did so with foresight while others coasted in economic backwaters.

Recognizing and adjusting to structural change and colonial disabilities, however, represented only part of the challenge facing colonial business people. Like their British counterparts, many were also cut of a particular mould and tended to operate by a set of ethics not necessarily compatible with the dictates of an industrial order. In order to succeed, colonial entrepreneurs had often to ape cultural values prized by their British commercial correspondents. For some, as we shall see, those values came to condition their entrepreneurial strategies. Countervailing pressures did however exist. The economic growth of the United States seemed less hampered by old world aristocratic habits: the historian, Anthony J. Perkins, has asserted that American 'colonial society reflects a culture permeated with market values and capitalist principles.' While, especially with relation to the agricultural sector, this is a highly contested proposition, it is nonetheless fair to say that most historians see the United States as exhibiting a much less culturally fettered type of entrepreneurship than that displayed by Great Britain. In fact some, like Perkins, see the dominance of an aggressive entrepreneurial spirit in the United States as its unique identifier and as a primary explanation for its economic growth.[3] Given the proximity of the United States it would be surprising if such an ethic did not have some discernible impact on business behaviour to the north. Sometimes, given either long-standing or fresh rivalries, this impact could be negative, something to be spurned, not adopted. At other moments Americans themselves moved north and participated directly in the process of business development.

The notion that industrial change proceeded at a gradual rather than a revolutionary pace means that the traditional hero of industrialization, the entrepreneur, inventor, and innovator is no longer centre stage. The 'Great Man' theory of history, so appropriate for explaining sudden change, is less useful for understanding gradual development. Business historians have begun to refocus their attention from presumed 'movers and shakers' to an assessment of the cumulative contributions made by a wide range of middling level petty producers. From this perspective industrialization was, in terms of its determinants as well as its effects, a social phenomenon. To comprehend that process, the socio-cultural as well as economic context within which such change occurred must be delineated.

A word or two of caution is appropriate here. Generalized definitions of a nation's culture are of only limited worth in understanding the particular behaviour of a business or any other activity. There is no substitute for close analysis of specific interactions between structures and agency. Yet no person is totally free, just as no structure is totally impermeable. And beliefs can contain freedom even as they can aid in dissolving structure. Business behaviour in British North

America evolved within socio-economic contours set by the British mother country, their American neighbours, and local conditions. The resulting behaviour was not all of a piece throughout the various colonies. To some extent each region exhibited distinctive practices and for that reason our analysis will proceed on a regional basis, resisting the imposition of an over-arching time frame.

Notes

[1]Julian Hoppit, 'Understanding the Industrial Revolution', *Historical Journal* 30 (1987), 211–24 and Maxine Berg and Pat Hudson, 'Rehabilitating the Industrial Revolution', *Economic History Review* XLV (1992), 24–50 are useful introductions to the debate. Quote is from John Smail, 'Manufacturer or Artisan: The Relationship Between Economic and Cultural Change in the Early Stages of the Eighteenth Century Industrialization', *Journal of Social History* 25 (1992), 792.

[2]For characterization of the business class, see P.J. Cain and A.G. Hopkins, 'Gentlemanly Capitalism and British Expansion Overseas: 1) The Old Colonial System, 1688–1850', *Economic History Review* 39 (1986), 501–25; M. J. Daunton, '"Gentlemanly Capitalism" and British Industry 1820–1914', *Past and Present* 112 (1989), 117–58, and the resulting debate in ibid. 132 (1991), 150–87; W.D. Rubinstein, 'The Structure of Wealth-holding in Britain, 1809–39: A Preliminary Anatomy', *Historical Research: Bulletin of the Institute of Historical Research* 65 (1992), 74–89. For discussions of artisanal persistence and input into industrialization, see Smail, *op. cit.*, and Maxime Berg, *The Age of Manufacturers: Industry, Innovation and Work in Britain, 1700–1820* (Basil Blackwell, 1985).

[3]E.J. Perkins, 'The Entrepreneurial Spirit in Colonial America: The Foundations of Modern Business History', *Business History Review* 63 (1989), 160–86; for a survey of recent literature on the agricultural economy in the United States, see Allan Kulikoff, 'The Transition to Capitalism in Rural America', *William and Mary Quarterly* 46 (1989), 120–44.

7 THE BUSINESS OF FUR: 1763–1871

Canada's business historians have, arguably, been overly fascinated with the fur business. Agriculture far outpaced the fur trade in its contribution to New France's gross national product, and from the perspective of metropolitan European countries the Old Regime fur trade was of minimal economic value. The Conquest changed none of this. Fur continued to be 'the most inconsiderable of all trades', accounting for under half a per cent of the total value of all English imports during the first seventy-five years of the eighteenth century. The British state, like the French state before it, cultivated the fur trade in order to maintain and extend alliances with Natives in the interior until after the War of 1812, when they severely curtailed the policy. The potential of expanding American markets stood in stark contrast to crumbling Native confederacies. Yet the fur trade did continue to expand and to enlist even more Native nations within its compass.

Business historians' penchant for case studies has justifiably been criticized. Too often the study of one entrepreneur or firm barely touches on the surrounding economic, social, and political contexts. As David Monod put it, business history 'has remained fundamentally self-referential'.[1] Yet a focus on the expansion and evolving organization of the colonial fur trade need not fall into that trap. Fascinating as a study for its own sake, from a business history perspective it is especially significant as a harbinger of business change in the preindustrial era. In fact, a close study of the fur trade can shed light on the nature of European expansion across Native territories in what was to become western Canada; unveil the bitter corporate rivalries that characterized the early years of such expansion and that give lie to the myth of a peaceful frontier; highlight business/legal/state interaction in the preindustrial era; pinpoint regional variations in business enterprise; and, in general, provide a specific context for evaluating entrepreneurial strategies, managerial change and the nature of labour relations in an era spanning merchant and early industrial endeavour. The fur business and indeed the conduct of business in general can be viewed as a crucible within which economic, social, and cultural relations were shaped and reshaped. In an era of dramatic specialization within the discipline of history, it is on the above premise that business history should stand or fall.

STRATEGY AND STRUCTURE DURING THE COMPETITIVE ERA, 1763–1821

Despite the best hopes of Hudson's Bay Company (HBC) traders at Fort York and Albany, the Conquest of 1759 did not mean the end of competition from Montreal. The traditional trade was gradually taken over from the French by Scots and

Loyalist merchants. By 1779, Hudson's Bay traders complained that 'the country northward of Lake Superior is poisoned with [Montreal pedlars].' '. . . the pedlars are in every hole and corner where there are any Indians to be found.'[2]

By 1790 it seemed that the St Lawrence trade had been firmly grasped by one enterprise, the North West Company (NWC), a result of a series of mergers of nine smaller competing Montreal partnerships. That Company shipped four to five times the value of fur shipped by the Hudson's Bay firm. Yet the latter had long since ceased to sleep by the sea. From the late 1760s to the mid 1770s, the HBC had sent some forty-four expeditions into the interior to attract natives to trade at the Bay. In 1775 it began to establish inland posts. Following 1790 the Company expanded dramatically, operating fifty-nine interior posts by 1798. Yet it was unable to manage this ambitious expansion effectively: in 1795, for example, of five trading posts in one Saskatchewan area, two were Hudson's Bay Company outlets in direct competition with each other.[3] Trading goods tended to be of mixed quality. Ultimately the substantial costs of expansion pushed the Company to the wall. By 1804 the Napoleonic War was exacerbating these problems: the HBC's charter required that the enterprise adhere to the Navigation Acts and this meant that it could ship furs only to England and from there trans-ship their product to Europe. The NWC was not so restricted and was better able to find alternative markets; the European war had therefore less impact on it. By 1804, the issue seemed hardly in doubt: the NWC employed over twice the number of workers—950 to 435. It operated nearly twice the number of interior posts — 108 to 57. Moreover, it controlled the west's richest fur-bearing areas. In 1804 the HBC seriously entertained the possibility of a buy-out by the NWC.[4] Few contemporaries would have predicted that a scant seventeen years later, the NWC would lose its identity and that the company on the Bay would emerge with a monopoly over the fur trade.

Most often, historians point to two factors which facilitated the HBC's ultimate victory: cheaper and swifter transportation into the interior, and a more modern managerial/corporate structure. Both are nicely deterministic: given geographical realities and, as Michael Bliss put it 'a loose, ramshackle, pre-modern' business structure, the NWC was doomed to die.[5] Such an explanation, however, tends to create a false polarity. Such a polarity blurs somewhat when one looks closely at the actual managerial structures of the two companies and at the way in which each company operated its transport system. In fact, it can be argued that only when the HBC moved closer to the managerial and transport systems of its rival, did its success become possible. The difference between modern and pre-modern stuctures was never absolute, and locational advantage is, by itself, rarely sufficient to explain much.

The managerial structure of the Montreal-based enterprise differed in several significant ways from that of the HBC. The Montreal concern divided the *pays d'en haut* into a number of regional departments, each one managed by a partner who wintered in the area. Each year these men met with their counterparts from Montreal at Grand Portage, above Lake Superior, where furs, goods, and information were exchanged and policy matters decided. Careful consideration of European market demands, of competition in the interior, and of the condition of each department's fur-bearing supply underlay strategy decisions for the conduct of the next season's trade. Costs would be cut, posts shifted, specific furs targeted and appropriate trade goods ordered in a reasonably efficient, flexible, and rational manner. Since the wintering partners as well as the Montreal merchants all shared in the annual profits, all had a common end in view, and incentive was high.

The HBC's managerial structure was much less responsive to the changing nature of fur trade competition. Most of the significant decisions were made in London by the Company's governor and advisory committee. Certainly some of those policies could be and were modified by chief factors at the Bay posts and those factors did have input into decisions made in London. But such input and modifications were rarely ever the result of head-to-head discussion. Moreover, as the Company began its expansion into the interior, those men who ran interior posts rarely visited the Bay to report in person to the chief factor who oversaw regional operations. Instead communication between interior posts and the Bay forts and London was by mail. Any significant changes in fur-trade strategy could take two to three years to put in place, in sharp contrast to the more responsive system employed by their chief rivals, the NWC.

It is commonly pointed out that unlike the NWC, before 1809 the HBC did not pay its traders any portion of the firm's yearly profits. They were salaried employees and as such, many historians have argued, probably did not work as hard for their company as did their counterparts in the NWC who depended on profits for their income. This comparison is true as far as it goes. In reality, under the payment system employed by the HBC those who managed the inland posts were given incentive money in the form of premiums calculated on the value of their yearly fur shipments. This policy had two serious consequences. In the first place it encouraged competition between district clerks. While wintering partners for the NWC shared in overall profits, inland clerks for the HBC made money on the amount of fur shipped from their post. Raiding the territories of company posts became common practice. Such a payment system also encouraged trading at any cost. The inland clerks, after all, made money on the value of fur, not on the ultimate profit made from the sale of that fur. As one Nor'Wester wrote in 1805, 'Those people do not care at what price they buy or whether their employers gain by them so long as they have their premium, which sets them in opposition to one another almost as much as they are to us.'[6]

In an era of intense competition, matters of company loyalty and employee competence were especially important. The NWC benefited enormously from the heritage of skill built up over several centuries of fur-trade endeavours out of Montreal. While almost all of its partners were of Scottish or British heritage, eighty per cent of the company's employees in 1805 were French Canadians from parishes along the St Lawrence River. By contrast, seventy-one per cent of the HBC's employees in 1805 were from the Orkney Islands, although its managerial structure was predominantly Scottish and English. Very early in the competition, the chief factors at Fort Albany pointed to the NWC's advantages:

The people of Canada whose principal commerce arises from the inland trade, have studdied everything for its convenience and by long experience have arrived at great perfection in conducting it, having tradesmen on the spot for every branch, some packing the bales properly for the canoes, others making baskets, cases, rundlets etc. in which the necest attention is paid to the stowage, and weight. The Canadian peasants are brought up to the service from their infancy so that a trader may engage any number of men ready trained and experienced to his hand. These are all great advantages which your Honours have not. When a servant comes first into this service as a labourer, he is akward and clumsy as it is possible to conceive, and by the time he [is] rendered useful for inland, he goes home, and we have to begin anew.[7]

In particular, the HBC lacked men who could match the Nor-Westers' skill in navigating inland waters. Time and again inland traders from the Bay commented on their competitors' greater skill in this area. Orkney men proved to be much less suitable for the interior trade than their French counterparts. While the HBC did develop the shallow draught York boat, which could carry more men and material than the voyageurs' canoes, it was slower and much more cumbersome to transport over portages than the birch bark canoe. In a time of competition, such drawbacks were crucial. For the construction and operation of the canoes the HBC was dependent on natives, the country-born, and on those few French voyageurs whom they could entice from the NWC into their employ. From this perspective the different skill levels of the two work forces went far towards negating the HBC's geographical advantage.

Clearly, then, the North West Company's organizational structure would seem to have been less 'ramshackle' than some have thought. Even after they absorbed their last St Lawrence rival, the XY Company in 1804, and, in order to accommodate their new wintering partners, embarked on a sustained attempt to develop trade west of the Rocky Mountains, the expansion took place in the context of general retrenchment. The NWC reduced its work force from 950 in 1805 to 711 in 1811. The NWC also attempted to establish a peaceful and rational working relationship with the HBC. It entered into a series of negotiations with the Hudson's Bay Company and between 1804 and 1810 ordered its interior clerks to co-operate with their rival wherever possible. Even as the North West enterprise expanded to the Pacific, they sought peace in order to consolidate and profit from their extended affairs.

The environment within which the fur trade rivals operated, however, did not permit such luxury. The Napoleonic War affected the HBC in three ways: it disrupted markets; it made very difficult hiring suitable employees at cheap wages; it stimulated a steep rise in the cost of provisions and trade goods. The NWC also had difficulty in hiring cheap labour: rural Lower Canada, the source of their workers, was, in the early part of the century, enjoying an agricultural boom, thus increasing labour costs. The War of 1812 upset the North West's trade and supply routes and cut off all provisions from Detroit and other American ports, thus forcing the Company to rely on its internal provisioning system—hunting and trading for food with natives. Finally, and of crucial importance to both companies, traditional stocks of beaver, the only fur which remained in high demand in Europe, declined precipitously. If demand was to be met and profit made, new fur sources had to be mined.

In this changing and challenging environment the HBC reacted first. It undertook a major managerial retrenchment and structural reorganization. New personnel assumed control. In significant ways they began to ape NWC operations. A profit-sharing incentive system similar to that of the Nor'Westers was introduced. The Company began to recruit workers from the St Lawrence parishes in the heart of the NWC's territory: by 1819 only fifty per cent of its labour force were Orkney men. Conscious of the NWC's ability to react more quickly to changing fur trade conditions, the new Governor attempted to streamline and standardize the transmission of fur-trade news to London. Covert plans were laid to expand into the fur-rich and North West-controlled Athabasca region. Most importantly, at the insistence of one of the new directors, the Scottish peer and philanthropist, Lord Selkirk, a scheme to establish an agricultural colony at Red River, astride the Nor'Westers' transport system, was set in motion. If Selkirk saw the colony as a way to provide a decent life for hardpressed Scottish agriculturists, the HBC believed the colony could be the source of cheap labour and cheap food and help satisfy one of the original conditions in its charter, that of western colonization.[8]

These moves initiated a period of bitter and bloody competition. Post construction escalated and new personnel were hired. By 1819 the HBC had over 554 employees and the NWC over 900. Battles broke out in the Red River colony culminating in the death of its governor, Robert Semple, and twenty of his men. Bloodshed also occurred in the Athabaska region. Both sides hired 'bully-boys' to intimidate the local Natives and rival traders. The Nor'Wester's adopted an official policy not to assist 'Hudson's Bay servants . . . in case of starvation'. One Nor'Wester expressed 'exultation' when 'no less than 15 men, 1 clerk with a woman and child died of starvation going up Peace River.'[9] Both companies attempted to acquire furs destined for and prepaid by their rivals. Both suffered large financial losses due to depredation by the other. NWC-related judges and sympathetic juries in Upper and Lower Canada consistently thwarted Selkirk's attempts to enlist legal help in what had become the waging of a private war for control of the North West fur trade.[10]

By 1819 neither company was in good financial shape. Although the NWC had defeated competition from an American entrepreneur, John Jacob Astor, on the Pacific coast, they were still unable to turn a profit from their west coast affairs.[11] Poor relations with Natives, unsuitable personnel, weak market demand in China, and high transport costs to Montreal contributed to financial losses. The HBC also felt financial pressures. The Company owed its banker £100,000 in 1819, about twice what it had owed in 1816. Yet at least the HBC could still borrow money. For the NWC that possibility was becoming increasingly problematic.

The NWC's Achilles' heel did not lie in its decision to expand and to engage in brutal competition with its rival. The Company's real problem was of a latent sort: few contemporaries understood it, but it existed nonetheless. The problem

Hudson's Bay and North West companies' forts at Pembina on the Red River. Peter Rindisbacher's early 1820s painting neatly symbolizes the competitive era. *(National Archives of Canada/C1934)*

centred in the Company's management of its financial affairs. In this sense the enterprise did reflect the weakness of its limited partnership structure.[12] The partners demanded an accounting at the end of each year's trading season. That in itself was not exceptional. What rendered such an accounting problematic was the fact that the long-distance trading system relied on the preferment of credit by British merchants whose accounts might not be closed for up to two or three years after the finish of a particular trading season. The limited partnership arrangement, however, encouraged the partners to see each season as a separate business venture. Thus charges incurred in one season would, under this system, not necessarily be met or provided for from that season's returns. Similarly, outlays for capital costs like canoes and new interior posts were charged during the year expended. No system of amortization or policy for carrying money over in anticipation of future capital renewals—canoes lasted less than three or four years on average—existed. Thus in years of small capital costs, profits were inflated and totally distributed with no thought to future capital expenditure. The result was a near-total inability to know with clarity the real financial condition of the Company's affairs. By contrast, the corporate structure of the HBC facilitated long-term financial planning and resulted in a much more stable and clearly understood accounting system.

Did anyone realize the financial morass into which the NWC's accounting system and limited partnership structure had led it? It would seem that several of the

Company's partners were so aware. Even more significantly, Edward Ellice, a rich British-based merchant who was a long-time supplier and creditor of the NWC, had long realized that a merger of some sort was necessary. Towards that end, he had been buying some HBC stock even as he continued to lend money to the NWC. He urged the companies to meet and encouraged the British government to apply pressure to see that a resolution of conflict took place.[13] The two companies merged in 1821: the Hudson's Bay Company retained its name, but of the 53 trading partners, the NWC supplied 32. More significantly the merger meant the end of Montreal's century-long link to the fur trade. Provisions, goods, and furs now flowed only through the Bay: 'the fur trade,' as one old Nor'Wester exclaimed, 'is forever lost to Canada.'[14] In terms of trade, so it was. Yet, as had the NWC before it, the Hudson's Bay Company continued to hire stalwart and poor peasants from 'voyageur parishes' in rural Lower Canada. At both the managerial and labourer levels, the HBC benefited from the experience and skills of the Nor'Westers. The victor defeated but did not discard its rival and therein lay the basis of its success. The HBC showed itself able at strategic moments to appropriate some of the best elements of its rivals' strategy and structure and to assimilate those elements within an already tested and sound corporate edifice.

GENDER, ETHNICITY, AND CLASS IN THE FUR TRADE: 1763–1821

Well before 1760 most Natives who traded directly with the HBC and the St Lawrence traders did not themselves trap fur. Rather they were middlemen who traded European goods to inland Natives (often after having used the goods for a lengthy period) at a substantial mark-up for furs with which to trade at European posts. Cree and Assiniboine Natives were especially adept at the middlemen role. European inland expansion after 1760, however, swiftly undercut that function. Increasingly Native trappers and European trading posts were cheek to jowl. The Cree and Assiniboine adapted by providing food for the ever proliferating European traders, and in that manner retained a measure of autonomy and power. They could and did threaten to withhold provisions from traders pending acquiescence to their demands. They often burned grasslands surrounding interior posts so that the traders could not easily hunt game. But inland expansion did affect relations and power balances between Native groups. The Cree and Assiniboine, as the first prairie Natives to acquire guns, had also acquired much power over inland tribes. Now these inland tribes had equal access to this deadly technology. This equal access, combined with struggles to control the southern based horse trade, threatened dramatic change to long-standing power and trade relations between prairie Natives.

In addition to altering the structure of the Native fur-trading system and Native power relations, European inland expansion after 1760 irrevocably changed the lives of those new tribes with which they came in contact. When Native traders travelled to distant posts with furs their contact with Europeans was of limited duration. Their consumption of alcohol and tobacco took place within a time period dictated by seasonal demands. Close proximity between posts and trappers coupled with fierce competition resulted in a dramatic increase in the use of alcohol to attract Natives. At York Factory alone, the distilling of high-proof rum increased from 1600 gallons in 1798 to over 6000 gallons in 1821. Easy availability and less pressure of travel contributed to increased consumption. The results were debilitating.[15]

Alcohol addiction was one insidious result of more frequent and prolonged contact. Social violence was another. And this violence affected some much more than others. It is often claimed that during this period of intense competition Native trapper/traders benefited by playing one company off against another in their pursuit of better terms. Without doubt Natives did take advantage of this opportunity. Increasingly they traded less for more whenever they could. North West, XY and Hudson's Bay traders constantly lamented that reality. But in their vicious response, they reflected and accelerated changing power relations within the fur trade frontier.

Native women, who in the early years of the fur trade played a central and pivotal role in economic and social affairs, were among the first to suffer the effects of such change. Fur traders, desperate to control commerce, began to replace country marriages with kidnapping. They abducted Native women and children in order to force Natives to trade with them rather than with their competitors. As one Athabascan trader explained,

> it will assist to discharge the debts of a man unable to do it by any other means . . . the second is that it may be the means of thickling some lecherous miser to part with some of his hoard. I therefore kept the women to be disposed of in the season when the Peace River bucks look out for women, in the month of May. . . .[16]

Some Athabascan Natives met this tactic with violence. Others turned away from the trade altogether and resumed, for a time, their traditional hunting and gathering ways.

The offspring of Native women and white traders—mixed-blood or Métis children—had become common features around all interior and bay-side posts. Even as Native women were being abducted in the zones of fiercest competition, they were being replaced throughout the fur-trade frontier by their mixed-blood daughters. Before the close of the competitive era, mixed-blood rather than Native women became the preferred choice of white traders. Of fairer skin, and having generally been brought up by the mother outside of the post possessing similar economic and trading skills, they assumed increased status during this period. So, too, did mixed-blood males. Proficient in the hunt and skilled in war and, at times, educated at eastern schools, they began to challenge Natives as providers of food to trading posts, transporters of fur trade goods, and, in general, prized employees of the fur trade companies.[17]

Changes in working conditions also took place within the heart of the hierarchically structured companies. Both companies began to cut back on their workforce following 1804. Even when they rehired following 1811, wages were low.

In addition, the NWC would seem to have so increased the costs of provisions and equipment to its inland workers that many fell into hopeless debt, and some of those simply quit the company. The HBC adopted a similar practice. When it introduced a profit-sharing system in 1809, only those at the upper level of the managerial structure could participate. The Company's servants — a name the company used to describe the Orkney men and others who worked on three- to seven-year contracts — lost all access to incentive pay and, moreover, were required to purchase from the Company items which had in the past been provided free of charge. Increasingly, it made little difference for whom an inland fur-trade labourer worked: in the competitive era retrenchments and cost-cutting first and foremost affected the voyageur from the St Lawrence parish and the Orkney man from overseas. The social and ethnic gulf which existed within both companies was further widened by harsh fiscal exactions during the competitive era. Some have called this a system based on paternalism, a term which implies some sense of reciprocity between manager and employee and some sense of mutual comradeship. At the height of the competitive era, such sentiment was hard to find. Moreover, alternatives for inland labourers at the bottom rung were few: as David Sanderson, a mixed blood who had worked over a decade for the HBC explained in 1817: 'he will not come into the service . . . because he is not used well, and is always starving and will only do the same when he goes like an Indian.'[18] Nor were many of these trends of brief duration: they were about to undergo further transformation during a period of monopoly and consolidation of economic and social power within the fur trade.

MANAGING THE MONOPOLY: 1821–1871

As manager of its northern department—and soon of all of its departments—the Company selected George Simpson, an illegitimate son of a Scottish minister who had spent less than one year in fur-trade affairs. The appointment signalled an important departure from recent practice. The thirty-three-year-old Simpson had had experience working for an internationally focused sugar trading company in England. This background in marketing, rather than fur collection, set him apart from inland fur-trading contenders. During the period of intense competition, the primacy of the market place had been overshadowed by the desire to outdo rivals in the collection of fur. Following 1821, the HBC directors, acting through and advised by Simpson, began to redirect focus from product collection to product marketing. Such an orientation had existed in the early years of the HBC's monopoly, but never, before 1821, had the implications of such a strategy been as rigorously pursued.

Before all else, Simpson had to deal with the unwieldy result of the 1821 merger: most historians have concluded that the new company had three times the number of workers that it could usefully employ on its payroll. The Hudson's Bay company would succeed, Simpson believed, not 'by Prize Fighting, but by persevering industry, Oeconomy in the business arrangements and a firm maintenance of our rights not by the fist but by more deadly weapons'.[19] 'Oeconomy'

THE MÉTIS

BUSINESS ON THE PLAINS, 1830–70

George Simpson had little good to say about the work habits of the Métis people. His pejorative depiction coloured a traditional historiography that viewed the Métis as a people who tragically failed to adopt to a civilized and capitalistic way of life.[1] Historians have now gone far towards correcting that view. Clearly, many of the Métis people adopted early and astutely to market opportunities provided by the Hudson's Bay Company and, after the mid-1840s, by their competitors on the plains.[2] Pemmican production is a case in point. Pemmican, or dried buf-

falo meat, was the staple of the fur trader's diet. In relation to weight and bulk it was more nutritious than alternative foods, easily transportable, and nearly imperishable. Métis became quite skilled at the hunting of buffalo and the production of pemmican. Every summer and again in the fall hundreds of Métis families set out for the buffalo plains of northern North Dakota with horses, oxen, dogs, and Red River carts; each cart could transport up to 900 pounds of meat. In 1820, 54 carts accompanied the hunt; in 1840, 1210 carts left Red River, capable of returning with one million pounds of meat. Expeditions on that scale required meticulous organization. For each trip a Provisional Government and president were elected and the hunt was mar-

Métis encampment photographed at Elbow River in Saskatchewan shows two of the ubiquitous Red River carts. *(National Archives of Canada/PA138573)*

shalled behind a flag. Groups were formed and each member of each group had his or her specific duty to perform. In 1839, 1840, and 1841, the Hudson's Bay Company spent £5000 on buffalo products.

The production and sale of pemmican was probably the first industry west of the Great Lakes. Women played pivotal roles in this process. One eyewitness in 1854 left the following description:

> The meat, when taken to the camp, is cut by the women into long strips about a quarter of an inch thick, which are hung upon the lattice-work, prepared for that purpose, to dry. This lattice-work is formed of small pieces of wood placed horizontally, transversely, and equi-distant from each other, not unlike an immense gridiron, and is supported by wooden uprights (*trepieds*). In a few days the meat is thoroughly dessicated, when it is bent into proper lengths, and tied in bundles of sixty or seventy pounds weight. This is called dried meat (*viande seche*). Other portions which are destined to be made into *pimikehigan*, or pemican, are exposed to an ardent heat, and thus become brittle, and easily reducible to small particles by the use of a flail; the buffalo-hide answering the purpose of a threshing-floor. The fat, or tallow, being cut up and melted in large kettles of sheet-iron, is poured upon this pounded meat, and the whole mass is worked together with shovels, until it is well amalgamated, when it is pressed, while still warm, into bags made of the buffalo-skin, which are strongly sewed up, and the mixture gradually cools and becomes almost as hard as a rock.

Experience gained in the pemmican trade prepared the Métis well for an emerging trade in buffalo robes in the early 1840s and for the freeing of market conditions later in the decade. Returns from the production and trade in buffalo robes and leather goods far exceeded that available in the pemmican industry and in uncertain subsistence farming, with the result that many more Métis families left farming and camped in the plains over the winter to hunt buffalo and prepare their robes for fall marketing. In so doing, as one historian has noted, '[a]ll the functions of a modern packing plant and tannery were performed by the hunters, their wives and families, using traditional labour-intensive methods.'[3] Some Métis became, themselves, middlemen, purchasing prepared robes and selling to the Hudson's Bay Company, Norman Kittson, and a number of other outlets. The value of the buffalo fur trade at St Paul alone rose from $1,400 in 1844 to $300,000 in 1865.

Some took advantage of other spin-offs from the buffalo trade. The manufacture and sale of Red River carts assumed heightened importance throughout the 1850s and 1860s. In 1835 there was only one blacksmith in Red River. In 1849 there were eight, along with eleven carpenter shops, three cooper shops, and thirty merchant ventures. Some Métis specialized in freighting goods to St Paul. This specialization and commercialization extended as well to the buffalo hunt itself. Increasingly Métis began to hire wage labour to carry out the hunt and robe production. And as buffalo became even more scarce around Red River, Métis left the colony to hunt and trade on a permanent basis on the great plains.

Not all Métis left Red River. In fact, the commercialization of the buffalo

⟶

trade led to splits within the Métis community. Métis of Scottish ancestry tended more often to farm; those of French-Canadian background participated more in the fur trade. Within the fur trade group, class interests emerged: during the Riel Rebellion of 1871, the merchant and entrepreneurial class tended to oppose Riel, and the hired labourers and carters proved to be his allies. In a more general sense, Gerhard Enns, an historian, has argued that most Métis in the buffalo trade remained locked in a proto-industrial milieu characterized by the 'retention of the family economy', with its emphasis on 'consumption and leisure, through feasting, playing and drinking'.[4] Given more time the Métis might have reconciled the tension between family economy and a more acquisitive industrial capitalism. But such time was not available: coinciding with the near extinction of

the Great Plains buffalo, a second immense herd began to flood the prairies and the Métis proved unable to stem that flow of white Anglo-Saxon Protestants from the east.

Notes

[1]G.F.G. Stanley, *The Birth of Western Canada* (Toronto 1937, reprint 1960).

[2]G. Enns, 'Tripman, Trader, Plainsman, Chief: The Social and Economic Worlds of the Red River Métis' (PhD diss., University of Manitoba, 1991).

[3]Irene Spry, 'The "Private Adventures" of Rupert's Land' in J.E. Foster, ed., *The Developing West: Essays on Canadian History in Honour of Lewis H. Thomas* (Edmonton, 1983), 54.

[4]G. Enns, 'Tripman, Trader . . .', Conclusion.

necessitated retrenchment: by 1825 operating posts numbered 45, down from 109 in 1821; employees numbered 900, down from about 2,000 at the time of merger. While one old Nor'Wester threatened to shoot the bearer of the news that he was to be let go, most acquiesced silently, if sullenly.[20] Many were given land and some minimal assistance to homestead at Red River. Those let go tended to be at the lower ranks of employment and were most often Natives and mixed bloods. Those eased out of the upper ranks tended to be the most bellicose of the 'bully boys'. To succeed in the new company required different skills and attitudes; desk men or as one caustic subordinate referred to the successful chief factor, James Keith, those with a temperament of 'a dried spider' got promoted.[21]

And, in fact, under the new regime post activity became more and more routine and directed from the centre. Individual posts took on a variety of specialized functions: some gathered fur; some gathered food; some acted as transhipment points; all were subordinated to and in effect simply cogs of a larger process the dynamics of which were increasingly charted and controlled by a central bureaucracy. While a council of Chief Traders and Factors met with Simpson annually at Red River, most often, as one Chief Factor noted, Simpson had 'everything cut and dry for us'.[22] While these men retained control of the profit-sharing system introduced in 1809, they were, following the merger, perceived and treated less as partners and more as employees.

Between about 1821 and 1871 business and social arrangements in the North

West reflected a hardening of racist attitudes towards non-white peoples. Following Simpson's reorganization only 16 of the 140 clerks — the lowest rank that could hope for promotion to chief trader—were Natives of the country. By 1832 the number had increased, but only by three. Capitalist calculations, however, tempered racial stereotyping in the work force. Mixed bloods and Natives increasingly dominated the labouring ranks. Twenty per cent of the servants were mixed-blood in 1832; fifty per cent were non-white in 1850. Despite believing that mixed bloods were 'indolent and unsteady', Simpson soon recognized that it was a 'good policy to have about an equal proportion of each [mixed-blood, Irish and Scottish], which will keep up a spirit of competition and enable us to deal with them on such terms as may be considered necessary and proper.' A racially mixed workforce weakened the possibility of collective resistance and increased the ease of managerial control.

Hiring mixed bloods as labourers, however, failed to alleviate growing dissatisfaction amongst the ranks of traders and chief factors, many of whom had mixed-blood sons, often educated at Montreal and London, and desired for their male offspring a managerial career within the fur trade. Simpson, in partial defiance of a rather intransigent governing council in London, instituted a new personnel category, the apprentice postmaster, which facilitated upperward movement for mixed-blood sons of chief factors and traders. In the last decade and a half of Simpson's tenure (1845-1861) mixed bloods made up about twenty per cent of new appointments to the rank of chief trader. Two factors facilitated the appointment of mixed bloods to positions of power over whites within the HBC. The first is simply the power of patronage. Almost all who were so appointed were sons of white Chief Factors. The second emerges from the context of the devaluation of posts as administrative units in the fur trade following 1821. As the historian Philip Goldring noted, well connected bi-racial men experienced some upward mobility 'because real authority resided in London, and was shared with only two or three influential men — invariably whites — in the Indian country'.[23]

Racist attitudes affected the status of mixed-blood and Native women. Here too Simpson played a central role. Although he had at least two mixed-blood wives as per the custom of the country, to him they were just 'bits of brown' to be discarded at the appropriate time. Anglican ministers at Red River and elsewhere in the 1820s ignored the existence of country wives until their marriages had been solemnized by the Church, and even forbade mixed-blood mothers to visit their children at the church-run school in Red River. In 1830, the forty-three-year-old Simpson returned to Scotland to marry his eighteen-year-old Scottish cousin, Frances Ramsay Simpson. Others followed suit and as the historian, Sylvia Van Kirk, has noted, these actions 'reduce[d] the status of country wife to that of mistress'.[24]

Yet a cautionary note is required here: not all Hudson's Bay officers mimicked Simpson; some in fact, objected strongly to his callous conduct and many provided for their mixed-blood children and wives in their wills. Especially in the more remote areas of the fur trade, marriages *à la façon du pays* continued as the

LIMITS TO CONTROL
TRADERS, WORKERS, AND THE HUDSON'S BAY COMPANY, 1821–71

HBC officers like George Simpson McTavish believed that '[R]egular hours of work were as essential in the wilds as in business city marts and factories.' But such aspirations to clock-like efficiency were seldom realized. Despite the ringing of bells at posts to signal the stop and start of various functions, natural rather than factory time conditioned work patterns throughout the fur trade. Much work—hunting, cutting and transporting firewood, and transporting fur—took place free of direct supervision. Almost all work took place in accordance with seasonal opportunities. Few workers were specialists: most were expected to do a number of different tasks. This was work as it had existed in preindustrial England and, within that context, the desire of officers like McTavish to instill factory type discipline met with limited success and significant worker opposition.[1]

Simpson's attempt to create a heterogeneous work force did not always lead to quiescent labour relations. In fact, some have argued that ethnic groupings may have differed from post to post but remained relatively homogeneous within each post. Certainly on the west coast, ethnic mixing within each post was the norm. But whatever the reality across the expanse of fur-trade territory, one fact remains clear: labour unrest was common. Strikes and mutinies occurred throughout fur-trade country. That, at least, the mixed-blood labouring force benefited from such tactics is suggested by their success in commanding wages higher than those offered recruits in England and Scotland throughout most of the Simpson era.[2]

The Company had particularly acute problems in dealing with Native workers. Natives who manned the essential transport brigades to York Factory were especially troublesome. Many had other options: traditional foraging, fishing and hunting and, for some, farming to fall back on. For them casual employment in the Company was a luxury, not a necessity. 'Tis a perfect plague,' one Chief Factor lamented, '. . . knowing that [they know] they have it in their power to distress you.' Indeed the wages demanded by Native workers acted as a catalyst for the modernization of the Company's transport system when it turned to steam powered boats in the years following 1860.[3]

By far the most troublesome to the Company, however, were its dealings with Native trappers and traders, people who did not consider themselves to be in any way employed by the HBC. For the post-1821 period, historians are far from unanimous in their characterization of such relations. Some argue that the monopoly era was a time of increased dependency on the HBC for goods, food and jobs. The lament by the Cree leader, Chief Sweet Grass, in 1871 is often pointed to as proof of increased dependence: 'We are poor and we want help—we want you to pity us—our country is no longer able to support us.'[4] Yet others claim that such pleas were rhetoric, designed as a first step in a series of bargaining moves. They point, instead, to examples—as at Norway House north of Red River—of Native groups who profited from a variety of pursuits, not all of which were related to the HBC.

The issue of credit nicely encapsulates the essence of this debate. Was credit the means whereby the Company kept trappers and traders on a string? Did credit, as Christopher Hanks has argued was the case with the Swampy Cree around Oxford House, keep 'the Indians forever beholden to the HBC'?[5] Or was credit something that Natives wished to retain and were successful in doing so despite the efforts of the HBC, in a period of monopoly, to end it? A number of regional studies lend overwhelming support to the latter interpretation. It may be, as Toby Morantz has speculated, that native traders had become accustomed to credit. At some level it may have represented for them a moral obligation, an affirmation of trust to which both parties had to commit. Trade, in the absence of credit and given the possibilities of other survival tactics, would not be conducted.[6]

Should one conclude, then, that during the era of monopoly credit was a means whereby the Natives manipulated the HBC, and not the reverse? It is not necessary to take such an extreme position. Clearly, the existence of free land and free resources exercised severe constraints on the HBC's ability to control Native trappers and traders by credit, or other means. The Company resisted credit in part because it recognized that too much credit, and related present-giving, could foster apathy and laziness as much as respect and reciprocity. The Company agreed to continue credit-giving in monopoly conditions because it felt it could successfully alter mark-ups to compensate for poor or lazy hunters. In this sense benevolent paternalism—the seeming disinterested acquiescence to Native demands—facilitated covert exploitation. Good hunters, as Harold Innis long ago and Frank Tough more recently have noted, paid the debts of

poor hunters. Only in competitive situations could credit be of economic benefit to Native traders. The HBC adopted paternal methods because in many areas of fur trade country through much of this period the environment—free land and available resources—gave it few other options. Only when land and resources were securely under the control of others could wage labour be bought and sold and could credit make trappers and traders beholden to the HBC.[7] Just as one must contextualize credit in order to understand its role at a particular time and place, so, too, must one be sensitive to variable patterns of interaction and subordinacy in a far-flung and far from homogeneous fur-trade hinterland.

Notes

[1]Michael Payne, *The Most Respectable Place in the Territory* (Ottawa, 1989), 51-64.

[2]Carol Judd, 'Mix't Bands . . .' in *Old Trails and New Directions* (Toronto, 1980) and 'Native Labour . . .' *Canadian Review of Sociology and Anthropology* 17 (1980); G. Makahonuk, 'Wage-Labour . . .' *Saskatchewan History* XLI (1988); P. Goldring, 'Governor Simpson's Officers', *Prairie Forum* (1985), especially for wage rates, 281 fn. 39.

[3]Judd, *op. cit.*; R. Enns, 'Indian Subsistence and the Commercial Fur Trade at Norway House: 1821-1875', unpublished paper, CHA, Victoria (1990), 13.

[4]A.J. Ray, *Indians in the Fur Trade* (Toronto, 1974), 228.

[5]C. Hanks, 'The Swampy Cree and the Hudson's Bay Company at Oxford House', *Ethnohistory* 29 (1982), 107.

[6]Enns, *op. cit.*; McEachern, 'The Reorganization of the Fur Trade after the Merger of the HBC and NWC, 1821-26', Discussion Paper 39, Dept. of Geography, York Uni-

⟶

versity, 1988; Dallas Wood, 'The Hudson's Bay Company and the Peace River Fur Trade, 1821-1850: District Management in the Age of Monopoly' (MA thesis, University of Alberta, 1988); Ken Coates, *Best Left as Indians: Native-White Relations in the Yukon Territory, 1840-1973* (Montreal, 1991); Paul C. Thistle, *Indian-European Trade Relations in the Lower Saskatchewan River Region to 1840* (Winnipeg, 1986);

Toby Morantz, '"So Evil a Practice": A Look at the Debt System in the James Bay Fur Trade', in R. Ommer, ed., *Merchant Credit and Labour Strategies in Historical Perspective* (Fredericton, 1990), 203-22.

[7]Frank Tough, 'Indian Economic Behaviour, Exchange and Profits in Northern Manitoba during the Decline of Monopoly, 1870-1930', *Journal of Historical Geography* 16 (1990), 385-401.

norm. Nor should it be thought that Simpson and those of the British bourgeois class who followed his lead treated their white wives as equals, in any sense of the word. Simpson treated his wife as a child. Her role was that of a Victorian gentlewoman, as one of Simpson's associates noted, a 'pious creature who resigns herself patiently under all circumstances which will contribute to the Honor of her Gallant Knt.' White and mixed-blood women were objects to be used in ways determined by white men, and, no matter their colour, women were increasingly perceived to be help mates, not independent actors in business affairs.[25]

Retrenchment and the implementation of a labour relations system provided the foundation for broader policy initiatives. The policies were twofold: one was designed to minimize competition; the second emerged as a multi-faceted attempt to bring Company policy in line with market demands. While both sets of strategies had weaknesses, the HBC, in the forty-year period following the merger, enjoyed average annual profits of £60,000 and annual dividends of ten to twenty per cent.

Simpson's actions on the west coast provide a good example of company strategies for handling competition and protecting fur-rich trapping zones. He first sought binding and negotiated settlements. With the Russian-American Company in the north he succeeded in 1838, agreeing to a settlement which protected the HBC's coastal interests. The Columbia River region further to the south was more difficult to manage. There the threat arose less from the action of a single fur-trade company and more from the threat of American westward agricultural expansion. That moving frontier made it likely that the so-called Snake River country, south of the Columbia River, would fall into American hands. Accordingly, Simpson instructed his traders to trap the territory bare. This tactic would, he hoped, discourage trappers proceeding north where he was implementing a policy of selected conservation across British Columbia and the prairies. This frontier policy sacrificed profits in order to protect more controlled and managed resources from outside competitors. It also influenced British negotiators to cede the Columbia area to the United States in the Oregon Boundary Treaty of 1846: fur-rich British Columbia remained in British hands; the overtrapped prairie to the south fell to the United States.[26]

Effective on the coast, the policy had mixed results in the Red River country. Mixed-blood and other former Hudson's Bay employees defied company claims to monopoly by trading furs under their very noses at Red River. In an attempt to combat the growing competition at Red River and elsewhere, the number of operating posts increased from forty-five in 1825 to fifty-eight by 1841. So, too, however, did the competition. Indeed, affairs at Red River had not developed as Simpson and the Company had hoped. The colony could not be depended on as a provider of foodstuffs for the fur trade. Crop failures rather than successes were the norm. Yet population grew and with it demands for free trade which culminated in the arrest and subsequent acquittal of free trader Pierre-Guillaume Sayer and three others in 1849. After that date commercial freedom seemed unrestrained. By the mid 1850s hundreds of mixed blood, on their own and as employees of American companies, made their living in opposition to the HBC's fur trade.

The Métis could compete with the Hudson's Bay Company only because American competition provided alternative outlets for the sale and purchase of goods. Norman Kittson's re-opening of a trading post, in 1844, at Pembina, 70 miles south of Red River in American territory, signalled the beginning of the end of the HBC's western trading monopoly. Even before that date the American Fur Company was besting the HBC in the collection of buffalo robes. Behind this competition lay a revolution in transportation. In the buffalo trade the use of steamboats on the Mississippi and Missouri Rivers by the American Fur Company proved far superior to York boats, just as steam on the Red River would soon facilitate easy access to Red River commerce. In the 1850s rail and steamship lines linked St Paul, Minnesota and New York, facilitating the swift acquisition of trade goods and influx of itinerant competitors. The charter, Simpson complained in 1857, was 'almost a nullity' in the face of the increased competition.

As long as the HBC remained wedded to the York boat and to Hudson Bay as the main entry and exit point for their merchandise, they were at a ruinous disadvantage. As the historian Andy Den Otter has pointed out, the HBC had to finance carrying charges on its goods for a minimum of two years while their expanding competitors at St Paul 'needed to finance only a three-month inventory'. Accordingly the HBC began to send trial shipments via St Paul in 1858. When the Northern Pacific and St Paul and Pacific railways reached Red River in 1871, the HBC switched all its shipping from the York Factory route to the Red River and began to adopt steamboats at other points throughout the west.[27]

Historians have written a great deal about the Red River troubles.[28] Such an emphasis is easy to understand. The French-speaking mixed bloods at Red River had a strong sense of identity and were in reality challenging not simply the Company's economic prerogatives, but also its political and judicial powers in the fur-trade interior. As well, the transportation revolution which made possible a competitive commercial environment had a profound impact on the HBC's future. Much less emphasis has been put on evaluating the changes that occurred as a result of the second set of policy initiatives implemented in this era: those related to meeting changing market demands. In fact, those policies facilitated much of the company's financial success and, equally importantly, laid the foundations for a major corporate decision taken in 1871 when, as the historical geographer, Skip Ray, has put it, the Company found itself at a crossroads.[29]

In keeping with general mercantile practices in this era, the HBC after 1821 became less and less specialized. Diversification took place on two planes: within and outside of the fur trade. By the 1870s the Company marketed a much broader range of animal products than it had ever done before: in the Columbia Department, for example, species other than those like beaver, marten, and muskrat, which already enjoyed fairly well-established markets, grew from 8 per cent in volume in 1825 to 35 per cent in 1840 and, following the fashion shift from beaver to silk hats in the 1840s, to 48.5 per cent of the total in 1849. Throughout the period Simpson encouraged traders to send fur and skins of a wide range of animals to be 'market tested' in London. Some of those sent were discarded because, it was feared, they might compete with already established items. Others found an often small but steady foothold in the British/European market. By 1850, the research of the historian, Lorne Hammond, has shown, the Company collected twenty 'major forms of wildlife' in the Columbia District 'as well as a range of by-products and domesticated animals'. Increasingly, too, these various items were pre-packaged in standard ways and weights so that middlemen purchasers could be assured of a comparable and consistent product over time.

The collapse of the beaver market in the 1840s struck at the heart of one of the Company's major plans: that of besting its competitors in frontier price wars while encouraging the managed harvesting of beaver in inland zones, in the process acquiring control of both market and resource. Silk hats put an end to such aspirations.[30] The second policy, that of diversification within the fur trade, provided the means for survival in the dramatically changed market context of the 1840s and beyond. After a brief period of disbelief, the Company attempted to market beaver, not as a hat, but as a fur. This redefinition of use only slowly took hold. More significantly, the Company began to focus on the sale of other furs, especially the marten. Orders went to interior posts to encourage, via presents and high prices, the trapping of marten rather than beaver, wherever feasible.

The diversification in the marketing of furs other than beaver had its parallel in the increased export of non-fur items. Simpson was continually seeking potentially profitable trade for the Company. He encouraged the export of sheep, buffalo, whale, and seal products as well as fish, lumber, coal, and oil. That after the decline in the sale of beaver, Company profits and dividends remained at a stable level suggests that such exports played a positive role in the Company's operations. Indeed the estimates of one fur-trade historian, Richard Mackie, suggest that as much as twenty-three per cent of the Company's profits in 1855 derived from the sale of non-fur items. Small wonder that one bemused observer could write as early as 1848 that

A Fur Trader is now certainly a heterogeneous animal, at least the Fur Trade is a most curious compound of professions, Miners, Lumberers, Furriers and the *d—* *—l* only knows what else besides. By the power of St Patrick the Incongruity of the Fur Trade beats an Irish Medley all hollow.[31]

Or that J.W. McKay, a long-time fur trader could reflect in 1872 that he had 'been Sailor, Farmer, Coal Miner, packer, Salesman, Surveyor, explorer, Fur Trader and Accountant in Your Service'.[32] Moreover, especially on the west coast, these non-

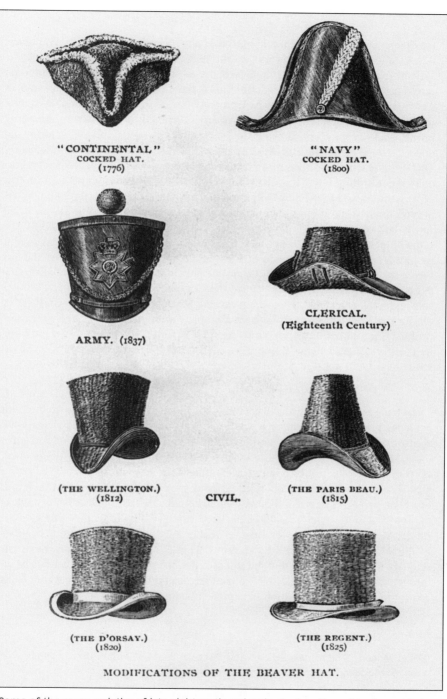

"CONTINENTAL."
COCKED HAT.
(1776)

"NAVY"
COCKED HAT.
(1800)

ARMY. (1837)

CLERICAL.
(Eighteenth Century)

(THE WELLINGTON.)
(1812)

CIVIL.

(THE PARIS BEAU.)
(1815)

(THE D'ORSAY.)
(1820)

(THE REGENT.)
(1825)

MODIFICATIONS OF THE BEAVER HAT.

Some of the many varieties of late eighteenth and early nineteenth century beaver hats.
(National Archives of Canada/C17338)

fur items were traded with regions other than Great Britain: San Francisco, Alaska, the Sandwich Islands and within the Columbia Department itself.

This extensive experience in marketing an increasingly diversified product range underlay a significant redefinition of the Company's *modus operandi* in 1871. By the end of the 1850s the Company had lost its legal right as a trading monopoly in western British North America. Probably stimulated by immense profits made by the Company and Company directors on the sale of Victoria land during the height of the British Columbia gold rush in the late 1850s and early 1860s,[33] a real estate-oriented enterprise, the International Financial Society, purchased controlling interest of the Company in 1863. In 1869 the HBC sold much of its western land to the new Dominion of Canada for £300,000. It retained lands around its existing trading settlements and one-twentieth of land in the so-called fertile belt of the western prairies. Many in the Company wished to sell all the remaining land. Others, especially the interior partners who could only earn money from profit on the sale of furs, argued for the continuance of the fur business. A third group argued for an intensification of the process of diversification already underway: they wanted the Company to become a general wholesale and retail enterprise. That group carried, albeit narrowly, the day. Until 1900, the fur trade continued to provide the Company with its greatest single source of profit.[34] But a corner had been turned in 1871, in a direction paved by the previous half century of gradual but significant experimentation in the marketing of a broad range of fur and non-fur products.

*   *   *

The changes effected by the HBC were not unique. In the context of Imperial business practice the Company was far from alone in centralizing managerial control, attempting to divide workers along ethnic lines in order to better control them, submitting workers to severe wage cuts, aspiring to monopoly dominance, diversifying product lines and experimenting with new transportation technologies. The Company did not enjoy equal success in all of these endeavours. It did, however, persist in an era of dramatic change. In the more limited colonial context the HBC's activities were, as a total package, replicated by few other single enterprises. Yet, as we shall explore, many smaller enterprises did adopt one or other of the strategies exemplified by the HBC. This is not to suggest that they consciously followed the model of the HBC. Rather, the point of the chapter has been, through a case study of the HBC's operations, to highlight themes and processes central to a period of transition in capitalist business activity.

Notes

[1]David Monod, 'The Iceman Selleth: The Business World of Milton Rous', unpublished paper, *CHA* 1990, 1.

[2]Victor P. Lytwyn, *The Fur Trade of the Little North: Indians, Pedlars and Englishmen, East of Lake Winnipeg, 1760–1821* (Winnipeg: Rupert's Land Research Centre, 1986), 36–7.

[3]F. Pannekoek, *The Fur Trade and Western Canadian Society, 1670–1870*, *CHA* Historical Booklet 43 (Ottawa, 1987), 5; D. Wayne Moodie, 'The Trading Post Settlement of the Canadian Northwest, 1724–1821', *The Journal of Historical Geography* 13 (1987), 360–74; R.S. Allen, 'Peter Fidler', *DCB* 6, 250.

[4]Ann Carlos and Elizabeth Hoffman, 'The North American Fur Trade: Bargaining to a Joint Profit Maximum under Incomplete Information, 1804–1821', *Journal of Economic History* XLVI (1986), 967–86; Ann Carlos, 'The Causes and Origins of the North American Fur Trade Rivalry: 1804–10', *Journal of Economic History* XLI (1981), 777–94; Ann Carlos, 'The Birth and Death of Predatory Competition in the North American Fur Trade, 1810–21', *Explorations in Economic History* 19 (1982), 156–83; R. C. Cole, *Historical Atlas of Canada* I (Toronto 1986), Plate 65.

[5]Michael Bliss, *Northern Enterprise . . .* , 105.

[6]Lytwyn, *The Fur Trade . . .*, 88.

[7]Ibid., 40–1; Cole, *Atlas*, Plate 65.

[8]Support for the last few paragraphs can be found in the articles by Carlos, *op. cit.*, and in Cole, *Atlas*, Plate 65.

[9]P. Goldring, 'William MacKintosh', *DCB* 7, 567.

[10]Hamar Foster, 'Long Distance Justice: The Criminal Jurisdiction of Canadian Courts West of the Canadas, 1763–1859', *American Journal of Legal History* 34 (1990), 1–48.

[11]J.D. Haeger, 'Business Strategy and Practice in the Early Republic: John Jacob Astor and the American Fur Trade', *The Western Historical Quarterly* 19 (1988), 183–202.

[12]R.A. Pendergast, 'The XY Company, 1894–1904' (PhD diss., University of Ottawa, 1957).

[13]J.M. Colthart, 'Edward Ellice', *DCB* 9, 234.

[14]Moodie, *op. cit.*, 370.

[15]A.J. Ray, *Indians in the Fur Trade: Their Role as Hunters, Trappers and Middlemen in the Lands Southwest of Hudson Bay, 1660–1870* (Toronto, 1974). For the alcohol output at York Factory, see Michael Payne, *'The Most Respectable Place in the Territory': Everyday Life in the Hudson's Bay Company Service, York Factory, 1788–1870* (Ottawa, 1989), 20.

[16]W.A. Sloan, 'The Native Response to the Extension of the European Traders into the Athabaska and Mackenzie Basin, 1770–1814', *CHR* LX (1979), 293.

[17]J. Brown, *Strangers in Blood: Fur Trade Company Families in Indian Country* (Vancouver, 1980); Sylvia Van Kirk, *'Many Tender Ties': Women in Fur Trade Society, 1670–1870* (Toronto, 1980).

[18]Lytwyn, *The Fur Trade . . .*, 144.

[19]J.S. Galbraith, 'George Simpson', *DCB* 8, 813.

[20]B.M. White, 'Joseph Cadotte', *DCB* 6, 100.

[21]P. Goldring, 'James Keith', *DCB* 8, 455. For a comprehensive review of changes in the Northern Department following the merger, see Ute McEachern, 'The Reorganization of the Fur Trade after the Merger of the HBC and NWC, 1821–26', Discussion Paper 39, Department of Geography, York University, 1988.

[22]Elizabeth Arthur, 'Far From the Maddening Crowd: Hudson's Bay Company Managers in the Country North of Superior', *Ontario History* LXXXII (1990), 11. On managerial tasks, see also P. Goldring, 'Governor Simpson's Officers: Elite Recruitment in a British Overseas Enterprise, 1834–1870', *Prairie Forum* (1985), 251–81.

[23]Carol Judd, '"Mixt Bands of Many Nations": 1821–70', in C.M. Judd and A.J. Ray, *Old Trails and New Directions* (Toronto, 1980); Judd, 'Native Labour and Social Stratification in the HBC's Northern Department, 1770–1870', *Canadian Review of Sociology and Anthropology* 17 (1980), 305–14; G. Makahonuk, 'Wage-Labour in the Northwest Fur Trade Economy, 1760–1849', *Saskatchewan History* XLI (1988), 1–18; P. Goldring, *op. cit.*, 273.

[24]R.A. Willie, 'John West', *DCB* 7, 900–2; Sylvia Van Kirk, 'Nancy McKenzie', *DCB* 8, 561.

[25]Michael Payne, 'Fort Churchill, 1821–1900: An Outpost Community in the Fur Trade', *Manitoba History* 20 (1990), 2–15; Sylvia Van Kirk, 'Frances Ramsay Simpson', *DCB* 8, 811–12.

[26]James R. Gibson, 'The "Russian Contract": The Agreement of 1838 between the Hudson's Bay and Russian-American Companies', in R.A. Pierce, ed., *Russia in North America: Proceedings of the Second International Conference on Russian America* (Fairbanks, 1990), 157–79; G. Williams, 'Peter Skene Ogden', *DCB* 8, 661.

[27]A.A. Den Otter, 'Transportation Trade and Regional Identity in Southwestern Prairies' *Prairie Forum* 15 (1990), 1–23 and Den Otter, 'Railway Technology, the Canadian Northwest and the Continental Economy', *Railroad History* 162 (1990), 5–19, quote p. 10.

[28]See relevant section in G. Friesen, *The Canadian Prairies* (Toronto, 1984) for sources and commentary.

[29]The following section has benefited from Lorne Hammond, '"Any Ordinary Degree of System": The Columbia Department of the Hudson's Bay Company and the Harvesting of Wildlife, 1825–1849' (MA thesis, University of Victoria, 1988); Richard Mackie, 'Not the Fur Trade in Canada: George Simpson and Resource Development, 1820–1860', unpublished paper, CHA, Kingston, 1991; A. J. Ray, 'Adventurers at the Crossroads', *Beaver* (1986), 4–12; A.C. Gluek, Jr, 'Industrial Experiments in the Wilderness: A Sidelight on the Business History of the Hudson's Bay Company', *Business History Review* 32 (1958).

[30]Hugh Grant, 'Revenge of the Paris Hat', *Beaver* (1988–89), 37–44; J.F. Crean, 'Hats and the Fur Trade', *Canadian Journal of Economics and Political Science* 28 (1962), 373–86.

[31]R. Mackie, *op. cit.*, 1.

[32]R. Mackie, 'J.W. McKay', *DCB* 12, 642–3.

[33]P. Baskerville, *Beyond the Island: An Illustrated History of Victoria* (Windsor, 1986).

[34]A.J. Ray, *op. cit.* See also A.A. Den Otter, 'The Hudson's Bay Company's Prairie Transportation Problem, 1870–85,' in J.E. Foster, ed., *The Developing West* (Edmonton 1983), 26–47.

8 ARRESTED TRANSITION: ATLANTIC CANADA

More so than was the case in central Canada, staple extraction dominated the economy of the Atlantic region. British mercantilist policies encouraged the extraction and export of staples and discouraged any diversification into staple processing or secondary manufacturing. The export of fish, wood, and coal provided the region with exchange to purchase food and manufactured imports from abroad. While many miners, woods workers, and fishers in the Maritime region were also farmers, agricultural production almost never generated enough food to feed the region's people. Most of those who farmed had to work also in one or other of the dominant staple industries in order to survive.

The extraction of staples in a mercantilist context has been seen by many historians as a sufficient explanation for the fact that extensive and lasting industrialization failed to take hold in the Atlantic region.[1] Such a perspective is too simple. Not only does this interpretation have about it a sense of inevitability, but it also absolves the region's inhabitants from any responsibility in the matter of arrested transition from a commercial to an industrial mode of production. It tends to depict the region's inhabitants as a passive people overwhelmed by and helpless in the face of locational constraints and exterior control. This is not to imply, however, that the staple/mercantilist perspective should be discounted out of hand. Rather the strong focus on staple extraction which developed within the context of mercantilist policies in the first half of the nineteenth century led to the emergence of a distinctive entrepreneurial culture. As mercantilism ebbed at mid-century this indigenous culture persisted and set limits to entrepreneurial behaviour throughout much of the rest of the century. In this sense indigenous social relations of production—the character and strategies of the entrepreneurial élites and their relations with those who they employed and with whom they traded—went far to determining the pace and nature of economic change. The activities of the region's business élite informed by a culture which was itself influenced by mercantilist policies from abroad helped mould a particular economic structure by the century's end. At certain points throughout the century, one or other of these several elements held sway. Yet it is only in their combination that one can find a satisfactory explanation for the reality of arrested transition. In the end, Maritimers made their own economic bed, but an understanding of why so few slept comfortably in it requires a close look at the historical evolution of the local business élite.

MARITIME MERCHANTOCRACIES

The mercantilist system spawned a particular type of colonial business élite. Throughout the Atlantic ports wholesale merchants became the 'co-ordinators of

109

colonial commerce'.[2] Within the protected free trade zone of the British Empire, colonial merchants shipped whatever they could and imported as much as possible. As the historian, Bill Acheson, succinctly wrote, 'the merchant's final objective was to create an entrepôt into which a dozen different forms of commerce would flow.'[3]

It should be emphasized that Acheson is making two points here. Both require elaboration. Merchants, especially the large wholesalers, rarely specialized in any single commodity: diversification of trade was one way merchants sought security in a volatile trading world. Some historians have argued that this is all that merchants did. They invested in movable goods, from which they looked for short-term rather than longer term returns. This capital, in other words, was of a floating rather than a fixed sort. The implications of such a characterization are immense and have been most completely, albeit controversially, elaborated in the writings of the economic historian, Tom Naylor. Naylor emphasizes the exchange relations role exercised by colonial merchants within an international context.[4] For him control of such relations always resided outside the colony, in Liverpool, Glasgow, London, or the Jersey Islands. Because colonial merchants owed their livelihood to satisfying the commercial needs of distant traders, they refused to invest in fixed enterprise, in colonial industrial development. To do so would, potentially, cut down on the flow of imports. Such investment seemed contrary to the mercantilist axiom that colonies existed as markets for items manufactured in the mother country. In the maritime context much of what Naylor says rings true. Yet, in the final analysis his characterization is overdrawn. He focuses too narrowly on exchange relations and external control and thus overlooks the implications which follow from Acheson's second point, that of creating a colonial entrepôt.

Maritime merchants wished to build ports capable of dominating the trade and credit needs of as large a hinterland as possible. Whether located in Halifax, Saint John, or smaller ports like Pictou and Yarmouth, merchants were in 'pursuit of development'.[5] They looked to establish something permanent and distinct in British North America. Over time they developed a sense of social allegiance to their port. Local pride's strong sense of fixedness is not recognized by perspectives which focus primarily on exchange and exterior control. In order to develop their local ports, merchants did regularly invest in fixed enterprises. Such investments related most often to the development of a social and structural infrastructure capable of supporting entrepôt growth: banks, schools, hospitals, water and electric services, and transportation improvements were among these.[6] Fixed investment did occur within a mercantilist frame. Some merchants, although always a minority, did invest in industrial enterprises. Local merchant élites would trade with any country or colony if prospects of profit seemed possible. Maritime merchants were the children of British mercantilism: while never completely outgrowing that heritage, they, like children everywhere, came to espouse ends uniquely their own. These general points gain specificity from two case studies of Maritime merchants in action and from brief sectoral studies of shipping, banking, coal mining, agriculture, lumbering, and fishing.

The Halifax Merchantocracy

David Sutherland's study of Halifax merchants in the first half of the nineteenth century provides an instructive entry into the world of a maritime port's merchantocracy.[7] Some five hundred men (he identified only one woman!) were active as major wholesale merchants at some period during that half century. In many ways these merchants exhibited the two fundamental attributes of a class: a similarity in economic structure, and strong internal recognition of common values and common aspirations. In the early years the major wholesale merchants were a blend of pre-American Revolution merchants, Loyalists who arrived after the Revolution, and immigrants from Scotland. Following 1815, however, that merchant class became increasingly composed of the Nova Scotia-born, often sons, cousins, and nephews of older merchants. Nor, with several prominent exceptions were these merchants birds of passage. Eighty-five per cent of the 393 merchants for whom a place of death could be found died in the colony. Only 14 per cent of those born outside the colony died outside the colony.[8] From the outset this merchant class established deep local roots. Intermarriage within the mercantile élite acted as a form of social closure, especially in the period from 1815 to 1840. So, too, did an extensive system of interlocking apprenticeships.[9] While some Halifax merchants, like William Black, would allegedly only trade with the Scots merchants, in fact, his ethnic focus was exceptional. Familial interlocking went far towards transcending ethnic and religious differences.[10]

In its beginnings Halifax had been a garrison town, founded as a fort to protect imperial property, not as a port to expand imperial trade. Early merchants, notably Joshua Mauger, grew wealthy serving the British army and navy and aping the social mores of the officer class.[11] While, following the American Revolution, and, especially during the years of the Napoleonic blockades, Halifax became more a port than a fort, old social aspirations persisted. In social terms merchants continued to aspire to be gentry: patterns of conspicuous consumption, as enumerated by wealth inventories at death, testify to the ongoing desire of wealthy merchants to live in the style of the British aristocracy.

The merchant-gentry were preeminently Nova Scotia-born. Those men dominated municipal politics, had links to provincial politicians, and participated in a wide variety of social and cultural affairs. They willingly underwrote the capital costs of entrepôt development: banks, insurance companies, electric and gas works, shipping, and interior transportation projects received their support. They had a strong commitment to developing Halifax as a port of trade and most of their collective, and at times quite ambitious, entrepreneurial activity went towards that end. They saw themselves competing with neighbouring Saint John for control of a common hinterland as well as competing with various American ports for control of the important West Indies trade.

If the Naylor interpretation misses the strong sense of place and the locally, as opposed to imperially, centred *raison d'être* exhibited by Halifax's business élite, he is, nonetheless, quite correct in his depiction of merchants being opposed to industrialization. Few major Halifax merchants invested in industrial concerns in the first fifty years of the nineteenth century. In part, such reluctance can be explained by the fact that Halifax lacked a populous hinterland for the sale of such items: the concentration of people per square mile was significantly below that for Quebec and Ontario in the mid-nineteenth century, for example. In part, too, Imperial policy opposed general industrialization within colonies. Some merchants did underwrite the production of nails, flour, sugar, and rope, but they were a decided minority. In Halifax, as in Saint John (which will be examined in more detail later) the manufacturing initiative emerged more from the city's artisans than from its merchants. In fact Halifax merchants as a group did not simply ignore industrialization: they actively blocked those who wished to develop the port in that direction. This obstructive policy is not explained by locational factors. Rather, merchants classified local industry as potential competition, in the sense that local production would diminish the flow of imported manufactured goods and thus cut into their profits. Halifax's Chamber of Commerce could, therefore, with perfect logic support drawbacks on duties on imported raw materials that might be processed in the colony while opposing any tariff on imported manufactured goods. The consistency lay in the fact that both measures could conceivably lead to increased trade, the bread and butter of merchant enterprise.

It is also interesting to note that even as British mercantile policies began to recede in the face of pressures exerted by those in England who desired free trade, Halifax merchants did not demonstrate much interest in local industrial production. When William Huskisson began to liberalize British trade laws in 1825, Halifax merchants began to increase their trade with the United States, Europe, South America and the foreign as well as British West Indies. This policy gained solid profits into the 1840s. During that decade a series of events undermined the props of traditional prosperity: trade with the British West Indies declined following the abolishment of slavery and the consequent weakening of the economy of Nova Scotia's primary trading partner;[12] the repeal of the protective Corn Laws (1846) and the Navigation Act (1849) ended the official policy of mercantilism; local competitors, like Saint John, increasingly appropriated parts of Halifax's trading hinterland; the merchant class, itself, was under pressure from emerging businessmen within Halifax, traders, retailers, and shopkeepers who were demanding access to portions of power and prestige within the city's commercial community. In the face of these upheavals, Halifax merchants continued to ignore industry. Instead, they looked to increased trade with the United States and paved the way for their acceptance of the Reciprocity Agreement of 1854. They also began to agitate for railroads to facilitate the development of a larger, perhaps even transcontinental, hinterland for their port. Yet when colonial spending for railroad development began to escalate, merchants were among the first to get cold feet. The city of Halifax threatened to renege on financial promises in 1857. In the same year many merchants deserted the reform government and helped unseat it in the election.[13] In all this, the development by Halifax merchants of an indigenous industrial base remained far from the centre of their priorities. Their concept of development remained constant: their city of residence was to remain an entrepôt, a place for the exchange of goods, not the production of goods.

112

Production statistics for the colony as a whole suggest that this entrepreneurial strategy extended to other Nova Scotia centres. The size of industry in Nova Scotia in 1850 compared favourably with that of Upper Canada. Twenty years later the growth of factory employment in six major industrial sectors lagged dramatically behind that of Ontario's. By 1870, per capita industrial output in Ontario exceeded that of Nova Scotia by 2.2 times.[14] This is a significant change because some literature suggests that Nova Scotia's, and by extension Atlantic Canada's, arrested industrialization can be best explained by the constraining control exerted by external forces. Great Britain, through the policy of mercantilism, held reign until the mid-century. Following 1867 the federal government of Canada, which supported central over maritime Canada, held sway for the rest of the century. Yet in the important years following the end of mercantilism and the beginning of Confederation, presumably a period of relative autonomy from outside state control, Nova Scotia's business élite remained aloof from industrial pursuits. This is not to conclude that that élite did not prosper. An analysis of the probated wealth of the colony's élite (composed of merchants, gentlemen, bankers, master mariners, ship builders, and ship owners) in 1852-53 and 1871 showed a 58 per cent increase in wealth after controlling for price inflation. In each year merchants accounted for one-half of all estates valued at over $15,000. No other single occupation or profession came close to this number. Craftsmen and tradesmen, the category closest to that of a manufacturing class, experienced only a 31 per cent increase in wealth. Indeed, in his study of Nova Scotia between 1850 and 1871, the historian, Julian Gwyn, did not mention a distinct manufacturing sector![15]

If it is clear that industrial production lagged in Nova Scotia between 1850 and 1871, it is perhaps less clear why such was the case. It has already been suggested that control by an exterior state seems an improbable cause. What, then, of the simple fact of location? Were other potentially competing centres like Upper and Lower Canada better situated in terms of markets and resources? If they were, then perhaps the slow process of industrial growth had little to do with the nature of the colony's commercial business élite. A simple and conclusive answer to these important questions is not possible here. It is true that the colony's and indeed the Maritimes' agricultural potential paled before that of Upper Canada and parts of Lower Canada. It is also clear that central Canada had, via the Great Lakes, access to iron and coal resources in the United States superior to those possessed by Nova Scotia. A more detailed study of the colony's commercial élite in the third quarter of the century is required before a conclusive answer can be given. It may be the case, for example, that the breakdown of exclusivity occurring within the merchant élite in the late 1840s allowed a new group of businessmen to gradually set a new agenda for development policies.

If such a new élite did take control, however, it is doubtful if any revolution in commercial policy occurred. Despite pressure from artisans and a minority of merchants, tariffs, for example, remained little altered from the 1840s until after Confederation. Manufacturing interests received little support from the colony's policy-makers. Moreover, two further sets of aggregate statistics suggest the important, albeit negative, role played by the commercial élite. In 1870, Nova Scotia imported about twice the per capita value of manufactured goods than did Ontario. These goods satisfied about one-half of the province's consumption of manufactured items.[16] While we do not know the economies of scale at the level of specific manufactured goods, at a general level there was clearly a large indigenous demand being satisfied by external sources. Low population densities compared to Ontario, then, are not a sufficient explanation for arrested industrialization. The point is that merchants profited nicely from the sale of those imports. Few others did.

The final statistic relates to population flows. There is growing evidence that people began to trek out of Nova Scotia in the late 1840s and continued to do so throughout the rest of the century. This exodus, one historian has concluded, 'was the most important socio-economic phenomenon for Nova Scotia in the third quarter of the nineteenth century.'[17] Part of this exodus can be related to regional failures in the agricultural sector. But much must also rest at the feet of the merchant élite. They, virtually alone in the colony, had wealth enough to diversify into job-creating enterprises, as their counterparts in the northeastern United States did, in such areas as textiles and boots and shoes. The existence of such enterprise would have stemmed the flow of people to similar factories in the States. They chose not to do so and, as a result, along with locational and extra-governmental constraints, they helped create a local social and economic structure that would make much more difficult any future movement into industrialization. Local colonial entrepreneurs did not construct the mercantilist frame within which the maritime economy emerged. They did, however, provide that structure essential support long after the Imperial Government had dismantled its legislative underpinnings. The case of Saint John, New Brunswick, offers further insight into the ways by which a Maritime bourgeoisie helped maintain a social and economic context resistant to industrial growth.

The Saint John Merchantocracy

In some ways the city of Saint John differed significantly from that of Halifax: including adjacent Portland, it contained, in 1840, nearly twice as many people (27,000 to 15,000); it possessed a more populous natural hinterland (accessible via the Saint John River and its tributaries); shipbuilding and the lumber industry were major parts of the city's economy, unlike Halifax where a small timber supply encouraged merchants to commission the building of boats at various outposts; manufacturing on a scale much greater than in Halifax provided significant local employment. Saint John, in sum, was the Maritimes' major metropolis and ranked as the third largest city in British North America.[18]

Despite these structural differences, the city's dominant business élite possessed many of the characteristics of the élite in Halifax. During the first half of the nineteenth century just over one-half of the forty most prominent businessmen in Saint John had been born in New Brunswick and possessed strong ties to the local community. Many of the rest hailed from Scotland. Like Halifax merchants, those in Saint John lived like British gentry. They also rose to prominence within and were fiercely protective of the British mercantile system. Unlike major merchants in Halifax who shipped and transhipped a variety of goods to the West Indies and sundry other markets, many of the major Saint John merchants focused almost exclusively on the timber trade, exporting logs and boats to Liverpool. But if produce and markets differed, policies and attitudes concerning manufacturing did not. Before 1840 most of the Saint John merchant élite did what they could to discourage the growth of local industry. As in Halifax, the merchants dominated the local banking structure; if at times they warred with themselves over financial issues, they were one in denying credit to non-merchants. Local producers of goods had to seek financial support elsewhere. The élite refused to support petitions for protective tariffs on manufactured or food goods. For them, as for their Halifax brethren, their right to buy cheaply and sell dear overshadowed all else.

The dismantlement of the mercantile system in the 1840s profoundly affected the power of the merchants. The movement towards free trade on the part of the mother country could be countered by exporting lumber and deals to the United States instead of timber to England. By 1849, New Brunswick exported £266,000 of lumber and deals compared to only £179,000 of timber.[19] More difficult to contain, however, were the reactions of what might be called the sub-élite of the Saint John business community.

Unlike Halifax, Saint John boasted, even before 1840, a relatively vibrant artisan/manufacturing class. Its strength lay in the woodworking/shipbuilding sector, although tanners, saddlers, and metal workers were also significant. The masters and journeymen who toiled in these crafts had by the mid 1830s achieved a meaningful level of class consciousness. On a number of social and economic issues they articulated positions at odds with those of the dominant mercantile élite. Intermarriage and interlocking apprenticeships further strengthened the bonds of the emerging class. Moreover, in a process common to nineteenth-century Philadelphia, Newark, and, indeed, to some British cities in the early eighteenth century, some artisans and masters began to expand into larger units: extended partnerships, at times but not often including minor merchants, created the capital base necessary for such growth. In the shadow of the dominant merchant élite, and virtually unconnected to that élite, a nascent indigenous manufacturing sector had emerged in Saint John.

As the mercantilist system disintegrated, the artisans began to demand the imposition of tariffs to protect and ensure the future of their manufacturing endeavours. Agriculturists, too, supported such initiatives in the hope of being able to secure some protection for the local sale of their produce. This combination of external and internal pressure led to the gradual fracturing of the dominant mercantile élite. Those most closely associated with the timber trade continued to block tariffs in areas which would make boatbuilding and feeding crews more expensive. In other areas they compromised and grudgingly allowed higher tariffs to be implemented. Those merchants, who were locally born and/or who were not as closely connected to the timber trade, began not only to support higher tariffs, but in some instances to invest in local manufacturing

115

enterprises. Following 1850 the not so wealthy among the élite also boosted railroads and by 1860 the 108-mile European and North America railroad from Saint John to Shediac opened for business.[20]

After 1850 merchants of a mercantilist persuasion, that is those in the lumber trade who continued to seek their fortunes in the export and import sectors, had to share space with a combination of more locally-focused wholesalers and ambitious masters and artisans. In effect the business élite in Saint John had split into two factions, each operating virtually independent of the other. The consequence was important although limited economic diversification. Certainly in comparison to Halifax and Nova Scotia, Saint John and New Brunswick boasted a much more dynamic and solid manufacturing base by 1870. While Nova Scotia imported just under half of its manufactured goods, New Brunswick imported just under one-third of the manufactured items consumed by its residents. Moreover, manufacturing in New Brunswick contributed 39 per cent of the province's commodity income in 1870, while manufacturing in Nova Scotia contributed only 27 per cent.[21]

Yet in several ways New Brunswick's economy at 1870 reflected the nature of its business élite. The colony continued to import the bulk of its foodstuffs. Protection for farmers was never implemented in any systematic way and, partly as a result, the import of food came close in value to the export of timber. Food industries like flour milling, distilling, and meat curing were almost non-existent. In fact, employment in flour and grist mills declined by 15 per cent in the twenty years following 1850. The great merchants had held firm on this issue: they wanted to profit from the import of agricultural produce, and they also believed that those imported goods were cheaper than home production, and thus they saved money on the victualling of the crews who sailed their timber ships. Manufacturing areas that received some tariff production developed; those that did not, stagnated. Significantly many of the items necessary to build and outfit wooden ships remained unprotected. Since shipbuilding was the most important manufacturing sector in New Brunswick and indeed throughout much of the Maritimes, potential linkages in the industrial sector were retarded, if not completely precluded by the existence of a tariff structure, the design of which continued in important ways to reflect the interest of the major import-export merchants at Saint John. A closer examination of the shipping industry reveals much about the nature of nineteenth-century business enterprise throughout the maritime region.

THE SHIPPING INDUSTRY IN ATLANTIC CANADA

Shipbuilding was extremely important to the maritime economy. Between 1815 and 1860, Prince Edward Island, New Brunswick, and Nova Scotia manufactured 212 million tons of shipping, about half of which was sold in the United Kingdom. Newfoundland purchased most of its ships from the other colonies. While total investment and profit figures are not available, the export of ships represented 80 per cent of Prince Edward Island's exports in 1825 and probably accounted for a positive trade balance in that colony for most of the pre-Confederation era.[22] In

New Brunswick, the shipbuilding industry was second only to timber in the nineteenth century. In the 1850s the sale of ships added £300,000 sterling to annual average exports of £900,000 in New Brunswick. Before 1850 the sale of ships brought some £72,000 sterling to Nova Scotia each year. In the 1850s some £253,000 sterling was annually invested in the shipbuilding industry in Nova Scotia and between 1853 and 1858 the sale of ships generated an average annual value of £110,600 sterling.[23] This return added about 10 per cent to the colony's exports in those years. These figures, it should be emphasized do not take into account returns to shippers from external trade, a figure Sager and Panting put at £80,100 sterling per annum for New Brunswick throughout the 1860s.[24]

The evolution of the shipbuilding industry stands as a central example of the ambivalent nature of Atlantic business enterprise. Shipbuilding was clearly an industrial pursuit; but in the Atlantic region it was an industrial endeavour which evolved under the aegis of merchant capital. In the first instance it developed within the protective confines of the mercantilist system. Colonial shipowners could sell their vessels duty free on the British market. They could sell their goods in a British market protected by preferential duties. By virtue of the Navigation Acts, which kept foreign shipping out of most colonial trade routes, they enjoyed privileges as general carriers. Small wonder that most major merchants in the important Atlantic ports were also major shipowners. Between 1820 and 1849, merchants owned 66 per cent of all tonnage newly registered in the major Atlantic ports. The rest was owned by a wide spectrum of small operators. While there were important exceptions like James Yeo, a Prince Edward Island merchant who built at least 155 ships between 1833 and his death in 1868, most merchant ship owners had their boats built for them by others.[25] Few of the major Saint John or Halifax merchants were shipbuilders, but many owned ships. For merchants, shipowning performed three functions. Ships provided another way to diversify capital investment and thus protect against sudden trade fluctuations. Ships were trading vessels, which could carry trade goods and could themselves be traded. Ownership of ships allowed merchants greater control of the dispatch of their trade goods and the opportunity to ship goods at a cheaper rate than would be possible any other way. For most merchants, vessels were adjuncts to a process of commercial exchange. They bought vessels from others to ship goods to and receive goods from others and to sell the vessels themselves to others.

All this may seem to be self-evident and simple common sense. And so from a merchant's perspective it was. When, however, it is recalled that merchants dominated the business communities of the major Atlantic ports, their perspectives and the policies that emerged therefrom set the contours within which the shipping and most other economic endeavours evolved. During the first few decades of the nineteenth century shipbuilding in the Maritimes was very much what economists call an enclave industry, an industrial pursuit that afforded little linkage to other regional development and that left ultimately only a minimal amount of capital in the region. With the exception of wood, most other material for the construction of ships, often including labour, was shipped from Britain to the Maritimes. James Yeo, for example, went so far as to set up a shipyard in England

Shipbuilding in Dorchester, New Brunswick: a sight typical of the Maritime coast in the nineteenth century. *(National Archives of Canada/C10103)*

near Bideford to which he sent his unfinished ships for completion. The experiences of the Pictou merchant and sometime shipbuilder James Crichton suggests that even those who wished to utilize local inputs faced rigid mercantile restraints. In 1824 Crichton entered into a mutual agreement with Cannon and Miller, a Liverpool mercantile concern, to construct a 460-ton vessel to be sold in Liverpool. Despite Crichton's opposition, the Liverpool merchants sent to Pictou up to a dozen ship's carpenters to construct the vessel. As well, all the rigging and sails came from England. While Crichton felt that 'as good ship carpenters and workmen could be obtained in the Province at as cheap a rate of wages and the work could be carried on in a more economical manner by employing only such numbers as the supply of timber and materials [allowed]', the Liverpool merchants felt that being able to advertise that the vessel had been built 'entirely with Liverpool workmen' overshadowed any increased labour costs.[26]

By the end of the mercantile system, shipbuilding had become much more under the control of colonial procedures. A more pronounced division between builders and merchants had taken place. But merchants controlled the ultimate output. They invested their capital in a colonial industrial product in order to, as Sager and Panting put it, operate an 'oceanic extension of the merchant's warehouse'. As such they happily continued the process of importing as many inputs for shipbuilding as seemed possible. These items included food for crews, mill engines for saw mills, rigging, tin and copper plate, sails, tackle, canvas, cordage, anchors, and other items for the vessels themselves. Had all metal inputs for New Brunswick ships been manufactured in that province the value of output from the local metal sector would have increased by close to 25 per cent in 1871. Between 1869 and 1878, Nova Scotia and New Brunswick shipbuilders imported, for every dollar of ship materials produced locally, $1.40 from abroad.[27] Merchants desired to build cheaply and augment their general carrying trade. The enhancement of exchange, not production relations, continued to be their collective goal. Even after the end of mercantilism, the maritime shipbuilding sector continued to exhibit many of the characteristics of an enclave industry.

There is a further point that any history of business enterprise in the shipping sector (or any other sector) must explore: the distribution of economic surplus or income. Julian Gwyn has demonstrated that shipbuilding in Nova Scotia was beset by sharp cyclical shifts. He estimated that between 1850 and 1871 ship's carpenters probably enjoyed a maximum of six full employment years.[28] Few artisans in any of the Atlantic colonies could depend on a single occupation for a living wage. Occupational pluralism was common throughout the nineteenth century. Most families farmed as well as worked in the woods, in the fishery, and/or in some seasonal craft endeavour like shipbuilding. In this context, merchants could profit from control of exchange and distribution. It was not necessary for them to invest in technological inputs in the production process, for occupational pluralism provided, in effect, a bank of cheap labour. As long as wood resources remained relatively abundant, the merchant capitalist could continue to import technologically advanced inputs and profit from the continuance of pre-capitalist social relations. Shipbuilding emerged from and interacted with local social relations, nicely at one with the local social and economic context. The potential for an industrial enterprise like ship construction to alter and transform that local context was often appropriated by merchants with their eyes on exchange, not production, value. When merchants helped fashion a tariff system that facilitated the import of building materials for ships, they stripped the industry of much of its transformative power. In this sense that industry was of a disarticulated character. It drew from the local context but it also drew from non-local contexts and to the extent that it possessed the power to alter economies, that influence was channelled to other places.[29]

This is not to argue that a smoother transition to industrial capitalism, a transition that would have encouraged the local development of linked enterprises and the growth of larger production units and the creation of a labouring class more completely focused on single pursuits, would necessarily have led to a higher standard of living throughout the region. It is to suggest, however, that the reasons why such a transition was an arrested or delayed process in Atlantic Canada cannot be understood without focusing on the role played by that region's mercantile businessmen in profiting from the maintenance of a pre-capitalist system of social relations. The shipping and shipbuilding industry, albeit only one component of that structure, was nonetheless an extremely important one whether measured by export value, carrying capacity for trade goods, or employment for artisans. Moreover, it illustrates the limits to which industry developed within the context of merchant capital: instead of encouraging the breakdown of pre-capitalist low-productivity economic enterprise, shipbuilding perpetuated and profited from its continuance.

THE LUMBER INDUSTRY

Like the shipping industry, the lumber industry emerged within the mercantile system. The closing of the Baltic, England's main source of timber, in 1807 by Napoleon forced England to institute a sliding protective tariff which guaranteed easy access for colonial timber. Although the Baltic opened after 1815, that preference was maintained until the early 1840s. New Brunswick's exports of ton timber increased from 5,000 tons in 1805 to 417,000 tons in 1825, averaging off to 200,000 tons annually until the 1840s. Commencing in the 1830s and continuing throughout the 1840s and 1850s, trade in lumber and deals to the United States gradually surpassed the export of ton timber to Great Britain. In this, the dismantlement of the mercantile structure accelerated a trend already visible.[30]

Merchants dominated the New Brunswick lumber industry. In the early years of the nineteenth century wholesalers located in Saint John extended lines of credit to numerous country storekeepers and brokers who, in turn, outfitted part-time lumberers. These men went into the woods and delivered their timber in the spring. Gradually these operations became consolidated within the control of several large companies. The granting of timber licences for five years enabled large well-capitalized merchant houses to dominate the trade. By the late 1840s four companies—three, branch enterprises of the Glasgow-based Pollock, Gil-

PROTO-INDUSTRIALIZATION: SHIPBUILDING IN RURAL REGIONS

Larry McCann, an historical geographer, has perceptively characterized rural shipbuilding as an example of proto-industrialization, similar to that which occurred in rural preindustrial Europe (see Chapter One). In some ways the typical rural shipyard anticipated modern factories: division of labour existed; blacksmiths, sawyers, joiners, and even carvers worked separately. But more significantly, that workplace stood apart from a modern industrial enterprise. A merchant class underwrote and often organized production; distant markets generally dictated output; seasonal operations fitted well with the wider preindustrial rural environment.

The shipbuilding operation of Colin Campbell, a merchant in the small rural town of Weymouth, Nova Scotia, is a case in point. Between 1854 and the late 1870s, he built at least twenty vessels. Almost all workers, with the exception of his foreman, were employed on a part-time basis and most were farmers or farmers' sons who lived within three miles of the shipyard. Many of these same farmers also worked for Campbell cutting wood in the winter. Generally the vessel was built between February and mid-May, thus allowing his workforce to return home to tend their farms. Seventy-five per cent of the heads of households in the Weymouth region depended on at least two jobs to earn a living.

Occupational pluralism became a way of life for many rural maritimers, a culture of work handed down from one family generation to the next. It was, as McCann put it, 'a strategy for survival in a marginal world of work'. It facilitated decentralized small-scale industrialization. It retarded the growth of cities or large central places. Technological upgrading could be sidestepped by the hiring of cheap rural labour and by taking advantage of cheap rural land. In this context, occupational pluralism became an established and accepted way of life, a manner of work which supported proto-industrialization, but which retarded both urban growth and the move to a modern industrial world.

Sources

Armour, C.A., 'Colin Campbell', *DCB* XI (Toronto 1982), 146-7.

McCann, L.D., '"Living a Double Life": Town and Country in the Industrialization of the Maritimes' in D. Day, ed., *Geographical Perspectives on the Maritime Provinces* (Halifax, 1988), 93-113.

mour and Company, and the other a local concern headed by Samuel Cunard—held 40 per cent of all the area licensed to be cut in New Brunswick! Especially in the northeast of the province, independent operators had become a rare species. Similar but less dramatic consolidation also occurred in the south with a few large wholesalers situated in Saint John emerging to dominate the valley. Much of this consolidation occurred during a time of unstable if not actually declining timber markets. Bankrupts were taken over by wealthier merchants. Sources of supply were controlled by few competitors. Collusion on prices became ever more pos-

Lumber mill at Stanley, New Brunswick, in 1835. *(National Archives of Canada/C3552)*

sible. Wage labourers rather than 'independent' contractors increasingly cut wood in the forests. Yet even wealthy magnates were at risk in the timber-dominated economy. It took up to two years to receive any return on timber exported to Britain. To engage in the trade in a significant way required large capital outlays. Moreover the British timber market fluctuated dramatically throughout the era. Joseph Cunard, a man who when returning to Chatham from a trip would send advance word so that he would be suitably fêted on his arrival, declared bankruptcy in 1847. Overly aggressive commercial strategies, effective competition from the Gilmour firm, and a swift decline in timber prices led to his concern's demise. The consolidation of timber operations in the hands of a few wholesale merchants who, often, also engaged in shipbuilding, sawmilling, and a general wholesale trade did mark a significant step away from decentralized pre-capitalist economic relations. Yet, at the same time, those who worked in the woods did so on a seasonal basis and continued to depend on other employment to survive the rest of the year. The occasional 'feasts' given workers by men like Cunard failed to compensate for low wages and time off work. In this sense, the lumber industry continued to be nestled within and depend upon the persistence of a pre-capitalist social and economic milieu.

In Nova Scotia the lumber industry took a different form. Nova Scotia had been settled at an earlier date than New Brunswick with the result that by the early nineteenth century easily obtainable timber stands had been exploited. In contrast to New Brunswick, rivers in Nova Scotia were smaller and did not facilitate large-scale lumber enterprise. A third factor which contrasts with New Brunswick relates to the pattern of Crown land grants. In New Brunswick the colonial government encouraged the development of large-scale enterprise through the granting of large blocks of land to a small number of timber entrepreneurs. The Nova Scotia government granted small lots to thousands of applicants, the result being a myriad of small scale timber operations.[31]

More study needs to be done of the reasons for and the effect of such a land policy on the colony's economic development. Certainly in the saw-milling section the effect was profound. By 1850 the structure of the sawmilling industry in New Brunswick differed greatly from that in Nova Scotia. Exports of boards and planks exceeded 160 million board feet in 1850, almost 4.5 times more than Nova Scotia exports.[32] Five hundred and seventy-five mills operated in New Brunswick, employing an average of seven or eight men and boys. Nova Scotia boasted twice the number of mills and two-fifths the number of employees, averaging 1.6 person per mill! By 1871 the contrast in structures was even greater. New Brunswick had ten fewer mills than in 1851 and 2,800 more workers, averaging 12.6 people per mill.[33] Nova Scotia continued to have double the number of mills and averaged only 2.5 people per mill. Clearly the lumber industry in Nova Scotia remained extremely dispersed and, for the most part, operated on a pre-capitalist craft and part-time basis. Many such small operations did persist in New Brunswick. Led, however, in the northeast by Gilmour Rankin and Co., and Joseph Cunard and Co. and by sawmillers in the region of Saint John, operations expanded and in some areas steam power was instituted. Joseph Cunard's Chatham operation typifies those of the large-scale sawmiller. As early as 1841, eighty people worked at his steam-driven sawmill. It was a company town, with a company store, and Cunard was the local important person who held most of the significant political appointments.

In New Brunswick the sawmilling sector was clearly becoming a significant industrial endeavour. Yet, as with shipbuilding to which it was obviously closely connected, the sawmilling industry had about it many of the characteristics of an export enclave enterprise. Even in the larger operations, like Cunard's, the most skilled workers were idle for the equivalent of three months a year. Many worked as well on farms, in the fishery, or in the woods. By mid-century even the large sawmills interacted with and helped to maintain pre-capitalist or non-wage subsistence patterns. Scattered evidence suggests that this symbiotic pattern prevailed for at least the next twenty years. Technological upgrading would seem to have proceeded slowly. In 1861 fewer than 10 per cent of the colony's sawmills operated with steam as opposed to water power. Saint John merchants did invest in some of the larger sawmills in and near the city and equipped them with up-to-date gang as opposed to sash saws, but they continued to support low tariffs that facilitated the importing of all sawmill machinery. As late as 1871 there was no engine-building firm in New Brunswick.[34] The products of this industry, although obviously used for local construction of buildings, homes, and ships, were primarily geared to the export market. As such this was an adjunct to the traditional primary resource-based wood sector, a sector that its historian, Graham Wynn, has described as being 'in a position of economic vassalage to its metropolitan market'.[35] Sawmilling moved New Brunswick only a small way from such a context. The United States provided, along with Britain, a major outlet for their products. Local consumption of boards and planks was significant, although no precise measurements of the relative size of that market are available. In the final analysis, however, sawmilling represented yet another instance of the limits to which industry could develop within a mercantilist frame.

COAL MINING

The existence of large coal deposits has often acted as a spur for regional industrialization. In the late eighteenth and early nineteenth century, coal-rich areas in England, Europe and the United States usually embarked on a swifter pace of industrial diversification than areas without easy access to that resource. Nova Scotia had rich coal resources: bituminous coal deposits in the northeast represented the largest coalfield on North America's eastern seaboard.[36] Colonial entrepreneurs were interested in developing this resource. The British crown, however, fearful of encouraging colonial industries which might compete with those at home, discouraged mining by imposing large royalty payments and short leases, and by retaining control of all coal on most land grants made after 1788 and on all land grants issued following 1808. As a result significant amounts of coal were not mined until after the crown granted a sixty-year monopoly to the British-controlled General Mining Association in 1827. By the late 1830s that company had invested $250,000 in Nova Scotia; it employed 1,500 workers with a monthly payroll of $5,000 and, according to one historian, it represented one of the few bright spots in Nova Scotia's economy prior to 1871. In fact, the company's operations at Pictou and in Cape Breton ranked as one of the largest concentrations of industrial workers and industrial investment in British North America.

The company, however, did very little to stimulate industrial development anywhere in the colony. About the only linkage that accrued to local interests was that to shipping and even then much of that benefit was funnelled to the company's local agent Samuel Cunard, very likely in compensation for Cunard's failed attempt to acquire a mining lease on reasonable terms a year before the General Mining Association received theirs. The Company's monopoly made it impossible for other local entrepreneurs to start up operations anywhere in Nova Scotia and thus thwarted potential regional industrial growth. Benefiting from its monopoly the company charged higher prices for the sale of coal in Nova Scotia than it did for coal sold in the more competitive American market. As late as the 1870s it continued to import from England most of the equipment needed for the industry. Skilled labourers were recruited in Scotland; general labourers, paid much lower wages, were enlisted from Newfoundland and Cape Breton. Miners worked about 200 days a year at the most. General labourers had to fend for themselves during down times. The company did, it appears, support some skilled labour until the restart of operations. The company constructed workers' housing and furnished food and supplies to workers from the company store.[37] As early as 1835 the mining manager stated that the 'greater part of the men in the concern were in debt' to that store. Some thirty years later 162 men at Sydney Mines owed $9,422 to the company. During strike activity in the 1870s, one of the first concessions made was to abolish (as it turned out, only temporarily) the company store and allow the workers to purchase goods wherever they chose. Tellingly, when neighbouring merchants evinced support for the miners, the mine's manager threatened to reinstitute the company store![38]

Finally there is evidence to suggest that the company mismanaged the exploitation of the local resources. Mining took place according to British methods. These methods were capital intensive and were probably appropriate to an area which was short on resources and strong on capital and skilled labour. The reverse was the case in Nova Scotia. Areas endowed with a rich resource but short on capital and skilled labour were generally developed on a less capitally intensive manner. Marilyn Gerriets, an economic historian, has compared operating costs of the General Mining Association's mines with those of its Nova Scotia rivals following the revocation of monopoly in 1858 and with those of its American competitors before that date, and found the General Mining Association to be by far the most expensive operation.

What should one conclude from this brief analysis of the coal mining industry in pre-1871 Nova Scotia? The General Mining Association was clearly an impressive industrial enterprise. Twelve smokestacks, one over 140 feet in height, dominated the Albion mine site at Pictou in the late 1830s. Mine shafts ran to depths of 400 feet. Steam engines ventilated the shafts. A railway took the coal to the harbour where a steam engine lifted a ton of coal at a time into waiting vessels.[39] The company did pay some royalties to the colonial government and its exports did contribute in a positive way to Nova Scotia's export-import ratio. Yet very likely more mining would have occurred at an earlier period had the General Mining Association not been granted a monopoly and to that extent the colony would have probably received greater royalties. Whatever the truth of the royalty issue, one is on firmer ground in stating that while coal took Nova Scotia to the brink of industrialization in this era, it was industrialization of a truncated sort. The owners allowed limited linkages and diversification to occur. Their charter prohibited the development of competing enterprises. Many workers became indebted to the company store and for many, especially of the colonial born, coal mining was simply one of several jobs needed to maintain a living.

The extent to which coal mining transformed traditional relations of production was limited to export-oriented coastal enclaves. Clearly the operators of the General Mining Association viewed coal as a product to be exchanged, not as an input into a process of production, a commercial orientation fitting neatly with British desires to limit colonial industrial growth. The General Mining Association fettered, it did not facilitate, colonial industrial development. Marilyn Gerriets cautions that a more dispersed and competitive coal industry might not have been enough to foster sustained industrialization in Nova Scotia. She points to the problem of a relatively small local market and underdeveloped agriculture as possible structural impediments. In the broader context, coal mining in this era is yet another example of disarticulated development. It typifies maritime business development throughout the pre-confederation period. Economic linkages that held the promise of diversification beyond commercial endeavours were curtailed within the colony and/or transferred outside the region. Equipment and other capital goods were shipped in from the outside. As the historian, Ian McKay, concluded, 'the regional economy in the nineteenth century never became more than the sum of its constituent parts.'[40] In the context of other economic development in Nova Scotia, the Albion Mine's twelve towering smokestacks were more symbol than substance, promising a future which their owners never intended.

THE FISHERY

The Newfoundland fishery always depended on the vagaries of external market demand, the pressures of international competition, and the availability of the natural resource. Unlike the sale of wheat from the Canadas and wood from New Brunswick, both primarily to Great Britain in the nineteenth century, Newfoundland's products were sold mainly in southern Europe and Brazil, areas over which England possessed little control. From 1815 to 1836, a period when population increased from about 40,000 to 75,000, the per capita export of saltfish declined from 23.4 to 9.8 cwt per person.[41] Increased Scandinavian competition, and protectionist policies in importing countries accounted for the difficult market conditions, conditions which, in the words of one scholar led to 'hardship, starvation, bankruptcy and depression in Newfoundland' in these years.[42] For much of the rest of the century the export of fish measured on a per capita basis continued to fluctuate 'around a declining trend'.[43] Sealing did offer one bright spot amidst the uncertainty. St John's merchants, even as they cut their investments in cod fishing fleets, built and outfitted, in the 1860s, steamers to exploit the northern seal fishery. But by the 1880s this resource, too, yielded rapidly decreasing returns.

It is easy to exaggerate the problems that beset the Newfoundland fishery in the nineteenth century. If per capita exports declined in the second quarter of the century, volume and prices per quintal did increase. Moreover Newfoundland remained, even in the early twentieth century, the largest cod exporting country in the world.[44] Profits were made. Capital was accumulated. Who, then, made that money and what did they do with it?

No central co-ordinating body oversaw the fishing industry in the nineteenth century. Initially, British-based merchant houses and, gradually, merchants and agents resident in St John's marketed the greater percentage of the catch. Yet by the end of the third quarter of the nineteenth century many of the most influential of these merchants began to invest instead in industrial pursuits and mainly in commercial exchange-related ventures. In this, the major St John's merchants behaved in a manner little different from that of their Halifax and Saint John counterparts. Shipbuilding took place but, as elsewhere in the region, much of the material used was imported from England. Merchants tended to invest in the process of exchange, rather than the process of production.[45]

Recent historical analyses have focused closely on the internal structures of the Newfoundland and Maritime fishing industries. While their findings are far from all of a piece one interpretive trend stands out. Properties inherent in the staple itself did not in any deterministic way lead to instability and underdevelopment.[46] Resource endowment and export markets were only part of the story. Institutional structures, whether put in place by governments for imperial interests unrelated to the fish business or by merchant capitalists and even by fishers themselves, led to, what was from the point of view of the vast majority of Newfoundlanders, at least, an unpalatable result. To approach an understanding of the fishery business, then, requires a close look at the social and economic relations of production in that industry.

The Newfoundland cod fishery developed within institutional constraints established by imperially-focused British policymakers. As Chapter Two discussed, the evolution of the salt fishery cannot be understood simply as a function of the properties of the staple itself. Throughout the eighteenth century the British government supported the migratory fishery in order to provide skilled sailors for the navy. Yet, despite official discouragement of year-long residency on Newfoundland, some settlement did occur and West Country merchants began to trade in provisions as well as operate shipping fleets. Further decentralization in the fishing industry took place in the mid to late seventeenth century when entrepreneurs, called byeboatmen, purchased passage on the West Country merchant-owned sailing vessels and contracted with those merchants to sell fish to them and buy supplies from them. The byeboatmen hired their own workers, or servants as they were called, and owned their (small) fishing vessels for use in Newfoundland. Planters—those who lived year round on the island—also entered into contractual relations of a similar sort with major West Country merchants. Planters and byeboatmen hired their fishing crews in England and, in part because of the competition for such labour, wages rather than the traditional shares gradually became the dominant mode of payment. The West Country merchants, more and more engaged in supplying provisions and transporting crews for others as well as fishing for themselves, also began to do away with the share system and to pay wages for their labour.[47]

The British government was, albeit reluctantly, willing to allow planters to reside year round on Newfoundland, but was not willing to allow the servants to do the same. Yet, by the third quarter of the eighteenth century, it seemed that many servants were doing just that. To British officials, at least, the reason they remained emerged directly from the exploitative and virtually unregulated nature of the credit system entangling merchant, planter, and servant. At the beginning of each season planters obtained credit from merchants for materials and provisions. But at season's end planters often shopped around in an attempt to sell their catch to other merchants at a better price. To forestall this ploy the extender of credit attempted to seize the catch as soon as possible. The losers in the ongoing drama between the planters and merchants were most often the servants, who would be paid less than they had contracted for—often so much less that they could not afford a return trip to Britain. It was this last consequence that the

British government could not suffer. Able-bodied seamen were needed at home, not on the barren rocks of Newfoundland. As a result, Palliser's Act (1775) required that when a merchant seized a planter's catch he had to pay the servant's wages before all other expenditures, and that money had to be made available for the return trip of all servants.[48]

During the Seven Years' War and especially the Napoleonic Wars the migratory fishery was fraught with risk and expense, encouraging the establishment of resident agents and the end of the yearly migration to the banks. Even as this trend developed, servants used the Palliser's Act to protect their wages against the planters and merchants. Northeastern Newfoundland courts found overwhelming in favour of the servants on issues concerning their right to first call or first lien on the year's catch. In 1802 such rights were formally extended to resident servants: the requirement of a trip home was dropped. The court's upholding of this Act, in the face of the increasingly acknowledged reality that the migratory fishery was close to an end, helped set the structure for relations between merchant, planter, and servant throughout the nineteenth century. The planters, who borrowed from merchants, had now to pay servants, repay merchants, and survive on what was left. Often what was left was too little to maintain a viable and independent presence in the fishery. The resultant squeeze intensified with the downturn in the fishing economy following the boom years of the Napoleonic Wars. Starting in 1817 merchants became less and less willing to advance winter credit for foodstuffs, forcing fisher families to mine small household gardens and apply for meagre government relief in order to survive. Secure in their belief that agriculture could never supplant but only support the fishery as the main economic endeavour in the outports, merchants supported this strategy.[49] After the Napoleonic Wars, therefore, planters increasingly relied on family labour rather than a wage-paying system. Household production sidestepped the wage-labour problem but made it virtually impossible for planters to do other than rely on merchant credit for all goods except whatever produce the household could grow in a very unfavourable agricultural environment.

Servants, who often married into a planter's family, also began to establish their own households as fishing units: father and son fished from small boats; wives and daughters did the shore work of cleaning, salting, and preserving the cod. For these ex-servants and their young families this transformation might have seemed a step towards demographic and economic independence. Yet the fishers were no longer guaranteed a wage by planters: they had now to risk their own savings. They looked to agents of St John's merchants for credit to purchase and outfit their boats and were dependent on those merchants for the sale of their catch and the provision of supplies. What had been a combination of credit and a waged cash economy in the seventeenth century and into the eighteenth century had become a credit, non-cash, and—although in some cases planters did persist —generally household economy by the middle of the nineteenth century.[50]

It must be emphasized that this transformation did not occur evenly or at the same time throughout Newfoundland. Indeed the structure of the fishery meant that many outport enclaves were more closely focused on Great Britain than on relations between their community and other outports. And within this structure, merchants remained at arm's length from the process of fishing: instead they were providers of credit, provisions, and capital equipment and buyers of cod, seals, and in the north, fur. By 1850 Newman and Co., a London-based and long estab-lished fishery enterprise, commented 'Our business is to offer Planters supplies at prices which will pay us, receiving their Fish & Oil in payment, because they cannot pay us in money.'[51] After 1850 they had increasing difficulty in doing this because of other mercantile competition and uncertain fish prices and, in some areas, other fisheries than cod to which the fishers could resort if Newman's provision prices were deemed too high or the cod prices offered felt to be too low. Fishers and planters, in some areas, continued to have some flexibility in playing merchants off against one and other. The response of Newman's and other merchants, like Bird and Co. who plied the Belle Isle fishery, was to restrict credit further and, perhaps as significantly in terms of any potential economic devel-opment in the colony, to refuse to engage in cash transactions, that is, refuse to pay fishers other than in goods and equipment even should they have a balance owing at the season's end. As Joseph Bird declared in no uncertain terms to his agent: 'you will not purchase any fish unless the payment be made in goods. You will not purchase any and pay cash for it as last year.'[52] The evolution of what has been called a truck system—the paying of wages or amounts due to producers by means of goods with high mark-ups—was a complex and protracted process throughout the colony.

However unevenly, what this business system tended towards and what mer-chants strove with varying degrees of success to attain is nicely illustrated by historian Rosemary Ommer's study of the Jersey-Gaspé cod fishery in the nine-teenth century.[53] On the Gaspé coast of the St Lawrence River, the Jersey-based Charles Robin & Co., one of the era's largest inland fishing firms in British North America, operated, even in the face of competition stimulated by the Reciprocity Treaty of 1854 with the United States, an exploitative truck system. Most of its transactions with fishers were in kind, and the goods the firms provided both for credit and for exchange for fish and fish products were regularly marked up between 25 and 40 per cent and often as much as 100 per cent. Ommer, on the basis of some comparison with mark-ups in other areas, concluded 'this kind of mark-up clearly reduced the fisherman's real wage below his nominal wage and was thus a deliberate means of defrauding workers of a part of their wages.'[54] Many Gaspé families were constantly indebted to Charles Robin and Company and attempted to pay—if they did not the company would cut off all supplies—with not just fish and fish oil, but also wood, hay, potatoes, cabbage, and manual labour. All along the rugged rocky coastlines, family gardens and household pro-duction helped stave off starvation and, ironically, in so doing facilitated the persistence of exploitation. Even when there seemed to be alternatives fishers remained with Charles Robin because, Ommer believes, that company promised a reliable source of supplies, even when the fishery hit a bad year. Other traders had no comparable track record. In a relatively isolated area an established mer-cantile firm could profit from monopsony—being a single supplier of goods—

and because of its stability, could withstand periodic competition. The company existed as a form of security for fishers who operated in an isolated export enclave.

Moreover Charles Robin & Co. had no interest in developing the area's general economy. Few roads existed. Most of the sailing vessels were built in Jersey. Coopering, cordage, and even garment making were developed in Jersey. Truck pay allowed the company to diminish returns to the local populace and virtually precluded local capital development and any possibility of economic diversification. Studies of the fishery in Nova Scotia and in Cape Breton have confirmed Ommer's more detailed analysis. According to an observer in 1858, Nova Scotia fishers were 'the most wretchedly poor of any class in the whole province', even though fish was Nova Scotia's primary export. Yet from the 1820s to 1870 exports barely kept pace with population growth, so real growth in that area was negligible. Moreover, as Julian Gwyn has noted, merchants refused 'to play other than a commercial role'.[55] As a result, the boats and capital equipment used by fishers deteriorated, especially compared to those used by their American competitors. Local fishers were led to the inshore fishery, where smaller and cheaper boats could be used. Merchants, by not investing directly in boats and sharing more equitably the returns on the fish sales, stifled development both within and outside the industry. The Newfoundland business system was certainly more varied and complex, but the merchants within it all moved towards establishing the Gaspé model. The impetus within the system, its internal dynamics, pointed away from local economic diversification and towards a narrowly focused and exploitative export enclave economic structure.

What is interesting here is the changing nature of the linkages between merchants and the fishery. At the outset merchants were themselves involved in catching and processing fish. Gradually they stepped back from such direct involvement, becoming sellers of foodstuffs and equipment, and purchasers and transporters of fish. Gradually, too, they began to restrict their credit connections, first in terms of supporting the food requirements of fishers over the winter and eventually in more general terms including the upkeep and purchase of fishing equipment. Merchants could restrict such linkages and continue to profit from an exploitative truck system, because poor resource endowments made it difficult for the local fishers to strike out in a different economic direction. As this business structure evolved, the relationship between merchant and fishers became more and more at arm's length. Over time merchants distanced themselves from the heart of the local economic process. This development stands in marked contrast to what the historian, David Vickers, discovered to be the norm in New England: 'the tight interdependence between he who provides the capital and equipment (what is being worked with) and he who does the working'.[56] To profit from business in the more richly resource-endowed regions of Massachusetts and, as we will explore, central Canada required a relatively tighter interdependence at the local level. This study of the Newfoundland and Gaspé fisheries suggests that areas characterized by one staple do not require such close connections between merchant and producer. Looked at this way it was easy for merchants to walk away when the fishery no longer seemed to promise adequate returns: after all they had long since ceased to regard their business as one of the production and processing of fish; for merchants fish was a commodity to be traded. If profits could not be made, then trade in other areas would be explored.[57] And by the late nineteenth century, an increasing number of Newfoundland merchants were doing just that, no matter the cost to the wider populace, who, much more economically disadvantaged, were much less fleet of foot.

AGRICULTURE IN ATLANTIC CANADA

Much is known about the flow of imports and exports of agricultural produce in Atlantic Canada. Less is known about the distribution of resources throughout the region. And less still is known about rural attitudes to production and agriculture as a commercial or 'moral' pursuit. A traditional historiography characterized the agricultural sector as primarily subsistence oriented and, to that extent, egalitarian in effect. Many suggested that farming played second fiddle to lumber, fish, and minerals and farmers tended to be casual in their farming methods, resulting in low per-capita production. Travellers' accounts, the critical analyses of improvement-oriented agricultural societies and, in the cases of Nova Scotia, New Brunswick, and Newfoundland, a chronic deficit in trade of agricultural products, seemed adequate support for such a general interpretation. Prince Edward Island, which throughout this period enjoyed a positive balance of trade in agricultural goods, generally received less attention, although when it did the terms subsistence and poor were prominent in most analyses.[58]

It is increasingly difficult to accept the perspective offered by the traditional interpretation. A spate of micro studies of agriculture in various localities throughout Nova Scotia, New Brunswick, and, to a lesser extent, Newfoundland point to a tremendous variation in output both across and within regions. Such variability renders substantive generalization problematic, especially so with New Brunswick and Nova Scotia. In Newfoundland, with the exception of a small area around St John's which produced food for sale in the city, agriculture was of a garden-plot subsistence nature, a helpmate for the fishery and little else.[59] But in Nova Scotia and New Brunswick, agriculture was for many much more than a secondary activity. At mid-century, over half the people in each colony farmed. Studies of the Upper Saint John Valley and the St David and Wakefield townships in New Brunswick, and of the Annapolis Valley in Nova Scotia, have argued that commercially-oriented agriculture characterized these areas. By 1861 in the Upper Saint John Valley, about 12 per cent of farmers produced a commercial crop, a percentage comparing favourably with the 16 per cent of Upper Canadian farmers in that category. Some of the earliest settled farmers in that region, in fact, sold directly to lumbering camps, in the process successfully competing with the country store keeper on a commercial level. In at least some rural communities, farmers, rather than merchants, dominated the social and economic hierarchy.[60]

But in the course of unearthing flourishing homesteads, micro studies have also laid bare what aggregate production and trade figures and contemporary observers

131

have hinted at, the reality and extent of rural poverty. T.W. Acheson's careful analysis of farming in two New Brunswick townships is a case in point. Due in part to remarkable soil variety, farming was not all of a piece in St David and Wakefield townships.[61] Instead Acheson discovered four levels of agricultural endeavour. Fifteen per cent of farms in both townships could not support one family. A further 25 per cent generally required some, probably regular, off-farm work to make ends meet. Thirty per cent of the remainder (more in St David) produced some surplus and the final 30 per cent (less in St David) produced significant surpluses for commercial sale. Bitterman's study of Middle River in Cape Breton also points to a strong commercial farming élite, approximately one-quarter to one-third of the farmers, and a much poorer one-half to two-thirds who in order to live had to travel to the woods, fisheries, or mines each winter. Other community studies demonstrate that the first settlers quickly monopolized the best land and practised social and economic closure through intermarriage, property accumulation and speculation, and withholding local credit from newcomers. Just under two-thirds of farms in six New Brunswick districts were worth less than $500 in 1861; 12 per cent of farms in those districts were valued at over $2,000. As early as 1791 close to 50 per cent of the labour force of one Nova Scotian rural county were wage labourers. Tenants and squatters comprised two-thirds of Prince Edward Island's population in the second quarter of the nineteenth century. One half of Cape Breton Island's population were without title to the land they farmed in 1837. Following 1827, both Nova Scotia and New Brunswick sold rather than granted land free, a decision which 'severely restricted' access to land by new settlers.[62]

Micro studies testify to the stratified nature of the agricultural sector in Atlantic Canada. Any use of aggregate data must, therefore, be situated within this context. For example, between 1851 and 1871, measured on a per capita basis, production in Nova Scotia of grain, peas, corn, hay, potatoes, butter, and cheese, and the ownership of horses, cattle, pigs and sheep either declined, remained the same, or with the single exception of potatoes, increased imperceptibly. In other words, production increases barely kept pace with local population growth. How should one interpret these findings? When situated against a backdrop of rural inequality, Julian Gwyn finds them to be persuasive evidence of continuing and extensive rural poverty. Other historians have been reluctant to accept such a conclusion. They argue that values as well as volumes must be considered. Certainly income figures would be extremely useful. However, as yet the only systematic attempt to consider output in terms of value has generalized from Pictou County prices, and Pictou County along with the Annapolis Valley was among the richest and most strategically placed of all agricultural regions in Nova Scotia.[63] Even if aggregate income from agricultural production did increase between 1851 and 1871, the real point is who profited from such an increase. Existing micro studies suggest that such income would have been distributed in a very unequal manner.

What, then, remains of the traditional interpretation of Atlantic agriculture? To the extent that the view encompassed an inward-looking, egalitarian, self-contained, subsistence-oriented agriculture, not much. Aggregate per capita output of agricultural commodities in Nova Scotia and New Brunswick compared favourably with Quebec's and Maine's output.[64] Far from homogeneous, rural communities were, at both ends of their income structures, firmly a part of and not apart from a wider and developing economic milieu. A rationally conducted commercial agriculture based on inter- and intra-regional trade existed throughout both maritime colonies. In Prince Edward Island, a flourishing export trade occurred as well. In some areas, commercial agriculture may have stimulated shipbuilding to carry produce to markets.[65] Probably, more often, however, agriculture provided workers for the construction of ships, rather than produce for transport in them. The Atlantic region's stratified farming structure allowed owners of staple-producing enclave industries to tap a rural proletariat at minimal cost to themselves.

In the sense that off-farm work was a regular feature of a substantial number of farm families and that inter-regional trade a marked characteristic of many farming communities, it seems clear that rural regions were enmeshed in a larger capitalist milieu. Despite such structural linkages, it is, of course, possible that farmers continued to strive for some more communitarian lifestyle. It could be that they, as Daniel Vickers has recently suggested was the case for Massachusetts farmers, aspired to a modest 'competency', an independence and inheritance to pass on to the next generation. Those few historians who have ventured an opinion on the Maritimes are split on this issue.[66] Very likely, as in much else concerning Atlantic agriculture, different mentalities co-existed within and across rural regions.

RAILWAYS

Many scholars see transportational developments as central to explaining the pace and extent of industrial growth. In most countries railways emerged as the primary means for the efficient and reliable transport of goods and people.[67] Yet in the Maritimes, railway construction, especially as compared to the Canadas, developed slowly. Nova Scotia and New Brunswick initiated railway building programs in the first half of the 1850s, but by 1866 only two hundred and eighteen miles of track had been constructed in New Brunswick and one hundred and forty-seven miles in Nova Scotia. Some historians have concluded that this seeming lack of interest reflected apathy, indifference, and a failure to embrace that century's most exciting technological development.[68] Such a perspective, with its implicit pejorative view of Maritime entrepreneurship, does little justice to the social and economic context within which Maritimers lived. Nor does it do justice to the emergence of a strong sense of public entrepreneurship in this period.

In Nova Scotia and in New Brunswick merchants divided over the need for railway construction. Many successful merchant entrepreneurs were riding a rising wave in world trade and continued, wisely, to invest their capital in shipbuilding and shipping. Such activity garnered substantial profits for these entrepreneurs well into the 1870s. Apathy had nothing to do with their investment decisions: good sense did.[69]

In the absence of a strong local entrepreneurial élite willing to invest in and promote railways, those who favoured such development looked, as they did in the Canadas, to the colonial state to provide the necessary support. This initiative met with strong opposition, not simply from the shipping interest, but also from regional entrepreneurial élites in towns like Yarmouth which stood little chance of benefiting from state-funded railway construction. Yet even in the Maritimes precedents for such involvement did exist. The City of Saint John, for example, issued city bonds as early as 1830 and by 1843 was over $100,000 in debt. The historian Rosemary Langhout has argued that this development initiative at the municipal level presaged a major reorientation of public policy: spurred by the proposals put forward by railway advocates, politicians in Nova Scotia and New Brunswick in the 1850s voted in favour (often narrowly) of allowing their governments to raise money in England for the construction of publicly owned colonial railways. While construction, compared to that in some other colonies, proceeded slowly, fiscal policies were nonetheless dramatically altered. Colonial governments traditionally raised most of their revenue from import taxes. Reluctant to increase such taxes, they turned to local banks and, increasingly, to the British bond market for the raising of capital. Provincial fiscal policies were completely restructured to meet the costs of railway construction. This restructuring took place against a backdrop of, at best, divided support. Many of the areas' richest and traditional economic élite stood aloof. But these activities did facilitate the support of a growing sector of landward-looking entrepreneurs and politicians, men like Charles Tupper in Nova Scotia, who wanted to develop coal and iron resources, and Samuel Tilley in New Brunswick.[70]

These politicians and their supporters were willing allies of their Canadian counterparts in the negotiations that led to Confederation in 1867. The landward continental-oriented business interests in the Maritimes certainly lacked the general support enjoyed by similar groups in the Canadas. As a result on the eve of Confederation their railway infrastructure was relatively underdeveloped. Yet despite the export-oriented, seaward focus of much of the Maritimes' business élite, and the dominant entrepreneurial culture which such an orientation fostered, other agendas did emerge. The mining of coal, the possibility of becoming entrepôt for a continent, and plans for indigenous industrialization sparked a sustained interest in developing land transportation, both to establish better links with their neighbours to the south as well as with their sister colonies to the west. By the eve of Confederation proponents of these views had gained valuable experience in the financing and managing of railways within the context of public enterprise. This experience informed and conditioned their participation in the Confederation agreement.

* * *

A distinctive entrepreneurial culture emerged in the Maritimes during the first half of the nineteenth century. In the first instance that culture owed its existence to a series of Imperial legislative enactments. Under Imperial protection merchants rose to the fore in local urban centres. The extent to which colonial merchants could maintain their privileged position following the Imperial Government's dismantlement of the mercantile system was strongly conditioned by the nature of local/regional resource endowments. From this perspective merchant control was greatest in the areas where natural resources were the least diverse. But in all regions merchants put a stamp on the form economic development took. Unless one wishes to adopt a model akin to environmental determinism, one must leave open the possibility of choice. Merchants did not have to pursue the closely focused and limited mode of activity that they, as a rule, did. Opportunities to diversify and encourage the local development of manufacturing enterprise did exist. For the most part these opportunities were not forcefully pursued. Indeed in some instances merchants opposed and effectively blocked such diversified development. It is in the combination of human agency, staple/resource endowment, and the power of historical tradition that Maritime business development must be situated. If the relative influence of each of these factors varied from one colonial locality to another, it is nonetheless only in their combination that a comprehensive understanding of the character of Maritime business endeavour can be approached.

Notes

[1] For an introduction to this literature, see Larry McCann, 'The Mercantile-Industrial Transition in the Metals Towns of Pictou County, 1857–1931', *Acadiensis* 10 (1981), 29–31.

[2] Graham Wynn, 'Industrialism, Entrepreneurship and Opportunity in the New Brunswick Timber Trade', in L.R. Fischer and E.W. Sager, eds, *The Enterprising Canadians: Entrepreneurs and Economic Development in Eastern Canada, 1820–1914* (St John's: Maritime History Group, 1979), 8.

[3] T.W.Acheson, *Saint John: The Making of a Colonial Urban Community* (Toronto, 1985), 57.

[4] R.T. Naylor, *Canada in the European Age, 1453–1919* (Vancouver, 1987).

[5] David Sutherland, 'Halifax Merchants and the Pursuit of Development, 1783–1850', *CHR* LIX (1978), 1–17.

[6] For a discussion of this activity in another colonial context, see Norman Long and Bryan Roberts, *Miners, Peasants and Entrepreneurs: Regional Development in the Central Highlands of Peru* (Cambridge, 1984).

[7] In addition to 'Pursuit of Development,' see David Sutherland, 'The Merchants of Halifax, 1815–1850: A Commercial Class in Pursuit of Metropolitan Status' (PhD diss., University of Toronto, 1975). See also his numerous biographies of merchants in the relevant volumes of the *Dictionary of Canadian Biography*.

[8] Calculated from information in Sutherland, 'The Merchants of Halifax', Appendix A.

[9] A.B. Robertson, 'John Wesley's Nova Scotia businessmen: Halifax Methodist Merchants, 1815–55' (PhD diss., Queen's University, 1990), 59–62.

[10]See Sutherland, 'The Merchants of Halifax', *passim*; Robertson, 'John Wesley's', 45; David Macmillan, 'John Black', *DCB* 6 60–1.

[11]D. Chard, 'J. Mauger', *DCB* 4, 524–8.

[12]Julian Gwyn, 'Commerce of Rum: West Indian Connections and Rum Runners, 1770–1854', in J.H. Morrison and J. Moreira, eds, *'Tempered by Rum': Rum in the History of the Maritime Provinces* (Nova Scotia, 1988), 111–33.

[13]Rosemarie Langhout, 'Developing Nova Scotia: Railways and Public Accounts, 1848–1867', *Acadiensis* 14 (1985), 16–17.

[14]Kris Inwood and John Chamard, 'Regional Industrial Growth during the 1890s: The Case of the Missing Artisans', *Acadiensis* 16 (1986), Table 4, 111; E.W. Sager with G.E. Panting, *Maritime Capital: The Shipping Industry in Atlantic Canada, 1820–1914* (Montreal/Kingston, 1990), 196–7, fn. 63.

[15]Julian Gwyn, 'Golden Age or Bronze Moment? Wealth and Poverty in Nova Scotia: the 1850s and 1860s' in D.H. Akenson, ed., *Canadian Papers in Rural History* 8 (1992), 202–3; J. Gwyn and F. Siddig, 'Wealth Distribution in Nova Scotia During the Confederation Era, 1851–1871', *CHR* LXXIII (1992), 435–52; K. Inwood and P. Wagg, 'Wealth and Prosperity in Nova Scotia Agriculture, 1850–70', unpublished paper, 1992.

[16]Calculated from information in Table 9:5, Sager with Panting, *Maritime Capital*, 191.

[17]J. Gwyn, 'Golden Age . . . ', 224.

[18]Unless otherwise noted this analysis draws on T.W. Acheson, *Saint John: The Making . . .* and T.W. Acheson, 'The Great Merchant and Economic Development in Saint John, 1820–50', *Acadiensis* 8 (1979), 3–27.

[19]Acheson, 'The Great Merchant . . . ', 18, fn. 67.

[20]C.M. Wallace, 'Saint John Boosters and Railroads in the Mid-Nineteenth Century', *Acadiensis* 6 (1976–77), 71–91.

[21]Sager with Panting, *Maritime Capital*, Table 9:5, 191; K. Inwood and J.R. Irwin, 'Canadian Regional Commodity Income Differences at Confederation' in K. Inwood, ed., *Farm, Factory and Fortune: New Studies in the Economic History of the Maritime Provinces* (Fredericton, NB, 1993), 102.

[22]Sager with Panting, *Maritime Capital*, 14, 176.

[23]J. Gwyn, 'Golden Age', 208–9; J. Gwyn, ' "A Little Province Like This": The Economy of Nova Scotia under Stress, 1812–53', in D.H. Akenson, ed., *Canadian Papers in Rural History* 6 (1988), 217.

[24]Sager with Panting, *Maritime Capital*, 177–9; Gwyn, 'Golden Age', Table 5, 208.

[25]Sager with Panting, 78; B. Greenhill, 'James Yeo', *DCB* 9 (Toronto, 1976), 855–7.

[26]Greenhill, 'James Yeo'; J. Gwyn, 'Nova Scotia's Shipbuilding and Timber Trade: David Crichton of Pictou and His Liverpool Associates, 1821–40' in P. Baskerville, ed., *Canadian Papers in Business History* 2, (Victoria, 1993), 211–33.

[27]Sager with Panting, *Maritime Capital*, 77, 189.

[28]Gwyn, 'Golden Age', 207.

[29]Peter McClelland, 'The New Brunswick Economy in the 19th Century' (PhD diss., Harvard, 1966), 168–239.

[30]The best source for the lumber industry in New Brunswick is G. Wynn, *Timber Colony: A Historical Geography of Early Nineteenth Century New Brunswick* (Toronto 1981). Chapters 1, 2, 4 and 5 were especially helpful.

[31]Barbara R. Robertson, 'Trees, Treaties and the Timing of Settlement: A Comparison of the Lumber Industry in Nova Scotia and New Brunswick, 1784–1867', *Nova Scotia Historical Review* IV (1984), 37–55.

[32]For Nova Scotia, see Gwyn, 'A Little Province . . . ', 218.

[33]Canadian Census, 1871, vols 3 and 4.

[34]Canadian Census, 1871, 4, 352; Acheson, *Saint John: The Making . . .* , 14 and Acheson, 'The Great Merchants', 25.

[35]Wynn, *Timber Colony*, 44.

[36]On the importance of coal, see A.D. Chandler, 'Anthracite Coal and the Beginnings of the Industrial Revolution in the United States', *Business History Review* 46 (1972), 141–81; for discussion of coal in Nova Scotia, see D.A. Muise, 'The General Mining Association and Nova Scotia's Coal', *Bulletin of Canadian Studies* 6/7 (1983), 71–87; Ian MacKay, 'The Crisis of Dependent Development: Class Conflict in the Nova Scotia Coalfields, 1872–76', *The Canadian Journal of Sociology* 13 (1988), 9–48; Ian MacKay, 'Class Politics and Regional Dependency: The Rise and Fall of the Working Class Movement in the Coalfields of the Maritime Provinces, 1830–1930', unpublished paper, Canadian-Welsh Labour History Conference, Gregynog, April 1987; Marilyn Gerriets, 'The Impact of the General Mining Association on the Nova Scotia Coal Industry, 1826–50', *Acadiensis* 21 (1991), 54–84; and S.J. Hornsby, 'Staple Trades, Subsistence Agriculture and Nineteenth Century Cape Breton Island', *Annals of the Association of American Geographers* 79 (1989), 411–34.

[37]Hornsby, 'Staple Trades', 424.

[38]MacKay, 'Class Politics', 11, 13, fn. 52.

[39]J. Gwyn, 'A Little Province', 220.

[40]Ian MacKay, 'Class Politics and Regional Dependency . . . ', 3.

[41]S. Ryan, *Fish Out of Water: The Newfoundland Salt Fish Trade, 1814–1914* (St John's, 1986), Table 2A, 39 (my calculations).

[42]K. Matthews, 'The Class of '32: St John's Reformers on the Eve of Representative Government' in P.A. Buckner and D. Frank, eds, *Atlantic Canada Before Confederation* (Fredericton, 1985), 216.

[43]S. Ryan, *Fish Out of Water*, Table 2A, 39 (my calculations); K. Matthews, 'The Class of '32 . . . ', 216.

[44]David Alexander, 'Development and Dependence in Newfoundland, 1880–1970' in E.W. Sager *et al.*, eds, *Atlantic Canada and Confederation: Essays in Canadian Political Economy* (Toronto, 1983), 12–13.

45E.W. Sager, 'The Merchants of Water Street and Capital Investment in Newfoundland's Traditional Economy' in Fischer and Sager, eds, *The Enterprising Canadians*, 75–96.

46Rosemary E. Ommer, *From Outpost to Outpost: A Structural Analysis of the Jersey Gaspé Cod Fishery, 1767–1886* (Montreal/Kingston, 1991); S.T. Cadigan, 'Merchant Capital, the State and Labour in a British Colony: Servant-Master Relations and Capital Accumulation in Newfoundland's Northeast-Coast Fishery, 1775–1799', *Journal of the Canadian Historical Association* New Series 2 (1991), 17–42.

47See Cadigan, 'Merchant Capital' and J.E. Crowley, 'Empire vs. Truck: The Official Interpretation of Debt and Labour in the Eighteenth Century Newfoundland Fishery', *CHR* LXX (1989), 311–36.

48The discussion of the Palliser's Act follows that in Cadigan, 'Merchant Capital'.

49Sean Cadigan, 'The Staple Model Reconsidered: The Case of Agricultural Policy in Northeast Newfoundland, 1785–1855', *Acadiensis* 21 (1992), 48–71.

50In addition to the above citations, see James K. Hiller, 'The Newfoundland Credit System: An Interpretation' in R. Ommer, ed., *Merchant Credit and Labour Strategies in Historical Perspective* (Acadiensis Press, 1990), 86–101.

51David A. Macdonald, 'They Cannot Pay Us in Money: Newman and Company and the Supplying System in the Newfoundland Fishery, 1850–84', in R. Ommer, ed., *Merchant Credit*, 118.

52Patricia Thornton, 'The Transition from the Migratory to the Resident Fishery in the Strait of Belle Isle' in R. Ommer, *Merchant Credit*, 158 and *passim*. See also Macdonald, 'They Cannot Pay', 118.

53R. Ommer, *From Outpost . . .* and 'The Truck System in Gaspé, 1822–77', in R. Ommer, ed., *Merchant Credit*, 49–72.

54R. Ommer, 'The Truck System', 59.

55J. Gwyn, 'Golden Age', 218–21. See also S. Hornsby, 'Staple Trades', 412–16.

56R. Ommer, ed., *Merchant Credit*, 82.

57Sager, 'The Merchants of Water Street', 91–3.

58For example, see A.R.M. Lower, *The North American Assault on the Canadian Forest* (Toronto, 1936); W.S. MacNutt, *New Brunswick: A History* (Toronto, 1963); and A.H. Clark, *Three Centuries and the Island: A Historical Geography of Settlement and Agriculture in Prince Edward Island, Canada* (Toronto, 1959). For a review of recent literature, see C.A. Wilson, '"Outstanding in the Field": Recent Rural History in Canada', *Acadiensis* 20, (1991), 177–89.

59Sean Cadigan, 'The Staple Model'; Robert Mackinnon, 'Farming the Rock: The Evolution of Commercial Agriculture and St John's, Newfoundland, to 1945', *Acadiensis* 20 (1991), 3–31.

60Béatrice Craig, 'Le Developpement Agricole dans la Haute Vallée du St Jean en 1860', unpublished paper, *CHA* (Charlottetown, 1992); 'Agriculture and the Lumberman's Frontier in the Upper St Jean Valley, 1800–1870', *Journal of Forest History* 32 (1988), 125–

37; and 'Agriculture in a Pioneer Region: The Upper Saint John Valley in the First Half of the Nineteenth Century', in K. Inwood, ed., *Farm, Factory and Fortune*, 17–36; T.W. Acheson, 'New Brunswick Agriculture on the Eve of Confederation: An Assessment' in ibid., 37–60; A.R. MacNeil, 'The Acadian Legacy and Agricultural Development in Nova Scotia, 1760–1861' in Inwood, ed., forthcoming. See also R. Bitterman, 'The Hierarchy of the Soil: Land and Labour in a 19th Century Cape Breton Community', *Acadiensis* 18 (1988), 33–55; and Nicolas Landry, 'L'Exploitation agricole à Caraquet: étude basée sur le recensement de 1861', *Acadiensis* 20 (1991), 145–57.

[61]Wakefield was located in the middle of the Saint John Valley. St David was located in southern Charlotte County.

[62]Jean-Roch Cyr, 'Aspects de l'agriculture chez les francophones du Nouveau-Brunswick au 19e siècle: le recensement de 1861', *Material History Bulletin* 27 (1988) 51–60; S. Hornsby, 'Staple Trades', 417–23; Wynn, *Timber Colony*; R. Bitterman, 'The Hierarchy of the Soil'; A.R. MacNeil, 'Early American Communities in the Fundy: A Case Study of Annapolis and Amherst Townships, 1767–1827', *Agricultural History* 62 (1989), 101–19; Debra McNabb, 'The Role of the Land in the Development of Horton Township, 1760–1775', in M. Conrad, ed., *They Planted Well: New England Planters in Maritime Canada* (Fredericton, 1988), 151–60.

[63]R. Mackinnon and G. Wynn, 'Nova Scotian Agriculture in the 'Golden Age': A New Look' in D. Hay, ed., *Geographical Perspectives on the Maritime Provinces* (Halifax, 1989), 47–60 and Kris Inwood and Phyllis Wagg, 'Wealth and Prosperity in Nova Scotia Agriculture, 1850–70', unpublished paper, *CHA* (Charlottetown, 1992), present a relatively favourable picture of the colony's agriculture. Julian Gwyn, 'A Little Province' and 'The Golden Age', is much more critical. See also J. Gwyn, 'Imports and the Changing Standard of Living in Nova Scotia, 1832–72', *Nova Scotia Historical Review* 11 (1991), 59–60.

[64]T.W. Acheson, 'New Brunswick Agriculture', Table 2.

[65]Bitterman, 'The Hierarchy of the Soil'.

[66]Daniel Vickers, 'Competency and Competition: Economic Culture in Early America', *William and Mary Quarterly* 47 (1990), 3–29; compare Béatrice Craig, 'Le Developpement Agricole', and T.W. Acheson, 'New Brunswick Agriculture'.

[67]Rick Szostak, *The Role of Transportation in the Industrial Revolution: A Comparison of England and France* (Montreal 1991).

[68]K. Pryke, *Nova Scotia and Confederation, 1864–74* (Toronto, 1979), IX; Donald Creighton, *John A. Macdonald* vol. 2 (Toronto 1955).

[69]Sager with Panting, *op. cit.*, 152–3.

[70]Rosemary Langhout, 'Public Enterprise: An Analysis of Public Finance in the Maritime Colonies During the Period of Responsible Government' (PhD diss., University of New Brunswick, 1989); A.A. Den Otter, 'Nova Scotia: Railways and Confederation', unpublished paper presented to B.C. Studies/Atlantic Studies, Victoria, November 1992.

9 FROM HINTERLAND TO HEARTLAND: UPPER CANADA/ONTARIO

Three and a half times the size of the British Isles, Upper Canada grew in population from 6,000 in 1784 to 60,000 in 1811, a growth rate similar to that of adjacent New York State. By the mid 1830s some 140,000 emigrants arrived, mainly from the British Isles where unemployment stimulated exodus. Between 1841 and 1851 population doubled from 450,000 to 952,000 aided by an influx of some 200,000, mainly fleeing the Irish famine, in the late 1840s. Emigration slowed after 1850, and by 1870 the province's population reached 1,962,922.

Like Maritimers most Upper Canadians farmed for a living. As late as 1870 urban dwellers constituted less than one-quarter of the population; close to two-thirds of all workers laboured on farms, a proportion little changed from 1850. By comparison, industrial workers represented some 13 per cent of the working population in 1850, and barely 14 per cent twenty years later.[1] In fact, in 1870, agricultural production accounted for just under 60 per cent of the province's per capita commodity income, some 10 per cent higher than that of its closest rival, Quebec, and a full 27 per cent more than did manufacturing.[2] Despite the fact that these figures point to the overwhelming importance of agriculture as a business pursuit, writing on Ontario's and, indeed, Canada's business history has often overlooked agrarian enterprise. As Gordon Darroch, an historical sociologist, recently wrote, 'it is widely assumed that rural smallholders can be safely ignored after 1860, while attention is turned to the face of the future in Canadian capitalism's nascent, urban industrial revolution.'[3] By the third quarter of the nineteenth century there were, indeed, signs of significant industrial growth but, as in England, the term revolution is inappropriate. Moreover, change was not simply of an urban, industrial sort. The persistence of agrarian enterprise as a dominant economic activity in nineteenth-century Ontario should not be equated to stasis or lack of development. In fact, commerce and industry wrought changes in rural as well as urban Ontario. Nor did such development occur in isolation. Business enterprise in Upper Canada/Ontario was neither completely rural nor urban: increasingly, such enterprise depended upon and profited from developments in both sectors.

AGRARIAN ENTERPRISE

Farming in the Upper Canadian bush was not a haphazard affair. It may have been that 'here,' as one settler exulted, 'we are laird ourselves.'[4] Yet transforming the social distinction of land ownership into the reality of economic security was a difficult and protracted process. A series of interrelated decisions had to be made in order to farm successfully. Decisions demanded the balancing of short-and long-term goals: How many acres should one attempt to clear in a year? Should one clear underbrush before chopping trees? How short should one chop a tree? How much labour should be allocated to burning, slashing, and weeding? Should one purchase hired help or rely on the energy resources of one's immediate family? What should one do with stumps?

British travellers often bemoaned the unsightly stump-strewn fields (and streets, for that matter). One traveller coined the phrase 'stumpology or the science of stumps' and advised that the first Canadian encyclopedia should contain an entry under that title.[5] While stumps took up on average one-quarter of usable tillage, farmers generally left them to rot for eight years before pulling them out. This did not denote carelessness or laziness on their part. For a bush farmer to survive, cropping had to begin as soon after arrival as possible. Six acres could be cleared and sown with Indian corn and pumpkin seed during the time it took to render one acre stumpless. Farming amidst stumps used only the top layer of the rich virgin soil. By the time that layer had been relatively depleted of fertility some acres would be cleared for ploughing and deeper soil used for the first time. This layered use of soil amidst stumps coupled with a lower seed density than in Europe reflected the measured way the bush farmer adjusted to the physical environment. The result may have looked haphazard, but it was the product of close calculation and systematic use of available resources.

The key resource was the nuclear family. Yet like the pioneer farm, the pioneer family was a resource in the making. Wives were also mothers, and children, while they very early learned how to tend oxen, helped plant root crops, and assisted in burning debris, were of limited assistance in chopping, clearing, and piling. Choppers could be hired but they were expensive and often performed poorly. Chopping more often than not fell to the lot of the male household head. Logging and piling often required more resources than the family could provide. Farming bees emerged from this context, not from some spirit of *bonhomie* and brotherhood bred from a presumed egalitarian frontier. Farming bees were a form of barter, a transaction, rather than a form of charity, of freely given labour. Labour was offered in return for copious food and drink (one yoke of oxen equalled one gallon of whiskey) and for the promise of labour in return.[6] At the outset, the environment necessitated interaction and precluded self-sufficiency. The exchange system that underlay that interaction was one indication of a form of counting-house mentality that facilitated the transformation of the wilderness.

To imply that some sort of commercial ethic underlay Upper Canadian farming is somewhat controversial. Doubters point to the prevalence of barter and argue that this symbolizes a pre-commercial or pre-capitalist era. Certainly Upper Canada, typical of most frontier communities, lacked cash. As a result many goods were exchanged for goods. A pound currency of wheat was exchanged for a pound currency of sugar, tea, or the equivalent sum in labour. No one owed two bushels of wheat: rather one owed a certain sum of money which might be paid off by its equivalent in wheat. In this sense from the very beginning Upper Canada's economy was cash-oriented. Farm produce was valued in monetary terms. Barker and Stevenson, a reasonably large country store at Picton, with annual sales in the 1830s of £2000, kept its local exchange accounts in a 'barter book', the existence of which testifies to the commercial basis of barter in rural Upper Canada. Moreover, cash played an important role in the settlement of rural accounts. One study of thirteen merchant enterprises operating at various times between 1792 and 1842 found that cash payments comprised anywhere from 3 to 30 per cent of the value of retail payments; for eight of those operations cash dealings represented 10 per cent or more of such payments.[7] Between January and August, 1833, one-half of the number of payments received by John Benson at his store in rural Napanee were in cash. During the same period he issued forty-four loans, most of which were also in cash.[8]

Nor were prices fixed on a haphazard, arbitrary, or atomistic basis. Several detailed studies by the historian Douglas McCalla have demonstrated that prices for produce and other commodities were fairly standard at any point in time throughout the economy. John Benson, for example, faced competition from two other stores in Napanee and a comparison of his price list for selected commodities with those of stores in Niagara, at the other end of Lake Ontario, reveal more consistency than difference.[9] This last point is of special significance. It suggests that prices in the rural area were sensitive to some sort of general market conditions, and rural merchants did not possess arbitrary price-setting power. By 1846 at least 160 Upper Canadian rural centres had two or more stores. Between 1807 and 1835 some nine hundred licences were issued to itinerant hawkers and pedlars, allowing them to traverse agricultural areas selling goods and bringing news. This level of local competition was complemented by rivalry between wholesalers situated in major urban centres like Hamilton and Toronto. If local merchants colluded on prices, farmers would often take their business to other localities.[10]

Indeed scattered qualitative evidence suggests that some farmers looked to settle in areas close to more than one market 'for the sale of our produce'. In 1835, one farmer in the region of Kingston wrote a sharply worded letter to the local paper warning Kingston's merchants 'to pay cash for merchantable produce [or] the remaining trade of Kingston will be driven to Belleville, where the needful can always be had. I say no more.' In that year he hawked his produce door to door in Kingston rather than trade with local merchants.[11] Farmers also evolved strategies that made it difficult for other rural entrepreneurs, like blacksmiths, to charge exorbitant prices. Thomas Priestman, a homesteader at Wainfleet in the Niagara region complained that 'blacksmithing is near as good as coining' and this discourages 'us . . . to go to the blacksmith before we be in nead [*sic*] of it.' In fact, Priestman was so dissatisfied that he wrote his brother in Newmarket, England, to send him three hundred weight of three- to four-inch nails and one hundred weight of two-inch shingle nails plus some other iron material.[12] Priestman, in other words, used Old World contacts to import on his own account, surely the ultimate way of circumventing unreasonably high local prices!

A system of long credit, whether expressed and ultimately settled in terms of goods or cash, underlay rural exchange. The rural merchant obtained his goods from urban wholesalers on, generally, twelve months' credit. Those wholesalers, themselves, imported from Great Britain on a similar credit basis. Transactions between farmers and rural merchants did not deviate from this pattern. For most stores the value of their debt quickly emerged as their principal asset. In this system, there can be little doubt but that most farmers were in debt to merchants for goods. Clearly merchants had much more leverage than did farmers. Yet there was a degree of mutual dependence. If enough farmers failed to pay or bought and sold elsewhere, rural merchants would also be unable to meet charges due. Credit shackled some more than others, but few were totally unfettered. Rural and urban merchants in Upper Canada, while at times suffering a significant rate of bankruptcy, were nonetheless generally better off than the farmers on whom they depended for business. But their economic control was decidedly less than that enjoyed by merchants in the Atlantic region. Greater competition and a more productive agricultural economy which facilitated the sale of more than simply one staple, allowed those who produced for merchants a degree of security and economic independence not enjoyed by their Atlantic counterparts. As noted on in Chapter Four on the fur trade, the significance of debt can only be properly understood by locating it within a particular set of local conditions. The nature of such relations could take various forms, not all of which were inimical to general economic growth and individual financial security. Moreover, the early existence and seemingly pervasive extent of credit in rural Upper Canada renders any notion of a communitarian, self-sufficient, or subsistence-based economy suspect. Farms were not self-contained units. Farms functioned on credit. While many transactions were of a local or regional nature, farmers did, when necessary, travel more widely to buy and sell and, on occasion, would import goods on their own account from Great Britain.

A further form of agrarian enterprise has thus far only been hinted at here: the buying and selling of land. The Proclamation Act of 1763 recognized Native rights to certain lands but it did not give Natives the freedom to dispose of that property other than to the British government. By 1806 much of southern Ontario had been purchased from the Mississauga Natives for a small amount of goods and cash. Some military commanders, such as at Detroit in the 1780s, ignored the Proclamation and personally appropriated extensive acreage from the Natives at low cost. The government ceded much of its land to Loyalists and their families and, after 1792, reserved one seventh of each township as a crown reserve and one seventh as a clergy reserve. In addition small but politically and socially well-connected groups of absentee landowners obtained rights to large blocks of lands in often potentially rich agricultural areas.[13]

A few examples illustrate what seems to have been a fairly pervasive pattern. By 1800, well before any major influx of settlers, between one-half and two-thirds of land in the Home District, the site of the colony's capital, York, was in the hands of primarily absentee owners. At any time between 1820 and 1840, twenty-three absentee landowners controlled from 10 to 30 per cent of all patented land in Peel County, one of the richest agricultural areas in the colony. Almost all of these men were highly visible in the colony's social and political life, and one historian has called them bona fide members of the local Family Compact.

When crown and clergy reserves are added to their holdings, then some 40 per cent of Peel County's land was not available to prospective settlers in 1820 and 1830, and in 1840, some 20 per cent. David Gagan, an historian, has estimated that these absentee owners could have realized a profit of from $7 to $9 per acre; collectively, they owned 42,115 acres in Peel County. A comparable alienation of a large block of property took place in southwestern Upper Canada. Of the 211,000 acres patented in the Western District by 1815, 43 per cent—much of the area's choicest land—was owned by absentee speculators (owners of 400 or more acres). The Baby and Askin families, long-time fur traders and merchants, owned about two-thirds of the lands patented by speculators in the Western District. These men exploited Natives: John Askin obtained Native land at a cheap cost because of his marriage to a Native woman. His activities so angered the prominent Native leader, Joseph Brant, that in 1796 Brant complained to D.W. Smith, a member of the local land board 'that Mr. Askins [sic] and some other merchants have been seducing several Indians to make over the lands to them . . . '.[14] It was a futile protest. Smith was a close confidant of Askin and when Smith became Surveyor General later in the 1790s he acted as Askin's intermediary and general fix-it person on land matters. The speculators routinely evaded taxes and kept good land off the market. As John Clarke, an historical geographer, has concluded, such extensive evasion 'must have had a dire effect upon the economic, social and educational development of the area'.'[15]

Similar activity seems to have occurred even in relatively less desirable agricultural areas. Montague Township in Lanark county, eastern Upper Canada, offered little prospect of remunerative farming. Yet by 1810 nearly one-half of its 112 square miles was controlled by absentee owners, speculators who only began to sell the land in the 1830s. Richard Cartwright, a wealthy and well-connected Kingston merchant, retarded settlement at Napanee by offering land at a high price. Not until his son took over the estate in the 1830s was that land made available on more reasonable terms. Similarly in the Collingwood area of north-central Ontario, wealthy absentee landowners controlled choice land and blocked effective settlement in the hopes of acquiring ever higher prices for their property. Bill Shannon, the historian who has most closely studied land development in Collingwood Township in the mid-nineteenth century, usefully distinguished between investors and speculators. Both types were absentee owners of large blocks of land. Investors tended to hold the land for a relatively long time period and upon ultimate sale realized a relatively smaller return. Speculators tended to buy at the time the market was about to rise and quickly sold at inflated prices, leaving the new property owner with an unrealistic debt burden and in that sense slowing further investment in regional infrastructural development by those who lived there.[16]

Several other intensive local studies have developed comparable distinctions and more studies of a similar sort would be useful.[17] Yet while motivations and strategies may have differed amongst major absentee owners and while some residents may also have speculated in local land, it is nonetheless clear that the buying and selling of large amounts of Upper Canadian land was a favourite business pastime of the colony's central and various regional élites. One estimate puts their collective holdings in 1841 at about one-third of the acreage south of the Laurentian Shield.[18] Indeed in the late 1830s, many of this élite publicly admitted that 'The great proportion of the land, especially in the older surveyed townships, comprehending the choicest locations in the neighbourhood of roads and navigable waters, now belongs to private individuals.' This admission was part of the prospectus for the Canada Emigration Association, a short-lived scheme to attract emigrants with the bait of fifty free acres of land. In that way these landowners hoped to promote development of their holdings and stimulate sales in the sluggish market following the short-lived Rebellion of 1837. Rising emigration in the early 1840s went far to render such a scheme redundant. Nonetheless its prospectus confirmed what the average settler knew only too well: much of the best land in the province had 'passed into the hands of private individuals' who left it untilled, 'with the view to their owner's obtaining higher prices'.[19]

While most activity in the land market took place on an individual or at best loosely linked group basis, there was one significant exception to that pattern. In 1825 the colonial government sold 2,500,000 acres of crown land to a private, British-based corporation, the Canada Company, for £295,000 payable over sixteen years. The steady influx of this money gave to the executive, non-elected branch of that government a great deal of independent power. The extent to which such a sale helped the prospective settler is a matter of debate. The Canada Company may have offered some benefits, in terms of roads and some other infrastructural development, to those prospective settlers who were relatively well off. Poorer emigrants had to rely on a system of auctions which the government implemented in 1826 for the sale of its remaining crown land.[20]

Too little is known about the way in which average settlers financed their property acquisition and farming operations. Some brought sufficient cash at the outset. The majority did not, however, and had to look to other sources for capital. Such sources were far from plentiful in Upper Canada. The chartering of the Bank of Upper Canada in 1821 and several other banks in the 1830s did not help because banks could not lend on the direct security of land, about the only asset most emigrants could offer. In the 1830s the Colonial Office disallowed the formation of trust and loan societies, fearing that such agencies might finance industrial growth which would compete with British enterprise.[21] When such societies finally received legal recognition in the mid-1840s, they tended to concentrate on urban markets. Most rural dwellers, therefore, had to look to the private market for credit. Local merchants, like the above mentioned Benson at Napanee, often provided credit. So, too, did successful regional farmers. On balance, however, the borrowing of money from land vendors or even from third parties in order to finance the acquisition or development of land, in other words financing by the granting of a mortgage, was undertaken in relatively few cases. One study of mortgaging in a rich agricultural area, Toronto Gore Township, found that no more than one-third of land holders had mortgages at any one time. Interest ranged far above the legal rate of 6 per cent, reaching in many cases 10 to 15 per cent.

The usury law which specified a 6 per cent maximum rate was often evaded by making mortgages at a discount, a procedure not restricted by law. A high percentage of those who mortgaged failed to complete their agreement. Indeed, court cases suggest that mortgage defaults were common in Upper Canada. Moreover, the law governing mortgages made it difficult for mortgagees to protect their investment. The mortgagee could foreclose but the mortgagor could apply for additional time to pay. Nor did foreclosure give the mortgagee absolute control over the land. The mortgagee could sell the property subject to transferring any money in excess of the debt owed to the original mortgagor. This made any sale of the land on credit very cumbersome to effect. Moreover, and perhaps most significantly, mortgage money was not abundant in Upper Canada. On balance, neither the prospective borrower nor lender were content with the nature of the mortgage system as a mode for the extension of rural credit.[22]

Bargain and sale contracts were a much preferable and more widely practised method of financing land sales in rural Upper Canada.[23] Settlers could purchase on an instalment plan, each payment being met from the sale of farm produce, and in this way the need for immediate access to a sizeable amount of capital was avoided. The vendor kept title to the property until receipt of the final payment. Payment defaults gave the vendor the right to evict and take over the property, including any improvements. At first glance, and despite the low initial payment made by the buyer, this system gave the seller enormous power. Some have argued that the Court of Chancery, established in 1837, and concerned with equity issues, carefully oversaw and contained such potential power. The Chancery Court, in effect, recognized the need for an equitable system for the buying and selling of rural land in order for any development to occur in Upper Canada. It did not permit a vendor to exercise swift redemption in cases where the occupant had substantially improved the property. In this respect the Chancery Court was not bound by a literal common-law reading of the contract. In general, the court extended rights of repayment to the settler even while protecting the vested rights of the vendor. Nor was this supervisory role at all inconsistent with the ends desired by major land holders. Indeed the first Chancellor of that court, R.S. Jamieson, was himself a major land owner and member of the Canada Emigration Association. If Upper Canada were to receive the image of a country of gouging speculators, than emigrants would certainly seek land in other jurisdictions. The key was to facilitate easy and reliable transferals of property: both buyer and seller desired that and the Chancery Court, sensitive to the importance of what it termed 'public convenience' in this area, acted as what would appear to have been an effective watchdog over property transactions in pre-Confederation rural Upper Canada.[24]

Indeed, in the area of land sales, Upper Canadian jurists seemed prepared to go beyond a generally conservative, precedent-based jurisprudence which followed British common law doctrines. Even John Beverley Robinson, Chief Justice of the Court of Queen's Bench in Upper Canada from 1829 to 1862, departed from British precedent in the area of land transaction. While ever the patrician—he never warmly supported a Court of Chancery, believing that gentlemanly landowners and lenders would, without court interference, honour an effort to redeem property even years after foreclosure had been instituted[25]—Robinson nonetheless recognized certain areas of sharp dealing, especially concerning land registration processes, and he did go beyond British common law to effect remedies. He did so in part because he felt that local conditions were so dramatically different that British precedents were inapplicable. In 1850, William Hume Blake, Chancellor of the Court of Chancery agreed:

> We are not dealing with the casual transfer of real property in a fully occupied and thoroughly cultivated country . . . it is [therefore] of vital importance . . . that, in this court . . . the numerous titles which depend exclusively upon this jurisdiction for their validity, should not be shaken by the introduction of doctrines, which, however suited to other states of society, have no application in our present social condition, but that they should be shown to rest upon settled and solid foundations.[26]

There were, as the historian John Weaver has demonstrated, even more compelling reasons for Robinson's support of Chancery.[27] Robinson and Blake were very much members of the wealthy élite. Robinson, in particular, owned considerable land around Toronto. A smoothly operating land market was a *sine qua non* for provincial development. Before 1834 most large landowners rested content without a Chancery Court. Existing practice seemed to sanction swift foreclosures without the right of real recourse on the part of the mortgagor. An 1834 Act changed that. It gave to mortgagors the clear right to exercise a power of redemption (i.e., paying off the mortgage and repossessing the land title if the foreclosee still owned the property) for a period of up to 20 years. For Robinson and other large landowners, this was close to unsufferable. A Court of Chancery, while allowing redemption, could be counted on to restrict that right to a period of some six months. In the context of the 1834 legislation, Chancery looked, to men of property, like a benefit and support, not an impediment to be overcome.

'Real estate', Robinson declared, '. . . passes in this country very rapidly from owner to owner.' So it did. As a result, in this more than in any other economic area Upper Canadian courts adopted an instrumentalist perspective, a willingness to respond in a creative fashion to what they perceived to be the needs of a developing local economy rather than passively following British doctrines established at another time and place. In this way, courts shored up a set of bounds to the process of land transactions; they facilitated the continuance of an active private land market by letting the game, from which they claimed all society would benefit, continue. In this context, it should be noted that while judges often referred to 'general welfare' and 'common good', they, and the law they interpreted, remained silent on the social distribution of economic power. Players could accumulate and speculate on land as much as they dared.

Bargain and sale contracts presupposed that at some level there would be a market for the sale of what the farm could produce. Many historians have assumed that such sales were limited to the export of wheat and flour. Recent studies, however, have conclusively demonstrated that before 1850, when most settlement occurred, Upper Canada was not an export-oriented, staple-driven economy.[28] In 1803, for example, wheat was indeed the most popular crop grown, but its production encompassed only 50 per cent of cultivated land, and the export portion took up only 20 per cent of that land. The account books of rural merchants provide an indication of the variety of produce generated by a farm. Of thirteen such businesses, six received more value from products like ashes, lumber, pork, rye, tobacco, or barley than from wheat, and two received the same value. Farmers generated such variety of items—one farmer planted thirty-nine different crops between 1819 and 1822—because there was at least a local market for them.[29] It is, of course, for that reason that merchants accepted such a variety of output as payment for debts. Rural growth bore little if any relation to the operations of the British Corn Laws, which promised, on paper and under certain conditions, a protected market for Upper Canadian wheat. Yet high transport costs and competing local demand in Upper and Lower Canada and in the Maritimes rarely made it sensible and profitable to ship much to Britain. Marvin McInnis, an economic historian, has shown that for over 60 per cent of the years between 1817 and 1850 British prices were significantly below prices for wheat in Montreal. For most of those years steady growth continued throughout the colony. The staple theory would, of course, not predict that. Moreover wheat was not the only potential export crop. As we shall see, the value of timber and wood exports from the St Lawrence-Great Lakes area equalled in value wheat and flour exports during the 1815-40 period. As well, demand for wood was strong in Upper Canada's internal economy—in most years more sawmills than grist mills were in operation.

Between 1842 and 1851 wheat output increased by nearly 300 per cent. Yet by 1851, on average, 80 per cent of a farm's cultivated acreage produced crops other than wheat. Even in the colony's wheat heartland, wheat acreage averaged less than 35 per cent of cultivated acreage. The 1850s marked the beginning of an era of intensive as opposed to extensive development in rural areas—some time in the 1850s most good agricultural land had been settled—and wheat exports doubled in volume and tripled in value between 1850 and 1856. While in 1861 more acreage was under wheat cultivation, wheat still averaged only about 22 per cent of all cultivated acreage. In fact, the acreage devoted to fall wheat, the preferred export crop, was far less. Close to 90 per cent of farms planted spring wheat, but only some 35 per cent planted a fall crop. Relatively few farms were in areas with a growing season long enough for a fall crop. Even farms which planted fall wheat allotted only an average ten acres to its production, about 20 per cent of cultivated acreage. One farm family could harvest eight to ten acres of wheat without hired help or mechanical assistance, and the two to three weeks between the harvesting of spring and fall wheat crops allowed family enterprise to handle both harvests economically. With the exception of some very large farms it would seem that few farmers had significantly mechanized their operation by 1861. Nor did many believe it to be economical to rely on hired

Table 9.1   Upper Canadian Farm Level Data, 1851 and 1861

	1851	1861
Average farm size	109 acres	110 acres
Average cultivated acres as % of total acres	37.5	45.5
Average acres in wheat	8.8	11
Average wheat acres as a % of total cultivated acres	21.6	22
Average net output per farm	$198	$403
Wheat as a % of net output	37	50
Livestock and dairy products as a % of net output	54	42

SOURCES: R. McInnis, 'Perspectives on Ontario Agriculture', Section 4, *CPRH* 8 (1992) and 'The Size Structure of Farming, Canada West, 1861', *Research in Economic History*, Supplement 5 (1989), 313–29.

labour. Although wheat accounted for a much higher proportion of net income than in 1851 (see Table 9.1), it is nonetheless clear that Upper Canadians conducted a mixed farming business. Even at the height of the colony's wheat boom, few specialized solely in the production of wheat as a cash crop. Bigger farms diversified more, rather than specialized more.[30]

By 1871 wheat output, due in part to poor weather and parasite problems, had declined by 42 per cent and Canada, as a whole, had become a net importer of wheat. In Ontario, wheat made a short comeback in the late 1870s. Probably because returns from wheat varied, however, from that point onwards Ontario farmers moved fairly steadily into beef, dairy, and general mixed farming, from which a more stable, if potentially less profitable, income could be expected.[31]

Was farming profitable in Upper Canada during the first three-quarters of the nineteenth century? Marvin McInnis has gone some way towards providing an answer to this important question. On the basis of a systematic sample of farms drawn from the 1861 census, he has suggested that only 16 per cent of Upper Canada's farm produced less than they consumed. A further 16 per cent produced enough to feed three families. Moreover he found that farming behaviour did not vary according to farm size. The greater the cultivated acreage, the greater the income, but small farms (*circa* 50 acres) and large farms (*circa* 170+ acres) farmed similar crops and, expressed as a percentage of total output, produced roughly similar quantities. Finally he has suggested that most farm families could live adequately without recourse to off-farm work.[32]

These findings clearly put Upper Canadian rural enterprise in sharp contrast to that of the Maritimes. This general context of prosperity helps explains why almost 40 per cent of central Ontario's labourers listed in the 1861 census who could be traced to the 1871 census had become farmers, and why 86 per cent of those who were listed as farmers in 1861 and could be traced to the 1871 census remained farmers.[33] For those who could afford to acquire land, farming did offer a realistic prospect for sustaining a livelihood. Yet farming was far from a quick way to wealth. A completed farm averaged about 80 per cent of its acreage cultivated. Farms in 1861 fell far short of that figure: Upper Canada's farming community was still very much in the process of development. And such development proceeded slowly: a producing farm cleared fewer than 1.5 acres per year.[34] Moreover, there is evidence that many of the recent entrants to the farming business were tenants, not owners. In 1871, 16 per cent of farms in Ontario were tenant-managed and this percentage increased over the next twenty years.[35] Several intensive local studies have found contrasting evidence to that offered at a more aggregate level by McInnis. In Peel County, a rich wheat-growing area, David Gagan found much evidence of rural poverty: he concluded that in 1861, 39 per cent of Peel's farmers had not 'moved beyond the primitive amenities of a pioneer society'. Remarkably he also discovered that 62 per cent of all freeholders in Peel County in 1861 had left by 1871.[36] Similarly, Chad Gaffield's study of Prescott County uncovered an extensive system of multiple occupations: in the eastern county, farmers worked in the lumber industry as well as farmed in order to support their families.[37]

Moreover, standardizing price data for the whole of the province, as McInnis does, blurs inter- and intra-county and township income variations. Not all farms were equally situated with respect to transport corridors and market destinations. Local prices and costs did, to some degree, reflect physical location. McInnis, himself, found that while average farm income for 1851 was $198, 35 per cent of Upper Canada's townships averaged less than $150 net farm income, a figure, in his words, 'well below the provincial average'.[38] Significant regional variations clearly existed. Some of this disparity can be accounted for by recency of settlement and the number of acres under cultivation. Darroch and Soltow, two historical sociologists, have argued that, in fact, a life cycle approach to the issue of land ownership and farm development is essential in order to understand the nature of rural development in this period. They have shown that in 1871, both the extent and incidence of farm acreage owned increased dramatically with the owner's age. Farmers in their twenties owned an average 28 acres, in their thirties 67 acres, and in their forties 106 acres, peaking to an average 118 acres in their fifties. They infer from this that a classic agricultural ladder was in place: young, ambitious farmers could start small and have reasonable hopes of expanding to at least moderate prosperity over the course of a lifetime. Yet even they acknowledge that only 52 per cent of rural men occupied two or more acres of land in 1871. Slightly over one in four rural heads of households were landless. Since township level analysis suggests that, as in the Maritimes, those settlers who arrived first and persisted had a greater chance of prospering than did later arrivals, in 1871 the deck seemed stacked against those new players.[39]

On balance, then, much still remains to be understood about the business of farming in Upper Canada/Ontario. While at this stage of our knowledge definitive generalizations are ill-advised, in relative terms it is clear that agriculture in Upper Canada was generally more prosperous than its Maritime and, as we shall see, Lower Canadian equivalent. This relative prosperity, many have argued, provided the basis for business development in other sectors of the economy. If Maritime agriculture facilitated enclave export-oriented development by supplying cheap labour, Upper Canada's more prosperous agrarian sector provided an important local demand for manufactured goods and thus contributed to the growth of a more diversified economy.

FOREST ENTERPRISE

From 1815 through the 1870s the export of Upper Canadian forest products rivalled in value that of wheat and flour.[40] Before 1840 sawmills outnumbered grist mills and such continued to be the case in 1871. Nor was the forest industry restricted to one geographical area in Upper Canada. Certainly the Ottawa Valley was prominent in the production of white and red pine, but exports via the Great Lakes-St Lawrence system were always significant in terms of potash, deal, oak, and staves. To a certain extent these were by-products of farm clearing, but overall the rate of exports bear little relation to the rate of land clearing, suggesting that this was an enterprise which existed separate from the farm. There is even evidence that significant lumbering took place in the western peninsula. As early as 1814, Thomas Smith, a land speculator, surveyor, and sometime Member of the House of Assembly who lived at Sandwich, claimed to have lost during the war a 'copse' measuring 7,785,720 square feet, which apparently contained 34,603 oak trees. Other merchants in the western peninsula area filed claims for lumber loss as well. In fact, Douglas McCalla has demonstrated that over one-third of the value of exports from the western peninsula into the late 1830s was from wood and its products.[41]

The export of these products via the Great Lakes and St Lawrence River had many benefits for the local economy: some 200-300 Great Lakes sailors received jobs shipping wood. Potash and staves could be produced by farmers during the winter and delivered to local merchants for transhipment out of the colony. Indeed, in 1846, the Grand River region of southern Upper Canada provided over 95 per cent of all the staves exported from Quebec, indicating that a specialized commercial system was in place. Merchant account books show that this kind of business was quite routine. Moreover, not all wood was exported. Country mills —which could be started for as little as £100-200—cut a great number of planks for local use. In 1826, according to one historian's estimate, the 425 sawmills in Upper Canada probably produced sawn lumber which in value equalled wheat exports. Distilleries—150 licensed in 1842—and steamboats—about 30 in 1840 —consumed wood, as did the construction and heating of buildings. As with farming, so too with the forest industry: diverse production, rather than a focus on one staple like wheat or squared pine timber, was the reality.[42]

More research is required before one can write confidently concerning the actual organization of the Great Lakes-St Lawrence business. For the early years the general impression is of a large number of small independent farmers, loggers, and sub-contractors selling their product, at less than one-half the Quebec city price, to merchant-forwarders located at the various Lake ports. Mossom Boyd, active from the 1840s in the Bobcaygeon region, sent his lumber to Lake Ontario via the Trent River system and by the 1860s had become one of the major operators outside of the Ottawa Valley. Dileno Dexter Calvin, however, by the mid-1860s had almost certainly become one of the biggest timber dealers in the Canadas. In the 1840s he located on Garden Island, two miles south of Kingston at the entrance to the St Lawrence, where Great Lakes timber could be conveniently rafted for the trip to Quebec City. As early as 1840, 236 vessels unloaded timber at the Island. While he did some logging on his own account, Calvin mostly performed the role of transhipper, for a set fee delivering to Quebec City wood for others. Huge timber rafts, often 120 feet wide by 1,200 to 1,500 feet long and weighing thousands of tons, were pieced together and floated to Quebec City by experienced crews composed of Natives and French Canadians. At peak times Calvin employed seven hundred. By the 1870s he had diversified into a wide variety of endeavours, including manufacturing, shipbuilding, tugboat operations, warehousing, and general mercantile pursuits.[43]

An indication of the power exerted by Calvin & Company on the Great Lakes-St Lawrence lumber trade is evident in the nature of its contracts with suppliers. For example, in 1846 the operations of a small supplier, John Grenier of Amherstburg, were overseen by hewers who Calvin had sent from Quebec. The French Canadians made sure the wood was being manufactured up to standard, and attested that Grenier was a 'fit and proper person, for carrying on the business'. In addition, one of the company's partners regularly travelled into the lumber areas to manage matters.

The contracts gave more than simply managerial latitude in the production process. Whenever possible, Calvin & Company negotiated deals which gave them control over production, shipping, and the ultimate disposition of the product. As John Keyes, an historian, has noted, 'this integration of services provided considerable leverage in dealings with producers.' One such supplier, having been forced to dispose of his winter cutting at a low price, swore that he would never again 'be dictated by any forwarder how much timber I must get in the face of a bad market . . . '. Yet he really had very little choice and several years later was once again shipping with Calvin & Company. Indeed, in 1847 Calvin & Company were part of a cartel which included prominent Upper Canadian oak producers as well as the three major St Lawrence rafting firms. These various companies controlled the production, shipping, and sale of about two-thirds of all oak shipped through Quebec City in 1848.[44]

Lumbering in the Ottawa Valley tended to be quite specialized, and the industry as a whole came under the control of a few large dealers at a much earlier date than would seem to have been the case in the rest of the colony. Squared white pine timber dominated the Ottawa Valley trade well into the 1850s and did not peak until the early 1860s. Yet significant trade in sawn lumber, sparked, in part, by growing urban demand and declining wood resources in the United States, predated the Reciprocity Treaty of 1854.[45]

To an extent greater than in the rest of the colony, Ottawa Valley lumbering depended on the export trade for its success. To succeed in that business, lumberers required access to large capital resources. Given the time it took to cut, manufacture, and transport, returns on investment often took over a year. Close ties of a financial and corporate sort to Quebec City forwarders reflected these requirements. While lumbering in the Ottawa region had been started by an American, Philemon Wright, by the 1830s many of the Valley's largest concerns were either branches of Quebec City companies or had been taken over by Quebec entrepreneurs who had then moved their main operations to the Valley.

George Hamilton, one of the most prominent early lumbermen in the Canadas, is a case in point. In 1811, when two Upper Canadian forwarders failed to meet the advances granted them by the Quebec-based Hamilton, Hamilton seized their deal mill at Hawkesbury which, following a fire, he rebuilt at a cost of over £15,000. The Hamilton operations point to the diversity of the export trade in wood even in the Ottawa Valley, since as early as the mid 1820s they shipped significant amounts of pine deals and standard staves to English ports. Throughout his career Hamilton fought for the rights of large companies to control the lumber trade. One way to achieve this was to restrict the entry of small producers to crown lands by instituting a state-controlled fee structure. Another way was by convincing the government that only selected large producers could afford to improve rivers and establish the necessary infrastructure for logging. In the 1830s the state 'listened' and granted river rights to Hamilton and other large producers who, in return for their monopolies, assumed all development costs. Under the management of his sons, the Hawkesbury firm benefited from increasingly high entry fees for the logging of Crown lands, and in the early 1850s, with five other firms (two of which, Allan Gilmour & Company and George B. Hall, were large Quebec-based dealers) it controlled over half the licences, half the area, and the best timber reserves on Ottawa Valley crown land. By 1860, the firm was appraised as being worth between $320,000 to $400,000. By 1870 the Hamilton Brothers operated the second largest sawmilling enterprise in Ontario and ranked as the eleventh largest industrial concern in the province.[46] Indeed, in 1870, seven of the nine largest sawmills in Ontario were located in the Valley and, reflecting the changing direction of trade flows, Americans owned at least four of them.[47]

The Hamilton brothers and other large lumber dealers, like the 'self-made lumber baron', John Egan, benefited from a form of what has been called the *système agro-forestier*. As in the Maritimes, agricultural enterprise did, to a degree, underpin forestry development. To meet the provisioning costs of their operations—in one case this amounted to one-third the cost of production — large lumberers owned and leased huge farms. In addition to this, however, those who the companies employed often themselves owned small farms. Income from these farms, although lessened by the existence of the large company farms, proved to be a necessary supplement to lumber work, especially given the fact that all big lumberers operated company stores which ate up much of the woods workers' wages. As Chad Gaffield has demonstrated, companies like the Hamilton brothers' operation exploited the relationship that existed between farming and woods work. They hired usually on only a temporary basis. They stocked their store at Hawkesbury with high price luxury goods and generally over-priced other items. Many who had hoped that money earned in woods work would be enough to start a farm were sorely disappointed.[48]

Economic linkages between the Ottawa Valley lumber industry and the rest of Upper Canada were not profound. French-Canadian labourers, often but not always migrants, dominated the workforce. Transportation, financial, and corporate links bound the area to Quebec in the east and New York State in the south. Some agricultural produce would have been purchased from the western region, although much was grown locally and meat, especially pork, was imported from the United States. Douglas McCalla has suggested that perhaps the most significant indirect link were the wages paid French-Canadian migrant workers. That take-home pay, estimated at £7,500 for the 1835-38 period, may have helped Lower Canada purchase more from Upper Canada during an era when much of Lower Canada's wheat and flour came from the upper province. This insight reinforces a speculation offered by Marvin McInnis. He has demonstrated that while Upper Canada produced more wheat than it consumed, it did not sell all of its surplus to Britain. Rather in some respects it had become British North America's breadbasket. How did Lower Canada pay for this produce? It may have done so, McInnis suggests, by money from the export of wood to Great Britain.[49] Taken together, the points raised by McCalla and McInnis suggest that the primary staple that helped condition the growth of both Canadas might well have been wood, not wheat.

COMMERCIAL UPPER CANADA

Even before 1791 merchants located at Kingston, Niagara, and Detroit exercised significant power in what was referred to as the up-country region. In some ways, the Revolutionary War provided a golden opportunity for astute merchants. Niagara is a case in point. In 1775 provisions and presents distributed to the Indians out of Fort Niagara cost £500. By 1781, such costs had escalated to £100,000. Between 1775 and 1785, the regular armed forces spent, on goods and services, another £150,000. It was a merchant's paradise. But to succeed merchants had to be of a special sort. Strong military contacts were one necessary prerequisite. Yet, as the career of John Butler, a Loyalist military leader from New York State suggests, even more was required. Extremely successful in attracting Iroquois support and engineering guerrilla raids, Butler aspired to a comfortable sinecure. The governor, however, considered Butler to be too 'deficient in Education and liberal sentiments' to merit significant preferment. The point was clear for those who chose to read it. To succeed, whether as a merchant, dependant on military contracts for success, or as a bureaucrat, breeding, respectability, and the proper social bearing were the *sine qua non*.

In this context a well-connected group of merchants emerged to dominate the fur trade and general forwarding business which flowed through Detroit, Niagara, Kingston, and Montreal. These commercial men moved to positions of prominence during a period of economic transition from an early pioneering economy, marked by the importance of military provisioning and the fur trade, to a more settled agrarian community following the War of 1812. Richard Cartwright, a New York-born Loyalist whose father hailed from England and mother from Holland, had before the Revolution studied 'the classics and higher branches of education'. In 1780 he entered into a trading partnership with the Scotland-born Robert Hamilton (no relation to the Hamiltons in Hawkesbury) who had previously worked for Edward Ellice, a prominent fur trader and land owner. Supplied by the Montreal firm of Todd & McGill, also prominent in the southern fur trade, and linked by them to John Askin, fur trader and merchant at Detroit, the young merchants emerged as the foremost suppliers to the military and the Indian Department. They triumphed over competition from some eighteen other mercantile concerns in the Niagara region primarily because they used their contacts and diversified out of a simply local trade to take control of the general forwarding business in fur and military goods. Since the military was determined to buy as much local produce as possible and wished to deal in bulk with larger established merchants, smaller merchants and farmers, often far from military depots, had to sell to Cartwright and Hamilton who, in turn, sold to the army. At times Hamilton, due to his close relationship with officers at the Niagara garrison, received payment in advance on the basis of what he thought he could supply. This payment was in currency and included, where appropriate, interest. By contrast Hamilton and Cartwright paid their suppliers with their own notes which they would redeem once a year in October with no interest. If a settler or small merchant wished the notes redeemed at any other date, they had to accept a 12½ per cent discount. Small wonder that in 1792 Cartwright could write, 'So long as the British government shall think proper to hire people to come over and eat our flour, we shall go on very well and continue to make a figure.'

As Hamilton's biographer has noted, these commercial links gave the ambitious duo control of what was one of the 'most highly developed organizations in the geographically fragmented and institutionally weak province before the War of 1812'. Nor were they slow in extending these links to non-economic spheres. As a first step in organizing for the up-country region a system of government separate from Quebec, in 1788-89 the governor divided the old Mississauga land into four districts, each district receiving Courts of Quarter Sessions and Common Pleas and a local land board, all to be administered under the rules of English law. While one should be cautious about attributing too much power to the merchant class—individuals within that class failed far more often than they succeeded—it is nevertheless the case that merchants, relative to their number in society, were substantially overrepresented in the law courts and land boards of this period.

An examination of the actual operations of these early courts underlines merchant dominance. Merchants played the leading role in adapting those institutions to the reality of local colonial conditions, especially to the reality of local economic conditions. Rarely learned in the complexities of British common law procedure, the merchants opted instead for informality, simplicity, and economy. These attitudes reflected mercantile ideas in New York and, to an extent, in England too. In addition to administering the courts, the merchants were the courts' heaviest users. They tended to be the initiators of suits at the other end of which were often retired Loyalist officers struggling to maintain payments. Merchants also tended to centralize court activities at Niagara, Kingston, and Detroit, thus making it impossible for rural settlers to enjoy equal ease of access. Costs, while cheap for merchants, tended to be high for rural dwellers. The general result was the strengthening and solidifying of merchant endeavours throughout the old Mississauga territory.[50]

The rules of the game changed somewhat following the passage of the Constitutional Act of 1791. It legislated the splitting of Quebec into Upper and Lower Canada, and the provision of an elected assembly and appointed councils in both colonies. The division hampered Upper Canadian commercial activity. Lacking a direct outlet to the sea, Upper Canadian merchants had to depend on Lower Canadians to handle imports from and exports to Great Britain, and in this situation the Upper Canadians were generally the junior partners. Moreover, the Upper Canadian commercial class had no means of developing port, canal, or general commercial infrastructures in the separate colony of Lower Canada. To the degree that such development lagged behind Upper Canadian needs (as it would), then local commercial growth was restricted.

From the merchants' point of view, a more immediate consequence of the Act was the arrival of Upper Canada's first Lieutenant Governor, John Graves Simcoe, a major in the Queen's Rangers during the Revolutionary War and a man who was determined to centralize control at the administrative capital (soon to be York) and in the process put merchants in their proper, subordinate place. This was no easy task. Although he tried, Simcoe was unable to alter significantly the structure of the provisioning trade. The army refused to buy small lots; many merchants were too distant from the posts to compete effectively; and established contacts and relationships were hard to break down. The core of the merchants' power lay outside Simcoe's political control. Men like Cartwright and Hamilton could to a great degree ignore the administrative capital: their power came from control of the developing economy with its links to army provisioning; from fur trading; and gradually after 1800, from the export to Lower Canada, the United States, and Great Britain of wheat and other food crops. Through their handling of debt and subcontracting of provisioning contracts, they could and did exercise patronage with which Simcoe, through his control of a relatively underdeveloped and nascent political system, could not as yet compete.

Simcoe, therefore, assiduously attempted to create a political system that would provide him with superior patronage powers. As a first step he restructured and centralized the old legal system based on regional Courts of Common Pleas. This system had permitted too much variance in decisions and allowed too much control to reside in the potentially self-interested hands of merchant jurists. Accordingly claiming that Upper Canadian settlers desired it (in Niagara bitter popular discontent did exist), he centralized the court system at York under the Court of the King's Bench, introduced British procedures and thus supplanted the regional and simplified structure which Hamilton, Cartwright, and other local merchants had operated since 1788.

Simcoe also implemented a centrally-controlled system of local government. To Courts of Quarter Sessions he appointed justices of the peace whose duties included some judicial responsibilities as well as administrative and patronage functions such as granting tavern licences and fair permits, appointing electoral returning officers, calling town and township meetings, and supervising financial matters, assessment collection and tax rates. At this point Simcoe came squarely up against the reality of merchant power. There were just too few people, other than merchants, of sufficient worth, talent and energy to fill the regional positions available. The structure Simcoe had hoped would provide the foundation for consolidating a patronage/clientage network exclusive of and competing with merchants had, ironically, to recognize commercial power as a prime criterion for place and prestige in early Upper Canada.

As in the Maritimes, Upper Canadian merchants exhibited a strong sense of regional loyalty. Men like Hamilton and Cartwright increasingly interpreted the wider world from the standpoint of a strong identification with local concerns, in contrast to British bureaucrats who struggled for preferment in York. York place-men looked almost exclusively to England for their current and, hopefully, future appointments. In this context they, rather than merchants, were the birds of passage. Despite these tensions, however, certain bonds united the emerging élite and separated it from the commonplace routine of Upper Canadian life. Large-scale land acquisition linked bureaucrats and merchants and separated them from most other Upper Canadian groups. The granting of huge land allotments to a relatively few well-connected and privileged Upper Canadians was part of a larger strategy. It reflected a concerted attempt on the part of Simcoe and the British government to create in rural Upper Canada a miniature replica of their understanding of British society. Land begot stability and denoted power. It could provide the foundation for the emergence of a landed gentry, if not hereditary then at least solidly entrenched, which could take its proper place atop a society characterized, in their words, by social gradations. This parcelling of land was meant to complement and buttress the political structure as set up by the Constitutional Act of 1791 (specifically the appointed councils and appointed Lieutenant Governor).

Initially Simcoe had no intention of including merchants within this landed élite. The fact that he did so reflected, not simply the realities of the local scene, but also the nature of élite life in Great Britain. By the late eighteenth century gentlemanly capitalism which linked large landed estates with market-oriented activity had become the touchstone for economic endeavour. Service sector enterprise—including government administrators, financiers and merchants—gradually became a part of this capitalist nexus. To the degree that an occupation or scale of income permitted a lifestyle similar to the conspicuous consumption practised by the landed nobility, the greater the place and prestige it carried.[51]

In Upper Canada a hereditary landed feudal class did not exist. It had to be created and if the result was only a pale reflection of British reality, the economic goals, social ideals, and political beliefs were similar. For all their differences, Hamilton and Simcoe were united in their pursuit of conspicuous consumption.

157

At Niagara, Hamilton owned what was reputedly Upper Canada's finest home. Simcoe could sup there at ease. A new Lieutenant Governor, Peter Hunter (1799-1805), had been commandant at Niagara and stationed at Montreal in the immediate post-Revolutionary years. He was well acquainted with the St Lawrence merchants, looking to them for assistance and providing them with appointments and patronage. These links between businessmen and bureaucrats were further solidified as relations with the United States deteriorated on the eve of the War of 1812. Merchants and York placemen rallied together to root out imagined and real American sympathizers within Upper Canada's largely American-born population.

Intermarriage further solidified the emerging élite and, at the same time, separated it from the mass of Upper Canada's settlers. Robert Hamilton, for example, constructed a closed network of family alliances centred at Niagara and linked by marriage to the Askins of Detroit. In addition to providing support for his large family of eight sons and one daughter, Hamilton brought four cousins over from Scotland and gave them a start in related commercial ventures. He also favoured a number of other recent Scots arrivals. Richard Cartwright dispensed favours to his cousins and son-in-law. Lesser merchants centred at smaller places, like the Nelles family at Grimsby and the Stone family at Gananoque, exhibited similar dynastic behaviour.

For many of these merchants, however, changing conditions had begun to undermine their economic base. In the early years of the nineteenth century the British military presence declined in Upper Canada. Moreover, with the growth of local agriculture, military needs could be more easily supplied by farms in close proximity to the posts. So, too, the fur trade began to wane. To survive, Hamilton had to extend his local trade; in 1803 he had 500 to 600 accounts scattered over 22 townships; by his death in 1809, 1,200 people owed him a staggering £69,000. Clearly his business had become much less focused on portaging goods along a southern frontier from Detroit to Montreal and supplying centrally located military depots. He may well have adjusted successfully had he lived, but his heirs failed to meet the challenge. The War of 1812 severed Upper Canada's link to the old western fur-trading outposts in the Michigan-Wisconsin region. Already weak, the Hamilton enterprises did not survive the physical devastation that the War wrought in the Niagara-Detroit region and they succumbed to bankruptcy.

Other merchants, resident in other posts of Upper Canada, did adjust to the economic transition and did, as Hamilton had in his early years, profit from war. Cartwright, who had moved his business affairs to Kingston in the mid-1790s, survived. Indeed, in the Kingston area, cross-border trade during the War of 1812 was facilitated by the fact that one of the men in charge of provisioning the British military was related to the officer in command of the American troops. They shared information and placed sentries at spots where commercial traffic never appeared. William Allan is a particularly interesting example. Like Hamilton and Cartwright, he cut his teeth on trade in the Niagara region in the late 1780s as a representative of a Montreal forwarding firm. Like Cartwright he moved in the mid 1790s, but to tiny York, the new Upper Canadian capital. As one of the first merchants there, with strong metropolitan connections to Montreal, he quickly prospered. By the War of 1812 he held many local posts, including that of post-master, and was well connected to the local and provincial political élite. During the War he profited handsomely from supplying the local commissariat with sup-plies at a 100 per cent mark-up. He assiduously rooted out dissenters and kept alert for treasonous activity. As the local government agent he felt frustrated that stronger measures for dealing with alleged spies, traitors, and the disloyal were not being implemented. For Allan and others at York, dissent could all too easily be equated with treason, political opposition with Americanization. His war activ-ities raised his value further in the eyes of the province's élite. Successful mer-chants around Burlington Bay at Dundas and Hamilton also benefited from strong metropolitan connections to Kingston, Montreal, and, often, Glasgow. The uncon-nected, inexperienced merchant had little chance of success in the small but devel-oping urban centres of Upper Canada. By the early 1820s, and in a fashion not at all dissimilar to the path taken by Hamilton, a new merchant élite stood close to the centre of the colony's power structure. Even as the fur trade and military provisioning were being supplanted by a more agrarian based economy, the road to preferment remained much the same. By 1820 a blend of bureaucrats and businessmen, not that much different from their pre-1812 predecessors, was plan-ning the colony's future.[52]

Before 1850, however, it would be misleading to speak of *a* business class in Upper Canada. As farming enterprise developed, throughout the colony nodes of commercial activity to service rural hinterlands emerged. Located in developing urban places like Hamilton, London, York, Kingston, Cobourg, Port Hope, and Port Stanley, these centres vied with each other for trade and economic power. While Hamilton, London, and Kingston, selected as regional administrative cen-tres, and York/Toronto as the province's capital and political centre were most favoured, all evolved similar urban élites and local governing structures at the heads of which stood men of commerce. In the 1820s merchants and other urban landowners throughout Upper Canada began to move away from Simcoe's system of civic rule by appointed magistrates operating through the Court of Quarter Sessions. A desire for increased efficiency — better roads, sanitation, regulated markets, fire control — underlay the community incorporation movement. Eight Upper Canadian centres incorporated in the 1830s and five more did so before 1847. Those who lobbied for incorporation quickly dominated the new structure. Two-thirds of the positions on the elected common councils and boards of police were held by merchants and lawyers in the 1830s. Between 1840 and 1860, 80 per cent of elected councillors in six urban centres were businessmen, just under 40 per cent of whom were merchants and 14 per cent of whom were manufac-turers, the rest being building contractors, other businessmen, and lawyers. High property qualifications kept the right to hold local office out of the reach of most urban dwellers. A high property qualification also restricted the municipal fran-chise. Well before 1850, and paralleling a similar development in Great Britain, the municipal state had become a closed preserve for business people and their allies.[53]

Business men acted swiftly to enhance their already considerable stature. In Hamilton in 1839 merchants headed over one-half of the 10 per cent of households with assessments totalling over £200; most of the rest were professional land developers and speculators. They dominated the Board of Police in the 1830s. They intermarried. They purchased pews and sat together at the respectable churches. They accepted, endorsed, and circulated each other's promissory notes. They lived apart from common labourers. When they finally succeeded in obtaining a chartered local bank, the Gore Bank, they treated it as York merchants treated theirs (see Sidelight, p. 174–5). In the 1830s they banded together to promote (unsuccessfully) a railroad. Some even began to sponsor the beginnings of some industry. Hamilton's commercial land-owning élite had its counterpart in emerging urban communities throughout Upper Canada.[54]

The issue of market regulation provides a useful perspective on the capitalist orientation of these urban élites. The honest and efficient sale of farm produce in growing urban centres was a central issue in town governance. The nature of regulations passed by town authorities, however, often benefited local businessmen more than local consumers. Market stall owners, not local consumers, lobbied most consistently for the apprehension and fining of unlicenced, non-market vendors. Many consumers, in fact, seem to have welcomed the decentralization and competition provided by itinerant salesmen. Yet for three reasons the town councils invariably supported the market. In the first place the town gained substantial revenue from the annual auctions and renting of stalls — this revenue represented 10 per cent of Toronto's income in 1838, for example. Secondly, by centrally locating the area's main mercantile business, the town consolidated its hold on the region's economy. Producers had to come to town to sell their produce. Finally, owners of many of the more prominent businesses surrounding the market — taverns, hardware and dry-goods stores — benefited from market activity and also sat on the town councils.

The emergence of a strongly regulated central market system in Upper Canada's towns occurred at the very moment when Great Britain and the United States were actively dismantling a similar system in favour of a more decentralized, *laissez-faire* commercial environment. This does not mean that Upper Canada was still rooted in a sort of medieval, pre-capitalist milieu. Rather the vitality of the market as institution reflected the wider processes of change sweeping Upper Canada in this period. These changes were actively desired by a middle class composed of market-oriented capitalist businessmen with eyes to the main chance. What was at work at the local level was the transmutation of medieval institutions — the incorporated borough and market — to serve élite needs in the context of an emerging modern economy.[55]

This trend to business dominance was also reflected in provincial politics. Before 1830 just under two-thirds of members of the house of assembly (MHAS) had been farmers at some stage in their career. Of those MHAS elected between 1830 and 1841, however, only a third had farmed and of that third, a full 50 per cent engaged in some other business pursuit. In fact, those who only pursued a commercial business career outnumbered by a two to one margin those who only farmed. Clearly MHAs reflected an emerging urban-oriented, business-minded, capitalistic society. It is especially interesting that businessmen predominated in the Conservative Party, a group often assumed to represent, in the Assembly, the presumed aristocratic 'non-capitalist' perspective of the office holding landed gentry. In the 1830s, 51 per cent of the elected Conservatives and only 26 per cent of the elected Reformers were businessmen or lawyers.[56]

From the outset merchants and their sympathizers sat on the appointed legislative and executive councils, the presumed preserve of the gentry. Hamilton and Cartwright were appointed councillors in the 1790s. William Allan was prominent on these bodies throughout the 1820s and 1830s. Gentlemanly capitalism permitted infrastructural development in the form of canals (the Welland and Rideau Canals), roads, and general public works. The government was even prepared to assist in the development of railways, conditional on the raising of private capital, which did not occur. Such development would facilitate rural growth. Between 1821 and 1838 the colonial government amassed a debt in excess of £1,000,000 in support of such ventures. The main purpose, as William Hamilton Merritt, a man adept at enlisting conciliar support for the Welland Canal, explained, 'was connecting the great chain of Lakes bordering on the Province with the Oceans'. Patrician landowners like John Beverley Robinson supported the emerging St Lawrence commercial system; for Robinson, that river had 'the pre-eminence over every other river in the world . . . it pursues its majestic course through fertile lands . . . which are distinguished by the language, the laws, the freedom, and the enterprize of the British race.' Far from being anti-development, Robinson, according to a recent study of his published law decisions, was 'a crucial . . . factor in the success of the St Lawrence commercial system'. He was knowledgeable concerning the general conduct of the wheat and flour trade and of land transactions and supportive of development in transportation, from roads to canals and railroads. While operating within the conservative and precedent-bound dictates of British common law, Robinson did help construct a standard legal framework within which Upper Canadian entrepreneurs could function. Firmly a member of the Family Compact, he also firmly believed that business growth was essential for Upper Canada's future.[57]

Upper Canada's historiography asserts the importance of the late 1840s and early 1850s as a significant turning point in the emergence of a modern economy and an expansive, speculative, thoroughly capitalist business élite. This perspective has merit. The dismantling of the old formal economic empire signalled by the ending of the Corn Laws, the Navigation Acts, and lumber preferences coupled with the introduction of responsible government seemed to shake old ways to the core. Railroads promised to revolutionize transportation and sense of time. As one aging member of the old ruling élite confessed, 'I find myself falling behind the age and cannot keep pace with the "March of Intellect".'[58] Yet Upper Canadian merchants and financial institutions survived the dismantlement of the old economic empire. While wheat exports to Great Britain shipped via the St

Lawrence decreased in 1847 and 1848, Upper Canadian wheat exports shipped to Great Britain via the Erie Canal more than compensated for that decline. Merchants and financial institutions experiencing some difficulty were those whose operations focused on milling and shipping wheat from the American mid-west to England via the St Lawrence. The Corn Laws had facilitated this by allowing all American wheat milled in the Canadas to be treated as Canadian wheat. With the repeal of the Corn Laws such privileged entry was no longer possible and, accordingly, some Canadian business financial interests lost money. But the St Lawrence canal system was not Upper Canada's Achilles' heel. The problem was rather one of focus. Those who overlooked Upper Canada's potential in favour of the seemingly richer fields of the American mid-west, had, in the late 1840s, to rethink their strategies.[59]

To a degree, dominant entrepreneurial styles did, however, seem to be undergoing change. William Allan, York's patriarchal merchant, had no patience with the speculative railroad promotions sponsored by merchants and landowners in Hamilton in the late 1840s. Clearly their attempt to raise money in England challenged his own initiative on behalf of Toronto. Yet more than traditional competition separated the Toronto and Hamilton promotional agendas. Hamilton promoters, men like Sir Allan Napier MacNab, a land speculator, general business promoter, and conservative politician, and wholesale merchants like Isaac and Peter Buchanan willingly associated with unscrupulous British promoters like George Hudson in their attempt to raise money for the Great Western Railroad. MacNab and the Buchanans speculated heavily in their railroad's stock. Allan, firmly in control of the Toronto and Lake Huron Railroad initiative, attempted to enlist the corporate backing of the Canada Company. All applicants for shares had to submit references testifying to their financial solidity and many would-be purchasers were refused. In the end, there was a downturn in the British economy, and both ventures failed to raise sufficient funds. While MacNab and Buchanan profited from their speculations and regrouped to form a new promotion, Allan determined to take all those who had reneged on their promise to purchase to court and, indeed, some were. This attitude parallels that of Robinson concerning mortgages: a gentlemanly capitalist should be as good as his word. It also echoes the pique felt by Allan when an earlier railroad promotion had failed in the 1830s. At that time, too, he had publicly stated that all defaulters should be sued.

The 'closed borough' style of entrepreneurship practised by gentlemanly capitalists situated at York was, indeed, being swept away. The next railroad scheme promoted by Toronto-based entrepreneurs was spearheaded by Frederick C. Capreol, an auctioneer and general businessman. He based his hopes for success on a 'Grand Canadian Railroad lottery'. Sons of old Family Compact leaders could support this, as one critic put it, 'temptation to attain wealth without labour', but the patriarchs themselves stood aloof.[60]

These moves to a more expansive and speculative business practice had their counterpart at the political level. Economic development increasingly became the major issue over which parties contended. Most members of the leading political party in 1854 could be classified as businessmen. So, too, could many of their opponents. Certainly men like the reformer, banker, and general financier Francis Hincks, or corporate lawyer, company director, and conservative John A. Macdonald, and others too numerous to mention emerged from a different socio-economic class than did many of those associated with the Compact. In this sense the Liberal leader in 1848, Robert Baldwin, gentry born and legally trained, remained closer to the politics and politicians of the pre-1840s than those of the post-1850s. Ambitious middle-class men moved even more to the fore in the 1850s. Old gentry families receded (some more slowly than others) from centre stage. Baldwin's resignation from politics and the assumption of reform leadership by Francis Hincks in 1851 neatly symbolize the transition from gentry to bourgeois rule. Some historians, however, push this notion of difference even farther and argue that a radically different set of policies accompanied the social transformation of political rule. The nature of these policies is most often encapsulated in the word, developmental. The easy assumption of state responsibility for railroad development and the attendant rapid growth of debt and rise of speculation, these historians argue, separate the pre-1840 from the post-1850 era. The former often is characterized as pre-capitalist, the latter as 'altogether capitalistic'.[61]

It is true that Baldwin exhibited a conservative stance on developmental issues. He opposed Hincks' measure to allow municipalities to borrow money for infrastructural growth. He spoke out against lotteries as a means for raising railroad capital and disagreed with Hincks' measures to support railroad development. Nor did he support a general Companies Incorporation Act even though 75 per cent of the MHAs from Upper Canada voted for it.

Baldwin represented one tendency visible in the pre-1840 era: a desire for moderate, balanced economic growth founded on landed property. Viewed from this perspective, the policies espoused by Hincks seemed reckless and speculative in nature. But did Baldwin and, indeed, William Allan, capture the spirit of the pre-1840 period any more completely than that of the emerging 1850 era? Even in the 1830s, under the shadow of York's leadership, speculative and shady investment schemes abounded. To take but one example, J.G. Bethune, a merchant and the Bank of Upper Canada's agent at Cobourg, invested money borrowed from the bank in a steamboat speculation despite Allan's express rules to the contrary. Bethune ended up in debtor's jail; the Bank lost some £9,000. In part because of this and other 'speculative' pressures, William Allan resigned as President of the Bank in 1835 and concentrated instead on the relatively sedate affairs of the British American Fire & Life Assurance Company.[62] At a broader level, a willingness to mortgage the state's future underlay even the Family Compact's economic policies. Canal and general infrastructural development depended on state money. Borrowing large sums from British sources began in the 1830s, not the 1850s. Not all pre-1840 political leaders were 'gentry' born. An important number had mercantile and financial expertise. Nor can differences between pre-1840 and post-1850 be caught by simply pointing to the nature of economic organization. In Upper Canada the use of chartered corporations for business purposes commenced in 1831—by 1837 the legislature had granted over forty such charters.

While the number of incorporations increased considerably by 1867, it represented a difference in degree, not kind.[63] Family Compact leadership presided over the beginning of a transformation in business organization from single owners, to partnership, to corporate entity. If the 1850s can be neatly represented by the steam engine, the 1830s were the decade of banks. In that decade no fewer than thirteen committees of the legislature investigated the workings of these financial organizations. In the 1850s even more committees focused on railroad operations. To subsume the characteristics of the pre-1840s under the term precapitalist is wrong. Capitalism was alive and well in Upper Canada before 1840. The political leadership of the 1850s reflected and reinforced the deepening of a trend evident at least by the commencement of canal construction in the 1820s, the transition from a commercial capitalist era to an industrial capitalist era. It is against the backdrop of continuity and gradual change that the business and political activities of the post-1850 entrepreneurial élite can be best understood.

RAILWAYS, INDUSTRY AND THE STATE, 1850–1871

The Canadas had failed in the late 1830s and late 1840s to raise start-up capital for railway construction. They could ill afford a third failure. Construction across the border to the south threatened the already beleaguered St Lawrence canal trade route. On a more local basis, railway lines represented the last hope that the many smaller Upper Canadian urban centres had of closing the widening gap between them and Toronto and Hamilton. Along Lake Ontario, Cobourg, Port Hope, Prescott, and Brockville entrepreneurs promoted railroads as did their counterparts in Hamilton and Toronto. Port Dover and Port Stanley on Lake Erie also joined in. These and other 'hinterland' lines represented about 20 per cent of the 1,411 miles of railway constructed in Upper Canada in the decade of the 1850s. The two major lines, the Great Western and the Grand Trunk, accounted for just over 60 per cent of that mileage, the rest being constructed by the Northern, out of Toronto, and the Buffalo and Lake Huron, linking Buffalo with the port of Goderich on Lake Huron. While these four lines did open up much local trade and stimulate hinterland development, their primary purpose was to link American routes on the eastern seaboard and New York State with lines running through Michigan and the Midwest to Chicago. Nor did the promotion of more local lines affect dramatically the structure of urban development. Rather those lines, for the most part, emerged from and consolidated the existing pattern. By 1860 the fifty largest urban centres in Ontario in 1981 were on at least one of the colony's rail lines.[64]

During the 1870s a second railway boom occurred. By 1871 the fringe agricultural areas of southern Ontario had developed sufficiently to warrant better transportation connections with established southern Ontario centres. If the 1850-57 period was characterized by the construction of large trunk or main line railroads—the basic structure of the Ontario system—the 1870s was the era of the feeder line. In that decade twenty-one new lines opened for business in Ontario, six of which radiated outwards from Toronto and Hamilton. By 1879, 3,250 miles of track overlay the province. Many of these lines had, even by the end of the decade, been taken over by the Grand Trunk or the Great Western, two fiercely competitive corporations. In the 1880s, with the construction of the Canadian Pacific Railway, the era of consolidation truly began. By the end of that decade, large national railways dominated the Ontario system.[65]

Railroads did facilitate some dispersal of urban peoples. An almost threefold increase of urban places between 1851 and 1871 testifies to that, as does the fact that Toronto and Hamilton's share of urban population declined from about one-third in 1851 to about one quarter in 1871 and 1881. Yet by the latter date, Toronto and Hamilton had maintained their positions as the largest urban centres while between 1861 and 1871 Kingston's population had actually begun to decline. Oakville, without a railroad, reached a peak in 1860 as did Brockville and Cobourg, even with railroads. By 1870 the urban pattern of contemporary southern Ontario was in place. Subsequent changes magnified rather than altered that pattern.

If railways did not transform urban patterns, they certainly challenged the collective abilities of the colonial business élite. An examination of that élite's response sheds much light on the strength and weaknesses of the local entrepreneurial community.[66] In the late 1840s, as the Toronto *Globe* remarked, many of the colony's 'active money-seeking businessmen' avoided railway promotion. This was especially true of the commercial community: only 15 per cent of railway directors before 1849 were merchants. This participation rate changed dramatically in the 1850s: during that decade merchants were never less than 42 per cent of all railway directors. Yet despite their numbers, many agreed with the wholesaler, Peter Buchanan, that 'To a man of business railway matters are a great curse.' Few stayed long in the director's seat: 32 per cent of the merchants left after one year, whereas only 16 per cent of the other directors stayed for less than two years. Nor did many merchants invest in railways: only two of the Northern railway's merchant directors had over £1000 invested in the road in 1857. T.C. Street, one of the wealthiest of Upper Canadian merchants, refused to invest in the Great Western, although he did in the smaller Erie and Ontario railway. While charters required that directors hold a minimum amount of stock, many railways attracted directors in part by giving or lending them stock free of charge.

What accounts for this rather cautious participation in the world of railway affairs? For many merchants, railways were simply extensions of their main business — as was shipping for maritime merchants. They looked on railways as a means of increasing their trade in the hinterland and making the import of goods more secure. Primary allegiance lay with traditional mercantile pursuits: Daniel MacNab, a wholesale hardware merchant in Hamilton, put his partner on the directorate of the Preston and Berlin railway simply, as he admitted, to represent the interests of 'Daniel MacNab & Co.'. This calculating nature is underlined when the rate of merchant participation is broken into time periods. Not until the government stepped in and passed the Guarantee Act in 1849, followed quickly by the creation of the Consolidated Municipal Loan Fund Act in 1850 and the further extension of government guarantees to principal as well as interest on railway bonds in 1852, did merchants become more actively involved. When prospects for substantial returns seemed reasonably secure, merchants lent a hand. Before that time few cared.

Merchant investment behaviour, it should be noted, differed not at all from that of other Upper Canadians. When Upper Canadians invested in railways, they did so for short-term speculative gain. Peter Buchanan made £3,500 in less than a month. Robert Harris said that he and his partners would invest £10,000 currency in Great Western stock: two years later he and his partner, Isaac Buchanan, held between them only 103 shares, barely half of which had been fully paid up. Of £622,700 of Grand Trunk Railway shares reserved for sale in Canada, few were purchased for investment: most were either defaulted on or dumped in London at reduced prices. In 1861 London investors believed that only one Canadian owned preference bonds, and that was to enable him to sue on behalf of the railway in a Canadian court.[67]

T.G. Ridout, longtime Cashier of the Bank of Upper Canada, was half right when he noted that local shareholders made most of their return by investing in areas opened up by railroads and thus could afford to sustain a loss on their shares. In fact, few even purchased shares. Smart local money went into areas developed by the railway, not into railways *per se*. George Brown, editor of the Toronto *Globe*, reform politician, and astute businessman, invested in the townsite of Bothwell and then successfully lobbied the Great Western Railway for a station on his undeveloped site. Not coincidentally, Brown's paper was an ardent propagandist for the Great Western. Nor is there any record of Brown ever investing in shares in that railway. Richard Juson, a Hamilton hardware wholesaler and a Great Western director for fifteen years, continually directed contracts his way. In the process, he diversified his operations from wholesaling into industry, as a manufacturer of nails and railway spikes. There are other examples of such diversification. Not investing directly in railways cannot be interpreted as being in any way opposed to industrial development.

If merchant participation was indirect and cautious, it was nonetheless significant. Benefiting from experience in the operation of their own businesses, merchant directors were adept at cultivating local financial support. The fact that 75 per cent of merchants were foreign-born and import-exporters broadened the networks upon which they could draw for assistance. Many successfully used contacts in England and the United States to draw in capital during the early years of railroad promotion. A particularly revealing example of such activity took place in the early promotions of the Great Western Railway. Peter and Isaac Buchanan and Robert Harris, partners in a wholesale firm at Hamilton, took advantage of the relatively loose links which existed between financiers on an international level to play American and British investors off against each other to their railway's advantage. In essence, they used a promised investment of $800,000 from American financiers, who assumed that they would then obtain firm control of the railway, as a base from which to gain entry into the lucrative British capital market from which, thanks to the American promises, they received far larger sums. The Americans had no idea that this was occurring until British commitments were firm and, more importantly, until they had invested all they had promised.[68]

The Great Western's promoters succeeded in large measure because of the nature of the international financial structure within which they manoeuvred. While financial links were developing between England and the United States, the era of coordinated international banking and investment projects was still some ten to fifteen years away. By then international banking houses, syndicate investment projects, and improved transatlantic communications severely limited such opportunities.[69] The absence of such systematic links and liaisons in the early 1850s facilitated a large amount of control on the part of shrewd Upper Canadian promoters.

When financing was in place, however, merchants were out of place. Few had the experience, time, or temperament to manage a railway in an operative state. Nor did the broader local entrepreneurial community offer much expertise in this respect. The commercially dominated Upper Canadian economy had spawned few large-scale companies before railways. Before 1840 British and American engineers had dominated canal construction and most of them had left the colony. Construction contracts for the Welland Canal were let by the government in small pieces: as a result in the 1840s few large locally-based contractors emerged within the country. With one or two exceptions, the local entrepreneurial community had to import expertise in order to construct and manage railways. In this sense, that community had yet to transcend its colonial roots.

Initially those experts were American engineers and contractors: they oversaw the construction of 50 per cent of all railroad mileage in Upper Canada (75 per cent if the British-constructed Grand Trunk is subtracted). American contractors hired American engineers who granted open-ended contracts. While it is difficult to find a definitive standard for measurement, it would nonetheless seem to be the case that the ensuing construction was unduly careless and expensive. Without doubt prices for wages and general supplies did increase due in part to the massive capital imports in the early 1850s. Yet such inflationary tendencies were unnecessarily exacerbated by, to take one example, the various manoeuvres of Samuel Zimmerman, an American contractor who built much of the Great Western's main line as well as playing a major role in the construction of six other Upper Canadian roads. Zimmerman used his power effectively. Aware, in October 1852, that the Great Western's merchant directors were being pressured by American investors to complete the road swiftly (in order to link Michigan and New York lines), he began to lag behind schedule. Although in violation of his contract, he was promised by the directors, on the advice of the Chief Engineer (a man Zimmerman had appointed) a bonus of $470,000 if he completed his section in a year's time. Beyond the fact that the bonus system encouraged others to 'bargain for it', the increased speed necessitated substantial hiring on short notice and thus contributed to a sudden and significant escalation of labour costs at a time of rapid inflation.

Indeed, Great Western costs were excessive even when measured against those of other Upper Canadian roads: it cost $66,700 to lay a mile of track on the Great

Western while other Upper Canadian railways averaged $49,000. A comparison with the per-mile costs in adjacent Ohio, Michigan, and Indiana suggests that high costs were systemic in Upper Canada: it cost the three American states an average of $35,000 per mile compared to Upper Canada's $51,000 per mile of track.[70] Moreover, the results did not warrant the high costs. A scant four years after completion, government inspectors deemed the Northern railway unfit for use, a fact not to be wondered at since the engineer, F.W. Cumberland, had received a $10,000 under-the-table payment from the contractors in return for which he sanctioned their speedy and careless efforts. The Great Western suffered a number of serious accidents during the first year of operation, many of which stemmed from poor construction. Nor were matters much better on the Grand Trunk, constructed under the aegis of Peto, Brassey, Betts and Jackson, a British-based and internationally experienced contracting company.[71]

Contractors and engineers were far from the only ones who padded their pockets at the expense of railway investors and the broader colonial public. By 1860 Sir Allan Napier MacNab had pocketed about $400,000 in modern values from a series of shady railway deals. Francis Hincks, John George Bowes, John A. Macdonald, Alexander Tilloch Galt, Luther Holton and other prominent Canadian politicians profited in similar ways from inside information and political positions. Even one Upper Canadian jurist, the old Family Compact member, John Beverley Robinson, was willing to condone the serving of two masters in order to facilitate railroad construction. Thus in a minority ruling he argued that John George Bowes, Mayor of Toronto, could keep profits derived from inside information because 'it was only by some such train being laid in advance of legislative measures . . . under the stimulus of personal gain, that the difficulty could have been met at the time.'[72]

This private peculation complemented profligate public spending. By 1852 the government, under Hincks' leadership, had put in place financial legislation which facilitated large-scale borrowing abroad. The Consolidated Municipal Loan Fund Act of 1852 allowed municipal governments to provide debenture aid for local transportation development, debentures that had the somewhat equivocal, but nonetheless real, backing of the provincial government. The Main Trunk Line of Railway Act in 1851 amended an 1849 Act which had provided government guarantees for the interest on all loans expended to construct roads of seventy-five or more miles and were half completed. The guarantee was extended to cover the principal and interest for the construction of the four largest railways in Canada.[73]

This enabling legislation certainly helped attract British capital in the favourable financial market of the early 1850s. Hincks had all along believed that, from the government's perspective, such debt would be indirect: the municipalities and railway companies would be sure to pay when due and the government would never be called as guarantor. How wrong he was! By 1859, acting under the Municipal Loan Fund Act, business leaders in twenty of Upper Canada's municipalities had borrowed 7.3 million dollars, representing a per capita debt ratio of approximately $81. Payments on 65 per cent of the 1.8 million dollars interest was overdue. For some municipalities, like St Catharines, borrowing under this Act represented only a fraction of total indebtedness. In 1859 St Catharines owed the Fund $238,535, but its local council admitted that the city owed more than $400,000 to its 'principal' creditors. The two largest cities, Toronto and Hamilton, borrowed immense sums under special legislation. When Hamilton's debt reached $50,000 in 1848 the local newspaper called for a stop: 'We should bless our stars that, like the tethered mule, they [the business-dominated city council] have gone the length of their rope.' By 1864 the province passed special legislation allowing the then nearly bankrupt city to issue debentures refinancing its three million dollar debt (a per capita debt ratio of $157). Clearly the 'mule' had run amuck in the 1850s. The provincial government also stepped in to protect Toronto's three million dollar indebtedness and the 7.3 million owed by other Upper Canadian municipalities. In the wake of this excessive expenditure urban services were cut back, less money was spent on sanitation, clean water, social assistance, fire protection, and health. Scattered evidence suggests that smaller municipalities may have been the most affected. Fires, for example, always a problem for mid-nineteenth century urban centres, devastated smaller, less well-equipped municipalities to a much greater degree than bigger centres. Impoverished municipalities had to increase taxes just to meet minimum payments on existing debt. The quality of life, especially for the urban poor, deteriorated as a result of excessive municipal expenditures made by urban businessmen on the eve of economic transition.[74]

Nor did railway companies fare any better. About $100 million was invested in Canadian railways during the 1850s, $70 million of which went to Upper Canada, most of which was expended between 1852 and 1856. This represented a per capita debt burden about 20 per cent in excess of the average for Ohio, Michigan, and Indiana in the same era. By the mid 1850s it had become clear that, like municipalities, railways could not meet their obligations. The three largest petitioned the government to pay their debt and provide them with new operating capital. Moreover, the Bank of Upper Canada, since 1850 the government's local banker, had become an essential component of a system that provided needed short-term financing for large capital intensive development projects. The government's London agents, Glyn Mills & Company and the Baring Brothers, relied on the colonial bank to supply capital when debentures could not be easily floated in England. By 1857 the government owed the Bank about $1.4 million and various railways owed it $205,000. Much of this debt was overdue and the Bank was on the verge of closing its doors. In order to maintain their own reputation in London, both Glyn and Baring underwrote debenture sales. Baring's personal investment reached $2,400,000, most of which related to the Grand Trunk. By the late 1850s, almost 50 per cent of government revenue went to meet interest payments on a large government debt, the greater part of which was occasioned by railway development. By that time private and public finances were, if not indistinguishable, well on the way to being so.[75]

In a context of escalating debt, careless workmanship, labour strikes, and a series of fatal railway accidents, the Canadian state began to clean its financial house. An audit department was created to control disbursements. A consolidated balance sheet, a statement which exhibited all the government's liabilities, was produced for the first time. Creative tariff measures were instituted which while raising revenue also paid particular attention to the developing demands of local industrialists for protection against foreign imports. Nor, in the context of these fiscal and social crises, were state measures restricted to traditional matters of public policy. It made no sense for the state to clean its own house and leave the operations of railways and banks, with which the state was intimately connected in financial and personal terms (many highly placed politicians sat on railway and bank boards), to run wild.

In the 1850s both the state and large private businesses were grappling with structural changes of a dramatic sort. Both railways and the government were beginning to professionalize and systematize their respective operations: to apply the method of the counting house and factory to their respective spheres. Managerial change and the implementation of a more bureaucratic procedure proceeded in both the public and private spheres. Indeed, British investors were swift in sending to the Canadas skilled British managers who, the investors hoped, would upgrade managerial control and operating systems. The Canadian state acted in a complementary fashion. The government passed legislation which pushed railroad management in the direction of more centralized and regimented control of labour and general operations. For a time the state's railway board employed a small staff of engineers to inspect and upgrade railway company procedures in these areas. The state also directly managed the reconstruction of the bankrupt Northern Railway and set general operating procedures for that road for the following twenty years.

In the first railway era the state supplied funds and acted as an ally to the self-serving interests of many railway promoters, financiers, and managers. The politician-entrepreneurs who headed the state often dabbled (some were immersed) in railway speculation and constantly safeguarded their own privileged positions in society. The legislation they passed facilitated the appropriation by management of past freedoms enjoyed by workers. Some legislation which moved in this direction was already in place. In 1845 the legislature had enacted 'An Act for the better preservation of the Peace and the prevention of Riots and violent Outrages at and near Public Works while in progress of construction'. The passage of 'A Master and Servant Act', in 1847, was designed to help control lumber workers in the Ottawa Valley and, more generally, to make any labourer or servant who quit work before the terms of his/her contract expired liable for criminal prosecution (should the 'Master' fire the worker without due cause, he was only liable for civil action).[76]

In the mid 1850s railway managers were ordered to construct detailed Rules and Regulations that spelled out exactly what each worker could and could not do. Railways could be shut down if such Rules were not published. Each Rule Book provided for fines and punishments to be exacted by the companies, not the state. Acting to protect the public from excessive carelessness, to maintain social stability in the colony as a whole, to safeguard its considerable investments, to facilitate further investment from abroad, and to protect its political future, the

Hamilton's Great Western Railway depot, 1860s. *(Stratford-Perth Archives)*

Canadian government helped move the colony from a predominantly commercial economic, social, and political environment to an increasingly industrial capitalist milieu.

It is important to emphasize that some restructuring of state and business enterprise did occur during the 1850s. The push for development capital emerged from within the colony and paralleled similar initiatives from nearby American states. The financial rules were set, to a surprising extent, by local political and merchant promoters. Once foreign capital reached the colony, British financiers held only a very limited control over its expenditure. Although many locals profited personally, they were unable to manage effectively capital expenditures during the construction era, or managerial processes during the early operational period. A combination of state legislation, regulation, and inspection and the importing of British managers helped to stabilize matters. Internal state procedures were also reorganized the better to meet the demands of an emerging industrial sphere and an increasingly complex international financial structure. The beginnings of an independent commercial policy, signalled by the implementation of a tariff structure that did not simply or solely favour British imports, was part of these changes.[77] Yet in all of this the state did not act as an independent broker, balancing the competing interests of labour, business, and general populist concerns within the contours of a market economy. In the pre-Confederation era, the business sector (while often divided amongst itself) had few real other rivals to contest its political influence. As a result, once the initial transitional crises were confronted the state was quite content to let its direct supervisory role lapse. As Ken Cruickshank has demonstrated, it was not until a coalition of opposed groups, that threatened political influence equal to that of railway corporations, emerged in the early twentieth century did the state once again, and on a more permanent basis, delegate significant power to a Board of Railway Commissioners to oversee affairs in that sector.[78] This is not to imply that a simple conspiracy theory can adequately explain the nature of business political development in this period. Such an interpretation would give too much foresight to those who participated in that process. Rather, local politicians and entrepreneurs (who were often but not always the same people) and British merchant bankers were, in effect, exploring new terrain. Out of that exploration emerged a more modern bourgeois state, one which provided the context for Confederation.[79]

In the 1850s, just as policies at the state and corporate level favoured various social groups at the expense of others, so, too, did the actual construction of railways alter the expectations of many locally or municipally focused businesspeople. Not all within the colony's broader business community benefited equally from the advent of railways. As railways broke down the relative geographic isolation of regional towns, local craftspeople were buffeted by competition from retailers selling similar products factory-produced outside the community. A few local producers could adapt and with the aid of railways ship and sell their products throughout the province. By 1870 the stereotype of a self-sufficient community producing goods for its own region had no basis in reality.

Structural changes facilitated the development of larger and more widely com-petitive business enterprises than those which had existed at the beginning of the 1850s. That these changes had a profound impact on the career expectancies of many artisans and prospective independent entrepreneurs can be demonstrated from the following case study of social transformation in the small industrializing town of Brantford.[80]

In Brantford at the beginning of the 1850s it was reasonable for an aggressive, ambitious individual to aspire to a career as an independent business person (4 per cent of the Brantford business community in the 1850s were women). As demand increased so, too, did the number of businesses. In fact, one study has concluded that the extent of self-employment in Brantford in the 1840s and 1850s blurred any class differences. The artisan and business classes were one. The depression of 1857 and the structural changes occasioned by railway expansion transformed this situation in the years between 1861 and 1880. Larger businesses resulted in a 40 per cent reduction in the number of business people active in the town. Increasing demand was now, more often than not, met by increased scale of operation rather than by increased number of operators. Smaller independent businesses and craft producers suffered most. Transiency in this group increased markedly. Rather than slip into the swelling proletarian ranks in the local area, failed entrepreneurs most often moved elsewhere— 'burst and gone' as the local credit reporter put it—perhaps to labour for a second chance.

It had always been a challenge to succeed in business. In the 1850s in Brantford and in Hamilton about 50 per cent of all businesses failed.[81] In Brantford, this percentage remained roughly the same for the next two decades. For Brantford, at least, these general figures mask a significant development: in the 1850s new and old businesses were equally likely to fail; in the 1860s and 70s two-thirds of all new businesses failed, whereas for the 1860s only about two-fifths and for the 1870s one quarter of old businesses went bankrupt.

These are suggestive trends. The high failure rate amongst established busi-nesses in the 1850s, the first era of railway building, points to the strains suffered by traditional businesses at a moment of structural change. This high rate of instability cannot be explained by referring to the cyclical and seasonal swings associated with a staple-based trading economy. Business failures affected more than individual entrepreneurs. For example, fifteen Upper Canadian chartered banks commenced operations before 1867. By 1870 only two remained in exis-tence. Nine of the thirteen failures occurred after 1850 and included the failure or takeover in a virtual bankrupt state of the colony's three oldest and largest banks: the Bank of Upper Canada, the Commercial Bank of the Midland District, and the Gore Bank. In other words, these failures occurred at a time when Upper Canada was moving from a mercantile-commercial to an industrial economy. Succeeding, in an era of transition, was by no means a sure thing.[82]

For the Commercial Bank and the Bank of Upper Canada, railway loans pre-cipitated failure. But both banks, and the Gore too, were over-extended to the wider mercantile community. Studies of the Bank of Upper Canada and the Gore Bank strongly suggest that major loans were made to well-connected friends, and

173

COMMERCIAL CAPITAL AT YORK/TORONTO

THE CASE OF THE BANK OF UPPER CANADA, 1821-34

The Bank of Upper Canada has most often been viewed through a political lens. Political connections are held to be responsible for its early success: nine of the first fifteen directors were on the Legislative or Executive Councils and several others held government appointments. There are two assumptions here: the first is that appointed councillors were never businessmen; the second is that the Bank profited primarily from government preferment. These assumptions permit a particular vision of a pre-capitalist agrarian-based society to remain unsullied. The reality is, however, somewhat different. Two-thirds of the fifty-three directors active between 1822 and 1840 had significant business and financial experience. Not only were merchants the largest single occupational group (21 of 53) but they tended to persist as directors for a longer period of time than those with other occupations. Merchants, along with men of other business experience, conducted the affairs of the Bank of Upper Canada.

In the period before 1841, the Bank of Upper Canada did not hold the main government account, that of the Receiver General, the rough equivalent of today's Minister of Finance. Rather the Receiver General kept those funds under his own personal control. In the late 1830s the Bank did receive the account of the Commissariat Department, but that account never represented more than 10 to 12 per cent of all deposits. It has often been alleged that the Bank loaned large sums to the government to finance casual and general infrastructural development and that these large outlays restricted mercantile business and thus retarded economic growth. In reality, the Bank acted as broker for government debentures. Between 1826 and 1834 it purchased some £180,327 of debentures and sold 94 per cent of them. Between 1824 and 1834, government debt fluctuated between 6 and 14 per cent of all debt owed the Bank. The Bank did benefit from government business, but such business was far overshadowed by its dealings with the general business community.

Some have argued that the Bank's commercial business dealings were conducted in a reckless and speculative manner. In fact, the Bank conducted its affairs in a manner very similar to that of other banks located in a frontier, capital-poor region. Banks in such areas tended to pay higher dividends and operate with lower specie reserve ratios (specie to notes outstanding: the so-called 'soundness school' of banking argues that reserves should be able to meet a high percentage of liabilities) than did banks in more established and developed centres. By creating money and credit in a capital-scarce region, such banks responded directly to local needs.

In the case of the Bank of Upper Canada, at least, the needs of those locals who lived in or around York-Toronto were looked after. York residents controlled much of the Bank's shares. Despite pressure from Kingston

In the pre-Confederation era banks printed their own money. The design of this Bank of Upper Canada bill captures the merging of agrarian and industrial worlds. *(National Currency Collection, Bank of Canada/James Zagon)*

and Niagara, William Allan, the Bank's president kept tight control over its agents' operations in those centres. This firm control over a small number of agencies served as a conservative counterweight to its expansive note issue policy. As importantly, it kept control of the colony's only bank at York. In times of economic downturn, discounts were suspended at the 'outposts' first and first recommenced at York. Very likely, too, York merchants benefited from a 'slow repayment' policy to an extent far greater than did merchants in other centres. A contemporary of Allan's once complimented him on his 'prudence in always having a *horse in the stable*', and the stable was the colony's capital.

Such control did not last. In the 1830s other urban centres like Hamilton and Kingston pressured the Legislative Council to pass enabling legislation sent to it from the Assembly to charter their own banks. Yet the Bank operated as a near monopoly in Upper Canada

for some twelve years. There can be little doubt but that York and its merchants and general businessmen benefited to a far greater extent than did their counterparts in other emerging urban centres. In fact one can safely conclude that this monopoly and its closed-preserve mode of operations contributed as much as York's rich hinterland and its position as capital, to that urban community's swift rise to dominance in Upper Canada.

Source

Baskerville. P., *The Bank of Upper Canada* (Ottawa, 1987).

to relatives of the bank directors. In this sense, one had to be of the right sort to receive significant financial backing.[83] Yet, after the economic collapse of 1857 many of those business people could not pay. In Brantford, alone, chartered banks lost $125,000 in 1858. David Burley, an historian, has argued that before 1857 loans were granted to applicants on the basis of their character, reputation, and community standing. This reflected a particular stereotype of the standard successful businessperson: an independent, hard-working family man. Credit reporters stressed personal qualities: if one were deficient in that sense, then, no matter how wealthy, the prospects for a good credit rating were slim. After 1857 the criteria for a good credit rating changed: one variable, that concerning one's financial and economic standing, dominated such evaluations. In order to receive credit even the wealthy had to provide collateral security, often in the form of real estate. Community standing and traditional measures of respectability were no longer sufficient in themselves to guarantee access to credit. Class standing measured by tangible indications of wealth rendered the pre-industrial business role model increasingly insufficient.

In this somewhat altered context, mortgage financing played an ever greater role in facilitating commercial and industrial expansion. In the past, banks had certainly loaned to commercial and industrial business people and received collateral security in the form of land and chattel mortgage. If Brantford is any guide, this practice became much more widespread following 1857. Mortgage debt increased as the city industrialized: in 1851 only 20 per cent of Brantford's business people had mortgages; by 1871, 35 per cent had mortgaged properties. Up to the early 1870s, mortgage debt financed the increase in the number of industrial enterprises. Some time in that decade mortgage debt began to facilitate the expansion of existing industries: by 1881 half the mortgage debt was owed by the wealthiest 10 per cent of the town's business people.[84] In the 1850s land acquisition could be thought of in two ways: it testified, in an eighteenth-century sense, to the business person's remaining a stable and permanent member of the community. Land acquisition could also be looked on as a way to bank one's capital. In a speculative atmosphere, what better prospective return was there than from land investment? A decade or so later land came to be viewed almost solely as a commodity, a form of economic rather than social collateral. And in this context land was less a place where one might bank one's capital and more a type of business capital, a means to facilitate general business ends.

One further implication might be drawn out of the Brantford experience. For those who survived the transitional era, future success was more assured. Most of those perched at the top in Brantford in 1881 had commenced their business careers in the 1840s and 1850s. As with agricultural success, an early start and persistence paid off. But also as in the rural sector, such upward mobility had, by the 1870s, become less and less possible. The gradually changing mode of credit giving gave the edge to existing wealth rather than prospective future success.

* * *

On the eve of 1870 most of Ontario's urban places retained their commercial orientation. While the number of industrial workers had doubled, between 1851 and 1871 their percentage of the total working population had increased by only one per cent. In 1850-51 manufacturing establishments were small, crafts-based, and dispersed throughout the agricultural population: only a little over 5 per cent were situated in the five largest urban centres and fully two-thirds of all manufacturing establishments listed in the 1851 census were saw or grist mills.[85] By 1870 thousands of small craft shops dominated the industrial landscape: 18,600 of Ontario's 21,730 industrial establishments employed five or fewer workers in that year. Four out of every five businesses produced less than $5,500 in goods per year and one-quarter of all firms produced less than $500. The average urban manufacturer employed only eight people and the average rural establishment employed only three workers. Moreover, two-fifths of Ontario's cities in 1870 employed less than 15 per cent of their population in industry. Finally, even as late as 1870 rural areas accounted for 68 per cent of industrial establishments and 42 per cent of the industrial labour force. Compared to modern day conceptions of industrial enterprise, Ontario's manufacturers remained small, dispersed, and relatively underdeveloped. Non-urban areas had not yet been 'ruralized'.[86]

But much had changed between 1850 and 1870. The industrial economy had become much more diverse. Saw and flour mills, for example, accounted for only 13 per cent of all industrial establishments. Local production of machinery, furniture, agricultural implements, boots and shoes, paper, woollens, and foundry products met close to 80 per cent of the province's needs.[87] This local production, it should be noted, greatly exceeded Maritime industry's ability to satisfy local markets. Moreover, industrial concerns were much less staple- and export-driven in Ontario than was the case in the Maritimes. Producer and consumer manufacturers, rather than export-staple industries, dominated the largest sixty industrial firms in Ontario in 1870. If small firms bulked large in terms of numbers, large firms dominated output: only 2 per cent of firms produced over $50,000 in annual output, but they accounted for 42 per cent of total production and 38 per cent of total value added.

By 1870, in fact, several distinguishing characteristics of twentieth-century Ontario's industrial structure were in place. Ontario had 51.8 per cent of Canada's total industrial production—by 1929 the figure was 53.3 per cent. Urban centres, in relation to population (under 24 per cent of the total population) claimed a disproportionate amount of industry: 38 per cent of establishments and 63 per cent of total industrial production. While in comparison to contemporary Ontario, industry was in 1870 still dispersed, it is nonetheless clear that concentration had begun: a pronounced trend existed towards the industrialization of urban centres. By 1870, two of these centres, Toronto and Hamilton, led in this area as they continue to do in the twentieth century: containing slightly less than one-quarter of Ontario's urban population, these two cities accounted for 30 per cent of urban industrial production, 31 per cent of urban industrial employment and 28 per cent of capital invested in industry in the Ontario urban system in 1870.[88] Larger firms tended to congregate in Toronto and Hamilton. Only one-third of urban industrial workers outside of these two cities worked in establishments employing more

Few pictures or drawings focus on the dismal working conditions inside such Victorian industrial establishments as this, the Toronto Rolling Mills in 1864. Most emphasize their sprawling exteriors; see the view of the Montreal Rolling Mills, p. 223. *(Metropolitan Toronto Library, J. Ross Robertson Collection/T10914)*

than fifty employees. In Hamilton, 55 per cent and in Toronto 58 per cent of industrial labourers worked in these large manufactures.[89]

During the next decade, industrial concentration increased even more dramatically. The Depression following 1873 led to many business failures in the agricultural implements, sawmilling, cotton, and foundry sectors, but while the number of firms declined, the number of employees and overall production increased in all of these areas. Consolidation and centralization of industrial capital characterized the 1870s and foreshadowed the more dramatic mergers and concentrations of the early twentieth century. Finally, in relative terms the present day distribution of manufacturing in southern Ontario had been put in place by 1880. A manufacturing belt from Oshawa west along the north shore of Lake Ontario into the middle of the Grand River Valley marked the zone of highest concentration. Relatively little industrial activity occurred in southwestern Ontario west of London and along the Lake Ontario-St Lawrence shorelines east of Oshawa, although, especially in eastern Ontario, many very small communities did centre on one or two industrial firms.[90]

Many historians have argued that a relatively buoyant agricultural economy up to the late 1850s created a demand for manufactured items.[91] Aggregate statistics are quite suggestive in this regard. By 1870 cash income per Ontario farm was 38 per cent greater than that for Quebec farms, 47 per cent greater than that for

New Brunswick farms, and 55 per cent in excess of that for farms in Nova Scotia.[92] It is assumed that this extra spending power had an impact throughout the economy. The fact that farm production of woollen textiles declined much more quickly in Ontario than in other British North American colonies tends to support this view.[93] Ontario farmers had money to buy, rather than make, their clothing and thus factory production was stimulated. Similarly, there are indications that farms mechanized more quickly in Ontario than elsewhere. By 1870 Ontario's farmers owned seven times as many reapers and mowers as their Quebec counterparts.[94]

While not doubting that the linkages between agricultural development and industrial growth are significant, there is some reason for thinking that other factors, yet to be systematically investigated, also helped to account for Canadian regional variations in business development. For example, in 1870 on a per capita basis manufacturing income in Ontario exceeded that of Quebec, New Brunswick, and Nova Scotia respectively by 18, 16, and 47 per cent.[95] These variations are not precisely what one might expect given the pattern of agricultural incomes. Kris Inwood and Tim Sullivan, two economic historians, comparing agricultural development and industrial growth for southern Ontario and selected border American states, have found that in relative terms between 1850 and 1890 Ontario's agriculture grew quickly, but its manufacturing grew slowly. They conclude that manufacturing growth cannot be seen as a simple response to agricultural growth.[96] Further work of an explicitly comparative nature, however, is required before one can say much more on the issues of causation.

In this context one would like to know more about the entrepreneurs who promoted industrial development in Upper Canada. Scattered evidence suggests that Upper Canadian merchants were more favourably disposed to industrial enterprise than their maritime counterparts appear to have been. Some merchants, like Isaac Buchanan, for example, were strong advocates of a protective tariff to encourage home manufacturers. While most historians believe that Upper Canadian merchants were quite willing to diversify into industrial endeavours or at least did not attempt to block such diversification, it nonetheless remains true that no study of a large group of Upper Canadian merchants comparable to that of Sutherland on Halifax and Acheson on Saint John exists. It may be that industrialists were primarily drawn from the crafts area, similar to the situation in Saint John. Given the data on industrial enterprise made available by the Bloomfield research, it should be possible to trace the background of industry owners and arrive at a more systematic answer to the merchant-industry relationship then is presently available.

The extent and pattern of railway construction was itself an important contributing factor to industrial growth. During the first railway era, Upper Canada received the lion's share of investment and laid more track than any other colony. Upper Canada's railroads, while far from profitable, did generate on average about twice as much revenue per mile as their much smaller Maritime counterparts.[97] Railways provided relatively cheap and efficient transportation which permitted manufacturers to extend their markets. Railways also created a demand for manufactured items. Rails, locomotives and all manner of hardware items began to be produced in the Canadas to help meet this demand. Perhaps most significantly, railways themselves became effective producers of many of the above items. The largest of these railroads, the Grand Trunk and the Great Western, ranked not only among the largest industrial plants in Canada before 1879, but were also in the lead in terms of managerial and technological expertise. They were the first large integrated — manufacturing, transportation, communication — industrial corporations to operate in the Canadas.[98]

If railways were a catalyst for industrial growth and to that extent help account for regional variations in such growth within Canada, railways might also help account for the relatively slow industrial growth in Ontario compared to that of many of its closest American border states. While at this stage of research this is a very speculative comment, it gains some credence when the amount of provincial subsidies for the construction of railways is taken into consideration. Recent work by Ann Carlos and Frank Lewis has suggested that the over 12 million in subsidies granted the Grand Trunk Railway by the provincial government 'might have been used more efficiently elsewhere in the economy'. Certainly the profitability of the Grand Trunk and the Great Western fell below that of many American railways for which comparable data is available. It may be, too, that the provincial guarantees encouraged investors to pour money into the Grand Trunk, not on the expectation that the company itself could provide a reasonable return, but rather that the government would ultimately honour its guarantee and protect the debenture investment, a scenario which did indeed take place. In this sense, the government encouraged a form of junk bond investment. Finally, Carlos and Lewis suggest that those who demanded railway services in the Canadas may not have received their money's worth from, especially, the Grand Trunk, at least compared to the larger 'social rates of return' generated by many American railways.[99]

Clearly the factors contributing to industrial growth take on different significances depending on the context within which they are placed. The role played by agriculture and railways in Ontario's early industrialization was undoubtedly important: the degree to which that relationship is seen as positive, however, varies according to whether such growth is viewed within a Canadian or an American frame.

It is sometimes implied, certainly in American business history literature, that railways were the first example of a large modern corporate organization and by implication, that other companies followed their lead.[100] In some ways, the Great Western and Grand Trunk railways do fit this model. They were in the forefront of managerial innovation and accounting control. They very quickly became large vertically integrated corporations which carried out their own repairs and constructed their own rolling stock, including engines. They managed large number of employees: in 1860 the Great Western employed 2,049 people and the Grand Trunk, 3,118. To control this large work force they utilized a combination of paternalism—uniforms, picnics, insurance plans, and housing—and strict regimentation—rule books and fines. In these respects railways were, indeed, at the vanguard of managerial and corporate change.[101]   Yet in the Canadian context, it would seem to have been a lonely position. There were few, if any, imitators. Only six of the sixty largest industrial firms in Ontario in 1871 were incorporated, and three of those were railroads. One of the others, the woollen enterprise of B.W. Rosamond and Co. of Almonte, remained firmly in the control of its family founders. Most were partnerships or sole proprietorships and in many of those cases kin relations played significant roles in managing the company.[102] Well over two-thirds of all incorporations before 1867 were in the areas of transportation or finance. None were in retailing or wholesaling and relatively few, between 10 and 15 per cent, were in manufacturing.[103] Moreover, only about one-third of the sixty largest industrial firms managed branch plants or a significantly diversified and extended operation. Most tended to focus on one enterprise in one central place. In this sense, their organizational structure remained simple and direct. For those who did expand into an integrated branch operation, managerial problems, as the case of Jacques and Hay outlined in the sidelight on pages 182–3 suggests, often proved close to insurmountable.

Nor, by 1870, had many industries followed the railways into the age of steam. Only 26 per cent of all establishments used other than hand power, and of those only 10 per cent used steam. But this statistic, by itself, understates the overall importance of steam and water powered industry: about one-half of all of Ontario's workers laboured in powered work places; such enterprises accounted for over three-quarters of fixed capital investment and over three-quarters of value-added output. In some cases, too, it should be noted, the use of steam may not have been the best economic choice. An interesting example of the persistence of old technology in the face of new is the longevity of the commercial sailing schooner on the Great Lakes. Grain, plaster, wood, and lumber of all sorts were primarily shipped in schooners, not steamboats, on the Great Lakes until late in the nineteenth century. Lower start-up costs, lower rates of depreciation and maintenance, and longer life made commercial schooners a better investment than steamboats. Sometimes the ignoring of technological change could be an example of sound entrepreneurial strategy.[104]

The industrialization process in Ontario did not follow a simple linear path from a small hand-driven artisanal craftshop to a large power-driven factory. In 1870 all industrial sectors contained a mix of craftshops, power-driven factories and manually-operated manufacturers. Some, like woollen, cotton and knitting mills and wood processing and paper mills, had a high proportion of operations in large power-driven factorylike settings. While most of these large factory operations were located in urban centres, there were important exceptions. In 1866, for example, the Rosamond family opened a new mill near Almonte, on the Mississippi River, which was six storeys high and 300 by 60 feet. A dye house, boiler house, business offices and warehouse complemented the central factory.[105]

Most other sectors, like cotton, chemicals, printing, furniture, and tobacco, contained a mix of large and small hand-driven manufacturers, artisanal craftshops, and some power-driven factories. The furniture sector is an excellent example of this mix and also raises some questions concerning the productivity gains

THE TROUBLED TRANSITION TO INTEGRATED MANAGEMENT

THE CASE OF JACQUES AND HAY

By 1870 Jacques and Hay, cabinet and furniture makers, had been in operation for thirty-five years.[1] Founded in Toronto, by the mid 1850s the company had become the largest factory in that city. Elizabeth and Gerald Bloomfield, using a multi-factor ranking procedure, classified Jacques and Hay (or Robert Hay and Company, after 1870) as the second largest industrial operation in Ontario in 1870.[2] Sandwiched between two railway companies—the Great Western headed the list and the Grand Trunk ranked third—Robert Hay and Company provides an excellent case study of managerial techniques in an era of economic transition. In terms of its personnel, business structure and managerial strategy, Robert Hay and Company reflects more accurately than do railroads the nature of industrial enterprise in Ontario at a time of transition from a commercial to an industrial milieu.

The company was founded and evolved to a position of stature in a fairly traditional fashion. Both of its founding owners were craftsmen who brought to the colony valuable cabinet-making experience learned in Scotland and England. Both worked in Toronto for several years under a master cabinetmaker before embarking on their own. This pattern of industrial development, especially in the cabinet- and furniture-making sector, was quite common, although Jacques and Hay were clearly exceptional in reaching the stature of enterprise they did. Jacques and Hay certainly had eyes for the main chance. They were quick to adopt technological changes in steam techno-

logy and implemented large-scale production methods wherever feasible. Yet the business structure within which they operated was also of a traditional sort. Despite the company's size—it employed 430 people, had a fixed capital investment of $400,000 and, in 1870, a production output of $500,000 —the business was run as a partnership. Jacques and Hay operated in the old-fashioned 'hands-on' way.

When the company decided, in 1854, to set up a branch at New Lowell, a village in Simcoe County forty-five miles north of Toronto, to supply the main operations with wood and furniture parts (a process of backward integration), Robert Hay sent his brother-in-law Peter Paton and his nephew, Robert Paton, to oversee the branch business. The intermixing of kin relations in business partnerships was, as we have noted elsewhere in this book, a well established *modus operandi*. In the case of Jacques and Hay, however, this very traditional strategy proved insufficient for the task of managing a newly 'integrated and spatially extensive enterprise'.[3] For the next nineteen years, Robert Hay sent letters decrying sloppy workmanship, careless ordering, poor packing, inefficient accounting, late order-filling, and a litany of other issues. Repeated personal visits seemed to do little good. Nor did the establishment of a telegraph office at New Lowell. The Patons were simply inefficient branch managers.

Yet, despite all, the Patons persisted. Kin triumphed over business efficiency. Both men hailed from Hay's hometown in Scotland. Traditional attitudes held that kin could be trusted, especially when business affairs were of a geographically extended nature. This almost perverse adherence to tradition is especially noteworthy in the case of Hay, because on other matters he had shown himself quick to adapt to change. Indeed the very experiment of backward linkage set his company apart from his competitors who located close to supplies or close to markets, but never close to both.

Ian Radforth has suggested that Robert Hay may have put up with the Patons because, in spite of the constant problems they caused, he may not have fully realized just how much their inefficiency was costing him. Not until four years after the branch had opened did Hay begin to keep a system of branch accounts. He admitted that 'the book-keeping part of the business has been too long delayed.' Yet, as Radforth notes, those books were probably insufficient. Cost accounting only began to be widely used in the 1880s: for the most part unit costs remained unknown to industrial managers in the mid-nineteenth century. In this respect, as in many others, railways were an exception. By at least the early 1870s, the Grand Trunk and Great Western managers had moved well beyond a simple double-entry bookkeeping system and had established a very effective set of cost accounting procedures that allowed them to chart costs at the unit level.[4] Despite his penchant for innovation, Hay failed to move in that direction. Nor did he establish any satisfactory means for managing at a distance. His experience was of the hands-on sort, and he adjusted only partially to a changing industrial milieu.

Radforth concludes his perceptive study of the Jacques and Hay firm with the speculation that the Patons may not have 'seriously affected' the business. Perhaps not. But another more qualified conclusion is possible. Jacques and Hay was by far the largest furniture- and cabinet-making concern in Ontario. Yet that it was not necessarily the most efficiently run and productively managed is suggested not only by the Paton problem but also by the fact that value added per worker in 1870 was $349, almost one-third lower than the industry average of $506 per worker.[5] Given the rudimentary accounting procedures used by the managers of Ontario's second largest business, this low rate of worker output may well have escaped their notice. Transition to modern industrial and financial management did not proceed at a swift, railway pace; rather, if the Jacques and Hay example is at all typical, even the most sophisticated and successful of mid-nineteenth-century industrial managers accomplished such change via a process of partial gains and slow advance: a process akin to groping in the dark.

Notes

[1]Ian Radforth, 'Confronting Distance: Managing Jacques and Hay New Lowell Operations, 1853-73' in P. Baskerville, ed., *Canadian Papers in Business History* (Victoria, 1989), 75-100.

[2]E. and G.T. Bloomfield, 'Industrial Leaders', *Canadian Industry in 1871*, Research Report #8 (Guelph, 1989), 12, Table 3.

[3]Radforth, 'Confronting Distance', 77.

[4]Paul Craven and Tom Traves, 'Canadian Railways as Manufacturers, 1850-1880', *CHA Historical Papers* (1983)', 279.

[5]Calculated from data in E. and G.T. Bloomfield, 'Industrial Leaders', 12, Table 3; 18, Table 12.

Table 9.2 Ontario's Cabinet and Furniture Making Sector, 1871

NO. OF WORKERS	NO. OF FIRMS	AVERAGE VALUE ADDED PER WORKER
Urban		
51+	4	480
26-50	9	406
6-25	56	589
1-5	164	528
Rural	333	489
Total Ontario	566	506

SOURCE: Condensed from E. and G.T. Bloomfield, 'Industrial Leaders: The Largest Manufacturing Firms of Ontario in 1871', *Canadian Industry in 1871*, Research Report #8 (Guelph, 1980), 49, Table 12.

generally assumed to be linked to steam and water versus hand power. Over one half of the 566 firms in this sector employed one or two workers and were located in rural areas. Seventy per cent of urban firms employed five or fewer workers. Only 21 per cent of firms operated with steam or water power, about the average for all Ontario industry. One might expect the technologically advanced and usually larger firms to be more productive, at least as measured by value added output per worker. But Hay and Company, the leading firm in this sector and the second leading industrial enterprise in Ontario, fell significantly below that sector's average output per worker. Interestingly, those firms powered by water or steam had an average value added of $498 per worker; those using hand power averaged $518 value added per worker.[106] Ontario's woollen mills, which were 100 per cent powered by water or steam, when ranked by size, also exhibit differences in value-added output per worker. The difference between those mills which were very large and the rest is suggestive. Contemporaries believed that small- or moderate-size mills were more efficient, and depending on what they meant by moderate-size firms, they may have had a point.[107] Those firms employing over 100 workers experienced an average value-added output per worker, $47 below the industry average. As Table 9.3 indicates, this output lagged behind that of all but the very smallest firms. (Not included in this evaluation are the numerous handloom weaving enterprises, which in Wellington County, for example, accounted for sixty-eight of some eighty-three textile enterprises.)

Clearly, studies of other sectors and more detailed studies of these are required. Current research cautions against generalizing too easily about the industrializing process in mid to late nineteenth-century Ontario. While in cities like Brantford (the seventh largest in Ontario in 1871) the business and labouring classes were significantly transformed by industrialism in this period, in many other cities and rural areas traditional craftshops persisted and prospered side by side with steam- and water-powered industrial factories. The change from a pre-industrial to a modern industrial structure did not occur at one time or in the same fashion whether one examines different industrial sectors or simply looks within a single

Table 9.3 Ontario's Woollen Industry, 1871

NO. OF WORKERS	NO. OF FIRMS	AVERAGE VALUE ADDED PER WORKER
100+	5	479
51-99	6	608
26-50	16	615
6-25	121	509
1-5	46	403
Total Ontario	194	526

SOURCE: Calculated from data in G.T. and E. Bloomfield, 'Water Wheels & Steam Engines, Powered Establishments of Ontario', *Canadian Industry in 1871*, Research Report #2 (Guelph, 1989), Appendix, Table A-9.

sector. The paths to the future were diverse and if by 1870 Ontario's industrial structure presaged that future, it also exhibited many links to the past. Ontario was truly at the point of economic transition.

Notes

[1]John McCallum, *Unequal Beginnings: Agriculture and Economic Development in Quebec and Ontario until 1870* (Toronto, 1980), 55, 129, 138–40. The best economic history of Upper Canada in this era is D. McCalla, *Planting the Province: The Economic History of Upper Canada, 1784–1870* (Toronto 1993).

[2]Kris Inwood and James R. Irwin, 'Canadian Regional Commodity Income Differences at Confederation', in K. Inwood, ed., *Farm, Factory and Fortune*, 102.

[3]Gordon Darroch, 'Class in 19th Century Central Ontario: A Reassessment of the Crisis and Demise of Small Producers during Early Industrialization 1861–71', *The Canadian Journal of Sociology* 13 (1988), 52.

[4]Cited in Peter A. Russell, 'Forest into Farmland: Upper Canadian Clearing Rates, 1822–1839', *Agricultural History* 57 (1983), 327.

[5]R. Ball, 'The Technology of Settlement and Land Clearing in Upper Canada Prior to 1840', (PhD diss., University of Toronto, 1979), 210. See also R.L. Jones, *History of Agriculture in Ontario, 1613–1886* (Toronto, 1946).

[6]Ibid., 184ff.

[7]Douglas McCalla, 'The Internal Economy of Upper Canada: New Evidence on Agricultural Marketing Before 1850', *Agricultural History* 59 (1985), Table One, 403.

[8]Jennifer Bunting, 'An Upper Canadian Merchant: John Benson of Napanee' (MA thesis, Queen's University, 1991), 57–9.

[9]McCalla, 'The Internal Economy . . . ' and 'Rural Credit and Rural Development in Upper Canada, 1790–1850', in R. Hall *et al.*, eds, *Patterns of the Past: Interpreting Ontario's History* (Toronto, 1988), 37–54; Bunting, 'An Upper Canadian Merchant', 45–7.

[10]McCalla, 'Rural Credit', 44; Brian Osborne, 'Trading on a Frontier: The Function of Peddlars, Markets and Fairs in 19th Century Ontario', in D. Akenson, ed., *Canadian Papers in Rural History* 2 (hereafter *CPRH*) (Gananoque, 1979), 63; Kenneth Kelly, 'The Development of Farm Produce Marketing Agencies and Competition Between Market Centres in Eastern Simcoe County, 1850–75', in *CPRH* 1 (1978), 67–88.

[11]Bunting, 'An Upper Canadian Merchant', 60–1; Kelly, 'The Development of Farm Produce', 71.

[12]Priestman to John Thompson, 13 January 1811, in '"Scratching Along Amongst the Stumps": Letters from Thomas Priestman, a Settler in the Niagara Peninsula, 1811–1839', ed. A.J.L. Winchester, *Ontario History*, 44.

[13]Laurie Leclair, 'The Huron-Wyandottes of Anderdon Township: A Case Study in Native Adaptation, 1710–1914' (MA thesis, University of Windsor, 1988) 20; J.K. Johnson, 'Land Policy and the Upper Canadian Élite Reconsidered: The Canada Emigration Association, 1840–41', in D. Keane and Colin Read, eds, *Old Ontario: Essays in Honour of J.M.S. Careless* (Toronto, 1990), 226–7.

[14]J. Clarke, 'Geographical Aspects of Land Speculation in Essex County to 1825: The Strategy of Particular Individuals' in K. Pryke, ed., *The Eastern District* (Essex County, 1983), 104–5.

[15]Laurie Leclair, 'The Huron-Wyandottes', 33; L.A. Johnson, 'Land Policy, Population Growth and Social Structure in the Home District, 1793–1851', *Ontario History* 63 (1971), 41–60; David Gagan, 'Property and "Interest": Some Preliminary Evidence of Land Speculation by the "Family Compact" in Upper Canada, 1820–40', *Ontario History* 70 (1978), 63–70; J. Clarke, 'The Role of Political Position and Family and Economic Linkage on Land Speculation in the Western District of Upper Canada, 1788–1895', *Canadian Geographer* 19 (1975), 18–34; and 'Geographical Aspects of Land Speculation', 69–112.

[16]G.J. Lockwood, *Montague: A Social History of an Irish Ontario Township, 1783–1980* (Kingston, 1980); Bunting, 'An Upper Canadian Merchant', 13–14; Bill Shannon, 'Brokers, Land Bankers and Birds of Evil Omen': Colonial Land Policies in Upper Canada, Collingwood Township, 1834–60' (MA thesis, University of Ottawa, 1990).

[17]Randy Widdis, 'Motivation and Scale: A Method of Identifying Land Speculators in Upper Canada', *Canadian Geographer* 23 (1979), 337–51; J. Clarke and Q.L. Brown, 'Pricing Decisions for Ontario Land: The Farm Community and the Speculator in Essex County During the First Half of the 19th Century', *Canadian Geographer* 31 (1987), 169–77.

[18]R.C.B. Risk, 'The Last Golden Age: Property and the Allocation of Losses in Ontario in the 19th Century', *University of Toronto Law Journal* (hereafter *UTLJ*) 27 (1977), 201.

[19]J.K. Johnson, 'Land Policy', 221–7.

[20]Clarence Karr, *The Canada Land Company: The Early Years* (Toronto, 1974).

[21]P. Baskerville, *The Bank of Upper Canada: A Collection of Documents* (Ottawa, 1987).

[22]David A. Bilak, 'The Law of the Land: Rural Debt and Private Land Transfer in Upper Canada, 1841–67', *Histoire sociale/Social History* (hereafter *Hs/SH*), 177–88, and David Gagan, 'The Security of Land: Mortgaging in Toronto Gore Township, 1835–1895' in

F.H. Armstrong *et al.*, eds, *Aspects of 19th Century Ontario* (Toronto, 1974), 135–53, are the main sources. But see also E. Brown, 'Equitable Jurisdiction and the Court of Chancery in Upper Canada', *Osgoode Hall Law Journal* 21 (1983), 279 and R.E. Ankli and K.J. Duncan, 'Farm Making Costs in Early Ontario', *CPRH* 4 (1985), 40.

[23]Bilak, 'The Law of the Land' and J. Clarke, 'Land and Law in Essex County: Malden Township and the Abstract Index to Deeds', *Hs/SH* 11 (1978), Table 2, 428.

[24]Bilak, 'Law of the Land', 186; P. George and P. Sworden, 'The Courts and the Development of Trade in Upper Canada, 1830–60', *Business History Review* 60 (1986), 273–4; R.C.B. Risk, 'The Last Golden Age', 208–9. For a somewhat different perspective, see M. Doucet and J. Weaver, *Housing the North American City* (Montreal/Kingston, 1991), 243–53.

[25]Doucet and Weaver, *Housing*, 248–9.

[26]P. George and P. Sworden, 'John Beverley Robinson and the Commercial Empire of the St Lawrence', *Research in Economic History* 11 (1988), 240, fn. 15.

[27]John Weaver, 'While Equity Slumbered: Creditor Advantage, A Capitalist Land Market, and Upper Canada's Missing Court', *Osgood Hall Law Journal*, 28, 4 (1990) 871–915.

[28]Douglas McCalla, 'The Wheat Staple and Upper Canadian Development', *Canadian Historical Association Historical Papers* (1978) 34–45; R.M. McInnis, 'Perspectives on Ontario Agriculture, 1815–1930', *CPRH* 8 (1992) 17–128.

[29]In addition to the citations in note 28, see McCalla, 'Internal Economy' and 'The "Loyalist" Economy of Upper Canada, 1784–1806', *Hs/SH* 16 (1983), 279–304; R. Ball, 'The Technology of Settlement'.

[30]Most of this argument can be found in sources cited in note 28. But see also Dennis Carter-Edwards, ' "Learning Soon the Modes of Carrying on Work Adapted to the County": Ethnicity and Agricultural Practices among the Glengarry Scots in 1851', unpublished paper, CHA, Kingston, 1991.

[31]McInnis, 'Perspectives on Ontario Agriculture', 86–8; R.E. Ankli, 'Ontario's Dairy Industry, 1880–1920', *CPRH* 8 (1992): 261–76.

[32]Marvin McInnis, 'Marketable Surpluses in Ontario Farming, 1860', *Social Science History* 8 (1984): 395–424.

[33]Darroch, 'Class in 19th Century Central Ontario', 60.

[34]Russell, 'Forest into Farmland', 328.

[35]W.L. Marr, 'Nineteenth Century Tenancy Rates in Ontario Counties, 1881 and 1891', *Journal of Social History* (1988), 753–63.

[36]D. Gagan, *Hopeful Travellers: Family Land and Social Change in Mid-Victorian Peel County, Canada West* (Toronto, 1981).

[37]Chad Gaffield, *Language, Schooling and Cultural conflict: The Origins of the French Language Conflict in Ontario* (Kingston/Montreal, 1987).

[38]McInnis, 'Perspectives on Ontario Agriculture', 56.

[39]D.A. Norris, 'Household and Transiency in a Loyalist Township: The People of Adolphustown, 1784–1822', *Hs/SH* 13 (1980), 399–416; Peter Russell, 'Emily Township: Pioneer Persistence to Equality?', *Hs/SH* 22 (1989), 317–32; Gordon Darroch and Lee Soltow, 'Inequality in Landed Wealth in Nineteenth Century Ontario: Structure and Access', *Canadian Review of Sociology and Anthropology* 29 (1992): 167–90, especially 177, 179–80. The landless household heads figure was obtained by subtracting this estimate of landless sons from total male rural landless.

[40]Douglas McCalla, 'Forest Products and Upper Canadian Development, 1815–46', *CHR* LXVIII (1987): 161, 167; C. Grant Head, 'An Introduction to Forest Exploitation in Nineteenth Century Ontario', in J. David Wood, ed., *Perspectives on Landscape and Settlement in Nineteenth Century Ontario* (Toronto, 1975), 78.

[41]J.K. Johnson, *Becoming Prominent: Regional Leadership in Upper Canada, 1791–1841* (Kingston/Montreal, 1989), 47; McCalla, 'Forest Products', 174.

[42]McCalla, 'Forest Products', *passim.*

[43]For Boyd, see D.J. Wurtele, 'Mossom Boyd: Lumber King of the Trent Valley', *Ontario History* L (1958): 177–89. For Calvin, see D. Swainson, 'D.D. Calvin,' *DCB* XI (Toronto, 1982), 139–41; C. Norman, 'A Company Community: Garden Island, Upper Canada at Mid-Century', *CPRH* 2 (1980), 113–34.

[44]John Keyes, 'The Dunn Family business, 1850–1914: The Trade in Square Timber at Quebec' (PhD diss., Laval, 1987), 149–55.

[45]Richard Reid, *The Upper Ottawa Valley to 1855: A Collection of Documents* (Toronto, 1990), xlvii–lxxiii.

[46]For Hamilton operations, see Peter Gillis, 'George Hamilton', *DCB* 7 (Toronto, 1988); 379–83; Gillis, 'John Hamilton', *DCB* 11 (Toronto, 1983), 379–81; McCalla, 'Forest Products', 190; Reid, *The Upper Ottawa* LXV, and E. and G.T. Bloomfield, 'The Industrial Leaders: The Largest Manufacturing Firms of Ontario in 1871', *Canada Industry in 1871* (Research Report #8) (Guelph, 1989), 12, Table 3; Robert Sweeny, 'Beyond the Staples: Firms and Functions of Lower Canadian International Trade' in R. Sweeny, *Protesting History* (Montreal, 1984), 93.

[47]Reid, *The Upper Ottawa* LXXII; E. and G.T. Bloomfield, 'The Industrial Leaders', 12, Table 3; R.P. Gillis, 'H.F. Bronson', *DCB* 11, 112–13.

[48]Reid, *The Upper Ottawa*, lxvi, lxix; McCalla, 'Forest Products', 186; Chad Gaffield, 'Boom or Bust: The Demography and Economy of the Lower Ottawa Valley in the Nineteenth Century', *CHA Historical Papers* (1982): 172–95.

[49]McCalla, 'Forest Products', 185–6, 194; McInnis, 'Perspectives on Ontario Agriculture', 47–8.

[50]Material in the early period is drawn from Bruce G. Wilson, *The Enterprises of Robert Hamilton: A Study of Wealth and Influence in Early Upper Canada, 1776–1812* (Ottawa, 1983); George Rawlyk and Janice Potter, 'Richard Cartwright', *DCB* 5 (1983), 167–72; W. Wylie, 'Instruments of Commerce and Authority: The Civil Courts in Upper Canada, 1789–1812', M.D. Flaherty, ed., *Essays in the History of Canadian Law* 2 (Toronto, 1983), 3–48.

[51]P.J. Cain and A.G. Hopkins, 'Gentlemanly Capitalism and British Expansion Overseas: The Old Colonial System, 1688–1850', *Economic History Review* 39 (1986), 501–25.

[52]Jean-Claude Robert, 'Horatio Gates', *DCB* 6, 278; 'William Allan', *DCB* 8 (Toronto 1985), 4–13; M. Doucet and J. Weaver, 'Town Fathers and Urban Continuity: The Roots of Community Power and Physical Form in Hamilton Upper Canada, in the 1830s', *Urban History Review* 13 (1984), 75–90; P. Baskerville, 'Entrepreneurship and the Family Compact, York/Toronto, 1822–1855', *Urban History Review* 9 (1981), 15–34.

[53]W.T. Matthews, 'By and For the Large Propertied Interests: The Dynamics of Local Government in Six Upper Canadian Towns during the Era of Commercial Capitalism' (PhD diss., McMaster University, 1985).

[54]Doucet and Weaver, 'Town Fathers and Urban Continuity'.

[55]Matthews, 'By and For the Large Propertied Interests', Chapter 3.

[56]J.K. Johnson, *Becoming Prominent: Regional Leadership in Upper Canada, 1791–1841* (Kingston/Montreal, 1980), 142, 159 (my calculations based on material in Appendix, 169–238). For 'anti-capitalist' view, see M.S. Cross, '1837: The Necessary Failure', in M.S. Cross and G.S. Kealey, eds, *Pre-Industrial Canada, 1760–1849* (Toronto 1982), 156–7.

[57]J.J. Talman, 'William Hamilton Merritt', *DCB* 9 (Toronto, 1976), 544–6; H.G.J. Aitken, *The Welland Canal Company: A Study in Canadian Enterprise* (Cambridge, 1954); P. George and P. Sworden, 'John Beverley Robinson and the Commercial . . . ', 218–19.

[58]Baskerville, 'Entrepreneurship and the Family Compact', 20.

[59]Baskerville, *The Bank of Upper Canada*; D. McCalla, *The Upper Canada Trade: A Study of the Buchanan's Business, 1834–72* (Toronto, 1979); J. McCallum, *Unequal Beginnings*.

[60]Baskerville, 'Entrepreneurship and the Family Compact'.

[61]Bruce Walton, '"We shall have plenty of money here": Francis Hincks, British Capital and Canadian Railway Policy, 1848–53', unpublished CHA paper (1987), 13; Cross, '1837: A Necessary Failure'; W.T. Easterbrook, 'Long Period Comparative Study: Some Historical Cases', *Journal of Economic History*, 17, 571–95; H.C. Pentland, 'How the Wealth was Won', *Canadian Forum*, (September 1972), 9.

[62]P. Baskerville, 'The Entrepreneur and the Metropolitan Impulse: James Grey Bethune and Cobourg, 1825–36', in J. Petryshyn, ed., *Victorian Cobourg: A Nineteenth Century Profile* (Belleville, 1976), 56–70 and P. Baskerville, 'Donald Bethune's Steamboat Business: A Study of Upper Canadian Commercial and Financial Practice', *Ontario History* LXVII (1975), 135–49.

[63]R.C.B. Risk, 'The Nineteenth Century Foundations of the Business Corporation in Ontario', *University of Toronto Law Journal* 23 (1973), 270–2.

[64]Douglas McCalla, 'Railways and the Development of Canada West, 1850–70', in Allan Greer and Ian Radforth, eds, *Colonial Leviathan: State Formation in Mid-Nineteenth Century Canada* (Toronto, 1992), 192–229, especially Table 7:1, 210 and fn. 47.

[65]P. Baskerville, 'Americans in Britain's Backyard: The Railway Era in Upper Canada, 1850–1880', *Business History Review* LV (1981), 314–36; P.J. Stoddart, 'The Develop-

ment of the Southern Ontario Steam Railway Network under Competitive Conditions, 1830–1914' (MA thesis, University of Guelph, 1976).

[66]Much of the following discussion is drawn from material in P. Baskerville, 'Americans in Britain's Backyard'; 'Professional vs Proprietor: Power Distribution in the Railroad World of Upper Canada/Ontario 1850–81', *Historical Papers* 1978; and 'Transportation, Social Change and State Formation, Upper Canada, 1841–64' in Greer and Radforth, eds, *Colonial Leviathan*, 230–56.

[67]D.C.M. Platt and Jeremy Adelman, 'London Merchant Bankers in the First Phase of Heavy Borrowing: The Grand Trunk Railway of Canada', *Journal of Imperial and Commonwealth History* 18 (1990): 219–20.

[68]For the British side of their promotional activities, see D. McCalla, 'Peter Buchanan, London Agent for the Great Western Railway of Canada' in D.S. Macmillan, ed., *Canadian Business History: Selected Studies, 1497–1971* (Toronto, 1972), 197–216.

[69]For the later period, see Dolores Greenberg, 'A Study of Capital Alliances: The St Paul and Pacific', *Canadian Historical Review* LVII (1976), 25–9.

[70]Calculation of expenditure per mile from data in D. McCalla, 'Railways and the Development', Table 7:3, 211.

[71]For the Grand Trunk, see A.W. Currie, *The Grand Trunk Railway of Canada* (Toronto, 1957), 51–6; for the other railways, see citations in footnote 53 above.

[72]Henry C. Klassen, 'Luther Holton: Mid-Century Montreal Railway Man', *Revue de l'Université d'Ottawa/University of Ottawa Quarterly* 52 (1981), 316–39; P. Baskerville, 'Sir Allan Napier MacNab', *DCB* 9 (1976), 519–27; Baskerville, 'Entrepreneurship and the Family Compact', 26. For a somewhat different perspective on Robinson and railways, see Paul Romney, '"The Ten Thousand Pound Job": Political Corruption, Equitable Jurisdiction and the Public Interest in Upper Canada, 1852–56' in D. Flaherty, ed., *Essays in the History of Canadian Law* 2 (Toronto, 1983), 143–99.

[73]Michael J. Piva, 'Continuity and Crisis: Francis Hincks and Canadian Economic Policy', *Canadian Historical Review* 66 (1985), 185–210.

[74]Data calculated from information in W.T. Matthews, 'By and For the Large Properties' Interests', especially 362–4. On fires, see D.A. Norris, 'Flightless Phoenix: Fire Risks and Fire Insurance in Urban Canada, 1882–86', *Urban History Review* 16 (1987).

[75]For the bank's involvement, see Baskerville, *The Bank of Upper Canada*; for Baring's, see Platt and Adelmar, 'London Merchant Bankers . . . '; for American debt comparison, see McCalla, 'Railways and the Development . . . '; for the nature of government debt, see Michael Piva, 'Government Finance and the Development of the Canadian State' in Greer and Radforth, eds, *Colonial Leviathan*, 257–83.

[76]Paul Craven, 'The Law of Master and Servant in Mid Nineteenth Century Ontario', in D. Flaherty, ed., *Essays in the History of Canadian Law* 1 (Toronto, 1981), 175–211 and 'The Meaning of Misadventure: The Baptiste Creek Railway Disaster of 1854 and Its Aftermath', in R. Hall *et al.*, *Patterns of the Past*, 108–29.

[77]D.F. Barnett, 'The Galt Tariff: Incidental or Effective Protection?', *Canadian Journal of Economics* 9 (1976), 389–407; A.A. den Otter, 'Alexander Galt, the 1859 Tariff and Cana-

dian Economic Nationalism', *Canadian Historical Review* 63 (1982), 151–78; and Michael Piva, 'Government Finance . . . ,' 270–4.

[78]Ken Cruickshank, 'The Transportation Revolution and Its Consequences: The Railway Freight Rate Controversy in the Late Nineteenth Century', *CHA Historical Papers* (1987), 112–37.

[79]The notion of collaboration which underlies British-colonial interaction in this period is explored in P. Baskerville, 'Imperial Agendas and "Disloyal" Collaborators: Decolonization and the John Sandfield Macdonald Ministries, 1862–64' in D. Keane and C. Read, eds, *Old Ontario*, 234–56.

[80]For Brantford, see D.G. Burley, 'The Businessmen of Brantford Ontario: Self-Employment in a Mid-Nineteenth Century Town' (PhD diss., McMaster University, 1983).

[81]For Hamilton, see M. Katz, *The People of Hamilton Canada West: Family and Class in a Mid-Nineteenth Century City* (Baton, 1975), Ch. 4.

[82]P. Baskerville, 'Banking on It: Banking in Pre-Confederation Canada', *Horizon Canada* 10 (1987).

[83]P. Baskerville, *The Bank of Upper Canada*; Doucet and Weaver, 'Town Fathers and Urban Continuity'.

[84]David Burley, ''Good for all he would ask': Credit and Debt in the Transition to Industrial Capitalism—The Case of Mid-Nineteenth Century Brantford, Ontario', *Hs/SH* 20 (1987), 79–100 and 'The Businessmen of Brantford, Ontario'.

[85]L.A. Johnson, 'Independent Commodity Production: Mode of Production or Capitalist Class Formation?', *Studies in Political Economy* 6 (1981).

[86]Elizabeth and G.T. Bloomfield, 'The Ontario Urban System at the Onset of the Industrial Era', *Canadian Industry in 1871*, Research Report #3 (Guelph, 1989), 63.

[87]The 13 per cent figure is computed from data in E. and G.T. Bloomfield, 'Water Wheels and Steam Engines: Powered Establishments of Ontario', *Canadian Industry in 1871*, Research Report #2 (Guelph, 1989), 12, Table 4 and 'Industrial Leaders: The Largest Manufacturing Firms of Ontario in 1871', *Canadian Industry in 1871*, Research Report #8 (Guelph, 1989), 43, Table 9. O.J. McDiarmid, *Commercial Policy in the Canadian Economy* (Cambridge, 1946).

[88]E. and G.T. Bloomfield, 'Industrial Leaders' 29–30.

[89]These figures can be found in E. and G.T. Bloomfield, 'The Ontario Urban System', 5, 29, Table 8 and 'Industrial Leaders', 14, Table 5.

[90]J.M. Gilmour, *Spatial Evolution of Manufacturing: Southern Ontario, 1851–91* (Toronto, 1972).

[91]Most notably, J. McCallum, *Unequal Beginnings*.

[92]Calculated from Inwood and Irwin, 'Canadian Regional Commodity Differences', Table 3, 105.

[93]Janine Grant and Kris Inwood, 'Gender and Organization in the Canadian Cloth Industry, 1870' in P. Baskerville, ed., *Canadian Papers in Business History* 1 (Victoria, 1989), 17–32.

[94]J. McCallum, *Unequal Beginnings*, 88.

[95]Calculated from Inwood and Irwin, 'Canadian Regional Commodity Income', Table 2.

[96]K. Inwood and T. Sullivan, 'Comparative Perspectives on Nineteenth Century Growth: Ontario in the Great Lakes Region', in P. Baskerville, ed., *Canadian Papers in Business History* 2 (Victoria, 1993), 71–102.

[97]McCalla, 'Railways and the Development', 203, 227.

[98]Paul Craven and Tom Traves, 'Canadian Railways as Manufacturers, 1850–1880', *CHA Historical Papers* (1983), 254–81.

[99]Ann Carlos and Frank Lewis, 'The Profitability of Early Canadian Railroads: Evidence from the Grand Trunk and Great Western Railway Companies', in C. Goldin and H. Rockoff, eds, *Strategic Factors in American Economic History* (Chicago, 1992), 401–26.

[100]Alfred D. Chandler, Jr, *The Visible Hand, The Managerial Revolution in American Business* (Cambridge, 1976).

[101]Craven and Traves, 'Canadian Railways as Manufacturers'. Employment figures from McCalla, 'Railways and Development', 211, Table 7: 3.

[102]E. and G.T. Bloomfield, 'Industrial Leaders'; R. Reid, 'The Rosamond Woollen Company of Almonte: Industrial Development in a Rural Setting', *Ontario History* 75 (1983), 266–89.

[103]R.C.B. Risk, 'The Nineteenth Century Foundation', 301, 304–5.

[104]G.T. Bloomfield and Elizabeth Bloomfield, 'Water Wheels', 8, Table One and 'The Hum of Industry: Millers, Manufacturers and Artisans of Wellington County', *Canadian Industry in 1871*, Research Report #9 (Guelph, 1989), 42, Table 13. M.E. Davidson, 'Changing Patterns of Great Lakes Vessel Ownership as a Factor in the Economic Development of Toronto, 1850–60', *Urban History Review* 16 (1988), 242–54.

[105]Reid, 'Rosamond Woollen Company', 270.

[106]See Table 2 and E. and G.T. Bloomfield, 'Industrial Leaders', 49–52.

[107]Reid, 'Rosamond Woollen Company', 277 and 288.

10 FARM, FACTORY, AND FINANCE: LOWER CANADA/QUEBEC

Traditionally, links to external, primarily staple-dominated trades firmly in the hands of anglophones in Montreal, Quebec, and British cities were assumed to have set the pace for business and economic growth in Lower Canada/ Quebec. There appeared to be a sharp contrast between anglophone and francophone entrepreneurship: the former was seen as aggressive, innovative, forward-looking; the latter more timid, conservative, reflective of a feudal past rather than a capitalist future. There seemed, as well, to be a sharp contrast between country and city and to an equally distinct demarcation within rural regions. Business action centred in cities; rural areas tended to be backwaters, for much of the period under review firmly in the grip of the Old-World, feudal-like seigneurial system. Anglophone farmers were thought to be at the root of any dynamism in rural regions; francophone farming habits were deemed to be wasteful, unproductive, and resistant to change. Constrained by the Coutume de Paris —which decreed that all sons and daughters must share equally in all estates— and excelling in fecundity, habitant farmers could not, the traditional historiography held, break a cycle of subsistence farming on ever smaller strips of land.[1]

This interpretative frame held sway until the 1960s, the era of Quebec's Quiet Revolution. After Quebecois began to take charge of their economy and political bureaucracy in the 1960s, historians sought for the past roots of such behaviour and found that those roots extended beyond the nineteenth century. Some provided a more nuanced picture within the traditional framework of staple-led business growth. Francophones as well as anglophones were credited with innovative and appropriate business behaviour in rural and urban contexts. Influenced by an international literature which attributes to peasant behaviour a rational and even entrepreneurial character, historians have argued that modernization did not bypass but transformed the habitant.[2]

Some argue that this transformation occurred quickly, that modernization was well in place by the eve of the Rebellion of 1837. Others argue for a less revolutionary development path, a route characterized by stops and starts and by much continuity even in the midst of change.[3] Historians, associated most especially with the Montreal Business History Project, have drawn on a related international literature which credits city-country regional relations with prime importance in influencing economic and business development and have applied these insights to an investigation of Montreal's economic and business evolution.[4] Increasingly, historians exploring the nature of entrepreneurial development within Lower Canada/Quebec see external forces and staple linkages as important, but by no means determinative: local human agency, operating within a context of 'bounded rationality', takes centre stage. Such a perspective sits well with a central orientation of this study of business in pre-Confederation Canada: an emphasis on the importance of regional context to an understanding of business relations. Such an approach can usefully highlight regional differences—as between the Maritimes and Upper Canada, for example. In many ways the situation in Lower Canada represented a mid point between those regions, a point defined more by staples and external linkages than was the case in Upper Canada and more by internal economic agency than was the case in much of the Maritimes.

RURAL BUSINESS: 1791–1850

Like nineteenth-century Upper Canadians and Maritimers, most nineteenth-century Lower Canadians lived in rural areas. Even in 1871, agricultural production accounted for almost one-half of all per capita commodity income.[5] While the number of industrial workers increased between 1851 and 1871, those workers still represented only a small percentage of the province's working population in 1871. As in the Maritimes and Ontario so, too, in Lower Canada, in order to understand the broad picture of business development an appreciation of rural business is essential.

That a crisis occurred within Lower Canada's farming sector in the early nineteenth century is a notion strongly embedded in the historical literature. Indeed most writing takes such a crisis as a point of departure, rather than as an hypothesis to be explored. In this context much emphasis has been placed on a presumed superiority of English over French Canadian farmers.[6] While two-thirds of all English-speaking Lower Canadians lived in rural areas in the mid 1840s, they only represented about one-fifth of all the colony's rural dwellers. If it could be shown that they farmed in a manner superior to the French, then one important factor in the crisis must reside in the nature of French Canadian farming practices. Some have attributed such a presumed superiority to the simple unwillingness of habitant farmers, content with a bare-subsistence life, to farm scientifically. More sophisticated proponents of the superiority argument point to a higher illiteracy rate among French Canadian farmers and to the fact that much information on 'modern' farming was being disseminated in English. Reference is also made to the alleged existence of smaller farm sizes and larger families in the French as compared to the English sector, the smaller sized farm being more difficult to exploit in a 'modern' manner. Marvin McInnis and Frank Lewis, two economic historians, have subjected these and related hypotheses to a systematic evaluation primarily based on a sophisticated reconstruction of information in the 1851 Canadian census. Their results, while not unchallenged, represent the most comprehensive evaluation of Lower Canadian agriculture yet available. Their most important finding was simply the great variability in production within both English and French areas. While, on average, they found the English to have a slight superiority in production, the significance of the average results was overshadowed by stronger variations within each ethnic group as opposed to between them. Agricultural production in Lower Canada was not all of a piece. Despite traditional literature's tendency to generalize broadly about farming, the reality is

194

Table 10.1 Lower Canada: Population Growth, 1791-1881

	TOTAL	% FRENCH		% ENGLISH		% URBAN		% RURAL	
1791	165,000	94	(155,100)	6	(9,900)	6	(9,900)	94	(155,100)
1815	335,000	88	(294,800)	12	(40,200)	11	(36,850)	89	(298,150)
1831	512,000	82	(419,840)	18	(92,160)	11	(56,320)	89	(455,680)
1844	691,200	75	(518,400)	25	(172,800)	12	(82,944)	88	(608,256) est.
1851	890,000	75	(667,500)	25	(222,500)	13	(115,700)	87	(774,300)
1871	1,191,516	80	(950,000)	20	(241,516)	23	(271,851)	77	(919,665)
1881	1,359,000	80	(1,080,000)	20	(279,000)	28	(378,500)	72	(980,500)

SOURCES: Serge Courville, 'Un Monde Rural en Mutation: Le Bas-Canada dans la Première Moitié du xixᵉ Siècle', *Hs/SH* 40 (1987), 244, Table 1; R.C. Harris, ed., *Historical Atlas of Canada* 1 (Toronto, 1987), 117; R. Rudin, *The Forgotten Quebecers: A History of English-Speaking Quebec, 1759-1980* (Quebec, 1985), 28, Table 1.1.

closer to one of significant variations in crops planted, in general net output figures, and in behaviours among rather than between francophone and anglophone farmers.

These findings are very useful but they do not confront the notion of crisis. The argument for such a crisis focuses on the declining state of Lower Canadian wheat production. Such production did indeed dramatically decline. Wheat production, from 60 to 70 per cent of field crop output in the late eighteenth century, fell to less than 15 per cent by 1844.[7] McInnis found that net output per farm in Upper Canada in 1851 was about one-third greater than that for Lower Canada. Two-thirds of Upper Canadian farms exceeded the average income for a Lower Canadian farm. He demonstrated that Lower Canadian farmers, on average, tilled a similar number of improved acres and profited in a similar fashion from animal products and miscellaneous crops. The disparity in income can be almost entirely attributed to the greater production of wheat in Upper Canada and this occurred because, as McInnis put it, 'they were more fortuitously situated for growing wheat.'[8]

The probable reasons for poor wheat production include infestations of wheat midge and the Hessian fly as well as declining market opportunities. Competition from Upper Canada proved to be a key factor in the latter situation. Due to shorter growing seasons, few Lower Canadian farmers could grow fall wheat, the crop most desired for export, so even in those few years before 1850 when a viable opportunity did exist in the British market, few Lower Canadian farmers could compete. But the problems of production would seem to have run deeper than that. Not only could Lower Canadian farmers not compete on the export markets but, in terms of wheat and flour, they were fairly consistently undersold in Montreal by Upper Canadian producers. Lower Canadians were not without company in facing this situation. The whole of the northeast region was being eclipsed by wheat production from the western interior. Farmers in the American borderland area, however, had a larger domestic market to which to supply other products than did their Lower Canadian neighbours.[9] Wheat was the cash crop without parallel in this period (even if not exported) and Lower Canadian farmers could find no adequate substitute for it.

In a relative sense, then, Lower Canadian agriculture experienced extreme difficulties in the first third to half of the nineteenth century. Before pursuing the implications of this relative difficulty, however, it should be noted that traditional historiography generally used the term crisis in an absolute, not relative, sense. Pictures are painted of general desolation, distress, and backwardness. It is this notion of crisis that more recent literature has rather decisively undermined. Indeed some historians have wondered if rural areas experienced problems of a significant nature at all. Serge Courville and, even more assertively, G. Paquet and P. Wallot have argued that the habitant began to shift out of wheat into animal and more diversified crop production as a rational response to market opportunities. Such diversification is not, they suggest, symptomatic of rural distress. Rather it suggests modernization of agricultural practice: the increased production of barley, peas, corn, potatoes, tobacco, and hemp reflected the variety of markets available to the habitant farmer—overseas, continental, urban/regional, and local village. Paquet and Wallot, on the basis of an analysis of inventories after death, suggest that the average peasant household grew wealthier between 1800 and 1835, not poorer. They also point to increased differentiation of income amongst peasant households in this period, an interpretation which has been corroborated by several other regional studies.[10]

On the basis of internally focused studies, it would seem that not all rural dwellers suffered distress during the first third of the nineteenth century. Jean Claude Robert, an historian, has demonstrated that both French and English farmers in the immediate vicinity of Montreal produced for the market, albeit English farmers produced somewhat more. While market prices in Montreal did increase in this period, a wide variety of foodstuffs seemed always available. Christian Dessaurault, in a detailed study of the economic behaviour and fortunes of habitants in the area of Saint Hyacinthe, found that during the first third of the nineteenth century about one-half of the area's farmers were market-oriented. Studies of merchant account books indicate that, as in Upper Canada, farmers desired and purchased a range of consumer items and credit was generally granted. In the Saint Hyacinthe region, in fact, many farmers loaned as well as borrowed: amounts owing farmers increased on average by some two-thirds between 1795-1814 and 1825-34. The sums involved, however, were minuscule compared to the amounts which passed through the hands of the traditional élite: the church, the seigneur, and the local merchants. Economic growth and social differentiation did take place in rural regions, but a traditional élite oversaw and reaped the most profit from such development.[11]

Some historians have seen the persistence of the traditional élite, a traditional land structure, and the socio-economic perquisites inherent in the seigneurial system as evidence of the failure of Lower Canada to break with its feudal-like past and enter a more capitalistic mode of social and economic production.[12] Some 80 per cent of Lower Canadians lived on the approximately 195 seigneuries in the

St Lawrence River region. Seigneurs did take advantage of their traditional rights: rents and dues extracted from the peasantry increased by some 36 per cent between 1790 and 1831. It was certainly the case that many seigneurs rested content with extracting wealth from peasant production and erecting mills for common use. In this sense those seigneurs participated only in an indirect way in productive enterprise. Yet there were, as well, numerous examples of direct investment by seigneurs in industrial enterprise requiring hired labour and producing for market consumption.[13] That the seigneurial system could be made to hold new wine in an era of transition is indicated by several case studies and by reference to some aggregate statistics which demonstrate the degree to which industrial enterprise found a comfortable home in Lower Canada's seigneurial heartland.

At the outset it should be noted that not all seigneuries were inherited. Even before 1791 a new breed of seigneur had begun to appear in the St Lawrence Valley: by that date two-thirds of all seigneuries were owned by French and English Canadian bourgeoisie. It is significant that each bourgeois group owned a third, with the remaining third owned by traditional French Canadian seigneurial families. In few areas did French capitalists compete on a level with English capitalists following the Conquest. In Montreal, for example, the French represented about 35 per cent of all businesspeople and 40 per cent of professional practitioners; they were a tiny minority of those who enjoyed government salaries, government pensions, and government contracts. It may well be that the one area in which they clearly held their own was that of land purchase and development. A preliminary study of land-holding in Montreal in 1825 suggests that such was indeed the case.[14] The following overview of business practice in seigneurial territory provides further evidence for that interpretation. This pattern of investment could be categorized as passive and conservative activity. Yet such a view is inconsistent with the fact that many French and English seigneurs did much more than sit back and collect rents. Rather they actively exploited their land holdings in a capitalistic fashion.

Specific credit instruments were developed to facilitate land sales in a colony where ready cash was a rarity. Louis Proulx, an ambitious merchant and seigneur based in Nicolet, Quebec, loaned money through a secured annuity system, taking possession of the security, often land, when the debtor failed in making a payment. He also purchased land under a contract *à réméré*, which allowed for repurchase by the vendor within a set time. These forms of lending netted Proulx some fifty lots between 1784 and 1798, all of which he later sold for nice profits. While many debtors lost all under the annuity system, that system allowed some speculators to amass a fortune. Pierre Foretier is a case in point. In the mid 1770s he was one of the largest Canadian investors in the fur trade. He was also an avid, but cash-short, land speculator. Thus for his early purchases he entered into several annuities, which allowed him to pay off the capital at a later and hopefully more propitious time. Foretier also used those annuities as a form of cash in many of his early transactions. As well he entered into a life annuity, an agreement which made the borrower liable to pay interest (usually 6 per cent) on the sum loaned until the lender died. For both parties this was, indeed, a gamble! By his death in 1815 Foretier had not only amassed a great amount of rural land, and had become a seigneur, but was also reputed to own the largest amount of land in the City of Montreal.[15]

These manoeuvres would seem to have been typical of a group of French Canadian capitalists operating in the late eighteenth and early nineteenth century. Jean Drapeau, a Quebec City merchant, shipbuilder, and seigneur, amassed a huge portfolio of rural property for which he only rarely paid cash. Instead he conducted his transactions through annuities and bonds. Once acquiring property he was quick to assess its worth and derive a profit from it by leasing to industrial concerns—bakeries, hat-makers, millers, and others. Other seigneurs, like Juchereau Duchesnay, a member of one of Lower Canada's élite families, constructed flour and sawmills and actively engaged in loaning money to habitants and potential entrepreneurs. His manor house became well known as a local credit establishment. Habitants who borrowed from him did so under the *à réméré* form of sale, further facilitating his personal acquisitions of landed property.[16]

Other French and English bourgeois spent more time developing rather than adding to their seigneuries. George Allsopp, a crusty Scots merchant often on the outs with the ruling British military class, purchased his seigneuries in 1773. By 1788 he had constructed the largest milling complex in the colony, one capable of producing 22 per cent of the colony's total flour output. He marketed his product locally, to the Gulf of St Lawrence fisheries, to government supply contractors, and to the West Indies. He continued to add to his manufacturing capabilities throughout the 1790s. Indeed, his biographer refers to him as a 'major industrialist'. Irish-born Henry Caldwell, an army officer and office holder, purchased his seigneurie a year after Allsopp. On it, he quickly built grist and sawmills. In 1810 alone, he sold over 1,775,000 pounds of flour to the government. He also ruthlessly used his seigneurial prerogatives to take advantage of the favourable British market for wood following the Napoleonic blockade. He bought out many of his censitaires (habitants) and required many others, when their leases came up for renewal, to grant him all rights to wood on the property, a practice his son continued.

John Young, a Scottish-born merchant, purchased his seigneurie in 1792 and soon oversaw a brewery and distillery complex that was large even by European standards. Much of his, at times, financially troubled enterprise came under the managerial control of his wife, Christian. And, in fact, several women seigneurs were active as entrepreneurs: Marie-Charles Joseph le Moyne de Longueuil, in 1823, had a steam mill built for carding and milling on her seigneurie. Marie-Geneviève Drapeau (born Nöel) administered her deceased husband's seigneury, although she acted in the more traditional stance of indirect participation in economic production by actively negotiating mill leases and the granting of wood rights to others.[17]

More significant were the operations of seigneurs like Barthélemy Joliette, Matthew Bell and J.T. Taschereau. Bell managed, on a seigneurial lease from the government, the Saint Maurice ironworks, an industrial enterprise which by 1807 encompassed 120 square miles and consisted of a blast furnace, foundry, two forges, coal crusher, flour mill, and sawmill. There were at least fifty houses for some two hundred to three hundred workers, along with, of course, the ubiquitous company store. Joliette and Taschereau established what were virtually industrial villages on their seigneuries. At Sainte-Marie-de-la-Nouvelle-Beauce, Taschereau's village was a complex of diversified industry which included saw and grist mills, a potasherie, a tannery and a brickyard. Joliette's operations were even larger: at the village of Industrie, a distillery, flour, saw, shingle, carding and fulling mill complex was in full operation. Lumbering was the centre of this enterprise and to transport his products to market, in the late 1840s Taschereau even built a twelve-mile railway.[18]

Undoubtedly these seigneurial enterprises relied to some extent on part-time labour from local censitaires. In that sense a form of production similar to that in the Maritimes was evolving: one that co-existed with, rather than supplanted, traditional preindustrial economic routines. Yet as Françoise Nöel has demonstrated in her study of the mills founded by Gabriel Christie on his seigneury, these enterprises affected not simply those who were directly employed but also provided opportunities for part-time artisanal labour from blacksmiths, coopers, carters, and others, and thereby acted as a spur to the growth of rural villages and towns throughout the seigneurial region. Jobs were created in the construction phase, the operations phase, and the general transport of the finished product.[19]

That many of those employed in these various pursuits did not in fact farm but relied on such opportunities for their livelihood, is suggested by a more widely focused and ongoing project initiated by Serge Courville. Via a close examination of census data Courville found that, in 1831, about 12 per cent of rural dwellers in the seigneurial territory of the St Lawrence lowlands did not farm. This represented some 40,000 people, almost as many as those who lived in the three largest cities—Montreal, Quebec, and Trois Rivières. Many of these individuals lived in some 210 hamlets and villages, a number which had increased fourfold since 1815, and worked in rural industries. Indeed in 1831 there were about 1,300 units of production (i.e., if a grist mill and sawmill were located in the same building, each was counted separately) operating in the seigneuries in the St Lawrence lowlands. Sawmills constituted just under half of all units, followed by grist mills, potash and pearl ash factories, fulling and carding mills, and a much smaller number of distilleries and foundries. By 1851 the number of productive units located in rural areas had more than doubled. Mills of various sorts represented only a third of all productive units, suggesting that significant diversification had taken place.[20]

What then, should one conclude from this evidence of productive business activity? These statistics clearly indicate that the seigneurial area was characterized by a wide diversity of business pursuits. Much of that activity was market driven, albeit most of the productive units would have been small operations. Courville has pointed out that the diversified structure of the rural economy resembled similar development in some European countries and in neighbouring New England where full-scale industrialization was preceded by decentralized

THE LAND BUSINESS IN THE EASTERN TOWNSHIPS

The seigneurial system did not extend to the Eastern Townships region of Lower Canada. There, land was held under the British system of free and common socage. Yet, perhaps even more than was the case in Upper Canada, large parcels of that land were held by a small number of wealthy speculators and land companies. Initially Americans settled in this border region, and many of the first American settlers acquired their land under what was called the leader and associate system common in the New England region. A group would petition for a whole township and each member or associate would usually grant 1000 acres of his 1200-acre allotment to a leader who, in turn, would be responsible for roads, surveys, mills, and general infrastructural support. That system had only a brief existence (1791-1809) before it collapsed due to disputes within Lower Canada's political and economic élite. One hundred and fifty-seven groups had actually been promised some eleven million acres of land but in the end fifty groups received about two million acres, most of which remained in the hands of absentee speculators.

In the anti-American climate following the War of 1812, the Colonial Office wished to encourage British, not American, emigration into the border townships. British half-pay officers and militia veterans received grants, but they often sold their rights to Lower Canadian speculators like Josias Wurtele and Henry Cull, the latter of whom entered the land market to, as he put it, make more in a short time 'than in ten years in the common routine of business with four times the sum'. Settlement proceeded slowly. By 1827 an exasperated British Government decided to auction off crown lands. In the Eastern Townships, even this system led to the acquisition of large blocks of land by a small number of speculators since the local Commissioner of Crown Lands auctioned 1200-acre lots to a number of individual purchasers, in the process ignoring the needs of small owners.

Such practice was quite consistent with Imperial policy. Impatient to see quick settlement, British ministers believed that wealthy owners of large blocks of land would be better able to facilitate local economic growth than would a large number of poorer holders of small lots. Moreover, the collection of payments seemed surer when only a few debtors owed the Crown. In this context, the government sold 876,661 acres to the British American Land Company (BALC) in 1835 for £120,000 payable in ten years at 4 per cent interest per annum. The Company was granted a monopoly and in return was expected to attract British settlers, construct roads, initiate surveys, and undertake other regional improvements.

In the 1830s, the Company did invest some money in infrastructural improvements; but it failed, in part because of the Rebellion, to attract enough paying customers so that by 1841 it gave back to the government 511,237 acres in recognition of payment arrears. Under the management of Alexander Tilloch Galt, the twenty-three-year-old son of John Galt, founder of the Canada Company and one of the originators of BALC, the land company turned to developing its remaining grant (the best of its initial holdings) and its private acquisitions (all of which amounted to over one-half a million acres) rather than spending money and time on recruiting settlers in the United Kingdom.

Galt tightened up the land sales and mortgage system, issuing (as did the Crown Lands Department) location tickets rather than land deeds prior to full payment. This procedure facilitated easy foreclosure and property repossession since the would-be purchaser did not have any legal document which required revocation by a court. He also allowed those who fell behind on their payments to enter into a leasing system, usually 6 per cent of the sale price per year. Finally, he ensured that the Company retained control of all lumber and mineral rights. This last proviso was important because from the late 1840s onwards the BALC became more a resource development sales company than a land and settlement company. Increasingly the BALC sold rural land in the Eastern Townships to lumbering interests (often American) and in that context settlement was usually perceived to be an impediment rather than an advantage. While the BALC did, under the initiative of Galt and his successor as Commissioner, R. W. Henecker, provide some land and capital for industrial development in the city of Sherbrooke, the directors, almost all of whom resided in London, were rarely favourably disposed to such activity, preferring instead to sit on undeveloped land until such property could be sold.

On balance, then, the land development strategies sanctioned by the state placed control of much of the region's best land and richest resources in the hands of a few companies and individuals: by 1838, for example, one local land agent estimated that 1.3 million acres were owned by 105 people or corporations and only six of those lived on their property. Close to 80 per cent of that land was in an unimproved state. The operations of the Colonial Office stood at the centre of this system. The needs of poor immigrant settlers were, as the historian Jack Little has concluded, sacrificed to meet the interests of 'short-term imperial expediency'. The Imperial government viewed colonial land as a commodity to meet immediate revenue needs and in the process ignored long-term consequences for local development. Land companies, individual speculators, and foreign-based resource companies understood well the rules of a game which favoured short-term gain over long-term development.

Sources

Cyr, Céline, 'Josias Wurtele', DCB 6 (Toronto, 1987), 819-20.

Déselets, Andrée, 'Henry Cull', DCB 6 (Toronto, 1987), 174-5.

Little, J.I., Nationalism, Capitalism and Colonization in 19th Century Quebec: The Upper St Francis District (McGill-Queen's, 1989).

————, 'Imperialism and Colonization in Lower Canada: The Role of William Bowman Felton', CHR LXVI (1985), 511-40.

————, 'Samuel Gale', DCB 6 (Toronto, 1987), 268-70.

McGuigan, G.F., 'Administration of Land Policy and the Growth of Corporate Economic Organization in Lower Canada, 1791-1809' in W.T. Easterbrook and M.H. Watkins, Approaches to Canadian Economic History (Toronto, 1967), 99-109.

Rudin, R., 'Land Ownership and Urban Growth: The Experience of Two Quebec Towns, 1840-1914', Urban History Review 8 (1979), 23-46.

industrial growth. Links between rural industry and the large-scale productions which would appear in urban areas have yet to be clearly established, but the strong evidence of productive activity in the rural areas points to the emergence of an increasingly integrated, localized market economy, one which some farmers were able, through their purchasing power, to support.

Clearly, then, if there was an agricultural crisis in rural Quebec in the first thirty to forty years of the nineteenth century, it was of a relative, not absolute, sort. In fact, in the years following 1850 Lower Canada's agricultural sector diversified in the same general way as did that in Upper Canada. The Grand Trunk Railway and the Reciprocity Treaty sparked trade in butter, cheese, wool, cattle, and horses as well as sawn lumber to American markets. Exports of butter and cheese from the Eastern Townships to the United States during the Reciprocity era grew especially rapidly. This agricultural sector continued to grow: by the end of the century close to two thousand cheese factories operated in the province. Quebec's agricultural output, relative to that of Ontario, however, continued to lag. In 1870 income per Quebec farm reached only about 70 per cent of income per Ontario farm. Nor did this ratio improve throughout the rest of the century.[21] In a relative sense, how significant was this lag for general business development in the colony? Let us examine another kind of business activity in Lower Canada's rural domain before we focus on business growth in the colony's emerging urban centres.

FOREST ENTERPRISE

The area of the seigneurial lowlands most prosperous in terms of agriculture and village growth was that surrounding Montreal. Other parts of rural Quebec were primarily linked to business of a different sort: around Quebec and Trois Rivières, the export of timber and lumber played a central role in the development of regional enterprise. In 1802, exports of masts and pine and oak products from Lower Canada to Great Britain were minuscule. By 1811, following the Napoleonic blockade and the institution of preferential duties which provided British North America a protected British market for forest products, exports of masts had increased from 50,000 cubic feet to 950,000 cubic feet, of pine, from 200,000 cubic feet to 2,450,000 cubic feet, and of oak, from 40,000 cubic feet to 1,250,000 cubic feet. Between 1805 and 1810 shipping out of the port of Quebec, the major export point for lumber products on the St Lawrence, increased from 170 vessels to 661 and overall tonnage increased fivefold. British North America timber exports to Great Britain represented in 1802 about one per cent of all such imports into the British market; by 1816, 66 per cent of all timber brought into the United Kingdom came from British North America. Nor did tariff reductions in the early 1820s and early 1840s have any long-term negative affect on the St Lawrence lumber trade. Indeed, by the mid-1830s St Lawrence lumber exports exceeded for the first time those of New Brunswick. Exports did drop in the year following the tariff reductions but in 1845, three years after the 1842 tariff reduction, the thirty coves along the St Lawrence from Cap Rouge to the Rivière Montmorency, where timber was received and sorted, shipped 1,499 shiploads of wood products; shipments of squared timber alone amounted to 24,000,000 cubic feet.[22] It was not until the late 1850s that the Baltic area once again surpassed British North America as the major supplier of squared timber in the British market. Moreover, in terms of the St Lawrence squared-timber trade, it was not until the late 1870s that the era of sustained decline commenced. For nearly three-quarters of a century the export of lumber to England and, somewhat later, timber products to the United States, dominated Lower Canada/Quebec's export trade.[23]

What impact did this trade in forest products have on the colony's business development? It is clear that English entrepreneurs based in the city of Quebec dominated the timber trade and shipbuilding and, at least until the early 1850s, used the city's Board of Trade as a platform for their own interests. This closely knit group of Anglo-Scots entrepreneurs lived in style in the upper town, and were members of similar social clubs, churches, and philanthropic institutions. Some among them, like William Walker, acted as spokesmen for lumber interests in the assembly and legislative council. Such representation proved useful in 1849, for example, when a petition to the assembly from lumber producers requesting the opening of one public lumber cove—all the roughly 30 coves then in operation were privately owned — was headed off by the powerful lumber merchants and defeated.[24] Others like Peter Patterson and John Sharples sat on the board of cullers established by the Assembly in 1819 to regulate the activities of those who carried out the all-important tasks of measuring and assigning quality grades to the timber and wood products shipped and rafted to the many coves in and around the port of Quebec.[25] Standard measurements could be better assured and foreign buyers could have more confidence in receiving a consistent product, but the board, itself, was in no way independent of those who shipped the timber. Quebec City's timber merchants kept close control over most of the operations relating to the timber trade throughout the nineteenth century.

Despite social and business linkages, competition was fierce. In the early years of the squared-timber trade Quebec merchants bid on rafts sent down the St Lawrence by independent lumberers and forwarders. Some Quebec merchants employed spotters up-river who would warn them of the approach of the rafts. In the early 1830s one Quebec firm purchased a large number of the rafts before they reached Quebec, thus pre-empting its city rivals and profiting nicely in the process.[26] This free-wheeling practice was relatively short lived. Centralized controls and compartmentalized functions soon became the norm. By at least the 1840s Quebec timber dealers generally contracted with timber manufacturers to send a prescribed amount of squared lumber or deals and planks to Quebec by a certain date. The Quebec merchant would often advance the cutters money throughout the winter on the security of the timber cut.

For example, in the autumn of 1846 W.J.C. Benson, a Quebec lumber merchant, contracted with James Jardine of Pembroke, Upper Canada to advance £1200 at 6 per cent interest for the delivery of 50,000 cubic feet of white and 50,000 cubic feet of red pine. Typical of these contracts, the risks and costs associated with delivery were borne by Jardine. Benson had the option of accepting the pine at a

Timber raft on the St Lawrence, *c.* 1838. *(National Archives of Canada/C40326)*

current price at the time of arrival in Quebec or of selling it to another merchant at a cost of 5 per cent commission. This meant that Benson would refuse to purchase in a poor market but that he would nonetheless sell the pine to another merchant for a low price and still pocket a 5 per cent commission. In addition to paying all costs, Jardine had, of course, to repay the winter advance and, if the markets were poor, would end up in debt to Benson or, worse, go bankrupt.[27] Winter contracts also gave Quebec merchants more control over the amount of product scheduled to arrive in Lower Canada each year. This control, however, was never absolute as, following good years, small independent operators would ship rafts on speculation, often flooding the market and depressing prices in the process.

Many of the more prominent of these merchants were themselves junior partners of businesses with head offices located in Liverpool or another British port. One of the largest of such enterprises was that of Pollock, Gilmour & Company, established in Glasgow in 1804. Commencing operations on the Miramichi River in New Brunswick in 1812, by 1833 the Company oversaw separate partnerships at Saint John, Quebec, Montreal, and the towns of Bathurst, Dalhousie, and Campbellton in New Brunswick. Each partnership was financially separate in order to minimize liability on the parent firm in England. Yet these operations enjoyed little other independence: family members headed each partnership; the Glasgow head office provided supplies, employees, and financing; and all exports went to the parent company. Most of the Gilmours, after making their fortunes in British North America, retired to and died in Scotland.

The linkages exemplified by this firm have often been considered typical of the British North American timber trade: the cutting and shipping of squared timber to England by large British-dominated mercantile partnerships. Certainly there were many other such firms in operation in Lower Canada. Yet other very large enterprises operated on a more independent basis. And not all successful timber dealers specialized in the squared-timber market.

Timothy Hibbart Dunn was born and died in Lower Canada. Following a valuable apprenticeship with the Calvin Company operations as Quebec agent in the 1840s, Dunn branched out on his own in the early 1850s. He did operate as a timber merchant, purchasing timber on his own account for resale, but most often he acted as a broker, entering into a contract with a Quebec timber merchant for the delivery of a specified amount of timber at a certain date. He would then arrange for this to be cut, generally in western Upper Canada, and he would receive an agreed upon commission on the completion of the transaction. Dunn thereby avoided the uncertainties involved in shipping to Britain where, in times of poor markets, cargoes could remain unsold for several years. Over a thirty-year period, Dunn's annual sales often exceeded $250,000. He was generally regarded as the major dealer in the squared oak trade. Not until the 1880s, a decade of poor markets and rapidly declining resources, did some other Quebec shippers begin to bypass Dunn and move directly into the production sector. By that time, however, the trade in squared timber was itself nearly over.[28]

Not least among the factors accounting for that decline was the rapid rise of the trade in sawn lumber, especially with the United States after the Reciprocity Treaty of 1854. In 1850, Great Britain purchased over 80 per cent of the wood products exported from Canada. By 1885 the United States had become Canada's most important market for wood products. In the early years of the timber trade, when rich stands of the large and straight trees necessary for the squared-timber market were easily accessible, start-up costs for entrepreneurs were low compared to sawn lumber endeavours which necessitated fixed capital costs in mills, machinery, and upkeep. By the 1850s, however, the growth of American and internal markets for sawn lumber, however, coupled with the increasing difficulty of finding suitable stands of trees for the squared-timber trade made investment in mills seem much more palatable. Moreover, more trees were suitable for cutting timber for planks, deals, and boards than for squared timber. Nor was as much of the felled tree wasted as in the squared-timber process where the best part of the tree was trimmed by axes. Thus, given suitable markets, the cost of leasing limits could be more easily recovered by manufacturing deals and planks than by exporting squared timber.

It would be wrong, however, to think that significant entrepreneurial activity in sawn lumber awaited the development of an external market. This was far from the case: in the 1820s some 23,000 cords of hardwood were sold as firewood in Montreal alone. Historians Brian Young and John Dickinson estimate that local markets consumed as much wood as the colony exported. The Canadian-born merchant Louis Roy Portelance did well enough supplying woodworkers, carpenters, and other Montreal entrepreneurs with boards and planks, to retire in the early 1820s and live off his earnings. Peter Patterson and Henry Usborne, two of the first British lumber dealers to establish operations in Quebec City, were quick to realize the value of that local market. While they initially focused on the squared-timber trade, they soon diversified into the manufacture of deals and planks for export and local sales to shipbuilders, cabinetmakers, and timber merchants. By 1818 they operated perhaps the largest sawmill complex in North America. Similarly, in the early nineteenth century Henry Caldwell, using money embezzled from a government account, set up a comparably large complex known as the Etchemen Mills. After Caldwell's illegal siphoning of money was uncovered, his bankrupt enterprise was eventually purchased by Patterson and his partners.[29]

William Price, born in London, England, is an excellent example of an astute entrepreneur who realized the value of local as well as export markets. An analysis of his career as a lumber merchant and manufacturer of planks and deals provides a graphic illustration of the power that successful businessmen could exert over the lives of their employees and, indeed, of those who lived in areas close to timber limits and centres of lumbering activity. In 1810, at age twenty, Price arrived at Quebec City to act as a clerk for a general import-export firm. By 1815 he had become that firm's local manager, and in the early 1820s he entered the timber export trade. The structure of the business closely resembled that of the Gilmour enterprises. Three separate, but overlapping, partnerships were formed: one in London, providing financing and selling colonial goods; one in Montreal, primarily concerned with the wheat trade; and one in Quebec City, managed by Price and handling the timber trade. In the squared-timber trade Price operated as did most of his competitors, providing advances for winter cutting and felling, receiving shipments at coves near Quebec where culling, packing, and loading cargoes for England took place. His operation had, perhaps, more solidity than that of many others due in part to his good fortune in receiving the British Admiralty contracts for masts and ship material for most of the years between 1830 and 1850. These contracts often exceeded £150,000 and were low-risk, high-return operations.

It was, however, Price's systematic diversification into the manufacture of deals and planks that set him apart from most of his contemporaries. As early as 1843 he had some £130,000 tied up in sawmills. By 1850 he owned at least forty sawmills, most of which he obtained from sawmillers he had bankrolled who could not repay on time. By this process of debt foreclosing he acquired control of an immense timber reserve and the best mill sites in the Saguenay and Lake St Jean region of Quebec. He shipped up to 500,000 planks yearly to England and sold fence posts, shingles, railway ties, boards and other products to local and American markets. By 1851 some 2000 colonists and 2000 workers in the Saguenay region were to a greater or lesser degree tied to the fortunes of Price's business.[30]

The nature of the power exerted by Price over the Saguenay region has been a matter of some historical debate. Historians Normand Séguin and Gaston Gagnon have argued that agricultural development suffered, taking second place to lumber activity. Gerard Bouchard, however, has pointed out that many single young men and some young married men worked in the woods for a few years in order to accumulate money for marriage and for starting up a farm. In this way, forest and farms were complementary, not competitive, enterprises. As well, Bouchard and others have noted that woods work and farm work peaked in different seasons, so that it was at least possible for a person/family to engage in both operations during the course of one year. Henry Usborne and John Hamilton, in their testimony before a British Parliamentary Committee in 1821, underlined the complementary nature of farming and woods work. Hamilton believed that lumbering was 'the only employment to which the emigrants could have recourse during the winter'. Usborne informed a somewhat sceptical Committee that only a 'very few' were devoted to full-time timber cutting and rafting. Most farmed in the summer. And, he continued, 'frequently many farmers procure a small quantity [of wood] which he exchanges for rum and clothes and provisions, and all the necessaries that he requires, with the merchant, who, in the country, retails out different things which are imported into Canada . . . .'[31] Moreover, farmers could sell their produce to lumber camps, further augmenting family income.

Undoubtedly some Saguenay farm families benefited in the ways outlined above. In fact, at a general level, the argument seems logical and persuasive. When close attention is paid to the strategies employed by Price in the management of his businesses and, by extension, of the wider Saguenay region, some qualification seems warranted.

Price brooked no opposition to his methods, nor did he permit any economic endeavour not firmly tied to his enterprise. Employees were paid in vouchers or tokens redeemable only at the company store or the firm's head office. Thus Price could and did determine both the salary received and the cost of goods purchased with that salary. The potential for exploitation was obviously great and at least one missionary in the region, Jean-Baptiste Honoré, argued loudly for change. In fact, he tried to establish what he termed a 'liberating' venture, an attempt to set up an agricultural colony separate from Price's control. Price, however, appealed to Honoré's Oblate superiors for his recall. Since the colonization venture incurred heavy expenses, Honoré was in a vulnerable position and ultimately had to quit the area much to the relief of, as Séguin put it, the 'champions of clerical-capitalist collusion in the Saguenay'.[32]

Workers adhered to a strict regime: if they were ill too often, they were fined five shillings per day; repairing of tools had to be done after work and axes had to be provided at the worker's expense. Work days extended from 'dawn until nightfall: the men must,' Price's manager instructed a foreman, 'leave the yard before daybreak in order to be at their site as soon as it is light enough to work, and they shall not leave the site until it is too dark to continue.' Even foremen, managers, and agents fared poorly at Price's hands. Peter McLeod, one of Price's foremost managers in the Saguenay region, died in 1852 owing Price £4520. Since his two sons could not be proved legitimate, Price took over McLeod's whole estate. A similar story concerns a somewhat lesser agent, Alexis Tremblay *dit* Picoté, who managed Price's affairs at La Malbaie. As Picoté's biographer put it, after some twenty years of working with Price, Picoté died owning one small mill and providing in a modest way for his sons, surely 'a meagre recompense for a man who had helped build the empire of William Price'.[33]

Another perspective on the relationship between forest, farms, and regional development is provided by the historian Jack Little, in his analysis of the Upper

St Francis district in the Eastern Townships. Little argues that farming and logging were, in principle, compatible enterprises and that, especially in marginal agricultural zones, some such mix of business and economic activity was necessary for regional growth. He is however, quite critical of the manner in which such an interaction emerged. Governments routinely granted large timber companies monopolistic control over wood resources. To do otherwise — to allow many small entrepreneurs access—would make collection of government fees tenuous and difficult. Under the small leasehold system that developed in some Scandinavian countries, farms could be taxed for general government revenue purposes; in Lower Canada/Quebec such a taxation system was not in effect. Fees from lumber concessions were the only revenue sources for local infrastructural development. In this context, governments looked to major companies to log the region, and often faced a further problem: the propensity of such companies to evade such payments.

Certainly William Price was past master at such manoeuvring. So, too, were the managers of the major lumbering company in the upper St Francis region, the American-owned C.S. Clark & Company. Clark & Company enjoyed close relations with J.H. Pope, a sometime partner and a member of the local assembly. The company routinely ignored settlers' cutting privileges and generally managed to overcome many lawsuits filed against it by disgruntled colonists and small-scale lumber entrepreneurs. The government made very little return from the Company's cutting fees, and colonists made only short-term gains from employment in the company.

Little concludes that the government and most other nineteenth-century groups viewed forests as temporary obstacles to agricultural growth.[34] The rapid destruction of local forests not only drained the regions of capital but also made future regional development more problematic. After all, the notion of a renewable resource was not part of the nineteenth-century business mind. Conservation and sustained development played little role in the forest industry of the nineteenth century.[35] For a time many rural regions in Lower Canada/Quebec developed within a mixed business environment of farm and forests. For some of those regions such mixed enterprise proved necessary for sustained development. The nature and structure of the forest industry, however, militated against such a scenario. In its place, systematic exploitation of forests with little thought for the region's future bequeathed to local colonists a heritage of not much more than bare subsistence, rather than development.

*   *   *

The most obvious conclusion from this overview of rural enterprise is the danger inherent in generalizing too widely from particular local environments. Lower Canadian farming was not all of a piece. Yet relative to Upper Canada, few farmers engaged in large-scale commercial production, and even in Upper Canada, as we have seen, only a minority were strongly commercially successful. Climate and location problems bedevilled Lower Canadian agricultural production. So, too, however, did institutional constraints. The seigneurial system was a real burden not faced by Upper Canadians. The operation of the Petite-Nation seigneury, owned by the Papineau family and the Beauharnois seigneury owned by one of the richest British capitalists to invest in Lower Canada, Edward Ellice, nicely illustrates the general point. In 1832 only ten of sixty-one occupied lots on Papineau's seigneury were free of debt: most settlers owed their seigneur the equivalent of a half year's labour in the local sawmills. Indeed, by 1850 the lessee-operator of one of the local sawmills, Stephen Tucker, had acquired forty-four lots almost all from hapless debtors who failed to meet dues on time. Papineau often took his censitaires to court for non-payment of dues. Few, however, were more exacting in this regard than Edward 'Bear' Ellice. Acting through his agent, John Forsyth, one of the most prominent of Montreal merchants, in 1826 alone Ellice took seventy-one of his censitaires to court for non-payment of *cens et rentes*. In one case, the censitaire owed only ten shillings![36]

One might have thought that the abolition of seigneurial tenure in Lower Canada in 1854 would have eased such burdens and opened the way for farmers to invest more capital in their farms. Some historians have indeed argued that such was the case. They point to the fact that *lods et ventes*—the 12 per cent of the selling price of any seigneurial land to be paid to the seigneur—was now abolished and that this and several other minor reductions represented an average savings to the habitant of at least one-third of his regular payments. The major part of such savings, however, would only be realized when the habitant sold his farm. Moreover, for most habitants the cost of acquiring total control of that farm remained prohibitive. Habitants were allowed to buy from the seigneur the land they farmed at a price pegged to the old annual *cens et rentes* and other casual dues. Since few could afford the price, they paid instead an annual rent equal to an interest charge on the property's value to the 'former' seigneur. As late as 1935, 60,000 farmers in Quebec continued to pay a rent to the last seigneur's heirs. The 'former' seigneur and his/her family benefited in other ways as well. The government indemnified them for the loss of *lods et ventes*. Now that hidden dues were no longer possible, it became easier for seigneurial and merchant families to speculate in rural land, to control timber reserves, and to acquire unfettered right to mill sites on regional waterways.[37] At one level, all of this may well have increased the possibility of business development in the old seigneurial areas. But it clearly stacked the entrepreneurial deck in favour of the land-owning élite. That, of course, was the Act's intent. The road to capitalist business enterprise in rural Lower Canada was far from what some scholars refer to as the revolutionary way. Nor, as some historians do, is it proper to speak of a division between a seigneurial and a commercial class in Lower Canada by the middle of the nineteenth century. As early as 1800 some two-thirds of all seigneurs were of bourgeois origins. As in England, land-owning and commerce were increasingly indistinguishable. Old élites were not put out to pasture. Business developed in rural areas even before the abolition of the seigneurial system, but it evolved for the most part firmly in the hands of those accustomed to control.

Forest enterprise followed a similar pattern. A few, like John Egan in the Ottawa Valley, rose from the ranks of shanty dweller to major lumber producer, but most lumber magnates were already well connected merchants. Financial and market-ing control rested firmly in the hands of a small élite centred in Quebec City and, in London, Liverpool, or Glasgow. Rural residents, whether in the Saguenay or the Eastern Townships, could combine farm and forest work, but their horizons were limited by the generally oppressive and exploitative presence of powerful urban-based merchant producers. Independent sawmills certainly persisted, but, as the Price example illustrated, the choicest of such operations were usually entangled in a web of credit and debt and, ultimately, were acquired by larger well-financed operations. The business activities of seigneurs and urban-based merchant producers did facilitate spin-off enterprises of a mercantile, farming, and industrial sort. But such enterprises tended to be small and to operate in the protective shade of the larger concern.

Viewed from a somewhat broader perspective, the nature of business devel-opment in rural Lower Canada accords with the notion of gradual rather than sudden or revolutionary change from a preindustrial to an industrial world. In that sense, gentlemanly capitalism set the contours for business change.[38] Seig-neurs, whether francophone or anglophone, of Old Regime families or bourgeois *nouveaux riche*, could acquire the trappings of feudal status — manor houses, landed property, a subservient peasantry, and, in the case of William Price, a statue dedicated to his memory—even while encouraging and profiting from industrial growth. This form of gentlemanly capitalism, perhaps even more strongly than in England, set the pattern of social, political and business change in rural Lower Canada/Quebec through the greater part of the nineteenth century.

FRAMING THE TRANSITION:
State, Law, and Business Development, 1815–1871

The abolition of seigneurial tenure occurred within a wider frame of gradual but significant legislative and legal change. Reflecting the social and economic ambi-tions of an urban-based business élite, those changes paved the way for the tran-sition from a commercial to an industrial society. Before the Constitutional Act businessmen from both ethnic groups could act together in the fur trade, and could sign common petitions demanding an elected assembly. The granting of an Assembly in 1791, with minimal franchise requirements permitting most rural and urban workers to vote, drove a wedge through that tacit alliance, and it has since become commonplace when discussing the nature of economic power in Lower Canada to refer to two élites: French and English. By 1805, in the Assem-bly, English merchants were outnumbered by French bourgeois, habitant farmers, and local tradespeople. Increasingly English merchants curried the support of British governors and dominated the appointments to the two non-elected coun-cils. In the early nineteenth century the French-dominated assembly blocked attempts to tax land for the jail, road, and canal developments favoured by the import-export oriented British merchant class. They proposed instead a tax on imports, a measure which the merchant-councillors vetoed. As well, the group that controlled the Assembly, the Parti Canadienne, resented the control by English speculators of large blocks of Eastern Township land, making rural expansion into that region financially burdensome.

Some historians, like Paquet and Wallot, have argued that the resulting stalemate blocked the emergence of an activist state and caused general economic development in Lower Canada to drift in a virtual policy vacuum.[39] This comment follows logically from the perception of two resolutely opposed blocs, each having well-defined and clearly demarcated socio-economic strategies. British merchants looked to enhance import and export business by the construction of canals, the establishment of large merchant banks, and the siphoning of trade from a developing continental interior down the St Lawrence river. This broad policy had support amongst many of Upper Canada's economic and social élite. Far from being anti-development (as some historians, like Fernand Ouellet, have argued), the Parti Canadienne offered an alternative economic program, one predicated on local and regional growth, small and numerous banks as in the United States, land availability, and canal linkage with New York rather than the midwest. Indeed, the strategy of taxing imports rather than land was the fiscal and operational heart of this economic platform. It commanded much political support amongst the habitants. It would not result in increased land prices. Some of the Parti Canadienne believed, as well, that high import taxes might restrict the flow of British-made manufactured goods to the colony and stimulate in their place locally owned manufactories.

The emphasis by Paquet and Wallot on the existence of two developmentally oriented entrepreneurial groups in Lower Canada in the early nineteenth century is a useful corrective to a traditional historical literature which, following Donald Creighton, focused only on British merchants and their collective dream of an Empire of the St Lawrence. That perspective privileged the business activity of the old fur-trade families who founded the Bank of Montreal. Anglo-Scots entrepreneurs tended to be centre stage. John Redpath played a major role in the construction of the Lachine Canal and in the mid 1850s constructed the first sugar refinery in the Canadas. John Molson, father and son, founded the Molson brewery and were among the first steamboat operators on the St Lawrence; for a brief period in the late 1820s they virtually controlled shipping on the Ottawa, the Rideau Canal and the Richelieu, in addition to dominating river transport between Montreal and Quebec City. George Moffatt, who received his start in the fur trade, by the early 1820s was a partner in Gillespie, Moffatt & Company, one of Montreal's major import-export houses. The list could go on. Nor can there be any doubt concerning the power that accrued to these men as a result of their business success. Indeed many lasting fortunes were established at this period of Lower Canada's history. And many who did succeed, like the Scots-born Hugh Allan, in the words of his biographers, owed their start to 'as was so often the case in the Montreal merchant community . . . family connections, social bonds and access to capital'. Allan used his privileged status well: by his death in 1882 he had become one of the wealthiest of Canada's entrepreneurs, a noted shipping magnate, railway developer, financier, and general businessman.[40] Clearly the Anglo-Scots business élite cannot be ignored. The point is, however, that their successes (and failures) did not reflect, as the traditional historiography would lead one to believe, the whole of Lower Canada's business activity. There were other 'realities'.

Business historians following the leads suggested by Paquet and Wallot have uncovered surprisingly strong evidence of locally oriented industrial production, especially in the Montreal region. Interestingly, one indication of the existence of industrial production comes from the close analysis of trade flows. A much more diversified trade flow existed than the traditional staple/mercantilist model of raw materials being shipped to the mother country in return for British-made manufactured goods indicated. Not all wood exports, for example, consisted of squared timber. In 1825, in fact, export value of such wood products as planks, boards, deals, staves, spars, and masts exceeded the value of exported square timber. If one were to add the value of the sixty-one vessels constructed in Lower Canada in that year, worth about £140,000 or almost equivalent to the worth of square timber, then the extent of value added accruing to timber in the province can be clearly appreciated. Even more at variance with what one would predict from the staple/mercantilist perspective is the nature of the material imported. The two most important import sectors, textiles and metal goods, consisted for the most part of unprocessed or semi-processed goods. To a great extent the making of clothing and the production of metal goods took place within the colony.[41]

Much of such production occurred in crafts shops. In Montreal between 1820 and 1842, for example, at least 53 dressmakers and 67 tailors hired 348 apprentices and 30 foremen and journeymen tailors. Most of these crafts shops were small, engaging only one or two apprentices and workmen and producing for a local and regional market. Many others, however, hired up to 14 and the largest dressmaking shop engaged 33. Within the needle trades, as the historian, Mary Anne Poutanen, has demonstrated, gradual change from a preindustrial to an industrial workplace took place. The nature of those changes can be illustrated by the following case study. Margaret Major owned the largest dressmaking shop in Montreal in the 1830s. Between 1833 and 1836 she provided board and lodging for seven of her eight apprentices. Their parents provided clothing and a bed. After 1838, Major no longer provided room and board. Moreover, after 1836, all apprentices were bound to work according to time standards set by Major: seven in the morning until noon and one o'clock until eight o'clock every day except Sunday. In the 1830s, Major and many other dressmakers and tailors rid themselves of the paternalistic trappings of the old guild system. Major provided training and in return received the unrecompensed labour of 33 apprentices. These changes were roughly paralleled by the gradual and uneven proletarianization of labour in other craft sectors in the first half of the nineteenth century.[42]

In Montreal in the 1820s, historian Robert Sweeny has argued, some fifty different craft sectors were the most dynamic element of the local industrial economy. He suggests that some of these producers imported on their own account and were able, because of their ties to local and regional markets, to avoid the effects of the first major international commercial crisis which took place in 1825-

26. Those sectors of the economy tied to export markets were more vulnerable. Those often overlooked sectors producing for local consumption were relatively untouched. While more research is required in this area, Sweeny's conclusions are nevertheless suggestive. Some craft producers, at least, were able to develop free from control by an established mercantile élite and to prosper even as some of the central personages of that élite declared bankruptcy.[43]

This is not to suggest that merchants in Montreal operated in a sphere somehow separate from sectors of production. In fact, those merchants who suffered most hardship from the international downturn were those who had invested in shipbuilding for export markets. Nor should one conclude that Montreal merchants simply invested in production sectors which were closely linked to export markets, like timber and wood products, and wheat and flour milling. Many, often former fur traders, did restrict their investments to such enterprises. Yet many other merchants carefully appraised the growth of potential markets in and around Montreal and invested money in the local manufacture of appropriate consumer goods.

It is difficult to be precise about the extent to which merchants controlled or, at least, invested in industrial production in Montreal in the early nineteenth century. In the leather trades, one of the largest of the craft sectors, it was not uncommon for a merchant and a tanner or bootmaker to enter into partnership. Normally each person contributed an equal amount of capital: in addition, the merchant brought to the concern his bookkeeping and sales experience and the crafts person his manufacturing skill. Profits tended to be equally shared. Poutanen suggests that cloth production was firmly in the hands of craft producers: only two Montreal merchants hired tailors between 1820 and 1842.[44] Sweeny suggests that merchants may have controlled production in the areas of brickmaking, distilling, nail manufacturing, and oil and paint works. Given the fragmentary nature of the historical evidence, however, it would be unwise to be too conclusive. Contemporaries labelled men merchants who were, in fact, like Henry Joseph, engaged as well in the production of snuff and tobacco. Historians have been content to call the Montreal businessman, Levy Solomon, a fur merchant when, in fact, in his last will and testament in 1792 he called himself a 'manufacturer'. And, as the following extract from his *inventaire après décès*, indicates, so he was:

> ... in the garret of said house is established a manufactory for carrot, pig tail, plug tail and other kinds of tobacco .... At a small distance from the house is erected a large and spacious building ... in this building are fixed complete starch and hair powder manufactory with a bake house and two very large brick ovens .... A complete well finished grist mill, built of wood, made to work with horses with four pairs of stones .... A small house ... in the upper part is established a complete snuff manufactory and underneath is a capital oven this place having been originally intended for a bake house ....[45]

In Montreal in the first thirty or forty years of the nineteenth century, therefore, business was not simply tied to an export market. Local craft manufactories did

The transition from craft to mechanized production. *(J.H. Walker, wood engraving, ink on paper, M930.50.5.262 and M930.50.5.142. Collection: McCord Museum of Canadian History, Montreal)*

exist and were gradually evolving into factory-type capitalist work relationships. Such manufactories flourished in part because of the market opportunities which existed both within the growing city and also beyond, in a regional countryside characterized by wealth differentiation and diversified economic endeavour. Anglo-Scots merchants in Montreal dominated the wheat trade, just as their counterparts in Quebec City dominated the lumber trade. Many invested in shipbuilding for export markets and in canal construction for the promotion of the St Lawrence waterways. Yet many others invested in and serviced local centres of production. The city and its environs were in the early stage of transition to an industrial economy: a stage at which merchant and producer did not simply co-exist but overlapped; a stage when the beginnings of a capitalist work place can be discerned.

These observations allow us to see Paquet and Wallot's initial insight in a different light. Clearly the socio-economic spheres they sketch overlap at crucial points. Local and regional markets were of interest to British merchants as well as French bourgeois. Local production also attracted British merchant capital and control. In the 1830s about 80 per cent of measures relating to economic development—construction of roads, bridges, canals, and railways—passed without opposition in the Assembly. Some anglophone businessmen in the Assembly supported the development aims of the Parti Patriote (the new name of the Parti Canadienne). The Assembly and Councils were indeed as one on the need to pass legislation which would 'discipline' an emerging industrial workforce and thus strengthen the power and economic well-being of emerging industrial employers. As early as 1802 the government passed repressive legislation aimed at controlling apprentice activities. Strikers were jailed in 1815.[46] On some economic and social issues, the state could and did act in a direct way with the backing of its constituent parts.

An examination of the loan activities of the Bank of Montreal also suggests that some qualification of Paquet and Wallot's insight is necessary. The bank, which commenced operations in 1817 and was chartered in 1822, was firmly in the hands of the British merchant class, most especially those merchants with extensive international contacts and business dealings. Active import-exporters like the fur trade veterans John Forsyth, John Richardson, George Gardin, Peter McGill, Samuel Gerrard and his partner, George Moffatt, dominated the bank's board of directors in the early 1820s. Gerrard, president from 1820 to 1826, ran the operation as if it were a mercantile partnership. He did the hiring and even loaned money in his own name to his friends and business associates. A few prominent francophone merchants like Austin Cuvillier actively supported and borrowed from the institution. But between 1818 and 1835, only 10 per cent of directors were francophones. For the most part, the francophone bourgeoisie looked on it with suspicion and few invested in its shares. Yet despite anglo-merchant control, the bank did support local commodity production, as well as shipbuilding, distillery, and construction enterprise by both short-term (three month) and long-term (three year) loans. Indeed, much of its heavy losses in the 1825-26 international financial crisis occurred because of loans to shipbuilding operations.[47] There was no simple division in economic ambition between anglophone and francophone business élites. Nor was there a simple division between merchant and industrial capital.

The Banque de Peuple was established in 1835 with the avowed purpose of supporting the enterprise of the French Canadian *petite bourgeoisie*, a group allegedly ignored by the Bank of Montreal. Its chief clients would, indeed, seem to have been farmers and artisans. Yet despite the notoriety that the Bank gained through the close affiliation of some of its leading directors with Papineau, the leader of the Parti Patriote, only seven of the twelve founding members of the Bank were French. Jacob De Witt, the bank's primary financial manager, was an American. Clearly, those businessmen who supported the bank felt that they required a friendlier financial institution than the Bank of Montreal. That group, however, defies the drawing of any simple ethnic line. Montreal's business community was simply too complex for that.[48]

While qualified, the essence of Wallot and Paquet's characterization remains intact. The business activity of the young Patriote lawyer, George-Étienne Cartier suggests as much. The son and grandson of prominent merchants from the Richelieu Valley, Cartier was admitted to the bar in 1835, whereupon he opened an office in Montreal. He had articled with the Patriote, Edouard-Étienne Rodier, the son of a small retail merchant in Montreal. Rodier's wife was a cooper's daughter. Cartier's clientele reflected the socio-economic sphere of the Parti Canadienne:

some seigneurs, small businessmen and merchants, retailers, local forwarders, and craft producers. Many were friends and contacts of his merchant family and like that family had links to the country as well as the city. The leaders of the 1837 rebellion came from this group. Men like Louis Marchand, who was born Levi Koopman in the Netherlands and who, by the late 1820s, had gained a local recognition as a merchant in the Saint-Mathias and Chambly region; Rudolphe Des Rivières, the son of a retail merchant at Lac-des-Deux-Montagnes, who was a bookkeeper with the Banque du Peuple in 1837; and Jean-Baptiste Dumou- chelle, born in Sandwich, Upper Canada, who was by 1808 a respected merchant at Saint Benoît in the Deux Montagnes region, were typical. 'Urban villages' were the centres of rural revolt. Local merchants and local professionals led the regional uprisings. Emerging industrialists in the countryside allied with Montreal lawyers like Rodier who openly campaigned for an economy focused on the development of small, independent producers and local industries. For these entre- preneurially-minded activists, trade with England was far from a prime concern, and was often directly opposed.[49]

*   *   *

British military force put a decisive end to the Lower Canadian Rebellion of 1837- 38. Many Patriotes were arrested, over a hundred were court martialled and over fifty were deported. A Special Council ruled the province between 1838 and 1841. That Council reflected the interests of an industrially minded and developmentally oriented bourgeois class. The Council took special pains to protect the rights of landed property and mortgage creditors. Within the district of Montreal the Coun- cil abolished seigneurial tenure (with ample compensation, thus retaining the allegiance of the Catholic Church; see the sidelight on pages 218–19). Outside Montreal, it set up county registry offices for the more efficient and public record- ing of property transactions; encouraged local transportational improvement by subsidizing road, bridge, and some canal construction; and strengthened munic- ipal and local government. While some of these measures were temporary and regional in application, the Council, nonetheless, set the stage for a more active state presence in the area of business growth.[50]

The Church was not the only pillar of preindustrial Lower Canada to benefit from the emerging business state. Patriote lawyers like Cartier, Louis La Fontaine, and Augustin-Norbert Morin moved to positions of legal and political prominence as spokesmen for an active French Canadian bourgeoisie. Typical of the lawyers who came to dominate assembly representation from Lower Canada, these men advocated what has been termed positive law: the maintenance of peace, protec- tion for property, and commercial freedom. Lawyers accepted the ideas of such contemporary writers as Jeremy Bentham and John Stuart Mill who emphasized the good which an active state could do in structuring social relations. In this sense, lawyers became 'retailers of ideology'. Believing that 'property is the ele- ment that must govern the world', Cartier acted as a tireless intermediary between government and capital, francophone and anglophone ambitions, and industrial and preindustrial structures. He was the lawyer for the Seminary of Montreal and the Grand Trunk Railway, of which the Seminary was the second largest shareholder in Canada. He actively supported the creation of a strong central federal power. As Attorney General in the 1850s he took prime responsibility for implementing a new law code, a code which, while preserving French civil law, clarified contract law to meet the needs of francophone and anglophone capitalists. He streamlined judicial procedures, supported the end of seigneurial tenure, and assisted in defining labour-management contract processes.

Anglophone law firms, like that of Frederick William Torrance and William Morris, acted in a similar if less politically public fashion. As the legal historian Blaine Baker put it: 'they were important participants in fundamental ideological and institutional change undertaken as a joint venture by Montreal's post-Conquest commercial community, its élite bar and the provincial assembly.'[51] These men formed an interconnected élite, linked by marriage, business ventures, and ideology. While Cartier argued for railways, shipping, and general development in the public forum, lawyers like Torrance lobbied the Legislative Committee on Railways Canals and Telegraph Lines and the Committee on Banking and Commerce. On behalf of their clients the Molsons, Redpaths, and other emerging Montreal industrialists they pushed legislators to do away with the seigneurial system.

It may well be that Patriote lawyers saw in responsible government and the Union's elected assembly an opportunity for upward mobility that had been denied to them under the 1791 Constitutional Act with its powerful appointed councils. Yet those lawyers also continued to promote business development and were able to work increasingly comfortably with representatives of the very commercial élite against which they had rebelled in the 1830s. That élite could no longer block their access to power. Alliance with it, in fact, made such access all the more possible. Thus, to a commission for the recoding of Quebec's laws, Cartier could appoint Charles Dewey Day, a judge who had sentenced rebels to hang and who was a prominent member of the Montreal commercial-legal élite. And so, too, Cartier could be nominated for elections in 1867 by a Molson and opposed by a person who espoused the socialist ideas of Proudhon. The emerging entrepreneurially minded and individualistically oriented men of politics, law, and business allied themselves with a similarly oriented group from Upper Canada. Under the aegis of the business-political-legal nexus, the transition from a preindustrial to an industrial society took place. And, during this era of transition in business practice and directly linked to that process, the modern Canadian nation emerged.[52]

*   *   *

This is not to suggest that those engaged in Lower Canadian business between 1840 and 1870 should be seen as an undifferentiated whole. It is to suggest that relative to the pre-Rebellion era, certain Lower Canadian business interests, allied with like-minded Upper Canadians, were able to use the state in a positive way

THE SEIGNEURIAL SYSTEM, THE CATHOLIC CHURCH AND BUSINESS GROWTH IN LOWER CANADA/QUEBEC

THE SÉMINAIRE DE SAINT SULPICE

Along with the seigneurial system, the Catholic Church is often cited as an institution inimical to business development in Lower Canada/Quebec. Michel Brunet, an historian, has argued that after the Conquest the English blocked French access to the business sector and in this context the Church provided French Canadians with a spiritual rather than material purpose to life. This alleged emphasis on non-worldly pursuits prevented the creation of an entrepreneurial mind set and so helped to retard the growth of a strong French Canadian business sector. A case study of the economic activities of one arm of that church, the Séminaire de Saint-Sulpice, owner of the seigneuries of Montreal, Two Mountains, and Saint Sulpice, qualifies such a perspective.

A central institution during the pre-industrial era, as industrialization emerged in mid-nineteenth century Quebec the Seminary became more a helpmate and supporter of new central actors. During the first three decades of the nineteenth century industrialists, land speculators, and even censitaires increasingly ignored the Seminary's traditional feudal rights, selling land without paying the *lods et ventes*, poaching on seigneurial lands, milling at non-banal mills, and reneging on accumulated debts. In this context, the Sulpicians pushed for legislation which would clarify their economic powers. The Ordnance of 1840 did just that. The Seminary received corporate status, strengthening its control over rural holdings, and making choice urban industrial land available for sale. All who could afford to pay seigneurial arrears could commute their land to freehold tenure, and many urban industrialists and general land speculators took immediate advantage of the opportunity. From the Seminary's point of view it had obtained legal rights rec-

to realize their entrepreneurial ends and to institute a set of legislative enactments which went far to institutionalizing the world view that underlay those ends. In this, lawyers, legislators and entrepreneurs acted together.

On a regional level, Montreal and Upper Canadian business interests profited the most directly from such enactments. While supportive of the ideology underlying the thrust for industrial expansion, entrepreneurs in other areas fought with less success for an adequate piece of the economic pie. The ambitions and interests of Quebec City's commercial élite, for example, were not always synonymous with nor as well served as those of Montreal's. In fact, Quebec City gradually entered an at first relative and then absolute economic decline as lumber exports increasingly went to the United States; as railroad development, in Lower Canada, primarily the Grand Trunk, favoured Montreal over Quebec, thus increasingly isolating the latter on the North Shore; and as Montreal's links with developing Upper Canada increased the fortunes of that city's sugar, tea, ognized by urban industrialists and in the process had re-obtained financial control over its traditional seigneurial rights.

Over the next thirty years the Sulpicians adopted the role of helpmate to the urban bourgeoisie, selling and/or commuting much of their urban and suburban properties. Because the 1840 Ordnance exacted restrictions on the amount the Seminary could invest in land, the Sulpicians began to invest in railroad and municipal bonds. At the same time, they maintained an urban presence as a social and religious benefactor, thus helping to diffuse potential resistance to industrialization on the part of the growing number of urban poor. The Sulpicians retained restrictive control of seigneurial rights in rural areas for a much longer period. Nevertheless, by 1890 only 1 per cent of the Seminary's revenue came from seigneurial income; in 1834 some 90 per cent had come from that sector.

This accommodation to economic change transformed the Seminary's internal organization and, perhaps, its *raison d'être*. Administration became more systematized and bureaucratic.

Land and debts were treated as commodities to be sold, rented, and developed. In fact, a measure of just how completely the Sulpicians internalized the emerging industrial ethic can be seen in the sale of hundreds of overdue debts to third parties. In this way, the Seminary avoided direct adverse publicity in exacting dispossession procedures. From a landholding institution in the early nineteenth century, the Seminary had become a significant investor in stocks of transportation companies and municipal bonds; it acted as a bank of deposit; it was an active player in the urban and rural mortgage markets; and it had restructured its internal management system in the direction of a more 'secular, specialized, professional and centralized' operation. Nor was this arm of the Church unique. By the late nineteenth century such behaviour was commonplace within Quebec's Roman Catholic Church.

Source

Young, Brian, *In Its Corporate Capacity: The Seminary of Montreal as a Business Institution, 1816-76* (McGill-Queen's, 1986).

coffee, cotton and hardware forwarders, and receivers of wheat and lumber. Moreover, the final initiative of those who adhered to the dream of the Empire of the St Lawrence—the expansion and revamping of the Lachine Canal system in the late 1840s—had little to offer Quebec City entrepreneurs. In the end that reconstruction altered American trade flows not at all: the Erie Canal-New York-Great Britain route would always be cheaper, safer, and more reliable. But the Canal's expansion did result in increased hydraulic power potential, a potential quickly seized on by Montreal industrialists like John Redpath who built a seven-storey sugar refinery worth £40,000 in 1854 along its banks; or like Augustin Cantin, a steamship builder whose fully integrated plant occupied fourteen acres near the entrance to the Lachine Canal; or like dozens of smaller enterprises engaged in flour milling, sawmilling, coopering, woodworking, and manufacturing nails, saws, and axes. By 1871 forty-four industrial enterprises abutted the canal.[53]

Nor, of course, were divisions within the Lower Canadian business community simply regional. Even as industrial processes, powered by steam and organized into ever more integrated manufactories — the huge Grand Trunk shops at St Charles employed close to a thousand workers in 1871 — emerged, so too did similar changes take place within traditional craft shop enterprises. The proletarianization of labour within these sectors commenced before 1840, but such change accelerated in the 1840s and 1850s. Traditional job descriptions were redefined; skilled workers were gradually being stripped of long held shop-floor autonomies. In response to such curtailments, in the 1840s and 1850s trade unions emerged among traditional craft sectors: printers, bakers, shoemakers, painters, stonecutters, carpenters and tailors. Bargaining and contract rights were codified in 1866, marking the end of the preindustrial apprenticeship system.

Francophone entrepreneurs continued to complain about problems in acquiring credit from the largest of Lower Canada's banks. To address this situation, between 1835 and 1875, francophones founded six banks in addition to the Banque de Peuple, which received a charter in 1844 and had a capital stock of £200,000. The direction of these banks was generally controlled by francophones, and their clients drawn from French sectors of the economy. By 1875, those banks commanded assets of nearly 18 million. As the historian Ron Rudin points out, this is a substantial sum when set beside the pronouncements of a traditional historiography which has generally ignored francophone enterprise. It is small, however, when compared to the assets of the English banks. Moreover, many shareholders were English. And, finally the operations of those banks tended to be locally and regionally oriented, whereas the operations of most English banks tended to a provincial, and, after Confederation, national orientation.[54]

Within Quebec City, entrepreneurial groups contended for power. Anglo-Scots entrepreneurs controlled the traditional economy based on the British lumber trade and wooden shipbuilding. A group of *moyen bourgeoisie* men like Eugene Chinic, who had inherited a substantial fortune from his family's hardware business, and financier François Vezina, began to challenge the old élite's traditional dominance. Gradually, these men gained control of the Quebec Board of Trade and began to implement a different vision of the City's economic future. Instead of viewing Quebec as a centre for export-oriented enterprise, they saw the city as the hub of a regionally focused economy developed by railways and fuelled by financial institutions which would funnel capital into the creative hands of the *moyen bourgeoisie.*

Although this group actively promoted railways along the North Shore, links which they hoped would tie local hinterlands to Quebec City, they were only marginally successful. By 1871, Quebec had 1235 kilometres of railway, but almost none ran on the North Shore. An attempt in the early 1870s to link Lake St Jean to Quebec City via a wooden track railway proved to be a spectacular failure. The Quebec entrepreneurial élite simply could not compete against the strength of Grand Trunk interests centred in Montreal, Upper Canada, and Portland, Maine. Not until the 1880s were the North Shore railways finally completed.[55]

The emerging francophone business group was more successful in the financial sector. Vezina and Chinic established a number of successful credit institutions ranging from the Quebec Permanent Building Society and the Notre Dame Provident and Savings Bank, to the Banque Nationale. The first two institutions were not designed to serve the needs of a commercial-industrial business class, but the Banque Nationale, founded in 1860, had that class, especially its francophone component, directly in mind. Indeed Vezina believed that the Banque acted as a powerful stimulant to francophone entrepreneurship: it 'has led our fellow citizens to have more confidence in themselves and not to leave to others sources of revenue which can be as usefully and easily exploited by themselves'.[56] Perhaps it did. But it is also clear that the institution relied on and met the needs of anglo entrepreneurs as well. By 1873 nearly 30 per cent of the bank's stock was in English hands and, in addition to serving the city's most important manufacturing sector, the francophone-dominated leather industry, the Banque Nationale also financed English lumber operators to the extent of setting up a branch to facilitate their needs and to admitting at least one such entrepreneur, Henry Atkinson, to its board of directors.[57] Ethnic and business interests were rarely completely synonymous.

* * *

By 1870, Montreal dominated industrial activity within Quebec. In fact, 39 of the top 150 industrial firms in Canada were located in Montreal: its closest rival was Toronto with 14. Containing 9 per cent of the province's population (107,225), it produced 43 per cent of the province's total value of industrial output. By comparison, Quebec City, with 5 per cent of the province's people (57,699), accounted for 9 per cent of the total value of industrial output and all other urban places accounted for only a further 12 per cent.[58] Quebec manufacturing activity was extremely centralized, compared to that in Ontario. Moreover, the nature of industrial work places differed significantly between Montreal and Quebec City. Only two of every five industrial employees in Quebec City worked in a powered setting, while slightly more than one out every two employees did so in Montreal.

The artisanal and hand-powered nature of industry in Quebec City is clearly apparent when one compares the operations of its largest industrial sector, the leather industry, with its counterpart in Montreal. In both cities, leather production was the most important industrial pursuit in terms of number of firms, employees, and value added in manufacturing. In Quebec, it was also first in total value of output; in Montreal, the leather sector ranked second in that category. As Table 10.2 demonstrates, Quebec City's leather firms were, on average, considerably smaller than those in Montreal; used less steam and water power; and realized a much lower value added in manufacturing. Leather producers in Quebec City served a fairly limited local region; those in Montreal, better served by railway links and enjoying proximity to a more prosperous hinterland, sold to a more broadly based market. This brief look at Quebec City's leather industry is instructive in yet another way. In 1870, the city was facing a continuous decline in its traditional business, the export of squared timber. The leather industry was not a

Table 10.2 Leather Industry in Quebec City and Montreal, 1870

	QUEBEC CITY	MONTREAL
No. of firms	107	162
Average non-manual horsepower units	.80	3
Average fixed capital ($)	2,999	10,135
Average no. of employees	21	35
Average value of ind. production ($)	24,887	40,706
Average value added in manufacturing	9,407	20,104

SOURCE: Calculated from information in E. and G.T. Bloomfield, *Patterns of Canadian Industry in 1871*, Research Report #12 (Guelph, 1990), Appendixes A-9 and A-11.

comparable substitute: it attracted little foreign capital; it generated only modest profits and thus could lead to only minimal investment diversification; it experienced a high rate of bankruptcies. But in the end, it was the best that Quebec City could do: as the historian Jean Benoit concluded in his study of that industry:

> son développement est à l'image de l'évolution de la vièlle capitale. Isolée géographiquement, elle detient des positions secondaires au sein du nouvel échiquier des échanges.[59]

No Quebec urban centre came close to Montreal's industrial concentration. Yet it is important to note that only 8 per cent of all the province's industrial establishments were located in that city. In fact, 10,923 of the 14,467 industrial establishments counted in the 1870 census were not located in any urban centre. Rural firms, as Table 10.3 (page 224) indicates, tended to be smaller, to employ fewer and to produce less. But, as in 1831 and 1851, they continued to be a fixture of rural life.

Did industry in Quebec lag behind that in Ontario in 1870? Measured by number and variety of industries, by total output and value added, and by number of industrial employees, the answer is yes. Even when we express the data in Table 10.5 in per capita terms, the difference is evident: Ontario's per capita production exceeded Quebec's by $6; and her value added per capita exceeded Quebec's by $4.40. Morris Altman, an historical economist, has argued that this differential increased during the next thirty years. It did so, he suggests, because industrial employees in Ontario received, on average, a higher wage than their Quebec counterparts and this fact, coupled with the higher income experienced by Ontario's farmers, created a richer market for consumer goods in Ontario than in Quebec.[60]

Altman bases his interpretation on income data averaged for the whole of each province. By breaking down aggregate industrial output figures into firm and regional categories, it is possible to provide an even clearer picture of the pattern of industrialization within each province and of comparisons between the two. Some similarities can be noted. In both provinces one in seven of urban dwellers and one in twenty-nine of rural dwellers worked in industrial firms. Moreover, the dominant metropolises in both provinces far exceeded all other urban centres

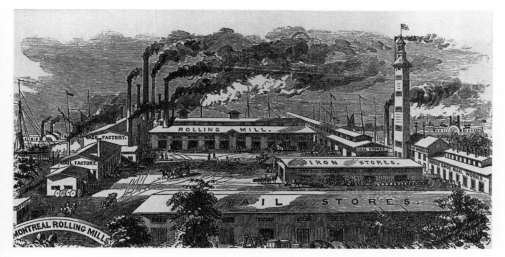

Incorporated in 1868 with a fixed capital of $200,000, the Montreal Rolling Mills ranked among the top one per cent of Canadian industrial establishments in 1871. By using the latest American steam-powered technology, its directors—prominent Montreal businessmen like Peter Redpath and William Molson—hoped to 'bid defiance to all foreign competition'. *(National Archives of Canada/C117867)*

in average total production and average value added per firm (Tables 10.3 and 10.4). Beyond these two points, however, the process of industrialization was markedly different within each province. Montreal had almost half as many firms as did all other urban centres in Quebec. In Ontario, urban industries were much more widely dispersed, reflecting in part the greater number of urban places in that province: 110 incorporated centres compared to 74 in Quebec.[61] By almost all measurements Montreal dominated industrial development in Quebec to a far greater extent than did Hamilton and Toronto in Ontario.

The suggestion that a relatively richer agrarian sector played a significant role in Ontario's industrial lead is not new. The data presented in Tables 10.3 and 10.4, however, further advance that interpretation. Canada's business historians have virtually ignored the nature of business development in rural areas. This is especially true of Ontario. As a result the extent to which the industrial process in Ontario was not simply dependent on a rich farming sector, but was itself a rural phenomenon, has been all but overlooked. In fact, much of Ontario's industrial lead can be accounted for by its small-town and rural enterprise, rather than by activity in the larger cities, the area so often focused on by historians interested in industrialization.

Rural industry in Ontario performed, on average, better than its Quebec counterpart. In value added per rural firm, Ontario's rural firms exceeded Quebec's by close to 25 per cent. In the urban context, the situation was virtually reversed: the value added per Ontario urban firm was about 18 per cent lower than that of Quebec urban firms. Montreal, however, accounted for all of Quebec's lead in the urban sector. Industry was not only more prevalent in small-town Ontario, but it also significantly outperformed its Quebec counterpart. Ontario, for exam-

223

Table 10.3   Firm Level Data: Urban and Rural Quebec, 1870

	MONTREAL	ALL OTHER URBAN CENTRES	ALL URBAN CENTRES	RURAL
No. of firms	1,150	2,394	3,544	10,923
Average total production per firm ($)	29,712	7,331	14,594	2,594
Average value added per firm ($)	12,333	3,275	6,215	1,011
Average no. of employees	19.3	6.4	10.6	2.9
Value added per employee ($)	640	509	586	349
Output per capita ($)	319	113	197	31

SOURCE: Calculated from information in E. and G.T. Bloomfield, *Patterns of Canadian Industry in 1871*, Research Report #12 (Guelph, 1990), Table 1, p. 19; Table 13, p. 53; and Appendixes A-9 and A-11.

Table 10.4   Firm Level Data: Urban and Rural Ontario, 1870

	TORONTO AND HAMILTON	ALL OTHER URBAN CENTRES	ALL URBAN CENTRES	RURAL
No. of firms	894	5,275	6,169	15,554
Average total production per firm ($)	23,568	9,380	11,436	3,178
Average value added per firm ($)	11,892	3,953	5,103	1,327
Average no. of employees	19.3	6.9	8.6	2.7
Value added per employee	650	573	597	486
Output per capita	254	363	198	39

SOURCES: Calculated from information in E. and G. T. Bloomfield, *Patterns of Canadian Industry in 1871*, Research Report #12 (Guelph, 1990), Table 1, p. 19; Table 13, p. 53; E. and G. T. Bloomfield, *The Ontario Urban System at the Onset of the Industrial Era*, Research Report #3 (Guelph, 1989), Appendix A-4.

Table 10.5   Industry in Quebec and Ontario, 1870

	QUEBEC	ONTARIO
No. of firms	14,467	21,723
No. of employees	69,182	95,215
Total production ($)	80,064,082	119,982,070
Value added ($)	33,070,990	52,123,830
Population	1,191,630	1,619,583

SOURCE: Calculated from information in E. & G.T. Bloomfield, *Patterns of Canadian Industry in 1871*, Research Report #12 (Guelph, 1990), Table 1, p. 19.

224

ple, had a 17 per cent advantage in average value added per firm in this sector. The smaller the urban centre, the greater the advantage Ontario enjoyed. Only 11 per cent of Quebec centres under 5,000 population (11 of 97) had at least one in four of their inhabitants employed in industry; the comparable Ontario figure was 62 per cent (43 of 69). It is not enough to point to Ontario's richer farming sector as a factor in the industrial advantage held by that province over Quebec in 1870. Perpetuating a stereotypical vision of rural equalling farming and urban equalling industry does justice to neither province in 1870. While both provinces exhibited significant industrial enterprise in rural areas, Ontario far overshadowed Quebec in that regard. By focusing too narrowly on industrialization as an urban phenomenon, Canada's business historians have, for too long, left the real nature and importance of rural enterprise in the shade.

Notes

[1] Two classic works which exemplify this trend are: D.G. Creighton, *The Commercial Empire of the St Lawrence, 1760–1850* (Toronto, 1938) and F. Ouellet, *Histoire Economique et Sociale du Québec, 1760–1850: Structures et Conjuncture* (Montreal, 1966). On farming, see R.L. Jones, 'French Canadian Agriculture in the St Lawrence Valley, 1815–50', in W. Easterbrook and Watkins, eds, *Approaches to Canadian Economic History* (Toronto, 1978), 110–26.

[2] Gerry Tulchinsky, *The River Barons: Montreal Businessmen and the Growth of Industry and Transportation, 1837–53* (Kingston, 1978); G. Paquet and J.-P. Wallot, *Lower Canada at the Turn of the Century: Restructuring and Modernization*, CHA Historical Booklet #45 (Ottawa 1988); S. Courville and N. Séguin, *Rural Life in Nineteenth Century Quebec*, CHA Historical Booklet #47 (Ottawa 1989). The last two contain good bibliographies.

[3] Paquet and Wallot are examples of the first. Courville is an example of the second.

[4] See, for example, Robert Sweeny, *Protesting History* (Montreal, 1984), and Sweeny, 'Paysan et ouvrier: du féodalisme laurentien au capitalisme québécois', *Sociologie et sociétés* 22 (1990), 143–61.

[5] K. Inwood and J.R. Irwin, 'Canadian Regional Commodity Income Differences at Confederation', in Inwood, ed., *Farm, Factory and Fortune*, Table 2, 102.

[6] For the notion of 'crisis', see Ouellet, *op. cit.*; R.M. McInnis, 'Perspectives on Ontario Agriculture, 1815–1930', *CPRH* 8 (1992), 77–83; F.D. Lewis and McInnis, 'Agricultural Output and Efficiency in Lower Canada, 1851', *Research in Economic History* 9 (1984), 45–87; R.M. McInnis, 'A Reconsideration of the State of Agriculture in Lower Canada in the First Half of the Nineteenth Century', *CPRH* 3 (1982), 9–49; Lewis and McInnis, 'The Efficiency of French Canadian Farmers in the Nineteenth Century', *Journal of Economic History* 40 (1980), 497–514. For critiques of the McInnis and Lewis position, see Robert Armstrong, 'The Efficiency of Quebec Farmers in 1851', *Histoire sociale/Social History* 17 (1984), 149–63 and Jack Little, 'Agricultural Progress in Canada East/Quebec: Problems in Measuring Relative Productivity during the Grain-Dairy Transition Period', *Histoire sociale/Social History* 18 (1985), 425–32.

[7] Armstrong, 'The Efficiency of French Canadian Farmers . . .'. 160.

[8]McInnis, 'Perspectives . . . ', 81.

[9]J. McCallum, *Unequal Beginnings: Agriculture and Economic Development in Quebec and Ontario until 1870* (Toronto, 1980), 42–3.

[10]Paquet and Wallot, 'Lower Canada at the Turn . . . ', and Paquet and Wallot, 'Les Habitants de Montréal et de Québec (1790–1835): Contextes geo-économiques differents, même strategie foncière', in F. Lebrun et N. Séguin, eds, *Sociétés villageoisies et rapports villes-compagnes aux Quebéc and dans la France de 21 ouest* (Trois-Rivières, 1987), 101–12.

[11]Jean-Claude Robert, 'Activities agricoles et urbanisation dans la paroisse de Montreal, 1820–40', in Lebrun and Séguin, *op. cit.*, 91–100; C. Dessureault, 'Crise ou modernisation: la société rurale Maskoutaine durant le premier tiers du XIXe siècle', *RHAF* 42 (1989), 359–88; Claude Desrosiers, 'Un aperçu des habitudes de consommation de la clientèle de Joseph Cartier, marchand général à la fin du XVIIIe siècle', *CHA Historical Papers* (1984), 91–110; Claude Pronovost, 'L'économie marchande au Bas-Canada: Le bourg de Terrebonne dans la première moitié du XIXe siècle' (MA thesis, University of Montreal, 1986).

[12]Daniel Salée, 'Seigneurial Landownership and the Transition to Capitalism in Nineteenth Century Quebec', *Quebec Studies* 12 (1991), 21–32.

[13]David Schulze, 'Rural Manufacture in Lower Canada: Understanding Seigneurial Privilege and the Transition in the Countryside', *Alternate Routes* 7 (1984), 134–67.

[14]Paul-André Linteau and Jean-Claude Robert, 'Land Ownership and Society in Montreal: An Hypothesis' in G.A. Stelter and A.F.J. Artibise, eds, *The Canadian City: Essays in Urban and Social History* (Toronto, 1984), 39–56.

[15]R. Chabot, 'Louis Proulx', *DCB* 5 (Toronto, 1983), 710–11; J. Burgess, 'Pierre Foretier', *DCB* 7 (Toronto 1988), 321–5; C. Pronovost, 'L'économie marchande . . . ', 90–1.

[16]C. Cyr and P. Dufour, 'Joseph Drapeau', *DCB* 5 (Toronto, 1983), 269–72; R. Brisson, 'Antoine Juchereau Duchesnay', *DCB* 5 (Toronto, 1983), 462–4.

[17]D. Roberts, 'George Allsopp', *DCB* 5 (Toronto, 1983), 19–23; M. Caya, 'Henry Caldwell', *DCB* 5 (Toronto, 1983), 130–3; A.R.M. Lower, *Great Britain's Woodyard: British America and the Timber Trade, 1763–1867* (Montreal, 1974); P.N. Moogk, 'John Young', *DCB* 5 (Toronto, 1983), 877–82; L. Lemoine, 'Le Moyne de Longueuil, Marie-Charles Joseph', *DCB* 7 (Toronto, 1988), 500–1; C. Cyr, 'Noël, Marie-Geneviève (Drapeau)', *DCB* 6 (Toronto, 1987), 546.

[18]J.C. Robert, 'Un seigneur entrepreneur, Barthélemy Joliette et la fondation du village d'industrie, 1822–50', *RHAF* 26 (1972–73), 375–95; R. Sanson, 'Une Industrie avant l'industrialisation: le cas de forges du Saint-Maurice', *Anthropologie et sociétés* 10 (1986), 85–107; M. Bedard *et al.*, 'Matthew Bell', *DCB* 7 (Toronto, 1988), 64–9; H. Provost, 'Jean-Thomas Taschereau', *DCB* 6 (Toronto, 1987), 750–1.

[19]F. Noël, 'Chambly Mills, 1784–1815', *CHA Historical Papers* (1985), 102–16.

[20]S. Courville, 'Croissance villageoise et industries rurales dans les seigneuries du Québec, 1815–51' in Lebrun and Séguin, eds, *Société villageoises . . . *, 205–19; S. Courville *et al.*, 'The Spread of Rural Industry in Lower Canada, 1831–1851', *Journal of the CHA* (1991), 43–70.

[21]B. Young and J. Dickinson, *A Short History of Quebec: A Socio-Economic Perspective* (Toronto, 1988), 133–4; M. Altman, 'Economic Development with High Wages: An Historical Perspective', *Explorations in Economic History* 25 (1988), 215–18.

[22]John Keyes, 'W.J.C. Benson', *DCB* 7 (Toronto, 1988), 70–1.

[23]Unless noted otherwise, this paragraph relied on John Keyes, 'The Dunn Family Business, 1850–1914: the Trade in Square Timber at Quebec' (PhD diss., Laval University, 1987).

[24]B. Young, 'James Bell Forsyth', *DCB* 9 (Toronto, 1976), 273–6; J. Benoit, 'Le Developpement des mecanismes de credit et la croissance economique d'une communauté d'affaires: Les Marchands et les industriels de la ville de Quebec au xixᵉ siècle' (PhD diss., Laval University, 1986), 426.

[25]John Keyes, 'Peter Patterson', *DCB* 8 (Toronto, 1985), 684–92; P. Landry, 'John Sharples', *DCB* 10 (Toronto, 1972).

[26]D.S. Macmillan, 'Allan Gilmour', *DCB* 11 (Toronto, 1982), 348–50.

[27]J. Keyes, 'W.J.C. Benson', *DCB* 7 (Toronto, 1988), 70–1.

[28]J. Keyes, 'The Dunn Family Business . . . ', and Keyes, 'T.H. Dunn', *DCB* 12 (Toronto, 1990), 277–81.

[29]Young and Dickinson, *A Short History . . .* , 132; Lise St-Georges, 'Louis Roy Portelance', *DCB* 7 (Toronto, 1988), 762–3; J. Keyes, 'P. Patterson', *DCB* 8 (Toronto, 1985), 688–92; A.J.H. Richardson, 'Henry Usborne', *DCB* 7 (Toronto, 1988), 872–5; M. Caya, 'Henry Caldwell', *DCB* 5 (Toronto, 1983), 130–3; A.R.M. Lower, *Great Britain's Woodyard . . .* , 68–9.

[30]Louise Dechêne, 'William Price', *DCB* 9 (Toronto, 1976), 638–43 and Dechêne, 'Les entreprises de William Price, 1810–50', *Histoire sociale/Social History* 1 (1968), 16–52.

[31]N. Séguin, *La Conquête du sol au 19ᵉ siècle* (Sillery, Quebec, 1977); G. Gagnon, 'Peter McLeod', *DCB* 8 (Toronto, 1985), 570–3; G. Bouchard, 'Introduction à l'étude de la société saguenayenne aux xixᵉ et xxᵉ siècles', *RHAF* 33 (1977), 3–28; R. Reid, ed., *The Upper Ottawa Valley to 1855* (Toronto, 1990), 87.

[32]N. Séguin, 'Jean-Baptiste Honoré', *DCB* 9 (Toronto, 1976), 397–9.

[33]G. Gagnon, 'Peter McLeod', *DCB* 8 (Toronto, 1985), 570–3; M. Lalancette, 'Alexis Tremblay dit Picotte', *DCB* 8, 892–4.

[34]J.I. Little, *Nationalism, Capitalism and Colonization in Nineteenth Century Quebec: The Upper St Francis District* (Montreal, 1989).

[35]Peter Gillis, 'The Ottawa Lumber Barons and the Conservative Movement, 1881–1914', *Journal of Canadian Studies* 9 (1974), 14–30, and Gillis, 'James Little', *DCB* 11 (Toronto, 1983), 521–2, for examples of some concerned businessmen.

[36]R.C. Harris, 'Of Poverty and Helplessness in Petite Nation', in J. Bumsted, ed., *Canadian History Before Confederation* (Toronto, 1979), 329–54; R. Sweeny *et al.*, eds, *Les relations ville/campagne: le cas du bois de chauffage* (Montreal, 1988), LIV–LV.

[37]J. Little, 'L.T. Drummond', *DCB* 11 (Toronto, 1982), 281–3; Daniel Salé, 'Seigneurial Landownership . . . ', 25.

[38]P.J. Cain and A.G. Hopkins, 'Gentlemanly Capitalism and British Expansion Overseas: The Old Colonial System, 1688–1850', *Economic History Review* 39 (1986), 501–25.

[39]Paquet and Wallot, *Lower Canada at the Turn of the Century* . . . .

[40]G. Tulchinsky, 'John Redpath', *DCB* 9 (Toronto, 1976), 654–5; A. Dubuc, 'John Molson', *DCB* 7 (Toronto, 1988), 616–21; A. Dubuc and R. Tremblay, 'John Molson', *DCB* 8 (Toronto, 1985), 630–4; G. Tulchinsky, 'G. Moffatt', *DCB* 9 (Toronto, 1976), 553–6; G. Tulchinsky, *The River Barons*, *passim*; B. Young and G. Tulchinsky, 'Sir Hugh Allan', *DCB* 11 (Toronto, 1982), 5–15.

[41]R. Sweeny, 'Beyond the Staples' in *Protesting History*, 88–99.

[42]Mary Ann Poutanen, 'For the Benefit of the Master: The Montreal Needle Trades During the Transition, 1820–42' (MA thesis, McGill University, 1985).

[43]R. Sweeny, 'International Dynamics and the International Cycle: Questions of the Transition in Montreal, 1821–28' (PhD diss., McGill University, 1985).

[44]J. Burgess, 'Work, Family and Community: Montreal Leather Craftsmen, 1790–1831' (PhD diss., University of Quebec at Montreal, 1986), 289–97; Poutanen, 'For the Benefit . . . ', 160.

[45]J. Lafleur, 'Capital marchand et transition vers le capitalisme: étude sur les marchands montréalais au cours du premier tiers du XIXe siècle' (MA thesis, University of Montreal, 1988), 105–7.

[46]D.T. Ruddel, 'La main d'oeuvre en milieu urbain au Bas-Canada: conditions et relations de travail', *RHAF* 41 (1988).

[47]G. Tulchinsky, 'John Forsyth', *DCB* 7 (Toronto, 1988), 309–11; J.M. Greenwood, 'John Richardson', *DCB* 6 (Toronto, 1987), 639–47; R. Sweeny, 'Peter McGill', *DCB* 8 (Toronto, 1983), 540–4; Peter Deslauriers, 'Samuel Gerrard', *DCB* 8, 320–2; R. Rudin, *Banking en français: The French Banks of Quebec, 1835–1925* (Toronto, 1985), 24; R. Sweeny, 'Colony and Crisis', in Sweeny, *Protesting History*, 8–52.

[48]Rudin, *Banking en français*, 25–37; Michel de Lorimier, 'Louis-Michel Viger', *DCB* 8 (Toronto, 1983), 913–17; Jean-Claude Robert, 'Jacob De Witt', *DCB* 8, 219–20.

[49]Brian Young, 'Dimensions of a Law Practice: Brokerage and Ideology in the Career of George-Étienne Cartier' in Carol Wilton, ed., *Beyond the Law: Lawyers and Business in Canada, 1830–1930* (Toronto, 1990), 92–111; R. Chabot, 'Édouard-Étienne Rodier', *DCB* 7 (Toronto, 1988), 757–9; Michel De Lorimier, 'Louis Marchand', *DCB* 11 (Toronto, 1982), 585–7, and 'Rodolphe Des Rivières', *DCB* 7 (Toronto, 1988), 247–9; B. Chassé, 'Jean-Baptiste Dumouchelle', *DCB* 7, 258–9.

[50]Brian Young, 'Positive Law, Positive State: Class Realignment and the Transformation of Lower Canada, 1815–66', in A. Greer and I. Radforth, eds, *Colonial Leviathan: State Formation in Mid-Nineteenth Century Canada* (Toronto, 1992), 50–63.

[51]G. Blaine Baker, 'Law Practice and Statecraft in Mid-Nineteenth Century Montreal: The Torrance-Morris Firm, 1848–1868', in C. Wilton, ed, *Beyond the Law . . .* , 49.

[52]Young, 'Dimensions of a Law Practice' and 'Positive Law, Positive State'; Baker: 'Law Practice and Statecraft . . . ', 45–92.

[53]G. Tulchinsky, 'Augustin Cantin,' *DCB* 12 (Toronto, 1990), 158–9; Young and Dickinson, *A Short History*, 123.

[54]Rudin, *Banking en français*, 44–5.

[55]H. Filteau and J. Hamelin, 'Guillaume-Eugène Chinic', *DCB* 11 (Toronto, 1982), 189–91; J. Hamelin, 'François Vezina', *DCB* 11, 901–3; Young and Dickinson, *A Short History*, 119.

[56]J. Hamelin, 'F. Vezina', *DCB* 11 (Toronto, 1982), 902.

[57]J. Hamelin, 'F. Vezina', *DCB* 11 (Toronto, 1982); R. Rudin, *Banking en français*, 33; J. Benoit, *Le Developpement des mecanisme de credit*, Ch. 6, Tables 1–5.

[58]E. and G.T. Bloomfield, *Patterns of Canadian Industry in 1871: An Overview Based on the First Census of Canada*, Research Report #12 (Guelph, 1990), 48, 57, Appendix A-9 and A-11.

[59]J. Benoit, *Developpement des mecanisme de credit . . .* , 741.

[60]M. Altman, 'Economic Development with High Wages . . . '.

[61]E. and G.T. Bloomfield, *Patterns of Canadian Industry* 51, fn. 29.

11 TIES THAT BIND: RAILWAYS, TARIFFS, AND BUSINESS, 1867–1885

The two Canadas came together with Nova Scotia and New Brunswick to form Canada in 1867. In 1870 Manitoba and in 1871 British Columbia followed suit, and Prince Edward Island joined in 1873. Traditional historiography argues that a group of farsighted politicians and businessmen put in place policies which went far to create a national economic structure within which the new nation could develop.[1] Railways and tariffs were two of the central props of that structure. A more recent historiography suggests that the promotion of railways, especially the Intercolonial (completed in 1876) and Canadian Pacific (completed in 1885), and the initiation of the so-called National Policy tariffs (in 1879), affected regional businesses in varied ways.[2] The new nation was a fragile alliance of many competing interests. Business was arguably the single most powerful of those interests, but regional, sectoral, and even personal agendas cut across any united business front. Some may have had 'National Dreams' but most visions were firmly rooted in sectoral, regional, and metropolitan contexts. Business people generally viewed Confederation, railways, and tariffs as a means for achieving provincial and particularistic, rather than national, goals. A closer examination suggests that the varied pattern of regional business development before Confederation was instrumental in structuring the goals of economic and business policies after 1867.

THE INTERCOLONIAL RAILWAY

By 1864, the idea of an intercolonial railway had been much debated. One historian has traced the notion back to the late 1830s.[3] In the early 1850s railway advocates in the Maritimes turned to the promotion of local lines only after they had failed to convince Imperial authorities and their Canadian neighbours of the desirability of a grander intercolonial line. Neither Canadian governments nor Imperial legislators were prepared to foot the bill for such an enterprise: Imperial loan guarantees either were not forthcoming and/or Canadian financial participation fell far short of Maritime expectations. In the early 1850s expansion-minded entrepreneurs and politicians in the Canadas looked to Portland, Maine, for a much shorter rail link to the Atlantic. Others argued for westward rather than eastward extensions. Still others favoured southern links with New York and Michigan. The rhetoric of Joseph Howe, Nova Scotia's native son, extolled the virtues of Halifax as the emporium for a continent but fell on deaf ears west of Quebec City.

Even within the Maritimes, the intercolonial concept divided reactions. Businessmen in Saint John could hardly be enthusiastic over a railway which promised to enhance the prospects of its primary urban rival, Halifax. Other towns offered moral support only if they were on the proposed route. Small wonder that when Maritime entrepreneurs turned to local roads the lines they built reflected the commercial competition of those two rival ports. Nova Scotia's publicly owned road ran, in part, from Halifax to Windsor, on Fundy's Minas Basin, in an attempt to cut traditional trade ties between Saint John and Windsor. Similarly, New Brunswick's state-owned enterprise ran from Saint John to Shediac, on the Gulf of St Lawrence, a community that had provided Halifax an entrée to the wood and fishing communities on the Gulf.[4] By the 1860s both New Brunswick and Nova Scotia had constructed a small network of local lines. Neither colony had been able to link those lines to larger through connections. It was becoming increasingly obvious that to be without such links meant becoming a backwater on the North American continent.

Yet many Maritime business people did not share that belief. Merchants involved in ocean trades — shipping, exporting, building vessels — continued to profit handsomely from such endeavours and remained relatively uninterested in continental linkages. Others, especially in New Brunswick, argued that the most sensible connecting link was with the United States, via Saint John westward to the Maine border. Advocates of the Western Extension correctly argued that trade flows were much stronger from the south than from the west, and that even flour and wheat from Canada West reached the Maritimes in bond over American railways. The strongest support for an intercolonial line emerged from those entrepreneurs and politicians involved in coal mining and the coal trade. By 1865 coal accounted for about a third of the value of Nova Scotia's exports. Four-fifths of the coal exported went to the United States: some Nova Scotia politicians hoped to diversify that trade by opening up rail links with the Canadas.[5]

In the Maritimes one could, therefore, generally find at least pockets of support for the idea of an intercolonial railway. By the 1860s several Canadian regional and sectoral interests had also begun to look favourably on the project. Quebec City entrepreneurs, increasingly restive about being cut out of the Canadian railway stakes (see Chapter Ten), began to press for a rail route which would connect that city to Halifax and other Maritime communities. Even without such a railway, Quebec enjoyed extensive trade links with Maritime communities. In the early 1850s two dozen Quebec City mercantile firms traded with the lower colonies, sending them pork, flour, and other foodstuffs and receiving, in exchange, sugar, molasses, and fish. Between 1847 and 1851 the port of Quebec exported to the Maritime 2.3 times the value of the goods it received, enjoying a trade balance of £183,000.[6] Flour exporters in Canada West also shipped, generally in bond via American roads, a substantial quantity of flour to Maritime markets. This trade increased significantly when in 1865 the United States abrogated the 1854 Reciprocity Treaty; exporters of flour wondered if the right to ship in bond would be cancelled next. Accordingly they grew more supportive of the notion of an intercolonial road on British North American soil as a back-up to the traditional and swifter routes.

231

Even more significant than these sectoral and regional interests were the changing attitudes of influential members of Canada's and Britain's political and economic élite. By the early 1860s the Canadas' most important railway, the Grand Trunk, was on the verge of bankruptcy. To men like the railway's new president, Edward Watkin, a well-connected British railwayman; G.C. Glyn and T. Baring, British bankers heavily financially committed to the Grand Trunk and, in the case of the Barings, British bankers for New Brunswick, Nova Scotia, and with the Glyns, the Canadas; and prominent Canadian politicians and railway promoters like Alexander Galt, George Cartier, and John A. Macdonald, one way out of the Grand Trunk's financial troubles was to expand to each ocean. The Grand Trunk already had a swift outlet to the Atlantic via Portland, Maine. In order to satisfy Lower Canadian interests, the Grand Trunk had also laid some track in eastern Quebec. For this section to have any chance of gaining a profit a Maritime link was essential. More deviously, the Grand Trunk management hoped that a government-operated Intercolonial would buy that mileage from them and thus save them from future deficits. Their hope was, indeed, realized in 1877 when the government purchased the Rivière du Loup line for $1,500,000, money which the Grand Trunk used to gain direct access to the lucrative Chicago market.[7] These Canadian and Imperial business groups lobbied a reluctant British cabinet. The cabinet, aware also of the need for a British rail route for the military security of the colonies, especially in the face of the Civil War raging to the south, voted to provide loan guarantees.

These varied interests converged at the historic Charlottetown and Quebec Conferences of September and October 1864, conferences which laid the foundations for Confederation in 1867. The debate over the Intercolonial was more than simply a sub-text at those conferences. As Samuel Tilley, a New Brunswick politician and banker from Saint John put it, 'We won't have the Union unless you give us the Railway.'[8] Tilley pushed successfully for the right to increase the colony's debt before Confederation, and for the right to borrow money at a lower rate of interest pending the assumption of debt by the new Canadian government. The representatives from Canada could hardly complain: their debt far overshadowed that of the Maritimes, and besides, they were extremely desirous of a larger political union in order to break some six years of political deadlock, where no coalition of political interests could command enough support to govern effectively. Even George Brown, editor of the Toronto *Globe* and leader of the Upper Canadian Reform group, a strong advocate of westward, not eastward expansion, realized that an Intercolonial route was necessary in order to achieve Confederation. These concessions allowed Tilley to raise money immediately for the Western Extension and thus to go some way toward pacifying opposition from that quarter. Charles Tupper, from Nova Scotia, also pushed for debt increases. Together they made certain that one of the clauses passed at the Quebec Conference promised the building by the new government of an Intercolonial railway.

Completed in 1876, the Intercolonial was the largest state-run transportation company in North America. Its subsequent history reflected the nature of its origins. 'In the end,' as Gene Allen, the Intercolonial's most recent historian, has remarked, 'the railway reflected a combination of different economic aims. Most of all, it was a way to pursue goals that each province had previously sought on its own. Any expression of a common national purpose was considerably harder to find.'[9] For nineteen of its first forty years the line failed to meet operating expenses.[10] Dictated in part by military considerations, its meandering route along New Brunswick's North Shore and up the Matapedia Valley to Rivière du Loup made it the longest route from the Canadas to the sea. Following its completion Maritimers regularly complained that its through rates did not sufficiently reflect Maritime interests, but the reality was that the Intercolonial was never in a favourable position to set through rates. Shipping interests provided brisk competition in non-winter seasons. The Grand Trunk and somewhat later the Canadian Pacific Railway exchanged traffic with the Intercolonial and went far to controlling the rates at which that traffic was carried.[11] But perhaps even more significantly, continental traffic was more and more being carried by continental railways.[12] The 1870s were an era of great consolidation among North American railways. Rate and traffic consortia composed of many small and independent roads were being superseded by amalgamations under unified managements. Cost savings followed and rates dropped. Those who persisted under the old system generally succumbed to their better organized and more efficiently run competitors, or rested content with carrying local trade and traffic. Many Maritimers realized the need for through links. What they had not anticipated was that links were now no longer enough. To compete effectively required a managerial structure unified at the continental level. For the Intercolonial, that did not take place until well into the next century. Looked at from this perspective it is perhaps understandable that by far the greater proportion of the Intercolonial's traffic was of a local sort. If that reality rankled Maritimers, it bothered few other Canadians and it nicely reflected the particularistic rather than national concerns that lay behind the railway's origins and, indeed, the origins of the nation of which that railway was a part.

THE CANADIAN PACIFIC RAILWAY

Few Canadians historians have resisted the temptation to see the Canadian Pacific Railway (CPR) as a primary agent of national integration. Such a perspective is easy to understand. The Riel Rebellion of 1870 convinced the Canadian state that a swift Canadian route to the west was necessary, if only in order to maintain control over the Métis. The agreement facilitating British Columbia's entry into Confederation stipulated that a railroad would be built to link the Pacific colony to the rest of the Canadian nation. The rhetoric of Sir John A. Macdonald and the Conservative supporters of the Canadian Pacific continually emphasized the national importance of such a railroad. Moreover, in some respects, a case can be made for seeing that road as an integrative force, a technology successfully challenging American business expansion into western Canada in the 1880s. In the end, however, such a perspective obscures more than it enlightens. It sidesteps the question of which groups and regions in the nation were most advantaged or disadvantaged by its construction. That issue can only be briefly considered in this chapter. Of more relevance here is the point that the nationalist perspective does scant justice to the nature of the road's origins: it casts a shadow over the primary importance of international capital markets, American financial and railway expertise, and the role played by a central government fully aware of and receptive to the demands of those capital markets and expertise. Clearly the CPR had political roots. Nationalist historians, however, have privileged those roots to the near-exclusion of more economic and pragmatic considerations. The point is that, as the historian Albro Martin has noted, 'the influence of political ends is obvious from the earliest stages of the railroad age in America.'[13] In that respect the Canadian Pacific Railway was in no way unique. Railway promoters, financiers, and managers understood this and worked within that context to achieve often very different ends. Indeed, it is tempting to assert that the political background of the railway's origins is, given its commonplace nature, the least interesting aspect of its early history. State policies were clearly important, but to consider their implications primarily at a national level is to miss those aspects of the railway's promotion that put it at the leading edge of nineteenth-century railway and financial behaviour. A closer look at the interests behind the activities of those businessmen most involved in the promotion and construction of the CPR is necessary if one hopes to understand its origins and its ultimate impact.[14]

Even in the 1850s the building of Canadian railways responded to the needs of far more than simply colonial interests. The Great Western, the Grand Trunk, and even the Northern were as much links in American railway networks as they were lines designed to assist colonial development. As Isaac Buchanan, a Great Western promoter, admitted, 'Ours is not simply a Canadian road.'[15] Nor, from its inception was the Canadian Pacific. By the late 1860s Boston interests associated with a complex of rail lines known as the Vermont Central were considering how to gain control of a rail system that would link their city directly to the midwest and thus enable them to compete effectively with New York and its existing New York Central, Great Western, and Michigan Central lines. One possibility was to acquire a route through Canada to run to Sault Ste Marie and then south of Lake Superior to connect with the Northern Pacific. An existing arrangement with the Grand Trunk was proving far too circuitous, especially in the face of a series of amalgamations by their New York competitors. Vermont Central interests, accordingly, enticed the Minnesota-based entrepreneur Jay Cooke to acquire control of the Northern Pacific. Cooke did so and in order to forestall competition from the St Paul and Pacific, he also acquired control of that line, in the process severely overextending his financial capabilities.

For the Vermont Central interests, Cooke was an important partner primarily because of his experience—gained during the Civil War—in selling bonds on the international financial market. By the late 1860s methods of raising money for large capital-intensive projects had evolved considerably since the early 1850s. Investment bankers now rarely acted alone in the purchase and sale of bond issues. Rather, they entered into syndicates which cut across national lines. These syndicates expected national governments to be in a position to provide grants and/

or other support to facilitate the project's completion and make more palatable the sale of securities. Nationalist historians lead one to believe that the Canadian government under Sir John A. Macdonald, a government pledged to construct a railway to the Pacific, was somehow naïve and ignorant of American developments and the mechanics of international finance. Nothing could be further from the truth. In fact, Macdonald and other government members had themselves encouraged Cooke to become involved with the Northern Pacific. Even more importantly, Macdonald and others encouraged the Vermont Central group to enter into an agreement with Hugh Allan, a prominent Montreal ship owner and perhaps the wealthiest businessman in Canada, who had become dissatisfied with the service of the Grand Trunk Railway, to form a company for the construction of the new Canadian railway. Moreover, by providing, in an act of June 14, 1872, 50,000,000 acres of land and $30,000,000 in cash subsidies to the contracting company the government met the prior demands of Allan and his American associates. All of this had, nonetheless, to be conducted in secret. Macdonald's constant public pronouncements of an all-Canadian route controlled by Canadians, which would allegedly protect Canada from the grasping Americans, stood in dramatic contrast to the realities of the deal. When details became public and when it also became clear that Macdonald had squeezed Allan for about $350,000 to spend on the recent election campaign, Macdonald got cold feet. He looked instead to a rival company headed by a different group of Canadian capitalists, but one which also quietly proffered American backing, to either amalgamate with Allan's company or conduct the business itself. For Macdonald, however, it was a case of too little, too late: his government was overthrown and the first attempt to construct a Canadian continental road collapsed with it.

Most nationalist accounts stop at this point: domestic politics and nationalist sentiments are seen as the crucial variables. But other forces, pressures that can only be appreciated by broadening one's analytical perspective, also played a role in the company's and the government's fortunes. The attempt by Cooke, Allan, and the Vermont Central promoters to raise capital on the international market was being thwarted by a combination of Grand Trunk Railway interests and rival investment bankers. Sir John Rose, a past finance minister in Macdonald's government and long a confidant of British financial backers of the Grand Trunk, was himself a partner in an interlinked British and American investment banking operation. To protect Grand Trunk interests and to weaken Cooke, a rival player in other bond flotations, Rose spread false rumours in Britain and Europe which effectively undermined the Cooke/Allan attempt to raise international capital. These activities, coupled with the international economic downturn of 1873, led to Cooke's bankruptcy. Interestingly, those who moved in to pick up the pieces of Cooke's transportational schemes — J.J. Hill, a Canadian expatriate living in the American mid-west; George Stephen, sometime president of the Bank of Montreal; J.S. Kennedy, a New York investment banker, and several others — joined with Sir John Rose's banking interests to acquire the contract for the construction of the new Canadian Pacific Railway as offered by none other than John A. Macdonald, following his return to power in 1878!

Macdonald did insist on the construction of an all-Canadian route, but to make the prospect of building a line across tundra and swamp north of Lake Superior palatable to contractors and international investors, his government granted $25,000,000 and 25,000,000 acres of land, completed sections worth $38,000,000, and a twenty-year monopoly prohibiting the building of any railway south of the CPR's main line without its consent. On the strength of these guarantees, these men created a syndicate to purchase and sell CPR securities to British, French, Dutch, German, and American markets. Even then the financing and construction proved troublesome in the extreme. The talents of George Stephen in raising funds and of the American manager William Van Horne in overseeing construction coupled with the timely assistance of Macdonald saw the venture through to completion in 1885.[16]

If the Intercolonial Railway reflected more the ambitions of certain regionally-based entrepreneurs than those of nationally-motivated business/statemen, the CPR reflected as much the agenda of internationally focused railway men and financiers as that of nationally focused Canadian politicians and capitalists. About half the common shares were owned by Americans. The banking interests with which Sir John Rose was affiliated were, according to the historian Dolores Greenberg, 'intimately involved in the decision affecting the Canadian Pacific, and those roads such as the Ontario and Quebec, the Toronto Grey and Bruce, the Credit Valley and the Soo which had ties to the transcontinental'.[17] The promotion, financing, construction (often by American contractors and, in British Columbia, Chinese workers), and management of the CPR point to the international rather than purely national nature of its origins. All of these factors reflected what one writer has termed 'the latest stage of capitalist development'.[18] Large capital-intensive projects could not be floated without having recourse to international investment syndicates. Such syndicates required the effective support of a strong state government before they would participate. Even labour requirements were partly met by tapping an international labour market. Looked at from this perspective, the promotion and construction of the CPR marked Canada's coming of age in an era of international financial capital.

* * *

The CPR and other railways also marked a new era in the business and economic development of British Columbia and the prairie west. The CPR's impact on industrial development in British Columbia was especially dramatic. By 1890 British Columbia's major urban centres boasted substantial industrial activity. Measured by per capita manufacturing output, Victoria, for example, ranked fifth in 1890 of the twenty Canadian cities with a population in excess of 10,000. By 1900, however, it had dropped from the top 25 per cent to the bottom 20 per cent in that ranking. Urban competition from its mainland rival, Vancouver, does not account for that change. By 1900, as a study by John Lutz has demonstrated, British Columbia, as a whole, was becoming deindustrialized. In several ways the CPR played a major role in this change. Firstly, the company established rates which, in 1901 facilitated the shipment of goods from Winnipeg to Golden, B.C.

In the mid-1880s the Albion Iron Works, Victoria's largest manufacturing enterprise, employed about 260 men and occupied an entire city block. Its existence belies the notion of Victoria, and indeed British Columbia, as a peripheral 'frontier' zone with little industrial capability. *(British Columbia Archives and Records Service/16775 A-6220)*

(1620 km) at the same cost as the shipment of goods from Vancouver or Victoria to Golden (765 or 845 km). Moreover it was approximately 13 per cent cheaper to send any item from Toronto to Vancouver than it was to send the same item from Vancouver to Toronto.[19] In this context British Columbia industries were restricted to a purely local business. In this sense locational constraints were artificially, not naturally, created.

But the CPR played a further role in the province's deindustrialization. As part of a program of aggressive expansion the railway purchased a number of locally owned transportation enterprises. Prior to the CPR's takeover, those companies had generally purchased their vessels, boilers, and other equipment from local manufacturers, like the large Albion Iron Works at Victoria. Following the take-over, the CPR routinely ignored local manufacturers and purchased supplies and material inputs from eastern Canadian companies. Non-local owners appropriated manufacturing inputs as well as corporate profits. In yet a third way the Company proved pivotal in redefining, at least, Victoria's economic future. Even as it helped strip Victoria of its manufacturing base, it contributed to the development of a relatively new enterprise, tourism, via the construction of the elegant and centrally located Empress Hotel.

Prior to railways, the Hudson's Bay Company had continued to enjoy strong if not absolute control over trade and development on the prairies. The beginning of the end was signalled in 1878 when the St Paul, Minneapolis and Manitoba Railway reached Winnipeg. Winnipeg merchants could now receive eastern goods by an all-rail route. The CPR further integrated the west into a competitive inter-national business milieu. Capitalists from Britain, eastern Canada, and the United States flocked to the west. By 1886, in Winnipeg, some nineteen large mercantile firms specialized in western commerce. To compete, the Hudson's Bay Company hired a new and aggressive ex-railway manager, C.J. Brydges, and he further diversified and decentralized the company's operations, establishing individual sales or retail/wholesale shops along the route taken by the CPR. Extensive cattle ranches, owned by British and eastern entrepreneurs, were established throughout southern Alberta.[20]

If the CPR helped open up the west to business competition, it nonetheless favoured some players over others. The Ogilvies, owners of a long established flour merchant firm in Montreal, entered into exceptional rate and traffic deals with the railway, as did the Hudson's Bay Company. In general, traffic rates favoured goods moving from eastern shippers and manufacturers to the west and British Columbia rather than the eastward flow of especially western manufac-tured items. The rates of the CPR and other railways also tended to favour rela-tively established businesses and commercial centres over newer regional points and smaller competitive firms. In the western context, Winnipeg benefited the most from such a bias. That city's business community pressured the CPR to grant shipping rates allowing it to compete effectively with Toronto and Montreal inter-ests throughout Western Canada. From the CPR's perspective, such favouritism facilitated the growth of stable and strategically located business centres in the developing west and thus made possible more efficient and centralized shipping operations. Even as the CPR helped open the west to competition and capitalist expansion, so, too, by exerting great control over the flow of commerce, the road went far to tying western entrepreneurs to Winnipeg and eastern economic interests. In this sense, freight rate structures played an important role in the pattern of regional economic development. Tariff rate structures promised to do the same. Yet, as the historian Ken Cruickshank has put it, '[u]nlike the formal and informal bargaining that went into the revision of customs tariffs . . . the final decision about freight rates rested with a private interest, the railway corporation.'[21]

TARIFFS, BUSINESS, AND THE STATE

Nineteenth-century British North American governments did not draw on income taxes of a personal or corporate sort to help finance their operations. Despite intermittent debate, politicians consistently shied away from this policy, fearing the imposition of such taxes would bring about the end of their political careers. This limitation on state income has often been downplayed by historians who argue that the state had little direct role to play in the social and economic affairs of nineteenth-century colonies and countries. Such a view has recently come under significant revision.[22] Starting in the second quarter of the nineteenth century, colonial governments became increasingly active in not only economic but also selected social areas of development. We have already outlined the importance of state activities in canal, railway, land, and resource development throughout British North America. The limits on income resources often proved crucial to policy formation in these sectors.

Moreover, as work by the historian Michael Piva has persuasively demonstrated, '[t]he critical role played by the state . . . went beyond tariffs, canals and railways; the state also kept this economy going.' It did so by balancing the Canada's consistently large trade deficit (it averaged about $10,000,000 between 1850 and 1866) by importing loan capital from Britain. After 1856 those loans were no longer used to finance real growth: they were increasingly spent to service the interest on an already existing debt.[23]

In the context of increasing pressure on state finances, tariff policies assumed an ever more central position on state agendas. Before Confederation the Canadas drew about 80 per cent of their revenue from customs duties. Between 1867 and 1879 the federal government raised about 60 per cent of its income from that source. Tariffs, of course, were far from benign instruments: their increase or decrease directly affected the livelihoods of many British North Americans. Export- and import-oriented merchants generally favoured low tariffs. The growing industrial sector, in common with their counterparts in the United States and Germany, applied pressure for higher tariffs in order to provide protection for 'infant' industries and facilitate job creation in the industrial sector. In various decades (among them, the 1830s and 1870s) farming interests also pushed for tariff protection. Gradually business tactics became more sophisticated, evolving from relying on individual friendships, to petitioning, to the formation of associations and groups for the express purpose of lobbying governments. By the

ENTERPRISING WOMEN IN URBAN BRITISH COLUMBIA, 1863–96

Historians tend to overlook the activities of women who were self-employed or employers of others, reflecting an approach to women's history embedded in the notion of 'separate spheres', a rhetoric which emerged in the nineteenth century as part of a process of subordinating and containing much of the behaviour of women in society. Yet a closer look suggests that the behaviour of a significant number of women in the late nineteenth century fails to fit a model which stresses the separation of work from home; the notion of home as a residence for family only; and the seclusion of women within the private bounds of family while males operated as the sole transactors of public activity outside that sphere.

Using 1870 census data, one historian has identified 30,087 midwestern American businesswomen, 10.5 per cent of all working women. A study of self-employed women in Victoria and Vancouver found that they represented 20 per cent of all working women. A little over 80 per cent of the 293 individuals operated in what has been called the traditional sphere of women's activities: accommodation-related ventures; dressmaking and millinery work; teaching—music, art, dancing, and cooking; and selling women's goods.

Probably 75 per cent engaged in these entrepreneurial activities out of sheer economic necessity. Indeed a full 40 per cent of married businesswomen (30 of 75) in Victoria and Vancouver in 1891 had no husband living in the home. For many of these women independent entrepreneurial activity represented a course of last resort, rather than a conscious choice to pursue an independent career.

Yet a somewhat broader context suggests that some women at all class levels were consciously carving out independent economic roles for themselves. For those who had some capital, the passage of a series of Married Women's Property Laws in the 1880s facilitated such independence. After 1887, British Columbian women were, as one federal judge put it, 'completely emancipated from their husband's control both as regards the enjoyment and the disposition of their real estate'. The changing composition of landholders in Victoria, B.C. suggests that married women took advantage of this legislation. In 1863, of every 25 non-institutional property holders only one was a women; by 1882, women were one in ten, and by 1891 one out of every five non-institutional property holders was a woman. Moreover an analysis of the

third quarter of the nineteenth century, tariffs could never be structured simply for revenue purposes. The interests of an increasingly dynamic, albeit diversified and regionally disparate, business class had also to be closely considered.

Even the Reciprocity Treaty of 1854 (which lasted until the US abrogation of 1865) reflected the dual pressures of state finance and industrial development on tariff formation. That Treaty provided for free trade in natural products: most goods imported into the Canadas were of a manufactured sort, thus revenue

240

loans granted by two large trust and loan companies in Vancouver and Victoria in the early 1890s revealed that one out of every eleven dollars loaned went to a woman. Some women, like the wife of R.G. Tatlow, a Vancouver businessman, thoroughly appreciated the power commensurate with owning her own land. On the eve of moving into a new house erected on *her* property, she, her husband ruefully admitted, 'has already hinted at "board"'!

Young married women were especially active as land-owners, credit takers and businesswomen. Some of these women would seem to have been consciously limiting family size in order to manage the demands of an alternative career, thus challenging a central prop of the cult of domesticity. Nor were such ambitions limited simply to bourgeois or upper-class women. Class position did condition motivation and constrict activity patterns. Yet even within poorer families independent ambitions died hard, as the following petition to the judicial court from fourteen-year-old Eva Clarke on the eve of her mother's death demonstrates. With her father's business verging on bankruptcy, Eva feared for her economic future:

I have been learning to play the piano for about eighteen months altogether. My present teacher is W. Sharpe of Victoria. It is my intention to qualify myself for a teacher of music of which I am very fond. It is necessary for me to have a piano in order that I may practice. I practice on the piano daily about two hours but it will not be possible for me to continue this practice unless I have a piano in the house where I live.

Eva's reaction to the death of her mother in 1888 provides a poignant illustration of individual perspectives within families and underlines the possibility that many young women in late-nineteenth-century Victoria openly sought independent career goals. Historians have ignored the existence and indeed realization (however constrained) of such ambitions for far too long.

Sources

Backhouse, C.B., 'Married Women's Property Law in 19th Century Canada', *Law and History Review* 6 (1988), 211–57.

Baskerville, P., 'She has already hinted at "Board": Enterprising Urban Women in British Columbia, 1863–96' *Histoire social/ Social History*, 1993.

Cohen, M.G., *Women's Work: Markets of Economic Development in Nineteenth Century Ontario* (Toronto, 1988).

Murphy, L.E., 'Business Ladies: Midwestern Women and Enterprise 1850–1880', *Journal of Women's History* 3 (1991).

sources were relatively untouched and at least 'incidental protection' to industry could be promised.[24] In the context of dramatic fiscal shortfalls and increasingly articulate industrial pressure the Canadian state increased tariffs on manufactured goods in 1858 and 1859. Some historians have seen these increases as primarily in the interests of industry; others have viewed them as fashioned to meet the financial needs of the government.[25] Those tariffs, especially that of A.T. Galt in 1859, in fact attempted to meet both needs. Revenue considerations may have been paramount, but with a sophisticated mix of *ad valorem* and specific duties, Galt went far to meet the demands of Lower Canadian importers, railways, and industrialists. The revenue so generated fell short of need, and the precarious state of the Canadas' finances represented a major spur for Confederation.

At a more general level it also seems plausible that those tariffs, combined with more efficient and cheaper internal transport costs, provided sufficient protection to facilitate significant manufacturing growth in the Canadas during the 1850s, 1860s, and early 1870s. Politicians were increasingly sensitive to the needs of the manufacturing sector. L.H. Holton, for example, in charge of government finance in 1863, was reluctant to lower tariffs because he feared that such action would 'raise a storm of enraged special interests about our head'.[26] High duties clearly commanded significant support from an important local sector.

One of the main assumptions lying behind Canadian fiscal policy before Confederation was the notion of a limitless frontier. By the late 1850s that notion was running up against the rocks of the Precambrian Shield. Rich agricultural land was at a premium in the Canadas. The sticking point, however, was that in the past the frontier vision had blinded the eyes and loosened the pockets of British financiers. By the 1860s, as the limitless frontier evinced finite boundaries, those investors were becoming increasingly tight-fisted and sharp-sighted. In this sense, too, Confederation offered a possible solution. The untapped west could become the new frontier, a hazy, ill-defined, but seemingly limitless horizon of opportunity. 'It would re-create,' as Piva put it, 'those visions of grandeur waiting to be realized through immigration and settlement, stimulated by the transportational projects that an expanded state would encourage.'[27] In this context, too, tariff policies would retain their central importance.

Not until the downturn in the economy following 1873 was there sustained pressure to raise duties to a significantly higher level than those established during the immediate pre-Confederation era. In fact, the first federal tariff simply copied the last tariff from the Canadas. New Brunswick and Nova Scotia interests had little input into that process. Even facing a faltering economy and declining revenues the Liberal Government headed by Alexander Mackenzie in the 1870s stood firm against any tariff increase. This gave Macdonald his opportunity. Taking advantage of an increasingly organized industrial lobby and a growing sympathetic labour movement, Macdonald came out strongly in favour of higher tariffs, a National Policy which would provide protection to industry against the dumping of products by American competitors. In a telling speech in 1877, Macdonald promised that:

> We will give a sufficient protection for every industry and we will be governed by evidence which we will carefully collect and gather regarding every manufacture and every trade. We will make every manufacture, every industry, produce the evidence of what is necessary for the purpose of protecting them in their present struggle into maturity; and gentlemen, that protection will be given them.[28]

Partly on the basis of the National Policy platform and partly due to the lacklustre performance of the Liberal Government, Macdonald swept back to power in 1878. Samuel Tilley, his Finance Minister, did, indeed, sift through industrialists' demands with painstaking care. Ben Forster, an historian, has demonstrated clearly that the Conservative government exercised a great deal of autonomy in creating its tariff policy: business interests were divided on regional and sectoral levels. New Brunswick industrialists were sharply divided on the tariff question. In Nova Scotia, manufacturers and coal producers supported higher tariffs, shipping and importing interests argued for the reverse. Industrialists in Quebec and Ontario failed to work closely as a united front. Individual manufacturers' demands were often in conflict with the demands of others. Business disunity gave the government much leeway and, while strong Conservative supporters were indeed rewarded, the government, in the end, acted on what it perceived to be its own interests.[29] Manufacturers were gaining power within the economy and the polity, but they were not yet dominant.[30] Agrarian, mercantile, and especially revenue interests also figured prominently in the government's calculations. Amidst competing and interacting interests, compromise not control, brokerage not imposition, characterized the tariff policy-making process.

Forster argues that loftier goals, those related, for example, to fostering western development and a nationally integrated economy, occupied a back row during this process. Linking the tariff to western development is more the product of later historians' imaginations than the considered policy of nineteenth-century governments. It is difficult to disagree completely with this interpretation. As an instrument for nation building, the National Policy tariff was ambiguous at best. High tariffs were viewed as necessary, but only temporary. Once 'infant' industries matured, tariffs would presumably have served their purpose. For some, tariffs existed simply as bargaining ploys designed to force the American state to lower duties and re-enter a reciprocity agreement. Moreover, when American industrialists, barred competitive entry, hopped over the tariff wall and set up branch plants in Canada, politicians cheered. The potential hazards involved in branch plant development were not a consideration.

Even more significantly, historians have yet to confront the probable complexity of tariff impacts. Just as the industrial lobby was not all of a piece, so, too, the tariff was a variegated instrument. To generalize about its effect is unwise, and not simply because it dealt differently with different industries. Canada was itself a nation of regional and intra-regional contrasts. As we have seen, by 1870 industrial development had proceeded at a different pace between and within regions. Not only did the pace of development differ, so, too, did the evolving industrial structure. In New Brunswick and Nova Scotia in 1870, industrial firms were smaller in size, less well financed, and paying their workers a lower wage than was the case in Ontario and in the Montreal region of Quebec.[31] These differences are rooted in the pre-Confederation era and have been discussed extensively in earlier chapters. Suffice it to say that household production and enclave development constrained industrial growth in the Maritimes to a far greater degree than was the case in much of central Canada. It may be that the small size of Maritime firms made it difficult for them to benefit in the long term from tariff policies.[32] Confederation, the Intercolonial, and the National Policy tariff were not the only and probably not even the primary reasons for Maritime industrial problems. One cannot hope to understand regional industrial differences by ignoring what occurred before and what was in place on the eve of the passage of the National Policy in 1879.

In one region of Canada, however, tariffs may indeed have made a significant difference. As A.A. Den Otter has pointed out, tariffs, in conjunction with railways, did effect a revolution in the transaction of trade in the prairie west. The Canadian Pacific Railway could not, by itself, rechannel trade into an east-west rather than north-south axis, but the railway did spark the westward movement of a large number of Canadian merchants, thus cutting into what had fast become an American preserve. But the CPR still had to compete with American transcontinentals, roads with direct links to Winnipeg. Eastern manufacturers in Canada would still have had to compete for the growing western market with larger and better financed American competition. The imposition of a 'deeply protective' tariff made such competition less possible. It also, as Den Otter has illustrated, forced American wholesalers, like T.C. Power and Brother Company and I.G. Baker and Company of Fort Benton, Montana, to purchase their supplies in Canada, often in Montreal, and ship them in bond over American railways to the west. The tariff, therefore, did not preclude American mercantile competition in the west. Nor did the tariff necessarily facilitate the shipment of goods over the CPR. But it did force American competitors to buy in Canada, if they wished to sell in Canada. That requirement, coupled with the dramatic increase in competition, undercut most American wholesalers and contributed to making the prairie west and British Columbia a hinterland market for Winnipeg and eastern business interests and a favourable investment frontier for British capitalists.[33]

Despite the rhetoric of nineteenth-century politicians and twentieth-century nationalist historians, railways were not the unalloyed steel of nationalist dreams and tariffs were not the sharp instruments of industrialists' hopes. Railways and tariffs were not conceived, constructed, and/or implemented in a vacuum. The evolution and impact of both reflected and were conditioned by interacting pressures of local, regional, national, and international origins. Even as Canada attempted to integrate its regions into a national whole, it was itself becoming integrated into a wider capitalist world. Canada's business communities stood at the interface of such pressures. How they balanced these complex and often countervailing forces is a central theme of subsequent chapters.

Notes

[1]D.G. Creighton, *John A. Macdonald: The Old Chieftain*, vol. 2 (Toronto, 1958); Pierre Berton, *The National Dream: The Great Railway, 1874–1881* (Toronto, 1970); H.A. Innis, *A History of the Canadian Pacific Railway* (Toronto, 1930). For a review of this literature as it relates to railways, see P. Baskerville, 'On the Rails: Trends in Canadian Railway Historiography', *American Review of Canadian Studies* 9 (1979).

[2]See, for example, Ken Cruickshank, 'The Intercolonial Railway, Freight Rates and the Development of the Maritime Economy', *Acadiensis* 22 (1992), 87–110; Cruickshank,

'The People's Railway: The Intercolonial Railway and the Canadian Public Enterprise Experience', *Acadiensis* 16 (1986), 78–100; Gene Allen, 'The Origins of the Intercolonial Railway' (PhD diss., University of Toronto, 1991); K. Inwood, 'Transportation, Tariffs and the Canadian Iron Industry', Discussion Paper #89–3 (Department of Economics, University of Guelph, 1989); Ben Forster, *A Conjunction of Interests: Business Politics and Tariffs, 1825–79* (Toronto, 1986); A.A. Den Otter, 'Nationalism and the Pacific Scandal: A Re-examination', *Canadian Historical Review* LXIX (1988), 315–9.

[3]Allen, 'Origins of the Intercolonial . . . '.

[4]Gene Allen, 'The Intercolonial Railway and the Economic Aims of Confederation, 1861–67', unpublished paper, CHA, Charlottetown, PEI (June 1992), 3–4.

[5]D.A. Muise, 'The Federal Election of 1867 in Nova Scotia: An Economic Interpretation', *Nova Scotia Historical Society* 36 (1967), 329.

[6]Allen, 'Origins', 160–1. Figures calculated from Tables 1 and 2, Chapter 5.

[7]P. Baskerville, 'Sir Joseph Hickson', *DCB* 12 (Toronto, 1990), 432–5.

[8]Allen, 'The Intercolonial Railway', 16.

[9]Ibid., 34.

[10]Cruickshank, 'The Intercolonial Railway', *passim.*

[11]Cruickshank, 'The Intercolonial Railway', *passim.*

[12]On this general point, see Baskerville, 'Sir Joseph Hickson', and Baskerville, 'Americans in Britain's Backyard: The Railway Era in Upper Canada, 1850–1880', *Business History Review* 55 (1981), 314–36.

[13]Albro Martin, *James J. Hill and the Opening of the Northwest* (New York, 1976), 238.

[14]For some work which is critical of the nationalist perspective, see L.B. Irwin, *Pacific Railways and Nationalism in the Canadian-American Northwest, 1845–1873*, 2nd ed. (New York, 1968); A.A. Den Otter, 'Nationalism and the Pacific Scandal'; Dolores Greenberg, 'A Study of Capital Alliances: The St Paul and Pacific', *CHR* 57 (1976), 25–39; Karen Anderson, 'The State, the Capitalist Class and the CPR' in R.J. Brym, ed., *The Structure of the Canadian Capitalist Class* (Toronto, 1985); Peter George, 'Foreword' in H.A. Innes, *A History of the Canadian Pacific Railway* (Toronto, 1971); Albro Martin, *James J. Hill and the Opening of the Northwest.*

[15]Cited in Baskerville, 'Americans in Britain's Backyard', 33.

[16]This discussion of the CPR is primarily drawn from works cited in footnote 14.

[17]Greenberg, 'A Study of Capital Alliances', 39.

[18]Anderson, 'The State', 126.

[19]John Lutz, 'Losing Steam: The Boiler and Engine Industry as an Index of British Columbia's Deindustrialization, 1880–1915', *CHA Historical Papers* (1988), 168–208.

[20]A.A. Den Otter, 'Transportation, Trade, and Regional Identity in the Southwestern Prairies', *Prairie Forum* 25 (1990), 1–23; Den Otter, 'Railway Technology, the Canadian Northwest and the Continental Economy', *Railroad History* 162 (1990), 5–19.

21Donald Kerr, 'Wholesale Trade on the Canadian Plains in the Late Nineteenth Century: Winnipeg and Its Competitors' in H. Palmer, ed., *Settlement of the West* (Calgary, 1977); Ken Cruikshank, *Close Ties: Railways, Government and The Board of Railway Commissioners, 1851–1933* (Montreal, 1991), ch. 2 (quote, 21).

22Allan Greer and Ian Radforth, eds, *Colonial Leviathan: State Formation in Mid-Nineteenth-Century Canada* (Toronto, 1992).

23Michael Piva, *The Borrowing Process: Public Finance in the Province of Canada, 1840–1867* (Ottawa, 1992), 174–5.

24L.H. Officer and L.B. Smith, 'The Canadian-American Reciprocity Treaty of 1855–66', *Journal of Economic History* 28 (1968), 596–623.

25For examples of those who stress the protective effects, see D.F. Barnett, 'The Galt Tariff: Incidental or Effective Protection?', *Canadian Journal of Economics* 9 (1976), 389–407, and A.A. Den Otter, 'Alexander Galt, the 1859 Tariff and Canadian Economic Nationalism', *CHR* LXIII (1982), 151–78. Examples of those who stress either revenue or a combination are: Ben Forster, *A Conjunction of Interests: Business, Politics and Tariffs, 1825–1879* (Toronto, 1986), and M.J. Piva, *The Borrowing Process*, ch. 6.

26Cited in Baskerville, 'Imperial Agendas and "Disloyal Collaborators": Decolonization and the John Sandfield Macdonald Ministries, 1862–64' in D. Keane and C. Read, eds, *Old Ontario: Essays in Honour of J.M.S. Careless* (Toronto, 1990), 247.

27Piva, *The Borrowing Process*, 220.

28Ben Forster, 'The Coming of the National Policy: Business, Government and the Tariff, 1876–1879', *JCS* 14 (1979), 45.

29Forster, *A Conjunction of Interests*.

30Paul Craven and Tom Traves, 'The Class Politics of the National Policy, 1872–1933', *JCS* 14 (1979), 14–38.

31Kris Inwood, 'Maritime Industrialization from 1870 to 1910: A Review of the Evidence and Its Interpretation', *Acadiensis* 21 (1991), 132–55.

32Ibid., 151.

33Den Otter, 'Transportation, Trade and Railway Technology'.

4

THE AGE OF BUSINESS CONSOLIDATION 1885–1929

12 COMMANDING HEIGHTS

In the late nineteenth century the investment banker emerged as the virtual embodiment of capitalism. In the editorial caricatures of the new mass-market newspapers, he appeared as the 'bloated plutocrat' replete with pin-stripe trousers, black frock coat, diamond stickpin, and top hat. In the works of radical social critics, 'finance capitalism' represented an advanced form of concentrated economic and political power: from their position on the 'commanding heights' of the economy, investment bankers consolidated industrial monopolies and maintained their control through interlocked directorates of commercial banks, manufacturing firms, and the older merchant houses.

From the 1880s through the First World War the great finance capitalists of the era—J.P. Morgan in the US, the Rothschilds in England and Europe, Hikojiro Nakamigawa in Japan—were the most visible elements in a complex process of industrial growth and business consolidation. The networks of rail and wire erected in the late nineteenth century presented opportunities for commercial and industrial entrepreneurs to exploit national and international markets. The development of new technologies in chemical, electrical, and metallurgical processing enhanced the capabilities of manufacturers to expand production while reducing unit costs, achieving economies of scale. But the expansion of marketing and manufacturing required substantial capital investment. In the early nineteenth century the relatively modest capital needs of manufacturers came from savings of individual entrepreneurs or partnerships, augmented by short-term commercial loans and reinvestment of earnings. These sources were insufficient to cover the heavy initial costs of large-scale manufacturing and distribution. To meet these needs a wider capital market had to be tapped, and new financial institutions emerged to mobilize money on the scale required.

The mechanisms for mobilizing large-scale capital varied widely across the industrializing world. In Germany and Japan, national governments encouraged big commercial banks to move directly into financing long-term investment in railways, manufacturing, and export trade ventures and often to exercise proprietary control over these enterprises. In the US, where commercial banking had become more decentralized since the 1830s, a different, more informal pattern emerged. After the American Civil War, a small number of investment houses appeared. They were often linked to but functionally separate from commercial banks, and located for the most part in eastern seaboard cities where they could tap foreign, principally British, money markets. These investment houses, such as Jay Cooke's in Philadelphia or Morgan's in New York, would underwrite entire issues of stocks and bonds for railways—and after the 1890s, industrial enterprises—reselling the securities at a profit to investors in New York and London. Unlike the German or Japanese banks, however, these investment houses acted primarily as middlemen rather than exercising direct control over the companies they financed.

In Britain a more complex system of capital financing had developed by the late nineteenth century. In contrast to the US, where banking across state lines was legally banned and small local banks proliferated, commercial banks in Britain established branches throughout the country, and by the end of the 1880s a few large institutions dominated the scene. British entrepreneurs used these banks for a variety of services. These banks did not generally engage in long-term investment or underwrite security issues; but British businesses could go into the stock and bond markets for these needs, tapping the savings resources of the wealthiest nation of the age. A variety of financial agents, stock and bond brokers and portfolio managers facilitated securities issues which were marketed to assorted savings institutions, investor syndicates and wealthy individuals. The availability of capital for investment, and the large number and variety of investors enabled British firms to expand without significantly altering the prevailing pattern of small and medium-sized industrial enterprises well into the twentieth century. At the same time, the size of the London money markets attracted capital seekers not only from the United States but also from Canada and other Dominions of the British Empire.[1]

FINANCE CAPITALISM IN CANADA

The Canadian financial community developed mechanisms for capital mobilization that represented a unique configuration of institutional arrangements, influenced by the patterns of the metropolitan centres of the Atlantic economic community, but also reflecting its colonial heritage and the particular needs of an underpopulated, resource-rich economy. Completion of the Intercolonial Railway linking the Maritimes and central Canada in 1876 and of the Canadian Pacific Railway in 1885 offered the prospect of a national market to aspiring entrepreneurs, and the National Policy tariffs promised protection to domestic manufacturers. By the mid-1890s, the potential resources of the western and northern interior regions were becoming visible to Canadian and foreign business observers.

It is important to keep a sense of perspective about the pace and scale of Canadian capital development. Even in the early 1900s, most capital formation was carried out by individuals through reinvestment of earnings or by small-scale partnerships. Although growing, Canadian urban centres were small by international standards: in 1890 the combined population of 400,000 of the two largest cities, Montreal and Toronto, was less than half the size of Chicago in the United States, only slightly larger than Dusseldorf, a medium-sized German industrial city. Most business enterprises in the country were small proprietary firms operating in local markets, and the emergence of large consolidations in some industries over the next two decades did not wholly transform this pattern.

The major holders of Canadian savings — approximately 60 per cent of the total in 1890 — were the chartered commercial banks. Authorized by the Bank Act of 1871, these banks, like their British counterparts, were allowed to establish branches throughout the country, and the Act set substantial capital reserve requirements, thus restricting competition in the field. Business slumps in the late 1870s and early 1890s further reduced their numbers. Between 1890 and 1920 the number of chartered banks shrank from 41 to 18, while the survivors extended a network of more than 4600 branches across Canada. Smaller proprietary banks serving local communities steadily gave way to the national joint-stock enterprises that could more readily ride the fluctuations in the business cycle.

The chartered banks, reflecting their origins and the influence of British commercial banks with whom they did business, were principally oriented to serving the needs of merchants for short-term credit to finance inventories and shipping costs. As they advanced into the western farming communities, the banks extended credit on a seasonal basis to wheat growers, but only to cover operating costs.

In the latter part of the nineteenth century, mortgage loan companies emerged to finance farms and residential construction, benefiting from the expansion of cities and filling a need that the commercial banks neglected. By the 1890s almost 20 per cent of Canadian financial assets were held by mortgage loan companies. The banks responded to this challenge by moving into the savings deposit field, offering rates competitive with the mortgage companies, but well into the twentieth century they remained relatively minor participants in the residential construction market (see Table 12.1).

The mortgage and loan companies provided a source of longer-term credit than the commercial banks, but only in a specialized area. By the early 1900s another source of domestic finance capital was developing with a more liberal approach to the longer-term credit needs of the economy. Between 1870 and 1890 Canadian life insurance companies made inroads against foreign-owned firms in that market, controlling over 60 per cent of the business by 1890 with assets of $20 million. That figure doubled over the next decade and more than tripled again between 1900 and World War I. In an era when pensions were provided to few people outside the government service, life insurance found a growing demand among the urban middle class. The earnings of this booming service industry initially moved into mortgage financing; but the life insurance companies also diversified into railways and other corporate securities, either directly or through loans to brokers and securities underwriters.

Although mortgage companies, life insurance firms and other smaller institutions such as trust companies — which at this time catered primarily to a small wealthy clientele — attracted an increasing proportion of Canadian savings, the chartered banks continued to command the bulk of the country's domestic capital resources through World War II. In *The History of Canadian Business, 1867–1914*, the political economist Tom Naylor advanced the argument that the dominant position of the chartered commercial banks in Canada, with their preference

Table 12.1 Canadian Financial Institutions: Distribution of Assets

YEAR	BANKS	INSURANCE	OTHER[a]
1901	75%	6%	19%
1929	50%	13%	37%

[a] (Includes savings & loans, trust companies, etc.)

for short-term lending principally for merchants and staple exporters, stunted Canadian manufacturing by diverting depositors away from local private banks and loan companies that were more inclined to support fixed capital investment. The chartered banks were more likely to invest abroad, particularly in the United States and Britain, rather than in home-based industries. As a result, Canada's manufacturers remained small and inefficient, vulnerable to foreign competition without tariff protection and equally vulnerable to foreign takeovers that the National Policy encouraged.[2]

Naylor's arguments have been challenged by Canadian business historians as based on faulty premises and inadequate evidence. In developing his thesis, Naylor treated railway investment, in which large chartered banks such as the Bank of Montreal played a major role, as distinct from industrial investment— even though both types of activity required substantial amounts of fixed initial capital; and railways not only stimulated manufacturing of iron and steel, but also developed their own machine shops and factories to produce locomotives and rolling stock.

While commercial loans may have constituted the bulk of the business of chartered banks, general conclusions about their investment practices need further study. An examination by James Frost of the policies of the Bank of Nova Scotia, for example, provides evidence on both sides of the controversy. Established in the 1830s, the BNS extended branches throughout the Maritimes in the 1880s and by the early twentieth century had become a national institution with its head office in Toronto. Through the 1880s the BNS invested substantially in Maritime industries, but shifted its emphasis thereafter to investment outside the region, in Caribbean utilities and US real estate among other fields. Although the Bank's directors appear to have become disenchanted over the prospects for industrial growth in the Atlantic Canada region during the depression of the 1890s, it continued to underwrite some manufacturing ventures there as late as 1910, particularly in the coal and steel industries.[3]

The lending and investment policies of particular financial institutions, however, provide a rather misleading picture of the structure of Canadian finance. While chartered banks, mortgage houses, life insurance and trust companies functioned as separate organizations, they were interlinked by ownership ties into a few cohesive 'communities of interest' which initially formed in the various regional metropolitan centres in the 1880s and 1890s. The most important groups were in Montreal and Toronto; by the 1920s they had extended their financial tentacles throughout the country, eclipsing other aspirants in the Maritimes and western Canada.

Montreal was the site of the first such assemblage of finance capitalists, who retained a dominant position in the field through the 1930s. Under George Stephen and Donald Smith (Lord Strathcona), the Bank of Montreal played a central role in the financing of the CPR; the fruits of that venture helped to underwrite expansion into a variety of industrial, commercial and financial endeavours. By the early 1900s the Bank of Montreal/CPR group held substantial investments in, and colonized the boards of (among others) Sun Life, the largest insurance company in Canada; Consolidated Mining and Smelting, a direct spin-off of the CPR; Ogilvie Flour Mills and Lake of the Woods Milling Co., which dominated that market and controlled networks of grain elevators across the prairies; Montreal Loan & Mortgage Co.; and numerous cotton mills, fire and marine insurance companies, trust companies, and ventures in emerging fields such as pulp and paper production.

In Toronto, the central figure of the turn-of-the-century financial community was George Cox, president of the Imperial Bank of Commerce and Canada Life Assurance, second only in their respective fields to the Bank of Montreal and Sun Life. Cox and his associates controlled other major insurance firms in Ontario, National Trust, and Central Canada Savings & Loan; through links with enterprising railway and industrial entrepreneurs such as William Mackenzie and Joseph Flavelle, they were also involved in meat packing, hydroelectric power and urban tramways, iron and steel, cement manufacturing and retail merchandising.

Although there was an element of rivalry between the established financial centre of Montreal and the growing industrial metropolis of Toronto—enlivened in the first decade of the twentieth century by railway competition between the CPR and the Canadian Northern Railway which had financial ties with the Bank of Commerce—members of both groups joined forces from time to time in investment ventures. The relationship of Herbert Holt and William Mackenzie is instructive in this regard. Holt began his career as a subcontractor for the CPR, then consolidated electric utilities in Montreal, and eventually became president of the Royal Bank of Canada—which, like the Bank of Nova Scotia, had moved from its original base in the Maritimes, and during Holt's era (although not necessarily through his exclusive leadership) developed into the largest bank in the country, surpassing the Bank of Montreal by 1929. (See Table 12.2.) Although maintaining his ties with the CPR group and operating from a Montreal base, Holt also took an interest in Latin American utility ventures promoted by Mackenzie (another CPR veteran) who had joined Cox in Toronto, developing electric utilities in that city before moving on to direct Canadian Northern's challenge to the CPR in the west.

Montreal and Toronto were the major centres of high finance in Canada, but other regionally-oriented groups congregated in some of the older commercial cities of the east. In Halifax, for example, John F. Stairs, scion of a long-established merchant family, sought to build a Maritime-based financial domain. An

Table 12.2   The Ten Leading Financial Institutions Ranked by Assets

1901	1929
Bank of Montreal	Royal Bank of Canada
Canadian Bank of Commerce	Bank of Montreal
Merchants Bank of Montreal	Canadian Bank of Commerce
Dominion Bank	Royal Trust Co.
Canada Life Assurance Co.	Public Utility Investment Co.
Bank of Nova Scotia	Bank of Nova Scotia
Imperial Bank	National Trust Co.
Bank of Toronto	Toronto General Trust Co.
Molson Bank	Canada Life Assurance Co.
Royal Bank of Canada	Dominion Bank

SOURCE: Compiled from *The Canadian Annual Financial Review* (Toronto), 1901, 1930.

advocate of the National Policy, Stairs envisioned an industrial future for his region, based on its position on the transatlantic trade routes and its coal reserves, and energetically promoted ventures in sugar refining, textile production, and iron manufacturing. His ambitions were cut short by his sudden death in 1904. Even before that point, however, financial interests from Boston and Montreal had begun to move into the Maritimes, and the shifting locus of regional control was signalled by the departure of Stairs' protégé, Max Aitken, to Montreal in 1907.

Another group remained outside the orbit of the metropolitan financial centres: French Canadian banks in Quebec. Although initially dependent on anglophone capital, by the late nineteenth century these banks had large savings reserves from French Canadians, had established modest branch operations across the province and in French-speaking communities in the Maritimes and the west, and were dominated by francophone directors. They provided commercial loans to businesses in these communities and, through affiliated trust companies, invested in local industries, although out of necessity a greater part of their investment went into non-francophone Quebec firms. The larger chartered banks of Montreal did not seek to impinge on these activities and anglophone shareholders in the 'French' banks were content to leave the French Canadian managers to their own devices.

Although small and localized operations in comparison with the powerful institutions of Toronto and Montreal, the francophone banks were sufficiently important in the Quebec economy to induce the provincial government to support a merger in 1924 of the two largest entities, the Banque d'Hochelaga and the Banque Nationale, to protect the interests of francophone depositors and businesses dependent on their credit. The leading figures of the French Canadian banking community in the early twentieth century, F.L. Beique and Joseph-Marcellin Wilson of the Banque d'Hochelaga, were tied in with the anglophone financial community of Montreal through Holt and Joseph Forget.

By the end of the first decade of the twentieth century, the aspirations of financial groups outside central Canada were declining, with Montreal and Toronto bankers entrenched as the heart of finance capitalism in the country. Ensconced in awe-inspiring neoclassical bastions of marble and masonry along King Street in Toronto and Saint James Street in Montreal, a group of no more than 40 or 50 men—bankers, lawyers and securities brokers—presided over a financial community with assets of over $1.6 billion. The ties that bound this élite were essentially personal and social rather than institutional: links forged by shared experiences, values, and kinship. Common to more than half of them was a Scottish heritage: 25 per cent were immigrants, a larger proportion second- or third-generation Scots. The overwhelming majority were Anglican or Presbyterian with a rising number of Methodists. Members of the same private clubs, their children attending a select circle of boarding or day schools, they encountered one another regularly at charitable events, weddings, graduations, funerals, and other social occasions as well as in the boardrooms of the numerous companies whose fortunes they commanded.

The financial élite of Canada evolved from small, closely-knit merchant communities in an underdeveloped colonial society, isolated from one another and from their transatlantic political masters and trading partners for long periods of time due to poor communications and transportation, and thus very much dependent on ties of kinship and mutual personal trust to survive. The telegraph, steamship, and railway were breaking down these barriers by the end of the nineteenth century, and the corporate structures they were erecting introduced an element of bureaucratic formality into business activities; but for the money men of Montreal and Toronto, many of them born a decade or more before Confederation, the older patterns of personal loyalty persisted.[4]

MONEY MARKETS AND MERGERS

Given the informal nature of their business relationships, personal contacts among Canada's financial élite played a major role in the processes of capital mobilization. In the absence of institutional arrangements such as investment banks, financiers formed private syndicates to underwrite large capital outlays, drawing upon the assorted agglomerations of savings at their disposal. In exchange, the syndicates took large quantities of corporate bonds with some common stock thrown in as a bonus, to be sold later if and when the undertaking became profitable. The securities would then be marketed through specialized companies affiliated with the syndicates: in Toronto, for example, Cox relied on the brokerage house of A.E. Ames, which was presided over by his son-in-law; and Dominion Securities, run by another protégé, E.R. Wood. The Bank of Montreal fielded securities through Louis J. Forget, one of the few French Canadians to successfully breach the anglophone financial bastions in Quebec, and several other brokerage houses. Both the Bank of Montreal and the rising Royal Bank worked closely in the great merger movement of 1909–13 with Max Aitken's two organizations, Royal Securities and Montreal Trust.

The immediate sites of activity were the stock exchanges in Montreal and Toronto. Both had emerged in the mid-1870s; as might be expected, neither was particularly impressive in comparison with the metropolitan exchanges of New York and London which absorbed the largest security issues, government and railway bonds. The Toronto exchange was located, until 1913, on the second floor of the Ames brokerage house, with Cox as its landlord. Nevertheless, the exchanges did benefit from the growth of the economy between 1900 and 1914, and the diversification of financial institutions. Trust, insurance, and loan companies provided call loans to brokers and investors; and even the chartered banks entered the market in a small way, although they preferred lending to investors in New York where the volume of business ensured greater liquidity in times of crisis as, for example, in the short but sharp market panic of 1907, and the slump engendered by the outbreak of war in Europe in 1914.

The two exchanges competed for business, probably to the detriment of both, although there was a certain amount of regional specialization. The Toronto exchange did a much larger volume of business in shares of non-banking financial companies and speculative mining ventures than Montreal, which had a virtual stranglehold on railway stocks traded in Canada. But Toronto mounted a strong challenge in the first decade of the twentieth century to Montreal's hitherto dominant position, acquiring over 50 per cent of shares in banks by the end of that period and competing vigorously in the growing field of hydroelectric utilities. Nevertheless, Montreal remained the leading securities market in Canada through World War I, particularly in the lucrative bond trade.[5]

But Canadian exchanges picked up only the odds and ends of the market. The big money was sent—or came from—elsewhere. The larger brokers like Ames traded heavily on the New York exchanges, and promoters of major underwriting ventures like James Dunn and Aitken headed for London. Virtually all federal and provincial government bonds were marketed outside Canada, and the large railways followed suit. In 1913 the bulk of CPR shares was held by British investors, with Canadian participation at about 13 per cent. The Grand Trunk remained an even more British undertaking, and Canadian Northern, the Canadian 'west's own product', was critically dependent on inflows of capital from London. The industrial mergers of 1909–13 were carried out by Canadian financial entrepreneurs using mostly British money. Of these, perhaps the most flamboyant was Max Aitken.

The prewar merger movement, the dramatic expansion of government securities issues to finance Canadian participation in World War I, and rather exaggerated expectations about the growth prospects of the 'new staples' — newsprint and metals—in the 1920s all contributed to the development of more specialized and diversified techniques of financial underwriting. By this time a number of companies were emerging that labelled themselves investment banks, such as Nesbitt Thomson and Wood Gundy. Their clients were increasingly found in Canada: the British investment market never fully recovered from the losses of World War I, and the Americans tended to focus on particular areas such as mining and petroleum and to use US brokers or to invest directly in Canadian firms,

MAX AITKEN

'The little fellow with the big head'—this was how Bank of Montreal president Edward Clouston described Max Aitken following their first encounter in 1904. Clouston was (probably) referring to Aitken's physical characteristics, but to other contemporaries it would have been an apt description of the brash young promoter's massive ego. Restlessly ambitious, Aitken alternately intrigued and exasperated the financial leaders of Halifax, Montreal, and London in the first decade of the twentieth century. Yet his achievements matched his ambitions. In Britain, where he settled in 1910, Aitken became Lord Beaverbrook, one of that nation's leading press barons, held Cabinet posts in both World Wars, and left a $40 million estate at his death in 1964. In Canada his legacy—besides a $12 million Beaverbrook Foundation supporting universities and museums—included major industrial consolidations and, more significantly, a host of innovative techniques for mobilizing large blocks of capital.

Born in 1879, son of a Scots Presbyterian minister, Aitken grew up in the isolated hinterland of New Brunswick where he formed early links of friendship with two other ambitious young men: James Dunn, who like Aitken would become a major figure in Canadian and British finance and ultimately salvaged Algoma Steel; and R.B. Bennett, later to become one of Canada's leading corporate lawyers and then Prime Minister of Canada. After several years of adolescent aimlessness, Aitken wound up in Halifax in 1902

Max Aitken, the little man with the big head. *(McCord Museum of Canadian History, Notman Photographic Archives)*

where he began a career as a stock and bond salesman for John F. Stairs. His success in these endeavours—and his penchant for simultaneously doing business on his own account—induced Stairs and his associates to set up Royal Securities Co. under Aitken in 1903. Following Stairs' unexpected death a year later, Aitken chafed under restraints placed on him by other investors in Royal Securities, and he sold out his interest in 1907 and moved to Montreal, where he bought Montreal Trust Co. In 1909 he sold Montreal

Trust to the Royal Bank of Canada and resumed control of Royal Securities.

Up to 1909 Aitken's promotional activities had focused on electric utility ventures in Latin America, and consolidating industries in the Maritimes. Riding a tide of investor optimism as the economy recovered from the Panic of 1907, he turned his attention and skills to mergers in the industrial heartland of central Canada. During one frantic year, 1909-10, Aitken assembled a series of major consolidations, including Canada Cement, Canadian Car & Foundry, Canadian Consolidated Rubber, and the Steel Co. of Canada (Stelco). A multimillionaire at age thirty, he then left Montreal, seeking greater worlds to conquer across the Atlantic.

'I created all the big trusts in Canada,' Aitken later boasted to Winston Churchill. This was a characteristically exaggerated claim, but he was a major figure in the transformation of the Canadian financial scene. When he began his promotional career, the market for Canadian securities was small, the instruments of capital mobilization limited, and even the most prominent bankers had little experience in underwriting the large flotations required to finance corporations that could operate on a national scale. During his apprenticeship in the Maritimes, Aitken developed sales techniques for luring small investors into the market; and along with Dunn and other financial entrepreneurs, he created a network of contacts in the larger and more varied London investment community. With a broader view of economic possibilities than many of his contemporaries, Aitken assessed both the market prospects and internal capabilities of the companies he assembled. Since he rewarded himself with large quantities of bonus stock from these mergers, his aim was to create logically coherent business structures that would dominate their markets, and his expectations were generally borne out.

Finally, Aitken both inspired and trained a new generation of financial investment specialists who refined, elaborated, and expanded on his techniques. Among the recruits to Royal Securities in its early years were C.H. Cahan, later a minister in the cabinet of Conservative Prime Minister R.B. Bennett; Arthur Nesbitt who later established a major investment and brokerage house; Ward Pitfield, whose descendants included the founder of Pitfield McKay Ross, and one of Pierre Trudeau's closest government advisors. Aitken's chosen successor at Royal Securities, Izaak Walton Killam, assembled even larger (though less durable) mergers in the 1920s when he became known as the 'mystery man of high finance'. When Killam died, he left an estate four times the size of Aitken's, and a tax bill sufficient to help establish the Canada Council.

Sources

Armstrong, Christopher and H.V. Nelles, *Southern Exposure* (Toronto, 1988), 107-47.

Marchildon, G.P., 'John F. Stairs, Max Aitken and the Scotia Group: Finance Capitalism and Industrial Decline in the Maritimes, 1890-1914', in Kris Inwood, ed., *Farm, Factory and Fortune: New Essays in the Economic History of the Maritimes* (Fredericton 1993), 197-218.

Taylor, A.J.P., *Beaverbrook* (London, 1972), 1-42.

especially in manufacturing. Canadian brokers coaxed hitherto private family firms, such as Massey-Harris, to go public and spun off specialized investment companies that held large quantities of common stocks as well as bonds in a variety of industries.

A second merger boom, larger than the prewar episode, took shape in 1925–29, generating 315 consolidations accumulating assets of nearly $1 billion, three times the size of the earlier mergers. The economic collapse of 1929–32 destroyed many of these speculative endeavours and chastened the survivors; market activity stagnated through the Depression and World War II. But mutual funds made an appearance in the 1930s, representing a less risky opportunity for small investors; and trust companies became more significant players on the financial scene, managing a growing body of public and private pension funds in the 1940s and 1950s. The investment community remained small, but the instruments of capital mobilization became more diverse, responding to both the growth of the Canadian economy and the broadening of the market for securities among middle-class investors.[6]

WEALTH AND POWER IN CANADA

How powerful were the finance capitalists in this era of dramatic economic development and industrial consolidation? To be sure, they had at their disposal vast reservoirs of money—'other people's money', as their critics pointed out—and used their strategic position in the investment process to maximize their profits. From the proceeds of these investments they enriched themselves and their families, procured lucrative employment opportunities for their children, in-laws and cronies, and erected tasteless late-Victorian palaces: Henry Pellatt's pseudo-Gothic castle in Toronto remains as a classic example of this form of conspicuous consumption. But did they exercise real control over the multitude of companies whose boards they populated, and did they determine the long-term direction of the industrial economy?

Much of the recent scholarship on the role of investment bankers in other countries suggests that their domination of the corporate empires they assembled was transitory and incomplete. Most of the merger titans of the turn of the century, like the conglomerators of the 1960s or the corporate take-over artists of the 1980s, were interested primarily in short-term profits, not enduring responsibility for these enterprises. The few who sought to translate financial leverage into operational control of companies or whole industries, like Morgan in the United States, experienced mixed fortunes. Many of their corporate agglomerations collapsed under the weight of excessive debt; control of those that survived passed into the hands of professional managers, who could be periodically purged, but represented a permanent feature of life in the upper echelons of twentieth century capitalism. Finance capitalists thus represented a phase in the evolution of the corporate economy, playing a significant role in the mobilization of capital and creation of large-scale enterprises, but a group whose influence was ultimately hedged about by other contending forces in the industrial system: managers, government regulatory bodies, unions, and financial competitors with innovative techniques for tapping a larger and more diverse capital market.

Was this the case in Canada? Opinions differ, both on the question of the extent of influence of the finance capitalists over the economy and the durability of their power. Certainly there is an enduring popular conviction that Canadian business has been dominated by a close-knit élite whose seat of power shifted from Montreal to Toronto but remained otherwise intact. Western agrarians complained mightily about the political as well as economic influence wielded by the Montreal/CPR clique at the turn of the century. In the 1930s the Social Credit guru of Alberta, 'Wild Bill' Aberhart inveighed against the 'fifty big shots' who ruled the country. Forty years later the journalist Peter C. Newman popularized the concept of a 'Canadian Establishment'—admittedly a somewhat broader group, encompassing bankers, lawyers, holding company titans and a sprinkling of industrialists — perpetuating their domination through interlocked directorships, cultivating each new generation through their private schools and social networks. The corporate managers whose significance bulks large in contemporary portrayals of the American business system were dismissed as 'the frightened men in corner offices', constantly harried by the bottom-line demands of their investors.

In academic circles, the notion that an entrenched financial élite dominates Canadian business found a secure niche among political economists and sociologists who generally rejected the view that 'managerial capitalism' displaced the finance capitalists, or that wealth and political influence had become more widely distributed and competitive in the industrial world in the mid-twentieth century. As noted earlier, Naylor traced the roots of this financial oligarchy back to Confederation while others, such as Wallace Clement, explored the linkages between Canadian and American financial leaders who formed a 'continental corporate élite'.

This interpretation provided a certain intellectual respectability for widely-shared popular opinions in Canada, but has encountered criticism from several directions. The Quebec sociologist Jorge Niosi challenged the assumption that the turn-of-the-century financiers established lasting domination over the corporate entities they sired or that the Canadian economy was dominated by a single cohesive élite. Although Niosi's 'ruling class' was small and concentrated in central Canada, it was never fully entrenched, as new groups emerged in the twentieth century—professional managers, Jewish and French Canadian financial and industrial entrepreneurs, western Canadian oilmen—to undermine the power of the older Anglo-Scots establishment. Similarly, Canadian business historians have drawn a more complex picture. In *Northern Enterprise*, Bliss dismissed the economic power of the finance capitalists and professional managers—and for that matter virtually all groups aspiring to control the Canadian market—as transitory at best. Assailed by public critics of big business, frustrated in their attempts to perpetuate family dynasties, many of the financial barons of the early twentieth century succumbed to the remorseless pressures of competition, changing markets, unforeseen or irresistible economic disasters, or their own misjudgements.[7]

Regardless whether they exercised substantial and enduring domination over the Canadian business scene, did the country's finance capitalists focus on certain sectors of the economy while neglecting others, particularly manufacturing? On this point, there is more agreement. As noted earlier, the large chartered banks preferred short-term commercial loans over long-term fixed commitments of capital, although they provided an increasing volume of call-loan money to investors in the early twentieth century. Canadian investors in turn generally preferred to channel their money into the securities of financial institutions and electrical utilities at home and abroad, particularly in the US and Latin America. British portfolio investment in Canada, much of which flowed through the hands of the financial syndicates in Montreal and Toronto, tended to concentrate on government bond issues, railways, and the mining industry. During periods of investor optimism, as in 1909–13 or the late 1920s, some of this money went into industrial investment, particularly to finance mergers, but in general industrial securities (if railways and utilities are excluded from the definition) were embraced with less enthusiasm.

Canadian industrial ventures were not, however, starved for capital. A substantial amount of direct investment—establishment of Canadian affiliates by foreign firms—flowed into the country in this era. The asset value of this direct investment more than doubled between 1897 and 1913, by which time it represented almost one-third of the total value of publicly-owned corporate stock in Canada. The largest volume of this investment came from the United States, totalling $254 million in 1910, of which 43 per cent was in manufacturing (including pulp and paper processing) and a large part of the balance in mining and smelting. From British sources came another $120 million in direct investment, almost 50 per cent of which was in manufacturing and mining.[8]

There were, then, distinctive patterns of investment and consequently of ownership in the various sectors of the Canadian economy apparent by World War I. Banks, financial institutions and utilities were financed by Canadians through domestic and British sources, and these companies for the most part remained in Canadian hands. Industrial and mining ventures depended more heavily on foreign direct investment and the extent of foreign ownership was proportionately greater.

These distinctions were of little consequence to most contemporaries. Domestic or foreign capital, portfolio or direct investment, all of it was welcome to help finance Canadian economic growth in the early years of the twentieth century. In the 1970s and 1980s, as Canadians worried over the consequences of a branch-plant economy for their industrial competitiveness and national economic independence, the origins of these problems were traced back to this era and the indifference of Canada's financial élite toward industrial investment, a view advanced in particular by the political economists. But the argument rested on the assumption that these attitudes were unique to Canada's finance capitalists; this was not necessarily the case. In Britain, for example, many of the chartered banks and the largest private merchant banks, Baring Brothers and Rothschilds, were wary of industrial investment, preferring to finance commercial undertakings and back government bonds. In Japan, the banks that sprang from established merchant houses like Mitsui were equally reluctant to finance industrial ventures. Even in the US, the big investment banks pursued security, not risk: railroad and industrial mergers were promoted when they seemed likely to dominate or monopolize markets; the small entrepreneur with a bright idea had to look elsewhere for initial capital. The common thread is that finance capitalists in general were cautious men, trusting only the judgement of their close associates, looking for a sure thing and sceptical of innovation.

The turn-of-the-century finance capitalists of Canada and other countries deserved much of the opprobrium heaped upon them by contemporaries and historians. They formed tight exclusive groups hostile toward those not of their own social background. To enhance their personal wealth and power, they helped themselves freely to the savings of thousands placed in their trust. They formed investment syndicates that engaged in insider trading, deceptive marketing of securities, and other practices of questionable legality even in their own time. To augment their short-term profits, they saddled companies with burdens of long-term fixed debt that often drove these enterprises to ruin, leaving bankruptcies and unemployment in their wake. They rarely supported innovative entrepreneurship, and siphoned scarce capital resources to sectors of the economy that were already operating at excess capacity. At the same time, these financiers performed tasks of capital mobilization that were beyond the means of individual businesses and many governments; assembled an international network of institutions that could channel money from established commercial centres to promote development of remote hinterlands; and developed increasingly diverse techniques for financing large and complex corporate organizations that would populate the heartland of the industrial world through the late twentieth century.

Notes

[1] On investment banking in the US, see Vincent Carosso, *Investment Banking in America* (Cambridge, Mass., 1970), and *The Morgans: Private International Bankers, 1854–1913* (Cambridge, Mass., 1987). On German banks and industrial investment, see Richard Tilly, 'Mergers, External Growth and Finance in the Development of Large-Scale Enterprise in Germany, 1880–1913', *Journal of Economic History* 42 (1982), 629–58. On British financial techniques, see R.C. Michie, 'Options, Concessions, Syndicates and the Provision of Venture Capital, 1880–1913', *Business History* 23 (1981), 147–64.

[2] On various Canadian capital-mobilizing institutions, see W.L. Marr and D.G. Paterson, *Canada: An Economic History* (Toronto, 1980), 243–64; E.P. Neufeld, *The Financial System of Canada: Its Growth and Development* (Toronto, 1972); K.A.H. Buckley, *Capital Formation in Canada, 1896–1930* (Toronto, 1955); Ian Drummond, 'Canadian Life Insurance Companies and the Capital Market, 1890–1914', *Canadian Journal of Economics and Political Science* 27 (1962), 204–24. On banks' attitudes toward industrial investment, see R.T. Naylor, *The History of Canadian Business, 1867–1914* vol. I (Toronto, 1975). For critiques, see L.R. Macdonald, 'Merchants Against Industry: An Idea and Its Origins', *Canadian Historical Review* 56 (1975), 263–81; Paul Craven and Tom Traves, 'Canadian

Railways as Manufacturers, 1850–1800', *Canadian Historical Association, Historical Papers* (1983), 254–81; Kris Inwood, *The Canadian Charcoal Iron Industry* (New York, 1986), 5–7; Gerald Tulchinsky, 'Recent Controversies in Canadian Business History', *Acadiensis* 8 (1978/79), 133–9.

[3]On the Bank of Nova Scotia, see James Frost, 'The "Nationalization" of the Bank of Nova Scotia, 1880–1910', *Acadiensis* 12 (Autumn 1982), 3–38. Neil C. Quigley, Ian Drummond and Lewis T. Evans, 'Regional Transfers of Funds Through the Canadian Banking System and Maritime Economic Development, 1895–1935' in Kris Inwood, ed., *Farm, Factory and Fortune: New Essays in the Economic History of the Maritimes* (Fredericton, 1993), 219–50, also finds little evidence that banks in that region neglected or discriminated against local manufacturing investment.

[4]On the Toronto and Montreal financial élites, see Christopher Armstrong and H.V. Nelles, *Southern Exposure*, 3–23; A. Ernest Epp, 'Cooperation Among Capitalists: The Canadian Merger Movement, 1909–13' (PhD thesis, Johns Hopkins University, 1973); Bliss, *Northern Enterprise*, 278–81. On the aspirations of the Maritime financial community, see T.W. Acheson, 'The National Policy and the Industrialization of the Maritimes, 1880–1910', *Acadiensis* 1 (1972), 3–29. On the 'French' banks, see Ronald Rudin, *Banking en français: The French Banks of Quebec, 1835–1925* (Toronto, 1985); and Paul-Andre Linteau *et al.*, *Quebec: A History, 1867–1929*, trans. Robert Chodos (Toronto, 1979), 351–5. On the social fabric of finance capitalism in late nineteenth century Canada, see T.W. Acheson, 'The Social Origins of the Canadian Industrial Élite, 1880–1910', *Business History Review* 47 (1973), 189–217.

[5]On the Canadian exchanges, see John F. Whiteside, 'The Toronto Stock Exchange and the Development of the Share Market to 1885', *Journal of Canadian Studies* 20 (1985), 64–81; R.C. Michie, 'The Canadian Securities Market, 1850–1914', *Business History Review* 62 (1988), 35–73. On stock markets generally, see Michie, *The London and New York Stock Exchanges, 1850–1914* (London, 1987); Thomas Navin and Marian Sears, 'The Rise of a Market for Industrial Securities, 1887–1902', *Business History Review* 29 (1955), 105–38.

[6]On Canadian merger movements, see Epp, 'Cooperation Among Capitalists'; Gregory Marchildon, 'Promotion, Finance and Mergers in Canadian Manufacturing Industry, 1885–1918' (PhD thesis, London School of Economics, 1990): J.C. Weldon, 'Consolidations in Canadian Industry, 1900–1948' in L.A. Skeoch, ed., *Restrictive Trade Practices in Canada* (Toronto, 1966), 232–6.

[7]On the changing role of finance capitalists, see Louis Galambos and Joseph Pratt, *The Rise of the Corporate Commonwealth* (New York, 1988), chs 1–2. For various efforts to assess the Canadian business élite, see John Porter, *The Vertical Mosaic* (Toronto, 1961); Peter C. Newman, *The Canadian Establishment* (Toronto, 1975); Frank and Libbie Park, *Anatomy of Big Business* (Toronto, 1973); Wallace Clement, *The Canadian Corporate Élite* (Toronto, 1975), and *Continental Corporate Power* (Toronto, 1977); William K. Carroll, *Corporate Power and Canadian Capitalism* (Vancouver, 1986). For alternative viewpoints, see Jorge Niosi, *The Economy of Canada* (Quebec, 1978), and *Canadian Capitalism*, trans. Robert Chodos (Toronto, 1981); Bliss, *Northern Enterprise*, 358–78.

[8]On US direct investment in Canada, see Mira Wilkins, *The Emergence of Multinational Enterprise* (Cambridge, Mass., 1970); Herbert Marshall *et al.*, *Canadian-American Industry*

(New Haven, Conn., 1936). On British direct and portfolio investment, see D.G. Paterson, *British Direct Investment in Canada, 1890–1914* (Toronto, 1976); and Matthew Simon, 'The Pattern of New British Portfolio Investment, 1865–1914', in J.H. Adler, ed., *Capital Movements and Economic Development* (New York, 1967), 33–60; and G.P. Marchildon, 'British Investment Banking and Industrial Decline Before the Great War: A Case Study of Capital Outflow to Canada', *Business History* 33, 72–92.

13 NETWORKS OF PROGRESS

Two technologies—one old and one new—occupied much of the attention of financiers, political leaders and the general public in Canada in the early twentieth century. By that time railways had become associated with big business, economic progress and national unification, and the period 1900–13 witnessed a dramatic overexpansion of Canada's rail network. In this same era the emerging technologies of electric power generation and distribution offered prospects of cleaner, safer cities, improved urban transportation, and more dispersed and diversified industrial development. Rail lines and electric power grids linked the scattered cities of Canada, encouraged the growth of new commercial and industrial centres, opened the resource-rich northern hinterland for exploitation, and could at least potentially alleviate the harshness and isolation of rural life.

The development of both technologies involved the erection of organizations of unprecedented size and complexity, characterized by large fixed capital costs, sophisticated technical capabilities, and bureaucratic structures. While communities initially welcomed the economic and social benefits bestowed by these organizations, those who controlled them were soon perceived as exploiters, gouging the public with high or discriminatory rates, enriching their owners with 'monopoly profits' and exercising behind-the-scene political influence. Consequently, the railways and utilities were among the first industries to become targets of political reform movements, and government intervention in the form of regulation and public ownership began to emerge early in the twentieth century. By the end of the 1920s, the Canadian railway, communications and electric power networks comprised a well-developed 'public sector' at the federal as well as provincial and municipal levels, a sector that contested, though it did not fully displace, the large private corporate enterprises that had established these systems.

ELECTRICAL UTILITIES

Of all the technological achievements of the late nineteenth century, the development of the electrical industry was probably the most publicized, due in no small measure to the vigorous self-promotion of its pioneers, particularly Thomas Edison. Although the inventions of Edison and other Americans received the most attention, technical improvements in the field took place in many countries and electrical technology diffused rapidly in the period 1875–95. During these years French and German researchers designed commercially viable electrical generators; the harnessing of electric power for lighting proceeded from the experiments of Edison and Elihu Thomson in the US, and Joseph Swan in Britain. Edison established the first central generating station for the distribution of electricity via direct current in New York in 1881. Five years later another American, George Westinghouse, developed the alternating current system which made it possible to transmit electric power over long distances. In 1887 Frank Sprague introduced the first electrified street railway in Richmond, Virginia. In the early 1890s an American investment syndicate, using Swiss-designed turbines, erected the first large-scale electric generating plant at Niagara Falls, providing power for lighting and streetcars in Buffalo, N.Y. as well as energy for the metallurgical and chemical industries that quickly clustered in the region.

While these technical feats enthralled the public, organizational developments of no less significance shaped the future of the electrical industry. In 1892 the two largest competitors in the field, Edison and Thomson-Houston, merged to form General Electric Co. and four years later negotiated a patent-sharing arrangement with Westinghouse. Meanwhile, Samuel Insull, a British immigrant to the US who had been Edison's personal secretary, devised the financial and organizational techniques for developing regional electric power grids, creating a Chicago-based system that dominated the American mid-west states through a structure of holding companies and interconnected transmission lines.

The companies that distributed electric power developed independently of the electrical equipment manufacturers, but in the early years of electrification in Canada, as in the US, the equipment makers initiated the establishment of distributing firms (which by the 1890s were designated, along with telephone, telegraph and railway companies, as 'utilities') in order to create a market for their products. During the 1880s salesmen from Edison and Thomson-Houston encouraged local entrepreneurs to set up companies, preferably with exclusive franchises or long-term contracts with municipal or provincial governments, to distribute electric power for streetcars, public lighting and domestic household uses. Since the initial costs of installing these systems were substantial, the equipment companies preferred not to participate directly, or at most to hold minority interest in the ventures, but they could provide a variety of inducements to attract investors. While the capital costs of utilities were high, operating costs, once the system was in place, were relatively modest and the profit potential was substantial. Participants in investor syndicates could be lured into underwriting bonds through liberal distribution of bonus stocks at below-par value, with the expectation that their market value would rise dramatically once the company was launched. Stock and bond salesmen also played upon the sense of public excitement generated by the inventive achievements of Edison *et al.*, and the expectation that electrification would usher in a new era of scientific progress and economic growth, creating what historians Christopher Armstrong and H.V. Nelles called a 'theatre of science'.[1]

Electrical equipment salesmen were not alone in adopting this strategy: American Bell of Boston, which secured the telephone patent of Alexander Graham Bell, also followed this route into Canada. In 1880 the Bell Company secured the services of Charles Sise, a transplanted New Englander involved in the Canadian insurance field, who assembled an investment syndicate to merge competing telephone systems in Montreal. Sise, who went on to run the company and extended Bell Canada into Ontario and the Maritimes, also took an interest in electrical utilities. In 1884 he participated in the formation of Royal Electric Co. in Montreal, a firm that established a central station for municipal lighting and also a plant manufacturing equipment under license from Thomson-Houston Co.

In Toronto another Thomson protégé, J.J. Wright, established a distributing company with financing organized by Henry Pellatt, a securities broker linked to the Cox group. In 1892 when Edison and Thomson-Houston merged in the US, Frederic Nicholls, another Cox associate, established Canadian General Electric, which in its early years was an independent Canadian-owned venture that manufactured electrical equipment under license from the Americans; CGE was absorbed by the American firm after Nicholls' death in 1923.

The development of these Canadian ventures in the 1880s and early 1890s took place in a highly competitive context. Rival American patent-holders in various technologies jockeyed for market position; meanwhile the older utilities such as gas companies fought to hold their existing position in the markets for public and domestic lighting, and some began to diversify into the electrical illumination field. Mergers in the electric equipment industry in the US in the 1890s did not translate immediately into consolidations in the utilities but the introduction of alternating current technology and long-distance power transmission opened the way for larger-scale enterprises to exploit regional markets.

This trend toward larger formations in the Canadian electric utility field can be seen in the growth of electric streetcar systems—more generally called tramways or traction companies—in urban communities. The tramway market attracted the interest of a new group of entrepreneurs. Railway building contractors whose business had flourished in the era of CPR construction in the 1880s faced diminished prospects in the following decade and turned their attention to related undertakings. The construction of urban street railways seemed a logical step for men like William Mackenzie, James Ross, Donald Mann, Herbert Holt and others who had honed their contracting skills on the CPR project, and they could anticipate a sympathetic hearing from financial syndicates accustomed to raising large sums of capital for steam railways.

The market for electrified city tramways was also apparent. Horse-drawn railways had appeared in Canadian cities in the 1860s but after thirty years their limitations were painfully evident. Expensive to operate (in Montreal, for example, the system required stables and feed for over 1000 horses), unreliable in bad weather, and restricted largely to city centres, their systems served a relatively small market: in 1892 only 10 per cent of the Montreal population, 25 per cent of Toronto's. Electrification would dramatically cut operating costs and permit the extension of lines over much larger distances.

A central figure in the rapid expansion of electric tramways (and much else) in the 1890s was William Mackenzie, who would later figure prominently in the railway expansion in the west. Combining stalwart Presbyterian virtue with gregarious optimism and hard-driving ambition, Mackenzie was a prototype for the expansionist-minded business figures who flourished on the Canadian scene at the turn of the century. After learning the contracting trade on the CPR line Mackenzie returned to his home in Kirkfield, Ontario in the early 1890s, dabbling briefly in Tory politics before discovering a more interesting and lucrative outlet for his considerable energies.

That opportunity was provided by the imminent bankruptcy of several of Toronto's horse-drawn tramways in 1892. Forming a syndicate of former associates from his CPR construction days (including William Van Horne, now the president of that line), Mackenzie merged the companies, refinanced them with $2 million in bonds secured with an exclusive franchise from Toronto's city council and acquired controlling interest in the stocks of the new Toronto Railway Co. at a cost of only $10,000 in cash.

The success of the Toronto street railway encouraged Mackenzie and his associates to undertake similar ventures in Winnipeg, Montreal, and Saint John, N.B. Mackenzie also spread his interest into municipal lighting through investments in gas companies in Vancouver and Halifax. By 1895, according to Armstrong and Nelles, Mackenzie had come close to 'assembling a *de facto* national utilities conglomerate', with visions of expanding his empire into the British utility market. This last venture proved to be a fiasco, however, and by this time Mackenzie had turned to another suitably grandiose project, the Canadian Northern Railway. He continued to take an interest in utility investments, particularly in Latin America after 1900, but his imperial visions were increasingly focused on developing a transcontinental rival to the CPR.

Canadian railway entrepreneurs were not the only ones to find the undeveloped electric traction market in Canada attractive. Henry M. Whitney, a Boston capitalist who had established electric railways in that city, took an interest in reorganizing the Halifax system as a sideline to his investment in Cape Breton coal mines in the early 1890s. Perhaps the most significant result of this project was that Whitney brought with him a talented and ambitious young engineer, Frank Pearson, who would play a major role in organizing Canadian utility companies in Latin America. On the other side of the continent a British investment syndicate led by R.M. Horne-Payne, acquired a number of foundering utility companies in Victoria, Vancouver, and New Westminster, B.C. and reorganized them into B.C. Electric Railway Co. The name was misleadingly narrow, for BCER effectively controlled the province's utility industry and the charter it received from the B.C. legislature gave the company exclusive rights to provide services to municipalities that had not even been established.

As the B.C. example indicates, utility promoters were very adept at exploiting the Canadian federal system to procure the most advantageous corporate charters. As in the US, municipalities were initially the preferred jurisdiction since they were most likely to welcome providers of local services with few strings attached, and councillors could be bought relatively cheaply. After the first flush of enthusiasm for utilities wore off, however, municipal governments could prove troublesome; happily for promoters, municipal powers were subject to provincial laws. In provinces like B.C. this situation could work to the advantage of the promoters, but in other cases—particularly in Ontario by the early 1900s—provincial legislators took a more restrictive view of the powers to be granted private enterprises in charters. But the federal government also had chartering authority and an adroit promoter (or his legal adviser) could select the jurisdiction most likely to adopt a liberal approach to such matters. When Charles Sise was organizing Bell Canada, for example, he was careful to secure both a federal charter to permit the establishment of a system that could operate across provincial boundaries and special laws in Ontario and Quebec to enable Bell to erect its poles and lines with minimal interference from municipal authorities.

The structure of BCER also indicates a broader trend in the erection of Canadian utilities. Traction companies were indeed profitable, but in order to be cost-effective and reliable they established their own central generating stations. Since these stations produced electric power in excess of the volume required for running street railways, particularly during off-peak hours, the traction companies sought customers in other markets including public lighting as well as industrial and household uses. This strategy led logically to moves to amalgamate tramways and other electric utilities at the municipal level. By 1900 the development of alternating current technology, through which large areas could be provided power from a single or a few large generating sources, opened the way for amalgamation of utilities on a regional or provincial basis.

Montreal was the scene of one of the first dramatic large-scale consolidations of electric utilities. Through the 1890s rival groups of financiers had engaged in a complex struggle for control of various gas, electric power, and traction companies in the city, culminating in the creation of Montreal Light, Heat and Power Co. in 1901, built around the base of Royal Electric Co. Although the organization of MLH&P was engineered by financiers James Ross and Louis Forget, the figure who was to dominate the company was its hired manager, Herbert Holt.

Holt, like Mackenzie, had entered the utilities field from a background as a CPR contractor, but in other respects the two contrasted remarkably: Mackenzie was an optimistic, exuberant risk-taker; Holt was a dour, cautious technocrat. While Mackenzie created nation-girdling rail and utility empires that ultimately collapsed with melodramatic flair, Holt steadily erected an edifice of interconnected companies that made him the most powerful Canadian capitalist of his time, presiding over the giant Royal Bank as well as a multitude of utility and industrial ventures. By the time he died in 1941 Holt had become the symbol of Montreal's secretive, arrogant anglophone élite.

In 1901, however, the success of Holt and MLH&P was by no means a sure thing. In Montreal it faced strong competition from Lachine Rapids Hydraulic Co. Although Holt's company had a large power site at Chambly, in 1902 Lachine Rapids Co. brought a more formidable ally onto the scene, negotiating an agreement to purchase power from a huge project developed on the St Maurice River by Shawinigan Water & Power Co. The Shawinigan venture, which had been established in 1897 by American interests (joined by the ubiquitous L.J. Forget) was primarily intended to provide electric power to industries encouraged to locate on the St Maurice River, notably a Canadian affiliate of the American aluminum company, Alcoa. But Shawinigan produced far more power than could be absorbed locally and the Montreal market was attractive.

Although Holt had earned a reputation for ruthless cost-effective management, his strategy for dealing with these challenges involved co-operation rather than price competition. In 1903 MLH&P bought Lachine Rapids Co., and four years later Holt negotiated a comprehensive agreement with Shawinigan to share the Montreal market, and a long-term supply contract which enabled MLH&P to expand its distribution network and solidify its position in the city and its environs. Over the next three decades the two companies worked in tandem to turn back challengers to the Montreal market.

Similar pressures toward consolidation and oligopoly in the utilities field were at work in Ontario in this period, but there events unfolded in a dramatically different fashion. At about the same time as the Montreal merger, utility financiers in Toronto, their confidence bolstered by successful ventures abroad, turned their attention to the hydro-power potential of Niagara Falls. By 1903 all but one of the major sites for power generation on the Canadian side of the Falls were occupied by American companies. Mackenzie, joined by Nicholls of CGE, Pellatt and the Cox group, formed Electrical Development Co. (EDC) to acquire this last site which would not only expand their supplies for Toronto utilities but would also be in a position to market surplus power throughout southern Ontario.

Even before Electrical Development began work on the site, however, opposition surfaced both in Toronto and the smaller cities of the region. In Toronto high utility rates and the refusal of the tramway to extend lines into the burgeoning suburbs had antagonized domestic consumers. Hostility toward the utility barons of Toronto was even greater in the nearby aspiring industrial towns like Berlin (now Kitchener), Waterloo, and Guelph, who feared that EDC would establish a monopoly that would thwart their future growth. From both quarters a movement for public control of electrical utilities gained strength; the provincial opposition Conservative party took up the cause and swept into office, vowing to block expansion of EDC. The key figure in this movement was Adam Beck.

The public power movement was not restricted to Ontario; indeed by the 1920s, except in Quebec and British Columbia the private utilities faced some form of government intervention either through regulatory measures or crown corporations, or both. On the prairies government ownership appeared first at the municipal level: in 1905 Winnipeg authorized the establishment of a public hydroelectric system that went into competition with Mackenzie's company. By that time the small cities of Saskatchewan had set up municipally owned operations. During this period as well both of these provinces and Alberta had 'nationalized' their telephone systems, more or less with the acquiescence of Bell Canada which did not intend at that time to burden itself with the costs of developing rural services.

During the 1920s the electrical utilities of Manitoba and Saskatchewan were knitted into provincial-wide systems. In Alberta and the Maritimes, private electric utility companies maintained a firm hold on the most lucrative urban markets, leaving the rural and small-town hinterland to the modest public systems. In

ADAM BECK AND ONTARIO HYDRO

The virtual founding father and dominant figure of the Ontario Hydro Electric Commission in its early years, Adam Beck was also the first of a long line of crown-company entrepreneurs —including Sir Henry Thornton of Canadian National Railways in the 1920s and Wilbert Hopper of Petro Canada in the 1970s—who flourished in twentieth-century Canada. Officially the bureaucratic chieftains of government-owned corporations, they acted more like Rockefeller, Carnegie, and other private business empire builders of nineteenth-century America.

Beck began his career in the 1880s as a businessman, manufacturing wood veneers and cigar boxes in London, Ontario, a small but ambitious commercial and industrial city which was already the hub of Canadian petroleum refining, included two breweries— Carling's and Labatt's—and aspired to become a major financial centre as well. Like his future rival, William Mackenzie, Beck was restlessly competitive, in sports as well as business; and, like Mackenzie, he dabbled in local politics, with greater success. In 1900 he was elected mayor of London

The streets of Berlin (now Kitchener) festooned with electric lights in readiness for switching on Niagara power on 11 October 1910. *(Ontario Hydro/Metropolitan Toronto Library)*

and two years later became a Conservative member of the Ontario legislature.

As mayor of London, Beck attended a meeting in nearby Berlin, Ontario in early 1903 instigated by opponents of Mackenzie's Electrical Development Co. Reflecting the alarm of small-town southern Ontario businesses at the prospect of a Toronto power monopoly, Beck also quickly recognized the political opportunities presented by the issue for his own ambitions and those of his party. Within a year he emerged as the leading advocate of public control of the province's hydroelectric power which the Tory leader, Richard Whitney, made the centrepiece of his successful election campaign in 1905. As a reward for his efforts, Beck was appointed chairman of a committee to investigate Ontario's hydro power needs and resources.

Beck dominated the inquiry and assembled a bipartisan coalition to support its proposal for a Hydro Commission that would regulate rates charged by private power companies and would also sell electric power 'at cost' to municipalities in Ontario. A curiously hybrid entity—it was in theory owned by the municipalities as a public corporation but was financed by the provincial government which also enforced its regulatory decrees—the Ontario Hydro Electric Commission, with Beck at its head, commenced operations in 1910. Although the Electrical Development Co.'s attempt to secure control of all available waterpower from Niagara Falls had been foiled, Ontario Hydro depended entirely at this point on private suppliers, and Mackenzie's company was still the largest supplier. Beck's strategy for overcoming this problem was in the tradition of robber-baron entrepreneurship. Ontario Hydro embarked on a vigorous campaign to promote electric usage, offering cheap rates to industries and domestic users. The Commission relied on government subsidies to cover the difference between its costs and sales prices; and with an assured market, Ontario Hydro proceeded to develop its own power sites, culminating in the early 1920s with the construction of the largest power station of its time at Queenston. Meanwhile, Beck used the regulatory powers of the Commission to control the rates of its private competitors. By 1921 Ontario Hydro had ousted EDC from its major market, the Toronto utility system; by this time Mackenzie's financial empire lay in ruins. Before the end of the decade Ontario Hydro controlled over three-quarters of the electric power generated in the province.

Beck died in 1925, embroiled in disputes with the province's political leaders who were increasingly troubled by the autonomy and influence of what was supposed to be an arm of government. Although Ontario Hydro's independence was reined in after Beck's time, few politicians cared to challenge directly the power of this large, technologically complex organization whose channels of influence percolated across the province. Adam Beck's legacy thus embraced both an enduring tradition of public ownership in the Canadian utility industry and a classic example of bureaucratic imperialism.

Sources

Armstrong, Christopher, and H.V. Nelles, *Monopoly's Moment, The Organization and Regulation of Canadian Utilities, 1830–1930* (Philadelphia, 1986).

Plewman, W.R., *Adam Beck and Ontario Hydro* (Toronto 1947).

Calgary, Halifax, and Saint John, consolidations of utility companies were orchestrated by financial groups in Montreal between 1910 and 1930. None of them, however, aspired to control regional markets in the style of MLH&P and Shawinigan; and in none of these situations did an Adam Beck emerge with visions of building a public power empire.[2]

Public ownership of utilities limited the aspirations of private entrepreneurs in Canada but it was only one factor. As early as 1898 electric utility promoters had discovered another promising market for their skills and capital resources, and in the early years of the twentieth century investments in Latin American utilities to some extent diverted their energies. Political leaders in these underdeveloped climes proved, if anything, to be more accommodating than their Canadian counterparts toward foreign capitalists bearing the latest technologies. Canadian businessmen were small players in this region — British, Americans and Germans were acquiring mining and petroleum concessions and aggressively marketing their industrial wares from Mexico to Chile and Argentina—but they found lucrative niches in the utility markets of the burgeoning cities of Latin America and the Caribbean.

The earliest venturers in this direction were Mackenzie and James Ross of Montreal. Blocked in their effort to establish a foothold in British tramways, the two promoters encountered a more congenial welcome in Jamaica in 1897. Their modest success lured another railroader, Sir William Van Horne, into the Caribbean. The master builder of the CPR retired from active management of that enterprise in 1899, but at age 56 his energies were undiminished, and Van Horne spotted an alluring opportunity to develop electric railways in Cuba, recently liberated from Spain. Together with some CPR cronies, American streetcar promoters, and his old rival, Jim Hill, Van Horne organized a Cuban venture in 1900.

The Cuban railway was not particularly successful but it helped alert Canadian utility entrepreneurs and financiers to the possibilities of larger undertakings in the region. A key figure in this process was Halifax-based Frank Pearson. In 1899 Pearson turned up on Mackenzie's doorstep in Toronto with a prospective concession in hand to develop electric street railways in São Paulo, the centre of Brazil's coffee trade. He had already hawked it unsuccessfully to American investors who found it too small, and to his Halifax associates who found it too expensive. Mackenzie embraced the opportunity and sent Pearson off to explore the prospects of amalgamating all of the city's utilities. With the Cox group, Mackenzie then set up São Paulo Railway, Light and Power Co. with the usual distribution of bonds and bonus stock to the Canadian promoters.

Success in São Paulo led to a larger undertaking in 1904 in Brazil's capital city, Rio de Janeiro. Eight years later Mackenzie and Pearson reorganized the two operations under a holding company, Brazilian Traction, Light and Power Co., capitalized at $120 million. The largest Canadian multinational enterprise of the era, this company dominated Brazil's utility industry and was variously dubbed 'The Light' or 'the Canadian Octopus' by citizens of the host country. After World War II the Brazilian government began to undermine The Light's monopoly, ultimately buying out the foreigners for $380 million in 1978. At that point the company in Canada was reorganized as Brascan, a conglomerate that eventually passed into the hands of the Bronfman family.

The Brazilian ventures whetted the appetites of other Canadian observers. In 1901 Pearson discovered another prospective utility market in Mexico which interested his Halifax colleague, John Stairs, then attracted Ross and Van Horne, and ultimately roped in some Toronto investors and the Sperling Group in Britain which was involved in B.C. Electric. Mexican Light & Power was incorporated in 1902; three years later Pearson added the Mexico City trolley lines to the portfolio. Initially highly profitable, the Mexican utility ventures fell on hard times after 1912. Threatened by marauding armies during the Mexican Revolution, devastated by the loss of Pearson who went down with the *Lusitania* in 1915, Mexican Light & Power was threatened with nationalization in 1921. It survived these vicissitudes and by the end of World War II was supplying over half the country's electric power. In 1960 the Mexican government took over all foreign-owned utilities, although, oddly, Mexican Light & Power's charter remained in Canada.

The Halifax utility financiers had to share control of the Mexican venture virtually from its inception but Stairs and his protégé, Max Aitken, had already begun exploring other Latin American projects, including electric railways in Cuba (carefully leaving the big ventures to Van Horne), Puerto Rico, Trinidad, and British Guiana. After Aitken went on to greater things, his protégé, I.W. Killam, continued to accumulate properties through Royal Securities, including utilities in Calgary, Newfoundland, Bolivia, El Salvador, and Venezuela, organized into a holding company, International Power, in 1926. These were not truly big operations — International Power was only one-tenth the size of Brazilian Traction — but they maintained a traditional Maritime link with Latin America, and their profits cushioned Killam when his schemes to consolidate the Canadian pulp and paper industry collapsed in the Great Depression. While bigger fish like Mackenzie floundered amidst financial woes at the end of their careers, Killam went to his grave in 1955 one of the wealthiest men in Canada.

The Canadian utility ventures in Latin America indeed represented, as their chief chroniclers, Armstrong and Nelles, have put it, 'a curious capital flow'. Aside from Maritime trade with the West Indies, there was no historical tradition linking Canada to the region. The Canadians did not have any particular technological edge over others in the field: they simply brought together mostly American technology and mostly British capital, exploiting a modest vacuum neglected by their larger counterparts. Although the earnings from these utility ventures enriched some promoters, these enterprises did not leave any lasting mark on Canadian business development, aside from providing Canadian engineers with some international experience. A few lawyers and clerks monitored these operations in Canada on behalf of the investors. Unlike the Canadian mining and manufacturing companies that moved overseas in the more recent past, these 'utility multinationals' were a rather more ephemeral presence, at least in the Canadian context, reflecting primarily the wide-ranging ambitions of a handful

273

of enterprising contractors and financiers and the mobility of international capital in the era that preceded the First World War.[3]

RAILROADS

While the emerging field of electric utilities attracted adventurous investors, the established technology of steam railroads remained a staple element of the Canadian and foreign securities markets in the decades preceding World War I. Although the opening of the Canadian Pacific Railway did not immediately people the prairies with wheat farmers, by 1897 the company had weathered its early financial troubles. At the same time opposition in the west to CPR's monopoly stimulated provincial politicians to encourage expansion of the railway network, which in turn enticed entrepreneurial railway promoters into the region. As the Canadian economy recovered from the depression of the mid-1890s the groundwork was laid for a new boom in railway construction.

Between 1900 and 1914 railway mileage in Canada more than doubled, increasing from 17,824 to over 40,000 miles, reflecting not only expansion in the west but also the opening of lines into northern Ontario and Quebec and a thickening of the central and eastern networks of branch and feeder lines. By 1910 two new transcontinental systems were in the works, liberally endowed with government bond guarantees, subsidies and land grants. Meanwhile the CPR responded by expanding its own system and diversifying its activities into ocean transportation, hotels and mining. This orgy of railway promotion, that far exceeded the capacity and needs of the economy, began to disintegrate even before the outbreak of war in Europe in 1914 cut the flow of overseas investment.

During the war the Canadian government was obliged to keep the nation's rail lines running but also had to confront the long-term problems of rationalizing an overbuilt and overcapitalized network. Amidst bitter debates over the dangers of monopoly versus the hazards of public ownership, the government took over the two new (bankrupt) transcontinental lines and consolidated them into Canadian National Railways, the country's first major experiment with crown corporations (they were to become a far more pervasive feature on the Canadian business scene after World War II). During the 1920s the CPR and CNR embarked on a new round of competition that benefited shippers and rail passengers but proved ruinous in financial terms for both companies. Exhaustion and retrenchment marked the Canadian railway environment in the Great Depression, signalling the end of an era of expansion that stretched back to the years before Confederation and had been a major factor in the political and cultural life as well as the nation's economy for almost a century.

For many Canadians 7 November 1885 had marked the fulfilment of the 'national dream', the completion of the nation's transcontinental railway line. For William Van Horne, General Manager of the Canadian Pacific Railway, it had been another business day: a beginning rather than an end. This hard-headed approach to their tasks was characteristic of the dominant figures of the CPR, Van Horne and Thomas Shaughnessy, and the managers they assembled to operate

Donald Smith prepares to drive the last spike on CPR's railway line; Craigellachie, 1885. *(Glenbow Archives, Calgary, Alberta)*

this complex enterprise. Cautious, attentive to details, and competitive, the CPR managers weathered a decade of financial and political difficulties in 1885–95, and steadily erected a formidable and diversfied system of rail lines and associated undertakings that enabled the company to surmount strong competitive challenges from the Canadian Northern Railway and the Grand Trunk during the ensuing twenty years. After World War I the CPR, unloved but profitable, remained the dominant carrier of commercial and passenger traffic in Canada with offshoots in mining, urban real estate and oceanic shipping lines.

The immediate problem for the CPR after the 'last spike' had been driven at Craigellachie, B.C. was to rebuild and improve the existing line which had been hastily laid to satisfy the expectations of politicians and bondholders. In addition, branch and feeder lines, essential for increasing traffic and revenues, had to be fleshed out. Finally, there was the threat of competition, particularly from James J. Hill's Great Northern Railway as it extended westward from Minnesota, to goad the CPR to expand services and offset complaints from Manitoba over the company's monopoly.

But expansion required financing and the debt-burdened line could not anticipate a rapid infusion of revenues from its western traffic or sale of its land grant. Settlers did not at once pour into the Canadian prairies; indeed western settlement lagged until the late 1890s when the federal government mounted a vigorous campaign to boost immigration to Canada. In the interim the American Great Plains, with numerous competing railway lines, attracted more migrants; and the harsh economic depression of the early 1890s withered the confidence of investors as well as aspiring farmers.

Nevertheless, the CPR did expand, more than doubling its rail mileage between 1886 and 1896. This growth was not without pain: in 1894 earnings were insufficient to cover capital costs and in the following year the CPR cut dividends by half, leading its former president, George Stephen, to urge fellow shareholders to sell their securities. The company survived the crisis but this experience reinforced management's financial caution and preoccupation with cash flow during the decades of prosperity that followed.

Pressures for expansion were hard to resist. Manitoba farmers had been resentful of the CPR's freight-rate policies even before completion of the line, and several times during the 1880s the province sought to issue new railway charters to encourage competition. The federal government under Sir John A. Macdonald vetoed the Manitoba legislation, but by 1888 the CPR decided to give up the monopoly clause in its charter 'in the interests of peace in the northwest', as Stephen put it (and in exchange for further government guarantees of its bonds).

An American line, Northern Pacific, had extended into Manitoba in the 1880s, but the CPR was able to negotiate a rate agreement with that company to avoid a price war. The major threat to the CPR in the 1890s was posed by Hill's Great Northern; and to complicate matters for Van Horne, Hill was involved in assorted railway ventures in the US with Stephen and Donald Smith, who still held blocks of shares in the CPR. By 1893 the Great Northern had reached the US west coast and the government of British Columbia was prepared to charter a line that would link the Kootenay mining region in the eastern part of the province with Hill's railway.

To meet this challenge Van Horne decided to build a new line from Alberta well to the south of the original CPR route. To do this, the CPR would have to go through the Crowsnest Pass of the Rockies, a costly undertaking that would require a new infusion of government assistance. In 1896, however, a federal election brought the Liberals to power under Wilfrid Laurier, long-time critic of the CPR's monopolistic tendencies, freight rates, and Tory political connections.

Fortunately for Van Horne, other Liberal politicos, especially Clifford Sifton, Laurier's Minister of the Interior, were anxious to promote western settlement and the CPR remained the major instrument to achieve this aim. After some dickering, the government and the company concluded the Crowsnest Pass Agreement of 1897, under which the CPR would receive the cash subsidies it needed in return for concessions over freight rates, particularly on the eastbound grain traffic from the prairies to central Canada. This concession was to remain in effect for an indefinite period, and in fact the Agreement established the base rate for the next seventy-plus years for western railways.

Although the CPR had surmounted its financial difficulties by 1899 Van Horne decided to step down as president, his enthusiasm sapped by years of bickering with fellow directors as well as politicians. Even before his formal retirement, his successor Thomas Shaughnessy had emerged as the key figure in the company. Like Van Horne, Shaughnessy was an American; his talents, however, lay in organization and financial management rather than construction. Shaughnessy, a prototype of the professional corporate manager of the twentieth century, thus represented an ideal candidate for running the CPR during the era of consolidation and measured growth that came after 1900.

Under Shaughnessy the modern organization of the CPR took shape. As the company's chief financial officer in its difficult early years, he emphasized cost controls and maintained a centralized system for monitoring budgetary allocations and earnings while adopting the decentralized system of operational management pioneered by American railroads in the nineteenth century, under which regional division chiefs exercised autonomy over such matters as traffic control, with regular assessments by headquarters of their financial performance. The physical plant of the line was regularly upgraded, larger and more technically advanced locomotives and other equipment were introduced, and rolling stock was increased to handle the growing volume of grain traffic after 1900.

Shaughnessy was particularly committed to reorganizing the company's debt structure. The financial traumas that wracked the CPR in 1894–95 were to be avoided. In contrast to its future Canadian railway rivals (and many other Canadian firms in the early twentieth century), the CPR had always relied on equity rather than debt financing (except for government-backed bonds). In the early 1890s the cash-strapped firm had departed from this practice to raise funds for expansion; Shaughnessy was determined to eliminate this debt as quickly as possible. After 1906 the CPR was able to finance more than three-quarters of its capital needs from reinvested earnings and sales of common stock. Consequently the capital market crunch of 1913–14 that ruined its rivals, Canadian Northern and the Grand Trunk, left the CPR relatively unscathed.

Diversification also helped to cushion the CPR against the perils of an overbuilt railway system in this era. The company had never been exclusively a transportation enterprise: earnings from sales of its land grants had been intended from the outset to contribute to its revenues. But Shaughnessy regarded the land grants as a 'drag on the company' because of the costs incurred in improving the land through irrigation works to attract settlers. Other activities were more promising.

Under Van Horne the CPR had begun to diversify: hotels were established along the main rail route, notably the Banff Springs resort erected in 1888. By the end of the century the company had investments in urban real estate as well. Steamship services were inaugurated in 1886, and within twenty years CPR ships were plying the Atlantic and Pacific oceans as well as the Great Lakes and the B.C. coast (where they carried Klondike-bound prospectors in the gold rush of 1898–1902). In 1898 the company acquired a mineral smelter at Trail, B.C. along with a mining railway, an unsought investment that would turn into one of the CPR's most lucrative industrial subsidiaries, Cominco. Under Shaughnessy the company also promoted exploration of the petroleum potentialities of its western lands. While the combined earnings of these various activities in the period 1900–30 were far less significant for the company than revenues from rail traffic and land sales, they presaged the later evolution of the CPR into a diversified holding company. The divisional structure inaugurated by Shaughnessy provided the organizational versatility needed to hold together its increasingly wide-ranging operations.

The success of the CPR under Shaughnessy was due in part to its organizational and diversification strategies, but also reflected the improving economic conditions in Canada after 1896, the federal government's immigration policies, and the expansion of the wheat belt in the west. Shaughnessy did not neglect the basic mission of the CPR to promote western development; indeed, under his management the company's westward orientation became more pronounced. Van Horne had devoted considerable attention in the 1890s to developing an eastern network for the CPR through a 'Short Line' running from Montreal to Saint John, New Brunswick via Maine, in addition to the Crowsnest Pass line in the west. Shaughnessy, however, increasingly focused on the prairies, double-tracking the main line through the region as well as building more feeder lines, expanding repair and industrial operations in Winnipeg and Calgary, and increasing western rail mileage by 6000 miles between 1903 and 1912, by which point more than half the company's tracks ran west of the Great Lakes. While this westward tilt by the CPR was not surprising, given the explosive growth of the prairies during the wheat boom of the first two decades of the twentieth century, Shaughnessy's actions were also prompted by the emergence of two major competitors in the region, whose spectacular rise and fall punctuated the Laurier era and left the country with its first major experiment with government ownership of a national enterprise.[4]

278

Canada's second (more precisely, its third) venture in transcontinental railway building began modestly in Manitoba in 1895. As noted earlier, Manitobans were unhappy over the CPR monopoly in the west even before completion of that line and remained unmollified when the company surrendered its monopoly clause in 1888. While Jim Hill was probing northwards from Minnesota in the early 1890s, the Manitoba provincial government began hawking a charter to build a line from Winnipeg to Hudson Bay, promising bond guarantees, land grants and subsidies.

The Hudson Bay project attracted the attention of Donald Mann, yet another CPR subcontractor at loose ends. Mann got in touch with his erstwhile partner, William Mackenzie, whose aspirations to build a utility empire were temporarily stalled. Mackenzie and Mann took on the Manitoba charter but they were not particularly interested in constructing a line through the province's northern wilderness. Instead, they began piecing together a series of short lines from Lake of the Woods to the Saskatchewan border between 1896 and 1901, picking up some federal government support in the process.

At this time, Mackenzie and Mann moved carefully, building not just railways but a base of local support that would stand them in good stead in their subsequent, more ambitious undertakings. They selected routes that had good development prospects and constructed a network of feeder lines to ensure that their main line would ultimately carry substantial traffic at rates that would be competitive with the CPR. To control costs, they built their lines to standards appropriate to anticipated use: heavily travelled sections were well constructed while those sections covering unsettled areas were laid down quickly, to be upgraded if and when traffic increased. Rather than importing labour, they employed people in the local communities and their construction 'had something of the air of a barn-raising about it; everyone was allowed to pitch in and do what they could.'

Up to 1899 these activities had created what historian Ted Regehr characterized as 'unconnected projections of steel' lacing Manitoba with profitable but as yet unintegrated lines. In that year, Mackenzie and Mann reorganized their venture as the Canadian Northern Railway and began to unveil plans to extend into Saskatchewan and the Northwest Territories. Two years later they scored their first major coup, acquiring the Manitoba branch lines of the Northern Pacific Railway, which gave them direct access to a transcontinental main line in the United States. Between 1901 and 1903 Mackenzie and Mann accumulated more bond guarantees and land grants from the Manitoba government, which enabled them to market Canadian Northern securities in London and New York. With over $14 million in new capital, they were now prepared to build a prairie line that would compete directly with the CPR. As in the case of Mackenzie's utility ventures, neither of the promoters had put up their own money: one-third of the capital raised was guaranteed by governments at various levels which ensured Canadian Northern's attractiveness to foreign investors. Mackenzie's Toronto associate, George Cox, brought in the Bank of Commerce,and the insiders rewarded themselves as usual with bonus stocks.

Besides making money, what did Mackenzie and Mann have in mind for Canadian Northern? At this time, in 1903, they seemed most intent on consolidating their prairie network and advancing with caution, as had been the case in their early years in Manitoba. Both Regehr and Mackenzie's most recent biographer, R.B. Fleming, suggest, however, that as early as 1900 they were contemplating development of a transcontinental line to ensure an adequate traffic flow from east to west; but this was a long-term plan, not to be attempted until the western system was complete.[5]

Canadian Northern's success as a regional carrier, however, lured another player onto the field. Up to 1902 the Grand Trunk Railway, reflecting the conservatism of its London-based board of directors, had concentrated on exploiting the central Canadian market, foregoing new ventures to keep earnings and dividends high. The depression of the early 1890s cut into the Grand Trunk's revenues, leading to a management shake-up in 1895: Sir Charles Rivers-Wilson, a British diplomat with experience in financial reorganization, was brought in as president, and he in turn recruited a battle-hardened American railroader, Charles M. Hays, to be general manager. Rivers-Wilson and Hays devoted their early years at Grand Trunk to rebuilding the company's earnings on its established lines, but Hays had his eye on the western market.

Rivers-Wilson, who met Mackenzie in London in 1902, seems to have been inclined toward developing a co-operative arrangement between the Grand Trunk and Canadian Northern to challenge the CPR, but Hays proposed a takeover of Canadian Northern. Cox and Laurier were both enlisted to assist in the process, but merger talks deadlocked as Mackenzie and Mann refused to accept the terms. Hays now determined to build a western line, or at least to threaten to do so, in order to put pressure on Canadian Northern: 'railroading', as Regehr put it, 'in the American tradition' of aggressive and ruthless competition.

Laurier had his own reasons for endorsing this scheme. Although the Crowsnest Pass Agreement had harnessed the CPR's western freight rates, the prime minister wanted to strengthen the regulatory capabilities of the newly-established Board of Railway Commissioners. To that end competition between two (or better yet, three) strong transcontinental lines seemed desirable, and would also enhance the government's policy of encouraging western settlement. Consequently he was receptive to a proposal from Hays for cash subsidies and a land grant to the Grand Trunk to support a Pacific line. But a political Pandora's Box had now been opened and other interested parties gathered round to voice their demands. Quebec MPs wanted more rail service in their province; Maritimers clamoured for yet another line to the Atlantic coast; others demanded improvements in local Grand Trunk rail facilities. Meanwhile, advocates of Canadian Northern, including Sifton, insisted that pledges of support for that line be honoured.

Hays balked at meeting all these demands and Laurier's cabinet was split over the issue. As usual, a 'compromise' was worked out in May 1903. Under this complicated proposal, the Grand Trunk would form a wholly-owned subsidiary, the Grand Trunk Pacific Railway Co., which would construct a line from Moncton, N.B. to Winnipeg; this 'Eastern Division' would be owned by the federal government but leased to the Grand Trunk upon completion. A 'Western Division' from Winnipeg to the Pacific coast would be built, owned, and operated by the

Grand Trunk Pacific. The usual array of land grants, subsidies, and bond guarantees up to $100 million would be provided, but assorted safeguards were imposed, including the requirement that the construction of the Eastern Division would be subject to supervision by a government commission. The entire system would be called the 'National Transcontinental'.

In the parliamentary debates that ensued, this messy proposal was subjected to further criticism. The Conservative leader, Robert Borden, introduced an alternative under which the government would take over the CPR from Lake Superior west and lease carrying rights to all railways on equal terms. In the end, however, Laurier was able to push through his plan. In early 1904 Hays, despite his own reservations, persuaded Rivers-Wilson and the Grand Trunk board to accept it, and the nation's second transcontinental venture was launched. What had begun as a negotiating ploy by Hays had been transformed through political pressures and the momentum of events into a huge but poorly conceived and ultimately disastrous undertaking.

In 1904, however, the outlook was bright and even Mackenzie and Mann displayed little outward concern about the future; but they did initiate steps to extend Canadian Northern's links to eastern Canada. They were inadvertently assisted by the appearance of the National Transcontinental scheme which persuaded smaller railway promoters and investors in Quebec that their own ventures were imperilled; and Mackenzie and Mann proceeded in the east as they had on the prairies, acquiring at bargain prices short lines which could be knit into a trunk system to connect with the Canadian Northern line in the west.

Both Canadian Northern and Grand Trunk steadily expanded their systems between 1904 and 1907. At that point a sudden speculators' panic spreading from Wall Street to the London money market led to a short but sharp business recession. Mackenzie and Mann retrenched and survived the slump; Hays took advantage of the situation to delay the assumption by the Grand Trunk of the Eastern Division of the National Transcontinental. Hays was convinced that the contracts for work on that division had been let at excessively high costs due to the political influence of the government-appointed supervisory board. A Royal Commission established in 1911 to investigate this issue tended to bear out Hays' suspicions, indicating that over $70 million of the $160 million project had been wasted on extravagant construction. But in 1907 Hays' actions soured an already deteriorating relationship between the Grand Trunk and the Liberal government in Ottawa.

Sunny days reappeared in 1909, however, and the orgy of railway construction resumed as the full effects of Sifton's western settlement policy took hold. Mackenzie and Mann now felt confident enough to unveil plans to complete their own transcontinental line, floating new security issues of over $130 million in London. They were hailed as public heroes and knighted in 1911. Canadian Northern sprouted branch lines in all directions: the initial and long-neglected Hudson's Bay route was revived, lines were run deep into the Alberta backcountry, and further link-ups with American railroads were in progress. Meanwhile Hays went on a building and buying spree in the United States with plans to construct lines in New England and New York. He appears to have been contemplating an even more dramatic move in 1912, unloading the Grand Trunk Pacific onto the government and building an alternative western line from Chicago. At this point he booked passage across the Atlantic on the *Titanic* and his schemes went down with him on that vessel's fateful voyage.

Even before this tragedy, the railway boom was beginning to run out of steam. In 1910 labour unrest, which was reaching a peak of intensity in North America, swept across the Canadian railways, affecting both operating lines and construction projects. Time was lost in settling these disputes (or battling the unions, as Hays chose to do). Inflationary pressures drove up the costs of labour and materials; and the money markets, especially in Europe, were growing jittery over recurring war scares.

In 1911 the federal elections removed Laurier and the ever-generous Liberals from power; and the new government of Robert Borden was determined to bring some order to what many Tories regarded as an uncontrolled railway building and borrowing spree. As noted above, one of their first acts was to set up a Royal Commission to investigate cost overruns in the Eastern Division. Although the Commission exonerated the Grand Trunk of responsibility for these problems, members of Borden's cabinet, including the Minister of Railways, Frank Cochrane, were now floating proposals for government acquisition and rationalization of the debt-burdened projects.

Mackenzie and Mann were the first to encounter the winds of change in Ottawa. Unable to raise more long-term funding in London, in 1913 they reluctantly approached the Canadian government for $30 million in new subsidies and loans to complete the Canadian Northern's western lines. Borden and Cochrane agreed to provide half this amount, but demanded that the government receive an equity position in the company. Mackenzie grudgingly accepted the terms, but interest charges on short-term debt accumulated in New York quickly dissipated this infusion of funds and Mackenzie was back at Borden's door in less than a year, this time requesting $96 million to complete the entire transcontinental project. Again the government agreed to provide bond guarantees for half this amount, but required Mackenzie and Mann to reorganize all their far-flung enterprises under the Canadian Northern umbrella, transfer a much larger bloc of voting stock in the company to the government (raising its equity to 40 per cent), and secure the balance of funds from private sources.

The outbreak of war in Europe in the summer of 1914 now engulfed the hapless pair: the British government banned the export of capital, choking off that source, and the New York securities market, plunged into chaos by that action, was equally unreceptive to the Canadian promoters. In 1915 Wall Street bankers agreed to consider a loan to Canadian Northern but proposed a full examination of the properties and demanded that the Canadian government guarantee any new bond flotations.

Meanwhile, Cochrane had been vainly pressing the Grand Trunk to take over the Eastern Division as required under the 1903 Railway Act. Hays was gone, but his successor, Alfred Smithers, was equally obdurate on this point and also wanted $30 million in Canadian government bond guarantees to continue work on the Grand Trunk Pacific. At this point Borden decided to buy time by creating yet another Royal Commission to try to sort out the railway problem. Although the head of the commission was A.H. Smith of the New York Central Railroad, the dominant figure was Henry Drayton, chairman of the Canadian Board of Railway Commissioners and, like Cochrane, a strong advocate of government control if not ownership of all the nation's railways, including the CPR. Not surprisingly, in their 1917 report Drayton and the third member of the commission, W.H. Acworth, recommended that the government take over both the Canadian Northern and the Grand Trunk Pacific (along with its parent, the Grand Trunk). Smith dissented, arguing that the Canadian Northern was a viable entity, a view shared by the Wall Street bankers' review completed in 1916.

In July 1917 Borden, who had endorsed the idea of a government-owned western line back in 1903, moved quickly to take over Canadian Northern. This decision precipitated an emotional interview with Mackenzie who, disconsolate over the mortal illness of his wife as well as the disintegration of his business empire, 'completely broke down with audible sobs which were most distressing'.[6] Action on the other elements of the Drayton-Acworth report was delayed as the Prime Minister fought out the election on the conscription issue. With a strong majority for his 'Union' government, Borden proceeded toward a complete takeover of the Grand Trunk properties, amalgamating them in 1920 with Canadian Northern as the Canadian National Railway.

Although contemporary public opinion tended (as did Shaughnessy of the CPR) to assign blame for the debacle on all the railway promoters, historians have been more discriminating. The Canadian Northern, by most accounts, was a soundly-built line and served the needs of the west, not least by pressuring the CPR to expand its own operations in the region. Mackenzie and Mann may have been overly optimistic in attempting to create a transcontinental system, but their failure was due more to circumstances beyond their control: the outbreak of war in 1914 cut off the flow of capital 'when they were within sight of their goal', and the refusal of the Board of Railway Commissioners, under pressure from western farmers and other shippers, to allow freight rates to rise despite war-induced inflation, cut into their operating revenues. By contrast, the National Transcontinental/Grand Trunk Pacific is seen as an ill-conceived, wastefully-built system that ultimately dragged down the otherwise reasonably sound Grand Trunk Railway. Hays, in particular, built 'castles in the air' and antagonized politicians of all persuasions; his successors performed equally poorly in defending the venture before the Drayton Commission.

There have been some differences among historians over the motives and objectives of the Canadian government in dealing with the railway crisis. Traditional accounts see the Borden administration as reluctant nationalizers, taking over the bankrupt lines because no other option seemed possible — or no other option that would not have imperilled the Bank of Commerce and other financial institutions that had invested heavily in the railway ventures during the prewar boom. Regehr and John Eagle, however, have argued that Borden and his ministers embraced public ownership as a step toward a rationalization of Canada's transportation system that would provide more equitable service in the west and reduce the role of foreign investors in an essential sector of the nation's economy. Although this argument may impute a more long-term approach to economic planning than seems appropriate for politicians of the era, there certainly were other examples of government-owned railways in Europe for them to emulate; even in the US, the rail system was placed under government control, albeit only for the duration of the war. Borden, as noted above,had advocated government ownership of the western lines as early as 1903, and during the 1920s he professed regret that the CPR had not been integrated with the other railways to form a single nationalized system.[7]

Such an amalgamation did not come to pass, however, and the nation's railway system instead came to resemble the utilities industry, with a combination of publicly and privately owned enterprises. By 1920 the Intercolonial Railway had been folded into the Canadian Northern/Grand Trunk system, despite the protests of Maritimers, to form the federal government's first major 'crown corporation', Canadian National Railways. Sir Joseph Flavelle, the meat-packing millionaire who had headed Canada's Imperial Munitions Board during World War I, was the first chairman of the CNR; the chief operating officer was David B. Hanna, who in 1921 encountered what was to be one of the line's most troublesome features: the inevitable complications that partisan politics introduced in running the CNR.

In 1922 Hanna, a veteran manager from Canadian Northern, fell afoul of the new Liberal regime of Mackenzie King and resigned. To replace him, King recruited Sir Henry Thornton. An American by birth, Thornton had begun his railway career with the Long Island Railroad, a commuter line, then moved to Britain shortly before World War I to run the Great Eastern Railway. Thornton's talents in organizing passenger service led to his appointment as Inspector-General of Transportation for the British War Office. He came to Canada in 1923 with a formidable reputation, and assurances from the government that there would be no further political interference.

Thornton's tasks were equally formidable. The CNR comprised over 200 assorted railway lines and carried $1.3 billion in debt: in 1922 earnings were insufficient to cover the service charges on the debt. Canadian railway workers had pressed successfully during the war for wage rates equal to those of their counterparts in the US; then the Board of Railway Commissioners reduced freight rates in 1920–21 in response to the postwar recession. Finally, in the postwar era the automobile was emerging for the first time in Canada as a serious rival to railways in the transportation field.

The CPR faced many of these same problems, but did not carry a significant debt load, and Shaughnessy's successor, Edward Beatty, maintained his company's earnings by cutting expenditures on equipment maintenance, living for a time off the accumulated assets of the Shaughnessy era. Nor did Beatty have to face the sniping that the Conservative party, now in opposition, directed toward

Thornton — and the CNR contributed to the chorus, pointing out repeatedly that the CNR's access to public funds gave it an unfair advantage over the private line.

Despite these problems, in his early years at CNR Thornton was successful in at least restoring the public image of the government enterprise. Attentive to labour relations—in 1925 he introduced proposals for an employee pension plan —he was also able to bring some internal order to the sprawling CNR system with its heterogeneous management drawn from previously rival companies. Thornton diversified the company into radio broadcasting, introducing 'Hockey Night in Canada' in 1924; he was mindful of technological changes as well, bringing the first diesel locomotive into Canada in 1929. Not all his ventures were successful: an effort to revive western 'colonization' proved abortive, as the tide of population was moving off the land in the 1920s. Nevertheless, Thornton could point in 1928 to an increase in surplus operating revenues, from less than $4 million when he took over to $58 million within five years.

The revival of CNR's fortunes brought Beatty back into active competition in the late 1920s. Both sides indulged in hotel-building binges in the major cities as well as in the growing resorts such as Jasper Park. Resplendent palaces such as the CPR's Royal York Hotel in Toronto and the CNR's Hotel Vancouver were erected, neither of which earned enough to cover costs of construction for many years. A new round of railway construction also ensued, focusing on Saskatchewan, with almost 2000 new miles laid. The CNR also built, at long last, the Hudson's Bay Railway that Mackenzie and Mann had promised to the Manitoba government more than thirty years earlier. In the buoyant economic times of 1926–29 these various commitments seemed worthwhile if costly, but for Thornton in particular, they were to prove the sources of undoing.

The onset of the Depression caught both companies in a financially overextended position and both suffered severe losses in operating revenues. The CNR's surplus dwindled to less than $10 million by 1930 and the company ran a $60 million deficit in 1931–32. But Thornton's problems were aggravated by the departure of the Liberals from power in Ottawa in the election of 1930. The new Tory leader, R.B. Bennett, had been one of the CPR's chief attorneys and had vigorously criticized Thornton and the crown corporation for years. The CNR's accounts were subjected to a thorough investigation by a parliamentary committee in 1931 and by a Royal Commission the following year. Thornton's personal expenditures and salary came under fire, and amidst allegations of extravagance and mismanagement, he was forced to resign in 1932. A year later he was dead.[8]

Beatty pushed for an amalgamation of the two lines, under CPR control, or alternatively for the government to take over running all the money-losing rail services, leaving the CPR with its more profitable divisions, particularly Cominco. The Liberals' return to power in 1935 stymied these proposals, and the new Minister of Transport, C.D. Howe, reorganized CNR management. By this time, the era of the railway as the major transportation mode in Canada was passing. The combined effect of the Depression and the shift to motor vehicles cut freight and passenger sales by half for the Canadian railways. Although World War II resuscitated the lines, the CPR continued to pursue its strategy of diversification into air transportation and eventually into oil and gas, telecommunications, and other novel fields, transforming itself into a conglomerate. The CNR was restrained by its public-service position from pursuing ancillary ventures to this degree, but it expanded investment in communications and urban real estate, with the CN Tower in Toronto providing a suitable symbol: few tourists who visit it would be likely to immediately associate this edifice with a company that began as a railway builder for farmers on the Canadian prairies.

Notes

[1]Christopher Armstrong and H.V. Nelles, *Monopoly's Moment: The Organization and Regulation of Canadian Utilities, 1830–1930* (Philadelphia, 1986), 63. On the international electrical utility industry, see Thomas P. Hughes, *Networks of Power: Electrification in Western Society, 1880–1930* (Baltimore, 1983); on the electrical equipment industry, see Harold C. Passer, *The Electrical Manufacturers, 1875–1900* (Cambridge, Mass., 1953).

[2]On the electric power industry, see Armstrong and Nelles, *Monopoly's Moment*; H.V. Nelles, *The Politics of Development: Forests, Mines and Hydroelectric Power in Ontario, 1849–1941* (Toronto, 1974); John Dales, *Hydroelectricity and Industrial Development: Quebec, 1898–1940* (Cambridge, Mass., 1974); Ted Regehr, *The Beauharnois Scandal: A Story of Canadian Entrepreneurship and Politics* (Toronto, 1990); Patricia Roy, 'The Fine Art of Lobbying and Persuading: The Case of B.C. Electric Railway', in David S. Mac-Millan, ed. *Canadian Business History: Selected Studies 1497–1971* (Toronto, 1972), 239–54; Paul-André Linteau, 'Urban Mass Transit', in Norman Ball, ed., *Building Canada: A History of Public Works* (Toronto, 1988), 88–112. For an interesting study of the contrasting personalities of Mackenzie and Holt, see Ted Regehr, 'A Backwoodsman and an Engineer in Canadian Business', *Canadian Historical Association Historical Papers* (1977), 159–77.

[3]Christopher Armstrong and H.V. Nelles, 'A Curious Capital Flow: Canadian Investment in Mexico, 1902–10', *Business History Review* 58 (1984), 178–203 (the phrase is applicable to the entire process they described in *Southern Exposure*); see also Duncan McDowall, *The Light: Brazilian Traction, Light & Power Co., 1899–1945* (Toronto, 1988); Jorge Niosi, *Canadian Multinationals*, trans. by Robert Chodos (Toronto, 1985), 61–81.

[4]On the CPR, see John Eagle, *The Canadian Pacific Railway and the Development of Western Canada, 1896–1914* (Kingston 1988); W. Kaye Lamb, *History of the Canadian Pacific Railway* (New York, 1977); J. Lorne McDougall, *Canadian Pacific: A Short History* (Montreal, 1968); David Cruise and Alison Griffiths, *Lords of the Line: The Men Who Built the CPR* (Markham, Ont., 1988).

[5]The quote about Canadian Northern's railroad building practices is from G.R. Stevens, *History of the Canadian National Railways* (New York, 1973), 177. The 'unconnected projections' quote is from Ted Regehr, *The Canadian Northern Railway: Pioneer Road to the Northern Prairies, 1895–1918* (Toronto, 1976), 55. On the history of Canadian Northern, in addition to these two sources, see R.B. Fleming, *The Railway King of Canada: Sir William Mackenzie, 1849–1923* (Vancouver, 1991).

[6]Borden, quoted in Stevens, 278. See also Fleming, 222–3.

7Regehr, 428–9; John Eagle, 'Monopoly or Competition: The Nationalization of the Grand Trunk Railway', *Canadian Historical Review* 62 (1981), 3–30. See also Bliss, *Northern Enterprise*, 375–7.

8On the Beatty-Thornton years, see Stevens, 307–60; Cruise and Griffiths, 321–34; D.H. Miller-Barstow, *Beatty of the* CPR (Toronto, 1951); D'Arcy Marsh, *The Tragedy of Henry Thornton* (Toronto, 1935).

14 GIFTS OF NATURE

For both domestic and foreign investors, much of the attraction of railroad and utility securities reflected confidence that the development of Canada's infrastructure would open the way for rapid exploitation of the country's natural resources. While both supplies of and demand for Canada's traditional staples were apparently declining in the late nineteenth century, new resources were being discovered that would serve the needs of industries, especially in the United States, and thus provide export markets considered essential for economic revival and long-term prosperity.

Looking back from the perspective of the present, the exploitation of Canada's 'treasure house of resources' may seem to have been a mixed blessing. The rapid development of the country's mining and forestry frontiers in the early twentieth century did indeed generate wealth and create jobs, but left a residue of environmental problems and littered the northern interior region with isolated, vulnerable single-industry settlements. Harnessing the 'new staples' to a continental market perpetuated Canada's role as a resource hinterland, and the linkages forged by American corporate investment were, if anything, much tighter than the older economic ties with Britain.

But for Canada's turn-of-the-century business and political leaders foreign investment, natural resource exports, population growth, industrialization, and economic prosperity were all part of the same package. This vision of development provided Canadian business people with hope for the future in the depressed 1890s, and their optimism grew over the next decade as Canada, in its emerging role as supplier of essential materials, shared in the industrialized world's long boom that preceded the outbreak of the First World War. Sir Wilfrid Laurier reflected that confidence, while taking political credit for his role in the process, when he predicted in 1910 that the twentieth century would 'belong to Canada'.

THE WHEAT BOOM

The opening of the prairies for agriculture was of course the most obvious example of the interconnection of staple exports and economic growth. The depression of the early 1890s delayed prairie settlement but by the end of the decade world wheat prices were rising, transportation costs were falling as western rail networks proliferated, and the Canadian government embarked on a vigorous campaign to stimulate immigration to the region through homesteading and subsidized travel costs for settlers. Wheat production tripled between 1904 and 1914, at which point it was Canada's major export commodity, accounting for almost 15 per cent of total exports, principally directed to the British market. Despite the slump in world wheat prices from overproduction in the 1920s, Canada's share of global wheat exports rose from 14 per cent in the prewar era to almost 40 per cent on the eve of the Great Depression.

The 'wheat boom' of the period from 1901 to the First World War was a highly visible element in Canada's development, but economists differ over its significance in accounting for the nation's economic growth in this era. Estimates of the contribution of the wheat boom to real per-capita income growth for the decade 1901–11 have ranged from a low of 8 per cent to a high of close to 40 per cent. To some extent these variations reflect differences over the 'linkages' between prairie agriculture and other sectors of the economy. These linkages were numerous and in effect diffused the impact of the wheat boom throughout much of the Canadian business system, although the degree to which this single staple affected overall economic development remains a matter of controversy.[1]

The most direct links were formed in the grain handling and marketing arrangements that emerged in tandem with prairie settlement. Along the rail lines various companies erected grain warehouses to store wheat for farmers for a fee. At Fort William/Port Arthur on Lake Superior, the major transhipment point for prairie wheat destined for eastern Canadian and export markets, large terminal elevators provided bulk storage. The railway companies owned most of these terminal elevators directly—CPR built the first one in 1884—and dominated this phase of the process until co-operatives and government-owned elevators entered the field in the late 1920s. The 'country' or line elevators were independent of the railways from whom they leased the land and who set basic design guidelines for storage facilities. By 1900 there were over 400 line elevators and they continued to proliferate, reaching a peak of 5,733 by 1930 with storage capacity of 5 million tons.

The line elevator business attracted a variety of groups. During the 1890s grain merchants operating out of Winnipeg entered the field, as did some Ontario-based firms, notably James Richardson and Sons of Kingston, which remains one of the largest family enterprises in the business. It was also one of the few big companies presided over by a woman: Muriel Richardson took charge of the firm after her husband's death in 1938, and ran it for the next quarter-century. Meanwhile, two Montreal flour milling firms, Ogilvie and Lake of the Woods, established footholds in Manitoba line elevators as part of their strategy of vertical integration. After 1900 both also established western mills, and Ogilvie erected a terminal elevator at Fort William. Ontario mills began developing their own prairie elevator networks during this decade, and by 1912 almost half of Canada's wheat exports took the form of processed flour. The Canadian Northern railway promoters, Mackenzie and Mann, invited American capital into the field: in 1906 Frank Peavey, the 'Grain King of Minneapolis', set up an elevator network on the Canadian Northern route; within three years he had elevators along the CPR line as well.

After the First World War, mergers steadily reduced the number of line elevator companies and the amalgamated firms moved to integrate line and terminal elevator systems. By the end of the 1930s the number of private firms in the field had diminished by 50 per cent from the 1914 total. Long before this process of

Muriel Richardson, President of James Richardson & Sons Limited from 1939 to 1966. *(Department of Archives and Special Collections, University of Manitoba)*

amalgamation began, however, western wheat farmers had been agitating against what they regarded as 'monopolistic' behaviour by line elevator syndicates in collusion with the CPR. In 1897 the railway had begun dealing only with warehouses maintaining mechanized grain elevators. At this point only three firms controlled almost half the elevator capacity, and CPR interests were linked to the two milling firms that occupied much of the rest of the market. Furthermore, the line elevator companies functioned as middlemen in the marketing of grain: in addition to storing wheat, they were often the major or the only buyers available to farmers. The Winnipeg Grain Exchange, established in 1887, was heavily populated with brokers connected to the elevator companies; after 1903 and until the Second World War dealers on the exchange could trade in grain futures, to provide a hedge against grain price fluctuations.

The shift from warehouses to elevators helped cut transportation costs by reducing the turn-around time for cargo pick-ups, and the operations of the Grain Exchange provided a certain degree of stability to the market. But prairie farmers saw the lion's share of these benefits passing to eastern and Winnipeg business interests. The following two decades witnessed the rise of a powerful agrarian political movement in the west, a series of provincial and federal government investigations and attempts to regulate the grain trade, and the emergence by the 1920s of the co-operative wheat pools and elevator networks that within another decade controlled almost half the country's elevator capacity.[2]

On the supply side, western wheat farmers were heavily dependent on Canadian manufacturers for a wide range of consumer goods as well as production equipment, thanks in large part to the National Policy tariffs, another source of their discontent. The most direct beneficiaries of these arrangements were the makers of farm equipment. From the middle of the nineteenth century a number of technological improvements in farm implements appeared, from cream separators and seed drills to steam-driven threshing machines. Of particular significance for western wheat producers, as beneficial as the new strains of wheat, were the steel plow and mechanical reaper which enhanced the efficiency of planting and harvesting in Canada's short growing season. Many of these innovations originated in the United States and Canadian farm equipment manufacturers, who had liberally borrowed and adapted American designs up to 1870, became ardent protectionists as large US firms such as McCormick extended northward, lobbying for import duties that peaked at 35 per cent in 1883.

In 1871 there were over 250 farm-implement firms in Canada, most of them congregated in southwest Ontario close to the old agricultural heartland as well as the nascent iron mills of Hamilton. Unlike many other protected industries, however, small scale competitors were rapidly winnowed out, particularly during the depression of the early 1890s. In 1891, when the two largest companies, Massey of Toronto and Harris of Brantford, merged they controlled over one half of the market.

Both Massey and Harris were family firms that had emerged in the 1850s. In the ensuing decades they had pursued parallel and competitive lines, developing their own sales agencies, persistently searching for innovations on the American scene, licensing and then refashioning these products for the Canadian market. The Massey firm was the senior partner in the amalgamation with a foothold in the European market, thanks to years of exhibiting at international fairs. During the debates preceding introduction of the National Policy in 1879, Hart Massey, the architect of his company's development since the 1860s, had broken ranks with other Canadian farm implement manufacturers, arguing that higher tariffs would raise production costs for his industry and weaken Massey's competitive export potential. After the Massey-Harris amalgamation, Massey renewed lobbying for tariff reduction, and duties on imported farm equipment were cut to 20 per cent in 1894.

This level remained high enough, however, to attract a formidable competitor in 1903 when the McCormick Co., reorganized by J.P. Morgan as International Harvester with almost 90 per cent control of the US market for binders and reapers, established a subsidiary in Canada. In the meantime, Massey-Harris had erected a strong sales network on the prairies, enlarged its manufacturing plant, and moved into the European market which by 1901 accounted for more than one-third of its total sales. Export sales and development of overseas manufacturing, especially in France, provided a needed cushion for Massey-Harris because International Harvester's sheer size and production capabilities dwarfed the Canadian firm: by the mid-1920s Harvester held a 40 per cent share of the Canadian market and had moved with greater dispatch and efficiency into production of mechanized tractors. In addition to competition in its home market from Harvester and slumping sales overseas in the early 1920s, Massey-Harris suffered from a lack of leadership: Vincent Massey, the last direct descendant of the founding families, was more interested in politics and diplomacy than running the firm. In

1927 Massey-Harris was reorganized as a public joint-stock company. The ensuing Great Depression, which virtually destroyed the company's export business, took Massey-Harris to the brink of bankruptcy in 1931, but under James Duncan, who had managed Massey's French plant in the 1920s, the company was able to stagger through the slump.[3]

While the wheat boom of the early 1900s (and its subsequent collapse in the 1920s) had a direct impact on suppliers such as Massey-Harris and the grain marketing industry, its effects permeated the rest of the economy, and the aggregate of these indirect linkages greatly exceeded in macroeconomic terms the income generated by specific industries directly serving the farming sector. The fortunes of western urban businesses—wholesalers, small local merchants, savings institutions with heavy investment in prairie real estate—rose and fell with the wheat market. In the early 1900s railway construction, which in turn stimulated expansion of affiliated industries such as iron and steel, was intended primarily to provide capacity for hauling immigrants to the prairies and their wheat in the opposite direction; and as in the 1850s the inflow of foreign capital to finance railways percolated into other quarters.

But the western wheat boom provides only part of the explanation for the country's remarkable economic growth in this era. Even in the case of industries directly related to agriculture, as the Massey-Harris example indicates, some production was destined for export. As the economy diversified and urban populations expanded, merchants, manufacturers and other businesses served these markets; by 1911 the proportion of the labour force involved in agriculture was little more than one-third of the total, and by 1931 this had diminished to less than 30 per cent. Even at the peak of the wheat boom in the second decade of the twentieth century, with the western rail network essentially complete, farm products accounted for only one-quarter of the total volume of freight, with minerals providing another 25 per cent and forestry products slightly less.

The prairie wheat fields unquestionably provided a major staple export for Canada between 1890 and 1930 and stimulated the growth of the west with its major grain entrepôts across the region and its overbuilt railway networks, not to mention enriching financiers and investors in central Canada and Britain. Certain features of the wheat trade distinguish it from other 'new staples' of this era. First, the major market for wheat lay in Britain and later continental Europe, in contrast to minerals and forestry products that largely flowed southward to the United States. Wheat was thus very much a 'traditional' transatlantic staple, with Canadians competing with American producers, bolstering the older ties with Britain. Western farmers longed for cheap American manufactured goods and resented eastern control of the transport and marketing of their wheat, but the 'regional alienation' of that era did not reflect the pro-American tilt of more recent western protest movements.

Secondly, and to some extent for related reasons, American direct investment played a somewhat less significant role in the wheat boom than in the development of other natural resources. Canadian rail expansion into the west was largely financed with British capital. The American presence in the line elevator field was fairly substantial in the early years of the century, comprising about 50 per cent of capacity in 1911, but that proportion diminished after the 1920s: by the Second World War, US interests held only about one-fifth of the total. American farm equipment companies like International Harvester crossed the tariff barrier to set up branch plants in Canada, but this was part of a general trend in manufacturing, particularly after the defeat of Reciprocity in 1911.

MINING

The emergence of Canada as a major player in the North American mining industry by the 1920s was the result of the fortuitous convergence of shifts in demand for and supplies of minerals after the 1880s. During the 'First Industrial Revolution' of the early nineteenth century the major ore required had been coal for generating steam power and the charcoal residue needed for iron production. British North America had few known reserves of coal outside Nova Scotia and little if any of the hard, fast-burning anthracite that fuelled American industrial growth. In any case most of the Maritime coal flowed south to New England while central Canadians imported coal from Pennsylvania and Ohio. When prospects for developing Nova Scotia's coal mines and integrating them with iron and steel manufacturing beckoned in the 1890s, it was a Boston capitalist, Henry M. Whitney, who in 1893 took the initiative in consolidating the Cape Breton coal fields into Dominion Coal Co.

The technologies associated with the 'Second Industrial Revolution' of the 1880s–1920s, by contrast, required a wide range of special metals, many of which had to be extracted and refined through complex, capital-intensive techniques. The most dramatic applications were in the military field, stimulated by the international arms race that culminated in the First World War. Nickel alloyed with steel provided hard armour-plating for the Dreadnoughts and other warships developed by the navies of the Great Powers; during the war, tanks and other armoured vehicles were introduced. Zinc and copper were combined to make brass casings for lead bullets, produced in vast quantities in the war. At the same time, civilian commercial uses flourished: nickel-steel alloys produced corrosive-resistant steel coated with zinc for general industrial purposes, in particular in the automotive field. Motor vehicles also used fibred asbestos for brake-linings and clutch facings, and asbestos blended with cement for heavy-duty pipes and construction materials. The electrical equipment industry required large amounts of lead for batteries and copper wiring for transmission lines. Even precious metals —gold and silver—had industrial uses, though the major gold booms of Canada in the 1890s and 1930s were more notably tied to the use of the metal for currency.

This rising demand for industrial minerals coincided with the opening of the Canadian northern and western interior by railway construction and the development of hydroelectric capacity that was harnessed to the smelting and refining of metals. The Canadian Shield, stretching across northern Quebec and Ontario, hitherto regarded as useless real estate and a barrier to agricultural settlement, was discovered to possess vast reserves of a range of minerals. A substantial portion of the wealth generated by the mining booms between the 1890s and 1930s was siphoned off by Montreal and Toronto financiers to help underwrite ancillary ventures and industrial consolidations that solidified central Canada's position as the economic heartland of the country.

The Canadian west was, however, the scene of the first sustained sequence of development. It centred on the Kootenay valley in south central British Columbia. During the 1880s American miners had begun exploiting massive copper-ore sites in Montana and silver-lead deposits in Idaho and Washington states. Some of them began looking northward, among them F. Augustus Heinze, a Columbia University-trained geologist who by the early 1890s was embroiled in a struggle among the 'copper kings' of Butte, Montana, for control of the industry. To out-flank his rivals, Heinze in 1895 established a smelter at Trail, B.C. to process locally mined copper and silver ores; in the following year Heinze secured a charter to build a narrow-gauge railway to connect the Trail smelter to the minesites.

At this point the CPR entered the picture. Alarmed by the prospect that Heinze might extend his railway from Trail to link up with Jim Hill's Great Northern Railroad, Van Horne and Shaughnessy in 1898 decided to buy not only the railway but also the Trail smelter—an inadvertent first step toward diversification by the CPR, which also in the long run transferred control over the development of the region from American to central Canadian business interests.

At the turn of the century, however, the Trail smelting operation was only one of a number of mining ventures in the Kootenay region. By this time the most readily accessible sources of copper, silver, and gold had been played out and the CPR faced the problem of having a large smelter with no supplies of ore. Shaughnessy's strategy to deal with this problem was twofold. Using its growing financial resources CPR began buying up other mines, culminating in 1906 with the establishment of Consolidated Mining and Smelting Co. (a name later shortened to Cominco). At the same time, technical specialists were brought in to develop new processes for separating, purifying and refining the often intermixed ores encountered by miners as they moved further underground.

The 1910 acquisition and subsequent development of the Sullivan Mine at Kimberley, B.C. was the key to Cominco's eventual domination of the region's mineral industry. The Sullivan Mine consisted largely of mixed lead and zinc ores, both of which had potential commercial value but had defied various technical efforts by smaller local smelters to separate them. Cominco acquired a promising separation process and began erecting a zinc refining plant at Trail in 1914. At this point the outbreak of war stimulated demand for both metals for shell casings, and the Canadian government undertook to finance Cominco's research and development. As it happened, a completely satisfactory zinc refining process was not brought on stream until the early 1920s; but Cominco had both the technology and capacity to fully exploit postwar civilian markets. To provide necessary electric power Cominco had also taken over a local power system in 1917, providing the company with a fully integrated operation. During the 1920s more than half of B.C.'s mineral output was comprised of Cominco's lead and zinc production. Given its economies of scale, Cominco generated profits even through the Depression and deployed the earnings from its Sullivan Mine base to diversify into fertilizers, iron and steel, and direct investment in East Asia after World War II.

The CPR was not the only railway to invest in the mining industry—MacKenzie and Mann acquired coal mines in B.C. to supply Canadian Northern—but the most important impact of railway development was to open up mineral regions of northern Ontario. Even before the CPR completed its transcontinental line this process was underway. In 1883 residents of Sudbury, Ontario, a settlement about 80 kilometres north of Georgian Bay that had just been reached by the CPR line, discovered traces of what appeared to be copper ores. Although examination of the samples by the Geological Survey of Canada were not very promising, a few prospectors filtered into the region. Among them was Samuel Ritchie, originally from Cleveland, Ohio, who had earlier been involved in unsuccessful efforts to develop iron ore sites at Marmora near Peterborough in eastern Ontario. Despite pessimistic reports on the Sudbury ores, Ritchie and others were encouraged to purchase land for mineral exploration by the provision of Ontario's General Mining Act of 1869 which imposed virtually no constraints on mining development, offered mineral rights on crown lands for $1 per acre, and did not require royalty payments. By 1886 Ritchie had assembled claims to all unpatented land in Sudbury and organized the Canadian Copper Co. with $2 million from business associates in Ohio.

Initially this enterprise seemed fated to go the way of Ritchie's iron ore venture. As in the case of the Sullivan Mine's lead-zinc deposits, the copper from Sudbury was intermixed with nickel and other minerals—the result, apparently, of the intense heat created by a meteorite whose impact had formed the vast oval bowl of Sudbury Basin in prehistoric times. Nickel was an ore of little known commercial value and there was no established technology to efficiently separate it from copper, although refining experiments were underway in Britain. Ritchie had already contracted for copper refining with a New Jersey company, Orford Copper, and he persuaded Orford's owner, Col. Robert Thompson, to try to develop a separation technique. Meanwhile, stimulated by reports from Britain on the potential military value of nickel, Ritchie began lobbying the US Navy for contracts to supply nickel-plated armour.

By 1895 Orford had perfected methods of separating and refining the Sudbury ores, and a different but equally effective technique for purifying nickel had been developed by the Anglo-German chemist, Ludwig Mond. Meanwhile, there were major changes on the business side. In 1891, Ritchie, whose penchant for risk-taking alarmed his backers — he envisioned erecting a diversified industrial empire encompassing iron- and steel-making at Sudbury as well as mining at Copper Cliff—was ousted from management of Canadian Copper. Thompson of Orford had persuaded his erstwhile colleagues in the US Navy to award him an exclusive contract for refined nickel, and then used this coup to secure the bulk of Canadian Copper's output, buttressed by a significant equity share in the mining firm. The Orford/Canadian Copper combination turned back challenges from

THE KLONDIKE GOLD RUSH

Curiously, Canada's best known mining boom, the Klondike gold rush of 1896-1903, had relatively little impact on the economy and business community, although the publicity surrounding the Yukon gold fields may have lured unwary investors into other equally risky if not fraudulent ventures whose stocks were vigorously traded on the Mining Exchanges in Toronto and Vancouver. Canada had experienced modest gold rushes through the nineteenth

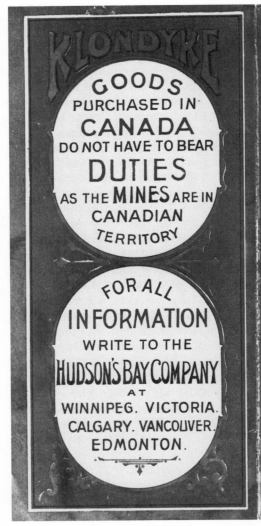 

The Hudson's Bay Company advertised supplies for the Klondike gold rush. *(Hudson's Bay Company Archives/Provincial Archives of Manitoba)*

century, most notably on the Fraser River and in the interior regions of the Cariboo and Kootenays in British Columbia in the 1860s. Another short-lived bonanza was discovered at Silver Islet on Lake Superior in the mid-1870s. It yielded $3.2 million in silver ore in a fourteen-year span, much of which flowed into the hands of a Detroit businessman, Alexander Sibley, who had acquired the venture from its despondent Montreal founders shortly before the strike.

Gold prospectors, many of them Americans, moved slowly from British Columbia into the Yukon wilderness in the 1880s, and the Canadian government had only just established its authority in the region when gold was discovered in the summer of 1896. The feature that made the discovery so attractive to the thousands of amateur prospectors who poured into the Yukon across Chilkoot Pass was that it was 'placer gold' that, at least initially, could be found along the bottoms of rivers and creeks and panned out rather than mined.

By 1898 over $8 million had been brought out in this fashion. Latecomers had to start tunnelling underground but the technology remained relatively straightforward although the vast majority of those who ventured to the Klondike never fulfilled their hopes. Those who exploited the prospectors—suppliers of equipment and transportation, and the array of gamblers, saloon keepers and other camp followers who congregated at Dawson City—probably found more reliable sources of income than the gold seekers themselves.

Large scale mining operations were not a major feature of the Klondike gold rush. In 1899 a British entrepreneur, A.N.C. Treadgold, persuaded the Canadian government to provide him with a large consolidated concession to permit more systematic mining operations, but the Treadgold concession stimulated a populist outcry among the small miners and was abandoned in 1904. Two years later the government imposed new regulations to encourage larger ventures and the Treadgold claim was taken over by a subsidiary of the American mining multinational, Guggenheims. Several other big firms mined the area for copper but by 1914 most of the gold was gone and Dawson shrank to a small outpost for government officials and mine employees.

The Klondike gold rush had some spill-over effects: in 1899 an Anglo-American group built a rail line (eventually acquired by the CPR) to connect the Yukon to the B.C. inland waterway, contributing to a dispute between the US and Canada over the boundary of the Alaska panhandle. But little in the way of long-term development came about in the region until the 1970s, by which time 'black gold'—the oil deposits of the Beaufort Sea—was the central lure.

Sources

Innis, Harold A., *Settlement and the Mining Frontier* (Toronto, 1936).

Zaslow, Morris, *The Grand Opening of the Canadian North, 1870–1914* (Toronto, 1971).

several British- and American-backed competitors (including a short-lived riposte from Ritchie), and reached an agreement with their only real international rival, the French company Société le Nickel which had mines in the Pacific, to divide world markets.

A more substantial challenger entered the field in 1899 when Ludwig Mond acquired mines in the Subdbury region, shipping output to his refinery in Wales. Growing military demand for nickel soon brought a much bigger player onto the scene. In 1901 J.P. Morgan consolidated US Steel Co., the largest merger of its time. Charles Schwab, who headed the new amalgamation, advised absorption of a nickel producer to ensure a reliable flow of supplies. Thompson, facing renewed competition from Mond, was amenable and in 1902 Morgan orchestrated consolidation of Orford, Canadian Copper, and assorted other producers into International Nickel Co. (later Inco) capitalized at $24 million.

Mond, whose refinery began production that same year, remained outside the amalgamation and over the next thirty years his enterprise maintained a strategy of advanced research, diversification of product lines, and aggressive marketing that outpaced Inco's performance. By 1925 Mond's mining output virtually equalled that of Inco and earnings had risen from one-fifth to one-half those of the American giant. But Mond generally avoided direct competition with Inco in the American market, and Inco's connection with Morgan helped thwart other potential entrants. Francis Clergue's venture into nickel in 1903 was easily suppressed when that ambitious empire-builder failed to secure American financing. In 1910 Fred Pearson, the peripatetic hydro-power promoter, formed a syndicate (that included, as usual, Mackenzie and Mann) to set up British-American Nickel Corporation using a new refining process developed in Norway. But Pearson was rebuffed by American bankers and the onset of war in Europe blocked British sources of capital. After the war another Canadian group that included John R. Booth, the Ontario lumber baron, and former Prime Minister Sir Robert Borden, tried to revive the venture but was driven from the field by a price war initiated by Inco and Mond. In 1928 Sir Alfred Mond, Ludwig's son, sold the family's nickel interests to Inco in order to devote more attention to his chemical enterprise. Although at the end of the 1920s another nickel company, Falconbridge, was assembled by Thayer Lindsley, an American geologist with Canadian backers and using the Norwegian process, the Inco-Mond merger left the American firm in virtual control of both the Sudbury field and the North American market.

The heavy capital costs and complex technology involved in extracting and refining nickel from Sudbury Basin established the conditions under which development would occur through large-scale corporations, although government policies encouraged the process as well—inadvertently before 1891, through mining regulations that permitted accumulations of claims on easy terms. After the Sudbury experience the Ontario government established a graded land price system and attempted, with limited success, to introduce royalty fees along with more formal procedures for establishing mineral claims. Both the provincial and federal governments also set out deliberately to attract foreign capital and foreign mining experts; there were no institutions in Canada for mining education until the mid-

1890s, and governments were always balancing the need to regulate (and raise revenues) against the need to promote economic development.

The American orientation in the Sudbury fields was more fortuitous. Ritchie's early arrival on the scene and hasty commitment to the New Jersey refiner, before he realized the technical problems involved in nickel production, were events not dictated by fate or forces of nature. Once the Morgan interests moved in, the integration of Canadian nickel production into the American steel industry proceeded steadily. At this point a degree of Canadian nationalist (or at least anti-American) sentiment surfaced, focusing not on the presence of foreign direct investment, which was generally regarded as desirable, but on the fact that virtually all refining and processing of nickel was carried out in the US, depriving Canadians of potential jobs and business opportunities. Not surprisingly, this theme was promoted by Ritchie after his ouster by Canadian Copper and by steel makers in Hamilton and Sault Ste Marie, Ontario, who were interested in developing their own integrated industry.

In 1897, emboldened by popular discontent over a highly protectionist US tariff law, these groups lobbied in Ottawa for an export duty to be placed on unrefined nickel. Frustrated by inaction at this level, they turned to the Ontario government in 1900, urging it to use its licensing powers to compel the nickel companies to establish the 'manufacturing condition' in that field, similarly to the province's undertaking for forestry products. Canadian Copper and Mond both resisted such pressures, threatening to close down Sudbury operations and draw their supplies of ore from New Caledonia, the French mine in the Pacific.

Although the government backed down, the issue simmered on through the next decade. The onset of war in Europe provided advocates of Canadian nickel refining with new ammunition. American neutrality in the war and the expansion of Inco's refineries in New Jersey fed rumours that the US company was supplying armour plating material to Germany, thus providing aid and comfort to Canada's foes. Although there was little evidence that significant quantities of nickel were running through the British blockade, Inco's owners (including the intensely pro-British J.P. Morgan) slowly succumbed to pressures from the Ontario and Canadian governments. Prime Minister Borden hinted that subsidies might be provided to Pearson's group, British-American Co., to build a refinery in Canada. In 1916 Inco announced plans to erect a refinery at Port Colbourne, close to the hydro facilities of Niagara Falls. Although the postwar slump temporarily closed all Inco's refineries, the company shifted the bulk of its nickel smelting to Canada in the 1920s.

The CPR had opened Sudbury basin for exploitation in the 1880s as an unanticipated by-product of its construction toward the Canadian prairies. Twenty years later a very similar sequence of events opened northeastern Ontario for mineral development, although the results were very different. Throughout the last two decades of the nineteenth century land speculators in Ontario and French Canadian missionaries in Quebec campaigned for construction of a railway between Lake Nipissing and James Bay to open that region to agricultural settlement. By 1900 some Toronto business interests joined the chorus, anticipating that rail access to Hudson's Bay would reduce their dependence on Montreal for shipping transatlantic goods; some even dreamed of linking Toronto to the Klondike via James Bay. Reflecting these various ambitions,the Liberal regime of George Ross in Ontario committed itself in 1902 to build a government-owned line, christened the Timiskaming and Northern Ontario Railway (later the Ontario Northland Railway).

By 1903 the line had been laboriously completed to Long Lake on the Ontario-Quebec border, about 160 kilometres north of Lake Nipissing. At this point workers on the line discovered veins of what proved to be pure silver. Within a short time there was a silver rush centring on a settlement named Cobalt, since that metal was found intermixed with the silver; Long Lake was renamed Cobalt Lake. By 1906 several thousand prospectors and their camp followers clustered at Cobalt, thanks to easy access via the railway (in contrast to the Klondike); silver-mine stock promoters from Toronto could trundle potential investors up for a day's viewing of the site.

In contrast to Sudbury basin, and like the Klondike, Cobalt was a 'poor man's camp'. Although the Ontario government tightened its regulatory procedures under the 1897 Mining Act, requiring a proved 'discovery' before licensing a claim, the intent of the measure was at least in part to streamline processing of claims and resolve disputes over claims, which to put it midly were frequent and spirited. By 1914 much of the silver was gone, but in the interim small prospectors could pry out the ores fairly easily without having to worry overmuch about separating mixed ores.

The Cobalt silver boom was short-lived but it spawned a number of millionaire prospectors who used their earnings to finance further ventures and to stake promising protégés. In 1909 gold discoveries at Porcupine, northwest of Cobalt, attracted the attention of the Timmins brothers who had developed one of Cobalt's early claims. Acquiring a site at Porcupine discovered by a fellow prospector, Benny Hollinger, the Timminses set up Hollinger Gold Mines, drew on their Cobalt profits to buy neighbouring claims, and laid out a townsite. Another set of brothers, Gilbert and Charles Labine, migrated from Cobalt to briefly join forces with the Timminses in the Hollinger mine, then moved westward, eventually opening the El Dorado gold mine in Manitoba—which proved to be more significant for its uranium deposits, leading to its acquisition by the Canadian government in 1944; the Labines used the proceeds to finance further lucrative mining ventures in Saskatchewan and Alberta in the 1950s. The Timmins and Labine brothers were only a few of the cohort of mining entrepreneurs who fanned out across the Canadian northern interior to exploit gold fields at Kirkland Lake and Red Lake in Ontario and more remote mining sites after World War I, their explorations made easier by small bush aircraft and the systematic topographical research of the Geological Survey of Canada.

For the most part the smaller operators at Cobalt and other mines were content to take out surface ores and ship them off in a relatively unrefined form. Eventually, however, the surface veins were played out and heavier equipment was needed. At this point metal mining became more capital-intensive and techno-

Table 14.1 Major Canadian Mining Companies, 1929

COMPANY	ASSETS	OWNERSHIP
International Nickel	$182 million	47% US; 31% UK
Cominco	$ 55 million	Cdn (CPR)
Hollinger Mines	$ 36 million	Cdn
Hudson Bay Mining & Smelting	$ 28 million	85% US
Noranda Mines	$ 21 million	65% Cdn; 30% US
Asbestos Corporation	$ 21 million	Cdn
Granby Consolidated Mining & Smelting	$ 17 million	majority US
Dome Mines	$ 13 million	majority US
McIntyre-Porcupine Mines	$ 12 million	majority Cdn
Mining Corporation of Canada	$ 9 million	Cdn

SOURCES: Compiled from *The Canadian Annual Financial Review* (Toronto), 1930; ownership data from E.S. Moore, *The American Influence in Canadian Mining* (Toronto, 1941); and H. Marshall *et al.*, *Canadian-American Industry* (New Haven, Conn., 1936).

logically demanding, and larger companies entered the scene, often consolidating a number of smaller claims and integrating mining and refining operations much like Cominco in British Columbia and Inco in Sudbury, albeit on a smaller scale. After World War I the pace of this expansion accelerated, driven by industrial demand for metals and a buoyant market for mining securities.

In 1922 two American mining engineers, S.C. Thomson and H.W. Chadbourne, set up a New York-based syndicate to develop some promising gold fields in Rouyn township on the western border of Quebec. On the advice of their Canadian lawyer, James Murdoch, the syndicate incorporated in Ontario as Noranda Mines to provide limited liability to the partners, and Murdoch became president. Noranda included both American and Canadian investors, among them the Timmins brothers. Recognizing that the copper sources of Rouyn were more abundant than its gold, Murdoch drew on capital from Hollinger Mines to set up a smelter near the mine and by 1930 had established a refinery in Montreal. By the end of World War II Noranda had acquired a brass factory and mining ventures in central America; its copper output and vertical integration made Noranda second only to Inco. As in the case of Cominco, Noranda devoted much attention to technological improvements, developing its own high speed ore roasters, as well as drawing on American and British processes through joint ventures.

Noranda was only one of a number of Canadian mining enterprises that integrated forward into refining, relying often on proximity to Canadian hydroelectric facilities and introducing technological innovations to achieve larger scale, lower unit cost production: in 1927, for example, Hudson Bay Mining and Smelting was set up to develop copper-zinc deposits at Flin Flon in Manitoba. In that same year Falconbridge Nickel appeared at Sudbury.

As indicated in Table 14.1, sources of capital and corporate control varied. Inco, which dwarfed all other Canadian mining entities in 1929 (particularly after its merger with Mond Nickel) was essentially an Anglo-American operation with a research unit in New Jersey and rolling mills in the US and Britain. While its near-monopoly position in the nickel industry declined after World War II, the company followed Falconbridge and Noranda into overseas direct investment. Cominco, the second largest firm in 1929, was controlled by CPR until 1986. The other major companies represented a mixture (sometimes an intermixture) of American and Canadian capital. The Ontario Northland rail link-up of Toronto to the Cobalt-Porcupine-Kirkland Lake region and the integration of the mining exchange into the Toronto Stock Exchange ensured that Toronto-based groups would play a major role in financing Canadian metal mining: Canadian historian J.M.S. Careless commented that the 'opulent suburbs of Toronto spell out a veritable progression of northern mining booms.'[4]

FORESTRY PRODUCTS

Between the mid-1880s and 1930 the lumber industry in Canada went through two overlapping cycles. With the rise of steamships the demand for squared pine timber declined and that development, aggravated by the disappearance of good pine through overcutting, eroded the position of the Maritimes, especially New Brunswick, in the industry by World War I. At the same time railways not only opened up new areas in Ontario and the west for logging but also provided a market for rail ties. The growth of cities in central Canada and the American Middle West provided another booming market, with the burgeoning rail network around the Great Lakes favouring development along the Ottawa River and Georgian Bay. Completion of the CPR in 1885 stimulated the rise of the lumber industry in British Columbia, particularly along the Fraser River, with Vancouver as its terminus and a centre for sawmilling. Much of this lumber went to the Canadian prairies, but the opening of the Panama Canal in 1910 provided B.C. fir and cedar products with new urban markets on the American east coast.

Meanwhile, a substantially new industry emerged after 1900 with the rapidly growing demand for pulpwood, using hitherto largely untapped stands of spruce, to be made into newsprint. By 1930 pulpwood accounted for over 40 per cent of total lumber production by value and processed and unprocessed pulpwood for over half of all lumber exports by value. The Great Depression severely damaged both the traditional Canadian lumber industry and the pulp and paper industry, but newprint emerged after World War II to become by the mid-1950s Canada's major export commodity, outpacing wheat as well as mineral and petroleum exports.

Although both construction lumber and newsprint flowed in the same direction —southward to the US market—in other respects there were significant differences between these two major components of Canada's forestry products industry. Traditional lumber production did not require major initial capital outlays, and although the introduction of steam-driven sawmills and log draggers at the end of the nineteenth century contributed to the growth of larger, integrated operations, there was still room in the industry for smaller firms. As late as the mid-

1920s the average capital cost of a sawmill was less than $100,000. Even the larger companies were run by individual proprietors or families: most notable among these was John R. Booth, the 'lumber king' of the Ottawa Valley who in the 1880s financed his own railway, the Canadian and Atlantic, to link his lumber tracts to Parry Sound, and later developed a Great Lakes steamer fleet to carry milled wood to Chicago. In Quebec the descendants of William Price expanded his timber empire in the Saguenay region. On the west coast in the 1890s James Hendry established B.C. Mills, Timber & Trading Co. which operated sales agencies as far afield as Australia and Britain. Hendry also pioneered in the production of an early version of prefabricated housing for prairie farmers. As usual, Mackenzie and Mann dabbled in this industry, establishing Canadian Western Lumber Co. in 1910 and erecting at Fraser Mills what was touted as 'the largest sawmill in the British Empire'. By this time foreign investors were entering the B.C. lumber trade: in 1909 Brooks-Scanlon, a Minneapolis-based family firm, built a large mill at Powell River that eventually became part of H.R. MacMillan's 'empire of wood'. A more exotic entrant was Vancouver Timber & Trading Co., set up by a German Junker, Alvo van Alvensleben, that reputedly included the Kaiser among its aristocratic shareholders; this enterprise was seized as 'enemy property' and its assets auctioned off in World War I.

In contrast, the pulp and paper industry required huge stands of woodland and large amounts of chemicals and hydroelectric power to operate high-speed continuous production mills. Although some of the larger individual lumber producers, including Booth and the Price brothers, moved into this field in the early 1900s, the substantial capital investment needed—by the 1920s an average paper mill cost several million dollars—encouraged the formation of large-scale joint-stock corporations and syndicates, attracting the interest of financiers in Montreal, Toronto, New York, and London as well as publishers and manufacturers in the US and Britain seeking to control the flow of paper supplies through direct investment. Overexpansion of the industry after World War I led to periodic crises and eventual rationalization of competing firms into a few large vertically integrated enterprises combining wood-cutting, milling, pulp-processing, and paper-making that dominated the market by the 1940s.

The development of an integrated Canadian pulp and paper industry was to some extent a by-product of government measures to protect the established lumber-milling industry. By the 1890s the focus of the lumber trade in Ontario had shifted from the Ottawa Valley to the Georgian Bay region. At this point conditions of relatively free trade in both logs and milled lumber prevailed between the US and Canada, and both American loggers and Canadian lumber millers exploited the situation. The Americans, and some small Canadian loggers, floated giant rafts of unmilled logs from Ontario to sawmills in Michigan, while larger Canadian lumber entrepreneurs like Booth competed directly with US sawmills for the lucrative Chicago construction market. Depression in the 1890s intensified competition, and in 1897 the American lumber milling industry successfully lobbied in the US Congress for restoration of import duties on milled lumber, while permitting duty-free entry of logs, provisions that were incorporated in the so-called 'Dingley Tariff'.

Ontario lumbermen turned naturally to the Dominion government for help in maintaining their US market position, but the Laurier regime proved reluctant to act on this specific case, hoping to negotiate a broader reciprocal trade agreement. Sawmillers then put pressure on the provincial governments in Ontario and Quebec to take action. In both provinces most of the land available for cutting was Crown property with timber rights leased by the government: in 1900 Ontario passed an act requiring all licensees to process wood from Crown lands in Canadian mills. Quebec was slower to respond but by 1910 it too imposed a similar restriction; New Brunswick and British Columbia followed in 1913.

The intent of the Ontario government of George Ross in initiating this measure in 1900—as in the case of the less successful concurrent efforts to promote nickel refining at Sudbury—was to encourage the 'manufacturing condition' in the province's natural resource sector. Although Ontario lumber interests supported this measure, their long-term aim was to regain access to the US market. When the Laurier government introduced a similar manufacturing requirement on Dominion-owned Crown lands in 1907, the latter objective may have been the key consideration, for by this time the attitude of the US government, hitherto stalwartly protectionist, was beginning to change. American lumber producers remained adamant on the need for high import duties on milled wood, but they now confronted a more formidable domestic foe: the American newspaper publishers' lobby.

In the late nineteenth century the American newspaper business had been transformed. The growth of big cities and the spread of literacy created a demand for newspapers at the same time that technological developments such as the rotary press enabled publishers to increase their output and reduce costs. Entrepreneurial publishers like William Randolph Hearst and Joseph Pulitzer exploited the opportunity, establishing mass-circulation newspapers and magazines designed to attract this growing audience with stories that emphasized drama and human interest. Newspapers had traditionally been organs of political parties and commercial interests, but the new mass-circulation media could exercise a much broader influence on public opinion, as well as amassing great wealth for their owners: Hearst, for example, took credit (with considerable exaggeration) for having pressured the US government to go to war with Spain in 1898.

A crucial link in the growth of mass-circulation newspapers was the technological revolution in paper-making that occurred in this era. Traditionally, paper was made from reconverted waste materials, such as rags and straw, which placed limits on supplies; in the mid-1800s new processes emerged in Germany and the US for processing paper from low-grade wood such as spruce or hemlock. The simplest process involved the mechanical grinding or chipping of logs. A more refined product was produced by cooking the pulped wood in a solution of calcium bisulphide, leaving cellulose fibres. The fibres would be matted into paper sheets or newsprint through steam-heated rolling machines: the most common was the Fourdrinier machine patented in England in the early nineteenth century.

The mechanical and sulphite pulping processes were most commonly used in Canada and the US for papermaking; other chemical processes were later introduced to produce a finer quality paper or a tougher paper that could be used for packaging material. After World War II Canadian paper makers began to diversify into production of this latter 'kraft' paper which by the 1980s became an important component of the industry as demand for newsprint slackened.

Since the Dingley Tariff imposed protective duties on imported paper as well as milled lumber, American newspaper publishers in the early 1900s faced problems not only of high current costs but long-term decline of reliable sources of supply of newsprint paper. By 1907 they were actively lobbying for reduction of duties to provide access to the cheaper and largely undeveloped pulp and paper resources of Canada. Reduction of duties on Canadian newprint and milled lumber were central features of the Reciprocity Agreement negotiated by the Laurier government and the Taft administration in the US in 1911. Although the broader trade agreement was stillborn when the Liberals lost the 1911 federal election in Canada, US duties on newsprint were virtually eliminated two years later.

The US tariff reductions of 1913 and the manufacturing requirements of provincial and federal licensing arrangements in Canada between 1900 and 1913 were followed by a dramatic growth of the pulp and paper industry. Newsprint production in Canada increased seven times over between 1913 and 1930; at the end of that period over 90 per cent of the output was exported, principally to the US although Britain and other markets absorbed a portion from Quebec and the Maritimes. The extent to which this expansion was the result of government trade and regulatory policies has been a matter of some controversy. Historians have generally assigned these measures a significant, if not necessarily critical role in setting the stage for the growth of the Canadian newsprint industry. Economist Trevor Dick, on the other hand, has argued that Canada's resource endowments were the major factors promoting growth. By the eve of World War I Canadian reserves of timber for newsprint were more plentiful than American supplies, so that market forces would have brought them into play sooner or later. Furthermore, since every stage of the pulp and paper process required massive inputs of water and electric power, the availability of large hydro sites in Canada and their proximity to the timber lands indicate, according to Dick, that cost considerations rather than government policies determined the location of newsprint manufacturing facilities.[5] It may be worth noting that after World War II the US newspaper industry began drawing more heavily on supplies from the Southern states which had experienced major expansion of hydroelectric facilities in the 1930s and had large, relatively unexploited timber lands.

In addition to the rapid development of vertically integrated firms, the period between 1912 and 1930 was punctuated by spasmodic phases of amalgamation, first in 1912–13, then in the immediate postwar period, and finally in the late twenties. Although in some cases these amalgamations reflected the growth of successful single firms, more frequently these were mergers orchestrated by Toronto and Montreal financiers like I.W. Killam, E.J. Nesbit and Herbert Holt, exploiting optimistic securities markets. As in the case of hydroelectric utilities, these mergers were financed through large bond issues, with the promoters picking up bonus stock; bonded debt in turn left these apparent industrial giants vulnerable to sudden downturns in newsprint prices, as occurred in 1921 and again in 1929–32: bankruptcies, reorganizations and rationalizations then ensued.

The largest of these boom and bust cycles came at the end of the 1920s. After the First World War the provincial governments in both Quebec and Ontario became increasingly generous in their forestry leasing policies in order to entice companies into the hinterland. Buoyed by the recovery of the North American economy from the postwar recession, American, British, and Canadian newprint manufacturers expanded their operations so that by 1926–27 production capacity had increased ten times over its level in 1920. By this time the larger firms began to worry about overcapacity and sought to control a potential price slide by voluntary agreements among sales agencies. When these efforts proved futile, a wave of amalgamations swept the industry, encouraged by security promoters in the bull market atmosphere of the time. Between 1926 and 1930 six gigantic mergers consolidated dozens of mills, controlling more than two-thirds of the industry's productive capacity. Two of the largest—Canada International Paper, a subsidiary of the American firm International Pulp & Paper, and Canadian Power & Paper, controlled by a Montreal syndicate led by Holt—were respectively the third and fifth largest industrial corporations in Canada in 1929.

Almost all of these mastodons carried far too much debt and lurched into bankruptcy when the Great Depression decimated investor confidence and newsprint markets. By 1932 four of the six leading firms were in receivership, including long-established companies like Abitibi Paper and Price Brothers, as well as the parvenu groupings. The only ones that escaped were companies tied to large foreign newspaper chains through long-term contracts, and smaller firms owned directly by newspapers, like Ontario Paper Co., a subsidiary of 'Colonel' Robert McCormick's Chicago *Tribune*.

Until the Great Depression the pattern of control of the largest newsprint firms resembled that of the mining industry: a mixture of foreign-owned (mostly American) and Canadian enterprises. During the 1930s two US firms dominated the devastated industry. But some British and European companies entered Canada in these years: Bowater Corp. acquired large timber reserves in Newfoundland, the Maritimes, and Quebec to supply the London press lords Beaverbrook and Rothermere. Domestic entrants also appeared, usually lumber companies diversifying into pulp and paper as their best sources of construction quality timber diminished: the most notable of these was H.R. MacMillan in British Columbia, who began his career as a government forester. Following World War I, he went into business as a lumber exporter; by 1930 he had acquired several sawmills to guarantee supplies for his British buyers. Subsequently he moved into newsprint, absorbing other B.C. firms, and emerged by the 1960s as one of the largest lumber and paper manufacturers in North America.

Although a great deal more research needs to be done on this industry, particularly on the internal structure of the big firms, certain general patterns prevailed at least up to World War II. The larger Canadian newsprint companies did integrate cutting, pulping and paper-making operations, but for the most part they did not diversify product lines. After the removal of US import duties in 1913, many American paper manufacturers shifted into fine paper and heavy-duty kraft products; American newsprint multinationals also rationalized operations, with their Canadian branches producing newsprint exclusively. In terms of technology, there was not a great deal of innovation in the industry from the late nineteenth century to the 1940s, and pulp and paper-making equipment was largely purchased from a small number of British and American-owned firms. While the newsprint companies represented large agglomerations of capital with integrated operations to achieve economies of scale in production, as single line producers they remained vulnerable to market shifts; the frequent boom and bust cycles in the industry may have worked against the development of managerial capabilities even in well-established firms.[6]

Notes

[1]See Robert Ankli, 'The Growth of the Canadian Economy, 1896–1920', *Explorations in Economic History* 17 (1980), 251–74, for a summary of this debate. See also the articles by E. Chambers and D.F. Gordon, and by G.W. Bertram in Douglas McCalla, ed., *Explorations in Economic History* (Toronto, 1987), 201–42.

[2]On the wheat boom and the grain handling industry, see C.F. Wilson, *A Century of Canadian Grain* (Saskatoon, 1978); Vernon C. Fowke, *The National Policy and the Wheat Economy* (Toronto, 1957) Charles W. Anderson, *Grain: The Entrepreneurs* (Winnipeg, 1991); Epp, 'Cooperation Among Capitalists', 204–43. The history of the co-operatives is discussed in Chapter 16.

[3]On Massey-Harris and the farm implement industry, see Merrill Denison, *Harvest Triumphant: The Story of Massey-Harris* (Toronto, 1948); E.P. Neufeld, *A Global Corporation: A History of the International Development of Massey-Ferguson Ltd.* (Toronto, 1969); Peter Cook, *Massey At the Brink* (Toronto, 1981).

[4]Careless, quoted in H.V. Nelles, *The Politics of Development: Forests, Mines and Hydroelectric Power in Ontario, 1849–1941* (Toronto, 1974), 118–19. For other studies of the Canadian mining industry, see D.M. LeBourdais, *Metals and Men: The Story of Canadian Mining* (Toronto, 1957); Philip Smith, *Harvest of the Rock: A History of Mining in Ontario* (Toronto, 1986); Peter George, 'Ontario's Mining Industry, 1870–1940', in Ian Drummond, ed., *Progress Without Planning: The Economic History of Ontario From Confederation to the Second World War* (Toronto, 1987), 52–76; Iain Wallace, 'The Canadian Shield: The Development of a Resource Frontier', in L.D. McCann, ed., *Heartland and Hinterland: A Geography of Canada* (Scarborough, 1982), 372–409; E.S. Moore, *The American Influence in Canadian Mining* (Toronto, 1941). On specific areas of the industry and companies, see Jeremy Mowat, 'Creating a New Staple: Capital, Technology and Monopoly in British Columbia's Resource Sector, 1901–25', *Journal of the Canadian Historical Association* (1990), 215–35; O.W. Main, *The Canadian Nickel Industry: A Study in Market Control and Public Policy* (Toronto, 1958); Leslie Roberts, *Noranda* (Toronto, 1956); articles by Alexander Dow and Robert Armstrong in Duncan Campbell, ed. *Explorations in Canadian Economic History* (Ottawa, 1985), 189–228; Alexander Dow, 'Finance and For-

eign Control in Canadian Base Metal Mining, 1918–55', *Economic History Review* 62 (1984), 54–67.

[5]Trevor Dick, 'Canadian Newsprint, 1913–1930: National Policies and the North American Economy', *Journal of Economic History* 42 (Sept., 1982), 659–87. Reprinted in McCalla, *Perspectives on Canadian Economic History*, 244–69.

[6]On the lumber and newsprint industry, see A.R.M. Lower, *The North American Assault on the Canadian Forest: A History of the Lumber Trade Between Canada and the United States* (Toronto, 1938); Nelles, *The Politics of Development*; Ian Radforth, *Bushworkers and Bosses: Logging in Northern Ontario, 1900–1980* (Toronto, 1987); G.W. Taylor, *Timber: History of the Forest Industry in B.C.* (Vancouver, 1975); Donald MacKay, *Empire of Wood: The MacMillan-Bloedel Story* (Vancouver, 1982); Patricia Marchak, *Green Gold: The Forest Industry in British Columbia* (Vancouver, 1983); J.A. Guthrie, *The Newsprint Paper Industry* (Cambridge, Mass., 1941); L. Ethan Ellis, *Newsprint: Producers, Publishers, Public Pressures* (New Brunswick, N.J., 1960); Carl Wiegman, *Trees to News: A Chronicle of the Ontario Paper Company's Origin and Development* (Toronto, 1953).

15 NATION BUILDERS

While the technological achievements of the Second Industrial Revolution—electric lighting and power, the automobile, the airplane, the sky-scraper—commanded the greatest public notice, business enterprises were experiencing organizational transformations of equal if not more lasting significance. The new technologies themselves and the expansion of national and international markets linked by steamships, rails and telecommunications contributed to business firms' growth in size and in complexity. The problems of running large or far-flung enterprises in turn stimulated innovations in company organization and administration.

This process of organizational change — the American business historian Alfred Chandler, Jr has called it the 'managerial revolution in business' — was most advanced in the US. There the rapid completion of a national railway system and the growth of immigration in the years immediately following the Civil War established the underpinnings for a large national market. Entrepreneurs such as Gustavus Swift, Andrew Carnegie, and John D. Rockefeller moved quickly to exploit this market, using the new technologies to achieve economies of scale in production and to develop national distribution networks, and new legal devices for corporate organization to integrate raw material extraction, manufacturing, transportation of goods, and marketing. As previously isolated local and regional markets became accessible, other businessmen sought to protect themselves by informal arrangements such as cartels and, later, through amalgamations with competitors. By the early twentieth century, the American business community was characterized by large-scale enterprises, the product of these processes of vertical and horizontal integration, reducing costs by eliminating middlemen.

Although many contemporary observers regarded such large enterprises as business juggernauts exercising monopoly or near-monopoly control over the economy, the people involved in running these firms found it difficult to exercise control over organizations' increasingly complex workings. Traditional methods of cost accounting, supervising workers, monitoring the flow of materials, maintaining product quality, and selling goods in distant markets often proved inadequate; production bottlenecks, disruptions in the workplace, unforeseen shifts in consumer demand and an array of related problems confronted even the most technologically advanced or prudently financed firm. In many cases these large enterprises, created to exploit a costly technology or national market, carried a heavy debt load while shareholders and bondholders clamoured for a quick return on their investment.

In the United States the railroads of the mid-nineteenth century pioneered techniques of managing large-scale enterprises: they were the first to have a body of salaried managers whose local supervisory authority was co-ordinated by a central office (using the telegraph system for that purpose), one that also monitored operations through standardized and regular statistical and financial reports. Building on this base, the large industrial and commercial enterprises of the early 1900s introduced a variety of measures to control costs, expand output, and enhance co-ordination and communication within their organizations. The most publicized of these innovations—the introduction of an assembly-line form of mass production associated with the auto manufacturer Henry Ford and the techniques of 'scientific management' of workers and workplace design developed by Frederick Taylor and his associates— were but two of a wide range of organizational changes characterizing American industry in this era. New methods of advertising and marketing products and services were developed to cater to an increasingly urbanized society. The organizational capabilities developed by US firms generated versatility and flexibility enabling them to move quickly and effectively into foreign direct investment, and to diversify their product lines and markets, achieving what Chandler calls 'economies of scope'.[1]

In other industrializing countries, similar processes of integration and managerial rationalization were taking place. In Germany economic and political unification and technological advances in chemicals and metallurgy contributed to the late nineteen-century growth of large-scale enterprises. In the US the Sherman Antitrust Act of 1890 banned cartels, so that industrial integration was shaped principally by mergers of smaller firms into large joint-stock corporations. In Germany, however, cartels were encouraged by the state so that large-scale industries often were dominated by confederations of nominally separate firms. Nevertheless the need for better instruments of communication and control of production and marketing encouraged close co-ordination among firms. In Japan, vertical and horizontal integration was carried out by family-based trading companies such as Mitsui and Mitsubishi investing in a wide range of interconnected industrial and financial enterprises, and recruiting managers from the samurai class as well as from merchant families.

In Britain, on the other hand, the processes of integration and rationalization were slow to take hold. Family firms and proprietorships from the earlier industrial era, particularly in established fields such as textiles, tended to remain small and independent. Capital requirements for these enterprises were relatively modest and financial services readily available, so that the pressures for cost control were correspondingly less severe than in the US. Market linkages to both local and overseas customers were already in place, reducing the incentive for innovation. Existing labour relations (and, perhaps, cultural attitudes of businessmen) tended to inhibit technological changes. Although British businesses joined in the merger mania of the early 1900s, these larger corporate enterprises clustered in the new industries of the time, such as chemicals or automobiles; even in these companies older traditions of organization persisted: management structures remained rudimentary and systems of internal communication and co-ordination loose and informal.

How does Canada fit into this picture? Did Canada experience a 'managerial revolution' similar to the US or Germany, or did it more closely follow the pattern of the mother-country, Britain? To some extent these questions cannot easily be answered without further study of the development of large-scale enterprises in Canada, particularly on their inner workings: structure of management, communications and accounting procedures, production and marketing practices, etc. Consequently, views on the subject vary considerably, depending on the perspective of the observer and the time-period observed. Canadian labour historian Craig Heron, for example, perceives a 'second industrial revolution' in place by the early 1930s, albeit with some special Canadian features: most of the major financial, manufacturing, and extractive sectors of the economy were dominated by a handful of large integrated firms with headquarters in central Canada. Political economist Glen Williams sees a more diffuse pattern: small and medium-sized manufacturers persisting in a wide range of industries serving the domestic market, their inefficiencies protected by the National Policy tariffs. Bliss tends to be sceptical of the achievements of 'managerial' rationalization in Canadian big business, particularly among firms cobbled together by merger promoters. These views are not necessarily incompatible, but they indicate the difficulties in describing the processes of change in Canadian business in this era.[2]

Certainly big businesses did emerge. In 1930 about 600 firms produced over $2 billion worth of goods, accounting for almost 60 per cent of total manufacturing output by value. One quarter of all employees worked in firms with over 500 people, of which 68 per cent were grouped in eleven industries. Growth occurred both through individual firm expansion and consolidation by merger. Between 1900 and 1930 there were over 500 mergers in Canada, absorbing almost 1200 firms. Mergers clustered in particular industries: consolidations in utilities, iron and steel, and wood products accounted for more than one-quarter of the total number of firms absorbed. Although most mergers involved horizontal integration, about one-fifth of the consolidations in iron and steel, wood products, and food processing produced vertically-integrated enterprises.

The pattern of big business shifted markedly between the early years of the twentieth century and 1930. Table 15.1 ranks the top twenty non-financial corporations by assets in 1909 (on the eve of the first big merger movement) and in 1929. Although the national railway lines remained the largest enterprises in Canada throughout this period (CNR, a crown corporation, was second only to CPR in assets in 1929) what is most notable is the rise of the extractive industries (mining and forestry products) and the relative decline of utilities *vis-à-vis* manufacturing in these years. Virtually all the manufacturing and extractive firms appearing in the 1929 ranking were at least in part vertically integrated. The CPR and the Hudson's Bay Co. had diversified investments in a range of fields.

'Bigness' is of course a relative term. The accumulated assets of the thirty largest non-financial corporations in Canada in 1909, for example, did not equal the asset value of the American giant, United States Steel Corporation. For Chandler, however, size alone is not a sufficient determinant: some degree of vertical

311

Table 15.1 Canada's Twenty Leading Non-Financial Corporations[a] (Ranked by Assets)

1909	1929
1) Canadian Pacific Railway	1) Canadian Pacific Railway
2) Grand Trunk Railway	2) International Power & Paper
3) Canadian Northern Railway	3) Imperial Oil Co.
4) Minnesota, St Paul & Sault Ste Marie Railway	4) Abitibi Paper Co.
5) MacKay Co.	5) Minnesota, St Paul & Sault Ste Marie Railway
6) Lake Superior Corp. (Algoma)	6) Bell Telephone Co. of Canada
7) Atlantic Railway	7) Shawinigan Water & Power
8) Commercial Cable Co.	8) MacKay Co.
9) Dominion Iron & Steel Co.	9) Canada Power & Paper
10) Montreal Light, Heat & Power	10) Dominion Steel & Coal Co.
11) Canada Cement Co.	11) Montreal Light, Heat & Power
12) Dominion Coal Co.	12) International Nickel
13) Amalgamated Asbestos Co.	13) Price Brothers
14) Bell Telephone Co. of Canada	14) Duluth, South Shore & Atlantic Railway
15) Canadian Car & Foundry	15) Twin City Transit Co.
16) Dominion Power & Transmission	16) Duke/Price Co.
17) Montreal Street Railway	17) Imperial Tobacco Co.
18) Ontario Power Co.	18) Massey-Harris Co.
19) Granby Consolidated Mining	19) Hudson's Bay Co.
20) British Columbia Electric Railway	20) Steel Co. of Canada

[a]Excludes proprietary companies (no public shares), crown corporations, and companies with exclusively foreign assets (e.g., Brazilian Traction Co.).

integration, the organizational capabilities to effectively manage such large agglomerations, and the capacity to develop strategies for long-term development rather than simply responding to market changes must also be considered.

In Canada in the period from 1900 to 1930 most companies that were advanced in this direction were linked to export markets. As noted in Chapter Fourteen, vertical integration was undertaken by flour millers, newsprint and mineral processors, and some export-oriented manufacturing firms such as Massey-Harris. Another (and related) feature of these large integrated firms was the significant and increasing role of foreign direct investment. In 1909, eleven of the top 30 non-financial corporations were wholly or partly foreign-owned, and this number increased to 15 by 1929. Foreign direct investment, mostly American, tended to concentrate in the mining, forestry and petroleum industries; but there were British as well as American firms in fields such as automobiles, electrical equipment and chemicals which represented the 'high tech' industries of the day. The Canadian firms in these industries were in effect integrated into larger corporate structures that a later era would designate as 'multinationals'.

Table 15.2 Canada's Thirty Leading Non-Financial Companies (Distribution by Sector)

SECTOR	% OF TOTAL, 1909	% OF TOTAL, 1929
Transportation	17	13
Utilities	40	27
Manufacturing	30	37
Mining & Forestry	10	20

SOURCE: *Canadian Annual Financial Review* (Toronto 1910; 1930).

REVOLUTION IN RETAILING

Even before industrialization took firm hold in Canada, traditional patterns of distribution and sales of goods were changing, and between the 1880s and the 1930s the transformation of wholesale and retail trade proceeded apace. The decline of both the general wholesaler and the small retailer, the growth of chain stores and mail-order catalogues, brand-name packaging, and the advertising industry were all part of this transformation. A number of social and economic developments contributed to this 'revolution in retailing'. The growth of cities enlarged markets, while improvements in city transit systems encouraged established merchants to build bigger stores in the downtown commercial centres. Urban workers, both blue-collar and white-collar, earned year-round cash incomes and had neither the time nor space to produce their food or clothing at home; rising incomes, particularly for the middle class, promoted a wider consumption of 'luxury' products. The railway network helped make possible direct linkages between manufacturers and retailers, and provided urban merchants access to rural communities. Standardization of products and product quality by manufacturers abetted the efforts of enterprising retailers seeking to build national market systems. For such entrepreneurs there were models to observe and improve upon, for large retail department stores and chains were appearing in all of the industrialized countries: when Timothy Eaton was developing his Toronto-based retailing empire in the 1880s and 90s, for example, he could and did study the pioneering efforts of companies like Macy's and Montgomery-Ward in the US and Whiteleys in Britain.

General wholesale merchants still dominated the flow of trade through the country; indeed they were the first to exploit the new opportunities for a national market presented by railway expansion. Wholesalers in Montreal and Toronto, using their financial resources for discount bulk purchases directly from manufacturers, deployed cohorts of drummers across the prairies and into the Maritimes to sell a wide range of dry goods and other manufactured products to local wholesale or retail merchants. While the Maritimes had large general wholesalers who drew on transatlantic suppliers, for the most part wholesale merchants and retailers outside central Canada ran relatively small establishments serving local markets, purchasing goods on credit from the general wholesalers and extending credit on fairly long terms to their customers. Credit sales were particularly entrenched in rural communities due to the seasonal nature of farming and fishing. In larger towns there was a certain degree of specialization among retailers while in rural Canada general stores carrying a wide range but limited stock of goods predominated.

By the 1880s, however, a larger and distinctively different kind of retail establishment was emerging in the bigger towns and cities of central Canada. Eaton was only one of a number of entrepreneurial retailers of his time, although in certain respects he had a broader vision of the potential market than did his rivals. Timothy Eaton had worked with his brothers in wholesaling ventures in small-town Ontario in the 1850s and 60s before moving to Toronto to set up a dry goods store in 1869. His experience as a wholesaler made Eaton leery of credit sales and the widely advertised policy of his new store was 'cash only' and a fixed price for all goods. With a steady flow of cash, Eaton could avoid debt (the company did not have to resort to large-scale borrowing until the 1920s when it expanded branch operations outside Ontario) and the volume of business enabled him to hold frequent 'bargain days'. Unlike his competitors who tended to focus on the upscale, middle-class market, Eaton targeted his sales toward lower-income buyers while stressing quality: like Sears in the US, Eaton guaranteed refunds for goods that were unsatisfactory, and worked hard to ensure that there would be few unsatisfied customers.

To that end, by the 1890s Eaton developed direct links with manufacturers, reducing costs over the long term by cutting out the wholesalers. By the end of that decade Eaton had buyers in London, Paris, New York, and even Japan. During this same time he also began to manufacture some goods in-house, particularly clothing, and eventually a wide range of products including horse harnesses, furniture, and camping equipment.

Eaton also took steps to establish internal controls over his increasingly complex business. During the 1880s the store began grouping related products for display into 'departments' which not only helped shoppers locate goods but also streamlined the management of records of procurement, inventory, accounts and sales. Eventually there were departments for groceries, drugs, and electric appliances as well as the traditional dry goods and home furnishings. Cash registers, adding machines, electric lighting and a pneumatic tube communications system increased the speed and efficiency of sales processing and accounting in the store. Naturally, much attention was devoted to enhancing marketing and sales. Advertisements became less cluttered, more oriented to piquing the reader's interest than simply conveying information. As early as 1884 Eaton began issuing a catalogue of goods for circulation through the Toronto metropolitan region. The mail-order catalogue quickly became a major part of the business, providing Eaton with customers deep in the heart of rural Ontario and eventually across the country. By 1903 Eaton had to set up a separate warehouse for mail orders; seven years later it became a separate division within the firm. Initially mail orders were handled through the postal service, but by 1916 the volume of business was so great the post office could no longer handle it, so Eaton's began establishing mail-order outlets in small towns. The Toronto store also established a full-scale branch in Winnipeg in 1905, although branch stores did not become a major part of Eaton's expansion until the 1920s under Timothy's grandson, Robert Y. Eaton, when new stores were established in Montreal, Hamilton, Halifax, and the major cities of the prairie provinces.

In 1930 with assets over $110 million (which would make it the twelfth largest non-financial company in the country) and a sales turnover of $172 million, Eaton's was the most successful of Canada's department stores, but it was by no means alone. Robert Simpson's store, virtually next door to Eaton's in downtown Toronto, quickly followed the lead into cash sales, departmentalization, direct purchasing, vertical integration into manufacturing some goods, and mail-order sales. Other large cities also featured large local department stores, usually family enterprises like Eaton's: Woodward's in Vancouver, Ogilvy's and Dupuis Frères in Montreal were among the most successful and enduring examples. But none of these stores were to move beyond their local markets or develop mail-order businesses on the scale of Eaton's and Simpson's.

The rise of the department store eroded the market position of small specialized retailers in the cities, and the growth of mail-order catalogue sales undermined the role of the general stores in small town and rural Canada. By the First World War another set of players was entering the field: the chain stores, ranging from general merchandise companies like the American-owned Woolworth's, which moved into Canada in the early 1900s, to grocery chains (soon to be dubbed 'supermarkets') which appeared in the 1920s: Loblaw's and Dominion Stores in Ontario and Quebec, Safeway in western Canada, and others. General merchandise or 'variety' stores resembled department stores, achieving economies through direct bulk buying from manufacturers, but they tended to locate in smaller cities and towns and to focus on volume sales of low-price goods, as indicated by their nickname, the 'five and tens'. The chains were seen as a particularly insidious threat by local wholesalers and small retailers since they encroached directly on traditional rural and small-town markets: resistance to the chains took political as well as economic forms, particularly in the grocery business, and persisted well into the 1930s.

While large retailers like Eaton were integrating back into manufacturing, the process also worked the other way, particularly in food processing. In the 1920s flour mills such as Ogilvie and Lake of the Woods began establishing bakeries to market their own brands in Canada. Long before this time large meat packers had moved into retailing. Among the most innovative of these entrepreneurs was William Davies, one of a number of pork slaughterers in Toronto in the 1880s when the city gained its reputation as 'hogtown', drawing supplies from the large agricultural hinterland of southern Ontario and packing salt-cured bacon for export, principally to Britain. Davies and his partner Joseph Flavelle expanded operations in the 1890s, introduced 'assembly line' techniques pioneered by American packers like Swift, and began retailing fresh and preserved meat through their own stores in Ontario and Quebec in the early 1900s. Flavelle became one of the wealthiest men in Canada, an influential figure in the Tory

315

THE HUDSON'S BAY COMPANY IN TRANSITION

Curiously, the company that was to emerge in the 1980s as the leading retailer in the country, controlling two of the largest department store networks as well as a fleet of smaller retail chains, was a relative latecomer in the field. Thanks to its vast real estate and resource holdings, the Hudson's Bay Co. continued to play an important role in northern and western development and to provide healthy dividends to its shareholders after 1870. But for more than a generation senior management was sharply divided over the best strategy for long-term development. In London two factions squabbled over whether to diversify into the general merchandise trade or to focus on land sales and immigration. Both sides agreed that the fur trade was a 'dying industry', but Canadian officers of the company argued that the fur trade could be resuscitated and sustained through the introduction of new management techniques, improved technology and the development of 'fur ranching' to supplement trapping.

As it turned out the fur trade was not on the verge of disappearance, although market demand had shifted from the traditional beaver and muskrat fur to fox, lynx, and mink. The advent of the bush plane and wireless radio after World War I opened the Canadian north to new competitors in the trade, particularly from the US. The divided Bay Co. leadership was slow to respond and gradually lost ground from the 1920s on. Meanwhile, however, the company had developed a network of general stores in the north and gathered a windfall supplying gold seekers bound for the Klondike at the turn of the century. In 1887 the Bay had opened its first urban outlet in Vancouver, but moved fairly slowly into this market. By 1914 there were stores in other cities of B.C. and Alberta and the company recruited a manager from the British department store, Harrod's, to run this unfamiliar operation. In the 1920s, the Bay opened a large store in Winnipeg but the timing was poor: Eaton's was already there and the wheat boom was collapsing. The Bay suffered serious losses in its foray into retailing and kept a low profile for a time thereafter, remaining principally in the north and west until the 1960s. But as a large firm with diverse investments, the Bay survived its setbacks in both the fur trade and

government of Sir Robert Borden and chief executive of Simpson's stores in the 1920s. The Davies firm merged with other slaughterers in 1927 as Canada Packers.[3]

MANUFACTURING PATTERNS

The wheat boom, the railway-building mania, and the dramatic expansion of mining and forestry have obscured the parallel growth of manufacturing, so that some popular histories have implied that Canada did not become an industrial nation until World War II. In fact, the development of both primary and secondary manufacturing was substantial and less susceptible to the rapid boom and bust

Delivery teams and vans at the HBC Winnipeg store, 1914

retailing, profiting from land sales and forming a partnership with E.W. Marland of Oklahoma, founder of Continental Oil, to develop its mineral properties through a joint venture, Hudson's Bay Oil and Gas in 1929.

Sources

Newman, Peter C., *Merchant Princes* (Toronto, 1991), part II.

Ray, Arthur J., *The Canadian Fur Trade in the Industrial Age* (Toronto, 1990).

cycles that characterized the extractive sectors. Even during the 1880s, long regarded as a period of stagnation for the Canadian economy, the level of capital investment in manufacturing doubled. The depression of the mid-1890s slowed growth in some areas, particularly in construction-related and consumer goods; but between 1896 and the eve of World War I expansion was general and more or less continuous, reflecting the buoyant economy. Manufacturing output by value almost quadrupled between 1891 and 1915, and the number of factories tripled from the turn of the century to World War I.

Ontario had perhaps the most diversified manufacturing base. In the 1880s the province's main industries were involved in processing agricultural products and

By 1890 women's millinery and dressmaking enterprises had increasingly to compete with general tailoring establishments and, especially, with department stores and their standardized production. *(Ontario Archives/F229-1-0/ File 22, top; Metropolitan Toronto Library/T13569, bottom)*

lumber. By 1910 foundries, machine shops, iron and steel fabricating mills, and clothing manufacturers accounted for almost one quarter of Ontario's industrial output by value, although meat packers, flour mills, dairies and bakeries continued, along with logging and mining, to be central to the economy. In Quebec food and beverage processing remained the dominant areas of manufacturing from the 1880s through World War I: Ogilvie and other large flour millers moved their centres of operations westward following the railways, but sugar refineries took the place of flour mills in Montreal in the 1880s. Cotton textiles became the most important of the new industries to emerge in Quebec in this era: by 1900 the textile and cloth manufacturing fields comprised the second largest industrial group in the province.

The Maritimes also experienced rapid industrial development between 1880 and 1900, especially in the cotton textile industry as mills proliferated in the towns of New Brunswick and Nova Scotia. Two industries—sugar refining, and coal, iron and steel — were seen as particularly promising. Maritime access to the Caribbean encouraged the growth of sugar refining and by the mid-1880s the region had 60 per cent of the capacity in this field. The coal mines of Nova Scotia and the proximity of iron ore from Newfoundland enticed foreign as well as local investment in the iron and steel industry.

For contemporary observers and many historians, a key factor in industrialization was the National Policy, combining protective tariffs for domestic manufactured goods and the development of a national market through the construction of railway systems. Economic historians are less certain of the direct connections between industrial growth and the National Policy, particularly before 1900; and, as will become apparent, there were some significant gaps in the protectionist bastions. Canadian manufacturers catering to the domestic market, however, entertained few doubts on the subject. Whenever the National Policy faced a challenge—in 1891 from advocates of 'unrestricted reciprocity' with the US, and in 1911 when Laurier negotiated a reciprocal trade agreement which encompassed natural products but seemed to open the door for reductions in rates on manufactured goods — the Canadian Manufacturers' Association could be counted upon to sound the tocsin and bankroll the party of protectionism.

Opponents of the National Policy, particularly among western farmers, assailed protectionism as an instrument of monopolistic big business, much as American Populists condemned the protective tariff in that country as the 'mother of trusts'. In the Canadian context, however, the relationship between the National Policy and the rise of big business is more complex. In the immediate aftermath of the introduction of the National Policy in the 1880s and 1890s small competitive firms proliferated in many of the 'protected' industries, and in at least some of these industries small-scale, localized production and marketing persisted well into the twentieth century. Even in those fields where large national enterprises emerged, the patterns of integration and managerial organization were uneven and incomplete. The evolution of two industries whose fortunes were linked closely with the protective tariff system—cotton textiles and steel—indicate the difficulties of generalizing about this relationship.

319

Textiles

In Britain and the US, small-scale enterprises predominated in the cotton textile industry until at least the period after World War I when integrated chemical firms producing synthetic fibres moved into the field. The basic technologies of factory production of both cotton and woollen textiles were well established in those countries by the early 1800s, and as a primarily labour-intensive industry, barriers to entry of new firms were relatively low. The diversity of products, in terms of both quality and range, also worked to the benefit of small manufacturers catering to special market niches. Furthermore, as would-be Canadian textile makers in the late nineteenth century discovered, the latest technology was readily available from equipment manufacturers: in many newly industrializing nations, textile factories made an early appearance, reducing the export markets for established firms in Britain and the United States.

In Canada, however, at least in the cotton textile field, big businesses appeared fairly quickly and established a stranglehold over the market for more than half a century. Prior to the National Policy Canadian textile manufacturing was mainly in woollen fabrics and centred in Ontario. These woollen mills relied generally on water power and were dispersed, serving local markets; their products were of coarse quality. During the 1860s and early 1870s there was a trend toward larger factories to serve an expanding market. The National Policy actually retarded this process, by allowing the smaller producers to hang on in a protected market. The introduction of Imperial Preference under Laurier in 1897, which opened Canada to much-desired British fine woollens, undermined this element of the domestic textile industry.

Cotton textile manufacturing emerged in Quebec and the Maritimes in the 1870s and 1880s. Both regions had readier access than Ontario to overseas supplies of cotton, and merchants in these communities (as in New England in the early 1800s) found textiles to be a logical field for diversification. The National Policy, which raised *ad valorem* rates from 17 per cent to 30 per cent for imported cotton products, persuaded Montreal dry goods wholesalers such as Andrew Gault and David Morrice to integrate back into textile production. In Nova Scotia and New Brunswick a more diverse group of import merchants and shipbuilders chose to move into cotton manufacturing as their traditional sources of wealth from the West Indies trade declined, and the Intercolonial Railway offered prospective markets in central Canada.

As in the woollens field, the National Policy initially produced a spurt of competitive expansion by small cotton cloth manufacturers leading to a crisis of overproduction by the mid-1880s. The Montreal manufacturers urged cartel arrangements to stabilize prices, but two of the largest mills, both in New Brunswick, held out and the scheme collapsed. By the early 1890s the Montrealers had shifted to a strategy of consolidation, abetted by the depression that fell particularly harshly on their financially overextended competitors in the Maritimes. A second round of mergers came in the period between 1897 and 1905 as Canadian manufacturers faced increased competition from British cotton imports under

Imperial Preference. It was not the National Policy, then, but rather its attenuation that stimulated the growth of large horizontal combinations in the Canadian cotton textile industry.

The big textile firms displayed some other curious features. Dominion Textile Co., the largest of these entities after its 1905 amalgamation with four other companies operating 12 mills, and possessing $10 million capital, specialized in 'grey and white cottons'. Just behind it came Canadian Colored Cotton Mills which in addition to its own Quebec operations acted as sales agent for several of the larger remaining Maritime companies in that particular line. Third came Montreal Cotton Co. which produced linings and dyed goods. This *de facto* division of markets has been described by one historian as 'complementary monopolies'. In effect it was a cartel in everything but name.[4]

The role of strong personalities and personal contacts among them may have been a major factor in creating this structure. During the 1880s and 90s, Andrew Gault presided, separately, over two of the major firms—Dominion Cotton Co. (the predecessor to Dominion Textiles) and Montreal Cotton Co. — and was linked indirectly, by marriage, to the Morrice family who controlled Canadian Colored Cottons. Gault's death in 1904 precipitated the formation of Dominion Textiles as a corporate entity, orchestrated by Montreal financiers. Several of these figures, including Holt and Louis Forget, were directors of Dominion Textiles, but the dominant figure over the next forty years was Charles B. Gordon. Although Gordon eventually became president of the Bank of Montreal, he was by training a textile manufacturer and retained Gault's connection with Montreal Cotton which was later absorbed into Dominion. The major new entrant in the white goods field was created by another strong-willed figure, Charles Whitehead, who had briefly been Dominion's general manager before departing to set up his own enterprise, Wabasso Cotton Co., in 1907. Whitehead chose to specialize in fine cottons, in competition with British importers rather than with the Canadian 'big three', so the market division arrangement remained more or less intact. Whitehead ran Wabasso until his death in 1953.

Under forceful leaders like Gordon and Whitehead, the large textile firms were centralized and rationalized. Marginal mills were closed down, and production increasingly centred in Quebec. Given the tariff wall and cartel-like structure of the industry, however, few of these firms moved toward full integration into marketing or more elaborate managerial organization. As their founders aged, the companies tended to become tradition-bound, reluctant to develop new markets or introduce new technologies, although Dominion did move gingerly into synthetic fibres. As protectionist measures actually increased in the Great Depression, there were few incentives for change before the abandonment of import duties in the 1950s.

Iron and Steel

The development of iron and later mass-production steel manufacturing was a central feature of industrialization in nineteenth-century Europe and North America. Indeed, although iron and steel were essential for a wide range of producer and consumer goods—machinery, ships, rails and rolling stock, stoves and pots, etc.— for many industrializing countries, developing primary manufacturing capability in this field took on a symbolic quality, demonstrating that the nation was truly modern and progressive. The introduction of new technologies such as the Siemens-Martin open-hearth furnace and the rolling mill in the mid-1800s made it possible to produce steel on a mass-production basis. By the 1890s entrepreneurs such as Andrew Carnegie in the US and Friedrich Krupp in Germany had assembled organizations integrating mining, smelting and metal fabricating with primary steel production that were among the largest corporate enterprises in the world.

Aspiring Carnegies in Canada, however, faced formidable obstacles. One problem was lack of resources: in the late nineteenth century accessible iron ore deposits were modest. Although the large reserves of Labrador were discovered in 1895, transportation costs from this remote region were prohibitive until after World War II. Substantial coal supplies existed in British Columbia and Nova Scotia, but were of relatively poor quality for efficient use in iron and steel making because of their high sulphur content. Finally, and most critically, the domestic market for primary iron and steel, at least up to the early 1900s, was too small to support production on the scale required to justify the substantial capital investment that an integrated steel industry needed. US tariffs barred them from that lucrative market; Canadian secondary iron and steel fabricators could satisfy their supply needs from the growing American industry, and during the debates over the National Policy in 1879 they successfully blocked the imposition of protective tariffs in this field.

Despite these obstacles entrepreneurs in Nova Scotia began to expand iron-making capacity in the early 1880s, supported by government bounties. In 1887, partly in response to Maritime complaints, some primary iron products were brought under the National Policy umbrella. But tariff protection was only gradually extended: steel rails were not included until 1903, and even in the 1920s Canadan steel manufacturers were lobbying with limited success for across-the-board coverage at 20 per cent rates. At that point more than half the structural steel and sheet-metal consumed in Canada was imported.

There were charcoal furnaces and iron foundries in Canada long before the time of the National Policy, but for the most part they operated on a small scale, serving local markets and depended on diminishing ore deposits: the St Maurice forges in Quebec, in existence since 1737, were finally closed in 1883. The first 'modern' iron and steel manufacturer appeared in New Glasgow, N.S. at about that same time. Several local merchants and blacksmiths joined forces to establish the Nova Scotia Steel Co. in 1882. Encouraged by federal bounties and the 1887 tariff revisions, in 1889 they expanded operations to produce a range of primary iron and steel products, established feeder rail lines to the Intercolonial, and by 1894 had acquired control of iron ore deposits at Bell Island in Newfoundland. In 1900 the company continued on this path of vertical integration by purchasing the old General Mining Association coal properties on Cape Breton Island, and reorganizing as Nova Scotia Coal & Steel, capitalized at $7 million. N.S. Coal &

Steel was owned by Maritime merchants and financiers—John Stairs was a director—and focused primarily on the regional market, expanding carefully under an experienced manager, Thomas Cantley. By 1909 the company's assets had doubled and central Canadian investors were eyeing it as a potential merger target.

N.S. Coal & Steel's success lured other players onto the field. In 1899 the Boston traction magnate, Henry Whitney, who had established the Dominion Coal Co. in Cape Breton six years earlier, set up Dominion Iron & Steel Co. (Disco) which, like N.S. Coal & Steel, would procure iron ore from Newfoundland and integrate its operations with Dominion Coal to sell primary steel products to central Canada and, perhaps, the European market as well. After several early blunders—presaging the future experiences of this unhappy enterprise—Whitney sold out his interests in Dominion Steel to a group of Montreal financiers, led by James Ross and including Strathcona and Van Horne. Meanwhile, in Ontario several new enterprises were being established. In 1895 a group of merchants and secondary iron manufacturers in Hamilton set up the Hamilton Steel & Iron Co. which merged with Ontario Rolling Mills four years later. Although this company, unlike the two Maritime firms, had no control over coal and ore supplies, which were imported from the US, from the outset it linked primary production with fabrication and was oriented toward developing a diversified line of products.

The most dramatic—or melodramatic—episode in the early history of the Canadian steel industry took place at Sault Ste Marie in Ontario. Here a young American entrepreneur, Francis Clergue, had appeared in 1893, offering to take over the city's debt-ridden electric power plant and link it to a nearby pulp and paper mill. Over the next several years, Clergue's enterprises in the area proliferated: in 1897 he acquired a mine that seemed to possess promising iron ore deposits, built a short rail line between the mine and Sault Ste Marie, and, in 1901, established Algoma Steel Co. But Clergue's ambitions did not stop at this point: like Sam Ritchie in Sudbury a decade earlier, Clergue envisioned creating an integrated and diversified industrial empire, embracing chemical and nickel production as well as newsprint and steel. A talented promoter, Clergue persuaded American investors to contribute to the $15 million venture, unveiled in 1902 and christened the Consolidated Lake Superior Corporation.

Clergue's vision exceeded his managerial abilities. The ore from the Helen Mine proved to be of poor quality, coal and pig iron had to be brought in from distant sources, the Algoma mill had a Bessemer converter rather than the more efficient open hearth technology, and transportation costs to the southern Ontario market were higher than projected. Within two years the Lake Superior Corp. teetered on the brink of bankruptcy, and Clergue's backers removed him from the scene. Before his departure, however, Clergue had spearheaded a successful lobbying campaign to bring steel rails—Algoma's major product—under tariff protection, and the company's fortunes were revived by the railway boom of the Laurier era.

The pre-World War I boom and the war itself stimulated moves toward consolidation in the Canadian steel industry between 1910 and 1920. In 1910 Max

Algoma Steel in a 1928 aerial view. *(National Archives of Canada/PA15588)*

Aitken orchestrated the formation of the Steel Co. of Canada (Stelco), combining Hamilton Steel & Iron with four secondary steel fabricators in Ontario and Quebec, capitalized at $25 million. Much of the capital was raised by Aitken from British investors, and the board included the usual prominent Montreal and Toronto financial figures such as Holt and Edmund Osler of the Dominion Bank. But the firm was managed by experienced steel makers: initially by Charles Wilcox and Robert Hobson from the Hamilton enterprise and later by Ross McMaster, whose father had run Montreal Rolling Mills before the merger.

Aitken had organized Stelco only after failing to consolidate the Nova Scotia iron and steel industry. In 1909 he had been able to recombine Dominion Coal and Dominion Steel (which had been separate since Whitney's departure), but N.S. Coal & Steel rebuffed his overtures. By 1917, however, the New Glasgow-Halifax group had been replaced by New York-based investors. Over the next few years a byzantine struggle for control of the Nova Scotia industry involving American, British and central Canadian financial interests, culminated in the creation of the British Empire Steel Corporation (Besco) in 1921 combining Dominion Coal, Dominion Steel, N.S. Coal & Steel, Halifax Shipyards and assorted other steel-consuming enterprises.

The chief figure in the merger, Roy Wolvin, a Montreal shipbuilder and financier, seems to have believed, mistakenly, that the Canadian government intended to underwrite a large expansion of the country's merchant marine fleet

324

after the war. Like many mining and newsprint agglomerations that sprang up at this time, Besco, capitalized at $500 million, carried a fair amount of 'watered' stock (new shares issued without corresponding assets). More critically, Besco was launched at a time when international steel markets were weak. This situation hurt all Canadian producers, but Besco was particularly vulnerable because of its relatively high production costs and peripheral position in the central Canadian market.

By the 1920s these three companies—Algoma, Stelco and Besco—controlled most of the country's domestic primary iron and steel output and a large proportion of secondary manufacturing as well, although there were some strong competitors in this part of the market, notably Dominion Foundries & Steel. Dofasco was established in Hamilton in 1913 by the Shermans, a Cleveland family who managed it carefully, introducing state-of-the-art facilities and diversifying product lines regularly. In the 1960s, Dofasco moved back into the primary steel industry, the first Canadian firm to use the basic oxygen process that replaced the open hearth technology. The 'big three' did not monopolize the primary market either, since more than half the country's supplies came from abroad; even after World War II over one-third of Canada's primary iron and steel was imported.

But the uneven tariff protection was only one factor affecting the Canadian steel industry. None of the 'big three' was a fully-integrated operation. Two of these firms experienced so many problems, ranging from inadequate resources to bad management, that they survived only through periodic injections of government largesse in the form of contracts or direct subsidies. Although Algoma performed reasonably well through World War I (thanks to rail and munitions contracts), much of its earnings were absorbed by debt payments on the original Lake Superior venture, and new capital raised in the war had to go toward replacing the Bessemer converter. Algoma's absentee owners were reluctant to seek new financing, fearing loss of control of the enterprise (and their dividends), so the company failed to diversify, remaining primarily a producer of steel rails.

When this market collapsed in the 1930s, Algoma careened back into bankruptcy. At that point it fell into the hands of James Dunn, a financier who, like his fellow New Brunswicker Max Aitken, had made his millions as a promoter of Canadian utility companies and similar ventures on the London money market. Returning to Canada in the Depression, Dunn salvaged Algoma by ruthlessly writing down its bonded debt, reorganizing its management, and using political connections to procure rail contracts that would carry it until full-scale diversification could be carried out. Although Dunn ultimately saved Algoma and made his mark as an industrialist, the company — facing high transport costs and dependent on external supplies of its raw materials—continued to rely largely on government assistance through World War II.

Meanwhile, Besco staggered through the 1920s from one crisis to another. By 1921 Wolvin's expectations of a postwar shipbuilding boom had glimmered away, and hopes for a transatlantic market never got off the ground as European steel producers, operating at excess capacity, cartelized to block North American competition. Increases in east-west rail freight rates reduced Besco's competitive position in the home market as well. To meet his debt obligations, Wolvin sought to reduce operating costs by imposing severe wage cuts in Besco's steel mills and coal mines, a move precipitating some of the bitterest labour conflicts of the era, and leaving a legacy of hostility and distrust that poisoned worker-management relations through to the present. Wolvin's harsh measures failed and in 1926 Besco collapsed into receivership. Reorganized in 1928 as Dominion Steel and Coal Co. (Dosco), the company was now under the control of Herbert Holt and the Royal Bank. Although nursed back to moderate health by the end of the decade, Dosco remained, like Algoma, primarily a producer of steel rails, even more distant from central Canadian markets and dependent on government contracts to survive.

Stelco, by contrast, weathered the postwar recession and performed well through the 1920s, doubling its sales volume and more than quadrupling net profits between 1921 and 1930. In part Stelco's success could be attributed to its strategic location in central Canada's industrial heartland, but there were other factors, not least among them good management. During World War I the company applied its retained earnings to updating its equipment and acquired iron and coal mines in the US to ensure its supply needs. Oriented from the outset toward secondary manufacturing, Stelco under McMaster in the 1920s continued its strategy of diversification in such products as sheet steel, machine parts and steel rods which were in demand by the growing Canadian auto industry. With a substantial amount of its output accounted for by fabricated materials, Stelco also benefited from the existing tariff structure and declined to join its rivals in lobbying for new duties except on products where it faced threats from U.S. Steel. Although Stelco suffered in the Depression, its diversity and careful use of its financial resources in the 1920s left the company the strongest in the industry.[5]

A FOREIGN PRESENCE

While the role of the National Policy in creating large integrated industrial entities is not entirely clear-cut, there does seem to be a strong relationship between the tariff system and the growth of foreign direct investment, particularly from the US, in Canada. Between 1879 and 1887, 37 American 'branch plants' sprang up in Canada, and this number increased to 66 by 1900. Provincial measures such as Ontario's pulpwood processing requirement brought more direct investment across the border in the first decade of the new century, and the defeat of Reciprocity in 1911 stimulated a new round of American entrants. As indicated in Table 15.3, by 1914 US direct investment in Canada exceeded $600 million, making that country the largest recipient of American capital, over one-third of that in manufacturing enterprises. During World War I the pace of US direct investment in Canada slowed, but between 1919 and 1929 the capital flow doubled, about half going into manufacturing. In 1929 the US Commerce Department estimated that there were over 1,000 firms in Canada that were wholly or partially owned by Americans. Between 1890 and 1913 direct investment flowed in from Britain as well, particularly in the utilities field, but the British generally preferred portfolio investment which entailed earnings without the responsibilities of man-

Table 15.3 Direct US Investment in Canada (in $ millions US)

	1914	1919	1929
Total	618	814	1657
Manufacturing	221	400	820
Mining/Oil	184	230	373
Utilities[a]	77	91	318
Sales	27	30	38
Misc.	109	63	108

[a] Includes railways

SOURCE: M. Wilkins, *The Maturing of Multinational Enterprise* (Cambridge, Mass., 1971), 31, 189.

aging enterprises. Americans usually wanted to exercise some control over the companies that they established in Canada, and after World War I American capital inflows grew steadily, surpassing British direct and indirect investment levels by 1926.

Michael Bliss and others have argued, persuasively, that this influx of American direct investment was not an accidental by-product of the National Policy. The architects of the protective trade system recognized that Canada desperately needed foreign capital and erected the tariff wall deliberately to entice American manufacturers to leap across and set up branch plants that would 'keep jobs at home'. Similarly, the Patent Act of 1872, which contained a 'working clause' requiring patentees to establish manufacturing plants in Canada within two years, was intended to bring foreign technology into the country. The central objective was economic growth and the questions of where the capital came from or who owned the factories operating in Canada were hardly raised. Certainly up through World War I the US, the world's largest debtor nation in 1913, had based its own dramatic industrial expansion on a steady inflow of foreign direct as well as portfolio investment.[6]

But the National Policy was only one factor in the process. As noted in Chapter Fourteen, from the 1890s on, Canada's mineral and forestry resources attracted investors from abroad. In the service sector, US and other foreign firms found it desirable to form affiliations with Canadian businesses that had well-established contacts in their local communities. Even in manufacturing, Canadian trade measures were only one consideration for foreign enterprises establishing branch plants. In the US many of the large integrated industrial firms that emerged in the early 1900s adopted a decentralized multidivisional structure in their domestic operations that was logically extended into a branch plant system when they moved into foreign markets. An examination of the expansion of American companies in Canada in two important (and related) industries — automobiles and petroleum — indicates the complex nature of the process of direct investment in this era.

Few businesses have been as well and fully chronicled (except in Canada) as those in the automotive industry. While the basic technology and earliest manufacturing in the field developed in France and Germany in the 1880s and 90s, American entrepreneurs, notably Henry Ford and William Durant, transformed the automobile into a major commercial product, combining assembly-line production and mass marketing techniques on an unprecedented scale between 1910 and 1920. During the following decade US auto makers expanded sales and operations overseas and those that survived the Great Depression consolidated the American position of domination in the industry until the 1970s. Much as the railway had exemplified industrial progress in the nineteenth century, the automobile became the symbol of the Second Industrial Revolution, and of America's preeminent economic role in the twentieth century.

Not surprisingly, given these circumstances, the Canadian automobile industry was rapidly submerged. Of the 40-odd auto manufacturers established in Canada between 1898 and 1933, only a handful were 'Canadian' in the sense of being both locally owned and using Canadian technology and few of these survived for long. More than half of the total were under foreign ownership from the outset and by 1933, 70 per cent were branch plants of American firms.

Various explanations have been presented to account for the weakness of the indigenous auto industry. Shortsighted bankers have come in for the usual round of abuse for ignoring budding Canadian Henry Fords; the underdeveloped state of paved roads, particularly in rural areas—due in part to the opposition of farmers to the taxes required to pave them—was an impediment to the growth of an already small market. Most Canadian auto manufacturers were drawn from the carriage and wagon industry. In the US auto makers more frequently began their careers building bicycles which familiarized them with the precision designing required for motor vehicles. In Canada the bicycle industry had fallen into the hands of a monopoly, Canada Cycle & Motor Co., at an early stage, blocking the dissemination of such skills. This particular situation reflected a broader problem: the absence of mechanical engineers and skilled machinists generally in Canada. According to legend, R.S. McLaughlin had to turn to an American manufacturer, Durant, when the engineer he hired became too ill to work and there were no other trained designers for him to fall back on.

One factor that contributed to the early arrival of Americans on the Canadian auto scene was proximity. Most American auto makers were concentrated in the Middle West, particularly around Detroit. Aspiring auto entrepreneurs on the other side of the border tended to congregate in southern Ontario; only a few auto manufacturers surfaced in Quebec and the Maritimes, and none lasted. While the tariff might lure Americans northward, they did not have far to go, and in many cases the initiative came from the Canadian side.

In 1904, Gordon McGregor, a carriage-maker near Windsor, Ont., crossed the Detroit River to call on Henry Ford. Ford, who had yet to win fame and fortune with his Model T, accepted McGregor's proposal to set up a company (in which Ford held 50 per cent interest) to manufacture Ford's autos in Canada; and, more significantly, to have exclusive rights to sell Ford products throughout the British

Empire, except in Britain where Ford had another potential partner. The 35 per cent duty of auto imports into Canada—an extension of National Policy tariffs on carriages—may have been a factor, but from Ford's vantage point, access to the 'imperial' market through a Canadian company that was virtually next door to his Detroit factory was a major attraction. Ford Canada held what in current parlance would be a 'mandate' to make and sell Ford cars on four continents.

Three years later another Ontario carriage maker, R.S. McLaughlin, struck a deal with Durant to build and sell Buicks in Canada. When Buick and Durant's other enterprises became part of General Motors Corporation (GM), McLaughlin's Oshawa-based enterprise acquired its Canadian manufacturing and marketing rights; and in 1921, when Britain extended special preferential duty remissions to Canada, GM gave McLaughlin the 'mandate' to the British Imperial market. By the early 1920s between one-third and one-half of Canada's auto production was exported, principally to other parts of the Empire. By this time many of the Canadian auto makers, including those that had made licensing agreements with American manufacturers, had disappeared: GM and Ford accounted for 60 per cent of the country's output.

The Canadian auto industry has been called 'a creature of the tariff';[7] but it would perhaps be more precise to say that it was a creature of the various preferential trade arrangements made between Britain and Canada between 1900 and 1920. The Canadian protective tariff structure did, however, have a major impact on the production arrangements made by American firms and their Canadian affiliates. Since import duties on auto parts and materials were considerably lower than the duty on the final product, the Canadian plants specialized in assembly operations. Also, despite the export orientation of the Canadian firms, their production runs were much smaller than those of their parent companies. Despite their inability to achieve economies of scale, the Canadian companies were cushioned by the 35 per cent tariff rate. By the mid-1920s, however, consumer discontent over the price differentials between American- and Canadian-made autos led the Liberal government of Mackenzie King to roll back the tariff to 20 per cent. At the same time the government introduced a 50 per cent 'Canadian content' provision on auto parts and materials, in effect playing off the big assembly firms against the suppliers. Although tariffs on assembled vehicles were raised again in the Depression, this proved to be a temporary measure. But the Canadian-content requirement remained.

Despite their fulminations over changes in Canadian duties, the big American auto makers did not dismantle their Canadian operations, in part because up to World War II these factories served markets that maintained barriers against direct US imports. There was, however, no particular incentive for them to significantly improve the production capabilities of their Canadian affiliates which remained miniature and relatively inefficient replicas of the American plants. The Canadian-content requirements encouraged the growth of domestic auto parts manufacturers, mostly in Ontario; but the combined forces of these regulations and the Depression drove most of the remaining smaller auto producers out of business in Canada in the 1930s, so that the parts industry was tied to a handful of US-

329

owned giants. By this time McGregor, McLaughlin and other Canadian partner-investors had passed from the scene, and the Canadian auto-making companies were effectively wholly owned subsidiaries of the Americans.[8]

Canadian trade policies also contributed to the entry of foreign firms in the petroleum industry; but here again other factors helped ensure that they would acquire a commanding position in the field, at least up through the 1960s. In the case of the largest of these companies, Imperial Oil, the corporate structure that emerged was probably influenced more by US antitrust laws than by anything that happened in Canada.

In the nineteenth century petroleum was used primarily as a base for fuel for illuminating homes and streets: kerosene, the refined product used for this purpose, was developed by a Nova Scotian, Abraham Gesner, in the 1840s. With the advent of electric lighting toward the end of the century that market died. Providentially, the development of the internal combustion engine, which by 1914 had become the major power source for automobiles, not only salvaged the fortunes of the petroleum industry but ensured that it would become one of the largest and most lucrative fields of enterprise in Canada and in the world.

As in the case of iron ore, Canada's large deposits of oil and natural gas in the west and off the east coast were either unknown or inaccessible in the nineteenth century. Some deposits of crude oil were, however, being worked in south-central Ontario from the 1860s, at the same time that the larger fields of western Pennsylvania were being opened. A number of small oil drilling companies surfaced at Oil Springs and Petrolia, and nearby London, Ontario, became the local centre for refining. As in the US, competition in the industry in the early days was fierce, and several efforts by refiners to establish cartels to control production and prices in the 1870s proved short-lived. In 1880, Joseph Englehart, an emigrant from Cleveland, Ohio, the refining capital of the US industry, joined with several London merchants to set up Imperial Oil, which took over much of the refining capacity in the region. One holdout, however, was McColl and Anderson, a partnership which continued to operate as one of the few Canadian-owned independent oil companies for more than seventy years. Imperial controlled only about one-third of the production of Ontario's oil and gas output through the late 1880s, but it established a distribution network in the prairies and moved into the more profitable Toronto and Montreal markets in 1888–90.

Meanwhile, in the US the industry was being consolidated by John D. Rockefeller. After acquiring control over the major refineries in Cleveland, Rockefeller created a huge vertically-integrated enterprise, Standard Oil, absorbing or eliminating most of his competitors. By 1890, Standard Oil controlled over 90 per cent of the US market and had begun moving into foreign markets, including Canada.

In 1885 the Canadian government imposed import duties on both crude oil and refined kerosene. The tariff on crude oil at 6 cents per gallon was not at a 'protected' level—and in fact Canadian refiners were soon to need crude imports to supplement the limited output from the Petrolia fields—but it was supplemented by 'inspection fees' charged on imports and a 50 gallon quota on 'bulk' imports of crude and refined oil. Between 1889 and 1896 Standard Oil set up three separate subsidiaries in Canada: in part these were intended to circumvent the tariff restrictions, but they also represented part of the American company's strategy of forward integration, establishing direct distributing outlets to the Maritimes, Quebec, and Ontario.

In 1893 the restriction on bulk imports was lifted, and four years later the Laurier government introduced moderate reductions of the duties on refined products. In 1898 Imperial Oil's Canadian owners sold their company to Rockefeller and in the following year the other Standard subsidiaries were merged with it. The new American-owned Imperial controlled virtually the entire Canadian market. While prospective changes in Canadian trade laws may have provided the occasion for the Standard takeover, this was not the only factor involved. Throughout the 1890s Imperial had faced serious difficulties raising capital to expand operations in order to compete with the Standard subsidiaries. The quality of crude oil from the Petrolia fields was poor and Imperial did not have the technology to overcome the problem. By the mid-1890s Petrolia output had peaked and Imperial was increasingly dependent on imported crude, much of it from Standard's American fields. The alternative to the Standard take-over might well have been the elimination of Imperial from the market. Like many of Standard's competitors in the US, Imperial's owners decided to merge instead.

In the years immediately following the Standard take-over, from 1899 to 1910, Imperial Oil existed as a company in name only: its refineries were largely closed down and the few that remained in operation were managed by another Standard subsidiary in Buffalo, New York. Many of the previously quasi-independent sales agencies were eliminated, and the entire marketing and distribution network was run from Standard's headquarters in New York City. In 1904, the Canadian duties on imported crude were removed, and Standard constructed a line to supply the Canadian market from its fields in Cygnet, Ohio. During this period, Standard/Imperial faced little competition for the Canadian market. A handful of small producers continued to operate in Petrolia, and two refining enterprises appeared between 1902–9, both controlled by American 'independents' in Ohio. In 1910, however, Standard still held over 80 per cent of the market and had extended its distribution network across the prairies to the west coast.

In that year the Anglo-Dutch company, Shell—Standard's major rival in international petroleum markets—announced its intention to establish a subsidiary in Canada, to be supplied from fields in the Dutch East Indies. At the same time, Standard Oil faced an even graver threat on its home front. Assailed by reformers since the 1890s as the virtual embodiment of a 'predatory monopoly', Rockefeller's empire became the target of US government antitrust action in 1907. Four years later the US Supreme Court upheld a decree ordering the dissolution of the Standard Oil 'trust'. In the ensuing division of the American corporation, Imperial passed into the hands of the Standard Oil Company of New Jersey. More significantly, Imperial's role was re-evaluated: it was now to be both a Canadian bastion against Shell and a vehicle for some of Jersey Standard's overseas investments that would be more secure from the potential scrutiny of US antitrust officials.

331

Accordingly, Jersey Standard dispatched their most vigorous executive, Walter Teagle, to take charge of reorganizing Imperial.

In the words of John Ewing, Imperial's historian, 'Teagle . . . took Imperial from the vassalage in which it had been since 1898 and gave it at least the status of a free man.'[9] Control of sales and distribution was shifted to Toronto and the network continued to expand, particularly in the west, to meet the challenge from Shell. The original Imperial refinery at Sarnia, Ontario increased production with a steady supply of crude via the Ohio pipeline, and five new refineries were established between 1914 and 1923. The company's capital base was significantly enlarged from $15 million to $50 million in 1917. A subsidiary, International Petroleum, was set up to develop oil fields in South America, and in 1918–19 another subsidiary commenced exploratory work in Alberta and the Northwest Territories. This last undertaking was prompted by the news that Shell was negotiating with the Canadian government for access to mineral concessions in the west. Shell did not, in fact, carry out any substantial exploration before 1939; but Imperial, as noted in Chapter Thirteen, acquired a concession from the CPR and began drilling for oil in Alberta in the 1920s. Altogether, Imperial spent over $18 million in exploration and drilling before striking a gusher at Leduc, Alberta in 1947.

Although Imperial had been resurrected as a vertically-integrated concern, it was very much a part of Jersey Standard's global system, as Teagle made apparent when he took charge of the parent company in 1918. Imperial's South American fields shipped oil principally to the American west coast and Caribbean markets, and its own supplies came largely from Jersey Standard's own fields up to the 1950s. More than 90 per cent of the company's net income between 1921 and 1939 was distributed to shareholders, with Jersey Standard as the main beneficiary. Aside from Shell, Imperial's main competitor in this period was McColl-Frontenac which focused on the central Canadian market; in 1938, it was taken over by the American giant, Texaco, so that by World War II Canada's three major integrated oil companies were all foreign-owned entities. There were a few smaller drilling companies operating in Alberta, and in the Maritimes K.C. Irving began to build a regional distribution system in the 1930s, benefiting from public discontent over Imperial's near-monopoly position there—although Irving also bought much of his crude from the US company. Ironically, the emergence of a vigorous indigenous group of entrepreneurs in the industry did not come until the 1950s, stimulated in large measure by Imperial's ultimate success in its long and expensive search for oil in the Canadian west.

Notes

[1]See Alfred D. Chandler, Jr, *The Visible Hand: The Managerial Revolution in American Business* (Cambridge, Mass., 1977), and *Scale and Scope: The Dynamics of Industrial Capitalism* (Cambridge, Mass., 1990). On British business organization, see Leslie Hannah, *The Rise of the Corporate Economy: The British Experience* (Baltimore, 1976). Also

see A.D. Chandler, Jr and Herman Daems, ed., *Managerial Hierarchies: Comparative Perspectives on the Rise of the Modern Industrial Enterprise* (Cambridge, Mass., 1980).

[2]Craig Heron, 'The Second Industrial Revolution in Canada, 1880–1930', in D.R. Hopkins and G.S. Kealey, eds, *Class, Community and the Labour Movement: Wales and Canada, 1850–1930* (Wales, 1989), 48–66; Glen Williams, 'The National Policy Tariffs: Industrial Underdevelopment Through Import Substitution', *Canadian Journal of Political Science* 12 (1979), 333–68; Bliss, *Northern Development*, 359–61. See also Ben Forster, 'Finding the Right Size: Markets and Competition in Mid- and Late-Nineteenth Century Ontario', in Roger Hall *et al.*, eds, *Patterns of the Past: Interpreting Ontario's History* (Toronto, 1988), 150–73.

[3]On the 'revolution in retailing' see Ian Drummond, *Progress Without Planning*, 274–93; Joy Santinck, *Timothy Eaton and the Rise of His Department Store* (Toronto, 1990); Peter C. Newman, *Merchant Princes* (Toronto, 1991). On the Davies company and meat packing, see Bliss, *A Canadian Millionaire: The Life and Business Times of Sir Joseph Flavelle* (Toronto, 1978).

[4]Epp, 'Cooperation Among Capitalists', 372. See also Barbara Austin, 'Life Cycles and Strategy of a Canadian Company: Dominion Textiles, 1873–1983' (PhD diss., Concordia University, 1985); *Report of the Royal Commission on the Textile Industry* (Ottawa 1938). On the woollen textile industry, see Forster, 'Finding the Right Size', 154–8.

[5]On the Canadian iron and steel industry, see W.J.A. Donald, *The Canadian Iron and Steel Industry* (Boston, 1915); Kris Inwood, *The Canadian Charcoal Iron Industry* (New York, 1986); Inwood, 'The Iron and Steel Industry', in Drummond, *Progress Without Planning*, 185–207; William Kilbourn, *The Elements Combined: A History of the Steel Co. of Canada* (Toronto, 1960); Duncan McDowall, *Steel At the Sault: Francis Clergue, Sir James Dunn and the Algoma Steel Corporation, 1901–56* (Toronto, 1984); Acheson, 'National Policy'; David Frank, 'The Cape Breton Coal Industry and the Rise and Fall of Besco', *Acadiensis* 7 (Autumn 1977), 3–34; Gordon Boyce, 'The Manufacturing and Marketing of Steel in Canada: Dofasco Inc., 1912–1970', *Business and Economic History* 2nd ser., 18 (1989), 228–37.

[6]Michael Bliss, 'Canadianizing American Business: The Roots of the Branch Plant', in Ian Lumsden, ed., *Close the 49th Parallel, etc.: The Americanization of Canada* (Toronto, 1972), 26–42. See also Stephen Scheinberg, 'Invitation to Empire: Tariffs and American Economic Expansion in Canada', *Business History Review* 47 (1973), 218–38.

[7]Tom Traves, *The State and Enterprise: Canadian Manufacturers and the Federal Government, 1917–31* (Toronto, 1979), 101.

[8]On the auto industry in Canada, see Tom Traves, 'The Development of the Ontario Automobile Industry to 1939', in Drummond, ed., *Progress Wihout Planning*, 208–23; Howard Aikman, *The Automobile Industry of Canada* (Montreal, 1926); Robert Ankli and Fred Frederiksen, 'The Influence of American Manufacturers on the Canadian Automobile Industry', *Business and Economic History*, ser. 2,9 (1981), 101–13; Donald S. Davis, 'Dependent Motorization: Canada and the Automobile to 1930', *Journal of Canadian Studies* 21 (1986), 106–32; Mira Wilkins and Frank E. Hill, *American Business Abroad: Ford on Six Continents* (Detroit, 1964).

⁹John Ewing, 'History of Imperial Oil', 1951, ch. 8: 15; Manuscript at Imperial Oil Archives, Toronto. See also Earle Grey, *The Great Canadian Oil Patch* (Toronto, 1970); David H. Breen, 'Anglo-American Oil Rivalry and the Evolution of Canadian Petroleum Policy to 1930', *Canadian Historical Review* 62 (1981), 283–320; Hugh M. Grant, 'The Petroleum Industry and Canadian Economic Development: An Economic History, 1900–61' (PhD diss., University of Toronto, 1986); B.H. Wall and G.S. Gibb, *Teagle of Jersey Standard* (New Orleans, 1974); Graham D. Taylor, 'From Branch Operation to Integrated Subsidiary: The Reorganisation of Imperial Oil under Walter Teagle, 1911–17', *Business History* 34 (July 1992), 49–68.

16 INTEGRATION AND DISINTEGRATION

The emergence of big business was never a painless process. Thousands of small enterprises succumbed to the rigours of competition, driven from the field or absorbed into larger, stronger firms. 'Rationalization' eradicated the roles of those who had functioned as middlemen in industries undergoing vertical integration, and new managerial structures challenged both the status and living standards of skilled artisans. Not surprisingly, this was an era punctuated by political upheavals, pitting small businesses against the new corporate organizations, and chronic labour unrest where the underlying issue was often not wages and working conditions but control of the workplace. In Canada these dislocations also took on a regional dimension: local industries in the west and the Maritimes confronted the centralizing strategies of Toronto- and Montreal-based corporations. For the small retail merchant in Winnipeg, the independent kerosene jobber in Montreal, the machine parts manufacturer in Amherst, or the iron puddler in Hamilton, the advent of the large integrated corporation threatened disintegration of their livelihoods and sometimes of their entire communities.

Those who were so threatened did not, however, meekly accept their fate; and although the triumph of big business is often seen as the era's prevailing theme in Canada, it was not a total victory. Skilled craft unions resisted the full-scale introduction of 'scientific management' and mechanization in industry with considerable effectiveness at least up through World War I; and in many fields industrialists continued to depend on skilled workers. Small and medium-scale family-owned enterprises persisted in the industrial as well as commercial and service sectors of the economy where consolidation could not produce economies of scale. Small-business owners resorted to trade associations and similar organizations to defend the *status quo*, often through pressure on local and provincial governments. Farmers adopted 'modern' business practices and also joined co-operatives and commodity marketing 'pools' that could compete more effectively with large corporate enterprises: here too governments played a role in responding to the pressures from small producers to constrain big business through regulatory measures imposed on the railways and grain merchants. The extent to which workers, farmers, and small businesses were able to 'countervail' the power of the large corporations through economic and political pressures has been the subject of continuing debate among historians and social scientists in the US and Europe as well as Canada. It seems reasonable to say, however, that the struggles for control of the workplace and the marketplace that accompanied the rise of big business in the early twentieth century helped lay the groundwork for more activist and interventionist roles for government in the fifty-odd years following the coming of the Great Depression.

CONTROLLING THE WORKPLACE

The Second Industrial Revolution transformed traditional relationships between employers and their workers in several critical ways. The sheer growth in size and scale of firms in industries where consolidation and integration took hold made it impossible for owners, even of proprietary or family firms such as Massey-Harris, to maintain effective and regular face-to-face contacts with their employees. Layers of salaried supervisors or 'managers'—a term rarely used in the nineteenth century business world—emerged to handle these and other routine tasks of administration. In corporate organizations, such as the CPR, salaried executives with little or no proprietary interest in the firms they worked for determined strategies and policies, subject at most to the sporadic intervention of major shareholders. By the early 1900s 'management' had become a recognized element in large industrial organizations, and no small part of the tasks of management encompassed establishing and enforcing rules and procedures under which work was conducted in the enterprise.

For larger integrated companies (and smaller ones aspiring to that status), reaping the benefits accruing from economies of scale in production required managers to devote constant attention to achieving 'efficiency' by controlling the costs of production and increasing the productivity of workers. Concepts of cost accounting, which enabled manufacturers to determine and monitor the cost per unit of production, migrated via branch plants and industrial journals from the US into Canada in the early 1900s. Productivity—higher unit output per input of capital, labour, and technology—could be increased by introducing labour-saving machinery, redesigning jobs to reduce 'waste', offering various incentives to workers to increase output, or a combination of these techniques, developed in their most elaborate form by the American engineer, Frederick W. Taylor and his fellow-advocates of 'scientific management'.

The extent to which employers comprehended and embraced these ideas is a matter of some debate. The American labour historian Harry Braverman in *Labor and Monopoly Capital* has argued that scientific management was a central element in a concerted effort by corporations to use technological and administrative methods to reorganize the workplace, reducing the autonomy (and pay rates) of skilled craft workers and replacing them with 'machine tenders' whose working environment was dominated by white-collar managers. Others have maintained that, despite the widespread publicity surrounding 'Taylorism' in the early 1900s, few employers adopted these ideas completely—although many did introduce specific techniques such as the piece-rate system and bonus incentives. Even skilled workers were willing to accept some of these innovations, particularly measures that reduced the arbitrary power of foremen and introduced more formal work rules, although they also bitterly and often successfully contested the imposition of more comprehensive schemes.

In Canada, many businesses embraced cost-accounting procedures and a few experimented with more elaborate scientific management plans. In 1910 the CPR brought in Henry L. Gantt, one of Taylor's disciples, to reorganize production in its locomotive repair shops in Montreal, later extending the system to its other facilities. The Canadian Manufacturers Association encouraged its members to follow suit, publishing articles on scientific management in its journal, *Industrial Age*. It is difficult to determine how deeply the movement took hold or how enduring the changes were among Canadian employers. The experience of Knechtel Furniture Co. of Hanover, Ont., indicates the rather mixed record of scientific management. A family firm established in the 1880s, Knechtel brought in 'efficiency' experts from Chicago in the early 1920s who introduced a quota and bonus pay scheme endorsed by the United Brotherhood of Carpenters which, like many Canadian craft unions, was an offshoot of an American organization. Resentful of what they perceived as a challenge to their competence as craftsmen, the employees engaged in covert opposition and eventually staged a strike in 1923. Knechtel subsequently abandoned the scheme and there were no further experiments with wage incentives until the 1950s. Similar episodes of effective worker resistance to ventures in scientific management occurred throughout this period, even at the larger corporate-owned operations such as the Canadian General Electric plant in Hamilton. To some extent, the limited impact of these techniques, particularly in industries such as furniture-making where proprietary firms were well-entrenched, reflected uneasiness on the part of the owners themselves over derogating their authority in labour relations to 'college boys' with no experience on the shop floor.[1]

Another route through which reorganization of the workplace proceeded, possibly with greater impact than the complicated planning operations of Taylor and his followers, involved introduction of new machines and machine processes, particularly in the branch-plant industries. Ford, for example, transferred his assembly-line system to the Canadian plants shortly after developing it at Highland Park in 1910–13. The American-owned mining and newsprint companies introduced continuous-flow processes into the new mills established in Ontario and Quebec in the 1920s.

The introduction of labour-saving technologies in these 'new' industries did not precipitate confrontations with displaced skilled workers. Mechanization was more troublesome in older established fields, such as iron production. A range of jobs, both skilled and unskilled, was eliminated or downgraded as the larger mills moved to open hearth operations in the early 1900s, in the face of dozens of strikes and slowdowns that sometimes affected the entire work force, as happened at Dominion Steel in 1904 and N.S. Coal & Steel in 1915. Nevertheless, as late as the 1930s a variety of skilled jobs persisted, particularly in the rolling mills, and the new technologies required trained machinists, electricians and crane operators who exercised more 'autonomy' than assembly-line workers. In this industry, the workplace had been reorganized, but it remained a complex system in which informal patterns of bargaining underlay the formal structure of managerial authority.

Although the degree of management control varied among industries and among firms within industries, the enlarged scale of industrial operations and elaboration of formal systems of management generated a massive increase in

337

administrative paperwork and a growing body of clerical workers to deal with it. Between 1900 and 1930, white-collar worker numbers rose from 2 per cent to 7 per cent of the total Canadian work force, and during the first two decades of the twentieth century clerical jobs increased at almost three times the rate of job creation for workers generally. Initially this growth occurred in the larger consolidated firms where increases in administrative overhead could be absorbed and offset by gains in productivity and reduced labour costs. The introduction of new technologies—adding machines and tabulators, stencils and mimeographs, vertical files and intercoms—not only improved the efficiency of office operations in larger firms but also enabled smaller enterprises to adopt 'modern' business methods without incurring substantial new administrative costs.

The recruitment of women into this emerging clerical work force reflected these advances in the mechanization of office tasks and the employers' interest in controlling the costs of administration. Between 1890 and 1930 the proportion of women in clerical jobs in Canada rose from 14 per cent to almost half the total. In the late nineteenth century women constituted only about 10 per cent of wage-earning workers, although in certain industries, notably cotton textile manufacturing in Ontario, the proportion was significantly larger. The expansion of white-collar clerical jobs in the early 1900s provided women with an entry into full-time paid employment. At the same time employers generally paid them less than their male counterparts, in keeping with prevailing social mores on the status of men as 'heads of households' and the main income-earners of their families. Scientific management techniques were probably more accepted in office organization than other areas of work, with increasing numbers of routine tasks of bookkeeping, typing, filing, etc. assigned to lower-paid female clerks. This picture can be overdrawn: both male and female white-collar workers earned higher than average wages (which includes pay for unskilled transient workers) throughout this period, although the gap narrowed during the 1920s. Secretarial and other office work was hardly unskilled labour: these jobs required literacy and training in running office equipment. The conditions of work were generally cleaner and safer than shop floors, not to mention mines and sawmills. Opportunities for advancement into management, however, were far more constricted for women than for men, both in administrative work and in retail sales, another area of growing employment of women by the 1920s.[2]

Both corporate managers and small business proprietors were preoccupied with cost control and improving efficiency, but some of them recognized that a discontented worker could be a less productive worker and a potential labour union recruit. One response to these dangers was adoption of a variety of measures that have been termed 'welfare capitalism', ranging from Christmas bonuses and annual company picnics to pension annuity plans and 'profit sharing' schemes for workers. Many of these initiatives represented extensions of policies followed by paternalistic employers in the nineteenth century, but they also reflected the influence of newer concepts of scientific management, seeking to stimulate greater productivity by encouraging worker 'loyalty' to the firm. Employees would be encouraged to purchase stock in their companies on an instalment payment basis in the hope that this would give them a vested interest in boosting profits. Measures of this sort did not always work out as expected: president Walter Teagle of Imperial Oil, for example, was outraged to discover that employees who had purchased shares in the company under a program introduced in 1915 were 'speculating', i.e., selling their stock as the market value increased during World War I. Most employers preferred arrangements under which 'profit sharing' took the form of bonuses calibrated to reward employees who had rendered faithful service for many years.

In the early 1900s mining and forestry enterprises in the northern and western interior began developing planned communities that reflected both their economic requirements and 'welfare' ideas. The early mining towns, like Sudbury, that had rail links to urban centres had grown more or less spontaneously as grubstakers and mine workers attracted by good wages (or at least steady jobs in the depressed 1890s) swarmed into these areas. Sometimes mine companies would erect primitive bunkhouses for their workers but there was little deliberate planning involved. After 1900 big firms began estabishing more stable communities of company-built houses on well-laid-out streets, with parks and playgrounds: Copper Cliff, developed by Inco after 1910 to replace an earlier shantytown, was a typical example. Meanwhile, corporations and entrepreneurs like the Timmins brothers, extending their operations deep into the wilderness, adopted similar town-planning methods in order to attract and retain workers in these remote settlements.

The larger, mostly foreign-owned firms also experimented with various forms of employee-representation committees during and after World War I. Although at their peak in 1920 these 'industrial councils' boasted 145,000 members (about 8 per cent of all industrial workers but equal to 50 per cent of all unionized workers), they clustered in a relatively small number of companies, mostly US branch plants, that were also engaged in 'welfare' activities. The model for these councils was largely the handiwork of Canada's first minister of Labour (and future prime minister) W.L. Mackenzie King, who devised an employee representation plan for the Rockefeller Foundation while in temporary exile from Canadian politics during World War I. He described his ideas in characteristically turgid fashion in a book entitled *Industry and Humanity*, published in 1918. Imperial Oil created an industrial council that was similar to one established by its parent, Jersey Standard (a Rockefeller firm) in 1919. Another innovator in this area was International Harvester, whose industrial relations chief Arthur Young proselytized the industrial council concept in the US and Canada in this era. Several larger Canadian-owned companies followed suit, notably Massey-Harris, which may have simply been keeping pace with its rival, Harvester. A more elaborate system emerged in the Canadian National Railways maintenance shops in the mid-1920s, involving formal co-operation between management and the rail workers' unions. CNR President Thornton's endorsement of this arrangement derived in part from his experience with the British industry where a similar system had been introduced in World War I.

ALCOA AND ARVIDA:
A 'PLANNED' COMPANY TOWN

Arvida, Quebec, erected from the ground up by the then Canadian subsidiary of Alcoa in the 1920s, was a prime example of a 'planned' town. In 1901 the Pittsburgh Reduction Co. (later the Aluminum Co. of America) established a plant on the St Maurice River in Quebec, purchasing electricity from the Shawinigan Water and Power Co. to run an aluminum smelter from processed bauxite shipped by rail from the United States. By the end of World War I industrial demand for aluminum had increased from less than 1000 tons/year in 1900 to over 130,000 tons/year, and Alcoa had secured a monopoly over aluminum production in North America. By the early 1920s, however, Alcoa's smelting capacity in the US had been reached. Shawinigan Water and Power, which was selling electric power to other industries and residential users in eastern Quebec, was also approaching full capacity.

At this point the prospect of a far larger power site on the Saguenay River, a major tributary to the St Lawrence, came to Alcoa's attention. A huge section of the best land for power development in the Saguenay region had been acquired shortly before World War I by James B. Duke, the American tobacco magnate who apparently hoped to develop a giant synthetic fertilizer complex there. Nothing much came of this scheme and in the early 1920s a portion of the area was leased to the Canadian newsprint company, Price Brothers. Duke's notion of using the rest of the site to develop his own aluminum enterprise brought Alcoa—alarmed at this prospective challenge to its monopoly—into the picture. In 1925 a merger of the three interests—Duke, Price Brothers, and Alcoa—was negotiated; Duke's death later that year led to a increased Alcoa commitment to what would become one of the largest aluminum operations on the continent and the foundation of the Aluminum Co. of Canada.

Even before the merger was officially completed, Alcoa had begun erecting a smelter near the Price Brothers mill at Kenogami, and in 1926 the company began to develop a model town, christened Arvida (in honour of Alcoa's president, Arthur Vining Davis). It was designed by architects from New York, who were advised to develop housing styles that would resemble French Canadian homes, to accommodate both the work force Alcoa wanted to attract from Quebec and the American managers and technicians. Catholic and Protestant churches, schools, a hospital and various recreational facilities were rapidly built by the company, although the onset of the Depression delayed street paving until well into the 1930s; and the houses proved to be poorly insulated and too small for many of the families that moved into the town.

In both its virtues and defects, Arvida reflected the perceptions of labour relations typical of many larger multinational enterprises in Canada: although Aluminium Ltd (later renamed Alcan Aluminum Ltd) was created as a nominally separate Canadian firm in 1928, ownership links with Alcoa remained through the 1950s. The American managers were encouraged to learn French, or at least enough to communicate with workers in the plant, which for the time represented an enlightened approach. In 1937 the company signed collective bargaining agreements with two 'Catholic' unions. But differences over wages and working conditions culminated in an angry albeit short-lived strike in 1941. During World War II the company began selling its houses to permanent workers on liberal terms, meanwhile extricating itself from full responsibility for the costs of running public facilities.

Sources

Campbell, Duncan, *Global Mission: The Story of Alcan* (Toronto, 1985), 85–133.

Igartua, Jorge, 'Corporate Strategy and Locational Decision-Making: The Duke-Price-Alcoa Merger of 1925', *Journal of Canadian Studies* 20 (Autumn 1985), 82–101.

Smith, George D., *From Monopoly to Competition: The Transformations of Alcoa, 1888–936* (Cambridge, Mass., 1988), 138–45.

The town of Arvida was planned to provide some employee accommodation close to the continuously operating smelter. Construction of over 250 houses began in the summer of 1926; all were ready by winter. *(Alcan Archives)*

Except for the CNR experiment, these committees functioned on an individual plant rather than company- or industry-wide basis, and trade union representatives were deliberately excluded. The independent unions castigated these councils as 'company unions', mere puppets of management, intended to preempt any genuine collective bargaining. The charges were not ill-founded: most industrial councils were dominated by managers; employee representatives were generally docile or loyal supporters of the 'company' position. Controversial issues such as wages, hours, or job security were rarely raised for serious discussion. Unwelcome proposals could be vetoed by top management, who could also unilaterally terminate the councils. At the same time, industrial councils did provide managers with an early-warning system on labour unrest, and some improvements in working conditions were achieved. During the 1920s when the independent union movement was badly devastated and demoralized, the industrial councils provided a means through which workers could express their concerns even though they were usually powerless to do anything more effective unless management chose to act.[3]

Many business people throughout this era had little use for 'welfare' schemes or industrial councils, sharing the view of the American industrialist Samuel Insull that the most satisfactory labour relations policy was 'a long line of men waiting at the gate'. From their perspective labour unions were at best parasites on the productive forces of capital and at worst dangerous radicals intent on destroying the free enterprise system. The rise of militant organizations such as the Industrial Workers of the World which flourished briefly (and was opposed by the established craft unions as well as by business) in Canada and the US in 1910–20, tended to confirm their worst fears. The hard-line approach was most entrenched among small- and medium-sized proprietary firms, such as those that banded together into the Citizens Council to defeat the Winnipeg General Strike in 1919. But this strategy of confrontation was not restricted to small business. Several of the most prolonged and bitter strikes of this era involved large corporations, notably the Grand Trunk Railway strike of 1910–11, and the Besco confrontations with coal and steel workers in Nova Scotia in the mid-1920s.[4]

The notion that collective bargaining agreements with trade unions could help ensure stability in the workplace was a view few employers were willing to accept before World War II. Smaller businesses feared the power that well-organized independent unions might exercise over their industries. Many of the larger companies established in the early 1900s carried heavy debt loads incurred by expansion and consolidation, and regarded control of labour costs as essential for their long-term strategies. The cadres of managers emerging in these firms were equally unwilling to concede to workers any substantial role in setting the pace of production or rates of pay for which they, as managers, were held accountable by their superiors and by shareholders. The economic downturns that punctuated the period of general growth from 1900 to 1930 perpetuated in the business community attitudes of caution and pessimism prevalent in the depressed 1890s. Even the CPR, which introduced some of the most sweeping 'welfare' programs in Canada and developed a working relationship with the skilled craft unions, resisted 'radical' unions that tried to establish industry-wide collective bargaining in 1902–3, and periodically advocated legislation to ban strikes on the railways.

Confrontation between labour and business and pressure from both sides, though for different purposes, brought more government attention and occasional intervention in industrial disputes after the 1880s. In 1886 the growth of the Knights of Labor, a movement originating in the US, induced the Macdonald government to appoint a Royal Commission to investigate labour relations in Canada. As is frequently the case, nothing much came of this exercise and the abrupt decline of the Knights diminished incentives for action. A new round of strikes on the railways and in the mines in the early 1900s led to the establishment of a federal Department of Labour; and in 1907 the Labour minister, Mackenzie King, introduced the Industrial Disputes Investigation Act (IDIA), which provided for conciliation boards to attempt to resolve labour-management disputes in advance of strike action by workers or employer lockouts in the transportation, utilities and resource industries. The IDIA was thus limited in its reach and could not, in an case, impose arbitration if conciliation failed (as in the case of the Grand Trunk strike of 1910–11). In its early years, however, King could boast of a 90 per cent success rate for conciliation. IDIA was less effective in dealing with confrontations between militant industrial unions and employers in the aftermath of World War I, and in 1925 the Act was held by the Supreme Court to have exceeded federal jurisdictional authority. By this time, the federal government and most of the provinces had worked out agreements to keep the system going.

Government involvement in labour relations was not consistently oriented toward conciliation. Courts at all levels tended to be hostile toward unions, and provincial governments joined employers in seeking injunctions against strikes, sometimes also using police power to quell labour unrest. During the Winnipeg General Strike in 1919, federal troops were deployed to maintain 'order' while local police and employers' groups suppressed demonstrations; strike leaders were subsequently arrested and deported. Provincial and federal forces were also used during the Cape Breton strikes of the 1920s, and the RCMP established a special unit to carry out surveillance of labour unions after World War I. In general even the conciliation measures were intended primarily to stem labour militancy. While King and other political leaders characterized government's role as that of 'impartial umpire' in labour disputes, the basic objectives of government policies were to maintain social stability and minimize the economic disruptions that strikes entailed, an approach that benefited employers more than workers.[5]

THE ROOTS OF REGIONAL INEQUALITY

Business consolidation and vertical integration were accompanied by significant shifts in the types of economic activities and distribution of wealth among the regions of Canada between 1890 and 1920. Although the case can be made that these changes were underway before this time, economic integration accelerated the concentration of finance and industry in central Canada at the expense of the

Maritimes and the west coast. The National Policy tariffs have been identified as a critical element in this transformation, but in the first decade of the National Policy the trend is less apparent. In 1890 British Columbia surpassed all other provinces in per-capita manufacturing output; and although the Maritimes lagged behind the rest of the country in per-capita manufacturing output, the region retained market shares commensurate with its proportion of the population in several industries—and its industrial growth rate in the 1880s had surpassed that of Ontario and Quebec. As late as 1901, two of the ten leading chartered banks in Canada were located in Nova Scotia, which also had the two largest iron and steel producers and the largest sugar refinery in the country. By the time Canada entered World War I, however, virtually all of the major financial institutions had relocated to Montreal or Toronto; and both B.C. and the Maritimes fell well below the national average in per-capita manufacturing while Ontario substantially exceeded this level.

Even within central Canada changes were apparent by this time. Although Quebec was the main beneficiary of Maritime decline, particularly in the cotton textile industry, and Montreal remained the financial heart of Canada through the 1930s, the province was losing ground in a range of traditional industries. Flour mills and railway equipment manufacturing shifted to the prairies and steel-making capacity concentrated principally in Ontario. The 'new' industries, such as electrical equipment and automobiles, developed almost entirely in Ontario. By the 1920s Ontario had become the centre for producer-goods manufacturing while Quebec focused more on light industry, some consumer goods, and financial services.

Although explanations for these shifts are varied, at a very simplified level they tend to move in two different directions. One line of interpretation focuses on the 'natural' advantages of central Canada over other regions, or at least those conditions that enabled Ontario and Quebec to become the main beneficiaries of industrial growth and consolidation in the early twentieth century. Even before Confederation these two provinces contained more than three-quarters of the population of British North America, and their territorial acquisitions between 1870 and 1914 provided a natural resource hinterland that attracted both domestic and foreign investment. Southern Ontario's proximity to the burgeoning industrial heartland of the American Middle West made it a logical site for industrial expansion through direct investment from the US. Railway development—generating financial crises in central Canada in the 1860s—in the longer term created a transportation network undergirding the growth of Montreal and Toronto as the centres of the emerging transcontinental rail system from the 1890s through World War I. Once the process of industrial growth took hold in central Canada, it became more or less self-generating, attracting capital and labour from other regions of the country as well as from abroad. The differentiation of industrial activities between Quebec and Ontario reflected variations in energy sources and in the distribution of skills in their work forces.

An alternative line of argument emphasizes the economic consequences of government policies which were in turn influenced by business élites in central

Canada and the votes of those who were dependent upon them for capital and jobs. The National Policy tariffs created a captive market for industries centred in Ontario and Quebec, and reoriented production and trade flows in B.C. and the Maritimes from export markets to a continental system in which higher transportation costs put both regions at a disadvantage. Government-subsidized railways were similarly intended to redirect trade patterns on east-west lines with Toronto and Montreal at the hub. Rail freight rates, set initially by the few large carriers and subsequently by government commission, discriminated in favour of central Canadian shippers. By the early 1900s, bankers and industrialists in the 'peripheral' regions recognized the trend of these developments and either sold out to central Canadian financial interests or relocated there, accelerating the process of regional change. In this context the consolidation of industry and financial institutions in Montreal and Toronto exploited competitive advantages conferred upon them by the federal government in the 1880s-90s, enhanced by provincial policies—most notably in Ontario—after the turn of the century.

The debate over uneven regional development, and the role of business groups and government policies in these processes, has been most advanced in the Maritimes. The controversy in fact can be traced back to the 1920s when the Maritime Rights Movement, backed by business interests in the region, protested allegedly discriminatory federal tariff and railway policies that benefited their competitors in central Canada. Although the Maritime Rights Movement disintegrated before the end of the decade, many of these arguments were resuscitated by regional historians in the 1970s–80s, and were elaborated upon by political economists who perceived the 'deindustrialization' of the Maritimes in the early twentieth century as presaging on a smaller scale the eventual fate of a Canada colonized by branch plants and financially integrated with the United States.[6]

During the 1880s merchants and shipbuilders in Nova Scotia and New Brunswick diversified into a range of industries, principally targeting on the central Canadian market, to exploit opportunities presented by the National Policy and the Intercolonial Railway. Even before the depression of the 1890s, some of these industries, notably cotton textiles, had succumbed to competition and take-over by Quebec firms, and regional financial institutions were beginning to redirect their investment into central and western Canada or overseas. Meanwhile, the diversion of Maritime capital into industrial pursuits limited investment in rebuilding the region's merchant marine to compete effectively in the new era of steamship traffic. Although general conditions of economic prosperity masked the decline of the region in the early 1900s, in the years following World War I the major remaining industries of the Maritimes faced a series of insurmountable crises. By this time more than half the manufacturing capacity and virtually all the financial institutions in the region had passed into the hands of central Canadian firms. During the 1920s, over 1100 Maritime companies disappeared, almost all of them locally-owned enterprises.

Some of the problems of aspiring industrialists in the Maritimes were of their own making, others were the result of economic shifts beyond the control of anyone in Canada. Industrial promoters in the Maritimes in the 1880s had little experience in or technical knowledge of the fields they were entering. As with traditional merchant ventures, financing was done on a short-term basis and in amounts sufficient only to cover initial start-up and operating costs. In some cases, particularly in textiles, mills were built on a larger scale than the prospective market would justify. The Gibson mill near Fredericton, N.B., for example, could have supplied the entire Canadian market if it had ever operated at full capacity. During the 1890s local and outside entrepreneurs began to focus on developing the coal and iron industry. Although these ventures proved to be more successful and durable, their long-term competitiveness was limited by the poor quality of local coal and iron ore and the geographically scattered locations of various stages of production in the industry. Ironically, local preoccupation with developing iron and steel capacity may have diverted capital from areas where there was substantial growth in the 1890s, as for example in pulp and paper milling and tobacco processing.

Changing conditions of demand and supply in the transatlantic world as well as in Canada constricted the range of opportunities for Maritime businesses and stymied their best efforts at critical points in this era. Declining demand in Britain for Maritime lumber exports from the early 1880s eroded the region's capital base and induced local entrepreneurs to shift into production for the domestic market where the long-term advantage lay with competitors in Ontario and Quebec. Sugar refining, in which the region held almost one-third of the market and 40 per cent of the country's exports through the early 1900s, thanks to its proximity and trade links with the Caribbean, suffered a serious setback with the entry of US and European competitors into Canada's domestic and export markets after World War I. In that same period, lumber shipped via the Panama Canal to the east coast from British Columbia compounded the problems of the Atlantic region's sawmilling industry. Throughout the period from 1880 through the 1920s outmigration, particularly of working-age males, depleted the Maritimes' population, contributing not only to the region's productivity problems but also to the steady decline of its political leverage in Ottawa.

Federal government policies influenced the region's economy, although not always to the detriment of Maritime businesses. As noted earlier, the National Policy provided new investment opportunities for the region in the 1880s when exports were declining. At the same time, as critics of the National Policy argue, this reorientation worked to the long-term disadvantage of the region. Perhaps more seriously, the federal government took no interest in rebuilding Canada's merchant marine fleet while committing large subsidies to developing the country's railway system. In export-oriented countries such as Japan and Germany, governments vigorously promoted merchant marine development; and even in the US, the merchant fleet began to recover in the early 1900s after a generation of neglect. The failure of Maritime shipbuilders to make the transition from sail to steam has sometimes been cited as an example of entrepreneurial lack of vision, but the incentives, such as they were, encouraged diversion of their resources and energies into other fields.

346

Transportation costs, particularly railway freight rates, were a central element in determining the competitive position of Maritime *vis-à-vis* central Canadian firms. The history of freight rates in this era is complex and controversial. During the mid-1880s, John Stairs, the Halifax industrial promoter, successfully lobbied the Intercolonial Railway to charge lower rates on westbound (i.e., to central Canada) shipments than it charged on eastbound shipments of refined sugar. Other interests jumped on this bandwagon and by 1899 the region's shippers enjoyed an average 12 per cent lower freight cost for their westbound goods over competitors from Ontario and Quebec. As a railway financed and operated by the federal government, the Intercolonial was highly susceptible to rate-setting based on political pressure, and whatever their deficiencies as business strategists, Maritimers like Stairs had well-honed skills as political horse-traders.

Understandably, shippers in central Canada were less delighted over the differentials, and the establishment of the Board of Railway Commissioners provided them with a forum for airing their grievances before an 'objective' audience. Their protests before the Board became more effective as Maritime parliamentary representation declined. In 1915, sugar refiners in Montreal and Ontario, alarmed by the threat to their traditional markets posed by an aggressive new firm, Atlantic Sugar of Saint John, N.B., renewed long-standing complaints over the sugar differential before the Board. The Board's authority over the government-owned railway was ambiguous; but following the merger of the Intercolonial and the CNR in 1918, the new crown corporation's management took steps to eliminate differentials for all freight. Maritime efforts to exempt the Intercolonial rates from this new policy were defeated in Parliament, and the Board rejected appeals from regional shippers, applying what one Maritime historian calls 'misguided symmetry', by maintaining that rates should be based on 'fairness' to all parties and commercial considerations. The increase in westbound freight rates combined with the postwar recession devastated the region's industries and contributed directly to the rise of the Maritime Rights Movement. Later in the 1920s the Liberal government of Mackenzie King partially restored the differential in order to defuse the movement, but by that time many of the region's factories had closed down. Those that remained soon would confront the harsh gales of the Great Depression.

Maritimers in the 1920s, and their more recent chroniclers, asserted that the Intercolonial Railway and its freight-rate differentials were linked to the commitment of the federal government to support their region made at the time of Confederation. *Laissez-faire* minded observers (and those from Ontario and Quebec) have regarded these claims with bemusement, as reflecting the self-interested wishes of Maritime businesses for special treatment not accorded other regions. It may be worth noting that the Maritime differential was not unique: the Crowsnest Pass arrangement imposed by the federal government on the CPR and other western carriers established differential rates to benefit western shippers. At the same time, changes in freight rates at the end of World War I were not the sole cause of Maritime economic troubles; at worst they were the culminating devel-

347

opment in a series of problems contributing to the region's decline that dated back to the 1890s.

The difficulties of Maritime business cannot be attributed entirely to the machinations of predatory capitalists on Saint James Street or myopic politicians in Ottawa; nor, by the same token, were they simply the victims of their own failings as entrepreneurs. The problems were deep-seated and cumulative, and many of the region's business figures contributed to the situation by responding in appropriately businesslike fashion. The Halifax directors of the Bank of Nova Scotia and the Royal Bank began moving their investments and eventually their headquarters out of the region in the 1890s. Ambitious entrepreneurs like Aitken and Dunn joined the tide of migrants to greener pastures. The local owners of N.S. Coal & Steel and Rhodes & Curry (later Canadian Car & Foundry) merged their enterprises with those of central Canadian capitalists. The federal government that eliminated the Intercolonial freight rate differential was led by a Halifax native, Sir Robert Borden; and the most vigorous foe of the Maritime Rights Movement in the 1920s was a transplanted New Brunswicker, R.B. Bennett. Their lack of regional 'patriotism' is hardly surprising. Few people thought of the Maritimes (or anywhere else in Canada, for that matter) as a 'region' before the 1920s. Aspiring industrialists and bankers sought footholds in the lucrative markets of central Canada which naturally led them toward relocation there as circumstances dicated.[7]

Historians of other 'peripheral' regions of Canada have sometimes joined forces with the Maritimers in denouncing the CPR/Bank of Montreal clique or 'Empire Ontario' for their centralizing strategies. To some extent, however, the Maritime situation was unique. As noted earlier, British Columbia had experienced a modest industrial boom in the 1890s, losing ground thereafter in part because of the high transportation costs to reach markets in the prairies and in part because of relatively high wage rates that reflected their small population as well as labour militancy. But industrialization in B.C. never developed on a scale equivalent to the late nineteenth-century Maritimes, nor did the region possess the financial houses that for a time graced the business centres of Halifax and Saint John. The prairie provinces were virtual colonies of central Canadian business from the time the Hudson's Bay Co. released its grip on that region. The largest private grain dealers, flour millers, mines, railway shops and wholesale merchant houses were branches of corporate and family firms in Ontario and Quebec; farmers, ranchers, miners and retailers operated on credit from the chartered banks of the east.

Perhaps the greatest misfortune for the Maritimes was that they never were a prospective hinterland for central Canada: in the 1880s and 1890s that region was a source of competition in the protected industrial markets. Later, after these competitors were vanquished or submerged, the Maritimes became essentially a neglected appendage of the emerging industrial and commercial heartland, populated (so it appeared to Ontarians) by exotic fisherfolk, kilted bagpipers, discontented coal miners and politicians perpetually seeking government handouts.[8]

THE PERSISTENCE OF SMALL BUSINESS

While the large corporations and family dynasties like Eaton and Massey commanded the greatest amount of attention of investors, politicians, and the public —not to mention future scholars—it should be kept in mind that most businesses in this era operated on a much smaller scale. As late as 1930, 89 per cent of all manufacturing firms in Canada had an annual average output of less than $200,000, and employed fewer than 50 people. Small independent retailers comprised more than 90 per cent of all enterprises and accounted for over 80 per cent of sales in this sector of the economy. More than one-quarter of the country's workforce was involved in farming or fishing, areas in which small-scale, decentralized operations predominated. In contrast to the US and Britain, where large integrated enterprises established themselves in consumer goods by the early twentieth century, in Canada these were principally found in the producer goods sector and in the processing of natural resources for export markets. Consequently, while most Canadians, particularly those outside major cities, may have read about big business in their newspapers, their usual everyday contacts were with pedlars and small shopkeepers, local realtors, insurance agents, and manufacturers.[9]

In some industries technological and market conditions made large-scale operations unfeasible or limited their ability to dominate markets: numerous small bakeries, clothiers, tanneries, sawmills and furniture factories could be found across Canada despite the growth of large companies in these fields. In other areas, vigorous efforts to achieve economies of scale through vertical integration and consolidation were at best only partialy met. The fisheries provide examples of this phenomenon.

Fishing itself remained a largely decentralized pursuit, at least until the introduction of seagoing freezer-trawler 'fish factories' by the Europeans and Japanese after World War II. But the development of new methods of preserving fish through refrigeration and canning in the late nineteenth century presented opportunities for larger-scale organization in processing and marketing fish products. This was particularly the case in the salmon fisheries of British Columbia where canneries thrived from the 1880s, exporting much of their output to Britain with relatively little competition—the American canneries on the Alaska coast were mainly oriented to the US market—until the Japanese entered the field after World War I. Canadian canneries, mostly locally-financed and owned, were concentrated along the Fraser River and on Vancouver Island.

In 1900 Henry Doyle, who managed a Vancouver branch of his family's California-based cannery, launched a scheme to amalgamate the B.C. salmon industry, which had suffered recurrent cycles of overproduction punctuated by periods of salmon stock depletion due to overfishing. The B.C. Packers Association, combining 39 canneries that accounted for over half the province's output, and financed with $2.5 million from US and central Canadian banks, was established in 1902. Doyle was ousted as general manager two years later following disputes with his backers, but B.C. Packers faced more serious difficulties. A loosely organized operation, the enterprise was unable to prevent its own members from engaging in independent selling of their output on the side; and the salmon boom that ran from 1905 to 1913 attracted new entrants, including Doyle himself, into the industry, setting up their canneries in the numerous bays and estuaries of the B.C. coast.

By the end of World War I, B.C. Packers controlled less than one-fifth of the province's industry, which was again experiencing falling prices as Americans and Japanese fought them for the British market and declining supplies of salmon. In 1928 a new effort at amalgamation produced B.C. Packers Ltd, a much more tightly structured enterprise that comprised (again) about half of the salmon canning output in the province. But several substantial operators remained outside the new organization, and other independent canners diversified into tuna and similar less expensive fish products. The Depression of the 1930s hurt B.C. Packers, but inadvertently improved its market position by eliminating many smaller rivals in remote sites. The success of B.C. Packers was thus more a result of general economic conditions than of its own strategic foresight.

A somewhat similar sequence occurred in the Great Lakes fishery. Although overshadowed by Canada's ocean-based industry, the Great Lakes fishery is one of the world's largest fresh-water fisheries, supplying both Canadian and US markets. In the nineteenth century most fishing and processing was carried out by small operators on both sides of the border, although the Hudson's Bay Co. controlled much of the packing and marketing of the catch from Lake Superior. The US imposition of protective duties on imported fish in 1890 transformed the situation as Canadian fishers formed linkages with American processing firms to circumvent the tariff. The Chicago packer, A. Booth & Co., established a trust in 1898 that eventually controlled 80 per cent of the western Great Lakes output, absorbing Canadian producers into a subsidiary, Dominion Fish Co. New York-based merchants moved in a similar fashion to dominate the eastern Lakes.

This trend toward consolidation and integration began to unravel after World War I. Improvements in transportation and methods of preservation enabled smaller packers to increase direct sales to the metropolitan markets of the American east coast, and the attenuation of import duties in 1913 reduced the influence of American firms in the Great Lakes fishery. Co-operatives and fishermen's trade associations emerged in the early 1900s to compete with the big packers and lobbied with some effect on provincial governments for introduction of regulatory measures to restrict American entrants. Meanwhile, overfishing and industrial pollution had depleted the Lakes of many of its most desirable types of fish, so that the decline of larger firms may reflect as well the relative deterioration of profitability in the fishery—much as the decline of the west coast salmon stocks limited the dominant role of B.C. Packers in that region.

During this period shifts in markets and the technologies of fishing and processing were also transforming the east coast fishery. By the 1920s large firms had emerged that integrated fishing, using steam trawlers, with on-shore packing and marketing. At the same time, however, decentralization and small-scale operations persisted in the industry. Although the number of people engaged in fishing and the number of independent packing enterprises diminished steadily, in 1930 there were still over 500 such ventures: 60 per cent of them had an average annual output of less than $10,000. By contrast there were fewer than 100 such firms in B.C., and more than two-thirds of these had an output in excess of $200,000 per year. Many of the larger-scale Maritime companies were family-owned or partnerships, notably the Zwicker family firm and W.C. Smith Co. of Lunenburg, N.S. and the Leonard Fishery Co. of Saint John, N.B.

Declining demand for dried fish products in the Caribbean and US import duties after 1886 threatened this traditional sector of the industry, although it experienced a renaissance during the period before World War I, before its final eclipse in the 1920s. By this time the market for fresh fish was emerging, enhanced by the development of refrigeration. After 1913, US duties on boned and skinned fish were reduced and other fresh fish were admitted free, reflecting in part the decline of the New England fishing fleets. Meanwhile, Maritime fishers and packers diversified into higher-value fish such as haddock, supplementing the traditional cod.

By the 1920s improvements in processing technology, including filleting and rapid freezing, had spread from the US into Canada. Before this time, the most significant developments had involved vessel design and fishing technology. Beginning in the 1880s, Maritime schooners became larger, sometimes with auxiliary steam power, permitting longer voyages and larger catches. Lunenburg in particular became the centre of the 'banker' fleet as well as the construction site for the racing schooners of the 1920s, of which the *Bluenose* was the most famous. During the early 1900s larger steam-driven trawlers made their appearance in east coast waters. By 1927 there were 10 trawlers operating in the Maritimes, each capable of bringing in between 150,000 and 300,000 pounds of fish per voyage.

The new technologies of fishing, processing, and preserving required substantial increases in capital investment. The average cost of outfitting vessels alone more than doubled between 1900 and World War I; a steam trawler cost close to $1 million. Some companies such as Smith's met these needs by enlarging their partnerships, integrating fishing and packing, and diversifying into fresh fish marketing. Others raised capital from central Canada, and American fish marketers also entered the Maritime industry. The largest operations in the early 1920s, based in Halifax, were the Maritime Fish Corporation and the National Fish Co., both of which owned or chartered several trawlers and had a number of cold-storage and processing plants at various Maritime outports. Both of these firms were taken over in 1928–29 by a New York company, Atlantic Coast Fisheries. During the 1930s, however, the properties were reacquired by H.G. Connor, who had founded Maritime Fish Corp. in 1910. Meanwhile, the Smith family in Lunenburg had expanded its position by acquiring a chain of packing plants from Ralph Bell, a Halifax merchant who would administer the Canadian aircraft industry during World War II, and return to Nova Scotia to amalgamate the Smith and Connor companies into National Sea Products Ltd in 1945.

Although the trend toward large-scale consolidations in the east coast fishery was underway by the 1920s, there were certain elements at work that slowed the pace of this process and limited its impact. From the early 1900s the traditional long-line fishers had assailed the introduction of steamer trawlers in their waters as a threat to their livelihood as well as an inherently wasteful practice, since trawler nets scooped up everything in their path, decimating the fish population. The Smith company, which relied on schooner fishing until the 1930s, joined in this protest. In 1930 the Canadian government introduced a trawler licensing system with high differential fees for foreign-owned vessels. The combined effect of this measure and the Depression reduced the trawler fleet to three ships by the mid-1930s.

In addition, some sectors of the fishery remained beyond the reach of big integrated firms. The lobster fishery, for example, identified by a Canadian government report in 1927 as 'one of the most important and valuable branches' of the industry, was characterized by small-scale operators, and regulated by the provincial governments. During the late 1920s the Antigonish Movement focused its efforts on developing co-operatives in the lobster fishery, with some financial support from the Nova Scotia government during the Depression.

In each of the fisheries, then, the growth of large integrated firms was offset to some extent by the physical and economic characteristics of the industry, by government measures in response to pressures from smaller producers, and by the emergence of co-operatives. These counter-trends were not sufficient to perpetuate or restore traditional patterns of small-scale individual enterprise, but they did set limits on empire-building in the industry. In general, the most successful ventures through the 1930s were medium-sized companies with some degree of vertical integration, predominantly proprietary or private limited-liability companies.[10]

A similar pattern might have been predicted for Canadian agriculture. Certainly in the US this was the case, particularly after World War I when the prolonged agricultural depression, aggravated by drought and insect invasions, decimated the ranks of marginal farmers. The survivors consolidated landholdings, introduced mechanization on a large scale and organized powerful lobbies to secure government price supports for their products. In Canada, a somewhat different process unfolded. Farmers on the prairies banded together into producer co-operatives and used their political clout to procure provincial government support for large quasi-public grain elevator and marketing enterprises. Canada's western farmers suffered the ravages of a depression that began long before the stock market crash of 1929, and many smaller operators went under. But the big storage and marketing structures remained and expanded as prosperity returned during World War II. There is a certain irony here, since many of the ideas about producer co-operation and government-owned elevators were originally devised by American farmers during the Populist era of the 1890s. In the US these 'radical' challenges to big business disintegrated in the early twentieth century, but took root and institutional form in Canada.

As in the US, farmers' journals and almanacs from the early 1900s urged their readers to adopt 'businesslike' practices, not just improved methods of cultivation and crop rotation and introducing machinery, but also more standardized book-keeping techniques and more efficient management of harvest workers. While the extent to which this advice was embraced is unclear, farmers, especially in the prairie west, were quite sensitive to the connections between their earnings and the prevailing commercial arrangements for storing, transporting, and marketing grain. As discussed in Chapter Fourteen, western ire centred initially on the CPR's freight rate policies and then on the large private elevator companies with their linkages to the Winnipeg Grain Exchange. Seeking redress for their grievances through political pressure on the western provincial governments, farmers also turned to more direct techniques of organization for marketing their products.

Ideas about co-operatives were percolating into Canada from the US and Britain in the 1890s. Farmers also had some immediate experience to draw upon: from the early days of prairie settlement, local communities had been making arrangements for shared use of equipment and labour at harvest time. In 1906 a British immigrant to Manitoba, Edward A. Partridge, proposed extending the idea of co-operation to grain marketing. Partridge's venture, the Grain Growers' Grain Co., was initially denied a seat on the Winnipeg Grain Exchange, but drew upon political support from farm pressure groups to secure its position on the Exchange in 1907. Meanwhile, farm groups were agitating for establishment of provincially-owned line elevators to challenge the private elevator 'combine'. While western political leaders were reluctant to enter directly into the business of running elevators, they were prepared to offer financial support to 'farmer-owned' companies. In 1911 the Saskatchewan Co-operative Elevator Co. was incorporated; and in the following year Manitoba, which had briefly experimented with a government-owned system, leased its 174 elevators to Partridge's Grain Growers' Grain Co., which in turn in 1913 provided financial guarantees to a Farmers' Co-operative Elevator Co. in Alberta. In 1917 the Alberta and Manitoba companies amalgamated to form United Grain Growers Ltd, with $2 million in capital raised from farmer-members, under the leadership of Thomas A. Crerar, who had succeeded Partridge as president of the Grain Growers' Grain Co. in 1912 and later headed the short-lived federal Progressive Party in the 1920s. The Saskatchewan Co-operative remained separate, but by the mid-1920s both companies were almost equal in size, and together they controlled more line and terminal elevators than any of the private firms.

Grain marketing and pricing continued to be a source of contention among western farmers. During World War I the federal government established a Board of Grain Supervisors which purchased wheat at fixed prices to supply domestic requirements as well as sales to Allied governments overseas. When the Winnipeg Grain Exchange resumed operations in 1919, the price of wheat promptly spiralled, leading the government to set up a Canadian Wheat Board that resumed fixed-price purchases of all grain. Farmers had initially been cool toward the Wheat Board since its set price was below the current market price; when market prices collapsed after the termination of the Board in 1920, many of them became vigorous advocates of its restoration. But opinions on the issue within the farmers' organizations were divided: Crerar, in particular, opposed reestablishment of a compulsory system. The Liberal government of Mackenzie King, elected in 1921, took the position that a peacetime Wheat Board would exceed federal constitutional authority, and proposed to revive it only if all the prairie provinces legislatures endorsed the plan. When Manitoba failed to do so (by a three-vote margin) the Wheat Board died—at least until the Great Depression.

Meanwhile, a movement spread across the west for creation of a system of controlled grain marketing through voluntary associations, called 'pools', modelled on the elevator co-operatives. Individual farmers would purchase shares (at $1 each) in the enterprise: when enough were signed on to account for 50 per cent of the acreage in a province, the provincial government would issue a charter authorizing the pool to purchase grain from the shareholders, at a contractually established price, and market it through a centralized sales agency with professional managers. Profits would be reinvested to strengthen the pool's asset base and enable it to maintain stable prices. Directors or 'trustees' would be elected by local shareholders on a proportional representation basis.

Prairie farm organizations supported the pool concept but it had some unusual advocates, notably Aaron Sapiro, a peripatetic lawyer from California (whose clients included the Hollywood producer Louis B. Mayer and the Chicago gangster Al Capone), who stage-managed a colourful campaign across the prairies in 1923–24 to persuade farmers to sign up for the pools. Another improbable supporter was the millionaire Calgary lawyer and future Tory prime minister, R.B. Bennett, who helped Sapiro draft the first wheat pool contract in Alberta in 1923.

Saskatchewan and Manitoba followed Alberta's lead in 1924, each province creating a Co-operative Wheat Producers Co. The pools contracted with the co-operative elevator lines for handling the crop. In 1926 the Saskatchewan wheat pool acquired the line elevators of the Saskatchewan Co-operative Elevator Co. for $11 million and commissioned a noted engineer, C.D. Howe, to design a new terminal elevator complex at the Lakehead. United Grain Growers declined a similar offer from the Alberta and Manitoba pools but continued to handle their output; these pools developed their own country elevator networks but avoided direct competition with United Grain Growers. By 1929 the three wheat pools owned more than 1600 line and terminal elevators, held cumulative assets of $29 million, and were handling and marketing more than half the country's wheat crop through a single central sales agency, Canadian Co-operative Wheat Producers Ltd. In the US, the newly-elected president Herbert Hoover established a Federal Farm Board closely patterned after the Canadian pools.

The Great Depression wracked prairie wheat growers and nearly destroyed the pools. Faced with global overproduction, the US, followed by Britain, Germany, France, and Italy, imposed prohibitive duties on grain imports in 1930–31. The 'dust bowl' drought and wheat rust decimated grain output later in the 1930s, reducing overproduction but ruining hard-pressed western farmers in the process: per-capita income in the three prairie provinces fell by more than 66 per cent in 1929–35, with farmers bearing the brunt of the decline. The pools' central sales agency, which had vainly attempted to prop up prices at the outset of the crisis, collapsed in 1931. Prime minister Bennett saved the co-operatives from bankruptcy by arranging for federal government guarantees of their liabilities, and in 1934 he proposed to reestablish the Canadian Wheat Board. The Liberals effectively blocked recreation of the Board with compulsory powers (which were finally conferred in 1943), but the co-operatives managed to stagger through the worst years of the Depression, marketing their wheat through the 'voluntary' Board and hanging on to their elevator networks. With the revival of export trade in World War II, the co-operatives recovered, with the Saskatchewan Wheat Pool emerging as the leading firm in the elevator and grain-handling field. The co-operatives also diversified, acting as purchasing agents and distributors of seed and fertilizer for their members.[11]

The wheat co-operatives overshadowed other ventures of this type in Canada, but they were not unique. The Depression stimulated the growth of the co-operative movement, although necessarily on a much smaller scale than in the wheat pools of the 1920s. In 1940, there were more than 1000 co-operatives, with 450,000 members in a range of agricultural fields, including dairy products, livestock and poultry, fruits and vegetables as well as the fisheries.

Much of the rhetoric of the co-operative movement, then and now, emphasized co-operatives and their 'democratic' decentralized structure as an alternative to 'capitalist' corporate organization. Some observers have questioned the extent to which these claims corresponded with the realities of co-operatives, especially in large organizations such as the wheat pools. The pools and elevator co-operatives necessarily relied on hierarchies of professional managers to run their operations effectively. Although the managers were accountable to directors or trustees elected by the co-operative membership, inevitably the directors would be obliged to allow a fair degree of latitude to management, as in most joint-stock corporations. Although members of co-operatives could play a larger role in the selection of directors through proportional representation than the average shareholder in a large corporate enterprise, as in other organizations incumbents tended to be reelected, creating a more or less self-perpetuating élite. One survey indicated that over one-third of directors in the large farm co-operatives served five terms or more. While the principles of organization of co-operatives differed from private corporations, in effect co-operatives — particularly the prairie farm co-operatives — essentially constituted a consortium of small profit-oriented proprietors. Although the wheat pools were sometimes denounced by their corporate competitors as 'bolshevik' experiments, impeccable conservatives like Bennett and Hoover saw them as alternatives to 'big governnment' and 'socialism'.

The disjunction between rhetoric and reality was also apparent in the history of Quebec's credit-union co-operatives, the *caisses populaires*. Alphonse Desjardins, a journalist and French Canadian proto-nationalist who established the first *caisse populaire* at Levis, Quebec in 1900 and tirelessly promoted the idea, envisioned these co-operatives as instruments for the preservation and advancement of the French-speaking communities of Canada: providing mortgages to lower-income homeowners, and loans to small businesses unable to secure credit from the large anglophone banks. There were 140 *caisses* in operation when Desjardins died in 1920. The movement slowed over the next two decades, but then grew rapidly during and after World War II, expanding from its rural and small town base into the larger cities, with 15 per cent of the French population of Quebec

Alphonse Desjardins, founder of
Quebec's *caisses populaires*.
*(La Confédération des caisses
populaires et d'économie
Desjardins du Québec)*

as subscribers in 1945. Although *caisses* also appeared in French Canadian communities in the Maritimes and the west, the movement centred in Quebec where by the early 1980s one-third of all personal savings were deposited in credit unions.

Ties of religion as well as ethnicity combined to promote the *caisses*. The Catholic hierarchy of Quebec vigorously supported the movement, which was seen as a development that might stem the migration of French Canadians from Quebec; and the church drew on the resources of the *caisses* to finance its construction projects in the province. The *caisses* were perceived as one of the social bastions preserving traditional French Canadian communities against the tides of secularism and industrialization.

While the movement stressed ethnic and religious solidarity, in practice the leaders of the *caisses* were predominantly French Canadian small businessmen and professionals. Although Desjardins advocated credit policies that would ensure that low-income earners qualified for loans and that most of the money loaned would remain in the local communities, as the *caisses* evolved more 'businesslike' criteria became the norm for loans, and investment gravitated toward larger, more profitable ventures. By 1945 almost half of the total assets of the *caisses* consisted of bonds, including provincial and federal government notes as well as corporate securities. During the 1920s a trend toward centralization emerged as the *caisses* grouped into regional confederations that drew on a portion of the asset base of their local members for investment, culminating in the formation of the *Federation de Quebec des unions regionales de caisses populaires Desjardins* (FQUR) in 1932. Under its first president, Cyril Vaillancourt, the FQUR operated much like a chartered bank with the local *caisses* as branches, although a number of these, particularly in the Montreal area, resisted Vaillancourt's

356

'dictatorship'. This development, like the founding of the *caisses* in 1900, reflected in part the tensions accompanying changes in Quebec society and the French Canadian middle class.[12]

Whatever their deficiencies as democratic institutions, co-operatives provided small business people with an instrument not only for gaining economic leverage against bigger competitors but also for enhancing their political influence. Other forms of direct political pressure were employed by small business groups throughout this era. At the federal level their power was limited and diluted, but in provincial politics small businesses could prove to be a formidable force, as the histories of Ontario Hydro and the prairie wheat pools demonstrate. Many of Canada's financial and corporate leaders were inclined to regard these small business pressure groups as retrograde forces, seeking to use government authority to perpetuate outmoded and inefficient practices. But institutions such as the co-operatives did represent an innovative effort by small businesses to accommodate the changing economic conditions while preserving their traditional independence.

Notes

[1] On scientific management, see Harry Braverman, *Labor and Monopoly Capital: The Degradation of Work in the Twentieth Century* (New York, 1974). For other assessments, see Daniel Nelson, *Managers and Workers: The Origins of the New Factory System in the U.S., 1880–1920* (Madison, Wisc., 1975), 55–78; David Montgomery, *The Fall of the House of Labor: The Workplace, the State and American Labor Activism, 1865–1925* (Cambridge, 1987), 214–56. On scientific management in Canada, see Bryan Palmer, *A Culture in Conflict: Skilled Workers and Industrial Capitalism in Hamilton, Ontario, 1860–1914* (Montreal, 1979), 216–22; Paul Craven, *An Impartial Umpire: Industrial Relations and the Canadian State, 1900–11* (Toronto, 1980), 93–100. On Knechtel, see Joy Parr, *The Gender of Breadwinners: Women, Men and Change in Two Industrial Towns, 1880–1930* (Toronto, 1990), 157–64.

[2] On workers in the steel industry, see Heron, *Working in Steel*, 53–72. On women and the development of clerical white collar occupations, see JoAnne Yates, *Control Through Communication: The Rise of System in American Management* (Baltimore, 1989); Graham S. Lowe, *Women in the Administrative Revolution* (Toronto, 1987).

[3] On welfare capitalism generally, see Gerald Zahavi, *Workers, Managers and Welfare Capitalism* (New York, 1990); Stuart Brandes, *American Welfare Capitalism, 1880–1940* (Chicago, 1970). On welfare capitalism in Canada, see Margaret McCallum, 'Corporate Welfarism in Canada, 1919–30', *Canadian Historical Review* 71 (1990); 46–80. On Imperial Oil, see Taylor, 'Imperial Oil, 1911–17', *Business History* 34, 63.

[4] On company towns, see Gilbert Stetler, 'Community Development in Toronto's Commercial Empire: The Industrial Towns of the Nickel Belt, 1883–1931', *Laurentian University Review* 6 (June 1974), 3–49. On industrial councils, see Irving Bernstein, *The Lean Years: A History of the American Worker, 1920–33* (Baltimore, 1966), 157–74; Bruce Scott, ' "A Place in the Sun": The Industrial Council at Massey-Harris, 1919–29', *Labour/Le Travailleur* 1 (1976), 158–92; Robert Storey, 'Unionization versus Corporate Welfare: The

"Dofasco Way" ', *Labour/Le Travailleur* 12 (1983); 7–42. The Insull quote is in Bernstein, 184.

⁵On government policies toward labour relations, see Craven, ch. 11; Craig Heron, *The Canadian Labour Movement* (Toronto, 1989), 60–2.

⁶For views of the Maritimes and regional disparity from 'mainstream' economists, see Marr and Paterson, *Canada: An Economic History*, 418–38; and Roy George, *A Leader and a Laggard: Manufacturing Industry in Nova Scotia, Quebec and Ontario* (Toronto, 1970). For a political economist's perspective, see Michael Clow, 'Politics and Uneven Capitalist Development: The Maritime Challenge to the Study of Canadian Political Economy', *Studies in Political Economy* 14 (Summer 1984), 117–40; and Paul Phillips, *Regional Disparities* (Toronto, 1982).

⁷For a summary of the history of Maritime industrialization and 'deindustrialization', see John Reid, *Six Crucial Decades* (Halifax, 1986), chs 4–5. On the achievements and problems of Maritime industrial entrepreneurs, see T.W. Acheson, 'The National Policy and the Industrialization of the Maritimes'; and Acheson, 'The Maritimes and "Empire Canada"' in David J. Bercuson, ed., *Canada and the Burden of Unity* (Toronto, 1977), 87–114; Eric Sager and Gerald Panting, *Maritime Capital: The Shipping Industry in Atlantic Canada, 1870–1914* (Montreal/Kingston, 1990), esp. chs 7–10; Kris Inwood, 'Local Control, Resources and the Nova Scotia Steel and Coal Co.', *CHA Historical Papers 1986*, 254–82; L.D. McCann, 'Metropolitanism and Branch Businesses in the Maritimes, 1881–1931', *Acadiensis* 13 (Autumn 1983), 112–25. On the freight rate issue, see Ernest R. Forbes, 'Misguided Symmetry: The Destruction of Regional Transportation Policy for the Maritimes', in Bercuson, 60–86; Forbes, *The Maritime Rights Movement* (Montreal, 1979); and Ken Cruikshank, 'The People's Railway: The Intercolonial and the Canadian Public Enterprise Experience', *Acadiensis* 16 (1986), 78–100.

⁸On 'deindustrialization' in British Columbia, see John Lutz, 'Losing Steam: The Boiler and Engine Industry as an Index of British Columbia Deindustrialization, 1880–1915', *CHA Historical Papers 1988*, 168–205. On prairie discontents, see chapters by Regehr and Bercuson in Bercuson, 115–42; J.F. Conway, *The West: The History of a Region in Confederation* (Toronto, 1984); Gerald Friesen, *The Canadian Prairies: A History* (Toronto, 1987), ch. 8, 12–13.

⁹See Elizabeth Bloomfield, 'Boards of Trade and Canadian Urban Development', *Urban History Review* XII (Oct.1983), 77–99; Alan F. Artibise, 'In Pursuit of Growth: Municipal Boosterism and Urban Development in the Canadian Prairie West, 1871–1913' in G.A. Stetler and A.F. Artibise, eds, *Shaping the Urban Landscape* (Ottawa, 1982).

¹⁰On the west coast fishery, see Dianne Newell, ed., *The Development of the Pacific Salmon-Canning Industry* (Montreal/Kingston, 1989); Patricia Marchak *et al.*, eds, *Uncommon Property: The Fishing and Fish Processing Industries in British Columbia* (Toronto, 1987). On the Great Lakes, see A.B. McCullough, *The Commercial Fishery of the Canadian Great Lakes* (Ottawa, 1989); and William Ashworth, *The Late Great Lakes: An Environmental History* (Scarborough, Ont., 1986), 112–22. On the east coast fishery—which still awaits a full-scale history (except for Newfoundland, which is well chronicled)—see Harold Innis, *The Cod Fisheries* (Toronto, 1954), 425–43; Stephen Kimber, *Net Profits: The Story of National Sea* (Halifax, 1989); *Report of the Royal Commission Investigating the Fisheries of the Maritime Provinces* (Ottawa, 1928).

[11]On farmers and 'businesslike practices', see Ian MacPherson and John H. Thompson, 'The Business of Agriculture: Prairie Farmers and the Adoption of "Business" Methods, 1880–1950' in Baskerville, ed., *Canadian Papers in Business History* (Victoria, 1989), 245–69. On farm co-operatives and wheat pools, see C.F. Wilson, *A Century of Canadian Grain*, 47–56, 211–26; Garry L. Fairbairn, *From Prairie Roots* (Saskatoon, 1978); V.C. Fowke, *The National Policy and the Wheat Economy*, chs VIII, XI–XII.

[12]On the issue of 'democracy' in the co-operative movement, see chapters by Christopher Axworthy, David Laycock and Brett Fairbairn in Murray Fulton, ed., *Co-operative Organizations and Canadian Society* (Toronto, 1990). On the *caisses populaires*, see Ronald Rudin, *In Whose Interest? Quebec's Caisses Populaires, 1900–1945* (Montreal/Kingston, 1990); and Paul-Andre Linteau *et al.*, *Quebec Since 1930*, trans. Robert Chodos (Toronto, 1991), 369–71.

5

THE AGE OF
THE ACTIVIST STATE
1930–1984

17 THE INCOMPLETE LEVIATHAN

As earlier chapters have made clear, government intervention in the market economy was hardly a twentieth-century novelty in Canada or in other industrializing countries. Long before Confederation, governments were involved in schemes to encourage the development of canals and railways, promote industry, and attract foreign investment through direct subsidies, public loans, tariff duties and drawbacks, and patent laws. Governments at all levels have continued to play this promotional role through the present. Regulatory measures — to restrict exploitation of child labour, prevent adulteration of food products and other commodities, and establish safety requirements in mines and factories — were also in place by the late nineteenth century, although the means of enforcement often left something to be desired. There were even ventures into public enterprise, usually the result of failures on the part of private companies to complete projects deemed to be essential to the economy: most of the canals wound up in government hands and the Intercolonial Railway linking the Maritimes to central Canada was undertaken by the federal government in the 1870s.

At the turn of the century, several new factors generated pressures for governments' more systematically activist role in the economy. The emergence of large-scale enterprises and the integration of local and regional markets into a national system presented novel and unanticipated problems for public authorities. Farmers, owners of small businesses, industrial workers, and urban consumers clamoured for measures to protect their interests against the perceived economic power of big business. In times of economic hardship, governments were pressed to assume greater responsibilities for alleviating distress. The demands of modern warfare, peaking around the middle of the century, required an unprecedented degree of economic co-ordination of the nation's resources. As the role of government expanded, public officials acquired increasing confidence in their ability to control the course of events, stimulating new interventionist initiatives. While business leaders continued to employ the rhetoric of *laissez-faire* liberalism, their enterprises were increasingly enmeshed in a web of governmental relationships, embracing public contracts, subsidy arrangements, regulatory agencies, and joint public/private undertakings.

The rise of the activist state was not a uniquely Canadian phenomenon, and in many respects governments in Canada were far less interventionist than those of other industrializing nations. In the realm of social welfare, for example, through the post-World War II era Canada lagged well behind continental European countries and even Britain and the US. Formal structures of collaboration between government and domestic businesses that emerged in 'late industrializing' countries such as Sweden or Japan were not explicitly followed in Canada—although informal networks of this sort were at work in federal policy-making in the late nineteenth century and in Ontario in the early 1900s. While the proliferation of Canadian crown corporations has projected an image of an intensely activist state, in other dimensions—particularly in the area of economic regulation—governments in Canada have been less obtrusive in the affairs of business than was the case even in that heartland of free enterprise, the United States.

For the most part, Canadian historians have focused on the promotional role of governments in the economy, with crown corporations representing a variation on this theme. There is a general consensus that our governments have been consistently interventionist, in contrast to Britain and (to some extent) the US, but views differ over the sources and purposes of this activism. Followers of Innis stress the interconnection of government policies and the development of staple-exporting industries, but they are not in agreement over the role of business *vis-à-vis* government in these pursuits. Hugh Aitken maintained that these policies represented 'defensive expansionism' on the part of governments, to encourage economic growth and to protect the east-west linkages that defined the country from the southward pull generated by the American economy. The political economists, on the other hand, see the initiative for governmental measures coming from the business community, particularly the staple-exporting merchants and their banking affiliates; in the more recent past these groups have had to share their influence on the state with representatives of the foreign (mostly American) multinationals in the extractive and manufacturing sectors.

Other scholars, deriving their ideas in part from proponents of the concept of 'corporate liberalism' in the US, emphasize the dominant role of big business in shaping Canadian governmental policies in the twentieth century. Not only overtly promotional measures but also government regulation of business were the result of pressures from the large industrial enterprises and banks anxious to create conditions of economic predictability and social stability through government action, to restrict markets and at least give the appearance of meeting the demands of farmers and industrial workers for a more socially equitable system. Far from being experiments in socialism (or instruments of nation-building), crown corporations played a necessary role in moderating the forces of the market on the one hand and political radicalism on the other.

Characteristically, Bliss offers a rather different view of twentieth-century developments, essentially dividing the business community into two general groups. 'Prudent' businessmen running established firms (large or small) tended to adhere to the traditions of *laissez-faire* although they were willing to accept useful departures such as protective tariffs or the National Banking Act. Arrayed against them have been a long line of 'adventurers, promoters . . . [and] visionaries' of the William Mackenzie/Francis Clergue type who have exploited the hopes and ambitions of Canada's political leaders for rapid economic development, and a general public convinced that government programs could translate economic growth into perpetual prosperity for all, free of market constraints and fluctuations. The legacy of these ventures is a country littered with bankrupt crown enterprises, cumbersome regulatory agencies and proliferating governn-ment bureaucracies whose history is punctuated by recurrent fiscal crises.[1]

All of these views reflect perceptions of a vigorous and expanding govern-mental presence in the economy characteristic of the post-World War II era. Many of the groups and pressures for an activist state — big business élites seeking stability, small businesses and others seeking to constrain big business, promoters with their schemes, ambitious government bureaucrats and intellectuals — were at work long before that point. But governments had neither the will nor the resources to proceed very far along on this course. Economic mobilization in World War I, as will be discussed in Chapter Eighteen, was limited in both its extent and impact. This chapter will focus on forays by the federal and provincial governments into regulation of big business in the early 1900s, and the haphazard responses of governments at all levels to the prolonged and devastating economic crisis of the Great Depression.

THE REGULATORY IMPULSE

As noted above, there was nothing unique about the movement for expansion of government regulation of business that emerged in Canada around the end of the nineteenth century: every industrialized or industrializing country was experien-cing similar pressures, although the responses varied considerably. Canadian gov-ernments could look abroad for models to emulate as well as for practices to avoid. Bismarck's Germany introduced major social welfare programs in the 1880s. In Britain, even in the heyday of *laissez-faire*, measures had been enacted to regulate health and safety conditions in factories and mines, and Canadian governments had followed suit in the 1870s and 80s. Just across the border, in the years after the Civil War American state governments had begun experi-menting with railroad freight rate regulation through quasi-judicial agencies, experiments culminating in the federal Interstate Commerce Commission Act of 1887. Three years later the US Congress passéd what appeared to be a sweeping measure against 'monopolistic' businesses, the Sherman Antitrust Act. Britain and continental European countries were less inclined to try to ban big business altogether, but they imposed certain constraints on 'unfair competition'.[2]

At the same time, Canada had its own distinctive regulatory patterns, reflecting its particular circumstances and traditions. In electric utilities and in railways, as discussed in Chapter Thirteen, government-owned enterprises coexisted with reg-ulatory agencies, and a similar pattern was to emerge in the air transportation industry. The Canadian government, unlike the American, did not engage in 'trust-busting'. It followed instead the European practice of attempting to police corporate behaviour, despite persistent pressures from farmers and small busi-nesses for more stringent measures against alleged monopolies.

Canadian constitutional arrangements had an impact on regulatory structures. A number of areas where regulatory initiatives occurred fell within provincial jurisdiction, and others were subject to concurrent federal and provincial author-ity. In the field of corporate securities, for example, both the Dominion and provincial governments had chartering (and implicit regulatory) powers: as noted in Chapter Thirteen, a shrewd businessman such as Charles Sise of Bell Canada could select the jurisdiction that would best serve his purposes. Provincial efforts to control the issuing of securities within their boundaries were held by the Judicial Committee of the Privy Council in Britain — effectively Canada's court of final appeals through the post-World War II era—to be inapplicable to Dominion-chartered companies. But the federal government was in turn restricted in its control over the resale of securities by brokers or investment houses. One way around this problem was for governments at both levels to pass similar laws, as in the Security Frauds Prevention Acts of 1931–32, although not every province was prepared to participate.

Jurisdictional disputes also complicated regulation of the insurance industry. From the 1870s on, both Dominion and provincial (primarily Ontario and Quebec) governments sought to control this field. The courts and Britain's Privy Council consistently ruled in favour of provincial regulatory priority, even over companies that operated across provincial boundaries. But the federal government persisted in efforts to maintain a foothold in the field, asserting its right to regulate Dominion-chartered and foreign insurance firms, with backing from larger companies who wanted the imprimatur of federal endorsement of their solvency to help them secure business outside Canada. After much bickering, the Dominion and provincial governments negotiated a compromise in 1934 under which the federal government would issue certificates of solvency to federally-chartered companies while leaving the balance of regulatory controls in provincial hands.

While federal-provincial divisions helped create a realm of legal ambiguity for businesses seeking to minimize regulatory constraints, the powers of the state at all levels over private property were far more extensive in Canada under the BNA Act than in the US where businesses could seek protection of their rights through the courts, at least up to the 1930s. Appeals by businesses of decisions made by Canadian regulatory bodies were thus stringently limited, so that the main arena for debate over these matters was in Parliament and the provincial legislatures. On the other hand, as will be seen, regulatory commissions and tribunals were inclined to be cautious about exerting their powers, and attentive to political pressures that could be brought to bear on the ministers and cabinets to whom they were accountable.

In Canada, both regulatory measures and crown corporations were sometimes initiated to advance overtly nationalist goals, particularly in the years after World War I when American economic and cultural influence was perceived to be expanding. From the late nineteenth century, some regulatory legislation was clearly designed to complement National Policy by protecting Canadian producers against foreign competition: licensing arrangements in the fisheries were intended to restrict American entry; 'inspection' fees levied on petroleum imports in the 1880s and 90s supplemented customs duties. In the 1930s crown enterprises such as Radio Canada and Trans-Canada Air Lines were created to head off the threat of large US entrants into these markets, and the regulatory bodies established in these fields used licensing and review powers to buttress the position of these national enterprises.[3]

The range of government regulation extended piecemeal between the 1880s and 1930s. Earlier chapters have touched on some of these activities, such as electric utility regulation, grain marketing, banking regulation and labour disputes arbitration. The federal government also monitored the production and distribution of food products, fertilizers, and drugs to prevent adulteration and false labelling, and regulated hunting, timber-cutting, and mining on Dominion lands. The first national park was established at Banff in Alberta in 1887. Between 1909 and 1921, a national Conservation Commission reflected the influence of the American conservation movement, but acted principally as an information-gathering body. Provincial regulatory measures encompassed mining and factory health and safety, workers' compensation boards, and mining and forestry on provincial lands. Outside the Maritimes, provincial governments controlled all subsoil resources. Regulation of insurance, trust and loan companies, and joint stock enterprises occurred at both federal and provincial levels. Jurisdictional disputes punctuated the history of water-power regulation with the federal government steadily retreating from assertions of control over navigable waterways from the 1920s on.

Along with banking, the Dominion government initiated measures in the early 1900s in two areas that impinged upon the operations of the largest corporate enterprises in the country: the establishment of the Board of Railway Commissioners in 1903, and the Combines Investigation Act of 1910. The history of these two laws and their enforcement indicates the complex character of regulatory politics and the limits of government intervention in the years before the Great Depression.

The federal government had, of course, been directly or indirectly involved in the development of the nation's railway system since Confederation. Regulation of railway operations, however, had been more haphazard in the late nineteenth century. In 1868 the federal Railway Act assigned such tasks to a cabinet committee, based essentially on pre-Confederation arrangements in the province of Canada. This Railway Committee was responsible for monitoring safety measures on rail lines, and, at least in theory, could review freight rates and establish limits on railway company profits.

In practice, there was relatively little governmental interference with the lines, even the publicly-owned Intercolonial Railway. Rates were set by company freight officials on a largely *ad hoc* basis, varying widely among routes and among shippers. In general, rates tended to fall in the late nineteenth century, but companies sought to compensate themselves for lower rates on competitive routes by charging higher tolls in areas where they controlled the market. In the most heavily competitive areas, such as southern Ontario where railways faced water-borne carriers as well as each other, major shippers could extort partial or total rebates of the tolls paid to the railways.

By the 1880s, disgruntled shippers were demanding more vigorous action by government to eliminate discriminatory freight rates and rebating. Rural communities in Ontario and the prairies who had initially welcomed the coming of railways now saw themselves as victims of monopolistic pricing and inadequate service. Merchants in the Maritimes and eastern Quebec, whose fortunes were declining as railways abetted commercial centralization in Montreal and southern Ontario, joined the chorus of complainants, along with retailers and small-scale manufacturers who felt they had to bear the burden of rebates granted their larger competitors.

With pressure growing from within his own Conservative party, Prime Minister Macdonald set up a Royal Commission in 1886. Two years later Parliament, following the Commission's recommendations, expanded the powers of the Railway Committee to resolve freight rate disputes, and also banned rebating. But shippers remained dissatisfied: few of them bothered to lodge complaints with the Railway Committee whose enforcement capabilities were limited. Meanwhile, the railway companies, emulating American lines, sought to stem the decline in rates by private negotiations among themselves. Although their efforts were not notably successful, rates did begin to stabilize in the late 1890s, and shippers were suspicious of these potentially collusive arrangements. Their suspicions seemed confirmed in 1898 by rumours of a secret agreement between the Grand Trunk and CPR to grant rebates to the American behemoth, Standard Oil Co., which had recently taken over Imperial Oil.

The Liberal regime under Laurier had undertaken to exert indirect control over railway rate decisions by encouraging competition—an approach that contributed to the chartering of new transcontinental lines, as discussed in Chapter Thirteen —and extracting concessions from the railways in return for subsidies, as in the Crowsnest Pass agreement with CPR. This was a time-honoured practice also followed by provincial governments: Manitoba, for example, imposed provisions for scheduled rate reductions and a ban on discriminatory rates in its 1901 contract with Canadian Northern Railway. But these methods were basically limited to situations where governments had some bargaining leverage over the companies. The Standard Oil episode helped convert Laurier's railway minister, A.G. Blair —with the Prime Minister as a reluctant follower— to the cause of regulatory reform. In 1903 the Board of Railway Commissioners replaced the Railway Committee, with authority over most provincial as well as federally-chartered lines, empowered to review and amend freight rates, and prevent discriminatory rates and rebating. Three years later the Board's authority was enlarged to cover telegraph and telephone companies operating across provincial lines.

Although Blair became the first chairman of the three- (later six-) person board, the central figure throughout its early years was Simon J. McLean, who had carried out a review of the railway situation for the government in 1899, drafted much of the original legislation, and served on the Board from 1908 to 1938. McLean, like Mackenzie King, represented a new element in Canadian governance, the intellectual academic-*cum*-bureaucrat: university-educated, usually in the emerging social sciences, and intent on bringing the skills of the nonpartisan 'expert' to the administration of public affairs. Although King quickly veered off into a conventional political career, McLean remained committed to the ideal of objective public service, providing an early example of the Ottawa 'mandarins' who flocked into the federal bureaucracy in growing numbers and with increasing influence on policy-making from the 1930s on. McLean (and King) were also, in the words of the Board's major historian, Ken Cruikshank, examples of 'policy entrepreneurs', bridging academic, political, and business communities to develop effective structures of public administration to deal with complex social and economic issues—much as professional managers were contemporaneously erecting systems of communication and control within the large corporate enterprises.

McLean, like Progressive reformers in the US, believed that regulatory agencies could be effective if shielded from partisan political influences, but he also concluded that American ventures into regulation were crucially weakened by a judiciary that, in America at least, was dominated by doctrinaire exponents of *laissez-faire* ideas. The act creating the Railway Board was thus carefully designed to limit appeals to the courts. At the same time, the Board was accountable to the cabinet, and its members had to be sensitive to the political as well as economic implications of their decisions. The Board's reviewing and discretionary powers were broad, but this characteristic was offset by the cautious instincts of the Commissioners who sought to mediate, if possible, rather than pass judgement on disputes, an approach that led critics to see them as defenders of big business rather than architects of a reformed transportation system.

In the US, many historians of government regulation subscribe to the 'capture theory', according to which regulatory commissions almost invariably have been transformed into creatures of the industries they were intended to regulate—with the Interstate Commerce Commission as a classic case. Dependent to a large extent on the information and technical expertise of the industrialists, often personally susceptible to blandishments offered by business (such as employment with large salaries after their terms end), government commissioners may end by sanctioning *de facto* cartels in the regulated industries rather than working on behalf of an ambiguously-defined 'public interest'. Some historians such as Gabriel Kolko have gone further, arguing that big businesses in the railroad and other industries promoted government regulation in the first instance in order to cartelize and eliminate smaller competitors.

Cruikshank and others who have examined the history of regulation in Canada are more cautious on these issues. The big railways did not vigorously oppose regulation, nor did they welcome it. Shaughnessy of the CPR, for example, lobbied unsuccessfully for the right of railways to appeal Board decisions to the courts on substantive as well as procedural grounds.

Board Commissioners were generally (with some exceptions, such as McLean) politicians or jurists with no direct ties to the industry either before or after their terms of office. At the same time, as politicians they were well aware of the crucial role of railways in the Canadian economy and consequently were willing to permit 'reasonable' differentials between long- and short-haul freight rates to help prop up heavily debt-burdened lines. More frequently, the Board found itself adjudicating disputes among shippers from different regions of the country—and its efforts to achieve 'equitable' results were perceived by those in the Maritimes and the west, as noted in Chapter Sixteen, as basically serving the interests of central Canadian businesses. During World War I, the government undercut the Board by directly authorizing rate increases. By the mid-1920s the Commissioners were badly divided over their appropriate role in resolving regional struggles, further undermining the Board's credibility.

By this time the federal government had taken over a substantial part of the railway industry, and all parties concerned with rates were turning to avenues of influence outside the Board to achieve their goals. The Board continued to function, however, reconstituted as the Board of Transport Commissioners in 1938 and reorganized again into the Canadian Transport Commission in 1967 with a broadened mandate — but still facing perplexing problems in determining its status *vis-à-vis* other instruments of government in the field: Parliament, the judiciary, and the crown corporations.[4]

If railway regulation provided at best a rather mixed record of effective government intervention, combines legislation represented an even more ambiguous example. Agitation against the 'trusts' spilled over from the US in the late 1880s and produced a measure against 'combinations' that acted 'to restrain or injure trade . . . lessen the manufacture of any article . . . [or] lessen competition'. The Liberal opposition in Parliament ridiculed the government's Act as meaningless as it attached the qualifier 'unlawfully' to its description of banned practices, and of no real consequence even to those businesses that might be prosecuted. Once in power the Liberals proposed in 1897 to give the measure some teeth by threatening to remove tariff protection from 'trusts' engaged in uncompetitive practices, but added their own weasel-word, 'unduly', to limit the likely application of the law, for which in any case enforcement provisions remained vague. Between 1889 and 1910 only eight cases were brought forward, all but one of them after 1903; five were successfully prosecuted, resulting in modest fines against the perpetrators.

Bliss argues that there was little real interest in this issue in Parliament, but this is not to say that opposition to cartels and 'monopolies' was nonexistent in Canada: western farmers campaigned against grain marketing 'combines', and small manufacturers railed against electric power companies throughout this period. Meanwhile, events in the US helped revive the energies of big-business critics in Canada. The Sherman Act had been rendered largely irrelevant in the 1890s by US Supreme Court decisions, but the American merger movement of 1899–1903 set the stage for a more vigorous antitrust effort. Although then (and later) the US government lacked the resolve and resources to systematically uproot big business, it was successful in 1909–11 in 'busting' two of the largest 'trusts': the explosives cartel dominated by Du Pont, and John D. Rockefeller's much-hated Standard Oil Co. Ironically, antitrust in the US simply spawned big business in tighter corporate forms, but at the time these events seemed to portend a more effective exercise of governmental control over business consolidations.

By 1909–10 the merger movement had spread to Canada and city dwellers experiencing inflation — which was attributed to the influence of these big consolidations on markets — added their voices to the agrarian chorus against

369

'monopoly'. In response, Laurier's ubiquitous Labour Minister, Mackenzie King, introduced the Combines Investigation Act in Parliament in 1910. King shared the view of many American as well as Canadian political leaders — including former US President Theodore Roosevelt—that antitrust was a blunt instrument which, if used rigorously, would destabilize the economy and penalize large enterprises that had acquired market power through technological and organizational innovations. It would be preferable to police 'abuses' of power rather than break up inherently efficient companies. In Britain at this time, there was a growing sentiment that their enterprises were, if anything, too small and inefficient, contributing to that country's declining industrial competitiveness. These arguments had a special resonance in Canada where even the largest industrial agglomerations were dwarfed by their American competitors.

Choosing regulation over trust-busting, King proposed to establish a typically convoluted process in which complaints about abuses of market power would be investigated by *ad hoc* boards convened for the occasion by the Minister of Labour. The definition of these abuses remained vague, but companies or 'combinations' found to be engaging in them could be subject to various penalties, including possible reduction of tariff protection. Perhaps not surprisingly, this law was enforced with less vigour than its predecessors: only one case was pursued between 1911 and 1923, and no action was taken.

Renewed concern over inflation in World War I led to the replacement of King's Act in 1919 by a Combines and Fair Practices law that empowered the short-lived Board of Commerce (see Chapter Eighteen) to initiate investigations of uncompetitive practices. After the 1919 measure, along with the Board of Commerce, was held unconstitutional by Britain's Privy Council, King—now Prime Minister—introduced a new Combines Act in 1923. Under this law a permanent official was installed in the Labour department with power to investigate mergers as well as collusive practices that might restrain trade 'against the interest of the public'. The continuing impotence of this regulatory venture is reflected in the fact that only 14 investigations were opened (in response to over 500 complaints) between 1924 and 1940, of which only one case involved a merger. Meanwhile the country witnessed a merger movement in the late 1920s of far greater magnitude than the pre-war consolidations.

The logical conclusion from this history is that Canada's political leaders had no intention of policing big business (much less busting trusts), but simply wished to de-fuse public outcries against 'monopolies'. The equally checkered history of antitrust in the US, and the experience of European countries and Japan with regulation of competition, suggests that the fundamental problem was not simply a lack of political will to enforce the law. Distinguishing 'good' from 'bad' trusts proved in practice to be a daunting task, and the 'public' was at best ambivalent about the evils (and virtues) of big business. During the 1930s public ire over economic hardships focused on large corporate enterprises, rekindling another outburst of antitrust enthusiasm; but World War II and the period of postwar prosperity muted much of this resentment. Canadians' sense of their vulnerability as a small, relatively open economy contributed to this ambivalence: in the 1970s a Royal Commission established in the wake of a new round of amalgamations concluded that the central problem for Canada was not the 'corporate concentration' it was set up to investigate, but rather the fragmented character of Canadian business which required more centralization and integration to prepare the country for the new era of global competition.[5]

In practice, government regulation was far less sweeping than the range of its activities would suggest. This outcome was not solely the result of pro-business attitudes on the part of Canada's political leaders—although they were inclined to be as solicitous of the interests of the large corporations their promotional policies had helped create as was possible while still responding to the demands of other constituents. The capabilities and financial resources of governments in the early twentieth century were quite limited. Before the introduction of income taxes their revenue sources were not substantial, and deficit financing was anathema to both the electorate and the business élites. Reliable statistical information about the economy was still rudimentary, focused principally on trade flows and government budgets: the Dominion Bureau of Statistics was not established until 1918, and employment levels were not measured until the Great Depression. Despite being less patronage-ridden than that in the US, government service in Canada remained a low-paid, poorly esteemed occupation, and university-educated figures such as S.J. McLean were exceptional. Universities in Canada were only beginning to mould themselves into centres for research and training in the natural and social sciences, and could hardly have supplied the recruits even if governments had sought them. For the most part neither political nor business leaders exhibited much interest in the academic world—with exceptions such as Joseph Flavelle who played a major role in reorganizing the University of Toronto and other institutions in the early 1900s. At a time when business people were just starting to wrestle with the problems of running large complex organizations, it is perhaps not surprising that governments proved less than fully capable of dealing with the equally thorny tasks of adjudicating economic controversies among a multitude of businesses and other pressure groups.

CONFRONTING THE GREAT DEPRESSION

What made the depression of the 1930s 'great' was not just its severity but also its long duration and seeming imperviousness to any remedial action. Canada and other industrialized nations had experienced downturns in the past—the depression of the 1890s was, arguably, even worse, at least for those who were unemployed and without access to the meagre relief that was provided in the 1930s. The short but steep slump following World War I had lasting effects, particularly on the Maritimes which never fully recovered from the collapse of their industrial base. But the Great Depression struck a Canadian economy that was already unstable, destroying the export markets and international capital sources upon which it was crucially dependent. Recovery from the catastrophic conditions of 1932–33, when over one-fifth of the country's labour force was out of work and gross national income was little more than half the 1929 level, was slow and incomplete up to World War II. The prolonged and debilitating slump reinforced the habitual caution of the business community, constraining new domestic investment and similarly limiting the willingness of political leaders to experiment with novel techniques of economic intervention. Ultimately, however, the sources of both the decline and recovery were well beyond the control of anyone in Canada.

The Great Depression was global in scope and in large part was the result of events stemming from unstable conditions in international finance and trade in the 1920s. The US stock market collapse in 1929 triggered a panic that spread to other capital markets world-wide but it was not in itself the 'cause' of the depression. By the late 1920s output of commodities—including wheat and newsprint, Canada's major exports—was exceeding demand; industrial investment as well was producing excess capacity in manufacturing, at least in terms of the existing consumer market, particularly in the US. These circumstances set the stage for a global trade war, inaugurated by the highly protectionist US Smoot-Hawley Tariff of 1930. Meanwhile, after the Wall Street crash, American bankers, whose credit had propped up the international economy in the late 1920s, began frantically recalling their loans. Other countries responded by imposing exchange controls and suspending the convertibility of their currencies: Britain and Canada left the gold standard in 1931, and the US did the same in 1933. By this point, world trade had collapsed to one-fifth of its 1929 level. Efforts to reconstruct the international system proved fruitless as countries scrambled to protect what was left of their domestic markets, dumping surpluses abroad. These developments fell particularly hard on the small, export-oriented Canadian economy.

Many of the actions taken by governments around the world proved inadequate or counterproductive. Protectionist measures and currency restrictions aggravated the rapid deterioration of international trade. As their revenue sources disappeared, governments retrenched, contributing to deflation and shrinking domestic consumer markets. Some social reformers looked as a model to the Soviet Union, where Stalin was introducing extensive state controls over the economy through his Five Year Plan. But none of the beleaguered capitalist nations chose this route, although the fascist states (and the US, briefly in 1933–35) experimented with enforced cartelization of industries to try to stabilize wages and prices. The remedies advocated by the British economist J.M. Keynes—a revamped international monetary system, and greatly expanded government spending to counter the decline in private sector investment and production—were not embraced until after World War II. Some countries, notably Nazi Germany and the US in the New Deal era, increased public outlays, but not as a result of conversion to Keynesianism. Germany's economic recovery in the mid-1930s was largely an incidental byproduct of Hitler's armaments program. In the US, President Franklin D. Roosevelt's New Deal was fashioned on an *ad hoc* basis, and his decision to cut spending in 1937 helped plunge the country back into depression until the outbreak of war in Europe restimulated the economy.

Canada's political leaders were no more, nor less, farsighted than their counterparts abroad. Mackenzie King and the Liberals were fortunate in that they were pitched from office in 1930 as the Depression's impact was just beginning to be felt, and returned to power in 1935 after the worst was past—earning an undeserved reputation for economic competence that helped stand them in good stead with the electorate for the next twenty-plus years. They also benefited from the fact that the Conservative leader, R.B. Bennett, was a virtual caricature of the bloated plutocrat, from his pince-nez to his spats.

Bennett had been one of the country's leading corporate lawyers, general counsel to the CPR, and board member of assorted other major enterprises before embarking on a political career. His initial program of action was very much in keeping with Tory traditions, combining protectionism with vague promises to 'blast' Canada 'into world markets'. When these remedies failed to show any effects, Bennett turned with increasing desperation to a variety of expedients in 1933–35. Many of these measures were torpedoed by the British Privy Council as unconstitutional, but several of his innovations—the Bank of Canada, Radio Canada and reciprocal trade negotiations with the US—were taken over, modified, and expanded by the Liberals after 1935.

Although Canada was badly battered by the Depression, some industries fared better than others and commenced recovery in advance of the economy as a whole. The staple-exporting sectors were particularly hard-hit and (except for minerals) slow to recover, acting as a brake on the rest of the economy throughout the decade. Wheat prices sagged from over $1/bushel in 1929 to little more than 50 cents/bushel in 1932. Drought and dust storms drove many farmers from the prairies in the mid-1930s and reduced overall output, but even with partial price stabilization through the Canadian Wheat Board after 1936, farm income was still only one-third what it had been in the late 1920s. Price declines in newsprint were not as dramatic, but in 1937 the industry was still operating at little more than half capacity: in this field market decline was aggravated by the overexpansion of investment in the merger boom of 1926–28. Other industries, including the railways, were similarly burdened with excess debt and capacity, augmented by the collapse of the wheat economy.

On the other hand, some of the domestic tariff-protected industries, such as textiles, were showing signs of life by 1933. The auto industry, which sank like a stone in the early 1930s, experienced a modest if incomplete recovery later in the decade, thanks both to protectionism and Bennett's push for Imperial Preference at the Commonwealth Conference in Ottawa in 1932—which also had the effect of temporarily redirecting Canadian exports toward Britain through World War II. The mining industries were also improving by mid-decade. The value of gold boomed in the deflationary conditions of the early 1930s, enriching speculators like Harry Oakes, and the arms race pushed up demand for nickel as the threat of war loomed in Europe and Asia. In striking contrast to the US situation, Canada's chartered banks survived the Depression without a single failure—reflecting the strength of the branch system, their orientation toward short-term commercial credit and a rapid liquidation of other debt, to the distress of the securities market, at the outset of the Depression.[6]

Pressures for government intervention in Canada reflected, in part, the varied fortunes of these industries in the Depression. Manufacturers and bankers in central Canada favoured protectionism (and later Imperial Preference) and balanced budgets. From the west and the resource industries generally emanated demands for more interventionist measures, expansion of the money supply, and reciprocal trade with the US. The unwillingness or inability of federal politicians in either of the major parties to accommodate these demands (except for trade agreements) stimulated the growth of more radical movements and experiments with interventionism at the provincial level.

But government intervention, such as it was, reflected more than Depression-stimulated pressures. The Bank of Canada, established despite opposition from most of the chartered banks, did not (as some westerners had hoped) inflate the currency; the economists who supported the idea stressed the role of the Bank as a source of long-term stability and representative of Canada's position in international dealings with other central banks (see Sidelight, p. 378). Likewise, the Canadian Radio Broadcasting Commission, established in 1932, functioned as a complementary National Policy, protecting Canada's airwaves. Renewed agitation against big business that led to the Price Spreads Commission in 1934 focused on small retailers' hostility to chain stores, a hostility antedating the onset of the Depression.

As in the case of the regulatory measures of the early 1900s, Depression-era interventionism was as much symbol as substance. In addition to hiking tariffs, when he first came to power Bennett initiated public works projects and relief aid to the provinces—a pointed contrast to King's miserliness. Imperial Preference was draped, as in the days of Sir John A. Macdonald, in the garb of Anglo-Canadian patriotism, even though the British were reluctant participants and the trade agreements had little immediate impact on the economy of either country.

The real intent of Bennett's abortive 'New Deal' proposals of 1935 is a matter of some controversy. By this point an election loomed and few of his earlier initiatives had produced much economic improvement. Bennett's brother-in-law, W.C. Herridge, stationed in the Canadian embassy in Washington, took note of the political benefits reaped by Roosevelt from his New Deal programs of 1933–34 and urged Bennett to follow suit. In January 1935 the Canadian Prime Minister, in a series of radio broadcasts, unveiled a variety of measures including unemployment insurance, old-age pensions, a new Combines law, and government marketing programs for wheat and other natural products. The proposals, when they came before Parliament, were rather less sweeping in substance, and in the next few years most of them were ruled by the courts to be unconstitutional invasions of provincial jurisdiction.

Many historians have dismissed Bennett's New Deal as largely a public relations ploy. But Bennett did not simply pull his proposals out of a hat. Many of the 'New Deal' and associated measures had been matters of considerable public debate before 1935 and had at least some support in the business community. The Wheat Board, which was reconstituted in 1935, had of course been set up originally by the Borden government at the end of World War I; Bennett had been involved in initiating the wheat pools in the early 1920s after the Liberal regime allowed the Wheat Board to lapse. Despite the virtual collapse of the pools in

1930, Bennett was at first cool toward reestablishing the federal Wheat Board, although he agreed to intervention in the form of government purchases of wheat surpluses in the futures market to try to stabilize prices.

In 1933 the Canadian government participated in an international wheat agreement negotiated in London which established export quotas and committed participants to try to impose production controls at home. Within a year, however, this agreement was unravelling, and western Canadian restiveness finally pushed Bennett to move toward direct controls. Still hoping to preserve the market system in some form, Bennett set up the Wheat Board as in effect a purchaser of last resort rather than a government marketing monopoly. Even this limited venture encountered stiff Liberal opposition, although King subsequently was obliged to retain the Wheat Board to keep his western political supporters on side.

Similarly the Natural Products Marketing Board established in 1934 was the culmination of a series of efforts by producers to stabilize commodity prices, first through voluntary agreements and then through provincial ventures into compulsory cartelization. In 1927 British Columbia fruit growers successfully lobbied for a provincial law empowering what was essentially a producers' co-operative to establish production controls and price floors for the industry; the arrangement was extended to dairy products in 1929. Two years later, however, these measures, along with a similar Saskatchewan law controlling grain production, were held unconstitutional by the courts since interprovincial sales were affected by them.

In this context the federal law was devised, under which local marketing boards would be authorized by a Dominion Board to control prices and output of various commodities entering interprovincial markets. To circumvent constitutional complications, similar provincial laws were passed to cover intra-provincial marketing. These arrangements were, however, insufficient to protect the Board from the British Privy Council which ordered its dissolution in 1937. Meanwhile, provincial governments in Nova Scotia, Ontario, and Quebec developed legally acceptable alternative measures for stabilizing prices in the dairy industry through the traditional exercise of licensing powers.

The theme running through all these complicated structures was the effort of the Bennett government to implement economic policies to combat the Depression while preserving the private property system. While Bennett was no more consistent in his philosophy than most politicians, there are continuities linking his support for the wheat pools in the 1920s to his Depression-era programs. As a big-business lawyer, Bennett was not doctrinaire about the sanctity of unrestrained competition and free markets: cartels and government intervention were acceptable in the interests of greater economic efficiency, or if necessary to head off more radical alternatives. Bennett was not unique in adopting this position: in the US both Presidents Hoover and Roosevelt (at least in the early phases of the New Deal) were prepared to sanction restrictions on the market system, preferably through 'voluntary' agreements in the private sector, with government providing appropriate incentives for their co-operation.

In Canada the Liberals were less inclined to tamper with markets, although perhaps more willing to engage in direct intervention through crown corporations, which maintained the distinction between public and private sectors of the economy. Even within the Conservative ranks, however, Bennett's views were contested, most notably by Harry H. Stevens. A Vancouver MP, first elected in 1911, Stevens was a long-time champion of B.C. business interests, which brought him into conflict with the CPR and other elements of the 'eastern' business establishment. In 1930 Bennett installed him in the cabinet as Minister of Trade & Commerce, a position of somewhat limited importance since Bennett tended to run the government as a one-man show. In 1934 Stevens took charge of a parliamentary committee (later reconstituted as a Royal Commission) to investigate charges that large retailers like Eaton's and the chain stores were using their market position to extort low purchase prices from small manufacturers while maintaining high mark-ups on prices to consumers. This 'Price Spreads' inquiry stirred up much interest and rankled a number of prominent (Tory) retailers. Before the end of the year Stevens and Bennett were at odds over the investigation, and Stevens resigned from the Cabinet.

One of Bennett's 'New Deal' proposals was the Dominion Trade and Industry Act which was intended to supersede the Combines Investigation Act. Although the new measure would prohibit discriminatory pricing, thus addressing the target of the Price Spreads investigation, the means of enforcement were (as usual) very weak. Essentially the Dominion Tariff Board—an agency set up in 1932 to monitor importers' appeals for relief from customs duties—was assigned the task of enforcement, removing the issue from the Labour department, where at least there were some knowledgeable officials on hand. In addition, the Board was authorized to allow collusive price agreements where it determined competition was 'wasteful'. Outraged, Stevens left the Conservatives altogether, forming his own Reconstruction party in the 1935 election. Although receiving only 9 per cent of the popular vote, the renegade 'party' cut into Tory support in Ontario and the west, which helped ensure Bennett's defeat.

Insofar as they were aware of these nuances of policy, members of the business community were not of one mind, except perhaps on the dangers posed by the CCF and other radical movements. Alvin Finkel in *Business and Social Reform in the Thirties* has argued that big-business élite were far more receptive to government intervention in the economy (at least on their terms) than many of the conventional political leaders in Canada. Not only government-sanctioned cartels but even social welfare measures found favour with at least some of these figures: in 1934 Sir Charles Gordon, president of the Bank of Montreal and Dominion Textiles urged Bennett, unsuccessfully, to have the federal government take over the burden of unemployment relief from the near-bankrupt municipal and provincial governments. Arthur Purvis, president of the Anglo-American chemical company, CIL, chaired the National Unemployment Commission, set up by the Liberal government in 1938, whose recommendations for national unemployment insurance, vocational education and public housing programs went far beyond anything contemplated at the time by Prime Minister King. For these businessmen, the need for social stability in the face of a prolonged depression took priority over fiscal caution and constitutional niceties.

A great deal more study needs to be done on business attitudes in this era before any firm conclusion can be drawn. If Purvis reflected a 'corporate liberal' viewpoint, this approach was rejected by others such as Joseph Flavelle, for whom government intervention permissible in wartime was unacceptable for a mere economic slump. In general it is fair to say that most businesses supported government measures that would help them survive the rigours of the Depression without necessarily endorsing interventionism in principle. As Finkel notes, Sir Herbert Holt promoted compulsory cartels in the newsprint industry to salvage his foundering venture, Canada Power and Paper, while denouncing a more conventional form of government promotion of the Beauharnois Power Co., whose project to harness the hydro power of the St Lawrence threatened Holt's control of the Montreal utility market. Small retailers who endorsed Harry Stevens' campaign against chain stores wanted the right to make their own price-fixing arrangements. Western business interests joined forces with farmers to urge the establishment of the Bank of Canada as preferable to the inflationary experiments advocated by prairie political spellbinders like Alberta's 'Wild Bill' Aberhart.

Bennett's last effort to salvage his political fortunes, the negotiation of reciprocity with the Americans, was expropriated by the Liberals (possibly with the connivance of sympathizers in the US government) and became for King the main instrument for pulling Canada out of the Depression. In 1934 the US Congress had opened a small gap in America's 'Chinese Wall' of tariff protection, authorizing the President to negotiate bilateral trade agreements that would reduce duties on imports from specific countries in return for appropriate reciprocal concessions. Despite his earlier advocacy of Imperial Preference, Bennett began testing the trade-negotiating waters in Washington as early as 1933. But talks moved sluggishly and remained incomplete when Bennett went down to defeat in October 1935. Within less than a month the new government of Mackenzie King had a reciprocity agreement in hand, the first major trade agreement between the two countries since 1866.

Reciprocity in 1935 involved only agricultural and other natural resource products, thus avoiding the wrath of the manufacturers lobby that had blocked Laurier's more ambitious initiative in 1910. Maritime fish processors were disappointed as the agreement excluded cod, in deference to New England interests; but by and large Canadian businesses were satisfied. US restrictions on Canadian whiskey imports were alleviated; in the 1920s they had been banned outright by American Prohibition laws—which had not prevented enterprising distillers such as the Bronfmans and Harry Hatch, owner of Hiram Walker's and Gooderham's, from participating in a thriving smuggling business. The repeal of Prohibition in 1933 opened prospects of a much larger trade.

In 1937–38, Canada negotiated a revised reciprocity agreement with the US, in the context of broader Anglo-American trade arrangements. The result of these convoluted negotiations—which involved talks with other Dominions as well as with the US and Britain—was that Canada lost preferential treatment in the British market for some (mostly agricultural) products, and removed some restrictions on US imports, including some industrial goods—thus arousing opposition from

377

THE BANK OF CANADA

The establishment of the Bank of Canada was the most substantial and enduring government measure of the Depression era; and although most of the chartered banks initially opposed it, in the long term they were probably the main beneficiaries. As with most other forms of government intervention in Canada, the sweeping powers allocated to the Bank were exercised cautiously by those entrusted with its administration.

Proposals for the creation of a central bank had surfaced before World War I, with support from at least some members of the banking community. During the brief but sharp Panic of 1907, many of the chartered banks had reached the limits of their capacity to issue bank notes as authorized under the 1871 Banking Act, stimulating demands for a more flexible system. When the outbreak of war in 1914 led to a run on the banks by alarmed depositors, the government passed a Finance Act which allowed banks to cover deposits with Dominion notes, issued as loans by the Minister of Finance, supplementing the banks' hard currency reserves.

Toward the end of the war there were proposals for a 'government bank' which would have exclusive powers to issue currency: this idea was particularly attractive to western Canadians who regarded the chartered banks as agents of 'eastern' business interests restricting their access to credit. Most bankers resisted the proposal, arguing that a government-controlled bank would be susceptible to political pressures to inflate the money supply; and of course they opposed the loss of their right to issue notes. A few, notably E.L. Pease of the Royal Bank, however, endorsed the concept of a central bank similar to the American Federal Reserve system, in which bankers exercised a substantial degree of influence over policies. But the Canadian Bankers' Association rejected a proposal along these lines in 1919 and successfully lobbied for continuation of the Finance Act arrangements through the 1920s.

The chartered banks weathered the worst of the Great Depression, but the methods employed to do so—foreclosing rapidly on delinquent debtors and maintaining high interest rates—rekindled western demands for government action to restrict their powers and expand the supply of credit. By 1933 several provinces were proposing to pass debt adjustment laws, and even Bennett recognized the need to take some action. As usual, a Royal Commission was set up, under a prominent British banker, Lord MacMillan, to review the alternatives. Meanwhile, one of Bennett's key advisers, Clifford Clark—like S.J. McLean, an economist and 'policy entrepreneur'—vigorously pushed for a central bank, on the grounds that it would provide a stable money supply, represent Canadian interests in the international banking community, and head off more radical demands for currency inflation. Despite continued resistance from the chartered banks, the MacMillan Commission found these arguments persuasive and Bennett's Finance Minister, E.N. Rhodes, introduced proposals for a Bank of Canada in early 1934.

By this time the bankers were isolated in their opposition. The Liberals under King, seeking to undercut the rising CCF on their left, criticized the Bennett proposal as insufficient in that it would establish the Bank of Canada as a private rather than government-

Prime Minister Mackenzie King and Graham Towers, Governor of the Bank of Canada, at the laying of the cornerstone of the Bank building in August, 1937. *(Courtesy Bank of Canada)*

controlled institution. The most contentious issue during the parliamentary debates focused on the question whether the Bank's notes would be issued in French as well as English. Although the Rhodes bill went through as originally drafted, after the Liberals returned to power, King proceeded to revise the Bank's charter in 1936 (and again in 1938), transforming it into a public institution issuing bilingual notes.

Meanwhile, the Bank of Canada opened its doors in 1935 under Graham Towers, a former official of the Royal Bank, whose training as an economist buttressed his credentials as an apolitical 'expert' with ties to the emerging public-service mandarinate. As Governor of the Bank from 1935 to 1954, Towers walked a fine line, seeking to preserve the institution from political influence and reassure the banking establishment of the essential 'soundness' of the Bank's policies while responsing to pressures for action to deal with the economic crisis. With British Columbia, Alberta, Saskatchewan, and Manitoba all sliding into bankruptcy in 1935-36, these pressures focused on demands that the Bank bail out the provinces through loans to cover their outstanding bonds. Towers feared that any such action would set a dangerous precedent for the Bank, carrying out

⟶

tasks more appropriate for the elected federal government. After much man-oeuvering, he persuaded King on this point, and also prodded the Prime Minister to initiate a Royal Commission to review the whole field of federal-provincial financial arrangements.

During World War II the Bank's role expanded beyond its initial mandate to cover seasonal fluctuations in the money supply to encompass exchange controls and wartime financing. Under Towers in the early postwar years the Bank used its powers to modulate the pace of economic growth, to the general satisfaction of both bankers and the government. Later, the Bank's position *vis-à-vis* the government would become more controversial as it sought to constrain inflationary pressures, leading to at least one occasion during the Diefenbaker era when the cabinet exerted its authority to remove an overly independent Governor, James Coyne. By the 1970s the Bank of Canada was perceived by the banking community, ironically, as a bastion of financial prudence besieged by spendthrift politicians rather than as a dangerous experiment in government economic intervention.

Sources

Granatstein, J.L., *The Ottawa Men: The Civil Service Mandarins, 1935-51* (Toronto, 1982), 49–61.

Granatstein, J.L. and Doug Owram, *The Government Generation* (Toronto, 1986), 210–15.

Grayson, Linda M.,'The Formation of the Bank of Canada, 1913-38' (PhD diss., University of Toronto, 1974).

Neufeld, E.P., *Bank of Canada Operations and Policy* (Toronto, 1958).

Watts, George S. *The Bank of Canada: Origins and Early History* (Ottawa, 1993).

the Canadian Manufacturers' Association. On the other hand, Canada gained greater access to the US market for a range of products, including codfish; and the 1938 agreement removed or raised American quotas on other imports the 1935 reciprocity deal had left intact. King could also point to the 47 per cent increase in US-Canadian trade, and a 27 per cent rise in gross national income in 1935–37 as results of reductions in continental trade barriers.

Although the renewed slump in the US economy in 1938 eroded these gains, the Liberals remained committed to trade policy as the main route to recovery. In 1938, King set up a Royal Commission to look into ways of streamlining government financing and services in the federal system. By the time the Commission's report came out in 1940, wartime mobilization and prosperity had replaced Depression-era concerns. But its proposals, which included a federal take-over of unemployment compensation and old-age pensions, laid the groundwork for Dominion-provincial revenue-sharing programs that flourished in the years after World War II.[7]

The disruption of trade between Canada and the US in the early 1930s did not destroy other business relationships that had been growing since the turn of the century. The tariff wars of the Bennett era stimulated an increase in the number of US manufacturing firms entering Canada from 534 in 1929 to over 800 by 1936, although the level of total investment declined. Reciprocity led to the departure of a few of these companies but improving economic conditions in the later 1930s brought an increase in investment as US companies in the auto and mining industries began to expand capacity in Canada. In 1939 the book value of US direct investment was back to pre-Depression levels at close to $2 billion (US), with manufacturing accounting for about 60 per cent of the total.

Although the badly battered newsprint industry remained in the doldrums throughout the decade, its continental character produced an unusual experiment in trans-national cartelization, involving governments on both sides of the border. Even before the onset of the Depression, the Quebec and Ontario governments had been backing efforts by pulp and paper companies to establish voluntary price and production agreements. With one of the largest firms, the American-owned International Paper, refusing to co-operate, the cartel disintegrated by 1930. When the US government embarked on its own venture into compulsory cartelization, the National Recovery Administration, in 1933, Canadian newsprint companies hastened to join their American counterparts in a 'code of fair competition'. US newspaper publishers, however, campaigned vigorously against the Canadian participants who were summarily excluded in 1934, shortly before the NRA was itself dissolved by US court order. At this point, the premiers of Quebec and Ontario joined forces with the Newsprint Association of America to reconstruct the cartel, using their control over forestry leasing permits to bring recalcitrant (and for the most part financially vulnerable) producers in line.

Direct investment did not flow only in one direction, although the American tide was inevitably more significant. Five Canadian banks, numerous insurance and trust companies and over 70 manufacturers had branch operations in the US by the mid-1930s, representing about $250 million (US) in direct investment. Most of these had been established before the Depression, but Canadian whiskey distillers and brewers set up shop in the US during the hiatus between the repeal of Prohibition and Reciprocity. Hiram Walker built the largest distillery in the world in Illinois. The Bronfmans followed this lead, acquiring full control over Distillers Co./Seagram's from their British partners in the process, eclipsing Hiram Walker as the largest whiskey producer in Canada by the 1940s and becoming the world's premier distiller in the post-World War II era. Although the US was the main area of Canadian foreign investment from the 1920s, some of the largest individual firms continued to be found in the utilities field in Latin America up to World War II. With combined assets of over $500 million (Cdn) in 1935, the three Canadian 'utility multinationals' in Brazil, Mexico and the Caribbean comprised one-quarter of the country's total overseas investment.

Despite its devastating effect on particular firms and industries, the Depression did not fundamentally alter the structure of business consolidation that had emerged in Canada between 1909 and 1929. As indicated in Table 17.1, the impact of the economic crisis was particularly hard on the newsprint and steel industries: by 1933 three of the largest pulp and paper companies and two of the three leading iron and steel firms were in receivership. Companies whose fortunes were tied to agriculture, such as Massey-Harris, or to consumer goods also suffered huge losses. At the same time the utilities and mining companies, despite

Table 17.1 Impact of the Great Depression on Canada's Twenty Leading Non-Financial Corporations[a] (Ranked by Assets, 1929)

RANK 1929	ASSETS, 1929[b]	EARNINGS, 1929[b]	ASSETS, 1935[b]	EARNINGS, 1935[b]
CPR	1,225	52	1,373	24
International Paper	393	5.1	270	n/a
Imperial Oil	223	23	199	25.7
Abitibi	178	7.9	121	c
Minn. & St Paul RR	177	9.9	172	−5
Bell Telephone Canada	151	9.3	212	8.5
MacKay Co.	122	5.4	125	−1.6
Canada Paper	117	5.3	83	c
Dominion Steel	106	6.4	42	−0.6
Montreal Light	103	3	175	0.5
International Nickel	96	14.5	198	18.5
Price Bros.	85	3.4	64	c
Duluth & South Shore RR	66	−0.8	70	−21
Twin City Transit	65	2	64	0.3
Duke-Price	64	3.9	62	4.3
Imperial Tobacco	63	4.8	70	5.8
Massey-Harris	59	2.7	31	0.2
Hudson's Bay Co.	57	2.4	36	0.2
Steel Co. of Canada	56	5.3	62	3.7

[a]Excludes crown companies, private firms (no public stock offerings) and companies with principal assets abroad (e.g., Brazilian Traction Co.)
[b]All figures in $ million (Cdn) at current values. 'Earnings' = net earnings before taxes.
[c]Companies in receivership in 1934–35.
SOURCE: *Canadian Annual Financial Review* (Toronto 1929; 1935).

relatively sluggish earnings compared to the 1920s, continued to dominate the economic landscape; and several, most notably Bell Canada and International Nickel, grew substantially during the Depression decade. Even in the most beleaguered industries, well managed firms such as the Steel Co. of Canada or Ontario Paper fared reasonably well.

At the same time, in contrast to the US in particular, the 1930s did not witness in Canada the emergence of new, technologically innovative enterprises: there were no Tom Watsons or Juan Trippes on the scene, and the successful entrepreneurs of the era, like K.C. Irving or Sam Bronfman, tended to move into established markets. As was the case with government policies, in the Canadian business community the Depression reinforced traditions of caution rather than experimentation, a return to the tried-and-true on the part of the investing public rather than pioneering into unknown markets with novel technologies.

Notes

[1]For staple-oriented views of business-government relations in Canadian history, see Hugh G. Aitken, 'Defensive Expansionism: The State and Economic Growth in Canada', in Aitken, ed., *The State and Economic Growth* (New York, 1959), 79–114; and W.T. Easterbrook, *North American Patterns of Growth and Development* (Toronto, 1990). The political economists' approach is reflected in R. Tom Naylor, *Canada in the European Age* (Vancouver, 1987), parts IV and V; see also Wallace Clement, *The Canadian Corporate Élite* (Toronto, 1975), ch. 2. The 'corporate liberal' interpretation has been most fully developed for US history. See, for example, Louis Galambos and Joseph Pratt, *The Rise of the Corporate Commonwealth*; and, for a left-wing version (probably more influential in Canada), the classic work by Gabriel Kolko, *The Triumph of Conservatism* (New York, 1963). Among Canadian studies often cited as reflecting this approach are Nelles, *The Politics of Development* and Traves, *The State and Enterprise*. A good succinct statement of this view is offered by Traves, 'Business-Government Relations in Canadian History', in K.J. Rea and Nelson Wiseman, eds, *Government and Enterprise in Canada* (Toronto, 1985), 8–19. Bliss's views are developed in *Northern Enterprise* (and his earlier writings), and summarized in Bliss, 'Forcing the Pace: A Reappraisal of Business-Government Relations in Canadian History', in V.V. Murray, ed., *Theories of Business-Government Relations* (Toronto, 1985), 106–19.

[2]For a survey of regulatory initiatives among industrial countries, see Morton Keller, 'The Regulation of Large Enterprise: The US Experience in Comparative Perspective', in A.D. Chandler, Jr and Herman Daems, eds, *Managerial Hierarchies* (Cambridge, Mass., 1980), 161–81. See also Keller, *Regulating a New Economy* (Cambridge, Mass., 1991). On US railroad (and other) regulation, see Thomas McCraw, *Prophets of Regulation* (Cambridge, Mass., 1984). On Britain's factory legislation, see Oliver MacDonagh, *Early Victorian Government, 1830–70* (London, 1977); and A.J.M. Taylor, *Laissez-Faire and State Interventionism in Nineteenth Century Britain* (London, 1972).

[3]For general overviews of Canada's experience with government regulation, see J.A. Corry, *The Growth of Government Activities Since Confederation* (Ottawa, 1939), a study prepared for the Rowell-Sirois Royal Commission; Carman Baggaley, *The Emergence of the Regulatory State in Canada, 1867–1939* (Ottawa, 1981), prepared for the Economic Council of Canada. See also G. Bruce Doern, *The Regulatory Process in Canada* (Toronto, 1978); and Margot Priest and Aron Wohl, 'The Growth of Federal and Provincial Regulation of Economic Activity, 1867–1978', in W.T. Stanbury, ed., *Government Regulation: Scope, Growth and Process* (Montreal, 1980), 69–149. On the regulatory conundrums of the insurance industry, see Christopher Armstrong, 'Federalism and Government Regulation: The Case of the Canadian Insurance Industry, 1927–34', *Canadian Public Administration* 19 (Spring 1976), 88–101. On the background to Radio Canada, see Frank Peers, *The Politics of Canadian Broadcasting, 1920–51* (Toronto, 1969). TCAL is discussed in Chapter 18.

[4]On railroad regulation in the US, see Ari and Olive Hoogenboom, *The ICC* (New York, 1976); Gabriel Kolko, *Railroads and Regulation, 1977–1916* (New York, 1965). An alternative view that sees the ICC as both 'uncaptured' and ultimately a destructive force in the railroad field, see Albro Martin, *Enterprise Denied: The Origins and Decline of American Railroads* (New York, 1971). On railway regulation in Canada, see Ken Cruikshank,

Close Ties: Railways, the Government and the Board of Railway Commissioners, 1851–1933 (Montreal/Kingston, 1991); and Baggaley, *Emergence of the Regulatory State*, 69–114. In *Monopoly's Moment*, Armstrong and Nelles offer an equally complex interpretation of the growth of regulation in the electric utility industry in Canada.

[5]On antitrust in the US, see William Letwin, *Law and Economic Policy in America* (New York, 1965); and Martin J. Sklar, *The Corporate Reconstruction of American Capitalism* (New York, 1988). On the Combines laws in Canada, see Michael Bliss, 'Another Anti-Trust Tradition: Canadian Anti-Combines Policy, 1889–1910', *Business History Review* 47 (1973), 177–88; Carman Baggaley, 'Tariffs, Combines and Politics: The Beginning of Canadian Competition Policy, 1885–1900', in R.S. Khemani and W.T. Stanbury, eds, *Historical Perspectives on Canadian Competition Policy* (Halifax, 1991), 1–52; Paul Gorecki and W.T. Stanbury, *The Objectives of Canadian Competition Policy, 1888–1983* (Montreal, 1984); L.A. Skeoch, *Restrictive Trade Practices in Canada* (Toronto, 1966), part I. *The Report of the Royal Commission on Corporate Concentration* (Ottawa, 1978) encountered mixed reviews and did not put to rest concern over big business influence, as reflected in such books as Diane Francis' *Controlling Interest: Who Owns Canada?* (Toronto, 1986)—which, however, emphasized family dynasties rather than corporations. Post-World War II developments are discussed in Chapter 20.

[6]On the international dimensions of the Great Depression, see Charles Kindleberger, *The World in Depression, 1929–39* (Berkeley, 1973); and John A. Garraty, *The Great Depression* (San Diego, 1986). On Canada, see A.E. Safarian, *The Canadian Economy in the Great Depression* (Toronto, 1970).

[7]Depression-era economic policies are discussed in Baggaley, *Emergence of the Regulatory State*, 163–204; see also J.H. Thompson and Allen Seager, *Canada, 1922–39: Decades of Discord* (Toronto, 1985), chs 10–12. Pierre Berton, *The Great Depression 1929–39* (Toronto, 1990) presents a particularly acidulous view of both Bennett and King, not to mention the business community in this era. On Bennett's policies, see Larry A. Glassford, *Reaction and Reform: The Politics of the Conservative Party Under R.B. Bennett, 1927–38* (Toronto, 1992), chs, 5–6. On King's approach, see H. Blair Neatby, 'The Liberal Way: Fiscal and Monetary Policy in the 1930s', in Michiel Horn, ed., *The Depression in Canada* (Toronto, 1988), 257–73. On divisions in the business community, see Alvin Finkel, *Business and Social Reform in the Thirties* (Toronto, 1979); Bliss, *Northern Enterprise*, ch. 15; Richard Wilbur, *H.H. Stevens* (Toronto, 1977), ch. IV–VI. T.D. Regehr, *The Beauharnois Scandal: A Story of Canadian Entrepreneurship and Politics* (Toronto, 1990) presents a fascinating glimpse of the internal workings of politics and business in Canada. On US-Canadian trade relations, see Richard N. Kottman, *Reciprocity and the North Atlantic Triangle, 1932–38* (Ithaca, N.Y., 1968); and Ian Drummond and Norman Hillmer, *Negotiating Freer Trade: The U.K., the U.S., Canada and the Trade Agreements of 1938* (Waterloo, Ont., 1989).

18 THE ARSENAL ECONOMY

War forced the pace of government intervention in the economies of industrialized nations in the twentieth century; not coincidentally, the requirements of industrial mobilization for war established close and continuing relations between governments and significant elements of the business community. Traditional methods of blockading trade were supplemented in the twentieth century by new instruments of economic warfare: the 'blacklisting' of merchants suspected of trading with the enemy, the 'freezing' of bank accounts and other forms of liquid capital held by citizens of an enemy state, and the confiscation of their fixed assets. The financial requirements of total war led to the imposition of income taxes, initially covering the wealthy and business corporations and eventually embracing virtually the entire population. Shortages of labour and materials created by the diversion of resources for war production prompted the introduction of wage and price controls to check inflationary pressures, and direct state involvement in labour-management relations. Ultimately, most governments established centralized controls over their economies to give priority to production for military needs, and state-owned enterprises sprouted in specific war-related industries.

Although these ventures into a command economy were usually dismantled when the emergency conditions of war abated, they provided government and business leaders alike with evidence of the potential capabilities of centralized economic organization. At the same time, those who had to deal with wartime bureaucracies became aware of the limitations of state power—although for many contemporaries the euphoria of victory may have masked these deficiencies. Finally, the mobilization of economies for war generated government subsidies to certain defence-related industries that by the 1950s had fashioned a system of special relationships popularly designated the 'military-industrial complex'.

The extent of war-stimulated government interventionism varied among industrial countries. During World War I, state controls were probably most advanced in Germany, France, and Britain: by 1915–16, these governments had imposed comprehensive wage and price controls and established centralized state agencies to allocate labour and resources for war production. The United States, which did not enter the war until 1917, moved with less alacrity toward a command economy; its major agency for economic mobilization, the War Industries Board, functioned primarily through 'co-operative' committees of private business leaders. Virtually the entire apparatus of direct government controls was dismantled after the war, although income taxes endured as a permanent feature of the economic landscape.

During World War II, European governments resorted again to direct controls, and even in the US a variety of centralized agencies (sometimes competing with each other) was in place by 1942. But perhaps the most enduring legacy of that war for Americans was the establishment of a system of indirect incentives — 'cost-plus' contracts, tax write-offs, and government loans—to encourage private sector conversion to war production. This system was resurrected as the primary mechanism for government economic mobilization during the prolonged arms race of the Cold War era, reaching its apogee in the early 1960s, and resurging in the 1980s, entailing major changes in the structure and location of American industrial activities.

The Canadian experience of wartime mobilization parallels that of the US, albeit on a much smaller scale and with some peculiarly 'Canadian' features, notably the extensive reliance on crown corporations to carry out tasks that private enterprise was deemed unable, or unwilling, to undertake. During World War I, after a fair amount of confusion and hesitation, the government moved to establish various economic control measures, although the major instrument of industrial mobilization, the Imperial Munitions Board, was linked to the British rather than the Canadian government. World War II featured a far more activist government effort, including a plethora of crown corporations, some of which continued to operate beyond the wartime emergency, particularly in the field of atomic energy. During the Cold War era, peaking in the mid-1950s, the government briefly ventured into erecting a mini-military industrial complex centred on the aircraft industry, only to abandon the effort amid great (and continuing) controversy.

One notable by-product of this century's war mobilization was a strengthening of links between US and Canadian industrial economies. During both world wars, but especially in 1941–45, continental economic integration was vigorously pursued by governments on both sides of the border. In the Cold War years, a more piecemeal integration of defence-related industries took shape, accompanied by development of Canada's 'strategic' raw materials principally for US military procurement agencies.

Business leaders played a major role in government programs to mobilize the Canadian economy for war. While the government gave lip service to the notion that war preparedness was 'everybody's business', and the Ottawa 'mandarins' retrospectively highlighted their own significance in these undertakings, the upper echelons of wartime agencies were dominated by 'dollar-a-year' men from private industry — not too surprisingly, given the close ties between big business and federal political parties in Canada since the age of Macdonald and the CPR, if not indeed throughout Canadian history.[1]

WORLD WAR I

In 1914 Canadians were no more prepared for war in industrial terms than they were militarily. After the Boer War—Canada's only significant military involvement since the Northwest Rebellion of 1885 — the government had contracted with a Scottish promoter, Sir Charles Ross, to manufacture a rifle for the Canadian militia; his factory in Quebec had yet to produce any volume of weapons when

Canada followed Britain into the European war. Aside from a Dominion arsenal in Quebec, Ross was the only military manufacturer in Canada. Following Laurier's Naval Bill of 1910—which had contributed to his political demise—the British arms maker, Vickers, had been lured into setting up a shipyard in Montreal; but as of the summer of 1914 delays in bringing the bill into force dissuaded Vickers from any major investment.

Not surprisingly, arrangements for military procurement took shape in a haphazard fashion. Shortly after the outbreak of war, Britain's War Minister, Lord Kitchener, contacted the Canadian Militia Minister, Sam Hughes, with an order for shell components for the British army. Hughes sought, unsuccessfully, to interest the U.S. Steel Corporation in the contract. American manufacturers were technically barred from such activities by US neutrality—although, curiously, Vickers was able to negotiate a deal with an American firm, Electric Boat Co., for assistance in the production of submarines in Canada. In any case, Hughes then turned to some 'reliable' associates, setting up a Shell Production Committee under Alexander Bertram, a Montreal steel maker. An assortment of contract brokers also turned up in London and New York, bearing letters from Hughes identifying them as 'agents' of the Canadian governmnent soliciting war orders; the most notorious of these characters was J. Wesley Allison whose alleged profiteering and shady dealing would contribute to Hughes' eventual downfall.

Rumours of profiteering, patronage, and mismanagement of military orders under Hughes' aegis prompted Prime Minister Borden to set up a War Purchasing Commission, excluding Hughes, in the spring of 1915. But procurement for British war orders remained in the hands of the Shell Committee despite increasing dissatisfaction with that agency's operations. Aside from complaints from Canadian businesses that Bertram and other cronies of Hughes were monopolizing contracts, the Shell Committee seemed demonstrably incompetent. Ten months after the outbreak of the war, the Canadians had only managed to deliver 3 per cent of British orders totalling $170 million. Problems of production were partly a consequence of Bertram's lack of organization—he tried to run the entire operation out of his own office, assisted only by an agent in London—but also reflected underlying weaknesses in Canada's industrial capabilities, particularly in quality control. Canadian manufacturers lacked the precision equipment and skilled workers necessary to produce munitions meeting the requirements of the British military.

Similar problems plagued the suppliers of Canadian arms. Ross proved unable to deliver on orders to supply rifles to the Canadian army: as late as 1916 only two-thirds of a 1914 contract for 100,000 rifles had been met. Troops in the field found the weapons faulty and unreliable. Despite Hughes' fulminations, in 1916 Borden cancelled the 'Ross rifle' and Canadian forces were resupplied with British-made Lee Enfield weapons.

Meanwhile, in Britain similar episodes of mismanagement and political favouritism in arms production had led to the establishment of a centralized Ministry of Munitions under David Lloyd-George in early 1915. The Canadian Shell Committee's failures generated pressure from London to place all arms production for

British needs in Canada under the control of the new Ministry, or at least to remove Hughes and his cronies from the process. In November 1915 Borden agreed to replace the Shell Committee with a new agency, the Imperial Munitions Board, which would be directly responsible to the British Ministry of Munitions rather than the Canadian government. Borden's choice as chairman of the IMB was Joseph Flavelle, head of the Toronto meat packing firm, William Davies Co., who had a reputation for disinterested public service and, of course, impeccably Conservative political credentials. Shortly thereafter, in the wake of scandals over the Ross rifle and Allison's activities, Hughes was forced out of the government altogether.

The IMB's achievements, in contrast to the sorry performance of the Shell Committee, contributed to Flavelle's reputation as an organizational genius. Defenders of Hughes have argued that, despite its failings, the Shell Committee laid the groundwork for Canadian industrial mobilization; in any case the period 1914–15 was a time of *ad hoc* experimenting and on-the-job learning for all the warring industrial states. In some areas, such as steel ship construction, the IMB performed with little more distinction than its predecessor. Furthermore, Flavelle's approach to organization was not too different from Bertram's, or for that matter most of Canada's industrialists. As Bliss points out, in running both the IMB and his private enterprises Flavelle consistently emphasized personal leadership, decentralization and teamwork among 'reliable' associates rather than the development of complex systems of organization. In contrast to the American situation, where the War Industries Board stimulated visions of close relations between government and business to promote national economic objectives, Flavelle and his fellow Canadian war mobilizers emerged with their views of a 'traditional' business-government relationship relatively intact.

At the same time, that 'traditional' relationship in Canada was not based on purely *laissez-faire* principles, and Flavelle was quite willing to extend government economic intervention when circumstances required. As early as 1904, Flavelle had endorsed Borden's proposal for a single government-owned western railway; and during the debates over railways in 1916–18, he continued to press for amalgamation and nationalization of the country's rail lines.

The IMB operated primarily through contracts with private companies, parcelling out over $1.23 billion in orders from Britain between 1916 and 1920. Nevertheless, Flavelle did not hesitate to set up government-controlled concerns to produce materiel unavailable from private suppliers, or to take over private companies (Ross's factory was 'nationalized' in 1917) that consistently failed to produce the quantity and quality of production required. Seven 'National Factories' were created during the war, producing such items as acetone for explosives, detonation fuses, and aircraft frames. These ventures were placed under managers recruited from the private sector and were all closed down or returned to private ownership after the war.

Flavelle also saw to it that orders were spread reasonably widely throughout Canadian industry, although (as in World War II) the major beneficiaries were in Ontario and Quebec, which received over three-quarters of the contracts.

Flavelle's efforts to avoid the charges of favouritism and corruption that had swirled around the Shell Committee were not always successful: in 1917, the Davies company was alleged to have profiteered on its sales of bacon to Canadian troops. Although the IMB had nothing to do with these transactions, Flavelle's presumed political influence and his reputation for unctuous self-righteousness fuelled the controversy. Notions about conflict of interest were at best rudimentary in Canadian business and political circles; indeed, the emergence of this issue as a matter of public debate was largely the result of wartime scandals.

Although the IMB was independent of the Canadian government, its operations helped impel that government to further forms of intervention in the economy. By diverting industrial resources to war production, the IMB contributed to shortages and inflationary pressures in the domestic civilian economy that ultimately required the government to play a role in controlling wages and prices—although these measures fell considerably short of centralized planning. At the same time, the IMB's links with US industrial suppliers, particularly in 1917–18, contributed to the country's balance of payments difficulties and led to at least a partial integration of the two economies to deal with the allocation of continental resources for war production.

In late 1916 a combination of factors—the IMB's activities, an unexpectedly poor wheat harvest, and abrupt increases in demand for Canadian newsprint—produced a rapid rise in consumer prices, precipitating strikes in some industries and general complaints against hoarders and profiteers. Facing the prospect of an election the following year, the Borden government moved gingerly toward establishment of economic controls. W.G. O'Connor, a Halifax lawyer and associate of Borden, was appointed Commissioner of the Cost of Living in the Department of Labour to investigate charges of hoarding and price gouging. While limited, the Commissioner's powers were not inconsequential: it was his report on meat packers, leaked to the press, that led to the public outcry against the Davies company and Flavelle.

By 1917 Controllers had been appointed to allocate food, paper, and fuel supplies. In 1918 a War Trade Board was in place to co-ordinate with a corresponding agency of the US government, with licensing authority over imports and exports to ensure the flow of essential materials to war industries. Government conciliation boards sprouted to deal with labour disputes on the railways and in the war plants. These various agencies engaged in unprecedented efforts to gather systematic statistical information on production output, the labour supply, wages, prices, and related matters.

The Armistice of November 1918 brought a halt to most of these experiments in state activism, but the immediate postwar period witnessed a brief resurgence of intervention in certain areas. As discussed in Chapter Sixteen, a Canadian Wheat Board operated in 1920–22 as a successor to the wartime Board of Grain Supervisors. A more ambitious though even more short-lived undertaking was the Board of Commerce, created in 1919 to cope with steeply rising prices in a range of consumer goods. Its controversial career was terminated in less than a

year, shortly before the courts ruled that it represented an unconstitutional extension of federal power.

Although the Board was meant to try to hold down prices, control profiteering
and, incidentally, block potentially monopolistic cartels, it was initially supported
by some business groups, most notably sugar refiners who hoped the agency
would impose price stability that the industry was unable to secure through voluntary agreements. In its early actions the Board did indeed prop up prices for
sugar and other commodities, seeking to ensure a steady flow of goods by guaranteeing producers reasonable profits. But it was subject to cross-pressures from
consumers and wholesalers demanding lower prices and other industrialists
opposed to any regulation. Newsprint producers,in particular, resented the Board's
efforts to restrict their exports in order to ensure adequate paper supplies to Canadians. By early 1920 the Board's inconsistent policies had alienated virtually all
interested parties. Ultimately the government refused to sanction the Board's decisions, the commissioners resigned, and the agency disintegrated even before the
British Privy Council demolished it as a legal entity. If nothing more, the Board's
unhappy history starkly revealed the limited nature of state power except in the
extremities of wartime.

A more enduring legacy of World War I was the strengthening of economic
links between Canada and the US, reflecting both the decline of British financial
power and the emerging continental nature of Canada's business relations. Here
also the IMB played a significant albeit less than enthusiastic role, a consequence
of Canada's increasing technological as well as financial dependence on the
Americans during the war.

In the early stages of the war the Canadian government turned to its traditional
source, the British money market, to finance anticipated increased costs. But by
the middle of 1915 it was apparent that British financial resources could not be
tapped further for Canadian needs. The Minister of Finance, Thomas White, sceptical of Canada's ability to mobilize domestic capital, turned—for the first time
in Canadian history—to the New York market, floating a $45 million loan. White
also issued $50 million in 'Victory bonds' in Canada which, to his surprise, were
oversubscribed by double that amount. By 1919 almost $2 billion had been raised
from the Canadian public. In 1916 the government introduced a business profits
tax, and followed with an income tax, purportedly only for the duration of the
war. Although domestic revenue sources thus became an important component
of war finance, the government continued to rely heavily on borrowing in the US.
By 1917, Canada's balance of payments deficit with the US was approaching
$400 million.

In theory, IMB contracts were financed by the British government, but in fact
all but a small proportion of this total was covered by advances from the Canadian
government to Britain at a rate of $25 million per month from July 1916 to the
end of the war. The Canadian government in turn had to depend on a steady flow
of US money to sustain these operations.

Beyond these circuitous financial connections, the IMB had more direct links
to US businesses. As the example of Vickers and Electric Boat indicates, Canadian

manufacturers relied on the Americans for a variety of needs. Coal, oil, and copper for industrial processes flowed in from the US, and the war plants also imported machine tools, gauges, chemicals for explosives, and aircraft engines. The war had substantially increased Canada's dependence on US imports at the expense of Britain, achieving in practice the goal the rejected Reciprocity Agreement of 1911 had sought to accomplish. The British never regained the share of the Canadian market they had occupied prior to the war.

While welcome from a military standpoint, American entry into the war in 1917 created a dilemma for the IMB and the Canadian government. The US military would now have first call on American producers, although in the short run Canadian war industries were better prepared to make use of these supplies. Of more immediate concern was the problem of financing. By 1917 Britain was largely dependent on American loans, and the Americans were in a position to demand preferential treatment for their suppliers. Even before the US officially declared war, American companies were filling British (and French) contracts; neutrality, as the Germans bitterly pointed out, was little more than a word. A full-scale shift of British orders to the US—which the British threatened unless the Canadian government took on the full burden of financing their IMB orders—would imperil the Canadian war economy. Compounding these difficulties was an American government ban on further foreign borrowing which raised Canada's balance of payments deficit with the US to a crisis situation. During the summer of 1917 some Canadian manufacturers began moving their operations across the border or selling their assets to Americans.

Flavelle, who had been a vigorous opponent of the Reciprocity Agreement in 1911, was a reluctant convert to continentalism. Nevertheless, in the fall of 1917 he dispatched emissaries to Washington to try to secure a place for the IMB in American economic mobilization arrangements. Fortunately for the Canadians, the US military faced a crisis of its own since it was having to compete for supplies with America's allies and the industrial mobilization effort was in chaos. An agreement was worked out under which the US Army Ordnance department would place orders with the IMB, although the Canadians would have to accept a 7 per cent differential, on the grounds that labour costs were lower in Canada (which was not in fact the case) and that the US government would forgo collecting war taxes on this production.

The IMB-Ordnance Agreement did not in itself significantly transform the IMB's operations. By the end of the war only $178 million, or about 16 per cent, of IMB contracts came from the US. It was offset by $130 million in orders that the IMB was obliged to parcel out to American manufacturers since the Canadians had also agreed to accept competitive bidding on British contracts. The agreement did, however, smooth the way for negotiations ensuring that a portion of US loans to Britain would be earmarked for financing British contracts with the IMB in Canada. In 1918 when the US War Industries Board was empowered to allocate all raw materials and industrial supplies for American war production, the Canadians were able to secure a portion of these supplies to keep their own industries running—thanks in large measure to vigorous lobbying by Lloyd Harris, scion of the Ontario farm machinery family and president of his own auto firm, who headed the Canadian War Mission in Washington. The sudden end of the war blocked further movement toward continental economic integration for the time being, and Canadian manufacturers were the first to suffer when the WIB began cancelling war orders. During 1919–20, enterprising Americans came to Canada to buy surplus Canadian industrial assets and inventory at bargain prices.

Michael Bliss has maintained that for Canada World War I was 'business as usual', leaving no deep or lasting imprint. This conclusion may be a bit exaggerated. Certainly by 1920 the IMB and most of the other wartime agencies had closed shop, and the government's forays into economic planning were brief and not very successful. After the postwar recession, manufacturing output was somewhat larger than at the peak of the Laurier boom, but there were no significant shifts in the size of the workforce in most industries, and prewar trends toward regional centralization of manufacturing and the growth of clerical occupations were, if anything, reinforced by the war.

There were, however, some enduring changes in the business community as well as in particular industries. Largely because of special wartime circumstances Cominco acquired a zinc process and Ontario a nickel refinery. Prairie farmers acquired at least a vision of the potential capabilities of centralized processing and marketing through wheat co-operatives. Corporate and income taxes, despite the promises of Finance Minister White, were here to stay. The War Measures Act, with its provisions for government economic controls, remained on the books for future emergencies. While continental economic integration flourished only partially and briefly, the war hastened trends that carried Canada away from its traditional orientation toward Britain as the major source of capital and market for its products. Although the Great Depression temporarily interrupted this process, it could be said that for Canada the 'American century' commenced at the very moment that Canadians were acquiring a sense of their national identity on the battlefields of World War I.[2]

WORLD WAR II

Although the outbreak of war in Europe in 1939 came with considerable forewarning, Canada was not much better prepared than it had been in 1914. This situation was due in part to the resolutely isolationist position of the prime minister, Mackenzie King, but other factors played a role. The Depression had eroded the morale as well as the assets of Canadian businesses, and a sharp slump in 1937–38 after the modest recovery of mid-decade left industrial production well below 1929 levels. Federal government efforts to develop national economic policies were stubbornly resisted by the premiers of the two largest provinces, Ontario and Quebec. Following the Munich crisis in autumn 1938, King increased government expenditures on military needs from $36 million to $65 million, and both the navy and air forces (such as they were) had begun upgrading after 1936; but King was deterred from more substantial measures by his sensitivity toward antiwar sentiments in Quebec that, as he could well recall, had helped topple Laurier from office in 1911.

In 1937 the British government, beginning its own belated military build-up, had arranged to underwrite the costs of production of Bren guns by a Toronto firm, John Inglis Co., generating an acrimonious debate in the Canadian Parliament over allegations of political favouritism by the Liberal government. This episode, with its overtones of World War I controversies over contracting, put yet another damper on King's enthusiasm for war preparedness. Aside from the Inglis contract, only National Steel Car Co. of Hamilton was engaged in munitions production on the eve of war in September 1939. The Bren gun affair did, however, persuade the government to establish a Defence Purchasing Board (later the War Supply Board) with guidelines in place for competitive bidding and a 5 per cent profit rate on contracts.

Meanwhile, National Steel Car had joined forces with other Canadian manufacturers in a project that laid the groundwork for what was to be one of the country's most successful ventures in war production. In the spring of 1938 the British Air Ministry dispatched a mission to North America to secure contracts for production of British-designed planes. Interested companies agreed to establish a joint venture, Canadian Associated Aircraft Ltd, to take on some of this work. Although King's response to the venture was initially cool, once the war began his views shifted. Canadian airframe manufacturing would fit in with the proposed British Commonwealth Air Training Plan (BCATP) to use Canada (and other Dominions) as training grounds for pilots and crews, a scheme that offered the advantage of limiting Canada's military contribution to the war effort while maximizing economic benefits at home. Although the Associated Aircraft operation was short-lived, a number of firms took over contracts to build trainer planes while King used the BCATP to secure re-election of his government in early 1940, confounding his provincial and pacifist rivals.

Spring 1940 also witnessed the fall of France and aroused fears that Britain faced invasion by the Axis powers. These events strengthened public support for the war effort and galvanized the Canadian government to mobilize the nation's resources. Military spending for 1940–41 increased tenfold over 1939 levels. A Department of Munitions and Supply with sweeping powers over industrial production and raw materials was established, absorbing the War Supply Board. To head this new department, King turned to Clarence D. Howe, his Minister of Transportation who had already established a reputation for effective, if abrasive, administrative leadership. An American-born engineer, Howe had run a successful firm designing and buiulding grain elevators and terminals at the Lakehead before embarking on a political career in the mid-1930s. In King's Cabinet from his first term, Howe had overhauled the Board of Railway Commissioners and the CNR, reorganized the government's administration of harbour facilities, sponsored the bill creating the Canadian Broadcasting Company, and established Trans-Canada Air Lines, the first of many of what Howe regarded as 'his' crown corporations.

Like Flavelle in World War I, Howe was to earn a reputation at the Department of Munitions and Supply as a master organizer, and went on after the war to run, directly or indirectly, so many departments and agencies that by the 1950s he was hailed (or denounced) as the 'Minister of Everything'. To his admirers, who included a number of businessmen he recruited to run war agencies, Howe was a Napoleonic figure: decisive, efficient, a master of details. To some historians, however — including Bliss — Howe's reputation is overinflated. Despite his image as a 'businesslike' minister, Howe functioned best in situations, as in World War II, where volume production rather than cost or quality control was the major measure of achievement. Like Flavelle, Howe's approach to organization involved selecting 'reliable' people to head his agencies and then leaving them to run things. But his criteria for choosing leaders was sometimes idiosyncratic—Ralph Bell, the Nova Scotia fish-packing magnate, was asked to run the Aircraft Division, for example, because he had experience flying a plane—and their effectiveness was linked, at least partly, to their personal relations with him. Howe feuded with other strong-willed figures, notably H.R. MacMillan, the B.C. timberman, who dared to question his methods of running the Munitions department in 1942; and he was openly contemptuous of critics in Parliament, displaying an arrogance that became even more apparent in the postwar era.

Whatever his failings may have been, Howe was an energetic and versatile figure who, through the force of his own personality, provided a sense of overall direction to the war mobilization effort. Business confidence was inspired not only by Howe's reliance on 'practical' businessmen to run the wartime bureaucracies but also by generous contracting policies, similar to those eventually introduced in the US to arouse corporate enthusiasm for the war effort. Government loans and subsidies to contractors were supplemented by provisions for accelerated depreciation of the valuation of war plants and other assets for tax purposes.

At the same time, Howe endeavoured to avoid episodes such as the Shell Committee scandal, adhering to the War Supply Board guidelines of 5 per cent profit rates, with efforts to recover excess profits. War production demands were sufficiently large that charges of favouritism, as in the Bren gun affair, were generally avoided though not absent. In 1941, for example, CCF critics in Parliament raised questions about the large number of war contracts awarded Canadian Industries Ltd, a joint subsidiary of the American company Du Pont, and Britain's Imperial Chemical Industries, whose president, Arthur Purvis, was on leave to serve as head of the British Purchasing Mission in New York.

Maritime businesses complained of regional discrimination in the disposition of contracts and government investment in manufacturing. Dosco's president, Arthur Cross, asserted in 1941 that the Munitions department had poured $4 million into steel companies in central Canada when his own firm had idle capacity. He attributed this situation to Howe's preoccupation with the postwar industrial interests of his home province, Ontario; others called attention to the close ties cultivated with Howe since the mid-1930s by Algoma Steel's chief, Sir James Dunn. Maritime shipyards protested the government's construction of new facilities on the Great Lakes and the reluctance of the Munitions department to

394

expand ship repair capacity on the Atlantic coast in favour of Montreal, contributing to the problems of naval convoys during the critical period of the Battle of the Atlantic in 1941–42. While shipbuilding and repair work represented the largest proportion of war contracts awarded to the region, only 6 per cent of all wartime ship construction was done in the Maritimes, while British Columbia accounted for almost half the total—perhaps not surprisingly, in the view of critics, since Howe's Director-general for Shipbuilding was H.R. MacMillan.

Howe had little patience with the CCF (or with Maritime manufacturers for that matter), but he also—again like Flavelle—had few qualms about using the full powers of the state, seizing private factories (National Steel Car among them) and creating a wide range of crown corporations. Forty-six such entities were established to produce aircraft, ships, chemicals, optical equipment, and targeting devices as well as munitions; to build houses for workers in the new war plants; and to allocate raw materials to contractors. Most of these crown corporations were intended only for wartime requirements, but Howe also deployed them to develop Canadian industrial capabilities for the postwar period in fields such as machine tools, metal fabrication, and aircraft engines.

One prominent example of this kind of venture was the Polymer Corporation. In the wake of Japanese conquests in southeast Asia in early 1942, North America faced serious shortages of natural rubber. Even before this point, Canada was experiencing problems: in 1940 Howe set up Fairmont Co. to stockpile rubber and other scarce materials through foreign purchases and acquisition of scrap materials for recycling. After Pearl Harbor, however, it was recognized that these sources would be inadequate, particularly since the Americans had mounted their own rubber stockpiling operation. In the 1930s petroleum and chemical companies in the US, Britain and Germany had been experimenting with processes to develop synthetic rubber from fossil fuel by-products, but little had been done in this field in Canada. To develop synthetic rubber capacity, Howe set up Polymer Corporation in 1942 and contracted with the Michigan firm, Dow Chemical, and a subsidiary of Imperial Oil (whose parent, Jersey Standard, had carried out the most advanced research in the field before the war) to provide technical and managerial assistance. Raw materials were acquired from the Rubber Reserve Co., a US government enterprise that was also engaged in a crash program to develop synthetic rubber. By early 1944 a plant was in operation in Sarnia, Ontario, at a cost of about $50 million. By the end of the war Polymer had produced over 785,000 tons of tires, tire cording, and other rubber products.

After the war most of the crown enterprises were closed down or sold to private companies. Polymer, however, was retained in government hands — in part because no interested buyers could be found willing to pay the asking price, but also because Howe regarded it as one of his great success stories and was reluctant to part with it. Polymer continued to operate at a profit through the 1950s, eventually diversifying into plastics and other petrochemical products. In 1972, as Polysar Ltd, it was folded into the Canada Development Corporation. Another wartime crown enterprise, Eldorado Mining, also remained under government control, initially for national security purposes, and was subsequently linked with

Atomic Energy of Canada Ltd to form the base of the country's ambitious venture into the nuclear power field.

Howe and his disciples asserted, with some justification, that these wartime measures ensured that — in contrast to the World War I experience — Canada emerged in 1945 with a strong and diversified industrial base. The comparison is not entirely clear cut, however, since the post-World War II era was one of generally sustained economic growth, unlike the unstable and uneven record of the 1920s. Altogether, $1.3 billion went into new capital investment in industry during the war, with the Munitions department accounting for $800,000, disposing of about half these assets to private enterprise when the war ended. The transportation network, the merchant marine and the construction industry also benefited from this wartime investment, enhancing the infrastructure as well as manufacturing capabilities.[3]

Without markets, the creation of this enlarged capacity would have been a formula for disaster, as indeed had been the case in the aftermath of World War I. Howe and other government officials were naturally preoccupied with the development of Canada's export trade as the war economy wound down in 1945–46. But exports were not the major ingredient in Canada's economic growth in the immediate postwar period. Wartime employment, a rising birth rate, and forced savings laid the groundwork for an enlarged domestic consumer market, augmented by an unprecedented net inflow of immigrants in the early 1950s.

As in World War I, the massive diversion of resources into war production contributed to shortages and inflationary pressures in the civilian market, pushing the characteristically hesitant prime minister toward imposition of economic controls. Shortly after the declaration of war in 1939, a Wartime Prices and Trade Board (WPTB) was set up in the Labour department; import and foreign exchange controls were introduced; and trade in some 'luxury' items was curtailed (whiskey was not so designated; even economic controllers needed their scotch). In 1940, wage ceilings were imposed and a range of new business profits and excise taxes introduced. By mid-1941, however, as the cost of living rose to 7 per cent, the Canadian Manufacturers' Association began supporting demands from the Bank of Canada for more substantial measures. In September of that year, the WPTB was transferred to the more politically formidable department of Finance, and placed under an energetic official from the Bank of Canada, Donald Gordon. The government then imposed a full-scale wage and price freeze.

Like Howe, Gordon recruited bankers and other businessmen to administer the WPTB system, which helped smother complaints from the private sector, and mounted a vigorous publicity campaign to secure public support for controls. Producers and distributors were offered subsidies to offset cost pressures, in order to prevent them from trying to pass costs along to the consumer. They were also tacitly encouraged to reduce the quality of goods and services if necessary to hold the price line. Rationing of gasoline, tires, some food products, clothing, and other items was introduced. Labour relations in war-related industries were brought under federal jurisdiction to keep wages in line with prices. Labour opposition, which spread through 1943, punctuated by strikes in steel mills and aircraft plants, was partially offset by provisions for union recognition in collective bargaining in the war plants; and this was extended to cover all industries under a 1944 law, optimistically dubbed the 'Magna Carta of Labour'. The right to strike was banned for the duration of the war (not entirely successfully) and compulsory conciliation boards were established.

Historians differ over the effectiveness of wage and price controls in Canada in World War II. J.L. Granatstein and others point out that from October 1941 to April 1945 the cost of living rose by less than 3 per cent; and that, whatever its faults, the Canadian controls were probably more successful than similar exercises in other countries. Bliss, however, emphasizes the wide range of exemptions and exceptions allowed by the WPTB and the precarious nature of public support which dwindled rapidly as the end of the war approached. Farmers, with Jimmy Gardiner a vigorous spokesman in King's cabinet, fought a rearguard battle against controls, and meat rationing was lifted temporarily in 1944–45 under pressure from this quarter. Other primary producers were able to get increases on the grounds that their prices were artificially low when the freeze was imposed. Contemporary critics argued that the subsidy arrangements benefited well-organized manufacturing groups and retail chains while smaller merchants were ignored. On the whole, however, it seems fair to say that controls were more effectively applied during World War II, and phased out in a more orderly fashion in 1945–46, than had been the case during and after World War I — due in part at least to the administrative and public relations skills deployed by Gordon and his 5000-plus controllers. Gordon's success led to his later recruitment to run the Canadian National Railways from 1949 to 1965. The effectiveness of controls and rationing helped create a pent-up consumer demand that buoyed the Canadian economy after the war.

In retrospect, probably the most significant development of World War II was the strengthening of economic links between Canada and the United States. The circumstances that produced this outcome were similar to those that prevailed in 1916–18, but in World War II they took effect more rapidly and with more enduring consequences.

As noted earlier, the British government had begun scouting the prospects for Canadian munitions procurement in 1938, and dispatched a British Purchasing Mission to Ottawa shortly after the outbreak of war with the Commonwealth Air Training Plan in hand. The British proposed that Canada should bear about 40 per cent of the costs (the other Dominions would absorb a smaller amount) and Britain would cover its share through purchases of Canadian wheat and other raw materials, and, if necessary, the sale of British assets in Canada. The Canadians insisted on a smaller financial commitment, which was achieved by reducing the estimated costs of BCATP. All this dickering shortly proved to be beside the point since all estimates were unrealistic and Britain's incapacity to pay was apparent even before the end of 1940. By this time most British investments in Canada had been liquidated and gold transfers were drying up. As in 1916, Britain wanted the Canadian government to effectively take over the financing of war production in Canada.

The Canadian government had been able to substantially increase its revenues by boosting income tax levels and expanding them to cover more than one-fifth of the population. Rising employment due to war production helped raise revenues from $467 million in 1939 to over $1 billion by the end of 1941, with corporate and business profits taxes contributing about one-quarter of this total. Additional revenues were raised through government bond and treasury certificate sales, totalling $745 million in 1940 and $1.3 billion in 1941. By this time, however, expenditures were running well over $1 billion a year with the end of the war nowhere in sight.

More critical was the problem of balance of payments. Even before the war, Canada had run deficits in trade and payments with the US, offset by exports to Britain. Wartime demand had of course boosted exports to Britain, particularly in value-added manufactured products, but the expansion of Canadian war production aggravated deficits in the American account. One third of parts and materials for Canadian industrial operations had to come from US sources. By the spring of 1941 Canada faced a $478 million balance of payments deficit with the US, with every indication that this would increase, and Britain made it clear that it could no longer cover the costs of imports from Canada.

The United States was (again) officially neutral, but President Franklin Roosevelt was openly sympathetic toward Britain, and had circumvented Congressional restrictions by arranging for sales of US goods to Britain (and Canada) on a 'cash and carry' basis since 1939, subsequently transferring 'surplus' warships to Britain in 1940. With British financial resources depleted by March 1941, Roosevelt sponsored a 'Lend-Lease' bill in Congress that would permit large-scale exports of war materiel to Britain without requiring immediate compensation — although Americans would later use this aid as a lever in postwar trade negotiations. The dilemma for Canada was that, as in 1916, Lend-Lease would incline the British to redirect all war production orders to the US, except those the Canadian government was willing to finance. The Canadians were also reluctant to request direct aid through Lend-Lease, as this might create pressures from the American side for liquidation of all Canadian assets in the United States.

There were two factors working in Canada's favour: first, thanks to Howe's Munitions department, Canadian industrial plants were geared up for war production while US economic mobilization was floundering. Secondly, Mackenzie King had directed much effort to cultivate ties with Roosevelt—who in any case was inclined to see Canada's welfare as vital to America's long-term interests: in 1940, the two leaders had established a Permanent Joint Board of Defence to co-ordinate continental military measures. In April 1941, shortly after passage of the Lend-Lease bill, King and Roosevelt negotiated the 'Hyde Park Agreement' under which the US would place up to $300 million in military contracts in Canada for 1941, and a portion of the $7 billion authorized under Lend-Lease for British war orders would be earmarked for the Canadians. Canada was not obliged to sell off American assets, and even the foreign exchange controls imposed by Canada in 1939 were left undisturbed.

Howe wasted no time exploiting the new situation, creating War Supplies Ltd to sell Canadian products in the US, and dispatching one of his prized protégés, E.P. Taylor, to wheel and deal for contracts among the chaotically disorganized procurement bureaucracies in Washington. Between May 1941 and the end of the war, War Supplies Ltd netted over $1 billion in US orders. Taylor went on to succeed CIL's Arthur Purvis as head of the British Purchasing Mission in the US, and after the war created Argus Corporation, that made him by the 1950s one of Canada's wealthiest figures, a mid-century Max Aitken. Meanwhile, US Lend-Lease aid to Britain rose to $30 billion before the end of the war, with Canada procuring orders that topped $1.4 billion. Altogether, Canada spent about $9 billion on military production in World War II, exporting more than one-third of this total.

The Hyde Park Agreement opened the way for more far-reaching economic links between the two countries, particularly after the US entered the war in December 1941. In contrast to World War I, a Canadian representative sat on the Combined (Anglo-American) Resources and Production Board established in 1942; and after some dickering, Canada also gained a seat on the Combined Food Board. Meanwhile, by the end of the war Canadian-US trade exceeded $2 billion a year, a figure larger than Canada's total trade average in the years just before the war. Almost three-quarters of Canada's imports came from the US, reflecting a trend underway since the negotiation of Reciprocity in 1935.

Under the umbrella of continental defence measures, the US government also constructed a variety of military installations and infrastructure, particularly in the Canadian west, including air fields, radar stations, and a highway to link Washington state with Alaska at a cost of $130 million.

Among the most controversial of these undertakings involved construction of an oil pipeline from Norman Wells in Canada's northwest to Fairbanks, Alaska. This 'Canol Project' was poorly planned and eventually abandoned, but it drew the attention of both Canadian and some American businesses to the potential resources of this wilderness region. During the 1920s, Imperial Oil had discovered oil and set up a modest refinery at Norman Wells on the Mackenzie River in the Northwest Territories. In 1942 the US War department decided to build a pipeline to link Norman Wells to planned air bases in the Yukon and Alaska. Despite advice from Imperial that the oil supplies were limited and of poor quality, the US military hastily embarked on the project at a cost of over $130 million over two years—by which time the strategic value of the pipeline had largely vanished. Excoriated by a US Congressional investigation, the War department decided to abandon the pipeline less than a year after it went into operation. Although Imperial had increased its estimates of the Norman Wells field's potential, neither the company nor the Canadian government were interested in acquiring the pipeline. At the same time, however, the Canadian government—irked by the arbitrary way that US authorities had gone about this project—decided to buy the Alaska Highway, in part to avoid further incursions. Meanwhile, Imperial Oil found the results of its role (subsidized by US government funds), modest through

399

they were, sufficiently encouraging to step up exploration and drilling in the less remote hinterlands of Alberta.[4]

Canada emerged from World War II with a greatly enlarged manufacturing base, including some industries that had not previously existed, and a potentially strong domestic consumer market. The federal government had extended its position in the national economy, and its leaders felt confident of their capabilities to play a major role in reshaping postwar Canada. Although the impetus for expanded social welfare programs introduced toward the end of the war was largely a political response to the growing popularity of the CCF, such measures as family allowances, old-age pensions, and an enlarged federal role in economic planning also reflected the ambitions and visions of Ottawa's bureaucratic mandarins.

The war also accentuated economic ties between Canada and the US. While the Hyde Park arrangements elapsed as the economies 'reconverted' to peacetime, close trade relations were maintained. American mining and petroleum companies took a renewed interest in Canadian resources. The Canadian political environment was hospitable to such investment, which spilled over readily into manufacturing and services. For a period of time after the war Canada was in the happy position of having both strong domestic and healthy export markets, enabling the country's businesses to solidify wartime gains, while new inflows of capital helped buoy the economy, especially after 1950. The roller-coaster conditions of the 1920s were thus avoided as the country enjoyed its most sustained growth since the Laurier era. The onset of the Cold War would extend that record of prosperity while accelerating the trend toward continental integration.

MOBILIZATION FOR COLD WAR, 1949–59

Even before the end of World War II, the 'Grand Alliance' of Britain, the US and the Soviet Union was coming asunder as the victors debated the future of Germany and eastern Europe. By 1947 the USSR and the western powers were on a collision course, and both sides prepared for a protracted era of tension. During the early stages of the Cold War, the US relied primarily on various forms of foreign economic and military aid to 'contain' what was perceived as Soviet expansion. By 1950, in the wake of the Soviet A-bomb test and the communist revolution in China, America began to rearm, and the outbreak of a shooting war in Korea hastened the pace of remilitarization. For the Canadian government, and for Canadian business, these developments presented both problems and opportunities.

While the most immediate issues in 1945 involved reconversion of the economy to peacetime levels, government officials were particularly anxious to sustain Canada's export trade. In 1944 at Bretton Woods the Americans had proposed to use their financial power to reconstitute the international monetary system and to pressure or cajole other countries into a multilateral reduction of trade barriers. Although Britain's 'sterling bloc' was one of the main targets of this effort, the Canadian government was in favour of measures that would also prevent a resurgence of US trade protectionism. To help resurrect British markets, Canada in 1945 offered a postwar loan of $1.25 billion.

Britain, however, was far worse off than anyone had imagined, and after the Canadian government dismantled economic controls and restored its currency to parity with the US dollar in 1946, American goods poured into Canada. By early 1947 Canada again faced balance of trade deficits with the US reminiscent of 1941, which the floundering economies of Britain and western Europe could not offset. Between 1945 and 1946, Canada's balance of payments with the US was transformed from a $30 million surplus to a deficit of $600 million.

At this point the US unveiled the Marshall Plan which would channel billions of dollars in aid to western Europe to help rebuild these economies, bolster the region against 'social unrest' (translated for the US Congress as Soviet subversion), and incidentally revitalize these markets for American exports. Again, as in 1917 and 1941, Canada faced a dilemma since US aid would not guarantee markets for Canadian goods. In the fall of 1947, Canadian officials once again trekked south, while King threatened to impose import quotas to demonstrate the gravity of the situation.

The Americans proved remarkably accommodating. As in the case of Lend-Lease, Canada was allowed to take over a portion of the Marshall Plan orders from Europe—which ultimately came to over $1 billion between 1948 and 1950. Howe, who had been 'Minister of Reconstruction' since 1944, added Trade and Commerce to his portfolio to spearhead the export drive. American trade officials also introduced a more dramatic proposal, to establish a US-Canadian customs union. Although Howe and other members of King's cabinet supported the proposal, the prime minister—who could still recall the fate of his mentor, Laurier, in 1911—ultimately demurred. Canada did, however, participate in the General Agreement on Tariffs and Trade (GATT), committing the country to dismantle its protective tariff system, although this process was to take thirty years.

Canada's participation in the Marshall Plan marked the beginning of a steady course of continental economic and military collaboration. The mining industry was an initial beneficiary of this trend. During World War II Canada had been a major supplier not only of uranium to the Manhattan Project but also nickel, lead, and zinc for America's military needs. Even before the onset of the Cold War, the US Congress had authorized development of stockpiles of 'strategic materials'. Unfortunately for Canada, this law gave preference to US suppliers and was buttressed by prohibitive duties on a range of minerals, measures that fell particularly hard on Alcan which had substantially increased its aluminum capacity in World War II. By 1948, however, American stockpiling authorities were increasing their purchases of Canadian minerals. After the outbreak of war in Korea, Congress quadrupled stockpile targets. In the following year a Materials Policy Commission chaired by William Paley projected an even vaster increase in US stockpile requirements. The prospect of this bonanza had already attracted US mining companies into Canada: $1.4 billion in new investment in mining and smelting facilities poured in between 1945 and 1955, most of it coming after 1950.

Growth in mining investment and exports was not restricted to stockpiled materials. World War II almost exhausted the iron ore reserves of Minnesota's Mesabi Range; and as early as 1942 the M.A. Hanna iron company of Cleveland was scouting the prospects for new iron sources in northern Quebec and Labrador. Seven years later, five American steel firms joined Hanna to form the Iron Ore Co. of Canada, investing over $250 million in the region between 1949 and 1954. The development of Labrador's iron reserves had an additional spin-off: American steel makers began to lobby vigorously for construction of the St Lawrence Seaway, a project dear to Canadian (or at least central Canadian) hearts since the 1920s, but which had been thwarted by opposition from American railroaders and eastern seaboard business interests. Despite their continued resistance, the measure was pushed through the US Congress as necessary for 'national security' in 1954; the Seaway opened for business five years later.

The Korean War also resurrected continental economic mobilization. After World War II the Permanent Joint Board on Defence engaged in desultory discussions of this issue and a Joint Industrial Mobilization Committee was set up in 1949. Canadian officials lobbied with modest success for a share in US military procurement provided under the Mutual Defense Assistance Act, that country's first step toward rearmament in that same year. Even after the outbreak of war in June 1950, however, the Americans, anticipating a swift victory, were only prepared to accept the principle of reciprocal arms purchases with Canada without attaching a dollar figure. Chinese intervention in the war in November of that year precipitated more vigorous activity on both sides of the border.

The Canadian government, with the Liberals still in power, announced a $5 billion rearmament program in 1951 and established a Department of Defence Production (DDP) with Howe, naturally, at its helm. As usual, Howe used tax concessions and other incentives to stimulate arms production, although there was little reliance on crown corporations; and, as usual, Howe relied on informal negotiations with his US counterparts to flesh out the reciprocal arms trade agreement made in October 1950. Although the Canadians continued to bicker with the Americans over aluminum exports—an issue of diminishing importance as the Canadian aircraft industry began to absorb more domestic output after 1951 —there were relatively few major controversies. In 1951–52 there was some cause for alarm as the DDP spent $500 million more in purchases from the US than it earned from arms sales; but by 1953 the trade balance was evening out, abetted by US stockpiling as well as more US procurement of military equipment in Canada. Conventional military spending began to tail off after the Korean armistice in 1953, but stockpiling continued to grow and the US began to develop a system of radar installations across Canada to protect the US against Soviet long-range bombers. These projects created some construction jobs although there was limited use of Canadian industrial suppliers.

There was one further by-product of the Korean War: what could be called an industrial development strategy that had been gestating in an *ad hoc* way since World War II. The basic premise of this strategy was that Canada had reached a level of competence sufficient to support development of a limited number of technologically-advanced industries—drawing, as in the past on foreign sources of capital and knowledge, but intended to establish the base for an innovative and diversified industrial economy. Atomic energy was one strand of this approach, but Howe, at least, focused on two interrelated pet projects—a Canadian airline and a domestic aircraft industry—although the centrepiece of the latter, Avro, proved to be more of a tar baby.

Howe's interest in aviation went back to his pre-World War II days as Minister of Transport. In the 1930s Canada had no cross-country air service, although the Winnipeg grain merchant, James Richardson, was trying to construct one, enlisting support from the two major railways. Howe, however, decided early on to develop a government-owned line, initially luring the presidents of CPR and CNR to serve on its board, and recruiting Philip Johnson, a former executive with Boeing Aircraft and United Airlines in the US to head the crown enterprise, Trans-Canada Air Lines, launched in 1937. Beatty of the CPR pulled out when it became clear that Howe would exercise real control over TCAL. In 1939 he acquired Richardson's network and created a subsidiary, CP Airlines, that established a strong foothold in the west. Canadian airlines thus duplicated the mixed public/private configuration of Canadian railways and utilities. Another potential rival emerged briefly in World War II when Lord Beaverbrook contemplated developing a British Commonwealth air line system—which, fortunately from Howe's viewpoint, never got off the ground.

Howe resisted efforts to privatize TCAL, and showered it with largesse whenever the opportunity arose, beginning with air mail contracts in 1938. The Air Transport Board, established in 1944 to regulate airlines, was under the authority of the Transport Minister and up to 1967 was in effect required to give TCAL any routes it applied for; CP Air, on the other hand, did not acquire a transcontinental route until 1959 after Howe and the Liberals had been thrust from power. The rationale for this apparent favouritism was that TCAL provided service to commercially unprofitable areas of the country.

Through the 1950s, CP Airlines focused on the international market while lobbying against the domestic routing structure. Although it acquired a firmer foothold in the domestic market in the following decade—by which time even the resurgent Liberals were persuaded of the virtues of 'competition', strengthening the independent regulatory powers of the Air Transport Board in 1967—both major carriers faced pressures from US airlines and from smaller companies seeking to establish regional commuter lines. Nevertheless, CP Air and Air Canada (as TCAL was renamed in 1964) maintained a dominant position in the Canadian market, swallowing up regional competitors through the 1980s, while the regulatory agency restrained American incursions.[5]

The aircraft manufacturing industry was largely a by-product of World War II. During the 1920s a few companies, mostly British, notably Vickers and De Havilland, had set up Canadian operations, lured by the prospects of providing small bush planes for mining and forestry companies as well as aircraft for the embryonic RCAF. Except for Vickers, briefly in the mid-1920s, none of them established plants to design as well as assemble planes, and there were no domestic engine

CANADA AND ATOMIC ENERGY

During World War II both the US and Britain initiated programs to develop an atomic bomb, assuming—incorrectly, as it turned out—that Germany was ahead of them in nuclear research. Canada's role in this effort came about inadvertently: during the 1930s the LaBine brothers had established one of the few existing uranium mining operations, Eldorado Mines, refining the ore into radium for medical uses. In 1944, Howe's Munitions department took over Eldorado to provide uranium for the Manhattan Project. Meanwhile, a British research team under an Austrian scientist, Hans von Halban, working on a nuclear reaction process using 'heavy water' (deuterium) as a moderator, transferred operations to Canada in 1942, partly on the assumption that the needed material could be procured from Cominco's smelting. Most of the heavy water was ultimately provided by the Americans, but a successful nuclear reactor was tested at Chalk River, Ontario in 1945 shortly after the end of the war. Upon these foundations, the Canadian government was to erect its postwar program to develop nuclear power through another crown corporation, Atomic Energy of Canada Ltd (AECL).

The Chalk River project had been carried out in co-operation with the British (although the Canadian government footed most of the $4 million bill), and Canada wanted to maintain that connection after the war. By the late 1940s, however, it was clear that the US would be a more reliable market for Canadian uranium; and C.J. Mackenzie, who as head of the National Research Council also presided over the country's nuclear power

ZEEP—Zero Energy Experimental Pile—at Chalk River. (AECL *Research, Chalk River Laboratories*)

research, was confident that Canada could develop its own reactors for 'peaceful purposes', primarily electrical power generation—a view shared by Howe. Eldorado Mines remained under government control, selling uranium to the US Atomic Energy Commission. In 1952, the Chalk River operation was reconstituted as AECL, which negotiated an agreement with Ontario Hydro in the following year to develop a larger-scale reactor at an estimated cost of $26 million. Less publicized were arrangements to sell plutonium produced by the reactors to the Americans for use in their accelerated nuclear weapons program. Although Eldorado and AECL remained legally separate, from 1953 to 1958 they were both under a Howe protégé, William J. Bennett; AECL took over Eldorado's commercial marketing of radioactive isotopes for industrial as well as medical purposes.

Bennett proposed a strategy of development by stages for AECL: a demonstration reactor was initiated with technical assistance from Canadian General Electric for completion in 1962. Meanwhile, however, pressure grew for a more rapid move to commercial development as the international nuclear power industry gained momentum. As in the case of the Avro Arrow, costs of prototype development were exceeding early estimates, adding to pressures for a faster return on government investment, particularly after Howe and the Liberals were removed from the scene in Ottawa in 1957. Howe's successor as Minister of Trade and Commerce, Gordon Churchill, pushed Bennett's successor, Lorne Gray, to announce in 1959 that AECL would move on immediately to a major project, the CANDU reactor at Douglas Point, Ontario, at a cost of over $100 million, in order to position Canada for the increasingly competitive export market. AECL would also take over most of the technical work rather than subcontracting to private enterprise, CGE having been assigned blame for many of the cost overruns on the demonstration project. The Douglas Point reactor went into operation in 1966, two years behind schedule and the subject of much controversy over design and construction problems.

Initially the CANDU was to be marketed abroad by private firms with AECL providing technical backup. CGE made several forays in this field in the mid-1960s but decided to abandon the effort in 1968, having made only one sale, to Pakistan, as it faced formidable competition from larger US, German and other companies, often with government-backed financing in hand. Technical problems involved in the Douglas Point project may also have been a factor. After 1968, AECL took over marketing as well, with similarly limited success until the 1970s; sales to Argentina and South Korea embroiled the crown corporation in scandals over bribery.

AECL transferred heavy-water technology to India in the 1960s (with the Canadian government assisting in financing); but Canadians and Americans were alarmed to discover that, despite safeguards, India had used plutonium from their plants to develop its atomic bomb in 1974. Public concern over nuclear reactor safety after the Three Mile Island accident in 1978 (and the far graver Chernobyl disaster of 1986) contributed to changing attitudes toward an industry that had once been seen as the most advanced of 'high technologies'—for many Canadians, the nation's adventure into atomic energy seemed from the perspective of the 1990s to have been costly and ill-advised, the result of scientists' infatuation and bureaucratic empire-building.

Sources

Bothwell, Robert, *Eldorado: Canada's National Uranium Company* (Toronto, 1984); and *Nucleus: The History of Atomic Energy of Canada* (Toronto, 1988).

Doern, G. Bruce, *Government Intervention in the Canadian Nuclear Industry* (Montreal, 1981).

manufacturers in 1938—by which time many of the existing airframe companies, battered by the Depression, were barely functioning.

As noted earlier, wartime demand not only stimulated production but brought technical and design experts to Canada, again mostly from Britain. Altogether Canadian manufacturers produced over 16,000 planes, half of them for export, and overhauled another 6,500. Two of the largest plants were set up (or taken over) by the government during the war: a Vickers-run operation near Montreal became Canadair Ltd, producing (American) Douglas DC-4s; the National Steel Car plant at Malton outside Toronto was reorganized as Victory Aircraft, one of the largest airplane makers, producing Lancaster bombers. In addition, the Munitions department joined forces with the National Research Council to form Turbo Research Ltd which worked with the British developing jet propulsion engines.

While Ralph Bell and others involved in the wartime aircraft program were vigorous proponents of a continued postwar government role in the industry, Howe was initially hostile. By 1945 he had become a partial convert, but believed the preferred route would be to encourage foreign aircraft firms with well-developed design capabilities to establish operations in Canada. To that end, the Canadair plant was leased to a US firm, Electric Boat (later General Dynamics); and Victory Aircraft's assets were turned over to Hawker-Siddeley Group, the British company that had developed the Lancaster, which set up a subsidiary, A.V. Roe (Avro) Canada in 1945. As inducements the Canadian government offered generous rental-purchase terms and the prospect of contracts to build planes for the RCAF and TCAL. In 1946, Avro was allocated Turbo Research Ltd, with the understanding that it would continue work to develop an 'all-Canadian' jet engine; Avro's British chief, Sir Roy Dobson, brought a number of airframe designers and engineers across the Atlantic to demonstrate Hawker-Siddeley's commitment.[6]

In effect, Howe set up Canadair and Avro as competitors for military and civilian contracts, envisioning a symbiotic relationship between Canada's public air carriers and the aircraft manufacturers that would put Canada in the forefront of developing jet airplanes, perhaps even ahead of the British and the Americans. These hopes proved premature: Avro developed a commercial jet transport, the Jetliner, in 1948–49, but had to use a British-made engine, and was unable to satisfy TCAL's requirements. The airline ordered less advanced modified DC-4s from Canadair, and Howe's Reconstruction department wound up absorbing the costs of the Jetliner, which was never brought into commercial production.

Avro was successful in developing a jet engine, the Orenda, in 1949, to be introduced in a military fighter plane, the CF-100, for the RCAF. With the coming of the Korean War, pressure mounted on Avro and other aircraft builders to step up production. Defects and production-line problems led Howe to push Hawker-Siddeley to bring in one of his protégés, Crawford Gordon, to take over running the Canadian operation. A hard-driving, abrasive figure in the Howe mould, Gordon strong-armed production increases, and even managed to export some CF-100s to Belgium, although the total costs of development and production, over $700 million, significantly exceeded initial estimates (a difference ranging from

The christening ceremony of the Canadian prototype of the Avro Lancaster 10.
(National Aviation Museum)

$200 to $350 million, depending on accounting methods). This was hardly a unique situation in the history of military aircraft, but it was one which the government was hard-pressed to defend as the atmosphere of crisis cooled following the end of the Korean war.

The Korean conflict had stimulated a mini-boom in the Canadian aircraft industry as other companies, still mostly British, flocked to Canada, concentrating largely in southern Ontario. The largest of these operations, after Avro and Canadair, was De Havilland which expanded its Canadian production and transferred research and design capabilities as well, wisely choosing to focus on smaller planes such as the Beaver and the Otter, suitable for short-range flights and wilderness conditions that required take-off and landing on water or small airstrips.

Even before the CF-100s were rolling off the line, the RCAF was laying plans for a more advanced fighter-interceptor, intended to counter the threat of Soviet long-range bombers. Despite the Jetliner fiasco and Howe's scepticism about the managerial capabilities of Avro, the company received favoured treatment as Canada's 'chosen instrument' for developing this new aircraft. In 1954 Avro submitted a proposal for the CF-105 (the Arrow), with an 'all-Canadian' engine, the Iroquois, at a projected cost of $118 million for 40 planes. From the outset, however, the Arrow was plagued with problems. Alarmed by rising costs, the DDP cut back on

407

its initial production commitments, which raised the unit costs. The RCAF was dissatisfied with the initial weapons control system, and Avro had to redesign the plane to accommodate a more advanced alternative. When the US Navy cancelled a missile program that Avro planned to use, the Canadian government decided to have the company take over development of this element as well. By 1957 the Arrow project had cost $146 million but Avro was still working on a prototype. To offset costs, both the company and the government looked abroad for buyers, but in vain.

At this point the Liberal government was defeated after more than twenty years in power. The new regime of John Diefenbaker was confronted with new cost estimates by DDP indicating that the Arrow would cost over $800 million to bring to full production. On the other hand, cancellation would devastate the economy of southern Ontario where thousands of subcontractors were dependent on a continued flow of public funds to Avro. Meanwhile, the Soviet Sputnik seemed to signal the end of the era of manned bombers which the Arrow was supposed to counteract. After some dithering, Diefenbaker cancelled the project early in 1959.

Defenders of the Arrow, then and later, denounced this decision, arguing that it effectively destroyed the nascent Canadian aircraft industry, demonstrating a lack of faith in Canada's technological potential. The Arrow was a state-of-the-art plane, and its escalating costs were the result of government vacillation and interference with the program. A number of historians, including Bliss and Granatstein, have maintained that the Arrow project was simply too big and expensive for a country of Canada's size to handle. Conclusions about Avro vary: the most charitable view is that it was a victim of circumstance, its reach exceeding its grasp; alternatively, the company is portrayed as a gathering of buccaneering opportunists, squandering public funds on technological white elephants. In many respects the Arrow controversy resembles the debate over Canadian Northern Railway, another project whose unhappy fate was shaped by changes in political as well as economic conditions.

The main beneficiaries of the Arrow debacle were foreigners. Many of the technical personnel from Avro migrated to the US to work in their aerospace industry. In 1961 the RCAF replaced the CF-100s with aircraft produced by General Dynamics; ironically, this arrangement paved the way for a US-Canadian Defense Purchase Sharing Agreement in 1963 which helped pry open the US military procurement market for Canadian manufacturers on a long-term basis. Meanwhile, Avro's British parent, Hawker-Siddeley, survived the Arrow cancellation reasonably well. Beginning in 1955, Dobson and Gordon had embarked on a diversification strategy, exploiting investor enthusiasm over Avro's high profile as Canada's major military contractor. Within two years Avro acquired Canadian Car & Foundry and a significant share in Algoma Steel, and, in 1957, swallowed up Dosco, making it for a brief period the third largest company in Canada. By this time almost half the earnings of Hawker-Siddeley came from its Canadian subsidiary. Diversification cushioned the shock of the Arrow and other cancellations of military aircraft by the British government at the same time. Dosco eventually proved to be a burden on the company (renamed Hawker-Siddeley

Canada in 1962) which dumped it into the laps of the Canadian and Nova Scotia governments in 1967.[7]

Despite their breezy self-confidence, Canada's political élite and their business allies left behind a rather mixed legacy. Their ventures into high technology benefited a small cadre of scientists and engineers and enriched foreigners—even the feckless British—at public expense. The stockpiling bonanza resulted in what some critics have characterized as rapacious exploitation of the nation's resources and environment. Even before the end of the 1950s, Canadian nationalists were expressing concern over the extent to which defence, trade, and investment policies were carrying the country into America's political and economic orbit—and these complaints grew in volume over the next decade as the US became enmired in an unpopular war in Southeast Asia. At the same time, the Cold War era was a time of unprecedented prosperity for Canada, produced a new crop of millionaires (some of whom linked their fortunes to government largesse), and encouraged provincial governments to emulate what seemed to be effective techniques for promoting economic development, combining government 'planning' with foreign investment.

Notes

[1]On economic mobilization in World War I, see Gerd Hardach, *The First World War 1914–18* (Berkeley, 1977); R.J.Q. Adams, *Arms and the Wizard: Lloyd George and the Ministry of Munitions* (London, 1978); Gerald Feldman, *Arms, Industry and Labor in Germany 1914–18* (Princeton, 1966); John F. Godfrey, *Capitalism At War: Industrial Policy and Bureaucracy in France, 1914–18* (1987); Ronald Schaffer, *America in the Great War* (New York, 1991); Robert D. Cuff, *The War Industries Board: Business-Government Relations in World War I* (Baltimore, 1973). On World War II, see Alan Milward, *War, Economy and Society, 1939–45* (Berkeley, 1977); John M. Blum, *V Was for Victory* (New York, 1976); Arthur Marwick, *Britain in the Century of Total War: War, Peace and Social Change, 1900–67* (London, 1968).

[2]On Canada in World War I, see Desmond Morton, *Canada and War* (Toronto, 1981), ch. 3. On Hughes and the Shell Committee, see Ronald G. Haycock, *Sam Hughes: The Public Career of a Controversial Canadian* (Waterloo, 1986), 225–57. On Flavelle and the IMB, see Michael Bliss, *A Canadian Millionaire*, 233–383; and David Carnegie, *The History of Munitions and Supply in Canada 1914–18* (London, 1925). On government economic controls, see J.A. Corry, 'The Growth of Government Activities in Canada, 1914–21', *Canadian Historical Association Annual Report* (1940), 63–73; Traves, *The State and Enterprise*, chs 2–4. On Canadian-American economic relations, see Robert D. Cuff and Jack L. Granatstein, *Ties That Bind: Canadian-American Relations in Wartime from the Great War to the Cold War* (Toronto, 1977), chs 1–3.

[3]On Canadian industrial mobilization in World War II, see C.P. Stacey, *Arms, Men and Governments: The War Policies of Canada, 1939–45* (Ottawa, 1970), 1–67, 485–528; Robert Bothwell and William Kilbourn, *C.D. Howe: A Biography* (Toronto, 1979), esp. chs 9–11; J.N. de Kennedy, *History of the Department of Munitions and Supply*, 2 vols (Ottawa, 1950); Morton, *Canada's War*, chs 4–5; John Schultz, 'Shell Game: The Politics of Defence Production, 1939–42', *American Review of Canadian Studies* 16 (Spring 1986),

41–57; H. Duncan Hall, *North American Supply* (London, 1955), chs 1–2. Bliss's comments on Howe are in *Northern Enterprise*, ch. 16. On Maritime complaints, see E.R. Forbes, 'Consolidating Disparity: The Maritimes and the Industrialization of Canada during the Second World War', *Acadiensis* xv (Spring 1986), 3–27. On wartime crown corporations, see Sandford F. Borins, 'World War II Crown Corporations: Their Function and Their Fate', in J.R. Prichard, ed., *Crown Corporations in Canada* (Toronto, 1983), 447–75.

[4]On wage and price controls in World War II, see J.L. Granatstein, *Canada's War: The Politics of the Mackenzie King Government 1939–45* (Toronto, 1975), 174–86; Joseph Schull, *The Great Scot: A Biography of Donald Gordon* (Montreal, 1979), chs 5–8. On wartime finance and US-Canadian arrangements, see Benjamin Higgins, *Canada's Financial System in War* (New York, 1944); Cuff and Granatstein, *Ties That Bind*, ch. 5; Granatstein, *Canada's War*, chs 4–5; Hall, *North American Supply*, ch. 7. On the Canol Project, see Mira Wilkins, *The Maturing of Multinational Enterprise* (Cambridge, Mass., 1974), 273–6; Richard J. Diubaldo, 'The Canol Project in Canadian-American Relations', *CHA Historical Papers 1977*, 179–95.

[5]On Canadian-US economic relations in the Cold War era, see R.D. Cuff and J.L. Granatstein, *American Dollars—Canadian Prosperity* (Toronto, 1978), especially chs 4–6; Dan Middlemiss, 'Economic Defence Co-operation with the United States, 1940–63', in Norman Hillmer, ed., *Partners Nevertheless: Canadian-American Relations in the Twentieth Century* (Toronto, 1989), 167–93; B.W. Muirhead, *The Development of Postwar Canadian Trade Policy* (Montreal/Kingston, 1992). On stockpiling, see Alfred E. Eckes, Jr, *The United States and the Global Struggle for Minerals* (Austin, Texas, 1979), chs 4–8; Melissa Clark-Jones, *A Staple State: Canadian Industrial Resources in Cold War* (Toronto, 1987), chs 3–4. On Canada's 'industrial strategy' see *A Science Policy For Canada* (Ottawa, 1970), ch. 4.

[6]Marsha Gordon, *Government in Business* (Montreal, 1981), 66–78 presents a jaundiced view of Air Canada's relations with the Air Transport Board. For other views on TCAL/ Air Canada and Canadian Airlines, see John W. Langford, 'Air Canada', in Allan Tupper and G. Bruce Doern, eds, *Public Corporations and Public Policy in Canada* (Montreal, 1981), 257–84; David Corbett, *Politics and the Airlines* (Toronto, 1965); and Garth Stevenson, *The Politics of Canada's Airlines: From Diefenbaker to Mulroney* (Toronto, 1987) which also examines the growth of smaller regional carriers.

[7]On Avro, see James Dow, *The Arrow* (Toronto, 1979); Greig Stewart, *Shutting Down the National Dream* (Toronto, 1978); J.L. Granatstein, *Canada 1957–67* (Toronto, 1986), 105–17.

19 'PROVINCE BUILDERS'

The Depression, World War II, and the Cold War not only extended the role of government in the Canadian economy but also enhanced the power of the central state. In the 1930s the virtual bankruptcy of many provinces in Canada pushed a somewhat reluctant federal government into areas hitherto regarded as largely or exclusively provincial responsibilities; financial arrangements made during and after the war confirmed this shift. By the 1960s and 70s, however, the centralizing trend was beginning to be challenged, reflecting changes in economic circumstances as well as political perceptions.

The postwar era's resource boom in the oil and gas industry, mining, and forestry provided provincial leaders, especially in the west, with a renewed confidence in the future, and rekindled traditional resentments against a federal government perceived as dominated by central Canadian interests. In the business community, regionally-based entrepreneurs and branches of foreign-owned multinational resource companies—neither of whom had close ties with central Canada's established financial and manufacturing élites—felt similar antagonism. Both regional entrepreneurs and multinationals were prepared to turn to provincial governments for various forms of promotional assistance as well as defensive actions against regulatory initiatives emanating from Ottawa. At the same time they were equally willing to take advantage of federal programs that worked to their benefit. Federal-provincial disputes over revenue-sharing and resource control that came to a head in the 1970s and early 1980s reflected these various divisions and cross-currents.

Provincial governments' action on behalf of their business constituents was entrenched in the Canadian political environment. Since the 1890s Ontario and, to a lesser extent, Quebec had built railways, offered subsidies, and used regulatory powers to boost local economic growth; the western provinces had also followed this path, albeit on a smaller scale. What was new in the post-World War II era was the extent to which provincial governments went about these activities in a deliberate and conscious fashion. At the federal level the C.D. Howe approach to economic development, blending traditional promotional techniques and crown corporations, provided a model of sorts, although this was not the only source of inspiration for aspiring province-builders. In their prairie strongholds the CCF experimented with social planning, eventually moderating their more ambitious visions and adopting a more conventional mix of government activism and incentives for private enterprise. In Quebec after 1960 French Canadian nationalists followed a unique course, deploying government policies to strengthen and diversify the provincial economy, but with the specific objective to promote the growth of a francophone business élite.

411

Deliberate province-building through government action had many of the same pitfalls as government-directed economic development at the national level. 'Targeted' industries that flourished under government largesse withered when forced to face the rigours of the market. Ambitious 'megaprojects' proved to be ill-conceived or poorly timed, conveying only their debts to future generations of taxpayers. Opportunistic business promoters and patronage-seeking politicians distorted the direction of government projects.

Underlying these problems was the circumstance that few provinces had the necessary resources or degree of control over their economic environment in order to carry out consistent and effective long-term development programs. These weaknesses were particularly apparent in the economically disadvantaged provinces of Atlantic Canada where one government project after another foundered, even when reinforced with aid from a procession of federally-financed regional development programs. Even the stronger provinces (and, for that matter, the federal government) had their share of white elephants and disasters. By the 1980s there was a growing appreciation—by no means restricted to the business community or to Canada—of the difficulty governments at any level face when seeking to direct or control events in an unpredictable and changing market system.

THE RISE OF THE WEST

'The west must pay tribute to the east,' the aspiring young financier James Dunn told his erstwhile New Brunswick colleague Max Aitken while the two of them were briefly domiciled in Calgary around 1900, 'and I'm off to the east to collect tribute.' This probably apocryphal remark neatly summarized the tensions many westerners perceived between their region and the emerging business élite of central Canada. Western antagonism toward the chartered banks, the CPR, and their political henchmen in Ottawa spawned not only political protest movements but also regionally-supported ventures such as the Canadian Northern Railway, and the elevator and grain-marketing co-operatives.

The early history of Confederation had left a curiously mixed legacy. A perpetual sense of regional grievance, never far below the surface, combined with a recognition by the west's political and business leaders of their ultimate economic dependence, was never more apparent than in the disastrous decade of the Great Depression. Traditions of labour militancy and agrarian unrest that produced the Progressives and the CCF existed alongside (and not infrequently at odds with) a strong regional entrepreneurial bent and 'open door' attitudes toward foreign, especially American, investment. All of these patterns shaped western Canadians' response to the opportunities presented by a renewed demand for the region's resources after World War II.

The postwar resource boom encompassed the established forestry and mining sectors as well as such new fields as uranium in the west and iron ore in Labrador and northern Quebec, but certainly the most dramatic developments occurred in the oil and gas industry centred in Alberta. In the nineteenth century Canada's only producing oil fields were in southwestern Ontario, although as early as 1719 explorers had noted the presence of petroleum deposits in the west, and in 1788 Peter Pond of the North West Company had come across the massive tar sands of the Athabasca River region. A century later the Geological Survey of Canada began mapping the resource potential of what was to become Alberta. Around the end of World War I, Imperial Oil began exploratory drilling on lands leased from the CPR, though with only modest success: one of its few finds, at remote Norman Wells, was the site of the brief-lived Canol Project during World War II.

Shortly before World War I, rumours of oil stimulated a mini-boom in the west after a local rancher, William S. Herron, discovered natural gas and light oil in the Turner Valley south of Calgary. Prospectors and promoters flocked to the region in 1913–14, but the Turner Valley proved to be more productive of stock swindles than commercial petroleum and the boom collapsed fairly quickly. Herron's enterprise, Calgary Petroleum Products, with the backing of prominent local business figures such as Senator James Lougheed and R.B. Bennett, prospered for a time but after a refinery fire in 1920 the company passed into the hands of Imperial Oil, whose subsidiary, Royalite, was the major producer in the area through the ensuing decade.

The pre-war débâcle did not, however, deter other entrepreneurs from prospecting in the region. In 1926, 'Major' Jim Lowery, a peripatetic Calgary businessman and sometime politician, cobbled together Home Oil Co. with financial support from Vancouver investors, benefiting from the buoyant stock market of the late 1920s. The Depression, dry wells, and a global oil glut in the early 1930s dampened Home Oil's future but the company diversified into gold mining in British Columbia to keep afloat. Another Calgarian, R.A. Brown, who ran the city's tramway and lighting systems, also entered the oil business, supporting his activities in the Depression by borrowing from Imperial and from British-American Oil Co., and introducing a scheme known as 'royalties financing' in which investors purchased direct shares in the revenues of producing wells. Brown's venture, Turner Valley Royalties, began full-scale production in 1936, which lured Home Oil back to the region. A third entrepreneur, Frank McMahon from B.C., entered the Alberta fields in the mid-1930s, establishing Pacific Petroleums Ltd which made a modest strike near Brown's wells in 1938.

Although by the end of the 1930s Royalite and independent production made Alberta self-sufficient in oil and gas, the big strike anticipated since 1914 proved elusive. As World War II ended both Imperial and Shell Canada stepped up exploratory work in the west, and Imperial's Leduc and Redwater finds near Edmonton in 1947–48 ushered in Alberta's 'age of oil'. Imperial's success brought other major companies into the region and rekindled investor enthusiasm in the smaller ventures as well. The Pembina field, discovered in the early 1950s, had proved resources of oil ten times the size of Leduc, which had in turn dwarfed the Turner Valley. By the mid-1950s the recoverable reserves of Alberta oil were reckoned to exceed 3.6 billion barrels, with the more remote fields of the north and the tar sands as yet untapped. Natural gas reserves were estimated at over 11 trillion cubic feet, equivalent to about 2 billion barrels of oil.

Waiting for Leduc No. 1 to blow in, 13 February 1947—the beginning of a new era in Western Canada. *(Provincial Archives of Alberta/P.2733)*

As in the turn-of-the-century mining industry in Ontario, the Alberta oil patch included both large-scale multinational firms and smaller independents of both Canadian and American vintage. Inevitably the 'majors' dominated the field. The most significant new finds of the 1940s and 50s were developed by these big companies and by the end of the following decade almost half of the province's crude oil production was accounted for by five firms: Imperial, Shell, Texaco, Gulf, and British Petroleum. All were linked into global corporate networks that integrated production, transportation, refining, and marketing. Most of the independents operated at the production end of the industry, although several branched further afield. The Hudson's Bay Co. resurrected its interest in its joint oil and gas venture with the US firm, Continental Oil, in the 1940s, and earnings from this source helped carry the firm through its transition into retailing. In 1949 Pacific Petroleums set up a subsidiary, Westcoast Transmission, to pipe natural gas from northern Alberta to Vancouver and—after years of lobbying with US regulatory authorities—to tap into the American west-coast market. In 1952 Home Oil passed into the hands of the Brown family of Calgary; under R.A. 'Bobby' Brown, Jr, the company expanded rapidly into pipelines, natural gas ventures overseas in Europe, and an ill-timed move into the Alaska oil fields in the 1960s. A Colorado-based family, the Nielsons, established a mid-sized integrated venture, Husky Oil, which developed its own western Canadian distribution network in the 1970s.

The complex structure of the oil industry helped preserve the role of both the larger independents and the numerous small ventures that sprang up in the wake of Leduc. The Big Five controlled more than one-third of the potentially oil-bearing lands (most of which were on crown property, leased from the Alberta government), but were willing to farm out their leases to small operators—at a stiff price to be sure—both to spread the risks involved in exploratory work, and to stem political difficulties by fostering the image of an open and competitive industry. Most of the larger firms also subcontracted drilling and supply operations to local companies, encouraging competition to keep costs down. Although relations between the majors and independents were hardly free of strife, an atmosphere of peaceful coexistence rather than Darwinian struggle generally prevailed.

While the subsidiaries of the multinationals were headquartered in Toronto or Montreal, the independents congregated in Calgary, where their shared values and experiences imparted a special regional flavour to the oil and gas industry. Many of these independents saw themselves as self-made men, imbued with a faith in entrepreneurial capitalism despite their dependence upon and interconnections with the oil majors; taking a proprietary view of their companies even when these were joint-stock ventures; and sharing the region's anti-eastern, anti-Ottawa sentiments even though they were far removed from both the small-farmer populists and the mercantile-ranching élite who had flourished in Alberta early in the twentieth century. Twenty years after Leduc, the oil industry had spawned a new generation of professional managers and technicians in the service of the multinationals and the larger regional independents, but replicating the 'free enterprise' ideas of their forebears, even as they turned to the provincial government as the instrument to protect and advance their interests.

The complex and contradictory nature of the oilmen's community was reflected in the politics and policies of Alberta's government. During the 1930s the Social Credit party had come to power, reflecting western grievances and expounding quasi-populist ideas. But even as he inveighed against the bankers of Bay Street, Premier Aberhart affirmed his party's commitment to support private property rights and business interests, especially in the oil fields. His successor, Ernest Manning, pursued this course through the 1940s and 50s, welcoming the oil multinationals, balancing the province's need for revenues against the industry's desire for profits, and seeking to smooth over potential conflicts between the majors and the independents. The main areas of government intervention involved the 'prorationing' of oil production in Alberta and the issue of natural gas pipelines to markets outside the province.

In 1930 Ottawa transferred control of subsoil resources to the prairie provinces; and during the mid-1930s intense exploitation of the Turner Valley fields—and competition between Imperial and the independents—aroused fears that these resources would soon be depleted, leaving the Depression-wracked province in perpetual poverty. The result was the creation of Alberta's Oil and Gas Conservation Board in 1938. During its early years the Conservation Board had little impact on the industry, particularly since Imperial Oil refused to adhere to its rulings and the government was reluctant to antagonize the one big company actively engaged in exploration. After Leduc and Redwater, Imperial Oil and the other majors entering the field became more receptive to government regulation, believing that it could stem a threatened production glut and keep small producers from siphoning off potential reserves from lands adjacent to their own leases—a practice that had worked very well for Pacific Petroleums in its early years. The independents too were supportive of an allocation system that would ensure them of a share in the field and protect them from unrestrained competition with the oil giants. In practice the enforced cartelization of oil production was of most benefit to the majors, particularly in the 1960s when changes in the original allocation formula encouraged production from higher-cost reservoirs. Nevertheless, a majority of oil producers, large and small, continued to endorse the Conservation Board as a mediator of disputes within the industry.

In the early 1950s the subject of natural gas exports, the most explosive political issue facing the Alberta government, encouraged another step toward intervention in the industry. Ottawa (meaning C.D. Howe) was now anxious to promote gas exports abroad to boost the country's trade position; meanwhile private companies, including McMahon's Pacific Petroleums, were lobbying for permits to move gas to the west coast or southward to the American middle west. Alberta voters, however, treasured this cheap and abundant energy source, and proponents of local industry argued that it must be preserved for economic diversification. In 1949 the provincial government gave the Conservation Board control over natural gas exports with the requirement that long-term supplies for Alberta should be protected. By 1954 Howe was pushing development of the Trans-Canada Pipeline (discussed in Chapter Twenty) threatening Alberta with the potential loss of markets in central Canada and the US if it persisted in hoarding its reserves. The province responded by creating Alberta Gas Trunk Line which would carry all natural gas produced for export. The company was not a crown corporation, although the province as well as representatives of Alberta's gas producers and utilities held shares in it. Voting shares could not be transferred to investors from outside the province.

Social Credit's interventionist forays had been primarily responses to particular situations. Conservatives who came to power under Peter Lougheed in 1971 pursued a more deliberate course of action, although they too preferred to proceed indirectly, relying on incentives to private enterprise to achieve provincial economic goals. Lougheed, grandson of the Calgary capitalist who had helped found Alberta's earliest oil venture, had close ties to the province's oil and mining leaders, most notably the Mannix family whose wealth from construction activities early in the century had created a diversified utilities and mining empire. During the 1960s Lougheed resuscitated the Tories as the political wing of indigenous business and managerial groups anxious to sustain Alberta's prosperity beyond the oil era. Providentially, the energy crisis of the early 1970s provided the new regime with leverage and opportunities to fulfil these ambitions.

Lougheed undertook to reset provincial royalties from oil production on crown lands above the ceilings established in 1951, and to push domestic oil and gas prices, which were regulated by the National Energy Board, toward rising world price levels. These efforts encountered stiff resistance from the oil majors, some of whom threatened to move their operations abroad, and from the federal government which continually squabbled with Alberta over pricing as well as tax and royalty-sharing arrangements. Despite their frustration over federal-provincial bickering and a forced withdrawal from the more ambitious designs to boost oil revenues, the Alberta government benefited from rising oil prices throughout the decade. In 1976 Lougheed announced the creation of the Alberta Heritage Fund which was intended to finance provincial economic diversification; within five years the Fund held over $8.5 billion. An Alberta Energy Company, with the province holding 50 per cent of the shares, was set up to invest in such areas as petrochemicals and tar sands development. Alberta Gas Trunk Line was allowed to move beyond its original role as a common carrier for natural gas. Under the leadership of Bob Blair it emerged as a major player on the western energy scene, outmanoeuvring the major oil companies in the early 1970s in bidding on the Alaska Highway Pipeline, acquiring control of Husky Oil in 1979, and diversifying into petrochemicals and production equipment for the oil and gas industry.

Provincial development was not without pitfalls, most notably in oil sands development. Despite the potential oil wealth, estimated in the hundreds of billions of barrels, buried in bituminous muskeg, the cost of extraction and processing deterred development before the oil-price hikes of the 1970s. A decade before, the American independent, Sun Oil, had begun pouring $130 million into a small project, Great Canadian Oil Sands near Fort MacMurray; it operated with continuous deficits until 1975. Despite this ominous precedent, in 1973 the Alberta government joined a consortium of four US major oil companies, including Imperial, to develop the Syncrude Project which anticipated an ultimate output four or five times that of Great Canadian Oil Sands at a cost of $1 billion. Within a year, Syncrude was floundering as projected costs soared to twice the original estimate and one of the partners pulled out. To avert disaster, Alberta brought the

417

Canadian and Ontario governments on board and made substantial royalty concessions to the remaining corporate participants. Syncrude lurched on, but the collapse of oil prices in the 1980s reinforced doubts about its long-term commercial viability.

The end of the oil boom ended much of Alberta's enthusiasm for province-building. To keep the oil industry from shutting down the government renegotiated royalty arrangements and issued new incentives. The disposition of the Heritage Fund was increasingly controversial. Whether industrial diversification, even into an area such as petrochemicals, was a realistic policy given the province's isolation from prospective markets, began to be questioned. Although Alberta remained a resource-rich and comparatively wealthy province, the 1980s marked the apparent end of more than thirty years of oil-stimulated growth and the confidence it fostered in Alberta's business and political leaders.

The post-World War II oil boom spilled over into neighbouring Saskatchewan which also benefited from discoveries of potash, a major raw material in chemical fertilizers, in the 1940s. The Great Depression and the dust storms of the 1930s had hit Saskatchewan even harder than Alberta and that experience, combined with a strong agrarian populist heritage, brought the CCF to power in 1944. The party was to remain in place for twenty years. Saskatchewan harboured virtually no mining or oil entrepreneurial elements, and so the socialist government might have been expected to adopt a resolutely interventionist approach toward these industries. The failure of early experiments with crown enterprises in other fields tempered the enthusiasm of provincial leaders for pursuing this course. Instead, the CCF focused its attention on social policies while encouraging private development of its resource industries.

In the potash industry a major investor was the American-based International Minerals & Chemicals Co., which established the world's largest potash mine near Esterhazy, Saskatchewan in the early 1960s. Other multinationals, British and German as well as American, held the lion's share of this market; Noranda entered the field through a joint venture with an Ontario co-operative, Central Canada Potash. Imperial Oil was initially cool toward development in socialist Saskatchewan. Independents such as Husky Oil, which began exploratory work there in the 1940s, were joined eventually by Imperial's former satellite, Royalite Oil (which was sold to Canadian investors in 1949), and Saskatchewan became a base for Royalite's western distribution network.

The CCF government was overturned in 1964 by a rejuvenated, business-oriented Liberal party under Ross Thatcher who essentially continued the pattern of encouraging foreign investment in the resource sector while seeking to dismantle other elements of the CCF program. The sudden collapse of the potash boom at the end of the decade — reflecting a slump in agriculture which also struck the farm implement firm, Massey-Ferguson, in the midst of a major international expansionary thrust — brought the CCF, now recycled as the New Democratic Party, back to power. The new regime under Allan Blakeney adopted a far more interventionist policy toward the resource industries, reflecting in part a growing anti-American, anti-foreign investment sentiment in Canada as well as a modest resurgence of populism in the beleaguered farming community.

Provincial crown corporations were established to give the government a foothold in the oil and uranium industries, and Saskatchewan joined forces with the Alberta Energy Co. (and Britain's government-owned steel corporation) to acquire control of Interprovincial Steel & Pipe Corporation, with the aim of providing the base for a regional steel industry. In 1975, after several years of bickering with the multinationals in the fertilizer field over royalties and taxes, the NDP government created the Potash Corporation of Saskatchewan (PCS) and proceeded to acquire a 40 per cent share of the industry in the province. The PCS integrated forward into marketing, setting up sales branches in the US and pursuing markets overseas, relying on its base as a producer of almost one-quarter of the world's potash output in the early 1980s. Meanwhile, in the oil and gas industry, Saskatchewan formed a somewhat incongruous alliance with Alberta to resist federal incursions in the 1970s. As in the case of Alberta, the Saskatchewan government, despite gestures toward economic diversification — and the establishment of a Heritage Fund — became increasingly tied to the fortunes of the province's resource sector, and vulnerable to the downswing in raw materials' prices in the 1980s.[1]

A resource-based strategy of province-building characterized the development of both leftward-leaning Saskatchewan and conservative Alberta during this era. In British Columbia, a similar pattern emerged: the Social Credit dynasty of the Bennetts, which controlled the province's political affairs with only one brief interruption between 1952 and the end of the 1980s, vigorously pursued pro-business (and particularly pro-foreign investment) policies, punctuated by forays into interventionism. The B.C. government was somewhat more successful than those of the prairie provinces in promoting diversification, particularly in the financial and service sectors, although the heart of the province's economy continued to be in the forestry and mining industries.

Even before World War II, the province's mines and lumber producers were beginning to recover from the worst ravages of the Depression, and the postwar era witnessed a dramatic expansion of capacity and technological change in both industries. New uses for pulpwood in synthetic fibres, film, plastics, and other products — and a revitalized construction industry — widened the market for wood products, while chainsaws, automated chippers, and waste recovery techniques improved productivity. In 1947 the province introduced a system of forestry management licensing intended to encourage sustained yield production through controlled harvesting and tree farming, and opened up the large reserves of the northwest coast and the interior. American multinationals such as Weyerhauser, Celanese Corporation, and Crown Zellerbach entered the province to exploit these new opportunities. At the same time, domestic producers expanded and consolidated. H.R. MacMillan merged his company with another large lumber firm, Bloedel, Stuart & Welsh, in 1951, and then took over the Powell River Co., the largest newprint producer in the region. MacMillan also joined the Ontario conglomerator, E.P. Taylor, in setting up B.C. Forest Products Ltd which scattered company mill towns across the hinterlands of the province. From its B.C. base, MacMillan-Bloedel transformed itself in the 1960s into a multinational with investments in US lumber mills, paper and box manufacturing in Europe and similar ventures in Latin America and the Pacific archipelagos.

In the mining field, Alcan established a smelter at Kitimat while Cominco continued to exploit its holdings at Trail. Cominco also diversified into steel and chemicals, and went the multinational route in the 1960s, principally through joint ventures in India, Australia and Japan. Japan in particular became a major market for B.C. minerals. Output of all minerals (plus, by the 1960s, some oil and gas) increased ten times over by value between 1950 and 1975, and more than doubled again in the following decade.

In its early stages the postwar resource boom in B.C. centred on the developed areas of the southwest coast. Transportation links into the northern coast and interior were few, and near-frontier conditions prevailed. The opening of the interior was largely the result of measures taken by the government of W.A.C. 'Wacky' Bennett. The New Brunswick-born hardware store owner in the Okanagan Valley led an insurgent Social Credit party which drew its strength from hinterland farmers, migrants from the prairies during the Depression and World War II. In the 1950s and 60s Bennett made development of the neglected back-country the heart of his economic policies. His rhetorical populism, like that of Aberhart and Manning in Alberta, was joined with vigorously pro-business attitudes apparent in his promotion of consolidation and foreign investment in the resource industries and his strident hostility toward labour unions which by the 1960s formed the nucleus of his main political opposition, the NDP. But Bennett's version of free enterprise embraced a willingness to resort to government activism, displayed particularly in the take-over of the province's ferry system in 1958 and of the utility industry three years later.

The 'provincialization' of the electric power system was an outgrowth of Bennett's desire to open up the interior for development. In 1957, Axel Wenner-Gren, a Swedish promoter whose international business empire included the Electrolux vacuum-cleaner company and a variety of banking and industrial projects in Latin America, unveiled before the receptive premier a scheme to develop a massive hydroelectric dam on the Peace River in northeastern B.C. This undertaking clashed, however, with a federal government initiative to reach an agreement with the Americans on the border-straddling Columbia River. Under the 1961 Columbia River Treaty, Canada would build storage dams in B.C., with the US guaranteeing that 50 per cent of the electric power generated in Washington state from the Columbia would be returned to Canada. Since Wenner-Gren's (and Bennett's) scheme was based on supplying B.C.'s power needs from the Peace, Bennett opposed the treaty, proposing instead that electric power should be developed on the Canadian side of the Columbia River for export to the United States.

In the 1960 election in the province the CCF/NDP had advocated a government take-over of B.C. Electric. Bennett skirted the issue, focusing on alleged 'communist' influences in the trade unions and the opposition party. But soon after his party's reelection, he proceeded to follow precisely this course, taking over both

B.C. Electric and B.C. Power, and establishing the B.C. Hydro & Power Authority. Bennett's venture into 'socialism' related directly to the convoluted Columbia/ Peace River situation. B.C. Electric had refused to agree to purchase power from the Peace River project (which was set up as a 'mixed' enterprise, with the Wenner-Gren group in a minority position), leading Bennett to conclude that the utility planned to draw its power needs from the US under the proposed Columbia River Treaty. Once the private utilities were in his control, Bennett focused his wrath on the federal government, summoning up ancient regional grievances against Ottawa. Faced with American threats that the entire treaty might be scrapped, the federal government gave in to Bennett. In 1963 it agreed to revisions under which the Columbia River power developed in B.C. would be exported to the US, and the proceeds would be used by B.C. Hydro & Power to finance the Peace River project, completed in 1967 as—of course—the Bennett Dam. Canadian nationalists fumed over this 'give-away' of the nation's resources, but Bennett solidified his political position at home and relied on Peace River power to attract industries (mostly pulp processors) into the province's hinterland.

Despite the sustained postwar boom, B.C.'s economy remained dependent on raw materials extraction for export markets, and sluggish demand in the early 1970s combined with growing dissatisfaction in Vancouver over Bennett's hinterland preoccupations brought the NDP temporarily to power. Political misjudgements by the NDP and rising inflation after the energy crisis of 1973, however, helped Social Credit rebound under W.A.C.'s son, Bill Bennett. Although renewed growth in the resource industry markets enabled the SoCred regime to stay in power for more than a decade and a half, exploiting bitter labour-business and urban-rural divisions at election time, the problem of long-term economic diversification began to loom larger in the 1980s.

During this period trade links with the Far East, especially Japan, were extended, augmented by an influx of both people and money from Hong Kong, which faced absorption into mainland China at the end of the century. The benefits of this migration centred primarily in the financial and service sectors of Vancouver, although Japanese companies such as Mitsubishi invested in B.C. mines and fisheries. Fluctuations in resource export markets—forestry products in particular, which were also affected by American protectionist measures both before and after the Free Trade Agreement—eroded many of earlier decades' economic gains in the province's hinterland. The diverging paths of business in metropolitan Vancouver and the interior, punctuated by debates over environmental controls in the resource industries, perpetuated a tradition of political and economic division in the province which had been muted during the decades of growth and prosperity after World War II.[2]

'MAÎTRES CHEZ NOUS'

French Canadian nationalism was a staple element in nineteenth-century Quebec politics and the province's political leaders of all persuasions had been emulating Ontario's promotional policies since the early 1900s. After World War II these

421

two traditions began to converge, and from 1960 on a formidable array of ambitious francophone business people, politicians and policy-oriented intellectuals set out to use the power of the state to advance their position in the provincial economy and to strengthen and diversify its industrial base. While the French Canadian business community was divided over the question of Quebec separatism, there was a broad consensus on the benefits accruing from government intervention on behalf of their economic and cultural interests.

Although there is a lingering popular notion that French Canadians traditionally avoided or were excluded from commercial pursuits, numerous francophone businesses did operate througout the nineteenth and early twentieth centuries. As noted in earlier chapters, 'French' private banks established networks across Quebec and the Maritimes and financiers such as Louis Forget and F.L. Beique emerged as millionaires in the early 1900s. Louis-Adelard Senecal built a diversified industrial empire by reinvesting profits from railway speculation, and entrepreneurs such as the Montreal book publisher Jean Baptiste Rolland and the banker J.E.A. Dubuc ventured into the pulp and paper industry in the late nineteenth century. Despite its reputation for hostility toward industrial and commercial development, the Catholic hierarchy in Quebec endorsed the efforts of the *caisses populaires* to promote manufacturing enterprises in rural communities in the early 1900s.

Historians of Quebec such as Paul-André Linteau have argued that for the most part these francophone businesses functioned on a relatively small scale: usually proprietary in nature, they served local markets and lacked the capital necessary to embark on larger, technologically advanced operations. During the merger era of 1909–29 many of these enterprises were absorbed into consolidations dominated by Anglo-Canadian capitalists in Montreal or were isolated in hinterland markets. The Great Depression hurt large and small firms alike but struck the smaller proprietary enterprises with particular force and reinforced the pattern of anglophone domination of the province's major industries: textiles, newsprint, metal mining, and banking.

Maurice Duplessis, who dominated the political scene and was premier of Quebec through much of the period from the mid-1930s to 1959, seemingly did little to reverse this process. Duplessis and his party, the Union Nationale, cultivated French Canadian voters and espoused Quebec's autonomy in its relations with Ottawa; his critics maintained that his policies encouraged a massive expansion of foreign direct investment in the province after World War II, generating economic growth but ignoring indigenous francophone business interests. Among the largest of the new investors was the Iron Ore Co. of Canada, a consortium of American steel producers and Ontario-based mining firms brought together by M.J. Hanna of Cleveland, Ohio in 1949 to exploit the iron reserves of the Ungava region on the Quebec-Labrador border. Duplessis, his opponents charged, had negotiated a generous royalty arrangement with the Iron Ore Co. in return for under-the-table contributions to the Union Nationale. Equally controversial were Duplessis' repressive labour policies, highlighted by government action to break a strike in 1949 against American-owned asbestos companies.

Conrad Black (in his capacity as biographer of Duplessis rather than as financier-conglomerator) has argued that criticism of Duplessis, in these matters at least, is overstated. There was substantial growth not only in the resource sectors of the economy but also in manufacturing, with output more than doubling between 1944 and 1959. Per-capita income increased by this same magnitude and standards of living improved in general, most notably in Montreal and the new industrial towns. Despite his reputation as a fiscal conservative, social benefits also improved under Duplessis, reducing the traditional role of the Catholic church. Furthermore, it is fair to say that Duplessis' efforts to attract foreign investors and promote rapid resource development were not noticeably different from those of his predecessors in Quebec or for that matter in Ontario earlier in the century.

French Canadian businesses were by no means quiescent in this period. Although most were found in the fields of financial services and retailing, some ranged further. The Simard family with earnings from dredging contracts procured through the federal Liberal government in the 1930s built a diversified shipbuilding and steel-fabricating duchy at their home base of Sorel, carefully keeping on good terms with Duplessis. Another family dynasty, the Vachons, developed a province-wide and then national market for their baked goods between the 1930s and 1960s; their firm eventually passed into the hands of a Quebec crown corporation, reorganized as Culinar Inc. At the same time the Vachons were beginning to sell their 'Jos. Louis' cakes, a talented mechanic in Valcourt, Armand Bombardier, was developing the snowmobile: originally intended as a kind of all-weather, all-terrain vehicle for rural households in Quebec, the Ski-Doo found a larger market as a recreational toy in the 1960s. Under the founder's son-in-law, Laurent Beaudoin, Bombardier Inc. diversified into subway cars for the Montreal Metro and then for mass transit systems in the US and overseas, becoming one of the largest suppliers in the world in this field. Another enterprising French Canadian of this era was Charles Trudeau who began supplementing his earnings as a lawyer in the 1920s by developing a small network of auto rental agencies and gas stations in the Montreal area. When he sold them to Imperial Oil in 1932, he used the profits to amass a fortune on the securities markets. His son Pierre, later prime minister of Canada, first entered politics in the 1950s as a vigorous critic of the Duplessis regime.

The example of Pierre Trudeau indicates one of the unintended legacies of Duplessis' development policies. As Quebec's economy grew and diversified in the postwar era, the rural power base of the Union Nationale was undermined. French Canadians moved into the industrial cities, joined by a rising tide of immigrants. Better-educated francophones aspired to move into professional and managerial positions, and they translated their frustrations over the dominance of the Anglo-Canadian and foreign business élite into demands for political change. The Liberal party in Quebec, moribund since World War II, was resuscitated by leaders like Jean Lesage to become the vehicle for this transformation, and came to power a year after the death of 'Le Chef' in 1959.

The Quebec Liberals were a composite of ambitious French Canadian professionals, intellectuals, trade unionists, and business people, an inherently unstable alliance. Eventually they split into factions over issues such as social reform and Quebec separatism, but in the early 1960s the Lesage regime was able to push through the 'Quiet Revolution', a sweeping program of economic as well as social and cultural reforms. Many of the measures of the Quiet Revolution were intended, directly or indirectly, to enhance the position of French Canadian businesses and thus welded their interests to the fortunes of the Liberal party in Quebec. Divisions in the Liberal party led to a Union Nationale resurgence in 1966–70; the exodus of left-wing Liberals to the Parti Québécois left the business element as the linchpin of the Liberals when they reemerged after 1970 under Robert Bourassa.

To a much greater extent than any of the other provincial governments of this era (including the CCF in Saskatchewan), the Lesage regime was prepared to resort to state intervention to achieve its ends. While C.D. Howe's development strategy had some influence, a more significant model was France after World War II with its panoply of nationalized industries and technocratic planning structures. At the same time there were limits to this ambitious interventionism. As in the case of the western provinces, Quebec ultimately had to confront the natural limits of its financial resources, and the province's ties to Ottawa and the national economy. In addition, francophone business leaders aspired to operate in national and international markets, and the Quebec government had to balance its provincial development orientation against these aspirations. The presence of large foreign-owned corporations in both the resource and manufacturing sectors also inhibited the manoeuvres of Quebec's government planners; although reduction of foreign control was an objective of the Quiet Revolution, it was necessary to balance this goal against the need to stimulate employment and maintain tax revenues. Government policies in the 1960s and 70s strengthened the position of francophone businesses, particularly in the construction industry and financial services. Nevertheless the foreign presence in mining increased significantly in this period and in 1978 almost half the province's largest manufacturing firms were linked to multinationals.

Crown corporations or mixed public-private enterprises provided one mechanism for province-building in Quebec, although (as in other provinces) results often fell short of expectations. In 1962 the province set up the Société Générale de Financement (SGF) as a provider of seed capital for new industrial ventures. The SGF included private financial institutions as well as the government, notaby the *caisses populaires*; private-sector investors held half the seats on the board of directors, although the government and *caisses populaires* group generally worked together. The SGF's particular mandate was to develop heavy industry in the province while also promoting French Canadian enterprises.

Initially, the Société hoped to achieve these goals through joint ventures, but over time the role of the government became predominant—the SGF itself became a wholly government-controlled affair after 1972. An early effort to set up an auto industry in partnership with the French firms Peugeot and Renault had disappointing results. An investment in the Simard family's Marine Industries in 1962 quickly took on the appearance of a bail-out rather than a development project, with SGF purchasing majority control of the floundering enterprise for $12 million. Somewhat more successful was Soquem, which undertook mineral exploration and development, but its general financial performance was poor and its role in the industry limited until the 1980s when the Quebec government expanded its capital base.

The Lesage government regarded the creation of a steel industry in Quebec as essential to its development program. Here again, however, the search for private partners, considered essential by SGF to guarantee commercial success, proved fruitless. In 1964 the government created a steel enterprise, Sidbec, without resolving the public-versus-private debate. In 1967 Sidbec began operations as a crown corporation, cobbled together from an assortment of unhealthy enterprises, including Marine Industries and a Quebec mill set up by Dosco, whose British owners — Hawker-Siddeley, of Avro fame — were anxious to divest themselves of their now-decrepit steel investment. Sidbec limped along, running chronic deficits through 1986, and embarking on an ultimately disastrous iron mining venture, undertaken at least in part as a result of political pressures to create jobs in the north St Lawrence shore region of Quebec. Although the company was able to provide a reliable supply of steel for provincial industries, it did not become the base for heavy industry envisioned by its proponents in the 1960s.

The best known interventionist measure of the Quiet Revolution was the development of Hydro Quebec as a government-owned utility monopoly, spearheaded by Lesage's Minister of Natural Resources, René Lévesque. French Canadian spokesmen had long advocated 'nationalization' of the province's utilities, and the Liberal party during its brief ascendency in Quebec in World War II had taken over the much-hated Montreal Light, Heat & Power, creating Hydro Quebec in 1944. For Lévesque, however, it was essential to 're-patriate' the much larger system operated by Shawinigan Water & Power, which was owned by the Power Corporation, a holding company established in 1925 by the investment house of Nesbitt-Thomson.

While other Liberals, including Premier Lesage, initially resisted his idea, quailing at the prospective cost of financing the take-over, Lévesque argued that a publicly-owned utility would be shielded from federal taxation — a consideration that had also weighed heavily with B.C.'s premier Bennett as he embarked on utility provincialization. In addition to making electric service more efficient by reducing duplication and thus controlling power rates, Hydro Quebec could be an instrument for industrial diversification and expansion of service into remote areas of the province. Lesage was eventually persuaded and staged the 1962 reelection campaign on the issue, invoking the slogan, 'maîtres chez nous' — a battle cry that would resonate for Quebec separatists in later years.

Like Sidbec and other such ventures, Hydro Quebec did not fulfil all the extravagant expectations of its proponents. Despite substantial expansion of capacity, the utility could not cover all the growing energy demands in the province in the 1960s and early 1970s. Nevertheless, it did provide many new technical and

425

managerial opportunities for francophones, and was able to hold the line on rates after the energy crunch of 1973 as it was less dependent than other utilities on oil. Well-managed, with indirect financial support from the Quebec government, Hydro Quebec's bonds achieved consistently high ratings. In the 1970s a reconstructed Liberal regime under Bourassa embarked on the huge James Bay hydroelectric development project which provided Quebec with surplus power for export when it was completed a decade later, although resistance by Native Canadians in the James Bay region and a sagging US energy market in the early 1990s curtailed Bourassa's plans for an even larger project. Of all the crown enterprises spawned by the Quiet Revolution, Hydro Quebec was the most enduringly successful.

René Lévesque also played a role in one further nationalizing foray, this time as premier of the Parti Québécois government in the province from 1976 to 1985. Despite his welfare-state rhetoric and the leftist base of the PQ, Lévesque as premier generally soft-pedalled interventionism: with independence as his main goal, he sought to avoid signals that Quebec would not be hospitable to private investment. Shortly after coming to power, Lévesque went to New York to reassure a sceptical audience of US bankers and industrialists that Quebec had not become a northern Cuba.

Nevertheless, the PQ government did move toward nationalizing the asbestos industry in 1978–80, with the declared intention of establishing an integrated processing and refining operation which the largely foreign-owned private firms refused to undertake. Although the initiative seemed plausible since Quebec's output accounted for almost one-third of the world's asbestos production at the time, serious problems soon emerged. The government was only able to acquire control of one of the four major producers and General Dynamics, the American parent of that company, the Asbestos Corporation, chose to contest the take-over in the courts, delaying the process. Meanwhile the industry itself slid into crisis, in part because of the health hazards of asbestos for workers in the industry: litigation over this issue drove the largest US producer, Johns Manville, into bankruptcy in the early 1980s. As the market remained sluggish even after the general economic recovery of the mid-1980s, the asbestos venture appeared to be yet another costly white elephant for Quebec.

While Quebec's experience with crown enterprises produced at best mixed results, other more indirect forms of intervention proved to be more significant. Along with Hydro Quebec, the most notable initiative of the Quiet Revolution was the creation of the *Caisse de dépôt et de placement* in 1965 which became a major instrument for expanding francophone businesses in Quebec and Canada. Initially set up to hold Quebec's pension fund—which provided the occasion for an early confrontation between Quebec and Ottawa as the federal government had its own plan for a Canada pension fund—the *Caisse de dépôt* also became the portfolio manager of revenues from a variety of government bodies, with assets of over $14 billion by the early 1980s.

In its early years the *Caisse de dépôt* invested primarily in provincial and Hydro Quebec bonds, thus assisting in the expansion of the crown venture and freeing the provincial government from reliance on anglophone financiers. But it also helped fund francophone enterprises such as Provigo, a provincial grocery chain set up by Antoine Turmel in 1969; by the 1980s Provigo owned a wide range of supermarkets, convenience store chains, and mail order houses across eastern Canada. The PQ government had broader ambitions for the *Caisse de dépôt*, pressing it to become more of a venture capital source for expanding francophone businesses such as Bombardier and the National Bank of Canada (the erstwhile Banque Nationale). The *Caisse* also bought into traditionally anglophone firms such as Dominion Textiles, and used its financial power to protect French Canadian firms from 'foreign' take-overs: in 1977 it blocked the Nova Scotia-based Sobey family from acquiring Provigo, although later the *Caisse* allied with the Sobeys to oust Turmel as chief executive of the retail company.

The *Caisse de dépôt* did not restrict itself to supporting French Canadian entrepreneurs in Quebec. In the 1970s the Ontario-born conglomerator Paul Desmarais, who had acquired and reorganized the Power Corporation, drew on the *Caisse* for assistance in his empire-building, to the point where in 1982 the federal Parliament restricted provincial companies from acquiring more than 10 per cent of a federally-chartered enterprise, in order to defend the CPR against a Desmarais/ *Caisse de dépôt* invasion. This episode naturally was seen by Quebec nationalists as confirming the tradition of anglophone bias in Ottawa.

Whatever their feelings on this issue, most francophone business people were not enthusiastic about Quebec separatism. Desmarais played a prominent role in opposing the PQ during the referendum on sovereignty in 1981, and the business community generally endorsed the return of the Liberals under Bourassa to power in 1986. Prosperity in the latter part of the decade induced some francophone business people to express more confidence about Quebec's ability to survive on its own during the debates following the collapse of the Meech Lake agreement. Recession in the early 1990s that hit Montreal particularly hard dampened much of this enthusiasm, and leading business figures such as Desmarais continued to argue that in economic terms French Canadians benefited more from decentralized federalism.

Despite the preoccupation of Quebec governments since the 1960s with creating a diversified industrial economy, manufacturing in the province declined, especially during and after the recession of the early 1980s, and despite examples such as Bombardier, most francophone businesses were concentrated in the financial and service sectors of the economy. These areas of course experienced substantial growth in this period, and reflected general shifts in the North American economy as manufacturers tended to migrate overseas. Overproduction and foreign competition also damaged the resource-based industries; multinationals such as the Iron Ore Co. phased out or scaled down their operations in Quebec, leaving pockets of high unemployment in the hinterlands even while Montreal prospered. The inability of the provincial government to achieve its diversification goals in the 1960s–70s or to do more than delay or cushion the impact of broader economic changes in the 1980s revealed the limits imposed on even relatively well-endowed provinces led by vigorous and talented technocrats. These problems were even more painfully apparent for Quebec's eastern neighbours in Atlantic Canada.[3]

THE PERILS OF PROVINCE-BUILDING

For the Maritimes the Great Depression descended in 1921 and its most enduring impact was on manufacturing. Federal government action to restore freight rate subsidies in the late 1920s and protectionism in the era of R.B. Bennett helped boost coal shipments to central Canada, and restrictions on trawlers enabled the local fish processors to regroup, as exemplified by the formation of National Sea Products by Ralph Bell in 1945. After World War II financial aid from federal and provincial sources contributed to the expansion of the long-liner fleet and the beginnings of a conversion by National Sea and other firms to trawler operations. While the traditional lumber producers faced growing competition from west coast suppliers after World War I, the pulp and paper industry expanded, particularly in New Brunswick where companies such as Consolidated Bathurst set up integrated mills.

Gains in the resource sector were offset by continuing problems in heavy industry, and in this area federal policies probably contributed to long-term decline. Although defence-related production in World War II helped Dosco, under pressure from Howe's ministry the company was obliged to close down its refurbished steel plate mill in 1946; the declining market for coal as railways and manufacturers shifted to oil-based power eroded its earnings from this source. The merchant marine which had expanded rapidly in World War II was equally rapidly dismantled: 74 deep-sea vessels were sold off to foreign shipping companies and the proceeds used by the federal government to help underwrite the expansion of the Great Lakes barge fleet. Rising freight rates after 1949 resurrected the old regional competitive problem for Maritime manufacturers. New capital investment in the region's industrial base lagged at half the national level in the early 1950s. Although the Maritimes experienced overall growth in the decade following World War II, the rate of growth was only two-thirds the national average. Migration out of the region, which had reached catastrophic levels in the 1920s, slowed over the next two decades, but Maritimers worriedly observed a renewal of this movement by the early 1950s, particularly among younger people.

Maritime political and business leaders agreed that the decline of manufacturing was the region's fundamental problem, setting the stage for a series of government initiatives to attract new industry, undertaken at first by the provinces and supplemented by federal regional development programs in the 1960s-80s. At the provincial level, Nova Scotia engaged in the most systematic and sustained effort, involving collaboration between the government and local business notables. In 1956 the Conservative party, after more than twenty years in opposition, returned to power under the leadership of Robert Stanfield, whose family had operated a successful textile firm in Truro since the 1800s. Stanfield's vehicle for re-industrialization was Industrial Estates Ltd (IEL), derived from a British experiment with regional development in the 1940s, and a forerunner of Quebec's SGF and the Bank of Canada's Industrial Development Bank. Although IEL was a crown enterprise with capital provided by the Nova Scotia government, it was run by business people; Frank Sobey, who had developed a regional supermarket chain from his base in Pictou, presided over IEL (along with his growing family enterprises) from 1957 to 1970. Stanfield vowed to ensure that IEL's decisions would be free of political influence. Its task was to provide seed capital and other inducements to industrial firms to locate in the province.

Altogether between 1958 and 1971 IEL provided over $150 million to 77 enterprises, many of them locating in rural and small-town communities in the province and over two-thirds of them employing fewer than 100 people. As a vehicle for hinterland industrial diversification the operation was a success: its most significant catch was the French company Michelin Tire which set up two plants in the early 1970s, attracted in part by the competitive wage rates advertised by IEL (and supplemented by a controversial provincial law passed in the 1980s to impede union organization of the plants). On the other hand, critics maintained that as a venture capital instrument IEL was unsound: even its successful investments represented a drain on a financially-strapped province—Michelin, for example, was provided $50 million in loans at interest rates well below those Nova Scotia was obliged to pay for borrowing the money. In addition, many of these manufacturers were chosen by IEL principally on the basis of 'creating jobs', perpetuating the labour-intensive aspect of the region's industries.

Two of IEL's largest undertakings proved disasters. In 1963 an American scientist-promoter, Jerome Spevack, persuaded IEL to help underwrite his enterprise, Deuterium Ltd, which was bidding on a contract to produce heavy water for Atomic Energy of Canada. Although Spevack seemed to possess strong technical credentials, the cost of the plant that was constructed at Glace Bay in Cape Breton was badly underestimated and there were serious design flaws. By the time the plant was completed an initial IEL commitment of $12 million had spiralled into a $140 million direct investment by the province. In 1971 the federal government took over the plant and poured another $225 million into its rehabilitation. By this time AECL had more heavy water than it was likely to ever use. The plant was closed down in 1985, never having achieved full production.

While this fiasco was still in its initial phase, IEL lured an Ontario company, Clairtone, to relocate to Nova Scotia. A small but rapidly growing manufacturer of high-fidelity phonograph sets, Clairtone needed funds to expand production and responded with alacrity to IEL's offer of $8 million. Partly under pressure from IEL to create more jobs and partly because its owners decided to diversify into a new market, the plant erected at Stellarton, N.S. in 1966 was set up to produce colour television sets. The bad timing of this move, and problems in quality control, rapidly undermined the venture. After several years of sustained losses totalling $20 million, Clairtone finally closed down in 1972. Although the major reason for its failure appears to have been a premature entry into an untried market, as in Deuterium's case mismanagement and labour problems were also factors in the débâcle.

K.C. IRVING

Despite the persistence of economic troubles in Atlantic Canada and the apparent inability of governments at any level to surmount these problems, in the post-World War II era the region produced a variety of entrepreneurs who erected family dynasties: the Sobeys and Jodreys in Nova Scotia, the McCains in New Brunswick, the Crosbies in Newfoundland, among others. The most prominent of these regional empire-builders was K.C. Irving. His networks of gas stations, lumber mills, newspapers, shipyards and shipping lines extended across his native New Brunswick through the Maritimes and into Quebec and the New England states. By the 1980s the Irvings' closely-guarded fortune, estimated at over $7 billion, made them one of the ten wealthiest families in North America if not the world—far greater than the more flamboyant and transitory millionaires of the era like Donald Trump or Robert Campeau. The founding father, still keeping watch over his enterprises in his eighties from a modest headquarters in Saint John, N.B., up to his death in 1992 seemed to embody the traditional values of proprietary capitalism that had flourished in the Maritimes a century earlier.

Kenneth Colin Irving was born in 1899, son of a prominent local merchant in the small town of Buctouche in eastern New Brunswick, a vigorous exponent of the Presbyterian virtues of relentless work, thrift, and paternalism. After serving with the Royal Flying Corps in World War I, K.C. became a local dealer for Ford Motor Co. and Imperial Oil. Like Charlie Trudeau in neighbouring Quebec, by the end of the 1920s Irving had set himself up as an independent agent, developing a network of auto service and repair garages across New Brunswick supplied with gas and oil by his own retail company, Irving Oil. During the Depression Irving's enterprises fared well, benefiting from the fact that car owners chose to hang on to their aging vehicles (inevitably requiring repairs), and from local resentment, shared by Irving, of Imperial Oil's 'monopolistic' pricing. Also during the 1930s K.C. inherited a paper mill from his father and used earnings from his auto repair business to acquire large timber holdings in anticipation of a resurging market for paper products. Among his acquisitions —which included a bankrupt bus line in Saint John, several local newspapers and the New Brunswick Power Co.— Irving picked up a small plywood manufacturer, Canada Veneers, in 1938. When the British Air Ministry (under Lord Beaverbrook) came shopping in World War II, Canada Veneers secured the contract for wood frames for over 6,000 De Havilland Mosquito aircraft for the RAF and RCAF.

After the war, K.C. parlayed his earnings from this enterprise into a much-expanded oil and gas operation, moving into refining in the 1950s; purchased corvettes from the navy to establish a cargo line that ranged across the western hemisphere; continued to expand his service stations and paper mills; diversified into home construction materials, and in 1959 took over the Saint John Dry Dock—whose business slumped when government contracts dried up after the Korean War— and substantially expanded its capacity just in time for a renewed naval buildup in the 1970s.

K.C. Irving's approach to business generally and to diversification resem-

K.C. Irving, Max Aitken, and E.P. Taylor vacationing in the Bahamas. (Provincial Archives of New Brunswick/p194/205 and courtesy of *The Daily Gleaner*)

bled that of one of the heroes of his youth, Henry Ford. Dedicated to vertical integration, Irving acquired enterprises that would either supply or provide markets for his main businesses: petroleum and paper products. Earnings were ploughed back into the business; external debt was held to a minimum. Irving sought to keep his companies under personal or family control: Irving Oil, founded in 1929 as a joint-stock venture, quickly passed back into K.C.'s hands as he used its profits to purchase most of the common shares—although later he was obliged to share ownership with the US firm, Socal, in order to finance his refinery. He reared his sons to take over running the businesses, but continued to spend as much time as possible overseeing affairs even after he established residence in Bermuda as a tax haven.

As the major figure on the local economic scene, Irving enjoyed public and political support in New Brunswick for many years. Even the noxious effluent from his Saint John paper mill was greeted as evidence of Irving's prosperity and jobs for New Brunswickers, although in the 1980s the Irvings did make efforts to control these emissions. By the 1960s, however, the extent of Irving's economic influence became a matter of political debate: K.C. feuded with the Liberal premier, Louis Robichaud, over the latter's efforts to roll back tax concessions granted in earlier years to Irving companies. Partly as an offshoot of this dispute, Irving came under fire in the 1970s from the federal Liberal government for allegedly creating a media monopoly in the province —a charge that was ultimately

⟶

dismissed by the Canadian Supreme Court. Although the arrival of Conservative regimes on the federal and provincial scene in the 1980s abated political tensions, the Irvings continued to encounter criticism from trade unionists and environmentalists.

The public image of this proverbially publicity-shy dynasty is ambivalent. On the one hand the Irvings can be seen as representing qualities which, in the conventional wisdom, are far too rarely found among not just Maritime but Canadian businesses: entrepreneurship, efficient organization, financial prudence, and dedication to quality in products and service. On the other hand critics portray them as secretive, ruthless, confrontational with labour, indifferent (at least until recently) to the environmental consequences of their operations, a dynasty whose far-flung enterprises have, paradoxically, blocked the growth of other regional entrepreneurs and have at best only marginally alleviated the population decline and high unemployment rates in their home province.

Sources

DeMont, John, *Citizens Irving: K.C. Irving and His Legacy* (Toronto, 1991).

Hunt, Russell, and Robert Campbell, *K.C. Irving: The Art of the Industrialist* (Toronto, 1973).

Nova Scotia was hardly unique in the field of publicly-financed disasters. The New Brunswick government in 1972 backed a promoter named Malcolm Bricklin who proposed to produce a sports car of novel design. By 1975 the Bricklin venture had gone under, along with the province's commitment of $23 million. During the 1960s Prince Edward Island poured over $9 million into a shipyard and fish-processing plant, a project that collapsed when anticipated foreign funding failed to materialize. Maritimers were not the only producers of white elephants: as we have seen, Quebec, Alberta, and Saskatchewan had their share, although their relative wealth cushioned the impact of these mistakes. During this period the government of Manitoba, seeking like Premier Bennett in B.C. to open up its northern regions, found itself with a money-losing forestry products complex at The Pas whose asset value was less than half the $150 million in loans extended to the project's foreign promoters.

By the 1960s the federal government was moving into the field, creating a series of acronymically euphonic regional development programs: ARDA, FRED, DREE, DRIE, ERDA, and ACOA. These agencies produced fewer dramatic disasters —although federal energy megaprojects foundered spectacularly in the 1980s— and could boast some modest successes. But overall the federal programs did not substantially alter the prevailing pattern of industrial location and development in central Canada. Provincial recipients chafed under the restraints imposed by Ottawa and levels of funding that failed to match the rhetoric that accompanied the unveiling of these programs. Federal bureaucrats and politicos in turn felt that the programs did not have the visibility desired to demonstrate Ottawa's commitment to reducing regional disparities in Canada.

While most chroniclers of provincial development schemes concur on their general lack of success, explanations for these failures vary. Some agree with Bliss that all such undertakings were fundamentally flawed: governments cannot be entrepreneurial, and when they attempt to do so fall prey to shady promoters and political interest groups. Other critics have been less categorical, emphasizing specific, if recurring, problems: those who made investment decisions, even experienced business people, often proceeded on the basis of hunches and guesswork. Details about development projects were shrouded in secrecy, excluding even the government officials ultimately accountable for the investment of public funds. The objectives of these province-building agencies were often ambiguous; the underlying goal was to create jobs (and thus grateful voters) in the short run, limiting the range of investment options and bypassing capital-intensive industries that could provide the base for a more diversified, growth-oriented economy in the long run. Finally, the concept of 'targeting' industries channelled government money away from areas where it could have been most productively used: as economist Roy George observed apropos of IEL, the $150 million expended by Nova Scotia to attract specific firms might better have been used to improve the province's infrastructure, education, and social services—which could have provided a stronger incentive for industrial relocation and private-sector investment.[4]

Few communities had a longer or more frustrating experience with the hazards of province-building than Canada's 'youngest' province, Newfoundland. During the nineteenth century merchants of St John's had wrested control of the local fishery from English companies and mobilized opposition to Confederation in 1867. Attuned to European markets for saltfish and in charge of the import trade, which was mostly from Britain and the US, the merchant élite controlled politics in the precariously-situated Dominion of Newfoundland and economically dominated the outports. A sharp break in fish prices in the mid-1890s precipitated a commercial crisis in St John's, aggravated political tensions in what was essentially a two-class society, and stimulated efforts on the part of the island's government to diversify the economy.

While St John's had produced entrepreneurial families such as the Bowrings who began in the 1850s to develop a transatlantic shipping and trading empire, most of the merchant community operated on a smaller, local scale. The collapse of the local banks in 1895 reinforced their inherent conservatism. Newfoundland's political leaders looked to foreign capital for diversification and growth, proffering land grants and tariff concessions to British, American, and Canadian enterprises that chose to invest there, principally in Newfoundland's mineral and forest resources. In the 1890s Henry Whitney developed iron mines at Bell Island to serve his Nova Scotia-based steel industry and in the early 1900s American and British promoters — including International Power & Paper — set up pulp and paper mills at Grand Falls and Corner Brook. The British Marconi company obtained a telegraph monopoly. Most controversially, a Montreal-based promoter-engineer, Robert Reid, undertook completion of a railway across the island in the 1890s, financed largely with public funds although Reid was assigned title to crown lands and a rail and steamship monopoly for his commitment. In 1921 the

Newfoundland government was obliged to take over the bankrupt line, reenacting on a smaller scale Canada's pageant of railway development.

Worse was to follow. Even before the Great Depression the island's newsprint operations were in financial straits, and the cod fishery which had boomed through World War I and the 1920s slid into crisis in 1931–33. By this point more than one-quarter of Newfoundland's population was on relief. The government, unable to cover the interest on its debts, voluntarily surrendered Dominion status to a British-appointed commission that governed it to 1949.

Military spending during World War II, particularly by the Americans who erected an air base at Gander, resuscitated the economy. The commission government promoted establishment of a co-operative fish enterprise, Newfoundland and Associated Fish Exporters Ltd (NAFEL), which could trace its roots to the fishermen's unions earlier in the century. But the prospects for the fishery were not promising: NAFEL faced competition from Iceland and Norway, the salt cod market was declining as demand grew for fresh-frozen fish, and European trawler fleets were soon to invade the Grand Banks. In 1949, prodded by an energetic political leader, Joey Smallwood, Newfoundland joined Canada. He was to be provincial premier for more than twenty years.

Like his predecessors in the 1890s, Smallwood sought to salvage Newfoundland's economy through diversification. He pinned his hopes particularly on development of Labrador, which had been divided between Quebec and Newfoundland (largely to the latter's advantage) by the British Privy Council in 1927. Anxious to attract manufacturing enterprises to the island portion of his domain, he recruited a self-styled economic expert from Latvia named Alfred Valdmanis to spearhead the effort. Valdmanis seemed to be a good choice, luring German and Swiss investors apparently apprehensive of the unsettled state of affairs in Europe in the early 1950s. Discovered to have been extorting bribes from his clients and submitting fraudulent accounts, Valdmanis was dismissed in 1954 and jailed. In short order many of the enterprises set up under his aegis collapsed and the Newfoundland government found that financing these ill-advised ventures had dissipated the surplus cash reserves built up in the 1940s.

Fortunately, Smallwood had other, grander irons in the fire. After Valdmanis' fall, he backed another promoter, John Doyle, who proposed to develop iron ore resources at Wabush Lake in Labrador; the establishment of the Iron Ore Co. astride the Quebec/Labrador border lent credence to his ideas. In this case Smallwood's instincts proved more sound. In 1957 an international consortium, that included both Dosco and Stelco as well as American and European investors, bought the project from Doyle and seven years later opened a $235 million iron mine at Wabush. Critics, however, argued that the direct benefits of this development to Newfoundland were considerably smaller than those accruing to the corporate participants.

The centrepiece of Smallwood's program was development of the electric power potential of Labrador's Hamilton River. In 1952 he travelled to London, procuring (through Lord Beaverbrook) an audience with Prime Minister Winston Churchill who in turn introduced him to the merchant banking Rothschilds. The Rothschilds organized the British Newfoundland Development Corporation (Brinco), a consortium of British firms, upon which was bestowed—in lieu of cash from Newfoundland—control over virtually all of the Hamilton River watershed with exclusive rights to develop hydro, mining, and forestry resources. Smallwood's expectations for rapid development of power at what was renamed Churchill Falls, however, were to be stymied for twenty years. To justify a project that would ultimately cost over $1 billion, Brinco wanted to secure power markets in the US and central Canada; the power would have to be transmitted through Quebec whose political leaders of all persuasions continued to contest the 1927 Labrador boundary settlement. For a time Smallwood promoted an alternative power transmission cable line through the Maritimes to New England, but by the mid-1960s it was clear that Brinco would have to negotiate with Hydro Quebec. After further bickering, in 1969 the two parties reached an agreement under which Quebec would purchase most of the power from Churchill Falls for 65 years at a fixed price (averaging around 2.5 mills per kilowatt hour); in addition Hydro Quebec took on $115 million in Brinco stocks and bonds. By 1974 Churchill Falls damsite, the largest such project undertaken in Canada, was in operation. Smallwood, who had been ousted from office two years earlier, was not on hand to take the credit.

In any case, Newfoundlanders were increasingly persuaded that there was little credit to be given. In 1974 the province acquired Brinco's shares in Churchill Falls for $160 million and integrated it into the government-owned Newfoundland & Labrador Hydro Corporation, partly in response to public dissatisfaction over rising electric power rates and resentment that Brinco (and Hydro Quebec) were reaping the lion's share of benefits. Subsequently the Newfoundland government challenged the validity of the 1969 contract between Brinco and Hydro Quebec, noting the vast discrepancy between the price paid Newfoundland for its power and the rates charged Quebec and US customers (which ranged up to 30 mills per kilowatt hour), but in 1984 the Supreme Court of Canada upheld the contract. Rather than stimulating a new era of economic growth for Newfoundland, Churchill Falls left a legacy of bitterness and frustration.

There were other setbacks. During the early 1980s the province's leaders looked to the development of offshore oil and gas as their source of renewal; another Supreme Court decision placed the Hibernia field under federal jurisdiction, the oil boom collapsed, and further offshore development came to at least a temporary halt. The expansion of the fishery under Canadian jurisdiction to 200 miles in 1977 seemed to portend better times for the province's oldest industry, but the cycle of boom and bust continued in the fisheries, aggravated by the increasing numbers of European 'factory trawlers' in the Grand Banks. By the early 1990s the rapid decline of the codfish stock led to international and Canadian governments to suspend fishing activities temporarily off Newfoundland; meanwhile fish processing companies such as National Sea Products that had expanded into multinational production in the US were obliged to retrench. Even the traditional staple of Atlantic Canada's economy seemed to be in peril.[5]

Notes

[1]On the development of the oil and gas industry, see Ed Gould, *Oil: The History of Canada's Oil and Gas Industry* (Vancouver, 1976); George de Mille, *Oil in Canada West: The Early Years* (Calgary, 1969); Earle Gray, *Wildcatters: The Story of Pacific Petroleums and Westcoast Transmission* (Toronto, 1982); Philip Smith, *The Treasure Seekers: The Men Who Built Home Oil* (Toronto, 1978); Eric Hanson, *Dynamic Decade* (Don Mills, 1958); Peter Foster, *The Blue Eyed Sheiks: The Canadian Oil Establishment* (Toronto, 1979); Bliss, *Northern Enterprise*, ch. 17. On the economic and political orientation of Alberta's oil community, see J.D. House, *The Last of the Free Enterprisers: The Oilmen of Calgary* (Toronto, 1980); and John Richards and Larry Pratt, *Prairie Capitalism: Power and Influence in the New West* (Toronto, 1979), chs 3–4, 7 and 9. On the business and development views of Social Credit, see Alvin Finkel, *The Social Credit Phenomenom in Alberta* (Toronto, 1989), especially chs 4–6. On the tar sands, see G.D. Taylor, 'Sun Oil and Great Canadian Oil Sands Ltd.: The Financing and Management of a "Pioneer" Enterprise, 1962–74', *Journal of Canadian Studies* 20 (Autumn 1985), 2–21; Larry Pratt, *The Tar Sands: Syncrude and the Politics of Oil* (Toronto, 1976). On Saskatchewan, see Richards and Pratt, *Prairie Capitalism*, chs 5–6, 8, 10–11; Jeanne Kirk Laux and Maureen Appel Molot, 'The Potash Corporation of Saskatchewan', in Allan Tupper and G. Bruce Doern, eds, *Public Corporations and Public Policy in Canada* (Montreal, 1981), 189–220; Laux and Molot, *State Capitalism: Public Enterprise in Canada* (Ithaca, N.Y., 1988), 107–14.

[2]On British Columbia generally, see Jean Barman, *The West Beyond the West: A History of British Columbia* (Toronto, 1991), especially chs 12, 14. On Bennett, see David Mitchell, *W.A.C. Bennett and the Rise of British Columbia* (Vancouver, 1983), especially chs 8–9; an alternative view is offered by Patricia Marchak, 'The Rise and Fall of the Peripheral State: The Case of British Columbia' in Robert J. Brym, ed., *Regionalism in Canada* (Toronto, 1986), 123–59. On B.C. industries, see G.W. Taylor, *Builders of British Columbia: An Industrial History* (Victoria, 1982); Taylor, *Timber: History of the Forest Industry in British Columbia* (Vancouver, 1975), especially chs 13–15; Donald McKay, *Empire of Wood: The MacMillan-Bloedel Story* (Vancouver, 1982); Patricia Marchak, *Green Gold: The Forest Industry in British Columbia* (Vancouver, 1983).

[3]On Quebec generally since World War II, see Paul-André Linteau, *et al.*, *Quebec Since 1930*, trans. Robert Chodos and Ellen Garmaise (Toronto, 1991). On the French Canadian business community, see Jorge Niosi, 'The Rise of French Canadian Capitalism' in Alain Gagnon, ed., *Quebec: State and Society* (Toronto, 1984), 186–200; Niosi, *Canadian Capitalism* (Toronto, 1981), ch. 3; Matthew Fraser, *Quebec Inc.* (Toronto, 1978); Paul-André Linteau and René Durocher, *Le retard du Quebec et l'inferiorité économique des Canadiens français* (Montreal, 1971); Pierre Fournier, *Le Capitalisme au Quebec* (Montreal, 1978); Norman Taylor, 'French Canadians as Industrial Entrepreneurs', *Journal of Political Economy* LXVIII (1960), 37–52; René Prevost and Maurice Chartrand, *Provigo* (Scarborough, Ont., 1988). On Duplessis, see Conrad Black, *Duplessis* (Toronto, 1977). On the Quiet Revolution, see Dale C. Thomson, *Jean Lesage and the Quiet Revolution* (Toronto, 1984), especially chs 10–12; Kenneth McRoberts and Dale Posgate, *Quebec: Social Change and Political Crisis* (Toronto, 1976). On particular crown enterprises and

projects, see Pierre Fournier, 'The National Asbestos Corporation of Quebec', in Tupper and Doern, *Public Corporations and Public Policy*, 353–64; Laux and Molot, *State Capitalism*, 114–21; Carol Jobin, *Les enjeux économiques de la nationalisation de l'électricité* (Montreal, 1978); Andre Bolduc *et al.*, *Quebec: un siècle d'electricité* (Montreal, 1984), chs 17–23.

[4]On Maritime economic affairs after World War II, see James P. Bickerton, *Nova Scotia, Ottawa and the Politics of Regional Development* (Toronto, 1990), which goes well beyond its title in covering the region. See also Roy George, *A Leader and a Laggard Manufacturing Industry in Nova Scotia, Quebec and Ontario* (Toronto, 1970); Henry Veltmeyer, 'The Restructuring of Capital and the Regional Problem', in Bryant Fairley *et al.*, eds, *Restructuring and Resistance: Perspectives from Atlantic Canada* (Toronto, 1990), which offers varying views of the roots of the region's problems. See also chapters 11–13 in Forbes and Muise, *Atlantic Provinces in Confederation*. On IEL, see Roy George, *The Life and Times of Industrial Estates Limited* (Halifax, 1974); Garth Hopkins, *The Rise and Fall of a Business Empire: Clairtone* (Toronto, 1978); and Harry Bruce, *Frank Sobey* (Toronto, 1985), ch. 9. Other studies of provincial development debacles include Philip Mathias, *Forced Growth* (Toronto, 1971); Sandford Borins and Lee Brown, *Investments in Failure* (Toronto, 1986); Tom Kent, 'The Brief Rise and Early Decline of Regional Development', *Acadiensis* 9 (Autumn 1979), 120–4.

[5]On Newfoundland generally, see James Hiller and Peter Neary, eds, *Newfoundland in the Nineteenth and Twentieth Centuries* (Toronto, 1980); Peter Neary, ed., *The Political Economy of Newfoundland, 1929–1972* (Toronto, 1973); David Alexander, 'Development and Dependence in Newfoundland, 1880–1970', *Acadiensis* 4 (Autumn 1974), 3–31; Brian C. Bursey, *A Half Century of Progress? A History of Economic Growth and Development in Newfoundland, 1930–1980* (St John's, 1980); Richard Gwyn, *Smallwood: The Unlikely Revolutionary* (Toronto, 1972); Forbes and Muise, *Atlantic Provinces in Confederation*, chapter 10. On Brinco, see Philip Smith, *Brinco: The Story of Churchill Falls* (Toronto, 1975); Thomson, *Lesage*, 248–88. On the problems of the fisheries, see David Alexander, *The Decay of Trade: An Economic History of the Newfoundland Saltfish Trade, 1935–65* (St John's, 1977); Rosemary Ommer, 'What's Wrong With Canadian Fish?' *Journal of Canadian Studies* 20 (Autumn 1985), 122–42; *Navigating Troubled Waters: A New Policy for Atlantic Fisheries* (Ottawa, 1983) [the Kirby Task Force Report].

20 MILLIONAIRES, MANDARINS, AND MULTINATIONALS

The quarter-century following World War II was an era of unprecedented economic growth for Canada. The average growth rate of the Gross National Product between 1950 and 1970, even taking into account inflationary pressures, rose 5.7 per cent per year, outpacing the Laurier boom of the early 1900s. While the benefits of prosperity were not spread equally across all regions, even in Atlantic Canada employment and income levels were rising and by the end of the period the country could boast the second highest standard of living in the world.

During the ensuing fifteen years, however, matters took a turn for the worse. Through the late 1970s inflation eroded real gains in income. National unemployment rates, which fell below 4 per cent of the work force in the late 1960s, hovered around 8 per cent through the next decade and rose to 12 per cent in 1981–83, marking the worst economic slump since the Great Depression. Chronic imbalances in Canada's balance of payments and rising government deficits, which had been a matter of relatively modest concern in the 1950s and 60s — when they were offset by booming commodity exports, new capital investment and employment growth—now became major issues for the public generally as well as for the business community.

Despite these dramatic shifts in the economy, certain features of Canada's business landscape remained constant between 1950 and 1980, although there were pressures for change that would become more apparent in the 1980s. The large corporations that had emerged in the years before World War II continued to dominate the national scene. Even though C.D. Howe's acolytes lauded gains in secondary manufacturing, the major industrial producers throughout the period were in resource extraction and processing, notably petroleum and paper products. The export staples remained the linchpins of the economy, but there was substantial growth occurring in the financial, retailing and service sectors.

At the same time, new patterns of ownership and control were taking shape. Increasingly through the 1970s and 80s the business community witnessed a bewildering sequence of mergers, consolidations, and reorganizations of the country's largest industrial firms, orchestrated by an assortment of financial entrepreneurs, some of them self-made millionaires in the Max Aitken mould, others the scions of dynastic wealth. To a great extent, however, these conglomerators and take-over artists were simply reshuffling and recapitalizing existing assets rather than creating new industries, and the ultimate impact of all this feverish activity remains to be seen.

Federal government policies, whether in the form of indirect macroeconomic 'planning' or through direct intervention in the marketplace via regulatory measures, crown corporations, or subsidies, played a greater role in the economy in 1945–84 than ever before. Fortified by their experience in World War II, and by an enlarged revenue base derived from income taxes, Ottawa's bureaucratic mandarins set out to introduce the techniques of Keynesian economics to smooth out business cycles—although their aspirations in this regard were hampered by the vagaries and resistance of politicians and business leaders. By the 1970s their task was supplemented by a variety of other missions, sought or unsought: revitalizing the industrial sector; protecting Canada's energy resources; reducing regional economic inequalities; promoting indigenous technological research; and, not infrequently, bailing out disasters in the private sector in order to limit the economic (and political) repercussions of industrial failures. Despite some successes, notably in trade negotiations with the United States and other nations, by the end of this era the Ottawa planners had become scapegoats for the manifold troubles of the economy.

None of these trends were unique to Canada. One of the most important features of the post-World War II era was the growing interdependence of the major industrial economies of western Europe and North America, fostered by monetary and trade agreements initiated by the US—with Canadian support—in the late 1940s and 1950s. These arrangements were intended to reduce economic barriers among nations and avoid a return to the trade wars of the Depression era. At the same time they encouraged the growth of multinational enterprises: in the first instance these companies were largely of American parentage and Canada was a recipient of a renewed surge of US direct investment in its manufacturing and resource sectors. By the early 1970s the degree of American economic influence had re-emerged as a major issue in Canadian politics and policy, its saliency reinforced by the energy crises of 1973–74 and 1979–81. By this time, however, American multinationals faced vigorous competition from European and East Asian firms, and Canadian enterprises were expanding abroad as well. Although Canada remained linked to the US through ties of investment and trade, the central issue was increasingly the long-term ability of both countries to compete effectively in the globalized economy.

COMMANDING HEIGHTS REVISITED

In North America the three decades following the end of World War II have been called the 'age of giant corporations'. Trends toward centralization, consolidation, and economies of scale production—underway since the turn of the century—accelerated. The achievements of big business in wartime mobilization and post-war prosperity reversed its bad image prevalent in the Depression, and subdued if not quite silenced its critics. In Germany and Japan big corporations resurfaced as enthusiasm among their conquerors for 'decartelization' waned in the Cold War; in Britain even socialists became advocates of private-sector consolidation to stem that nation's economic decline. In the US this was the era of the professional manager. Lip-service was accorded to the pre-eminence of the stockholder but real control was exercised by a self-perpetuating oligarchy of top management in giant firms such as General Motors and General Electric. In these institutions a 'civilized' relationship was fostered between business and labour, and big business leaders moved readily to and from Washington, D.C. to head giant public bureaucracies, notably the Defense Department and the Treasury. Meanwhile, business schools poured forth a new generation of managers aspiring to these heights of corporate grandeur. In 1967 the Canadian-born Harvard economist John Kenneth Galbraith proclaimed the arrival of a 'new industrial state' in which big corporations dominated their markets, engaged in long-range planning, and worked in tandem with Big Labour and Big Government to stabilize the economy.[1]

Even in the 1960s this was arguably a less than entirely accurate portrait of the business system, and during the next two decades rapidly changing economic conditions would reveal the limits and weaknesses of managerial capitalism. Nevertheless it was a persuasive perception, and in Canada the dominance of large corporations seemed, if anything, even more entrenched than in the US. This perception was due in part to the presence of subsidiaries of giant American firms, but even in the Canadian-controlled areas of the economy — banking, utilities, and retailing—bigness and stability seemed to prevail. In terms of size measured by assets, Canada's leading corporations remained at the top for more than a quarter century, albeit with some shifts in relative positions and the disappearance of some big utilities into the public sector. More than half the top twenty non-financial joint stock companies in 1955 were still at or near the top in 1980 (see Table 20.1). Their collective wealth had more than doubled, even taking into account inflation in the 1970s. Seven of the ten leading banks and financial institutions in 1955 remained at the head of the class in 1980 (two of the others were merged with larger firms in 1955–60): asset growth for them experienced an even more remarkable eightfold increase. Defenders of Canadian capitalism could point to the growth figures as evidence of the benevolent workings of the market economy; social critics focused on the persistence of a few big corporations to support their arguments against an entrenched business élite.

Behind this façade of stability, however, there were substantial changes in the Canadian business system. Asset size and growth are not the best measurements of business success, although at least up to the post-World War II era these figures are the most consistently accessible and reliable. In sales volume and net earnings (where the trends are relatively parallel, at least for the largest companies), manufacturing, mining, and forestry products accounted for almost two-thirds of the thirty leading non-financial firms in the 1955. Twenty-five years later most big firms were in the oil and gas field and in the 'other' category: retailers, media-related enterprises, construction, and real-estate (see Table 20.2). Even this snapshot is somewhat misleading since the 1980 rankings reflected the peak of the oil and gas boom. By the end of that decade, retailing and consumer products firms accounted for almost half of the fifty largest companies ranked by sales and earnings (see Table E.2 in the Epilogue). In the financial area, change was less apparent, in large measure because banks began, albeit with some reluctance, to expand into consumer credit in the 1950s–60s and investor services in the 1970s–80s.

440

Table 20.1 Canada's Twenty Leading Non-Financial Corporations[a]

RANK BY ASSETS, 1955	RANKING BY SALES, 1955	RANK BY ASSETS, 1980	RANKING BY SALES, 1980
1) Canadian Pacific	6	1) Canadian Pacific	2
2) Bell Canada	15	2) Bell Canada	6
3) Alcan	11	3) Alcan	7
4) Imperial Oil	3	4) Inco	12
5) Inco	7	5) Imperial Oil	4
6) Seagram's	2	6) Noranda	17
7) B.C. Power	b	7) Gulf of Canada	11
8) Shawinigan Power	b	8) Massey Ferguson	8
9) British-American Oil	13	9) Alberta Gas Trunk Line	b
10) Interprov. Pipeline	b	10) Dome Petroleum	b
11) Massey-Harris	12	11) Shell Canada	9
12) Hiram Walker	10	12) Seagram's	b
13) Stelco	18	13) Hudson's Bay	10
14) General Motors	1	14) Trans-Canada Pipe Line	16
15) Cominco	b	15) Stelco	b
16) International Paper	16	16) Genstar	b
17) Ford Motor Co.	9	17) Anglo-Canadian Telephone	b
18) Imperial Tabacco	b	18) Ford Motor Co.	3
19) Abitibi Paper	b	19) Texaco Canada	13
20) MacMillan-Bloedel	b	20) General Motors	1

[a]Excludes crown corporations.

[b]Information on sales unavailable or company not ranked in the top twenty by sales.

Table 20.2 Canada's Thirty Leading Non-Financial Corporations, Distribution by Sector (Ranked by Sales)

SECTOR	% OF TOTAL, 1955	% OF TOTAL, 1980
Utilities[a]	6	10
Manufacturing	46	27
Mining & Forestry	16	10
Oil & Gas	13	16
Other	19	37

[a]Includes railways. By 1980, two of the companies in this category (CPR, Bell Canada) could be classified as 'diversified' companies rather than simply utilities, raising the 'other' category to 44%.

SOURCES: Trott, Elizabeth, 'The Top 30 Canadian Corporations', *The Monetary Times* 125 (April, 1957), 34-6; *Canadian Business Magazine* 53, 27 (July, 1980), 63-4.

Equally significant were changes in patterns of corporate control. The period, particularly since the 1960s, witnessed the reemergence of financial swashbucklers whose empires encompassed many of the largest commercial and industrial corporations in Canada, with old-line companies such as Noranda and Algoma bouncing haplessly from one set of owners to another. Although their American counterparts inevitably captured greater public notice (even in Canada), Canadian take-over kings pioneered some of their techniques, and the Canadian business scene provided an environment more receptive to this renaissance of personal capitalism. As in the US, the growth of pension funds and mutual funds after World War II enlarged the domestic capital pool and spawned a subculture of fund managers prepared to move large blocks of money to maximize short-term earnings. In the US, however, the largest manufacturers were able to draw upon their own retained earnings for reinvestment; the big resource-based companies in Canada were more dependent on external capital sources to finance their expansion during the oil and mining booms of the 1950s and 1970s. Furthermore, since the days of Aitken and Dunn would-be Canadian empire builders were accustomed to travelling to richer money markets abroad to supplement the savings coaxed from cautious Canadians. There were also fewer regulatory or antitrust constraints in Canada and the community of financial movers and shakers was relatively small and cohesive.

One of the earliest proto-conglomerators of the postwar era was Canada's E.P. Taylor, who exploited all these opportunities. Even before service with Howe's Ministry of Munitions in World War II helped assure him of entry into the country's leading clubs and boardrooms, Taylor had erected a mini-empire in the Canadian brewing industry. Beer was (and remains) one of the more intensely regulated industries in Canada, with each province protecting its 'domestic' producers through price differentials and other restrictions on 'imported' (out-of-province) brands. After World War II the largest brewers, Molson's and Labatt's, developed national networks of plants and distributors, taking over many local producers, but in the 1930s the industry comprised a large number of small inefficient operators. Taylor formed an alliance with a British group who provided him with capital to assemble the Brewing Corporation of Canada by buying up small brewers at Depression-era prices. By the end of the decade Taylor's company held one-third of the Ontario beer market and had branched into soft drinks (Orange Crush), hotels and restaurants, and the Carling brewery with manufacturing and distributors in Britain and the United States.

Taylor's wartime activities brought him in contact with American businessmen, among them financier Floyd Odlum who specialized in acquiring and cultivating stocks in undervalued companies. From Odlum Taylor derived the idea of forming a 'closed' investment trust, essentially a venture capital enterprise that would acquire in a few companies blocks of shares sufficient to influence management decisions. The main criterion for selection was the growth potential of the target company, irrespective of its particular line of business: in this sense Argus Corporation, the investment firm set up by Taylor with several Toronto associates in 1945, represented a pioneering form of the conglomerate enterprise that would flourish in the US two decades later. Between 1945 and 1955 Argus acquired shares and board positions in a range of medium to large companies, including Dominion Stores, Dominion Tar, B.C. Forest Products (in association with H.R. MacMillan who sat on the Argus board), Hollinger Mines and, most notably, Massey-Harris.

The reorganization of Massey in the 1950s was a classic example of the Argus approach. After the war the farm implement firm rode the crest of a renewed agricultural boom and in 1953 merged with a British company, run by Harry Ferguson, that held a major tractor patent. Meanwhile, however, friction grew between the Argus group, which held about 28 per cent of the company's shares, and Massey's long-time chief executive James Duncan. In 1956 as the postwar market petered out, Taylor and his associates ousted Duncan and overhauled the company's management, bringing in a new team trained at the Harvard Business School, streamlining the sales force, reducing subcontracting to enhance inventory control, and transforming Massey-Ferguson into a full-scale multinational with more than half of its assets and sales outside North America. For a time Massey-Ferguson represented a major business success story whose dramatic growth reflected Canada's coming of age as an industrialized nation.

By the end of the 1960s other conglomerators were following the Argus path, buoyed by thriving stock markets in Toronto and New York—fuelled in part by US inflation in the Vietnam War era. Even the economic troubles of the following decade did not stem the acquisition spree. The energy crisis of 1973–74 seemed to portend a new age of growth for Canada's resource sector while sluggish performance in Ontario's manufacturing heartland left industrial firms opportune targets for take-overs and 'rationalizations'. Inflation boosted urban real estate prices. Banks and trust companies, legally separated after 1967, competed vigorously in the investment loan market, joined by financial institutions now springing up in western Canada.

Among the most prominent of the take-over kings of the era was Paul Desmarais, the French Canadian financial entrepreneur from Sudbury who transformed the Quebec utilities holding company, Power Corporation, into a vehicle for conglomerate expansion; by 1975 it held controlling interest in (among others) Canadian Steamship Lines, Consolidated Bathurst, Dominion Glass, and several major insurance firms. Desmarais' failed attempt in that year to take over Argus precipitated the creation of a Royal Commission to investigate 'corporate concentration' in Canada. While critical of conglomerates as instruments of real economic growth, the Commission concluded that they posed no danger of monopoly, and (in the spirit of Mackenzie King) that, if anything, the country needed larger, better integrated industries to compete effectively in global markets.

Conglomerators came from diverse backgrounds, with some exceptions such as Conrad Black, largely outside the Anglo-Scots Protestant community of the traditional 'Establishment'. In Desmarais' footsteps came another Ontario-born French Canadian, Robert Campeau, who specialized in acquisitions of retail chains. The Reichmanns, who emigrated from Austria via Morocco in the 1950s, established a foothold in the high-rise construction business in Toronto with their family firm, Olympia & York, went on into the skyscraper heartlands of New York and western Europe, and then diversified in the 1970s, acquiring strong interests in Gulf Canada, Hiram Walker and the pulp and paper giant, Abitibi-Price.

The Bronfman family produced two sets of rival acquisitors. Charles and Edgar, who inherited control of Seagram's from their father, Sam, explored the US merger market. Their explorations culminated in 1981 in an effort to take over Conoco (Continental Oil), one of America's ten major companies in the field and the former partner of the Hudson's Bay Co. in Canadian oil and gas development. Although Conoco ultimately wound up in the hands of Du Pont, the Bronfmans acquired a significant equity position in the American chemical giant. Meanwhile, their cousins Edward and Peter, who had been squeezed out of Seagram's, set up their own investment trust, Edper, and began shopping for companies. Their biggest acquisition, in 1979, was Brascan, successor firm to the Pearson/Mackenzie utility multinational Brazilian Traction. During the 1970s that company had sold off its electric system to Brazil for $450 million and transformed itself into a diversified holding company. While engaged in an extended struggle for control of Brascan, Edper also went after the even larger mining-*cum*-conglomerate Noranda (which had recently taken over MacMillan-Bloedel); the largest brewing company in Canada, Labatt's; and the usual assortment of real estate, insurance, and trust companies.

Another scion of wealth who entered the merger game was Ken Thomson whose father, Roy, had pioneered the radio broadcasting business in Ontario in the 1920s, then moved into newspapers. After World War II Roy Thomson migrated to Britain, establishing himself as a media baron and receiving the title Lord Thomson of Fleet. The most important accretion to his wealth was a fortuitous investment with the US firm, Occidental Petroleum, in British North Sea oilfields shortly before the first energy crisis of 1973. When 'young Ken' inherited the family fortune three years later (at age fifty-five), he deployed it not only into the expansion of the Thomson newspaper empire but also into more diversified areas. In 1979 Thomson acquired controlling interest in the Hudson's Bay Co., which had previously gobbled up a variety of competing retailers, including Simpsons, making 'The Bay' (as it was renamed) the largest department-store chain in Canada. While the harsh recessions of the early 1980s and early 1990s ruined or at least severely damaged the fortunes of lesser conglomerators, the 'Seagram Bronfmans' and Thomson remained among the twenty-five wealthiest billionaires in the world (surpassing the Irvings, as well as the sheikhs of Abu Dhabi and Dubai). Ken Thomson, however, perhaps preserving a Canadian tradition of wealthy miserliness, shopped for bargains at the sales counters of the discount stores that he owned.

While the proprietary empire-builders preempted media attention, among the largest of the era's conglomerates were two of Canada's oldest enduring corporate entities: the CPR and Bell Canada. After the expansion binge of the 1920s, the CPR had retreated for a time from its tradition of diversification. Apart from the creation of CP Air in World War II, the company stuck to railroading and managing its other established investments. During the buoyant 1960s, however, the company resumed its outward thrust, largely at the prodding of Ian Sinclair, who had joined the CPR in 1947 as a lawyer representing the firm in its perpetual freight-rate hearings before the Railway Commission, but soon displayed a talent for financial deal-making. In 1962 Canadian Pacific Investments (CPI) was set up to provide a vehicle for Sinclair's energies: non-transportation investments, including Cominco and CP Oil & Gas (established in 1957 to manage the CPR's mineral resource lands not already leased out), were assigned to CPI. In 1967 CPI began issuing its own public shares and embarked on a career of expansion into real estate through a subsidiary, Marathon Realty; telecommunications development (CNCP); and international investment in hotels, mines, and assorted other areas as well as industrial acquisitions that included Algoma Steel, Maple Leaf Mills and Canadian International Paper. When Sinclair took over as chief executive of the parent company in 1972, he arranged to remove the word 'Railway' from its corporate title. By the time he stepped down in 1981 more than half the company's earnings came from investments outside the transportation field.

Bell Canada also turned to diversification and multinational expansion in the 1970s, a novel move for what had traditionally been a profitable but conservative utility since its early years under Charles Sise. As in the case of the CPR, the central figure in this transformation was a lawyer, Jean de Grandpré, who had been hired in 1965 to help persuade regulatory authorities to liberalize the legal formulas under which the utility's profits were determined and later to combat Canadian Pacific's incursion into the telecommunications field. While de Grandpré was engaged in these tasks, Bell Canada's manufacturing affiliate, Northern Electric—whose links with AT&T's manufacturer Western Electric had been sundered in 1956 in a US antitrust case—was developing a strong base in microelectronic communications technology. By the 1970s the company, renamed Northern Telecom, was looking to foreign markets for its equipment, securing a major contract with Saudi Arabia in 1978 and a foothold in the heavily protected Japanese market in the following decade.

The Saudi contract, however, set the stage for a confrontation between Bell and the federal regulatory agency, the Canadian Radio and Telecommunications Commission, which rejected de Grandpré's argument that Telecom's overseas earnings should be considered separate from Bell's domestic business. This episode led de Grandpré to devise a legal strategy through which the utility's operations not directly tied to telephone service in Canada would be placed under a separate entity, Bell Canada Enterprises—BCE—(which also functioned as the parent of the telephone company). In 1983 de Grandpré became chief executive of BCE. Riding the mid-decade securities market boom made BCE the largest Canadian company in terms of assets with net earnings in excess of $1 billion in 1986; it acquired (among other enterprises) Trans-Canada Pipelines and other remnants of Dome Petroleum's empire and the former crown corporation Teleglobe Canada. At the end of the 1980s Bell Canada and Canadian Pacific remained, as they had been in 1955, the country's two largest private enterprises,

445

but both had been substantially transformed into 'diversified' companies operating in international markets.

Few of these conglomerates pursued E.P. Taylor's practice of 'hands on' control — and even the Argus approach was not without its shortcomings, as the later history of Massey-Ferguson would demonstrate. Mergers and take-overs created work for numerous lawyers, accountants, brokers, and business consultants, but the 'rationalizations' that usually followed eliminated managerial and manufacturing jobs in even greater numbers. The 1978 Royal Commission noted that the financial performance of conglomerates rarely matched expectations: as in the merger mania of 1909–13 and the late 1920s, many of these companies carried large debt loads and were vulnerable to economic downturns such as those in 1981–83 and again in the early 1990s.[2]

THE CARETAKER STATE

The years between the end of World War II and the 1970s have sometimes been designated 'the age of Keynes' in the industrialized capitalist nations. By this account, these countries embraced many of the policies advocated by the British economist during the Depression: the reduction of trade barriers among nations and the deployment by governments of fiscal policies at home that would, through indirect means, cushion the impact of fluctuations in business cycles. Focusing on the demand side of the market, governments fashioned taxing and spending measures to prop up consumer demand and encourage capital investment in periods of economic distress, and (in theory) to dampen inflationary pressures when economies were running at close to full capacity.

In actuality, this era was short-lived and Keynesian ideas were never fully embraced. Members of the business community, especially bankers, were less than whole-hearted in accepting government policies that produced regular budget deficits; politicians generally endorsed tax cuts and government spending to fight recessions but were reluctant to openly back tax increases and spending cuts to combat inflation. Even during the 1960s when political and business leaders achieved a certain level of consensus on the viability of Keynesian techniques, factors other than the pursuit of economic equilibrium were influencing policy-making, and that consensus eroded steadily during the 'Great Inflation' of the 1970s.[3]

In Canada a relatively early commitment to Keynesianism was achieved, thanks to the influence of the mandarin successors to Clifford Clark at the Finance Department, through the years of Liberal hegemony in Ottawa. Even C.D. Howe's Reconstruction ministry endorsed the countercyclical measures proposed in the White Paper on Employment and Income in 1945. Although emphasis was also placed on the traditional goal of boosting exports, in fact the main engine of growth in the immediate postwar years was the domestic market. At the same time, political considerations— federal bureaucrats' desire to expand into areas of provincial jurisdiction and the Liberal party's need to counteract CCF appeals

446

by co-opting their social welfare proposals—underlay the commitment to government spending programs.

During the 1950s 'macroeconomic management' showed signs of disarray. Graham Towers' successor at the Bank of Canada, James Coyne, began to tighten controls on the money supply in order to address what he perceived as the menace of inflation (which was growing at about 2 per cent per year at mid-decade). Friction between the masters of fiscal and monetary policies reached a head in the early 1960s when the Diefenbaker government sought to expand spending to cope with a recession beginning in 1958. Coyne's resistance led to his resignation-*cum*-dismissal in 1962, an event that met with a mixed response from the business community but one sufficiently negative to deter future prime ministers from taking similar actions.

Back in power, the Liberals introduced a new panoply of spending programs intended to do more than simply counteract a business slump: measures to aid 'have not' regions, a national health insurance program, and creation of an Industrial Development Bank. The decade of the sixties witnessed a major change in the scope and degree of government intervention in the economy, and not just in Canada. In Britain the Labour government unveiled plans to resuscitate that country's ailing industrial system. In the US, President Lyndon Johnson declared a 'war on poverty' which, unhappily for him, coincided with an escalating military conflict in Southeast Asia. In Canada, Prime Minister Trudeau proclaimed his intention to create a 'just society'.

All these heady visions disintegrated in the years that followed but governments did not abandon their hopes of managing economic affairs. In the 1960s the underlying aim was to redistribute the benefits of sustained economic growth; in the next decade governments sought to contain inflation through wage and price controls. By the middle of the 1970s, economists and government planners perceived inflation to be only one of a range of interconnected problems: declining productivity rates in manufacturing, particularly troubling in the face of new competition from the industrializing nations of the East Asia rim; apparent scarcities in energy resources which were exploited by the oil-producing countries' cartel, OPEC; and, finally, constraints on the ability of governments to deal effectively with these issues. Conservatives in Canada (and elsewhere) attributed this last problem to public deficit financing and the growth of long-term debt; resurgent nationalists in Canada focused on the alleged practices of multinational corporations, transferring jobs and investment away from North America and circumventing the regulatory and taxing powers of national states.

Between 1973 and 1983 much of the attention of federal policy makers was devoted to the subject of foreign direct investment in Canada and the development of the nation's energy resources. (These issues were increasingly perceived as interlinked, and will be discussed in more detail in the next section.) The government embarked on a series of what were essentially *ad hoc* arrangements but which in effect represented yet another interventionist thrust: propping up or taking over faltering large firms in troubled industries. 'Bail-outs' were by no means new to the Canadian economic scene; the Welland Canal and Canadian

Northern Railway, for example, had been kept afloat by government loans for years before finally becoming public enterprises, and even the mighty CPR had relied on injections of government funds in its early years. But the regularity with which public monies were used to salvage foundering firms in the 1970s inspired the CCF/NDP leader David Lewis to ridicule the private sector recipients as 'corporate welfare bums'—even as his party supported crown take-overs to preserve jobs.

Bail-outs were rarely justified simply as measures to save jobs. In 1967 when the British company Hawker-Siddeley (previously Avro Canada) decided to jettison its ailing coal and steel subsidiary, Dosco, government intervention was presented as a facet of regional development policy for the Maritimes. In fact the Cape Breton industry had been nursed along with freight subsidies and rail and defence contracts since the 1940s, although not in sufficient amounts to persuade Dosco's owners to undertake major improvements in the region's mills and mines. In the wake of Hawker-Siddeley's departure, the federal government and Nova Scotia worked out an arrangement under which the province would take over the steel mills while the mines were placed under a federal crown enterprise, Cape Breton Development Corporation (Devco), its mandate being to phase out coal mining and try to develop a more diversified industrial base for Cape Breton. Then the energy crisis of the early 1970s appeared to resuscitate prospects for coal markets, and diversification languished. Meanwhile, the steel operation (Sysco) limped along, propped up by provincial subsidies and continuing federal rail contracts. By the 1980s the region's coal industry too was largely dependent on government purchases as Nova Scotia converted its electric power system to coal-based generation. As instruments of economic development neither Devco nor Sysco had been particularly successful, and both remained vulnerable to shifts in government policies that could reduce or remove their financial support.

During the early 1970s the federal government intervened in central Canada's aircraft manufacturing industry. Again, this move was portrayed not as a bail-out but rather as a measure to support Canadian technological innovation and reduce foreign ownership; again, intervention followed years of government subsidization and took place in the context of a severe slump in the industry. Liberal leaders in Ottawa may have also have been mindful of their party's harsh criticism of Diefenbaker during the Avro Arrow débâcle in 1959. In 1974 the Canadian government purchased De Havilland Aircraft, another Hawker-Siddeley subsidiary (acquired at the tail end of Avro Canada's merger binge), and two years later, bought Canadair from its American parent, General Dynamics. Both companies were in financial difficulties but both were also developing new aircraft that the Canadian government touted as state-of-the-art technology. De Havilland's Dash-7 had the capability of landing and taking off from short airstips; Canadair was developing the Challenger, a small-scale jet suitable for the 'executive travel' market.

In addition to the $76 million paid to acquire the companies, over the next decade the federal government poured another $160 million into the Dash-7 and more than $1 billion in subsidies and loan guarantees into the Challenger. Unfortunately, both crown enterprises moved to full-scale commercial production of their aircraft during the hard recession of the early 1980s, and their consequent losses made them targets for critics as costly and allegedly mismanaged government enterprises. Both were subsequently re-'privatized': Bombardier took over Canadair after the federal government agreed to write off much of the debt incurred for the Challenger. De Havilland, ironically, passed into the hands of an American firm, Boeing Aircraft.

The recession of 1981–83 left its mark on more than the Canadian aircraft industry. In large measure the recession was a by-product of tough monetary policies imposed by the US Federal Reserve that drove interest rates up to 20 per cent and higher in order to break the inflation gripping the international economy in the late 1970s. The Bank of Canada pursued a similar course, perhaps more out of necessity than preference, given that Canada's balance-of-payment difficulties more than offset increases in exports after 1975. Inflation was brought down from 12 per cent per year in 1979 to under 5 per cent by 1984 by the 'old time religion' of credit restraint rather than Keynesian measures; national unemployment rates rose above 10 per cent of the workforce for the first time since 1939. Manufacturers, whose fortunes had been mixed at best in the 1970s, were badly hit by the monetary squeeze. Even the energy sector faced an uncertain future as the combined impact of recession, fissures in OPEC, and the development of new oil sources began to affect international markets.

The recession fostered a new round of bail-outs as well. The most spectacular involved Dome Petroleum, discussed on page 460. But there were other supplicants who seemed to demand action, given the potential impact of their demise on entire regions of the country. Massey-Ferguson had begun stumbling into crisis in 1978, experiencing in that year the biggest loss ($262 million) of any corporation in Canadian history. Massey's problems were partly the result of overexpansion abroad, entailing massive new debt in the early 1970s, and divisions among top managers. Conrad Black, who had wrested control over Argus Corporation in 1978, sought to turn the situation around, but within three years decided to pull his company out of Massey-Ferguson. By this time gloom had descended across the entire industry: even the US giant, International Harvester, faced bankruptcy. A Massey collapse would not only jeopardize thousands of jobs in Ontario but also the stability of several of the nation's largest banks, already a source of major anxiety over potentially bad loans overseas. Ultimately, Massey was refinanced at $700 million with loan guarantees from the Canadian and Ontario governments, and restructured as a much-shrunken firm—eventually to be shorn even of its historic Massey-Ferguson name, as 'Varity Ltd'.

At the same time a crisis loomed in Atlantic Canada. During the 1970s the beleaguered region had experienced a renewal, at least of hope for better times ahead, based in part on offshore oil and gas discoveries and also by the proclamation in 1977 of a 200-mile 'economic zone' off the coast, excluding foreign trawlers from much of the Grand Banks area. By the end of the decade Canada had become the largest exporter of fish in the world, and processing companies were expanding their fleets and plants: in Nova Scotia, National Sea Products was swallowed by a Cape Breton rival, H.B. Nickerson, in 1977. Expansion was costly, however, and the credit crunch of 1981–82 caught fishery companies heavily leveraged, particularly with the Bank of Nova Scotia.

By 1982 Ottawa, aware of the magnitude of the industry's debt troubles, established a Royal Commission under Michael Kirby, one of Trudeau's closest advisers, to search for solutions. The solution unveiled in the Atlantic Fisheries Restructuring Act in the following year entailed a substantial consolidation of enterprises in the region with an infusion of federal money accompanied by a significant degree of government ownership, to be shared with the banks. After much bickering with the Bank of Nova Scotia over the level of government financing required to make the enterprise viable and with the province over the social costs of closing down small plants in the outports, Fisheries Products International was set up in Newfoundland, with the federal government as the major investor.

In Nova Scotia, negotiations were equally complicated: local processors, backed by a consortium that included the Jodrey and Sobey families, and the provincial government resisted Kirby's plan for what was essentially to be a crown enterprise, and succeeded in reorganizing National Sea Products in 1984 as a private firm with minority government participation. National Sea then set out to become a multinational, establishing processing plants and marketing agencies in the US. Rapid depletion of the northern cod and other fish stocks later in the decade—which Canadian processors blamed on foreign fleets violating the 200-mile limit, and environmentalists blamed on general overfishing of the Grand Banks — precipitated a new crisis in the fisheries in the early 1990s, forcing National Sea to sell off much of its newly erected empire and to retreat to its original home base in Lunenburg, N.S.[4]

THE MULTINATIONAL STORM

While economic policy makers in Ottawa, Washington and elsewhere were primarily concerned with trade issues, the arrangements they negotiated with one another in the late 1940s and 1950s would have significant implications for international capital flows. Increase in world trade combined with the growth of international direct investment laid the groundwork for what by the 1980s was called the 'globalized economy'. The Bretton Woods system provided a stable base for currency exchanges for more than twenty-five years; US aid programs pumped billions of dollars into Western Europe and East Asia, resurrecting markets and stimulating new industrial growth. Paradoxically, multilateral tariff reductions encouraged companies in the US, and then in other industrialized countries, to develop sales and production facilities abroad. This was in part to ensure themselves of a foothold in emerging regional markets such as the European Economic Community, and later to circumvent non-tariff barriers that many countries, including the US itself and Canada, resorted to in the unstable economic climate of the 1970s. New technologies in communications, computers, and air travel provided the sinews of more closely knit multinational structures and brought hitherto remote areas into the global marketing networks — much as railways, steamships, and the telegraph spawned corporate integration at the national level in the nineteenth century.

While business leaders might hail the multinational enterprise as a symbol of progress and global prosperity, other observers were less sanguine. Critics in the Third World denounced them as instruments of a new 'Western imperialism', corrupting governments and consigning their countries perpetually to the role of 'hewers of wood and drawers of water' for the industrialized centres of Western Europe and North America. At the same time, trade unionists and social reformers in those industrialized centres warned that multinationals were exporting manufacturing jobs to low-wage nations in the Third World, concealing their profits in foreign tax havens such as Switzerland or Bermuda, and using their mobility and political influence to avoid regulatory measures imposed by national states. Perhaps not surprisingly, Canada, as a country traditionally dependent on exports of natural and semi-processed goods for foreign earnings but also with a small (though vulnerable) manufacturing base, produced critics of multinationals who offered both lines of argument simultaneously. During the Cold War era with its steady economic growth, these views had at best a limited audience. As economic conditions worsened in the ensuing decades, however, distrust of big business resurfaced, focused now on multinationals and reinforced by the continuing ambivalence of Canadians toward the United States.[5]

As noted in Chapter Fifteen, as early as 1926 American had surpassed British investment in Canada, with direct investment comprising almost half the total. Although the Depression curtailed the flow of new capital into Canada from the US, by 1940 growth had resumed, primarily in the form of branch plants in manufacturing. By 1950 Americans had over $6.8 billion invested in Canada (52 per cent in direct investment) and the rapid development of the country's mining and petroleum resources quickened the pace of growth in that decade. By 1960 US investment exceeded $17 billion, and that figure more than doubled over the next ten years, by which time direct investment comprised over 60 per cent of the total. Canada was the largest single-country recipient of US private capital throughout this period, and although inflows were beginning to pick up from other sources in the 1960s, at the end of that decade American investment still comprised over 80 per cent of the total figure of $35 billion.

This massive influx of American capital after World War II had a dramatic impact on patterns of ownership in Canada's industries, most notably in mining and petroleum where US firms controlled well over half the assets by 1967. American ownership in manufacturing also grew steadily if less dramatically: in specific industries, including automotive products, chemicals, rubber, and tobacco, foreign firms controlled between 80 per cent and 100 per cent of the assets. At the same time, the American and other foreign positions in railways and other utilities declined significantly, reflecting both the growth in crown ownership in these areas and shifts in investor interest as the Canadian domestic market expanded and its resource hinterlands were opened up for exploitation (see Table 20.3).

451

Table 20.3 US Direct Investment in Canadian Industry 1929-1977 (US-owned assets as % of total assets)

INDUSTRY	1929	1954	1967	1977
Manufacturing	30%	41%	45%	42%
Mining	32	49	56	40
Oil & Gas	n/a	67	60	51
Utilities[a]	23	9	7	5
All Industries	15	24	28	24

[a]Includes railway investments.

SOURCES: *Foreign Direct Investment in Canada* (Ottawa, 1972), 20-1; Jorge Niosi, *Canadian Multinationals*, 37.

By the 1960s other trends were becoming apparent. In the immediate aftermath of World War II, Ontario was the major recipient of US direct investment. By the end of the 1950s, however, the rate of new foreign investment, particularly in manufacturing, was levelling off there while western Canada was experiencing substantial new inflows — a circumstance that may have influenced the varying attitudes in the regions toward the benefits of foreign investment. In addition, US investors and companies were finding new opportunities, particularly in Western Europe following the creation of the Common Market in 1957 and in the burgeoning, capital-hungry economies in the East Asia Pacific rim. Canada's share declined from more than one-third of total US foreign investment in 1960 to about one-quarter by the mid-1970s, although American ownership remained substantial, particularly in the oil and gas industry. A similar pattern can be discerned in the distribution of control over Canada's largest private companies. In 1955 one-third of the country's thirty top non-financial corporations were partially or wholly foreign-owned; that proportion had declined to 25 per cent by 1980. Ironically, the debate over US economic control in Canadian industry took place at a time when that control was beginning to diminish.

Up to the mid-1950s the only debatable issue about foreign investment in Canada was how to get more of it. C.D. Howe's postwar reconstruction plans were predicated on fresh inflows of foreign capital, and the federal government offered numerous incentives to encourage such growth. Accelerated depreciation of assets for tax purposes, introduced in World War II, was extended to foreign direct investments (except in banking and trade) after the war. When Canada imposed exchange controls in 1947–48, repatriation of earnings by foreign investors was exempted in order not to deter new capital imports. The government also extended direct aid for specific projects that would develop Canada's natural resources and infrastructure. One such undertaking precipitated the first serious public controversy over the consequences of this 'open door' policy toward foreign investment: significantly, in light of the preoccupations of later years, this episode involved the oil and gas industry.

In the early 1950s a consortium of US and Canadian investors, led by the Texas oilman Clint Murchison, undertook to build a gas pipeline from Alberta to the American Middle West via Ontario. Like many such ventures the Trans-Canada Pipe Line Co. experienced numerous delays and unanticipated costs, but Howe, who was wedded to the scheme (which among other things offered jobs to his constituents in northern Ontario) kept the faith. In 1956 he agreed to set up a crown enterprise to build part of the line and to extend $80 million in new loans to Trans-Canada. With the Arrow débâcle looming in the background, the opposition in Parliament denounced the Liberal regime for its generous aid to foreigners seeking to deplete the nation's resources.

Although Howe forced his measure through, the 'pipeline debate' brought the issue of American economic influence to the fore and contributed to the government's electoral defeat in the following year. By this time, even the Liberals were badly divided on the issue: Walter Gordon, a Toronto businessman (and Liberal) who chaired a Royal Commission on Canada's Economic Prospects — created over Howe's protests—brought forth a report in 1957, shortly before the election, that focused on the dangers of foreign direct investment. Gordon emphasized in particular its impact on Canada's balance-of-payments problems; and, in terms reminiscent of Sir John A. Macdonald, warned that Canada faced possible economic if not political 'integration' with the United States.

Although Diefenbaker's squabbles with the US government over defence and trade issues — including a dispute over efforts by Washington to prevent US-owned subsidiaries in Canada from trading with Red China—strained Canadian-American relations, they did not disrupt the inflow of US direct investment, and Gordon's views represented a minority sentiment, especially in the Canadian business community. During the reshuffling among the Liberals after 1958, Gordon acquired influence with the new leader, Lester Pearson, and emerged as the Finance Minister when the Liberals returned to power in 1963. Gordon's initial budget, which included provisions for a 30 per cent tax rate on foreign 'takeovers' of Canadian companies, aroused such an outcry in Canada's financial quarters that it was hastily withdrawn, and Gordon himself departed from the cabinet shortly thereafter.

Although Canada's exports had rebounded from the recession, deficits in its trade balance with the US persisted through 1962–63. Automotive imports accounted for over half of the total, reflecting the predominance of American firms in the industry and the fact that most of their branch operations in Canada were assembly plants, importing vehicle parts from US suppliers of their parent companies. A Royal Commission set up under Diefenbaker had proposed establishment of what would in effect be a free-trade arrangement in the auto and parts industry between the two countries; after some protectionist manoeuvring on both sides, a formal agreement, the Auto Pact, was negotiated in 1965. Under this arrangement, Canadian affiliates of US auto makers would be able to export vehicles to the American market duty-free up to an amount equal to Canada's imports of parts, with the added provision that 60 per cent of the material and parts of those vehicles should be produced in Canada.

The Auto Pact encouraged expansion of US auto production with a concurrent increase in parts manufacturing in Canada, mostly in Ontario. Canada's trade deficit with the US was eased and the Canadian share of the North American auto market doubled to about 14 per cent over the ensuing decade. In the short term the Auto Pact could be lauded as a demonstration of the benefits accruing to Canada from the continental integration of the industry and the diplomatic friendship that followed economic connections. Later, when American auto companies faced rising competition from foreign manufacturers, Canadian nationalists could lament the longer-term consequences of Canada's industrial dependence in this area—although by the end of the 1980s the Auto Pact also provided an incentive for Japanese and Korean car-makers to set up branch plants in Canada in order to circumvent growing trade restrictions on their direct imports into the US.

Another episode, of considerably less consequence, demonstrated the peculiar configuration of foreign ownership in Canadian business. In 1963 Citibank of New York proposed to acquire the small Dutch-owned Mercantile Bank of Canada. The Canadian banking community, usually complaisant about the progress of American direct investment, exhibited alarm over the prospect of a foreign invasion of a sector that was overwhelmingly under indigenous control. Although ultimately unsuccessful in blocking the Mercantile Bank take-over, the industry's lobbyists were able to push through amendments to the Bank Act in 1967, limiting nonresident ownership of chartered banks while, incidentally, liberalizing restrictions on the ability of banks to offer competitive interest rates. Citibank eventually sold off its holdings in Mercantile Bank, and Canadian domination in this field remained largely unchallenged until the 1980s.

By the late 1960s public concern over the purported dangers of American economic influence was increasing. Several factors were at work: US involvement in Vietnam rekindled anti-American sentiments largely dormant since World War II. More material considerations were also involved: as US balance-of-payments problems emerged in the 1960s, Washington began imposing restraints on capital outflows, disregarding pleas from the Canadian government for special treatment which had been accorded in the past. In 1971 when the US faced deficits in both its trade and payments balances—for the first time since World War I—American President Nixon introduced import ceilings and surcharges, setting the stage for devaluation of the dollar (effectively ending Bretton Woods currency arrangements) later in the year. Although Canada was not the main target of these protectionist measures, as America's largest trading partner it would inevitably be affected. Canadian officials sought to negotiate exemptions from the trade restrictions, exemptions which were eventually provided, but the episode demonstrated Canada's economic vulnerability. The Trudeau government announced its intention to promote trade outside North America, which proved to be a rather quixotic quest: in 1982 more than two-thirds of Canada's exports and imports were with the US, a proportion essentially unchanged since 1971.

Meanwhile, Canadian nationalists had fleshed out their critique of the impact of foreign direct investment on the country. Branch plants in manufacturing, it was argued, were inefficient since their parent firms restricted them to short production runs for the small domestic market, rendering them unable to achieve economies of scale. The benefits of foreign technology, which supposedly would flow into Canada along with direct investment, were not apparent: the multinationals for the most part did not equip their subsidiaries with research capabilities or state-of-the-art products and processes. Although foreign-owned firms were recruiting and training more Canadians for technical and managerial positions than in the past, this trend too was seen as debilitating: the best and brightest Canadians were being inducted into multinational corporate organizations while indigenous entrepreneurship languished.

By the early 1970s significant elements of the federal Liberal party and most of the NDP embraced this critique and lobbied for measures to restrict further foreign direct investment. Although neither Prime Minister Pearson nor his successor, Trudeau, were stalwart economic nationalists, they recognized the potential political strength of the nationalists' appeals, particularly in Ontario's troubled industrial heartland. Pearson brought Gordon back into the government in 1967 and allowed him to set up a new Task Force on Canadian Industry that elaborated on the sins of the multinationals.

In 1971 the Canada Development Corporation, originally conceived by Walter Gordon, was created. The CDC was to be a 'mixed enterprise'—the government held a majority of shares but would presumably dilute its holdings to 10 per cent over the years. In practice this dilution was never wholly achieved. The CDC was mandated to 'help develop Canadian-controlled . . . corporations in the private sector' but also took over several crown enterprises, including Polymer and Eldorado Mines. In effect it was a kind of government-sponsored conglomerate. In 1973 CDC acquired a strong position in the US-owned mining and chemical firm, Texasgulf; and later the French gas company, Aquitaine. Although the CDC did not become the main instrument for 're-Canadianization' of the economy as its proponents hoped, by the end of the decade it had acquired a substantial asset base of about $2 billion — roughly equivalent to Brascan — and successfully resisted efforts by governments at various levels to turn it into a dumping ground for bail-outs.

In 1973 the Trudeau government, temporarily dependent on NDP support to stay in power, took a further step down the nationalist road with the establishment of the Foreign Investment Review Agency (FIRA). This agency, the brainchild of yet another federal task force chaired by Ontario MP Herb Gray, was proposed as a moderate alternative to the expansion of government ownership advocated by the NDP. FIRA would screen new foreign direct investments—with exemptions for small foreign firms (with assets under $250,000) and, more significantly, new investments by companies already operating in Canada. Although the introduction of FIRA generated much adverse publicity in the American business community (and it was 'defanged' in 1984 as part of the Mulroney government's effort to demonstrate that Canada was no longer 'hostile' toward foreign investment), many Canadian nationalists regarded it as a half-hearted affair. In practice, more than three-quarters of all applicants had their investment proposals approved; more applicants simply withdrew their applications than were rejected outright by FIRA. In retrospect it seems fair to say that, despite the plethora of commissions and task forces and the rhetoric of parliamentarians, the actual policies introduced by the federal government in this area were cautious, designed to placate public alarm without significantly jeopardizing the inflow of foreign capital that most Canadian political as well as business leaders saw as essential for continued economic development.[6]

In only one area (besides banking) did Canadian government policies approximate the nationalist rhetoric. Before 1973 most attention was focused on the foreign presence in manufacturing; from that point, the issue of American direct investment was increasingly linked to the development and control of Canada's energy resources. Developments on the international scene in the early 1970s set the stage for dramatic intervention by the federal government in the oil and gas industry and culminated with the National Energy Program of 1980–81—which in turn fell victim to abrupt shifts in global oil markets.

As had most of the other industrialized nations, in the 1950s, Canada shifted from coal to oil and gas as the major source of energy for both industrial and residential uses, with a modest increase in hydroelectric power. Canada also had large reserves of petroleum, and the National Energy Board, established in 1960 to regulate the market, consistently encouraged exports through the decade. Although western Canadian oil and gas looped through Ontario en route to the US market, Quebec and the Atlantic provinces depended on imports, principally from South America. In 1959 Home Oil had proposed construction of a pipeline from Alberta to Montreal, but Imperial Oil and Shell, the major suppliers for the eastern region, lobbied successfully against it. These elements comprised the 'National Oil Policy', such as it was, through the early 1970s.

But circumstances were changing. The United States—whose domestic producers had limited supplies from Canada and elsewhere through the 1960s—became a net importer of oil, and oil-producing countries, principally in the Middle East and Latin America, had set up a cartel, the Organization of Petroleum Exporting Countries (which did not include Canada or Mexico) to try to limit production and thus boost prices. The events of October 1973, when the Arab countries embargoed oil exports to countries that supported Israel and OPEC effectively jacked up the price of crude oil from $2 (US) per barrel to over $8 (US) per barrel, demonstrated the consequences of these changes. While Canada's immediate energy needs were not imperilled, two episodes in the 1973 crisis highlighted the role of foreign ownership in the energy sector. At the height of the crisis, tankers carrying oil to eastern Canadian ports were reportedly diverted to the US; moreover, the Canadian government learned that the country's potential oil reserves, based primarily on information from the industry, had been significantly overestimated.

In the wake of the 1973 crisis the Trudeau government, prodded by the NDP and by bureaucrats in the federal Department of Energy, Mines and Resources (who regarded the NEB as too closely tied to the industry), imposed controls and new taxes on oil and gas exports, froze domestic prices, announced its intention to build a pipeline linking Montreal to western supplies, and in 1975 established a crown corporation, Petro-Canada. As discussed in Chapter Nineteen, the export controls and tax measures infuriated Alberta and triggered a decade of federal-provincial bickering. For producers in the private sector, domestic and foreign-owned, the development of Petro-Canada generated an equally bitter controversy; when the crown corporation set up its headquarters in downtown Calgary, local oilmen promptly dubbed the spot 'Red Square'.

In fact Petro-Canada was initially a rather modest undertaking, intended primarily to explore for oil on Canada's northern frontier and to carry out research and development in synthetic fuels and other 'unconventional' energy areas. For these projects there would be little immediate commercial return and hence limited private investor interest, very much in keeping with the Howe tradition: the federal government transferred to Petro-Canada its share in Alberta's Syncrude project and also in a northern exploratory venture, Panarctic Oils. This strategy shifted, however, when Wilbert Hopper, a former energy consultant with the US firm Arthur D. Little and deputy minister of the Department of Energy, took over Petro-Canada in 1977. The original legislation required that Petro-Canada eventually become 'self-financing', and Hopper reasoned that this objective could not be met if the company restricted itself to unprofitable activities. Under Hopper, Petro-Canada began acquiring private companies involved in petroleum refining and distribution with the aim of creating an integrated system that (among other things) would be hard for a future government to dismantle. The earnings from these 'downstream' operations would be used to finance frontier development.

In Petro-Canada's initial expansionist foray, Hopper was outmanoeuvred by another quasi-public entrepreneur, Bob Blair of Alberta Gas Trunk Line, in a bidding war for Husky Oil. Subsequently Petro-Canada acquired Pacific Petroleums Ltd, a large western gas producer, from its American parent, Phillips Petroleum. After avoiding a privatization effort by the short-lived government of Joe Clark, Petro-Can took over the Belgian-owned Petrofina and then British Petroleum's Canadian holdings, which provided it with a network of refineries and service stations across the country. By 1985, when it acquired Gulf Canada's refining and marketing operations, Petro-Canada was the second largest oil company in Canada with over $8 billion in assets and one-fifth share of the country's petroleum retail market.

Most of these acquisitions were made after 1980; prior to that point, government policy and financing had emphasized Petro-Canada's frontier role. The $1.25 billion used to purchase Pacific Petroleums had been secured from Canadian banks in exchange for shares in a subsidiary, Petro-Canada Explorations. Developments in the international oil market and in domestic politics in 1979–80, however, loosened government restraints on financing Petro-Canada's expansion and also laid the groundwork for the National Energy Program (NEP). The overthrow of the Shah of Iran by Islamic fundamentalists in 1979 and the outbreak of war in the Persian Gulf a year later created an atmosphere of uncertainty about future oil supplies from that region. Once again OPEC exploited the situation, driving the price of oil to unprecedented levels, to $26 (US) per barrel and higher.

457

The sudden inflation in world oil prices and continued fear among Canadians over the long-term security of their supplies tilted public opinion toward a more nationalist and interventionist approach to energy issues—which helped protect Petro-Canada from the Clark government's privatization initiative in 1979 and contributed to the abrupt resurrection of the Liberals in the 1980 federal election. Reinstalled in power, the Trudeau government introduced a wide-ranging set of measures intended to expand Canada's energy resources, augment federal control over domestic prices and exports, and reduce foreign ownership in the nation's oil and gas industry.

The National Energy Program was a complex and controversial piece of legislation. The oil-producing provinces, particularly Alberta, were antagonistic. Even though the price of their oil and gas for the domestic market was allowed to rise toward world market levels, the NEP tax and royalty arrangements reduced their share of revenues. The Reagan administration in Washington, D.C. was outraged by Canada's affront to free-market principles and, more specifically, by the export restrictions and provisions of the NEP that discriminated against US companies. Within the industry, the reaction was generally critical, but the NEP had been designed to provide incentives to the smaller, Canadian-owned firms as well as Petro-Canada.

The Petroleum Incentives Program (PIP) provided subsidies and tax benefits specifically for companies with more than 50 per cent Canadian ownership that embarked on exploratory ventures. It reserved for them, as well, access to oil and gas deposits on federally-controlled crown lands—which encompassed most of the untapped regions of the northern interior and Beaufort Sea as well as the offshore areas. The government reserved the right to expropriate up to 25 per cent of any new oil and gas discoveries on these lands, with Petro-Canada as the logical beneficiary. At the same time Petro-Canada's capital budget was increased to almost $1 billion with the clear mandate to increase 'Canadianization' of the industry, and of course it qualified for the PIP grants.

Not surprisingly, Petro-Canada favoured the NEP while the multinationals, particularly Imperial Oil and Texaco Canada, were hostile. Somewhat surprisingly (to the government) many Canadian-owned companies were also opposed; their responses reflected a mixture of considerations. The Calgary-based oilmen were generally resistant to government intervention (at least in terms of regulation) on principle, and shared the Alberta government's resentment at the NEP's tax and export control measures that offset price increases. In addition, many of them were not involved in frontier exploration and lacked the capability to mount major ventures in this area, and not a few preferred to move their exploratory activities to the US which was busy deregulating its oil and gas industry. On the other hand a few, most notably the American-controlled Dome Petroleum, were prepared to work with the new energy regime; but Dome's fate (see Sidelight, p. 460) provided what seemed to be a salutary lesson to other potential collaborators.

Through 1981–82, the NEP was assailed from without by the US government while multinationals began reducing their Canadian operations. The federal government, however, with its base of support in the petroleum-consuming provinces of central Canada (and its renewed promise to extend pipelines to Quebec and the Atlantic region) remained committed to the program. Once again international developments were crucial to the course of events in Canada. By 1982 the recession and development of new energy resources weakened OPEC's ability to control prices and the cartel itself began to crumble. Since the NEP had been predicated on the assumption that oil prices would continue to rise, the steady decline in prices after 1982 undermined the program and eroded public support. By the time the Conservatives under Brian Mulroney came to power in 1984, vowing to dismantle the NEP, the energy issue had lost its saliency. The tar sands and offshore megaprojects were scaled down or virtually abandoned. The major legacy of the era of energy crises was Petro-Canada—which, as Hopper had anticipated, was so large and so embedded in the country's petroleum production and distribution system that even a government committed to privatization was unwilling to try to uproot it until the 1990s.[7]

The issue of foreign control of the Canadian economy had also lost much of its impetus, for a variety of reasons. As noted earlier, by the early 1980s the rate of American direct investment was falling: from an average growth of 11 per cent per year in the mid-1970s it dropped to less than 5 per cent per year. The US-Canadian Free Trade Agreement at the end of the decade would lead to the departure of some firms that had long operated in Canada. During the 1970s some European and Japanese multinationals established beachheads in Canada. Ironically, nationalist policies combined with the recession induced several of them, including the French gas company Aquitaine, Belgian Petrofina, and British Petroleum to sell their holdings to Canadian crown corporations. At the end of the 1980s American-owned companies continued to dominate the branch plant scene, particularly among the largest firms: Exxon's Imperial Oil was one of the top five firms by all rankings, and General Motors held its long-time position as the largest Canadian company ranked by sales up to the recession of the early 1990s. Nevertheless, public fears of an American economic 'take-over', at least through direct investment, had diminished.

Pressures of global competition were also producing structural changes in American multinationals. In earlier times industrial firms entering Canada had erected branch plants that were, in effect, miniature replicas of their home-based plants producing primarily for the Canadian domestic market: this had been one of the criticisms nationalists had focused upon. In the 1970s and 80s some of these companies began to overhaul their international production arrangements, reorganizing foreign subsidiaries to specialize in a few product lines for global or hemispheric markets and providing them with the technical capabilities needed to efficiently fulfil these 'missions' or 'mandates'.

IBM, for example, had set up a Canadian subsidiary before World War II, but it had largely been a sales agency for products made in the US, with modest local manufacturing capabilities. In the 1970s, however, IBM Canada acquired from the parent firm a western hemispheric 'mandate' in the microcircuits field, significantly expanding its manufacturing activities and exports. General Electric provided a similar mandate to its Canadian subsidiary for production of airfoils for

THE RISE AND FALL OF DOME PETROLEUM

Next to Petro-Canada, the company most closely associated in the public mind with frontier oil exploration and Canada's energy security in the early 1980s was Dome Petroleum. Ironically, this self-styled 'chosen instrument' of national energy policy was an American-owned enterprise. This was hardly a novelty in Canadian history: earlier 'chosen instruments'—Avro in the 1950s, the Grand Trunk Pacific in the Laurier era—had also been foreign entities. As in those earlier episodes, Dome was to soar spectacularly in the fevered days of the second energy crisis only to plummet into an abyss of debt and political controversy.

Dome Petroleum was a byproduct of Dome Mines, an enterprise founded in 1918 by the New York investment banker Julius Bache. By the 1950s Dome Mines was one of the largest gold-mining ventures in Canada; its subsidiaries included Sigma Mines in Quebec and Campbell Red Lake Mines in Ontario. The post-Leduc boom aroused the interest of Bache's son-in-law (and partner) Clifford Michel in the Alberta oil fields, and in 1950 Michel set up a small venture, Dome Exploration which in 1958 became a public joint stock company, Dome Petroleum. While Michel chaired the board of the firm until 1976, its chief of operations was Jack Gallagher, a Manitoban who had worked as a field geologist for Shell Oil in the US, Exxon in South America, and Imperial Oil. Initially, Dome Petroleum's activities were primarily in the natural gas fields in southern Alberta, but Gallagher showed an early interest in the potential oil wealth of Canada's northern frontier. Dome joined a consortium, Panarctic Oils, that had substantial federal government support (it was later taken over by the crown) in the early 1960s—an experience that brought Gallagher into contact with Ottawa's energy bureaucrats.

By the end of that decade Dome was one of the largest natural gas producers in the country, and this remained its major source of earnings. Meanwhile, Gallagher pursued his 'northern vision', centred now on the Beaufort Sea and reinforced by American oil discoveries at nearby Prudhoe Bay in Alaska. As a small player on the northern frontier, without the massive financial reserves of companies like Imperial, Dome depended on tax deductions for its Beaufort drilling ventures, and Gallagher cultivated his Ottawa connections, even joining the board of the Canada Development Corporation as a private sector representative. These efforts paid off in 1977 when the federal government authorized a Frontier Exploration Allowance under which companies incurring exploration costs in excess of $5 million per well (Dome was the only candidate at the time) could write off two-thirds of their taxable expenses. This measure, along with growing public interest in energy development, made Dome an attractive investment, abetted by 'Smilin' Jack' Gallagher's persuasive personality.

By this time Gallagher had become chairman of the board, and had passed on operating management of Dome to his long-time associate, William Richards, in order to devote his energies to the Beaufort development. Richards'

Dome Petroleum drill ships wintering close to the more traditional form of Arctic transportation. *(Canapress Photo Service)*

strategy for growth, however, was shaped more by the concurrent enthusiasm in the investment community for mergers and conglomerates. Under Richards, Dome embarked on an acquisition spree, taking over Trans-Canada Pipe Lines in 1978-79, Kaiser Resources in 1980, and Hudson's Bay Oil & Gas (HBOG) in 1981-82, making it (briefly) one of the ten largest (by assets) companies in Canada.

The unveiling of the National Energy Program initially posed some problems for Dome. The tax measures would affect its major cash source, gas exports; more ominously, the Canadian ownership provisions would restrict the company's access to grants and further drilling opportunities on crown lands. Dome and other producers lobbied suc-

cessfully to reduce the tax on gas exports, and Richards worked out a strategem for circumventing the 'Canadianization' obstacle by creating a subsidiary, Dome Canada, with more than half of its shares offered exclusively to Canadian investors. Dome Canada was launched with much fanfare in March 1981, raising $434 million in equity capital. The new company promptly applied for PIP subsidies to pursue its Beaufort project.

But Dome Petroleum's success in its dealings with the government could not long conceal its troubles on another front. Richards' acquisition strategy was proving expensive: prying HBOG from its largest shareholder, Conoco, cost over $2 billion and Dome was

⟶

already heavily leveraged with loans from a multitude of foreign and Canadian banks. Even to cover its interest payments, Dome had to increase revenues and Richards concluded that this required a complete takeover of HBOG, buying out the remaining shareholders for another $1.8 billion. By early 1982 the company had incurred debts of more than $6 billion.

At this point world oil prices began to slip and Dome's creditors took alarm. As in the case of Massey-Ferguson a year earlier, several major Canadian banks, particularly the Toronto-Dominion Bank and the Imperial Bank of Commerce, had large sums advanced to Dome; the company's possible bankruptcy would reverberate through the country's financial community. Through the summer of 1982 bankers and government officials scrambled to work out a debt rescheduling arrangement for Dome, with the banks and the government putting up $1 billion for debentures convertible to stock. The bail-out was the occasion for much acrimony. Existing shareholders complained about the dilution of their equity; Prime Minister Trudeau derided the banks for their lack of good judgement in leveraging Dome's expansionary binge; business commentators assailed the government for contributing to an environment of inflated expectations that influenced the behaviour of Dome's managers, the banks, and the investing public.

In the months that followed, Gallagher and Richards were forced out of Dome and its empire was dismantled: TCPL and other chunks of Dome's domain were picked up by Bell Canada Enterprises. Dome Canada, renamed Encor Energy, limped along as a much-diminished player in northern exploration; Dome Petroleum also continued to operate but oil prices fell steadily through the 1980s and there was little investor interest in frontier development. In 1988 Dome Petroleum was swallowed by Amoco Canada, subsidiary of a Chicago-based oil major, for $5.2 billion, the most expensive takeover in the country's history; Amoco in turn was to experience difficulties digesting its new acquisition in the recession that ensued.

To some extent Dome Petroleum, like the NEP, was a victim of circumstances. Had oil prices continued to rise in the 1980s its designs might have been judged as far-sighted and bold. But Dome also contributed to its fate. Richards' acquisition strategy was mistimed and driven, at least in part, by a desire to make Dome the largest oil company in Canada: the HBOG takeover in particular duplicated rather than complemented Dome's areas of strength in the industry and put Dome out on a financial limb. Dome's expansionary thrust was affected less by developments in the energy sector than by the merger fever that swept the business community in the late 1970s, fuelled by inflation and easy credit. As a final irony, that easy credit was provided in large measure by Canadian banks, eager to slough off their image as stodgy and conservative and to demonstrate their competitive vigour in the emerging global financial marketplace.

Sources

Foster, Peter, *Other People's Money: The Banks, The Government and Dome* (Toronto, 1984).

Lyon, Jim, *Dome: The Rise and Fall of the House That Jack Built* (Toronto, 1983).

jet engines. Westinghouse Canada and Litton Systems also developed specialized export operations for their parent firms' markets. Although relatively few foreign-owned companies were affected by these developments, many of them were in 'high-tech' fields whose expansion Canadian business and political leaders of all persuasions saw as essential for Canada's long-term industrial renewal. Overall, US-owned subsidiaries in Canada more than doubled their export sales from $11 billion to over $28 billion in 1976–84, with exports beyond the US averaging about one-sixth of the total.

Another development of the 1970s was the growth of Canadian multinationals, or, more to the point, heightened public awareness of their significance. There was of course nothing new about Canadian investment abroad: the 'utilities mul-tinationals' had flourished in Latin America in the early years of the century, and manufacturers such as Massey-Ferguson and Seagram's had had branch opera-tions in the US and overseas since the 1920s. During the 1960s the big mining and paper companies — Inco, Cominco, Alcan, MacMillan-Bloedel — had invested substantially abroad; and by the 1970s manufacturers as diverse as Bata Shoes and Northern Telecom were operating in foreign markets, while conglom-erators like the Reichmanns and Robert Campeau erected their jerry-built empires in the US and Europe. These were not all minor operators: some companies, including Cominco, Bata, and Seagram's, were the largest global producers in their respective fields.

Canadian banks also had a tradition of international expansion, through both foreign lending and branch operations abroad, principally in other parts of the British Commonwealth. The Bank of Nova Scotia and the Royal Bank had been active in the Caribbean, in tandem with the utility multinationals, as well as in the United States. Other financial institutions were involved in foreign markets: Sun Life, for example, was one of the largest Canadian investors in the US in the 1920s. At the end of that decade Canadian banks had 175 branches abroad, with the Royal Bank as the pace-setter. Depression, war, and the postwar expansion of the domestic economy redirected the attention of Canadian financial institutions closer to home, but after 1960 there was a renewed surge of activity abroad, stimulated by the growing interlinkages of global capital markets. In the years 1965–80, the foreign assets of Canadian banks increased from less than $10 bil-lion to over $90 billion (in part reflecting inflation, of course), and 160 foreign financial companies were absorbed by the big chartered banks, which were also diversifying their range of client services abroad as well as at home as federal regulatory measures were liberalized.

Canadian banks were relatively small players on an international scene popu-lated by giant institutions like Citicorp, Bank of America, and the Morgan group. Foreign loans sometimes proved hazardous undertakings for a financial com-munity that had prided itself on its stability and prudence. The international debt crisis of the early 1980s, which was in part a by-product of the energy crises, caught five of the leading banks with almost $20 billion in loans outstanding to countries such as Argentina, Brazil and Mexico that came perilously close to defaulting. Canadian bank expansion abroad weakened the case for protection of the home front as well, leading to the revision of the Bank Act in 1980 to permit foreign entrants, although they were still restricted to less than 10 per cent of the Canadian financial market, and would-be invaders like American Express faced continuing bureaucratic obstacles.[8]

Globalization of financial, commercial, and industrial markets undermined the regulatory and interventionist thrust of national governments that had been fostered by depression and war earlier in the twentieth century. While the National Energy Program marked the apogee of Canadian government activism (except in wartime), it seemed in retrospect to be a kind of last gasp rather than the logical culmination of a half century of interventionism. By the early 1980s new regimes were coming to power in the US, Britain, and elsewhere, espousing a reinvigorated credo of free enterprise, open markets and a diminished role for the state in the economy. By the end of the decade the command economies of the communist world were crumbling. In Canada the Conservative electoral victory of 1984 marked the eclipse of the age of the activist state. For some Canadians the events that followed portended the prospective disintegration of the country or, perhaps, its ultimate 'integration' into a continental economic empire that had long been displacing the older transatlantic empire within which Canada had first emerged.

Notes

[1]See J.K. Galbraith, *The New Industrial State* (Boston, 1967). For general overviews of business developments in this era, see Robert Sobel, *The Age of Giant Corporations*; Louis Galambos and Joseph Pratt, *The Rise of the Corporate Commonwealth: US Business and Public Policy in the 20th Century* (New York, 1988).

[2]On E.P. Taylor and Argus, see Richard Rohmer, *E.P. Taylor* (Toronto, 1978); Frank and Libbie Park, *Anatomy of Big Business* (Toronto, 1973), 162–91. The careers of other conglomerators are viewed by Peter C. Newman in the various volumes of *The Canadian Establishment*. See also Susan Goldenberg, *Canadian Pacific: A Portrait of Power* (Toronto, 1983); Lawrence Surtees, *Pa Bell: A. Jean de Grandpré and the Rise of Bell Canada Enterprises* (Toronto, 1992). The conglomerate phenomenon is examined in the American context in Robert Sobel, *The Rise and Fall of the Conglomerate Kings* (New York, 1984). On business consolidations and conglomerates in Canada see Gideon Rosenbluth, *Concentration in Canadian Manufacturing Industry* (Princeton, 1957); Jorge Niosi, *The Economy of Canada: A Study of Ownership and Control* (Montreal, 1978).

[3]General comparative analyses of government economic policies in the postwar era include Robert Lekachman, *The Age of Keynes* (New York, 1968); Andrew Shonfield, *Modern Capitalism: The Changing Balance of Public and Private Power* (New York, 1965). See also Robert Collins, *The Business Response to Keynes* (New York, 1981).

[4]On macroeconomic policies in Canada, see David A. Wolfe, 'The Rise and Demise of the Keynesian Era in Canada: Economic Policy, 1930–82', in M.S. Cross and G.S. Kealey, eds, *Modern Canada, 1930s–1980s* (Toronto, 1984), 46–80; Bothwell *et al.*, *Canada Since 1945*, chs 19, 23, 27, and 33; Richard Phidd and G. Bruce Doern, *The Politics and Management of Canadian Economic Policy* (Toronto, 1978). On bail-outs, see Marsha Gordon, *Government in Business*, 83–7, 150–4; Borins and Brown, *Investments in Failure*. On

Massey-Ferguson, see Peter Cook, *Massey at the Brink*, chs 12–15. On reorganization of the fisheries companies see Kimber, *Net Profits*, chs 15–17; and Laux and Molot, *State Capitalism*, 135–9. See ch. 19 for other references on the fisheries.

[5]For varying views on the rise of multinational enterprises and their impact on economic and political affairs, see Raymond Vernon, *Sovereignty At Bay*; Richard Barnet and Ronald Muller, *Global Reach: The Power of the Multinational Corporations* (New York, 1974); Stephen Hymer, *The International Operations of National Firms* (Cambridge, Mass., 1976); Wilkins, *Maturing of Multinational Enterprise*, chs 12–14. Among many critiques of multinationals in Canada, see Kari Levitt, *Silent Surrender*; I.A. Litvak and C.J. Maule, *Dual Loyalty: Canadian-US Business* (Toronto, 1971). A.E. Safarian, *Foreign Ownership of Canadian Industry* (Toronto, 1973) examined the internal structures and perspectives of Canadian subsidiaries; Eric Jackson, *The Great Canadian Debate: Foreign Ownership* (Toronto, 1975) looked at different viewpoints.

[6]On Canadian policies *vis-à-vis* foreign direct investment, see Michael Bliss, 'Founding FIRA: The Historical Background', in J.M. Spence and W.P. Rosenfeld, eds, *Foreign Investment Review Law in Canada* (Toronto, 1984), 1–11; Charles McMillan, 'The Regulation of Foreign Investment in Canada', *Journal of Contemporary Issues* 6 (Autumn 1977), 31–51; Richard D. French, *How Ottawa Decides: Planning and Industrial Policy Making, 1968–80* (Ottawa, 1980). (Ottawa, 1980). On specific episodes see William Kilbourn, *Pipeline* (Toronto, 1970); John Fayerweather, *The Mercantile Bank Affair* (New York, 1974); Carl Beigie, *The Canada-US Automotive Agreement* (Montreal, 1970); *The Canadian Automotive Industry* (Ottawa, 1978).

[7]On the origins and growth of Petro-Canada, see Larry Pratt, 'Petro-Canada', in Allan Tupper and G. Bruce Doern, eds, *Privatization, Public Policy and Public Corporations in Canada* (Halifax, 1988), 151–210. On the National Energy Program, see G. Bruce Doern and Glen Toner, *The Politics of Energy* (Toronto, 1985). For an acerbic view of the government's energy policies see Peter Foster, *The Sorcerer's Apprentices: Canada's Super-Bureaucrats and the Energy Mess* (Toronto, 1982); for different assessments, see David Crane, *Controlling Interest: The Canadian Oil and Gas Stakes* (Toronto, 1982); James Laxer, *Oil and Gas* (Toronto, 1983).

[8]On Canadian multinationals, see Jorge Niosi, *Canadian Multinationals*, trans. Robert Chodos (Toronto, 1985); Alan Rugman, *Multinationals and Canada-United States Free Trade* (Columbia, S.C., 1990); Science Council of Canada, *Multinationals and Industrial Strategy: The Role of World Product Mandates* (Ottawa, 1980); Pancras Nagy, *The International Business of Canadian Banks* (Montreal, 1983); James Darroch, 'Global Competitiveness and Public Policy: The Case of Canadian Multinational Banks', *Business History* 34 (July 1992), 153–75.

LEAPING IN THE DARK

By the mid-1980s the Canadian economy was rebounding from recession. Between 1984 and 1989 gross domestic product rose from $400 billion to nearly $700 billion and inflation had been wrestled down to a relatively tolerable rate of 4 per cent increase a year. Manufacturing output rose along with increases in forestry and mining production. Canadian business figures expressed new-found confidence in the country's prospects. Around mid-decade manufacturing export levels were exceeding those of the traditional staples (excluding energy exports) for the first time in the country's history. While Prime Minister Mulroney's 'open door' policy and the booming US capital market brought new investment into the country, Canadian businesses were also investing abroad, and earnings from these direct investments exceeded net outflows to foreigners in 1986–88, another reversal of past trends. The Reichmanns, Campeau, and other Canadian conglomerators joined in the American merger and acquisition binge, and there were even rumblings in the US Congress over the Canadian 'invasion' of their country's real-estate market. Canada's economic growth rate, averaging about 4 per cent a year in 1985–90 was well ahead of the United States and West Germany.

The recession of the early 1990s rapidly undermined much of this confidence; even before that point, some observers were calling attention to longer-term concerns. Unemployment rates lingered in double digits into 1986 and never fell below pre-1980 levels. As usual, the problem was worst in Atlantic Canada, but even British Columbia faced persistent high rates, and in Alberta the slump in energy demand held down activity in the oil patch. While the eighties resurrected Ontario as the nation's industrial heartland, there were problems for manufacturing as well. Improvements in productivity, in terms of both labour and capital inputs, lagged in comparison with rates in other major industrialized nations. Manufacturing, particularly in Ontario was tied to a relatively small number of product lines such as automotives and was vulnerable to shifts in market demand, a situation that became painfully apparent in the 1990s recession. Chronically high unemployment rates and low gains in real wages dampened the domestic market while export growth reflected the weakness of the Canadian dollar rather than the long-term competitive strength of the country's industries: devaluation actually worked against this result since Canada had to import much of the advanced technology needed to enhance productivity.

Pondering Canada's industrial problems and solutions became a cottage industry in its own right. Some critics, noting that small and medium-sized firms accounted for more than two-thirds of new job creation in the recession of the early 1980s, asserted that the age of large-scale vertically integrated industrial enterprise was ebbing, and that future growth would depend on smaller, more

467

versatile companies that could secure specialized 'niches' in increasingly splintered, diversified markets. Others argued that the essential element was not the scale of operations but the structure of organization. Economist Charles McMillan, who served for a time as an adviser to Mulroney, urged Canadian firms to adopt the methods of Japanese manufacturers, tailoring product lines to the specific needs of their customers and diffusing quality control practices across the workforce rather than leaving it as the exclusive prerogative of management. McMillan and others also emphasized that Canadian businesses had to invest more in development of new technologies that would improve production processes and enable firms to shift product lines in more rapid response to changing markets. The American 'competitiveness' expert, Michael Porter, also advanced these views and stressed as well the need for more investment in applied research, retraining workers and strengthening the country's educational system generally.[1]

These proposals indicated the need for a continuing role for government, although emphasis was placed on public investment in infrastructure, research, and education rather than the traditional practices of protectionism, subsidies, and regulation. The Conservative regime that came to power in Ottawa in 1984, however, was initially dedicated to dismantling government programs and reducing the federal deficit. The National Energy Program was a prime target along with FIRA, which was renamed Investment Canada to highlight its revised role as facilitator rather than watchdog of foreign investments. Related to these steps were measures to 'privatize' federal crown corporations.

While the impetus for privatizing derived in part from controversies over costly 'investments in failure' such as Canadair, ideological considerations played a major role and reflected international political influences. In Britain the Conservative regime of Margaret Thatcher had begun dismantling nationalized industries in the early 1980s, justified primarily as a means of restoring free markets rather than simply reducing government costs. In the United States where government-owned enterprises were less visible (though not nonexistent) deregulation of banking and the airline industry commenced in the 1970s, with support from both of the main political parties as necessary to rejuvenate competitive forces in the economy.

While the Mulroney government in Canada tracked these foreign developments with interest, it moved cautiously toward privatization, keeping in mind the politically disastrous consequences of Joe Clark's foray against Petro-Canada in 1979–80 (Petro-Canada itself escaped the privatizing drive until 1991). In addition, the government sought to avoid selling off crown corporations at distress prices, constraining its ideological enthusiasm with fiscal prudence. Nevertheless, in the sale of the aircraft manufacturers De Havilland and Canadair in 1985–86, Ottawa was obliged to absorb a substantial part of the debt.

In 1987 a more profitable if relatively obscure crown corporation, Teleglobe Canada, was privatized, eventually winding up under the effective control of Bell Canada despite the fact that the government had tried to avoid this outcome. In 1988–89 when Air Canada was placed on the auction block, institutional investors were wary. The airline had had a troubled history in recent years despite vigorous efforts to control costs and develop a competitive position in the transatlantic business and tourist travel market, but along with employees of Air Canada many individual Canadians patriotically bought shares in the company. Recession and the rising costs of financing a new fleet of airplanes, however, hurt Air Canada's earnings and led to a new round of cutbacks in the early 1990s. By 1992 both Air Canada and the equally-strapped Pacific West Airlines of Calgary (which had taken over CP Air in the 1970s) were looking towards amalgamation with American partners. In 1991, Petro Canada was finally privatized with its own employees taking on 80 per cent of the shares of the once-mighty crown, now seriously weakened by the extended slump in oil markets.[2]

Mulroney wisely held off on another controversial initiative until after the 1988 election: the elimination of federal sales taxes on manufacturing production—a relic of the 1940s that was now regarded as a constraint on the competitive capabilities of Canadian industry—and its replacement by a highly unpopular Goods and Services Tax on consumers, a measure that also enraged retailers and small business firms generally. The most significant economic development of the Mulroney era, however, was the negotiation of the Free Trade Agreement with the United States.

Curiously, the initiative for this undertaking came from the preceding Liberal regime. In 1982, with the country mired in recession, Prime Minister Trudeau followed the hallowed Canadian tradition of establishing a Royal Commission to consider Canada's economic prospects. The final report did not surface until long after the Liberals' departure from power, but in November 1984 the Commission's chairman, Donald Macdonald, began urging Canadians to take a 'leap of faith' and move toward comprehensive free trade with the Americans. Macdonald's call was quickly echoed by the Business Council on National Issues (BCNI), an organization set up in 1976 to represent the views of the country's large export-oriented corporations and banks, but it was also endorsed by the Canadian Manufacturers' Association, the traditional bastion of protectionist sentiment since the days of Sir John A. Macdonald.

Growing protectionism in the US stimulated the movement for free trade in Canada. Although the American government remained officially committed to multilateral tariff reductions under the GATT agreements, during the 1970s US manufacturers, facing rising competition in their home markets from the Japanese and other foreigners, lobbied for non-tariff restrictions on imports, and the recession of the early 1980s increased these pressures. Particularly vexing for Canadian exporters were the actions of the International Trade Commission, an agency of the US Commerce Department that had authority to impose countervailing duties against countries deemed to be engaged in dumping or other 'unfair' trade practices. Rather than acting as an impartial tribunal to settle trade disputes, the ITC in Canadian eyes was perceived to be acting in the interests of American producers; a controversial ITC ruling in 1986 against Canadian softwood lumber imports highlighted this problem. While Presidents Carter and Reagan rhetorically endorsed free trade ideas, the memory of the 'Nixon shocks' of the early 1970s lingered on and proposals for new protectionist measures circulated perpetually in the US Congress.

For Macdonald and other advocates of a US free trade agreement, growing American protectionism was not the only concern. With the emergence of regional trade blocs abroad, such as the European Economic Community, Canada ran the risk of becoming the only industrialized exporting nation without secure access to a market of more than 100 million people. The failure of Trudeau's 'Third Option' search for markets outside North America left Canada with few alternatives to the United States. Furthermore, it was argued, Canada's industries had to become more efficient and sales-oriented to survive in the globalized economy, and the 'cold bath' of competition in their own markets would hasten this process. Some critics, escpecially from the left wing of the Liberal party and the NDP, perceived a hidden agenda in this line of argument, maintaining that the thrust for 'efficiency' would result in wage cuts for Canadian workers and undermine social welfare programs erected over the past generation. After the Mulroney government took up the initiative, Canadian nationalists saw free trade as part of the new regime's continentalist tilt.

Encouraged by a largely supportive business community, the Canadian government embarked on its free trade quest in 1985–86. The Reagan administration in the US seemed receptive — Reagan had talked vaguely of creating a 'North American Common Market' in the 1980 presidential campaign — and arranged for a 'fast track' negotiating process that would circumvent Congressional delaying tactics. But the American business community was divided on the issue. Financial service companies such as American Express saw in free trade an opportunity to penetrate the Canadian market more readily, and US oil companies were interested in using an agreement as a means of blocking future NEP-type ventures by Canada. On the other side, American firms in direct competition with Canadians in fields such as lumber and food products were less receptive. The negotiations reflected these cross-pressures: the Americans pushed hard for inclusion of services and energy issues in the agreement but baulked at Canadian efforts to establish a system of rules that would in effect exempt their exporters from ITC actions and shield them from quotas and other non-tariff restrictions.

The negotiations deadlocked in the fall of 1987, requiring intervention at the highest levels on both sides. In the ensuing Free Trade Agreement the Americans achieved most of their objectives in the energy and financial areas, with further restraints on Canadian regulatory powers over foreign investment. The Canadians failed to get exemptions from countervailing measures but were able to secure agreement to a formal bi-national process for resolving trade disputes. Remaining tariff barriers between the countries would be phased out over ten years; the Auto Pact remained in place. On one of the thorniest issues, the definition of 'subsidies' (the existence of which could be deemed justification for countervailing measures), both sides agreed to defer a final determination until a later date.

After the US Congress ratified the Agreement, Mulroney decided to make it the centrepiece of his reelection campaign in 1988 — the first time a Canadian political leader had dared to risk his future on a trade agreement since Laurier's ill-fated Reciprocity venture in 1911. In contrast to 1911, however, in this case the nation's business figures were generally of one mind. The BCNI mounted a vigorous advertising campaign, combining assertions of confidence in Canada's competitiveness with ominous warnings of the economic chaos that would ensue if the Agreement were not approved. Opponents, including trade unionists, social reformers and nationalists, mobilized their forces, exploiting familiar themes of patriotism and anti-Americanism. But their votes were divided between the Liberals and the NDP, facilitating Mulroney's victory with less than 45 per cent of the popular vote (except in Quebec where all political leaders embraced free trade) but secure control of Parliament. In 1989 the Canada-US Free Trade Agreement went into effect, representing the most dramatic shift in the country's economic direction since the establishment of the National Policy more than a century earlier.

The onset of a new recession in the early 1990s complicated any assessment of the consequences of the Free Trade Agreement. Some American-owned branch plants closed down in Canada, but 'rationalization' was the order of the day in US industry as well. Cross-border shopping (mainly from the Canadian side) increased, but Canadian retailers blamed this development in part on the GST. Analysts of the trade disputes panels established under the Agreement maintain that in general they have functioned reasonably well, but controversial decisions continued to arouse alarm in Canada, most notably in 1991 when the US imposed countervailing duties against the Japanese auto firm, Honda, whose manufacturing subsidiary in Canada, it was alleged, was assembling cars for export to the US using parts largely made in Japan. Canadian critics disputed these claims and argued that the US government was acting under pressure from its beleaguered auto industry. Meanwhile, the American and Canadian government had commenced a new round of negotiations that included Mexico, looking toward establishment of a North American Free Trade Agreement (NAFTA).[3]

Trade competition was not the only challenge facing Canadian business in the 1980s. Environmental issues, largely ignored in the period of rapid growth after World War II, became a matter of public concern, dramatized by tanker oil spills off both coasts, chemical pollution of the Great Lakes, and the rapid depletion of natural fish stocks among other events. During the early 1980s US and Canadian authorities bickered over the issue of acid rain, with the Canadians blaming industries in the American Middle West for the problem while the Americans noted in particular the discharges of Inco's smelters in Sudbury. Ironically, Inco had erected extremely tall chimneys at its smelters in order to reduce local pollution levels.

Nor was the business community immune from changing patterns of gender relations in society. Women still faced formidable barriers to entry into the higher echelons of large corporations, but women were increasingly found running small and medium-sized enterprises, particularly in retailing and services. In the new competitive environment in financial services, banks were gradually abandoning conventional practices that restricted credit to male entrepreneurs.

The situation for minority groups remained more problematic, but the economic prospects for the most impoverished among them, the Native peoples of Canada, appeared to be brightening. During the 1970s a number of long-standing land claims issues were addressed by the federal and provincial governments, in part as a by-product of the search for new energy sources in remote northern regions. As discussed in Chapter Nineteen, in 1975 the Cree of the James Bay area, after years of litigation with Quebec over its plans for hydro development, procured an agreement that, among other terms, provided cash and royalty payments of $135 million over a ten-year period. An additional $90 million was pledged to the Inuit of James Bay who set up the Makivik Corporation to manage investments that ranged from local fishing operations to shares in Nordair. Meanwhile, in the Northwest Territories the federal government began negotiations with Native and Métis groups in the mid-1970s after a much-publicized Royal Commission report by Thomas Berger highlighted the social and environmental dangers of the proposed pipeline that would carry oil and gas south from the Beaufort Sea through the Mackenzie Valley. Although the pipeline project was later scaled down, in 1984 an agreement was made providing $45 million (in 1977 dollars) to the Native peoples of the region with pledges of additional funding for economic development.

Although these and other land claims settlements pumped much-needed capital into Native communities, proclamations of the advent of an era of 'red capitalism' were somewhat premature. Royalties to some bands from mineral leases fell off as energy demand eased in the 1980s. In 1981 the federal government announced the establishment of a Native Economic Development Fund but by the end of the decade only a fraction of the $345 million promised had been allocated. Access to private capital sources for both individuals and bands was limited because of government restrictions on their rights to transfer land titles. These issues along with protracted and inconclusive negotiations over other land claims fuelled renewed demands from Native groups for recognition of their powers of economic as well as political self-determination, but the defeat of the proposed Charlottetown constitutional accord in 1992 left these matters in limbo.[4]

One hundred and twenty-five years after Confederation, almost five hundred years after European seasonal fishing settlements first appeared in Newfoundland, the future direction of Canadian business seemed as uncertain as the future of Canada itself. The largest corporations (in terms of assets) in Canada bore familiar names: Bell Canada, Canadian Pacific, Seagram's, Noranda. But a number of these had been transformed over the preceding decade into diversified holding companies with subsidiaries abroad and operating in fields far removed from their original areas of concentration. Many of the behemoths of the manufacturing and resource sectors were suffering from the combined effects of recession and debt burdens incurred from expansion and diversification in the 1980s, while aggressive smaller firms in the retail and service fields, such as Canadian Tire and Moore Corporation, outpaced them in earnings. Companies in these areas comprised almost half of the fifty leading corporations ranked by sales (see Tables E.1 and E.2).

Table E.1   Canada's Twenty Leading Non-Financial Corporations 1992[a]

RANKED BY ASSETS	ASSETS (IN BILLIONS)	RANKED BY SALES	RANKED BY EARNINGS
1) Imasco Ltd	48.5	5	5
2) Bell Canada Enterprises	48.3	1	1
3) Power Corp.	27.2	21	18
4) Canadian Pacific Ltd	20.2	10	b
5) Noranda	14.4	11	37
6) Imperial Oil	13.2	8	12
7) Alcan	12.9	6	b
8) Seagram Co.	12.8	15	b
9) Thomson Corp.	10	16	9
10) Northern Telecom	9.4	12	4
11) Crownx Inc.	9	49	b
12) Carena Developments	8.3	96	b
13) Westcoast Energy	6.6	74	b
14) Trizec	6.4	133	b
15) Nova Corp.	6.2	41	16
16) GM Canada	6.2	2	b
17) Shell Canada	5.3	36	b
18) Inco Ltd	5.3	36	b
19) Brascan	4.9	13	b
20) Bombardier	4.3	28	19

[a]Excludes crown corporations, and privately-held companies.
[b]Not ranked in top 500 companies in category.

At the same time many features of Canadian business development persisted. On the financial scene the large chartered banks held their ground even as they absorbed losses from bad investments and overexpansion abroad. During the late 1980s two aspiring western institutions, the Canadian Commercial Bank and the Northland Bank, had gone under; as the recession took hold, the Maritime-based Central Trust, which had aggressively moved into central Canadian markets in the 1980s, skirted close to disaster, ultimately being taken over by the Toronto Dominion Bank.

The Porter study of Canada's position in international markets identified resource exporters—in forest products, petroleum, and metals—as the country's most competitive industries, with a few isolated pockets of strength in fields such as telecommunications and the beverage industry. Although foreign ownership was less salient as as a public issue (11 of the top 50 companies ranked by sales were partially or wholly foreign-owned, eight of them subsidiaries of US firms), the foreign presence remained substantial, particularly in export industries such as automotives, oil and gas, and mining products, with more than half of imports and exports between the US and Canada consisting of transactions within mul-

Table E.2 Canada's Top Fifty Companies (by Sector) Ranked by Sales, 1991

SECTOR	NUMBER OF COMPANIES	PER CENT OF TOP 50
Diversified	8	16
Manufacturing	11	22
Mining & Forestry	6	12
Oil and Gas	4	8
Other	21	42

SOURCE: *Canadian Business*, June 1993, 70-5.

tinationals. Canada's 'big businesses' for the most part remained relatively small in comparison with those in other major industrialized countries. The virtues of 'bigness' continued to be a matter of dispute: some observers noted the versatility of some Canadian firms, such as Bombardier and Spar Aerospace, in specialized markets, but others lamented the fragmented nature of many industries outside the resource sector and the general absence of technological innovation.[5]

In October 1992 Canadian trade negotiators joined their counterparts from the United States and Mexico in signing the North American Free Trade Agreement. In that same month Canadian voters in a referendum rejected the constitutional proposals drafted in the Charlottetown Accord, despite vigorous efforts by most of the country's business as well as political leaders to persuade them otherwise. The long-term impact of these two events remains to be seen, but for the Canadian business community NAFTA (assuming its ratification) would probably be of greater consequence. Even if rejection of the Charlottetown Accord paved the way for Quebec separation, Quebec would still be linked to the North American economy. Predictions about the consequences of NAFTA varied: for Canadian nationalists the agreement threatened to hasten the 'deindustrialization' of the country and its ultimate absorption into a continental system dominated by the United States. For most business observers the establishment through NAFTA of the largest common market in the world would enable Canadian businesses to expand and restructure their operations on a scale necessary to survive into the twenty-first century.

These contrasting views reflected very different perceptions of the essential character of the Canadian economy and the capabilities of Canadian business. One side saw Canada as a small, vulnerable country still fundamentally dependent on the export of staples. The other side focused on diversity in the Canadian economy and on the adaptability and versatility of its business community. In fact, the history of Canadian business provides some support for both views; yet it also suggests that Canada is an unusual amalgam: a country with a well-developed financial and manufacturing system resting on a raw-materials exporting base, whose future will be shaped by the talents of its people as well as the riches of its natural resources.

Notes

[1] The case for small business as the engine of growth was advanced by Michael Piore and Charles Schnabel, *The Second Industrial Divide* (New York, 1984). On restructuring, see Charles McMillan, 'From Quality Control to Quality Management:Lessons From Japan', *Business Quarterly* 47 (May 1982), 31–40, and 'How Japan Uses Technology for Competitive Success: Lessons for Canadian Management', *Business Quarterly* 54 (Summer 1988), 34–8. See also Stephen Waring, *Taylorism Transformed* (Chapel Hill, N.C., 1991), 160–86. Contrasting recipes for renewing Canadian competitiveness were offered by Michael E. Porter and the Monitor Company, *Canada at the Crossroads: The Reality of a New Competitive Environment* (Ottawa, 1991), and Alan Rugman and Joseph D'Cruz, *Facing Forward: Improving Canada's International Competitiveness* (Toronto, 1991). See also Porter, *The Competitive Advantage of Nations* (New York, 1990).

[2] On privatization see Tupper and Doern, eds, *Privatization, Public Policy and Public Corporations in Canada.*

[3] On the US-Canadian Free Trade Agreement, see G. Bruce Doern and Brian W. Tomlin, *Faith and Fear: The Free Trade Story* (Toronto, 1991); Gilbert R. Winham, *Trading With Canada: The Canada-US Free Trade Agreement* (New York, 1988). See also G.N. Horlick and F.A. De Busk, 'The Functioning of FTA Dispute Resolution Panels' in Leonard Waverman, ed., *Negotiating and Implementing a North American Free Trade Agreement* (Vancouver, 1992), 1–28. Sceptical (indeed hostile) views of the Free Trade Agreement, and the concept of globalization generally, are offered in Pat Marchak, *The Integrated Circus: The New Right and the Restructuring of Global Markets* (Montreal/Kingston, 1991); and Linda McQuaig, *The Quick and the Dead* (Toronto, 1991).

[4] On Native land claims and business activities, see Olive Dickason, *Canada's First Nations* (Toronto, 1992), 402–16; J.R. Miller, *Skyscrapers Hide the Heavens: A History of Indian-White Relations in Canada* (Toronto, 1989), ch. 14; John M. Parkinson, 'Sources of Capital for Native Businesses: Problems and Prospects', *Canadian Journal of Native Studies* VIII, 1 (1988), 27–58.

[5] See Duncan McDowall, 'Fin de Siècle: Canadian Business in the 1990s', *Business History* 34 (July 1992), 176–80. See also *Business Quarterly* 56 (Winter 1992), 55–75 for a variety of responses to Porter's *Canada At the Crossroads.*

INDEX

Date Due